THE MONCADA ATTACK

THE MONCADA ATTACK
BIRTH OF THE CUBAN REVOLUTION

Antonio Rafael de la Cova

The University of South Carolina Press

© 2007 University of South Carolina

Published by the University of South Carolina Press
Columbia, South Carolina 29208

www.sc.edu/uscpress

Manufactured in the United States of America

16 15 14 13 12 11 10 09 08 07   10 9 8 7 6 5 4 3 2 1

Library of Congress Cataloging-in-Publication Data

De la Cova, Antonio Rafael, 1950–
  The Moncada attack : birth of the Cuban Revolution / Antonio Rafael de la Cova.
    p. cm.
  Includes bibliographical references and index.
  ISBN-13: 978-1-57003-672-9 (cloth : alk. paper)
  ISBN-10: 1-57003-672-1 (cloth : alk. paper)
  1. Cuba—History—Moncada Barracks Attack, 1953. 2. Castro, Fidel, 1926– I. Title.
  F1787.5.D35 2007
  972.9106'3—dc22
                    2006100452

This book was printed on Glatfelter Natures, a recycled paper with 50 percent postconsumer waste content.

To the martyrs and political prisoners for Cuban freedom and democracy

The Cuban Revolution was born at Moncada.
Celia Sánchez

I am not going to say that we went to Moncada to make a socialist revolution. We went there with the idea of making a change, so that better men might govern and so that men would not steal. . . . We went to Moncada as disciples of Martí.
Haydée Santamaría

In our ranks in that period there was never talk about communism, socialism or Marxist-Leninism as an ideology . . . the problem of workers' exploitation was not discussed.
Melba Hernández

CONTENTS

List of Illustrations *ix*
Preface *xi*
Introduction *xxv*

ONE Growing Up under Three Different Names *1*
TWO "There is nothing unusual going on" *32*
THREE "On Sunday, Cuba will be in flames" *60*
FOUR "Shoot at those wearing tennis shoes" *81*
FIVE "We are going into history" *121*
SIX "That savagery cannot be blamed on Batista" *138*
SEVEN "You do not kill ideas" *174*
EIGHT "A leader is born" *203*
NINE "History definitively, will say it all" *228*
TEN The "Grand Task of Cuban Reconstruction" *249*

Abbreviations Used in the Appendixes *259*
Appendix 1. Rebel Participants in the Insurrection of July 26, 1953 *261*
Appendix 2. Casualties *267*
Appendix 3. Civilians Acquitted in Case 37 *271*
Appendix 4. Defense Attorneys and Their Case 37 Clients *273*
Appendix 5. "Manifesto to the Nation" *275*
Appendix 6. Gustavo Arcos, letter from Cuba, July 26, 2003 *279*
Notes *281*
Bibliography *353*
Index *363*

ILLUSTRATIONS

Figures

following page 120
La Demajagua Bell and student activists
Rebels at target practice
Fidel Castro
Raúl Castro
Renato Guitart
Eduardo Montano
Mario Chanes
Mario MartínezArarás
Mockup of the scene of the action
Post 3 side entrance
Post 2 main entrance
Post 3 side entrance from above
Upper-floor offices
Officers' Club
New military houses on Moncada Street
Palace of Justice
Bayamo garrison entrance
Lt. Angel Machado and executed rebels
Moncada courtyard and executed rebels
Government casualties
General Fulgencio Batista and Col. Alberto del Río Chaviano
Morales family
Pvt. Antonio H. Rodríguez Pérez and his brothers
Pvt. Armando Oliva López and Beralia Fajardo
Pvt. José Ferrá Mulet
Pvt. José Humberto Olivares

Pvt. Justo Ramón Martija
Fidel Castro in jail
Melba Hernández and Haydée Santamaría
Manuel Bartolomé
José and Juan Pujol
Orlando Castro García
Rebels exiled in Mexico City
Rebels at a Mexico City reception
Author with Sgt. Eulalio González
Former adversaries Ariel Matos and Orlando Castro García

Maps

following page xxx
Camagüey and Oriente, with Cuban island inset
Bayamo
Santiago de Cuba
Moncada garrison and vicinity
Saturnino Lora Civil Hospital
Siboney farmhouse and vicinity

PREFACE

All works dealing with the Cuban Revolution or Fidel Castro's rise to power will necessarily have to mention the Moncada and Bayamo garrison attacks of July 26, 1953. Prior studies of the Cuban Revolution have focused on the national civic, political, and guerrilla movement that surged after 1956. There is no profound scholarly analysis of the initial attack that provided the name for the 26 of July Movement that overthrew Maj. Gen. Fulgencio Batista on January 1, 1959, and seized power in Cuba for more than forty-eight years.

Until now, there have been only two views of the Moncada events, those propagated by the governments of Fidel Castro and Fulgencio Batista, each containing historical inaccuracies and exaggerations. This work disproves the persistent falsehoods propagated by both sides, especially the "Black Legend" created by Castro in his subsequently published defense speech *History Will Absolve Me*, in which he mentions prisoner torture, mutilation, and dismemberment and states that Batista ordered the murder of ten rebel prisoners for each soldier killed. Those statements have hardly been challenged by writers. The day after the Moncada attack, Batista said in a speech that "criminal hands . . . knifed our soldiers guarding the entrances of the garrison."[1] A decade later Batista wrote in his memoirs, *Cuba Betrayed*, that Castro "did not appear at the tragic scene of the fighting."[2] In 1968 Mario Riera Hernández published *Cuba Libre 1895–1958*, in which he purports that all eighteen soldiers in the Moncada garrison had been knifed to death. He also wrote that the rebels who seized the Civil Hospital had "slit the throats of soldiers and civilians in their beds" and that they "cut the bellies of pregnant women, slashing the neck of a young handicapped woman whom they first raped."[3] Col. Orlando Piedra Negueruela, Batista's chief of intelligence, stated in his 1994 reminiscences that Castro "did not participate in the attack" and that the rebels "massacred all the sick men who were in their beds."[4] Five years later Batista's brother-in-law Roberto Fernández Miranda indicated in his autobiography that during the Moncada attack "more than 20 soldiers had been killed, among them a few operated on in the nearby hospital, stabbed to death in their sickly beds."[5]

This work corrects these and other enthroned historical inaccuracies and describes why Fidel Castro chose to attack a citadel instead of attempting to assassinate Batista that same day at a Varadero Beach regatta festivity; how the Military Intelligence Service (SIM), through an informant, almost uncovered the conspiracy; exclusive details of the capture and murder of rebel prisoners; how Castro made no plans to initiate guerrilla warfare after the failure of the Moncada attack; how, after hiding for a week, the rebel leader initially made plans to flee the island and then secretly negotiated his surrender through a peasant family that contacted the archbishop of Santiago de Cuba; and the reasons why Castro was not summarily executed after his arrest, a fate which befell two-thirds of his captured followers.

After Castro seized power in January 1959, his regime's "official history" systematically modified the Moncada and Bayamo events, weaving fact and fiction, to foment Castro's personality cult. It focuses on the Moncada action and minimizes the role of the Bayamo attack, whose three leaders publicly broke with Castro in 1955. This propagandistic campaign, under the watchful eye of government censors, was spearheaded by *Bohemia* reporter Marta Rojas, who had initially reported the Moncada events and subsequent trials. She has written eight books and dozens of articles on the subject. Rojas's writings are heavily slanted, especially those written after Castro's closing speech at the Congress of Cuban Writers and Artists on August 22, 1961, where he admonished that their work should be constrained by the dogma "Within the revolution, everything; against the revolution, nothing." As a result, the names of twenty-seven of the ninety-nine surviving rebels, who became dissidents, have been erased from most Cuban history books or tersely labeled "traitor to the revolution."

The first Castro biography, published in Havana in 1959 by the journalist Gerardo Rodríguez Morejón, provides a cursory account of the Moncada attack, without citations, taken entirely from *History Will Absolve Me* and omits naming the Bayamo combatants. That year the journalist Jules Dubois, who covered the 1957–58 guerrilla war for the *Chicago Tribune,* rushed to publish Castro's biography. Dubois describes the insurgents as all under age thirty, although nineteen were thirty or older, and their total number as 200 instead of 160. The rebel Ernesto Tizol, a Sears clerk, is portrayed as a prosperous Miami businessman. Haydée Santamaría is wrongly depicted as having traveled twice to Santiago de Cuba, purchased supplies, and returned from Havana together with another female rebel, Melba Hernández. Raúl Martínez Ararás is correctly identified as a military leader of the movement, but most future writers ignored this important fact. Raúl Castro is erroneously portrayed as the squad leader storming the adjacent Palace of Justice. Dubois's biography describes twenty-six cars in the rebel convoy going to the Moncada attack, instead of sixteen. The vanguard vehicle that reached the Post 3 entrance without mishap is depicted as making a "wrong turn" and having "crashed into a curb." Fidel Castro is armed with a "shotgun" instead of a Luger. The assault is tersely described in one paragraph. Manuel "El Niño" Cala, a fifty-year-old veteran revolutionary killed that day, appears as "A child named Cala." Maj. Rafael Morales Alvarez, whom Castro later complimented for protecting the rebel prisoners, is falsely quoted as telling the arresting officer that "Fidel Castro was not supposed to be brought back alive." Castro's two-hour defense speech is stretched to "five hours," and Dubois dedicates thirty-two pages to quoting *History Will Absolve Me*.[6]

The first book about the Cuban Revolution was written by CBS newsman Robert Taber, *M-26: The Biography of a Revolution,* which was published in 1961 by the leftist press Lyle Stuart. Taber, portraying Fidel Castro as "anti-Yankee and nationalistic" and not a Communist, provides the most inaccurate version ever written about the Moncada attack. This includes calling President Carlos Prío a "former ABC revolutionary." In addition, Castro is "president of the FEU" university student federation, the rebel Ernesto Tizol is "a Miami restaurateur," and fifty-three-year-old Lt. Pedro Sarría, who arrested Castro and never attended college, appears as his university classmate. Raúl Castro is wrongly portrayed as the squad leader occupying the Palace of Justice. The Moncada attackers are intercepted by a lieutenant in a patrol jeep that has a mounted machine gun, instead of by two military police on foot. The rebel Gustavo Arcos is shot by the fictitious lieutenant and is also "riddled" by a machine-gun burst that "caught him full in the body," instead of being hit once in the lower back by friendly fire. "Fifty" rebels, instead of five, enter the compound, and Jesús Montané and Ramiro Valdés purportedly hold at bay fifty-five soldiers in a dormitory, while "Fidel appeared briefly in the barracks." The fallacy of placing Castro inside the citadel has never been repeated by other writers. In Taber's work the battle lasts nearly two hours, rather than under thirty minutes, and the number of military wounded is fifty-seven, instead of thirty. Taber exploits the Black Legend; he claims that Abel Santamaría had "his eyes gouged out, while in an adjoining cell his sister, Haydée, listened to his shrieks of agony," and that captured rebels were "tortured, castrated, and otherwise mutilated." Castro's two-hour self-defense speech is stretched to "five hours."[7]

In 1965 the French novelist Robert Merle published *Moncada: Premier combat de Fidel Castro* in Paris. The Moncada veteran and *Granma* expeditionary Jaime Costa Chávez states that Merle was hired by the Cuban government to write the book. Some of its chapters were later translated into Spanish and published in Cuban periodicals. Merle interviewed sixty rebel combatants, six civilian participants, and only one army officer, Lieutenant Sarría, who arrested Castro and later aided his guerrillas. He did not interview any other Batista military personnel or rebel dissidents and omitted from his bibliography works critical of the Cuban Revolution. That same year the regime's Ediciones Revolución published *Mártires del Moncada,* a compilation of sixty-eight brief hagiographies of Moncada and Bayamo rebels who perished on July 26 and during the subsequent guerrilla campaign. The work was produced by twenty-two government writers and coordinated by Marta Rojas. It mistakenly identifies as insurgents two civilians killed by the authorities in Santiago de Cuba, Eduardo Hernández and Francisco Viera Milián. *Mártires del Moncada* correctly describes its subjects as mostly poor or lower-middle-class Ortodoxo Party members with a primary education. It asserts that Mario Martínez Ararás said that he was ready to die for the new Socialist fatherland "that Fidel has envisioned for us." Mario's brother, Raúl, denounced that statement as an outright lie.[8]

The 1969 biography of Fidel Castro by *New York Times* reporter Herbert Matthews wrongly describes the rebels: "None of them was as much as thirty years old; most were university graduates.... Half of them were to die." The following year K. S. Karol, a Marxist Polish-French intellectual, published *Guerrillas in Power: The Course of the Cuban Revolution* with a brief but highly distorted Moncada version. Antonio "Ñico" López, who botched the Bayamo attack by forgetting the wire cutter for breaching the camp's rear fence, is erroneously elevated to "third in command" of the movement. The rebels went to the Moncada in "trucks" that were "decked out in gay flags—it was carnival night." Dr. Mario Muñoz, and not Abel Santamaría, led the group taking the Civil Hospital. After being captured, Santamaría's "eyes were torn out and handed to his sister." Fidel and Raúl Castro erroneously escaped together and a week later "allowed themselves to be taken prisoner." That same year Ernst Halperin produced *Fidel Castro's Road to Power: Cuban Politics from Machado to Moncada*. It was based on secondary sources, and the Moncada account relied mostly on Merle's *Moncada*.[9]

British historian Hugh Thomas's monumental *Cuba: The Pursuit of Freedom* appeared in 1971. Twenty-one of its 1,696 pages are dedicated to the July 26 attack and the events leading up to it. The author relied mostly on Merle and *Mártires del Moncada* and on the answers in a written questionnaire that he had mailed to Raúl Martínez Ararás, whose name he misspelled. He excludes the first names of many subjects and mentions the rebel Angel Díaz-Francisco only by his nickname "Patachula." Thomas erroneously places Castro at the university distributing arms on the day of the Batista coup d'état. The rebel José Ponce is wrongly identified as a Freemason, and the important role of Castro's paramour, Natalia "Naty" Revuelta, is insignificant. Jesús Montané is called the fiancé of Melba Hernández, although he was married to another woman. The sixteen cars of the Moncada attack convoy appear as twenty-six in Thomas's work. Raúl Castro is equivocally portrayed as an attack leader. The five-man rebel vanguard allegedly enters a dormitory full of soldiers. Inside the Moncada there are one thousand soldiers, rather than four hundred, and the rebel dead toll is sixty-eight, instead of sixty-one. Batista's secretary is depicted as meeting with the archbishop of Santiago de Cuba, although this never occurred. These errors were repeated in future accounts citing Thomas. The author claims that Abel Santamaría and Reinaldo Boris Luis were "apparently tortured to death." Thomas believed that "Had it not been for the repression, the Moncada attack would doubtless have been dismissed as one more wild and semi-gangster incident in the life of Fidel Castro."[10]

In 1972 Rolando E. Bonachea and Nelson P. Valdés, Cuban-American scholars and supporters of the revolution, edited *Revolutionary Struggle 1947–1958: Volume I of the Selected Works of Fidel Castro*. Their description of the July 26 insurrection repeats previous errors and adds others. The Bayamo attack leaders are wrongly identified as Antonio López and Juan Manuel Márquez, the latter of whom was a nonparticipant. The twenty-seven rebel dissidents and Naty Revuelta are omitted from this account. The insurgent Ernesto Tizol erroneously "owned a business in Miami," and Melba Hernández is mistakenly credited with "persuading an army sergeant" to obtain uniforms for the conspirators. The authors state that "most of the attackers" lived in Artemisa, although only 28 of the 160 rebels resided there. Raúl Castro incorrectly appears as the Palace of Justice attack leader. The insurgent convoy contains twenty-six cars instead of sixteen, rebel weaponry mistakenly includes "knives," and the convoy runs into "an army sentry jeep" instead of a two-man foot patrol. Two attackers who never left the Civil Hospital try to reach a non-existent "nearby radio station," and the thirty-minute attack on the Post 3 entrance lasts for "hours." The authors wrote, "Few revolutionaries had escaped the military roundup," although 48 got away. In addition, the tally of 53 prisoners murdered is inflated to "eighty men." Castro's trial, previously announced in the newspapers and opened to the press and the public, is held in "the greatest secrecy."[11]

For the twentieth anniversary of the Moncada attack, the History Section of the Political Directorate of the Revolutionary Armed Forces in 1972 began publishing a three-volume "official history," which was completed in 1983 and totaled 1,084 pages. Covering the revolutionary period 1952–55, the work is a compilation of segments of Cuban periodical articles, book chapters, documents, *History Will Absolve Me*, and original interviews with twenty rebels, Judge Juan Mejías and his daughter, and public defender Baudilio Castellanos. The combatants Juan Almeida and Mario Lazo added to the government's version by penning their memoirs.[12]

Two years later the Cuban exile scholars Ramón L. Bonachea and Marta San Martín published *The Cuban Insurrection 1952–1959*. In this work the July 26 account lacks new information and is based mostly on books and articles published in Cuba after 1959. Raúl Castro heads the Palace of Justice assault, and the Bayamo attack is mistakenly led by the martyrs "Mario Martínez Arará [sic], Ñico López and Hugo Camejo," although the latter deserted at the last moment. Oscar Alcalde, the Thion Laboratory bookkeeper, is described as owning the firm, instead of Dr. Filiberto Ramírez Corría. In the erroneous version of the Moncada attack, "Castro's car was fired on by a patrol car," and three surviving rebels "entered one of the barracks and exchanged fire with about 50 soldiers." Jesús Montané, who turned himself in on July 29, is depicted as surrendering with Castro three days later.[13]

In 1975 Herbert Matthews published *Revolution in Cuba,* without citations, and included a twenty-four-page Moncada chapter. He admits relying extensively on "the official story" for details of the attack. Thus, Matthews portrays the rebels who seized the Civil Hospital under gunfire and subversive shouts as being "welcomed by the nurses and staff," most of whom in reality hid with fear. The author honors revolutionary propaganda to the point of calling the three Bayamo leaders who broke with Castro in 1955 "traitors." He erroneously credits Castro, instead of Raúl Gómez García, with preparing the "Manifesto to the Nation." Castro's underground *El Acusador,* a four-page mimeographed bulletin, is called a "magazine." Melba Hernández is falsely portrayed as "the fiancée of Jesús Montané." Raúl Castro and Ñico López are erroneously given a commanding role. A nonexistent "patrol car" intercepts the rebel caravan at Post 3. The vanguard that enters the garrison allegedly holds "fifty unarmed soldiers prisoner." Haydée and Melba purportedly witness "prisoners being tortured and murdered." The rebel toll is sixty-seven dead, instead of sixty-one, and Castro's capture is erroneously credited to "an informer." The military commander of the district inaccurately appears as "General Martín Tamayo," who was stationed in Havana, instead of Col. Alberto del Río Chaviano. Matthews does place the events in historic perspective when quoting Castro's guerrilla secretary Celia Sánchez as saying, "The Cuban Revolution was born at Moncada."[14]

Another journalist, Lionel Martin, in 1978 published *The Early Fidel: Roots of Castro's Communism* with Lyle Stuart. It contains an eighteen-page Moncada chapter, with only one page describing the action in Bayamo and Santiago de Cuba, which lasts "two hours." The rest of the chapter mostly infers that Fidel Castro and Abel Santamaría "were convinced Marxists by this time," that some rebels had Communist inclinations, that Hugo Camejo's Marianao cell had "organized a Marxist study group," and that Fernando Chenard, head of La Ceiba rebels, had "educated other members of his cell along Marxist lines." These flimsy arguments, based on various articles published in the official newspaper *Granma* in July 1973, were negated by Raúl Martínez Araras, who led the Marianao group into combat at Bayamo, and Mario Chanes, the second-in-command of the La Ceiba cell. Martin states that his conclusions were reinforced by giving full credence to Castro's "retrospective statements," a minefield that most writers gingerly trod upon. The author relied on secondhand information from two Cuban army officers in the 1970s; they credited Castro with saying that a selected group of the movement's leadership held study sessions to analyze Communist books. Martin quotes another Castro government official as saying, "Only a Marxist could have written the Moncada Manifesto." The reader can judge if the document, reproduced in appendix 5, has the Marxist inclination that neither I nor other scholars have been able to perceive.[15]

Preface xvii

The most substantial tome on the events of July 26 is the journalist Mario Mencia's *El Grito del Moncada*, published in Cuba in 1986. Forty pages of the 706-page book are dedicated to the actual combat. It lacks a bibliography, some paragraphs are borrowed from Merle's earlier work, and the rest of the account relies heavily on the three-volume "official history." Surprisingly, Mencia omits the Black Legend by ending his work at the point where the attackers failed to enter the garrison.

That same year two Fidel Castro biographies were published by *New York Times* reporter Tad Szulc and the psychiatrist Peter G. Bourne, a former presidential assistant to Jimmy Carter. Six chapters (112 pages) of Szulc's 703-page *Fidel: A Critical Portrait* are dedicated to the revolutionary events of 1952–55. It is based on the "official" histories published by Marta Rojas, Robert Merle, and Mario Mencia and on interviews with the rebels Ramiro Valdés, Melba Hernández, and Pedro Miret. Szulc relied on the last two as "sources for the development of the military wing of the Movement," although Melba was not part of it. The author claims that "Moncada is the cornerstone of modern Cuban history." He points out that "Castro goes on weaving and re-creating his own myths about himself," adding, "If it suits him at a given moment, he embellishes memories and he manipulates them." Szulc falls into this fantasy trap by stating that as early as October 1947, "there was no question that [Eduardo] Chibás and the twenty-one-year-old Castro were Cuba's most important opposition leaders."[16]

Szulc repeats the Black Legend of rebel prisoner eye-gouging and torture and mistakenly has Castro, instead of Baudilio Castellanos, truncheoned by the police during a protest at the American Embassy in 1949. The third issue of the clandestine bulletin *El Acusador* is ballooned up to "ten thousand copies" instead of the five hundred printed. Ramiro Valdés, instead of Pepe Suárez, erroneously appears as the organizing leader of the Artemisa cell. The Artemisa group, which had twenty-eight combatants, gets inflated to "250 volunteers," and the rebel death toll of sixty-one is raised to sixty-nine. Abel Santamaría, a bookkeeper without a high school degree, is portrayed as an "accountant." Raúl Martínez Ararás is omitted from the core of the movement, and Ñico López substitutes for him in the leadership role. Aramís Taboada is incorrectly called a Moncada fighter, and Alfredo "El Chino" Esquivel is wrongly portrayed as a movement member. The Siboney farm, rented as a rebel safe house, appears as purchased by Tizol. A photograph of Castro with his son taken by a *Bohemia* reporter during a prison visit at the Isle of Pines is erroneously identified as a farewell snapshot before the Moncada attack. Szulc has geographic disorientation when he says that after leaving Havana, Castro had breakfast in El Cobre (Oriente Province) before reaching Las Villas. Raúl Castro is incorrectly given command of the Palace of Justice group at the last moment. The rebel vanguard that penetrated the garrison is depicted as being killed in front of the entrance gate. Teodulio Mitchel, who drove Castro to Siboney, is mistaken for a Bayamo combatant. Castro's captor, Lieutenant Sarría, is called a Freemason, although he never belonged to the fraternity. Col. Manuel Ugalde Carrillo, who was in Havana the day of the attack, is spuriously accused of having "ordered and carried out the murders of the captured *Fidelistas*."

Bourne's *Fidel* contains a fifteen-page chapter on the July 26 insurrection based on four rebel interviews and seven book sources. The author errs in giving Jesús Montané a leadership role and saying that he is wounded during the assault. The insurgent convoy has twenty-six cars, rather than sixteen, and Castro fights with a "shotgun" instead of a Luger. A perimeter foot patrol rides a nonexistent jeep; "fifty" rebels, rather than five, penetrate the Moncada; and they enter a dormitory, although they penetrate a different administrative wing. The archbishop of Santiago de Cuba and Batista's secretary hold a meeting that never occurred. Capt. Agustín Lavastida is called "Manuel" Lavastida, and credence is given to the Black Legend accounts of rebel torture and eye-gouging.[17]

The syndicated journalist Georgie Anne Geyer, who covered Latin America for twenty-five years, in 1991 published *Guerrilla Prince: The Untold Story of Fidel Castro*. It contains a fifteen-page chapter entitled "Moncada." Geyer interviewed Haydée Santamaría and four rebel participants to describe the events of July 26, 1953. She also relied on the Tad Szulc recorded interviews in the University of Miami Archives and other secondary sources. As a result, Geyer mistakenly has the Moncada chief Col. Alberto del Río Chaviano residing in Siboney instead of opposite the garrison, and Abel Santamaría's apartment, in a seven-story building, is portrayed as a "little house." Dr. Mario Muñoz is wrongly identified as the rebel radio operator for the uprising, and the insurgent convoy contains the wrong number of vehicles. Raúl Castro leads the Palace of Justice seizure, while his brother packs a "submachine gun" rather than a handgun. *Granma* journalist Tomás Toledo mistakenly appears as an attacker, and there are one thousand soldiers inside the Moncada, instead of fewer than four hundred. In addition, Geyer repeats the phony Black Legend of prisoner mutilation.

The historian Robert Quirk's 898-page *Fidel Castro,* published in 1993, erroneously places Raúl Castro in a movement leadership role, in command of the Palace of Justice squad, and later fleeing with his brother and others to the mountains. Quirk borrowed from Bonachea and Valdés's *Revolutionary Struggle* to repeat the mistakes of crediting Melba Hernández with "persuading an army sergeant" to get uniforms for the conspirators and having the rebel vanguard storming the Moncada "armed with knives." The author claims that there were no nearby buildings to provide cover for the insurgents. The main attacking force, in fact, entrenched itself in the military housing project adjacent to the garrison.[18]

In 1998 Gladys Marel García-Pérez, a research staffer at the Cuban government's Institute of History, published *Insurrection & Revolution: Armed Struggle in Cuba,*

1952–1959. It is part of the Studies in Cuban History series edited by Louis A. Pérez Jr., whose own Cuban history works mention the July 26 insurrection in scant terms. García-Pérez's 137-page book, in spite of its subsuming title, is limited to the events in Matanzas Province. She presents no new information on what she calls the "Moncada Project." Strictly adhering to the "official history" censorship agenda, García-Pérez omits Matanzas rebel leaders Raúl and Mario Martínez Ararás (the latter a July 26 martyr) and Héctor de Armas Errasti, who bought most of the rebel rifles. Dr. Mario Muñoz is incorrectly elevated to "chief of the movement in Matanzas and member of its national leadership," an allegation negated by his widow and other rebels and unsupported in scholarly work. The attackers, who disguise themselves with khaki army uniforms, are purportedly wearing "the rebels' olive green uniform." René Fraga Moreno, a nonparticipant not mentioned in any other Moncada account, "had joined the insurgency at the beginning, [and] was one of the principal participants."[19]

The latest Castro biography, by British diplomat Leycester Coltman and titled *The Real Fidel Castro* (2003), is seriously hampered by no citations. The first names of all pre-1959 military and police personnel are excluded, and none appears in the index. Fidel Castro is depicted as showing concern that when picking his followers for the attack, "none of those selected had children." In contrast, *Mártires del Moncada* points out that many of the rebels had offspring, dozens of whom became orphaned. The rebel Ñico López, an illiterate, unskilled laborer of Spanish parents, is twice erroneously identified as a black man employed as a printer. The name of Castros chauffeur, Teodulio Mitchel, is misspelled. The bookkeeper Abel Santamaría is described as an "accountant in a car dealership." The Bayamo attack is limited to only one paragraph. Coltman wrongly assumes that the blood-stained Moncada officers' barbershop, where the last skirmish occurred, had been "used for the torture sessions" of prisoners. The author claims that the army chief of staff, instead of Batista, issued the orders "to preserve the life of captured rebels." He repeats the fallacy that Lieutenant Sarría had studied at the University of Havana when Castro was a student. The book perpetuates the myth that after the Moncada attack failed, Castro, "with just two companions," was going to "start the slow process of building up a guerrilla force" in the Sierra Maestra Mountains. In fact, Castro had been secretly negotiating with the mining-truck driver René Celeiro to get him out of the region and had told his companions that he planned on going into exile abroad to save the revolution. Coltman wrongly states that the subsequent sedition trial had been censored in the news media and that during testimony, "an army witness disclosed that interrogators had extracted both Abel's eyes with a bayonet." These affirmations are disproved by contemporary newspaper accounts and the testimony of defense attorneys.[20]

My interest in the July 26 events developed when I was a history undergraduate doing an assigned review of *History Will Absolve Me*. I read Castro's denunciation of

Sgt. Eulalio González, whom he called "The Tiger," and described González as meriting distinction "in the annals of evil" for having "with his own hands murdered our comrade Abel Santamaría." Historical curiosity led me to look up his name in the Miami, Florida, telephone book and call the number. The gruff voice that answered suspiciously questioned my motivation. I then spent twenty minutes identifying myself and my historical interest in the topic before the listener acknowledged his identity. My inquisitiveness was further aroused when González stated that his moniker was "El Mulo" (The Mule) because he had worked with the army mule transport for two decades. He assumed that Castro called him "The Tiger" to depict him as ferocious. During the following year, I recorded various interviews with González on the front porch of his working-class neighborhood residence on S.W. Fourth Street. His wife Angelina always greeted me by providing an unsolicited glass of milk. Neither owned a car, and one day after González asked me to drive his wife to a relative's house, on the way there she told me privately: "My husband never killed anyone. He just talks a lot. When Batista fled, he wanted to turn himself in to prove his innocence, but I convinced him to seek asylum in the Chilean Embassy." This version of González as a harmless braggadocio was later confirmed by all the military personnel whom I interviewed and who knew him. The truth is that those who murdered the rebel prisoners kept quiet and let the opprobrium fall on González. Angelina's revelations prompted me during other interviews to include the input of family members, who sometimes filled in the memory gaps of the interviewee.

El Mulo indicated that former lieutenant Angel Machado Rofe had a barbershop on Twelfth Avenue and Flagler Street, where I became a regular customer. Machado, in turn, introduced me to some Moncada personnel, and I located others through the Miami phonebook, always mentioning when speaking with them that I had already spoken with their former comrades. Most of the interviews were audio-recorded, and the interviewees received a typed transcript copy. This allowed them to discuss, rectify, or add forgotten details. I also interviewed the funeral director who retrieved the rebel and military cadavers, physicians who treated the wounded on both sides and signed the death certificates, the rural family who arranged Castro's surrender, defense attorneys, codefendants, political leaders, and the judge who presided over the sedition trial. Almost all of these people had never been previously questioned about their historic roles. The 115 interviews were conducted by the author in Spanish between 1974 and 2005 in eight different states, Puerto Rico, and Cuba. Forty-one interviews were done via telephone due to travel constraints. Only four interviewees, three military men and the politico Raúl Chibás, requested not to be recorded but personally spoke at length while I took notes. Four others claimed to remember little or outright refused to talk about the events. Some military interviewees requested that I stop the tape recorder while they described the prisoner executions or provided other controversial information. Further information was obtained during unrecorded follow-up telephone conversations. Each interview was done with a combination of open-ended and specific questions and their corresponding answers, usually in the home or office of the interviewee. The interviews averaged about sixty minutes, ranging from under half an hour to more than six hours. The questions started with the persons' backgrounds and how those led to their involvement in the events of July 26, 1953. The respondents then generally moved the discussion to specific participation, most of it previously undocumented. The interviews gradually gravitated toward the controversial questions of casualties on both sides and allegations of prisoner torture.

Problems developed when some interviewees were deceptive, misleading, had faulty memory, or exaggerated their participation or that of others. At first these reactions prompted some confusion, until others clarified the discrepancy. For example, some soldiers affirmed that the Moncada attack ended by 8:00 A.M. while other interviewees indicated that "fighting" could be heard inside the citadel as late as 11:00 A.M. The inconsistency went unsolved for a year, until Pvt. Armando Oliva clarified that after the army resumed control at 8:00 A.M., a faction of unscrupulous officers carried out the vengeful execution of prisoners inside the garrison for the next three hours. To those outside the Moncada, the shooting sounded like an internal sporadic battle. Regimental intelligence chief Capt. Agustín Lavastida, who abetted the murders, falsely insisted that Abel Santamaría and the eighteen rebels captured in the Civil Hospital had died in combat inside the garrison. Soldiers who abhorred the massacre and Lavastida's dishonesty discredited his inaccurate version. Career officers informed me that army personnel had strongly divided loyalties between the corrupt Moncada chief, Col. Alberto del Río Chaviano, and the upright inspector general Maj. Rafael Morales Alvarez. The colonel promised during a 1974 telephone interview to send me his written version of the events but failed to do so before passing away four years later. I played both military antagonists against each other to arrive at the truth. All of the interview quotes in this book are generally substantiated by at least another oral or published account. My research interviews were not part of an oral history project, and I therefore obtained only verbal consent to record them. More than half of the interviewees have since died. Copies of the digitalized tapes and transcripts have been donated to the Cuban Heritage Collection of the University of Miami Library, Miami, Florida, and appear on the Internet at http://www.latinamericanstudies.org/entrevistas.htm.

In 1983 I located in Miami the Bayamo rebel leaders Raúl Martínez Ararás and Orlando Castro García, the latter recently released from a Cuban prison. They facilitated my interviewing their comrades in exile, including Jaime Costa Chávez, who initially evaded me. Raúl's perception of the impartiality of my work led him to admit after two years that his brother-in-law Ernesto Tizol, the rebel military strategist, had deserted on the way to the Moncada attack. As a result, one-third of the insurgents were deviated from the route and never reached their objective. This book could not have been completed without the crucial testimony of the rebels Gustavo Arcos and Mario Chanes. Arcos rode with Fidel Castro to the Moncada gate and was the first to shoot, while Chanes was one of the seven fugitives captured with the rebel leader a week later. When Chanes was allowed to leave Cuba in 1993, after completing a thirty-year prison sentence for seditious conspiracy, Raúl and Orlando arranged my interview with him, although Mario was rejecting all media requests. The recorded session lasted nearly seven hours, over a two-day period, and I later provided Chanes with a sixty-seven-page, single-spaced transcript to review. Four years later Orlando Castro and his wife Georgina Cid, a former political prisoner, were able to connect me on their telephone with Gustavo Arcos and Jesús Yanez Pelletier in Havana. Yanez was the army lieutenant and penitentiary supervisor who refused to poison Fidel Castro while Castro was in his custody. Orlando and Georgina had previously arranged for me to send smuggled questionnaires to both persecuted dissident leaders. Their replies were the basis for our lengthy telephone interviews, arranged through an intermediary, at a specific time via a private number. Orlando declined my offer to pay the expensive phone charges.

All the rebel interviewees were proud of their attempt to overthrow Batista and affirmed that their main motivation was to restore a democratic constitutional government. None expressed personal economic or social reasons for joining the cause. In retrospect, they regarded Fidel Castro as an ambitious manipulator who betrayed the promises of the "Manifesto to the Nation," which is void of Communist ideology and anti-American rhetoric. The military interviewees regarded themselves as doing their duty in repulsing a sneak attack that in some cases killed unarmed comrades and relatives. They denounced a revolution that upon victory established the longest dictatorship in Cuban history, employed kangaroo courts that executed thousands of its opponents, created a brutal prison system condemned by human rights organizations, turned the island into a Soviet outpost, sent its army to fight foreign wars for decades, and caused more than one million Cubans to flee their homeland, with thousands of rafters drowning at sea.

When this work was started, a dozen important interviewees were in Castro's prisons. Their memories proved to have retained the greatest details, possibly as a result of up to thirty years in isolation. These included the rebels Mario Chanes, Orlando Castro, Moisés Mafut, Manuel Suardíaz, Cpls. Norberto Batista Seguí and Néstor Reyes Martín, and Pvt. José Ferrá Mulet. The corporals and the policeman Evelio Xenis showed me the scars from the bullet wounds they received during the Moncada attack. Corporal Batista Seguí had for years filled out the Moncada payroll and vividly recalled most full names and ranks. The 115 testimonies I gathered are complemented by numerous other published Cuban sources and the declassified dispatches of the American Embassy in Havana to the U.S. Department of State.

On July 26, 2003, the fiftieth anniversary of the Moncada attack, Fidel Castro held a celebration in Havana with twenty-one of the thirty-one remaining Moncada veterans in Cuba. Gustavo Arcos and other dissident veterans were not invited. Instead, Arcos sent a letter to the international news media that appears in appendix 6. That same day my wife Carlina and I returned to visit eighty-four-year-old Moncada veteran Eduardo Montano Benítez in Passaic, New Jersey. Montano's tiny one-chair barbershop in Havana, where he lived in a back room with his wife Santa and his daughter Yolanda, had been a center of rebel conspiracy. He fought at Moncada and was among the last seven fugitives to be captured with Fidel Castro. When Castro began fomenting Communist indoctrination to his followers during their imprisonment in the Isle of Pines penitentiary, Montano became disillusioned, and he left the movement after the 1955 amnesty. After the rebels seized power in 1959, Montano, based on personal conviction and principle, turned down government job offers and special invitations to July 26 celebrations. In 1965 the Communist government nationalized his barbershop. Montano and his family went into exile in Spain in 1969, and two years later they migrated to Passaic. He continued the barber trade, and his wife obtained employment as a maid. Montano's daughter moved out after getting married, and his wife passed away in 1995.

Montano made the admirable choice of living modestly but with honor and dignity, rather than betraying his principles in exchange for the perks and comfortable lifestyle that he would have received as a Communist revolutionary hero in Cuba. He survives in abject poverty, with four cats, in an inner-city, third-floor walk-up, one-bedroom apartment. The foam cushions on his couch lost their covers years ago, and the armrests are worn down to the bare wood. In the apartment's rear balcony hang the tattered and faded flags of Cuba and the United States that were unfurled upon his arrival. Montano stays indoors most of the time because it is painful for him to walk. The dark veins in his lower legs are swollen and bubbled up, and they sometimes burst. The physicians have told him that they can do nothing short of amputation. Montano regrets that he is no longer useful to his homeland. He used to retrieve soda cans discarded along the roadside and recycled them for meager cash that he donated to Cuban exile organizations.

When my wife and I visited Montano's home on July 26, 2003, he greeted us with an effusive embrace, and with tearful eyes his first words were "Nos han quitado la patria" (They have taken our homeland from us). Montano spent most of that afternoon talking about Cuba. Yolanda regularly takes him newspaper accounts about Cuba that she prints from the Internet. Montano acknowledged his gratitude and love for America but yearns to see his homeland free from despotism before he dies. When told that this book was finally going to press, he exclaimed, "I probably will not live to see it, but my daughter and future generations will read it. That is what is important."

On July 26, 2004, I was invited to speak about this manuscript as part of Miami's WDLP-TV Channel 22 *María Elvira Confronta* program hosted by María Elvira Salazar. The other panelists were Bayamo attack rebel leader Orlando Castro García, Moncada insurgent Jaime Costa Chávez, Moncada soldier Ariel Matos, and the historian Enrique Ros. Prior to the start of the show, the former adversaries of the July 26 rebellion shook hands in a gesture of reconciliation. It reminded me of a similar event on the fiftieth anniversary of the Battle of Gettysburg, where aged veterans of the Civil War met to greet each other as Americans and to overcome their former animosities. During the TV program, Orlando Castro summarized the events of the birth of the Cuban Revolution by saying, "[I]f we continue with those errors, lacking maturity and a sense of historic responsibility, Cuba will never be a civilized republic. We have to tread the path of political solutions every time that it is possible." It is my hope that one day his vision will become a reality.

INTRODUCTION

In Santiago de Cuba at 5:15 A.M. every July 26 since 1959, 135 selected schoolchildren have arrived at the Moncada fortress in vintage American cars, dressed in khaki clothes, and wielding .22-caliber rifles with blanks to reenact the attack led by Fidel Castro in 1953. National Rebellion Day is Communist Cuba's most important national holiday marking the birth of the Cuban Revolution. The government organizes a massive rally, and Castro traditionally pronounces a major speech. At the time of the fifty-third anniversary celebration in Bayamo, on July 26, 2006, it seemed likely this would be Castro's final public oratory. The Moncada attack, aggrandized over the years to mythical proportions, distinguished Castro as a legitimate revolutionary and an independent political leader. It is exalted in the preamble of the Cuban Communist Constitution of 1976. The sixty-one rebels who died in the endeavor belong to the national pantheon of revolutionary martyrs. Their images appear on postal envelopes and billboards, and their names are emblazoned on parks, public buildings, municipalities, and industrial complexes named after them. Scenes of the assault of the Moncada garrison appear on currency bills and postage stamps. A one-cent stamp falsely depicts the Moncada enveloped in smoke and flames. Thousands of commemorative silver coins of the Moncada attack, in ten- and twenty-peso denominations, were issued in 1988 and 1993. Castro's subsequent trial defense speech, published as *History Will Absolve Me,* is the unquestionable scripture of the revolution and is mandatory reading for all Cuban students. The document, frequently interpreted and analyzed, is the most cited work in Cuba. Revolutionary minister of education Armando Hart states in his memoirs, "On an intellectual level, *History Will Absolve Me* stands as the highest achievement of Cuban thought in the 1950s." He adds that "Moncada forms part of the birth of the Cuban Revolution, which proclaimed its socialist character in 1961." The "26 of July Hymn," composed three days before the attack, is intoned at official functions along with the national anthem, and the red-and-black 26 of July flag is displayed alongside the national flag. The year 2003 was christened by the Cuban government as "Glorious Anniversaries of Martí and Moncada."[1]

Fidel Castro, a twenty-six-year-old attorney, assaulted the second-largest army citadel on the island with 135 followers lacking military skills. A simultaneous attack on the Bayamo army barracks was led by Raúl Martínez Ararás, a thirty-four-year-old accountant, with 24 insurgents. Their goal was to overthrow the dictatorship of Maj. Gen. Fulgencio Batista, who had seized power through a coup d'état sixteen months earlier, and restore the 1940 constitution. The insurgents, wearing ill-fitting army uniforms and armed with handguns, shotguns, .22-caliber rifles, and a fistful of bullets, fought soldiers equipped with machine guns and hand grenades and who outnumbered them four to one. After a brief skirmish, the attackers at Moncada and Bayamo fled in disarray. It was the only time in the history of the republic that one of the eight regimental headquarters had been attacked. The daring feat would not be repeated by Castro's troops during the guerrilla campaign of 1956–58. The uprising was not patterned after a traditional revolution. Fidel Castro's early efforts to attract the masses through clandestine, limited shortwave radio broadcasts and a mimeographed bulletin had had insignificant results. He clearly defined his motivation in a letter to Luis Conte Agüero on December 12, 1953, saying that his struggle had been carried out by Ortodoxo Party youths as a "heroic immolation to raise the faith of the people," and their purpose had been "to place power in the hands of the most fervent Ortodoxos." All political parties shunned the revolt, including the Communists, who denounced it as a "bourgeois putsch." In court, Castro portrayed his movement as nationalistic and democratic, devoid of Communist ideology. The "Manifesto to the Nation" and *History Will Absolve Me* lack the anti-American rhetoric, Marxist dogma, and totalitarian ideology that later permeated Castro's speeches. These works envisioned a democratic future for the Cuban Republic that was never fulfilled.

The Moncada and Bayamo attacks displayed Fidel Castro's ineptitude as a military tactician. There was hasty preparation, faulty attack strategy, excessive improvisation, and no contingency plan. In addition, some key targets were ignored. The rebels had inadequate arms and ammunition and no medical supplies, and some lacked training with the weapons issued to them. More than a dozen last-minute desertions occurred in Santiago de Cuba and Bayamo, although Castro tried dissuading them by purporting that army conspirators awaited inside the citadel. One-third of the Moncada attackers never reached their destination after being deviated from their route by a fleeing squad leader. At least four rebels were wounded by friendly fire. Castro had little control of his poorly trained followers, who gunned down in the military hospital a patient and an orderly. In addition, he abandoned on the battlefield more than a dozen dead and wounded rebels during a disorganized retreat.

Government casualties amounting to nineteen dead and thirty wounded prompted a faction of vengeful soldiers during the subsequent four days to murder more than fifty rebel prisoners and strew their cadavers in both garrisons and the countryside to simulate death in combat. It was the largest mass killing of prisoners since the War of Independence. The slaughter, halted after civic and religious leaders appealed to Batista, allowed Castro to turn a military disaster into a political victory. The rebel leader was sentenced to fifteen years in prison by an impartial tribunal, and thirty-one of Castro's followers received lesser terms. He then orchestrated from his cell a successful public-opinion campaign. The political-prisoner status of Castro and his followers granted them special privileges, including conjugal visits and an interview with a *Bohemia* magazine reporter and a photographer. Sympathetic turnkeys smuggled out letters and messages on a daily basis. As a result, Castro garnered sufficient national support to gain his and other rebels' release under a general amnesty after only twenty-two months.

While serving time, Castro wrote what became his revolutionary legacy, *History Will Absolve Me*. The pamphlet casts the "Black Legend" that captured rebels were tortured by soldiers who "shattered their testicles and . . . tore out their eyes" and "dismembered" their bodies. The tormentors purportedly did not spare one of the two female rebels, Haydée Santamaría, "and burned her arms with lighted cigarettes." In order to avoid implicating the real leader, Léster Rodríguez, who managed to escape, this legendary account falsely portrays Raúl Castro, who was captured, as the chief of a squad that seized the Palace of Justice courthouse.

Fidel Castro insisted to a reporter in July 2000 that his plan "was not ill conceived, it was well conceived. I assure you that Batista would have fallen."[2] This book challenges that contention. It analyzes the organizational aspects of the revolt, the rebels' backgrounds and ideologies, the combat strategy, the judicial process, the authenticity of the document *History Will Absolve Me*, the political imprisonment, and the successful amnesty campaign. I provide the testimonies, gathered during thirty-one years, of participants previously neglected by historians, including fourteen rebels, forty-seven military and government personnel, and fifty-four politicians and civilians. I also demonstrate how the soldiers had divided loyalties toward their high command. The military accounts are historically nonexistent, except for two brief interviews published in Cuba in 1963 and 1968. They were tailored with half-truths and falsehoods to fit revolutionary propaganda.

This work also demonstrates that United States policy toward Cuba in 1953 focused on a return to constitutional normalcy, the end of censorship, and cold-war concerns of Communist penetration in the Western Hemisphere. Castro, cognizant of this, had instructed his paramour Naty Revuelta to provide the American Embassy in Havana with a copy of the "Manifesto to the Nation." The document and *History Will Absolve Me* are void of criticism against the United States.

This work analyzes Fidel Castro's complex, out-of-wedlock childhood ruled by an authoritarian, unaffectionate father who did not legally recognize him until he was seventeen years old. He was raised in the rural shack of his maternal grandparents, a foster home, and strict boarding schools and was legally given three different names. His high school education and sense of personal predestination and mission were influenced by Spanish Jesuit priests mixing religious dogma with anti-Communism, anti-Americanism, and the Fascist ideals ruling their homeland. During Castro's university years, his political aspirations were frustrated after he lost a student government election. He then developed a propensity for political violence that filled a police rap sheet. By the time he was twenty-two years old, Castro had already been implicated in two gang murders and two assassination attempts. His revolutionary internationalism had its roots in the 1947 Cayo Confites expedition to invade the Dominican Republic and the 1948 Bogotazo riots in Colombia.

Cuba has a history of addressing political conflicts with violence. Narciso López led two military expeditions from the United States in 1850 and 1851 to overthrow Spanish colonial rule on the island. The Ten Years' War (1868–78) for independence ended in failure. In 1895 José Martí organized a renewed effort, but he died on the battlefield before Spain granted the island autonomy on January 1, 1898. Spanish loyalist riots in Havana and threats against the U.S. Consulate and the lives and property of American citizens prompted the visit of the USS *Maine* to the city. The mysterious explosion of the warship on February 15, 1898, killing 264 sailors, prompted the Spanish-American War. Spanish defeat ended nearly four centuries of colonialism and initiated the era of American protectionism.

The Platt Amendment, approved by the U.S. Congress in 1901 as part of the Army Appropriation Bill, was incorporated by the Cuban constitutional convention into its national charter. The amendment permitted American intervention to preserve peace on the island and to guarantee its independence. The United States could also veto foreign loans or treaties compromising its national security or Cuban sovereignty. A similar limitation was added to the 1904 Panama constitution, under article 136, granting the United States the same rights as under the Platt Amendment in Cuba.

Historians have generally viewed United States–Cuba relations during the republic (1902–58) from the narrow perspective of bilateral relations, instead of from the broader scope of America's regional policy. The United States, under the aegis of the 1904 Roosevelt Corollary to the Monroe Doctrine, militarily intervened fifty times in seven Caribbean basin countries between 1901 and 1928. Cuba, during its first three decades, was presided over by independence generals under the constraints of the Platt Amendment. In 1929 President Gerardo Machado initiated his second term, which was extended from four to six years after a subservient constitutional convention amended the nation's charter and abolished the vice presidency.

This prompted opposition protests, which Machado quelled with repression. As a result, the University Student Directorate (DEU) and the clandestine ABC organization resorted to urban terrorism and assassination to overthrow the government. The ABC manifesto, written by nationalist intellectuals, proposed agrarian reform, nationalization of public utilities, political freedom, and social justice.

The spiraling political violence and social unrest, fueled by the deepening Wall Street crisis that affected the Caribbean basin, led President Franklin Roosevelt to send Ambassador Sumner Welles to Havana on June 1, 1933, to defuse the situation. The ABC welcomed Welles's mediation, while the DEU opposed it. According to Rafael Guas Inclán, the former president of the Chamber of Representatives, when Welles failed to influence the Cuban Congress to impeach Machado, he warned the army high command that they would be dismissed under a Platt Amendment intervention. Machado, pressured by a general strike, went into exile on August 12, 1933, after the armed forces stopped supporting his regime. The military chiefs and Welles installed a provisional government, under the prestigious but irresolute Carlos Manuel de Céspedes, which included ABC members in the cabinet.

The DEU denounced the arrangement and joined forces with the dissatisfied army rank and file led by Sgt. Fulgencio Batista. Céspedes resigned on September 4, 1933, after being informed by anatomy professor Ramón Grau San Martín that the bulk of the army did not back him. The interim government ascended Batista to colonel and chief of the army and gave Grau the presidency six days later. The Grau administration decreed a series of nationalistic social, political, and economic reforms but was unable to restore public order. Batista, partly motivated by the American refusal to recognize Grau, forced the president to resign on January 14, 1934. The Roosevelt government approved the appointment of independence colonel Carlos Mendieta as the new president. The Reciprocity Treaty of 1934 and the Jones-Costigan Act reduced tariffs on Cuban products and created a favorable quota system for Cuban sugar. This established the base for United States–Cuba economic policy during the next twenty-five years. The Platt Amendment was abolished in 1934, when under the postulates of the Good Neighbor Policy the United States temporarily ended its former interventionist role in the Caribbean basin.

Colonel Batista and the army dominated politics through a succession of three presidents until 1940, when Batista won the presidential election under a coalition of political parties, including the Communist Revolutionary Union (URC). A constituent assembly, initially presided over by Grau, drafted the 1940 Constitution, which embodied the goals of the 1933 revolution. The government would have a large role in social and economic development, fostering agrarian reform and the national ownership of natural resources. The 1940 Constitution also proclaimed the right to revolt against illegal and oppressive governments and established a democratic road for Cuba.

The next twelve years were marked by economic prosperity, due to the growth of the sugar industry, as a result of demands created by World War II. New capital went into a nascent domestic industrial production and acquisition of sugar mills, which by 1952 totaled 113 Cuban-owned mills that accounted for 55 percent of all production. The Cuban economy was boosted by the establishment in 1950 of the National Bank of Cuba and soon thereafter of the Agricultural and Development Bank (BANFAIC). That year the Korean War prompted a sharp rise in sugar prices, leading to a proportional increase in wages. Social mobilization accelerated, although there were still inequalities to overcome, especially in the rural sector. During the previous fifty years Cuba had risen to the leading standard-of-living ranks among Latin American nations, although some social and economic ills persisted. By 1952 the country had enjoyed a twelve-year period of democracy and rising prosperity, which was disrupted by the Batista coup d'état. The Moncada attack was the nemesis of that unconstitutional act.[3]

The causes that led to the failure of the July 26 insurrection are probed in the concluding chapter, which also describes the fate of the rebel veterans and of the buildings comprising the scene of the action. The accusation by the Cuban Communist Party that Castro led a "bourgeois putsch" is subjected to a comparative analysis with Adolf Hitler's 1923 Munich beer-hall putsch. The conclusion also examines the outcome of the revolutionary goals proposed in the "Manifesto to the Nation" and *History Will Absolve Me.*

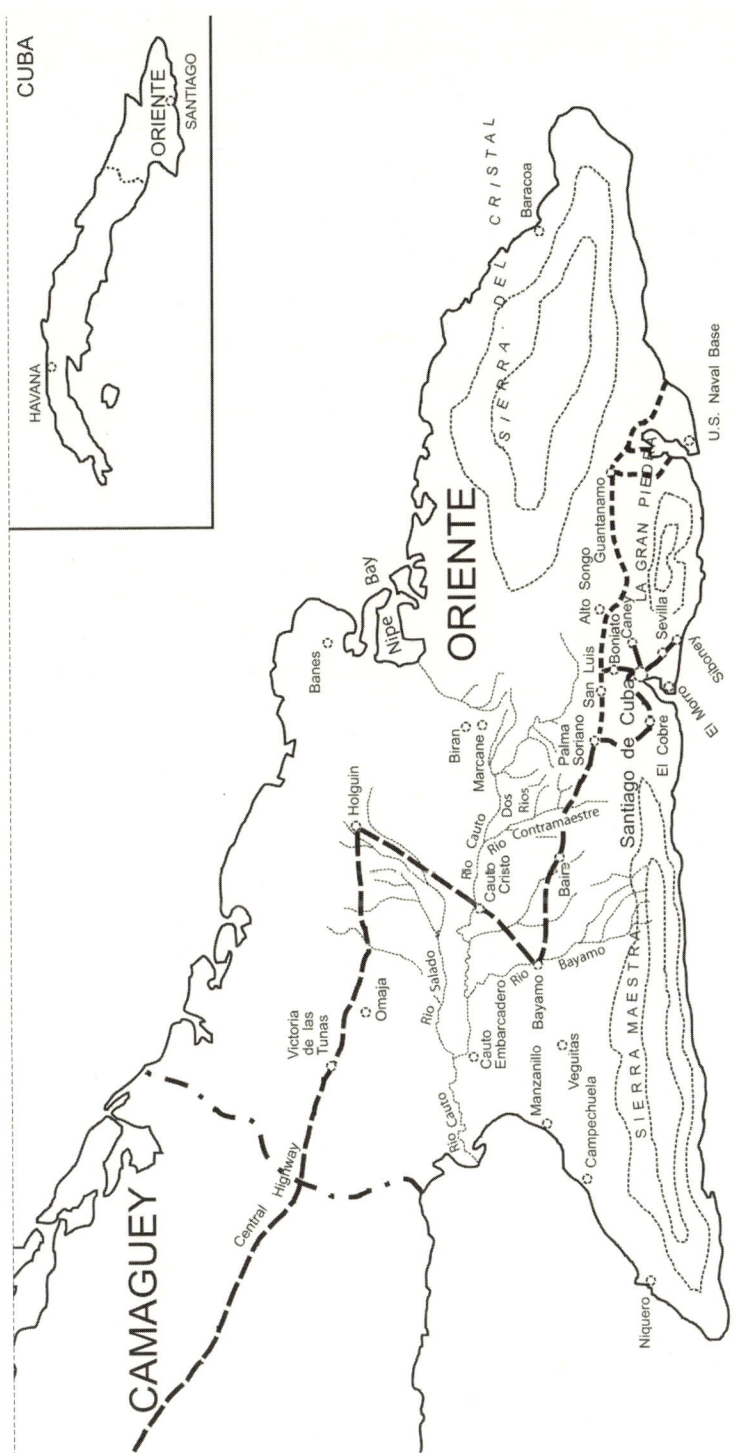

Camagüey and Oriente, with Cuban island inset. Map by N. L. Cooprider

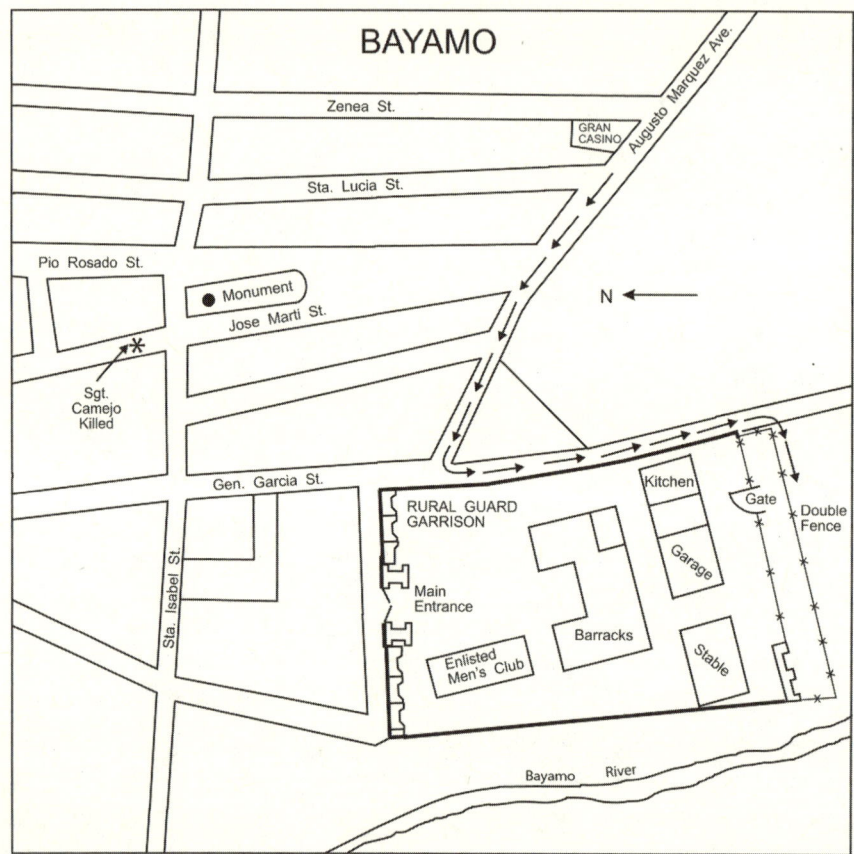

Bayamo. Map by N. L. Cooprider

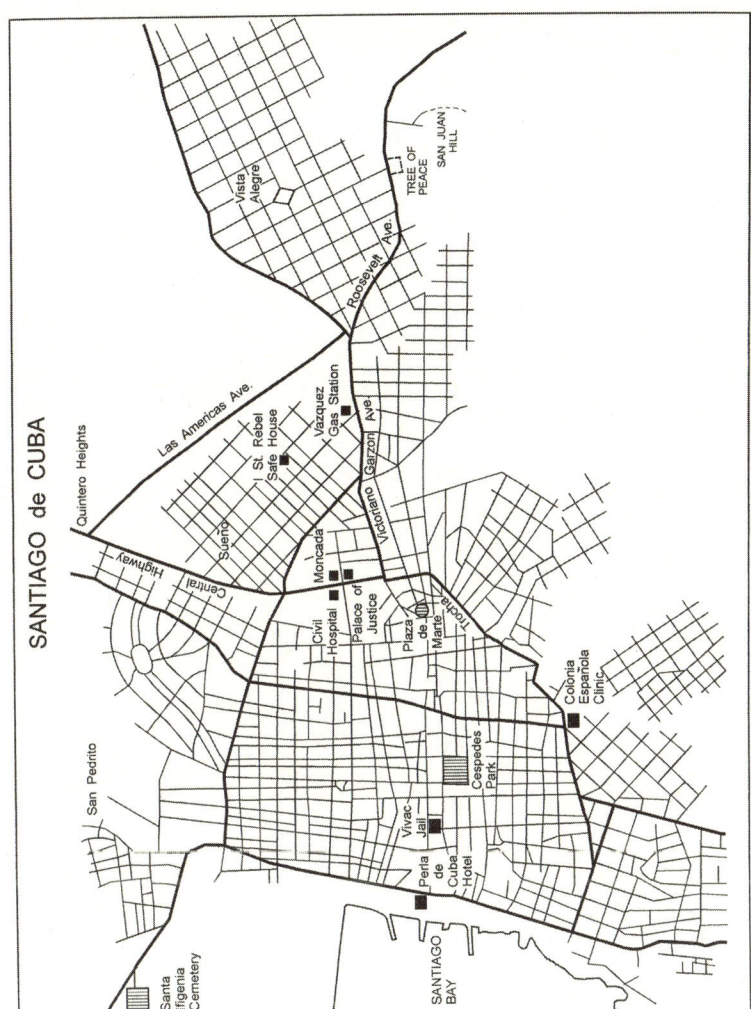

Santiago de Cuba. Map by N. L. Cooprider

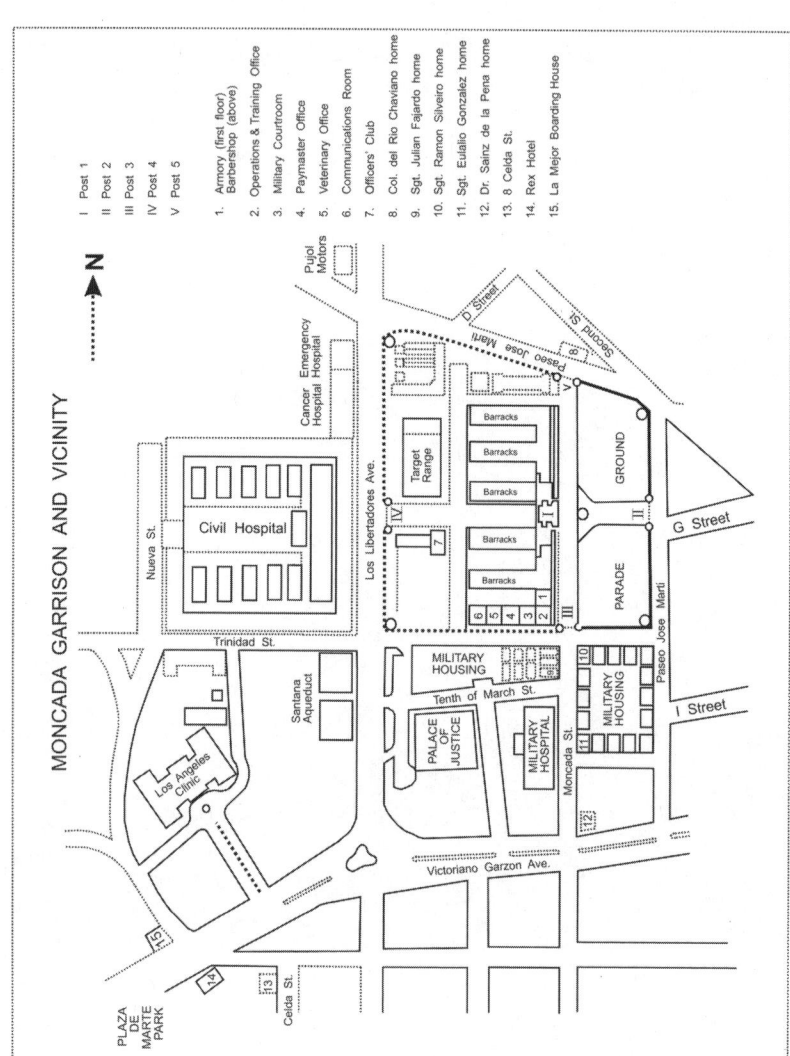

Moncada garrison and vicinity. Map by N. L. Cooprider

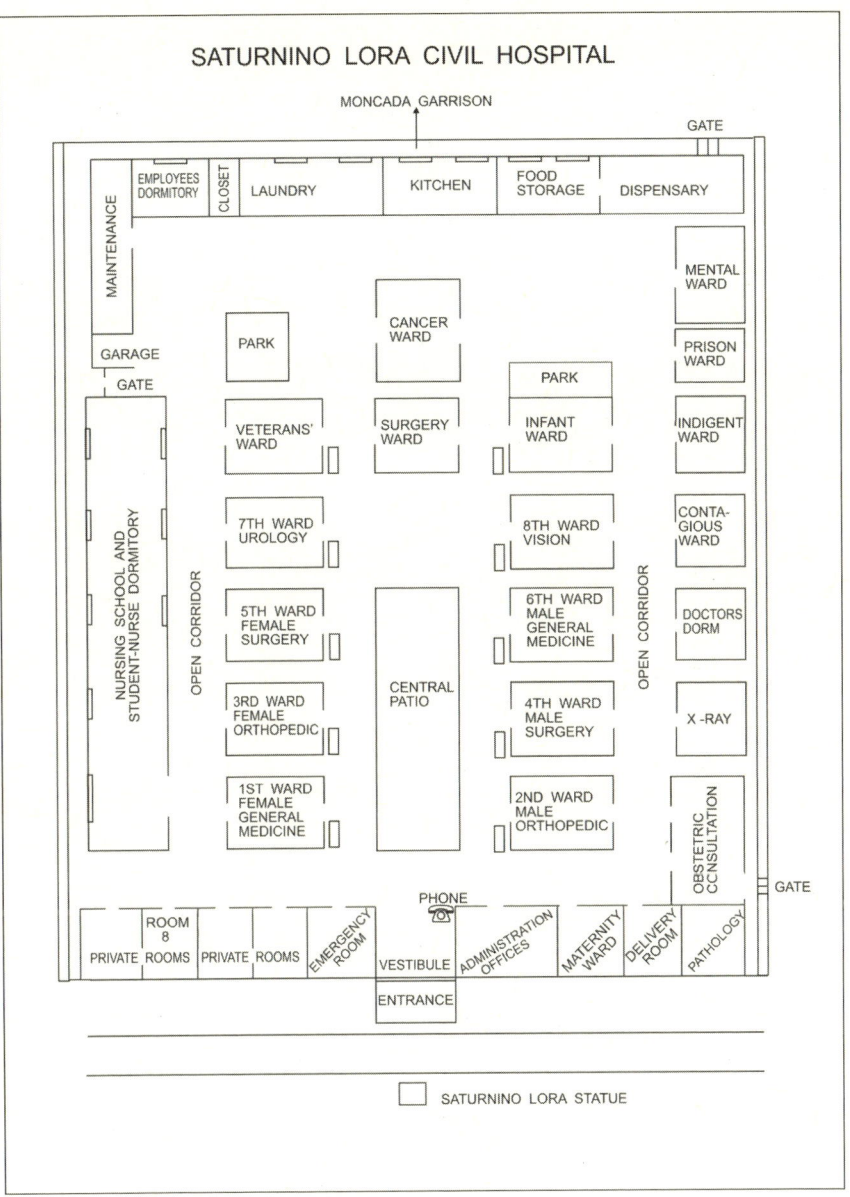

Saturnino Lora Civil Hospital. Map by N. L. Cooprider

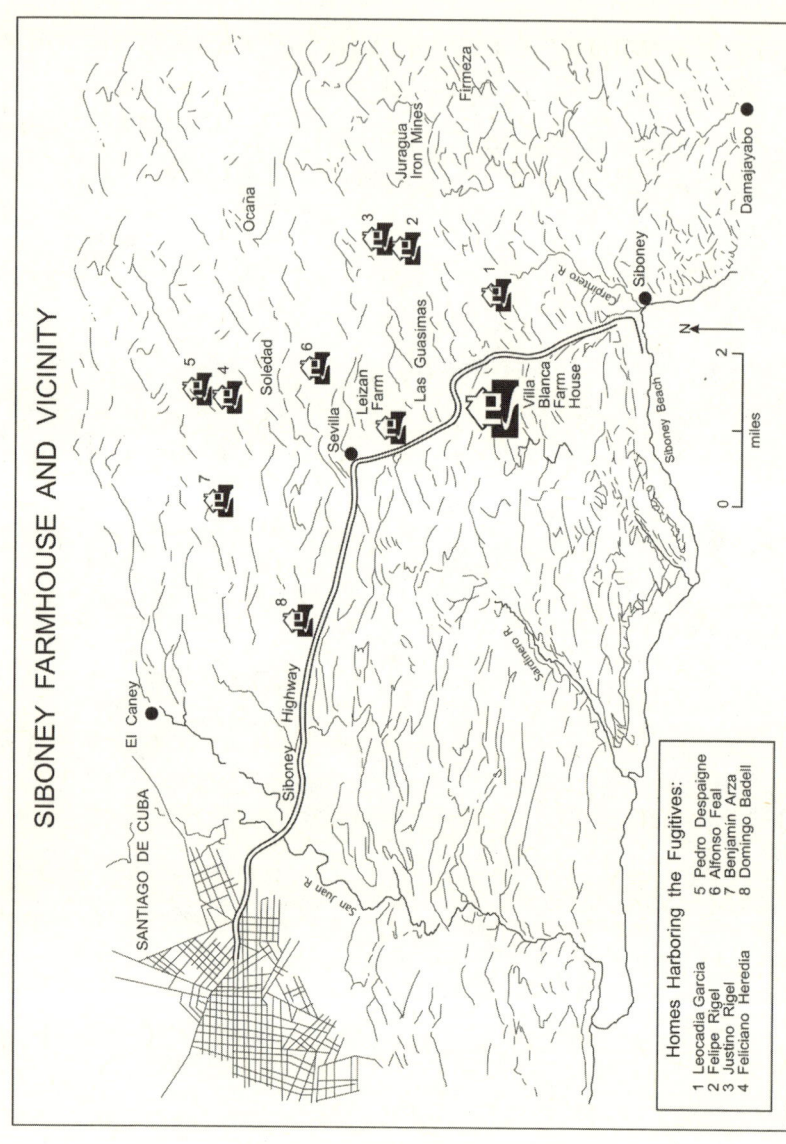

Siboney farmhouse and vicinity. Map by N. L. Cooprider

THE MONCADA ATTACK

ONE

Growing Up under Three Different Names

The pounding on the front door awoke Fidel Castro Ruz before dawn on March 10, 1952. The twenty-five-year-old attorney lived in a second-floor apartment on the corner of Twenty-third and Twenty-eighth streets in the fashionable El Vedado neighborhood of Havana with his twenty-three-year-old wife, Mirta Díaz-Balart Gutiérrez; their two-year-old son, Fidel Angel; Mirta's brother Waldo; and their paternal grandmother. It was his brother-in-law Rafael Díaz-Balart Gutiérrez who had come to warn him that Maj. Gen. Fulgencio Batista Zaldívar had just staged a coup d'état, thrusting him back into power in Cuba after an eight-year absence. "Rafael Salas Cañizares is the new chief of police," said Rafael, "but, do not worry, Batista has given orders not to bother anyone." Díaz-Balart, the national youth president of Batista's Unitary Action Party (PAU), recalled that "it was one of the few times that I ever saw Fidel frightened, but I assured him that nothing was going to happen despite his personal problem with Salas Cañizares." Castro then asked his brother-in-law to drive him to his half sister Lidia's apartment a few blocks away.[1]

Batista had been a third-place contender in the presidential elections scheduled for June, challenging the candidates of the incumbent Cuban Revolutionary Party (Auténtico) of President Carlos Prío Socarrás and the opposition Cuban People's Party (Ortodoxo). Batista, conscious of his electoral inferiority, had been dabbling in a military conspiracy prompted by the chaotic disciplinary situation in the armed forces, lawlessness, and rampant government corruption. Vice President Guillermo Alonso Pujol later wrote an article in *Bohemia* magazine stating that he had been invited the previous March to a secret meeting at Batista's Kuquine estate in Arroyo Arenas. Alonso, a Cuban National Party (PNC) leader, was a former Batista ally during the "Oppositionist National Union" campaign. He received the vice-presidential nomination in 1948 as a result of a political coalition between the PNC, the Auténticos, the Republican Party, the Democratic Party, and the Liberal Party. Batista told Alonso that junior army officers were planning to depose President Prío in favor of the vice president since gangsterism was leading the country toward anarchy. Alonso claimed that he tried dissuading Batista, who asked to be appointed minister of defense. A few days later Batista informed the vice president that he had defused the conspiracy. Alonso never explained in his *Bohemia* article why he did not inform Prío of the imminent danger.[2]

The coup began at 2:20 A.M. on Sunday, March 10, the last day of the Havana carnival festivities, when Batista departed Kuquine in a car escorted by two police cruisers commanded by Lt. Rafael Salas Cañizares. Other conspirators awaited in Havana at their command posts in Camp Columbia and La Cabaña army bases, the Aviation Corps, the Naval Headquarters at La Punta, and the National Police Central Division building. Batista, packing a .38-caliber pistol, was accompanied by various retired officers. They entered Camp Columbia at 2:43 A.M., and the two patrol cars headed for Havana to fulfill their objectives. The plotters occupied the control points of the base and arrested the post commanders. Batista had the four infantry battalions stationed there, which made up more than half of the Cuban army, ordered into formation to harangue them.[3]

La Cabaña fortress, at the mouth of Havana harbor, was taken over by its former chief, retired general Francisco Tabernilla Dolz, who entered with Manuel Ugalde Carrillo and three carloads of conspirators. They were joined inside by an armored company and soon had control of the Seventh Regiment. Other retired officers seized the Air Corps and the Naval Headquarters at La Punta. The only maritime unit in operation, the frigate *Antonio Maceo,* also defected. The forces supporting Batista in Havana also occupied the radio stations, the telephone and telegraph exchange, the airport, the railway and bus terminals, docks, the electric power plant, banks, and offices of government ministries. The takeover was completed within an hour and seventeen minutes. An official radiogram message was then sent to the chiefs of all eight army regiments, proclaiming that General Batista was in charge of the armed forces and that the government had been dismissed. The military commanders were to rally their troops and return acknowledgment of the fulfillment of orders.[4]

When Prío was notified at his suburban residence, he rushed to the executive mansion, where he found the naval high command and members of his cabinet, including the ministers Eduardo Suárez Rivas and Luis Casero Guillén, the latter of whom was also the Auténtico vice-presidential candidate in the upcoming elections. Prío telephoned the army regiments in the other five provinces at about 5:00 A.M. and learned that the sedition was limited to Havana. The president issued a press communiqué asking the military and the populace to remain loyal to the government. The leadership of the Federation of University Students (FEU) arrived at 7:30 A.M. and demanded weapons to defend the University of Havana. Prío quickly adjourned the meeting when told that Batista's tanks were en route from Camp Columbia, and he ordered that a shipment of arms be sent to his alma mater. The plotters were closely monitoring the Auténticos' activities through intercepted telephone lines.[5]

Prío headed for Matanzas in a car with four companions to take command of the provincial regiment. Half an hour before he arrived, the garrison chief was deposed and the regiment defected. The Moncada fortress in Santiago de Cuba was the last military unit to resist, until Capt. Alberto del Río Chaviano ousted his superior. When Prío realized that he no longer had the army's consent, he returned to Havana and at 1:00 P.M. sought asylum in the Mexican Embassy. The president and his family settled in Miami after a brief stay in Mexico City. The March 10 coup d'état surprised everyone, including the Eisenhower administration, which delayed recognition of the Batista government until March 27. By then, the American ambassador in Havana had received satisfactory answers from a Batista official regarding Cuba's fulfillment of international obligations, attitudes toward private capital, promises of constitutional reforms, and suppression of Communist activities.[6]

General Batista addressed the nation on the afternoon of March 10 after being appointed by the military junta in Camp Columbia as chief of state and supreme commander of the armed forces. He upheld his actions by purporting that Prío was planning to suspend the June elections and perpetuate himself in power. Batista referred to the coup as a "revolutionary movement." The Cuban Congress was disbanded, although legislators continued receiving their salaries for six months. Regional army commanders displaced governors and municipal mayors, and the military assumed censorship duties. The coup resulted in the resignation of the entire army command, while hundreds of Auténtico officers were purged from the armed forces along with anyone not supporting the new order. The openings in the ranks served to reward the coup participants.[7]

Public reaction oscillated from regret and joy to satisfaction and displeasure. The previous years of administrative corruption, gangsterism, and political crimes had left most of the populace weary of politics. The leadership of the Cuban Workers Confederation (CTC) called off a planned strike after Batista agreed not to rescind their labor benefits. Their headquarters and the Communist Party offices were placed under military supervision. A large number of political, economic, and foreign interests quickly supported the new government. Pledges of solidarity came from bankers, associations of landowners and cattlemen, the Chamber of Commerce, and the Veterans of Independence Organization. The opposition political leaders had either gone into exile, were hiding, or were suggesting patience and fortitude.[8]

The only opposition to the coup was from a group of activists who were gathered at the University of Havana awaiting the weapons promised by Prío. Student leaders used public loudspeakers to harangue the populace into resistance. Future Moncada rebels who rushed to the campus included the gun-wielding twenty-three-year-old law student Angel L. Díaz-Francisco, nicknamed "Patachula" after a childhood equestrian fall crippled his knee; Ortodoxo Youth member Gustavo Arcos Bergnes, who lived in a nearby boardinghouse; and Mario Chanes de Armas, a twenty-six-year-old bakery employee and secretary general of a labor syndicate at Puentes Grandes, Marianao. Congressman Rolando Masferrer Rojas, who derided Batista in his magazine *Tiempo en Cuba,* reached the university brandishing a machine gun and followed by an armed retinue. They departed after seeing that the Auténticos were not going to fight. The student holdout ceased after four days.[9]

Fidel Castro, hiding in his half sister's apartment to avoid arrest by Salas Cañizares, sent René Rodríguez Cruz to the university to appraise the situation since he was prohibited from entering the campus. Pedro Miret Prieto, an engineering student and future Moncada attacker, remembered that Fidel "was not precisely among the favorites on the university grounds." According to an Auténtico activist, "the FEU leaders looked upon Fidel Castro with suspicion, because of his unruly character and his reputed inclination of double dealing during his student days."[10]

Fidel Castro's genealogical roots burrow into the village of Armea, Láncara, in Galicia, Spain, where his father was born on December 4, 1875. Angel María Castro Argiz, an illiterate peasant, was the second of five children brought up in a one-room stone hut. In 1895 he accepted a one-thousand-peseta bounty to be an army draftee substitute and fight in Cuba against the independence insurgents. Angel Castro's character was hardened during three years by the cruelties of the guerrilla war, which included summary execution of rebels, pillage and destruction of separatist property, and massacres of peasants who aided the enemy. After the United States entered the conflict in April 1898 as a result of the Spanish-American War, Castro, like most defeated Spaniards, developed "a violent Hispanic antipathy towards the North Americans," which was later emulated by his sons.[11]

Angel Castro was repatriated with the Spanish army in September 1898 but returned to Havana on December 3, 1899. Years later he went to Guaro, Oriente Province, near Nipe Bay, beckoned by the labor opportunities at the Preston sugar mill of the United Fruit Company. Castro soon befriended the businessman Fidel Pino Santos, who became his benefactor. Pino assisted the Galician immigrant in establishing the small El Progreso eatery on November 26, 1906, although the establishment soon failed. Castro later lived and worked at Preston as a laborer and then as a warehouse checker of sugar before being fired with other cronies for systematic theft. In 1910 he became co-owner of El Deseo nickel mine. Castro was residing in Guaro in March 1911 when he married María Luisa Argota Reyes, a twenty-one-year-old biracial schoolteacher. Two of their four children survived infancy: Lidia, born in 1913; and Pedro Emilio, who arrived a year later.[12]

The former Spanish soldier organized a team of mostly black migrant laborers to clear forests and to harvest sugarcane for the American mills. He also established a rudimentary sawmill in Pinares de Mayarí that cut railroad ties and kindling for United Fruit. In November 1915 Castro bought land in the wilderness of Mayarí municipality, where he built his fiefdom near the village of Birán. Castro's Manacas plantation eventually expanded into one of the largest in the region, controlling twenty-six thousand acres. It had fifteen thousand orange trees, raised cattle, and cultivated sugarcane that was sold to the American-owned Central Miranda sugar mill seventeen miles away. Farm stock included 80 oxen, 22 bulls, 98 cows, 94 bullocks, 12 horses, 2 mules, 140 hogs, 15 sheep, and a variety of fowl. The Castros resided in a hardwood structure more than seventy feet in length, set on pylons over six feet high, with grand piazzas, floor-to-ceiling windows, and a cupola where the family slept. The abode, typical of those in Galicia, lacked a bathroom, plumbing, or electricity. Numerous animals lived below the floorboards.[13]

The estate grew to contain twenty-seven buildings clustered near the main house. These included a general store, a bakery, a blacksmith shop, postal and telegraph offices, a one-room public primary school, a billiard room, a bar, and a cockfight ring, where the laborers drank and gambled away their meager pay. Some five hundred peasants, mostly Haitian cane cutters, inhabited rustic *bohíos,* one-room, dirt-floor, thatched huts. Their numbers would double in twenty years. The village did not have a church and was visited by a priest only during the holidays. The peasants practiced popular religiosity emphasizing devotion to the saints and the Virgin Mary. Angel Castro almost never made religious manifestations and was described as a "skeptic" by Fidel Castro.[14]

The patriarch is described by Mario Llerena as "a bizarre, authoritarian Spaniard who could hardly communicate with or show affection for his family. He was not too scrupulous about the way he enlarged his property and increased the number of cattle in his herds." Dr. Emilio Núñez Portuondo declared that during the 1917 revolt in Oriente, Angel Castro led a Conservative militia and "took land belonging to supporters of the liberal cause and added them to his own holdings." Carlos Franqui concurs that Castro's rapid wealth was the product of stolen lands and cattle. A United Fruit manager stated that "every once in a while" he would have to retrieve from Manacas a purloined company tractor that had been painted a different color. A historian describes Angel Castro as "reticent, violent, hard-working, and rich." A machete and a Colt .45 revolver dangled from his belt, and he usually carried a silver-handled riding crop. According to Fidel Castro, his father acquired the estate by exploiting peasants and did not pay property or income taxes.[15]

In the early 1920s the peasant Francisco Ruz and his family arrived at Manacas looking for work and settled in a *bohío* half a mile from the main house. The plantation master employed their illiterate teenager Lina Ruz González as a household servant and quickly seduced her. When Lina was fourteen years old, she gave birth on April 2, 1923, to their daughter Angela, named after the forty-seven-year-old father. Ramón came into the world the next year, and Fidel, named after his father's benefactor, arrived on August 13, 1926. The children were born and raised in the Ruz shack, received their surname, and were prohibited access to the big house. In January 1931, when Lina was pregnant with her fourth child, Raúl, and the resemblance of her offspring to their progenitor was becoming evident, Angel Castro shunted the children to the home of his friend Luis Hyppolyte Alcides Hibbert, the Haitian consul, in Santiago de Cuba. The move may have been prompted by María Argota's objections to her husband's repeated infidelities. Hibbert and his spouse received a monthly stipend to home school the trio for two years. Fidel Castro recalled not receiving visits from his parents or relatives and often going hungry, and during three consecutive Epiphany holidays the only gift he received was a cheap toy trumpet. He regarded this as the worst period in his life.[16]

At the age of seven, Fidel Castro was enrolled as a first-grade boarding student in La Salle Catholic School in Santiago de Cuba, run by the Brothers of the Christian Schools, where he was later joined by his siblings Ramón and Raúl. The bishop of Camagüey, Enrique Pérez Serantes, a Galician friend of Angel Castro, arranged the enrollment because the children lacked baptismal and birth certificates. The patriarch donated a hefty amount to the institution, which created a "special grade" in order to place the three siblings in a classroom by themselves. Since Fidel Castro was not baptized and had not made his First Communion, some schoolmates mockingly called him a "dirty Jew." He responded to the taunts with violence and admitted being frequently disciplined during his five years there. Raúl Castro recalled, "And every day he fought. He had a very explosive nature." His mother tried to ameliorate the situation by having her son baptized in the cathedral on January 19, 1935. The document names him Fidel Hipólito, "son of Lina Ruz González," and lists the maternal grandparents and the godparents, Hibbert and his wife. His biological father and paternal grandparents are omitted from the certificate. Fidel Castro apparently received Hibbert's middle name as a form of gratitude. Five months later he made his First Communion.[17]

By January 1936 Lina Ruz had given Angel Castro two more daughters, Juana and Emma. María Argota then permanently left Manacas with her adult son and daughter, residing in Santiago de Cuba for at least five years before moving to Havana. The children of Lina Ruz now had access to the plantation home but were denied legitimacy. Their behavior problems continued in La Salle along with mounting complaints that they were "intractable fighters and bullies." In the fifth grade, eleven-year-old Fidel Castro punched and bit the school disciplinarian who rapped him on the head for misbehavior. Castro claimed that he then decided not to return to La Salle, but it appears that he and his brothers were expelled in November

1937. The principal of La Salle told Angel Castro that his sons "are the biggest rascals in the school."[18]

Thirteen-year-old Ramón "was delighted not to go to school anymore," and six-year-old Raúl was sent to a national civic-military school run by an army sergeant near Birán. Fidel Castro stated that he "threatened to set the whole house on fire" if he was not sent back to boarding school. Before he could be interned at the elite Jesuit Dolores School in Santiago de Cuba, his birth was inscribed in the Cueto civil registry on January 11, 1938, as Fidel Casiano Ruz González. His middle name had changed, and he still had his mother's surnames. Angel Castro, still married to María Argota, continued refusing to recognize his offspring with Lina Ruz. Fidel Castro became aware of his social inferiority among his new conservative Catholic and aristocratic classmates. He stated that their "social pride" made him suffer and that although his family was wealthy, they were peasants who did not belong to the upper class and lacked social influence and culture.[19]

On December 8, 1938, four months after Lina Ruz gave birth to Agustina, her seventh and last child, she wrote from Birán to Fidel Pino Santos, by now a Conservative Party member of the Chamber of Representatives in Havana. She pleaded that he convince Angel Castro to officially recognize their children, who were afflicted by their illegitimate status. Lina Ruz also felt insecure because the patriarch was "returning home late from the pursuit of fickle love affairs." For consolation, she would fervently pray to the life-size statues of the saints that she kept at home. After the Cuban divorce law went into effect under the Constitution of 1940, Angel Castro became a naturalized citizen on September 19, 1941, in order to benefit from it. Ten days later he filed for divorce from María Argota. On April 23, 1943, when the wealthy planter was sixty-seven years old, he married Lina Ruz before a municipal judge in Cueto.[20]

According to *Time* magazine, the marriage occurred "despite his loud-spoken accusations that Raúl had been sired by one of Lina's many other lovers. Neighbors remember that this gnawing suspicion later brought Angel to file, then cancel, a divorce suit." Raúl Castro's paternity has been credited in some written accounts to twenty-nine-year-old Pvt. Felipe Mirabal Mirabal, who with thirty-two-year-old Cpl. Narciso Campos Pontigo and another soldier, comprised the Rural Guard outpost at Marcané in 1930. Two former army lieutenants stated that Campos, not Mirabal, was Raúl Castro's biological father. Angel Castro waited eight months after his marriage before legally recognizing all of his children with Lina Ruz on December 11, 1943. Fidel Castro now shed his middle name of Casiano, for that of Alejandro, his maternal uncle's name.[21]

While a boarding student, the only time Fidel Castro spent at home was during the three summer months, the two-week Christmas vacation, and Easter week. He had to spend part of his vacation grudgingly working in the plantation general store while Raúl tended the bar, even though their father was annually making more than one hundred thousand pesos from his estate. Fidel Castro recalled in 2004 that "it was a hard house, of a very hard man, where we ate standing and where I still remember my mother chasing away the chickens from the sofas so that the scarce visitors could sit in a careful manner so as to avoid the usual shitty deposits of the fowl." He also stated that his father had a "bad temper" and was always reprimanding his children. José Pardo Llada, who visited the estate for six days, said that during that time he never heard a conversation between father and son. The psychiatrist Peter G. Bourne indicated that "Fidel's conflicts with his father were frequent and severe."[22]

As a result, Fidel Castro developed deceitful and manipulative traits. He once claimed to have lost his school report card and, after receiving a replacement, used the old one to give himself excellent grades and hoodwink his parents. The youth also devised "several schemes to get money" from his "tightfisted" father. Fidel Castro then wrote a laudatory letter to President Franklin D. Roosevelt on November 6, 1940, addressing him as "My good friend Roosevelt [sic]." The teenager falsely claimed to be only twelve years old and asked, "If you like, give me a ten dollars bill green american in the letter because never I have not seen a ten dollars bill green american and I would like to have one of them." The amount represented quite a sum, in today's dollars, especially for Cuba. Castro received only a Department of State courtesy reply, which was displayed on the school bulletin board for a week.[23]

In September 1942 Fidel Castro was sent to study in Havana, where Fidel Pino Santos enrolled him in the exclusive Jesuit Belén High School in the suburb of Marianao. He joined some two hundred boarders, out of one thousand students, who paid a fifty-peso monthly tuition. "It was the cream of the aristocracy and the Cuban bourgeois," affirmed Castro, who became sensitive of his own rural background when students mocked his rube vocabulary, manners, and wardrobe. He was called "El Guajiro" (The Redneck) and "El Loco" (The Madman) because of his unruly ways. Belén student Ramón Mestre Gutiérrez recalled how during a walk to a nearby cafeteria with a few classmates he saw Fidel Castro "flirting with a skinny blond girl on the porch of the San Pedro family residence across the street from the school entrance." When Mestre yelled to invite him along, "Hey, loco, come on," an enraged Castro briefly engaged him in fisticuffs. "Fidel bit me on the arm before running toward Belén," stated Mestre. The next day Mestre was told by the Jesuit teacher Miguel Larrusea that after the incident he had taken a handgun away from Castro, who was seeking revenge. Mestre questions why Castro was not expelled from Belén for such a serious violation. In contrast, Enrique Ovares Herrera, a teenage friend, never saw Castro with weapons while in high school. He recalled, "The need for weapons occurred later at the university."[24]

Ovares believed that the worst mistake Castro's parents made was sending him to a class-conscious elite school. As a result, Fidel Castro harbored contempt toward his parents, regarding them as "ignorant people without a proper education." According to Ovares, Castro's illegitimacy, lack of a social position, and inferiority complex led him to despise the wealthy social class that shunned him. Ovares stated that his neighbors, the brothers Jorge and Carlos Remedios Oliva, were the only Belén students who invited Castro to their home on the weekends. Their father, fifty-four-year-old Benito Remedios Langaney, a hard-boiled peasant, became a millionaire after being elected to the Chamber of Representatives. Members of this Cuban version of the Beverly Hillbillies were, according to Ovares, "the only ones Fidel could fit in with. The Remedios siblings had a basketball hoop at home and Fidel always played with them and me." The Jesuit teacher Amando Llorente recalled that "when the rest of the boys went to the movies, to a party or on vacation, Fidel stayed at school training himself in basketball, track and other sports to be the best when the competition came."[25]

Castro excelled in sports and was appointed chief of the Belén Explorers, similar to the Boy Scouts. He enjoyed winning in competition as a way of getting attention and demonstrating leadership. The student interns had to attend mass every morning before breakfast. Castro considered this daily obligation as negative and described religious meditation as "mental terrorism." He told the Brazilian Marxist Dominican brother Frei Betto in 1985, "I never really had a belief or a religious faith, in school they were not able to instill in me those values." Castro stated that all of his Jesuit teachers admired Spain's Fascist dictator Francisco Franco and that they had "a rightist, Franquist and reactionary ideology." They politically influenced him with the Fascist ideals of the Spanish Phalangist José A. Primo de Rivera. During a November 19 anniversary of Primo de Rivera's execution by Communists, Castro discoursed at a Belén rally. Decades later the Communist leader Carlos Rafael Rodríguez recalled an article in the conservative *Diario de la Marina* mentioning "Fidel speaking about fascism in a favorable way." The Communist newspaper *Hoy* disparaged Castro on December 14, 1944, for another school speech in which he criticized a political project by Communist senator Juan Marinello. He was called a "budding Jesuit, who for more than an hour talked nonsense and was being foolish."[26]

Castro was also imbued with the Spanish Jesuit teachings of Hispanidad, exalting Spain's moral and spiritual values and rejecting American liberal democracy, materialism, and cultural domination. Franco used Hispanidad partly as a strategic reply to Franklin Roosevelt's Pan-American designs. At Belén, Castro was inspired by the works of José Martí, and "From then on he would try to act, speak, and write" like the Cuban-independence leader. He graduated from high school in June 1945 with a sense of personal predestination and mission fomented by Jesuit teachings. Three months later Castro enrolled in the University of Havana Law School. He admitted that parental insistence, not vocation, prompted him to study law. Fidel Castro once stated having often "regretted that I was not made to study something else." He tried out for the university basketball team with Rafael and Frank Díaz-Balart, but all three were rejected. Castro, then measuring six feet in height and weighing 161 pounds, gave up sports, began smoking tobacco, and turned to student politics.[27]

The University of Havana had fifteen thousand students in thirteen schools. It was ruled by the University Council, comprised of the deans of all the schools and presided over by the rector. Tuition was free to students from low-income families. Each school had its own student association. Law School students had to take five courses annually during five years to graduate. Each course would elect a delegate, and the five delegates of each year would choose the course president. The five course presidents, one for each year of studies, would elect the president and vice president of the Association of Law Students. The other twelve schools used the same elective method. The FEU president and the executive board were then chosen by the thirteen school presidents. In March 1946 Fidel Castro was elected delegate of the judicial anthropology course. The professor who taught the class, René Herrera Fritot, had assigned Castro "the task of keeping the attendance role." Herrera had received a crate of "magnificent oranges" sent by Castro from his family's estate in January and another shipment in February before backing his candidacy. Castro was then chosen among the five delegates of the first year as the course president. According to then FEU secretary general Enrique Ovares and FEU presidential aspirant Luis Conte Agüero, this was the only student post Castro ever held.[28]

The University of Havana had been a hotbed of violence since the late 1930s, when thugs dubbed the *bonche* got control of the student government, obtained sinecures, falsified grade transcripts, ran gambling houses, and extorted industrialists and businessmen. "They were mostly elements involved in football and athletic activities, physically strong, but without any political talent," according to law student Rolando Masferrer Rojas. "They had pressured their teachers in the La Víbora and Havana Institutes into granting their high school degree without studying. When they arrived at the university without an academic background, they continued the same pattern by intimidating the professors, especially those in the Schools of Law and Medicine, to obtain their degrees." Their adversaries were led by thirty-year-old architectural-drawing professor Ramiro Valdés Daussá and his thirty-year-old adjunct Manuel "Manolo" de Castro del Campo.[29]

After Valdés Daussá was temporarily appointed chief of the University Security Corps in May 1940, he assigned Manolo de Castro, Oscar Fernández Caral, and others to assist in neutralizing the *bonche* on campus. This soon led to a confrontation in which twenty-six-year-old *bonche* leader Antonio Morín Dopico was wounded in a shootout. Five days later another *bonchista* was gunned down by twenty-six-year-old Mario Salabarría Aguiar during an argument in the university plaza. On August 15, 1940, Valdés Daussá was murdered by the *bonche*, and three months later Manolo de Castro killed an expelled professor who was a mentor of the *bonche*.[30]

The *bonche* and the revolutionary groups of the 1930s were repressed under the Fulgencio Batista presidency (1940–44). According to a confidential report from the American Embassy in Havana to the U.S. Department of State, shortly before President Ramón Grau San Martín was inaugurated in October 1944, he "met with all the so-called 'revolutionary' groups" and obtained their cooperation. The following month Grau appointed Mario Salabarría as major and chief of the Enemy Activities Investigation Service of the Police (SIAE) and thirty-one-year-old Eufemio J. Fernández Ortega as captain and chief of the Office of Police Control. Their opponent, twenty-six-year-old Emilio Tro Rivero, leader of the Insurrectional Revolutionary Union (UIR), became major and director of the National Police Academy and gave a dozen followers the rank of second lieutenant. *Bonche* leader Antonio Morín Dopico was appointed police chief of Marianao. The revolutionaries-turned-policemen rivaled for control of the black market, gambling, the "protection" business, and perpetrated armed robberies.[31]

Raúl Roa García, the dean of social sciences, indicated that the "terrorist organizations" that had fought against the Machado and Batista regimes had deformed into "pseudo-revolutionary gangsterism." Ernesto de la Fe Pérez, the thirty-one-year-old leader of Acción y Trabajo para un Orden Mejor (ATOM), defined the revolutionaries as mostly "rebels without a cause." Their frequent gang wars and running gun battles made the public sarcastically dub them the "trigger-happy lads." Most of their victims were policemen and army officers who had repressed political subversion and terrorism during the previous decade. The homicidal pattern was similar to the drive-by shootings of the Al Capone era in Chicago. The Central Intelligence Agency (CIA) station chief in Havana and the Federal Bureau of Investigation (FBI) legal attaché in the U.S. Embassy investigated these groups for possible Communist influence.[32]

Hundreds of revolutionaries got government sinecures called *botellas*. The UIR propaganda chief, twenty-six-year-old Vidal Morales Rodríguez, received a $250 monthly check from the Ministry of Education under Diego Vicente Tejera. He stated that Tejera's bodyguard "had 500 positions to parcel at $150 each." Grau acknowledged that the Ministry of Education had "an extensive payroll" for those he called "fire-eaters." Indeed, between 1943 and 1949 the number of government employees ascended from 60,000 to 131,000. During Grau's presidency there were sixty-four political assassinations, thirty-three people were wounded during these attacks, and more than two dozen persons were kidnapped for ransom to finance "revolutionary" activities. Five Havana police chiefs resigned under scandal or were assassinated in just one year.[33]

Emilio Tro, a U.S. Army World War II veteran, outlined the UIR's main objectives as punishing the henchmen of Machado and Batista and establishing a socialized economy. Vidal Morales described Tro as "a psychopath with a fourth-grade education. He was very likeable and pleasant but would kill anyone who disparaged him. He had war psychosis." According to Morales, the first UIR victim was fifty-six-year-old Desiderio Ferreira, former assistant chief of Machado's secret police, who was gunned down on his house porch on July 19, 1946. His killers left on his body the UIR calling card "Justice is slow but sure." Morales stated that nine days later Tro briefly left a poker game to murder two policemen.[34]

UIR opponents formed the Socialist Revolutionary Movement (MSR), led by Secretary General Rolando Masferrer and FEU president Manolo de Castro. Masferrer's magazine *Tiempo en Cuba* published confidential police information on rival UIR members, including their criminal records and lists of their automobile tags. According to Mario Salabarría, he and Eufemio Fernández were not MSR members but provided cooperation. Masferrer wrote the movement's thesis of "revolutionary socialism opposing Communism, imperialism and the incumbent Auténtico Party; neutralizing UIR and the other adventurism groups; and liberating the Dominican Republic from dictator Rafael Trujillo." Masferrer affirmed, "We projected with greater energy toward the workers' movement, the student movement, and the activities of peasants agitating in favor of agrarian reform." A CIA report indicated that Masferrer was seen "carrying a .45 automatic pistol of Argentine make and a collapsible .45 caliber machine gun with all identifying marks removed."[35]

UIR and MSR recruits had to prove themselves by first participating in "shooting an enemy of a rival group or engaging in terrorist activities against their critics." Fidel Castro initially sought acceptance with activists of both groups. His baptism of fire was on December 10, 1946, when, along with MSR members Angel "El Gallego" Vázquez, Isaac Araña Ahitú, and thirty-five-year-old electrical engineering student Fausto "Paco" Antonetti Fernández, he tried to kill rival Institute of Havana Student Association president Leonel A. Gómez Pérez, a twenty-year-old *bonchista* and UIR activist, after leaving the university stadium. Rafael Díaz-Balart affirmed that "Fidel and his companions awaited atop the wall on Ronda Street, where Leonel had no possibility of seeing who was shooting." Gómez was hit in the back of the left shoulder, and a twelve-year-old boy and two bystanders were wounded. Fernando Freyre de Andrade, nicknamed "La Vaquita" (Little Cow), was shot in the leg. FEU secretary general Enrique Ovares recalled, "The incident made Castro the laughing stock of the students who joked that he went gunning for the bull but instead hit the little cow." Castro, fearing a UIR reprisal, hid in the home of Díaz-Balart, who stated that "Vidal Morales later arranged a truce and, as a consequence, Fidel became a member of the UIR."[36]

Morales affirmed that mutual friends asked him to meet with Fidel Castro, who needed protection. Castro accompanied Morales to Tro's residence and greeted the UIR leader by saying, "I admire you as one of the greatest and most honest men in Cuba and I have always wanted to be your friend." Morales recalled that "Tro pulled out a UIR application form for Fidel that the three of us signed. The word went out that Fidel was now a UIR member, but Leonel Gómez disregarded the warning. A few days later Tro took Leonel out of his house at 6:00 A.M. and put him on a plane to Mexico City without returning until he cooled off toward Fidel." Gómez received a government grant to study abroad for more than a year.[37]

Castro acknowledged packing a gun while at the university. On April 27, 1947, police major Salabarría heard in his patrol car a radio dispatch bulletin describing a vehicle with two individuals who had fired shots at a meeting of the Association of Law Students at the university. The car and its occupants were spotted in front of Fidel Castro's rooming house on Mazón and San José streets, near the campus. Castro was arrested on the sidewalk with a .45-caliber pistol that Tro had given him. The driver, twenty-three-year-old law student Aramís Taboada González, was also detained, for possession of a .38-caliber revolver. A search of Castro's room failed to produce further evidence. Salabarría recalled, "That was the first time I encountered Fidel Castro. I was never called as a witness in that case because there was a court clerk named de la Ville, who, for $20, would take out certain parts of the weapon to make it inoperable, and when a gun expert testified that it would not fire, charges were dropped."[38]

The MSR, by way of FEU president Manolo de Castro, had clout within the University of Havana. The autonomous institution had a private police force paid by and responding to the University Council. The campus police, sympathetic to the FEU and the MSR, would frisk and disarm UIR members. "The UIR did not have strength within the university," recalled Rafael Díaz-Balart. "When we were assaulted by MSR members, the UIR backed us, which is why my brother Frank and I had certain militancy in the UIR. That is why I left Cuba in June 1947 with a scholarship for Princeton Theological Seminary in New Jersey, which included a position as a Spanish teacher, because if I stayed there, I would have had to form part of the spiral of violence. It was not so much that one would get murdered, but that one had to kill in an organized way."[39]

After Manolo de Castro left the university, he was appointed director general of national sports in the Ministry of Education. During the FEU presidential elections of June 1947, the aspirant Isaac Araña Ahitú, president of the Commercial Sciences School, was supported by Manolo de Castro and the MSR. The UIR promoted its own candidate, Humberto Ruiz Leiro, president of the School of Dentistry. The election was hotly contested because the FEU presidency guaranteed a future national political post. The presidency of the Association of Law Students went to Federico Marín Robaina, backed by the MSR, who defeated Fidel Castro, one of the five delegates of the second-year course, by a three-to-two vote. In an attempt to annul the election, UIR followers claimed to have impeached Marín and proclaimed Castro as president. According to FEU secretary general Enrique Ovares, the University Council ruled that Castro's petition was groundless and without precedent. *Bohemia* magazine reported that the University Council "left out" Fidel Castro and recognized Marín. Thirty-four years later Castro insisted that he had been the president of the Association of Law Students, an error that has been frequently repeated by writers.[40]

Marin agreed to be the sixth faculty vote for MSR candidate Araña, and UIR candidate Ruiz Leiro had the ballots of the other six schools. Ovares, who as president of the School of Architecture had the swing vote, remained neutral. The FEU Assembly met under armed guard for six hours on June 4 and broke the deadlock with a transitional candidate. Arquimides Poveda, a Communist and former FEU secretary, proposed that Ovares be elected FEU president because he was "outside of all the passions that surrounded the two candidates." Ruiz Leiro and Araña then renounced their candidacies. Ovares accepted the nomination and the next day was unanimously elected FEU president. He then backed a constituent assembly to establish a new FEU presidential electoral procedure by the direct vote of all students.[41]

The constituent assembly met on July 16, 1947, with only 891 students of 15,000 in attendance, to elect their leadership. A U.S. Embassy report noted "the apathy of the great mass of the students" and concluded that "only several hundred are rabid Communists." The MSR and the Communists promoted twenty-two-year-old Ovares, twenty-six-year-old José Luis Massó, and twenty-two-year-old Alfredo Guevara Valdés respectively as president, vice president, and secretary of the constituent assembly. Ovares recalled that "Guevara, who was very qualified and dedicated, was a Communist homosexual from a very poor family." The UIR backed Humberto Ruiz Leiro, Antonio G. Cejas, and Fidel Castro, who were supported by members of the Catholic Youth (JC) and the Catholic University Association (ACU), presided over by Humberto's brother. Castro carried out "a militant campus campaign" against the Communists opposed to his slate. He addressed the assembly, stating in part, "Let us not be subjugated by the pessimism and the disillusion provoked during the last years by the false leaders," whom he called "merchants of the blood of the martyrs." Student apathy and fear of violence prompted only 295 to participate in the election, in which 7 votes were annulled. Ovares won with 148 ballots, defeating Ruiz Leiro by 8 votes. Massó obtained 141 votes against 40 for his opponent, and Guevara trounced Castro 144 votes to19. Ovares recalled, "The University Council never approved our resolutions. Fidel, who never held an elected position in the FEU, felt very humiliated that an insignificant homosexual had defeated him by such a wide margin. After that loss, he did not run for elective student office again."[42]

That summer Castro and other students with revolutionary yearnings had the opportunity to join a filibuster expedition to overthrow Dominican dictator Rafael Trujillo. In March 1947 President Grau, who abhorred Trujillo, had ordered the chief of the Cuban navy to contact FEU president Manolo de Castro and provide weapons to the conspirators. Capt. Mario Gajate Erro, who had recently completed a general inventory of naval ordnance, was ordered to give surplus arms and munitions to the revolutionaries. The rebel leadership, headquartered at the Sevilla-Biltmore Hotel, included Dominican exiles Juan Rodríguez García, a wealthy septuagenarian planter and former diplomat, and Juan Bosch, a poet and novelist who in 1939 helped found the center-left Dominican Revolutionary Party (PRD) in Havana. Manolo de Castro, the link between the expatriates and the Cuban government, assigned command of the invasion force to Spanish civil war veterans Rolando Masferrer and Eufemio Fernández. Police major Salabarría claimed that he also played a key covert role in the plan.[43]

The new minister of education, José Manuel Alemán, donated more than half of the $1.5 million war chest, and Rodríguez García gave $400,000 of his own fortune. The Cuban navy provided thirty to forty 500-pound "blockbuster" aerial bombs, thousands of rounds of ammunition, and four 37-mm cannons. Captain Gajate recalled, "I would personally take this ordnance in navy trucks to the *América* farm of Alemán in Calabazar, where it was deposited in a huge garage. Alemán would personally receive it." To muster the invasion air force, Alemán purchased contraband arms and sixteen surplus U.S. combat airplanes. These included six P-38s, a B-24 Liberator bomber, two B-25 Mitchell bombers, and troop carriers. Salabarría arranged for the aircraft to land at the Mariel airport. Twenty-seven veterans of the U.S. and Canadian air forces, including three former Flying Tigers, were hired at $6,000 for the mission. The filibusters procured seven vessels, including two landing crafts and two patrol torpedo (PT) boats.[44]

In early July recruits began gathering at Havana's José Martí Park and other points. They were mostly unemployed, indigents, and a few romantic adventurers. Captain Gajate quipped that "The human quality of many of those enrolled was so bad that some citizens joked about what would happen to the banks and the jewelry stores in Santo Domingo if that army disembarked there." Fidel Castro acknowledged that due to hasty recruitment, antisocial elements were incorporated in the venture. Rafael Díaz-Balart, delegated president of the FEU's Committee for Dominican Democracy (CUDD), had previously introduced Castro to Dominican Liberation Army leader Juan Rodríguez García. Castro later purported that he was the committee's chairman. He then told FEU president Ovares, a major in the invasion force, that he wanted to participate in this "historic event" but worried that the rival MSR would kill him in the filibuster training camp. Ovares interceded with Manolo de Castro and exacted a promise from Rolando Masferrer that the MSR would not harm Fidel Castro. Masferrer later commented that "the crisis with the UIR was not produced until afterward. Until then, Fidel Castro did not have any outstanding actions, other than having shot at Leonel Gómez, and he was put in charge of an infantry platoon at Cayo Confites."[45]

On July 25 the Dominican ambassador in Washington, D.C., reported the invasion plans to the U.S. Department of State. Two days later the American ambassador at Havana met with the Cuban foreign minister on this matter. President Grau responded on the 28th to the diplomat that "energetic measures were being taken to suffocate the revolutionary activity based on Cuban soil." The next day thirteen hundred Cubans and two hundred Dominican and Latin American expatriates were transferred to the barren, half-mile-long Cayo Confites reef, on northern Camagüey Province. Food and water were transported daily by motor launch. Tempers were strained due to heat, unsanitary conditions, mosquitoes, thefts, and feuds ending in gunfire. Masferrer asserted, "I drew up the military plan and commanded the Augusto Sandino Battalion. Eufemio Fernández was in charge of the Antonio Guiteras Battalion." Two other battalions, named Máximo Gómez and José Martí, were commanded by a former Cuban army officer and a Dominican exile. The U.S. Department of State decided not to interfere and to let the United Nations handle the issue.[46]

The invasion plans unraveled six weeks later. On September 15 police major Salabarría received a judicial arrest warrant for murder against police major Emilio Tro, his chauffeur, and two police officials. Salabarría, the chiefs of the Secret Police and the Bureau of Investigations, and ten cops went to arrest Tro at the Orfila neighborhood home of Maj. Antonio Morín Dopico, the Marianao police chief and former *bonche* leader. A three-hour gun battle ensued as a CMQ Radio reporter broadcast the events live and Noticiario Nacional cameraman Eduardo "Guayo" Hernández Suárez filmed the action. Tro, his lieutenant, and Mrs. Dopico were killed, and another associate was wounded. Salabarría's force had seven casualties. President Grau ordered the army to intervene, and some twenty tanks and armored cars appeared on the scene. Salabarría, carrying fourteen one-thousand-peso bills in his shoes, was detained along with some subordinates.[47]

Gen. Genovevo Pérez Dámera, the thirty-seven-year-old army chief of staff, had the Military Supreme Court bring charges against Salabarría and nine of his men. Five days later he ordered the army to occupy the filibuster arsenal at Alemán's *América* farm. Salabarría claimed, "The Orfila events were used as an excuse to terminate the Cayo Confites expedition. Genovevo knew that I was a vital element in that affair and he insinuated that we had a conspiracy to overthrow the government. What really motivated him was a million-dollar bribe he received from Trujillo. Masferrer later denounced in the Cuban Congress the bank account number where the money was deposited in Cuba." Masferrer stated that General Pérez received the bribe from Dominican diplomat Roberto Despradel.[48]

Two Cuban navy frigates forced the expedition vessels to surrender on September 29 under the threat of being sunk. The invasion landing craft was towed into a Nipe Bay port in Oriente, and the filibusters were taken by train to Havana. Fidel Castro claimed that to avoid arrest, as "a question of honor," he dove off the ship and swam almost nine miles in shark-infested waters to Saetía, at the entrance of Nipe

Bay. In contrast, the ship's Dominican captain and an expeditionary stated that they helped Castro escape at night in a dingy that was lowered from the vessel. The fugitive later arrived at his family's estate with a machine gun. The filibusters were detained in Camp Columbia until October 3, when the supreme court ordered their release.[49]

In consequence of the Cayo Confites affair, Fidel Castro was unable to register in time at the university for the 1947–48 academic year and had to audit classes. He admitted that by not being a full-time student he had "no political rights" during that year and lacked official standing in student organizations. According to Ovares, Castro and other student agitators rarely went to classes since attendance was not mandatory for many courses. This gave Castro plenty of time for political activism. Ovares stated that Castro joined Alfredo Guevara and Lionel Soto Prieto, vice president of the School of Philosophy and Letters and international secretary of the Popular Socialist Party (PSP), in planning a campus antigovernment rally that would showcase the Bell of La Demajagua, which tolled the start of the 1868 Ten Years' War for independence. The minister of the interior had requested the use of the bell for official commemorative activities on October 10, but the guardians of the relic, the Manzanillo City Council, spurned him due to unkept public works promises.[50]

Castro and Soto, on behalf of the FEU, flew to Manzanillo, a city that had elected a Communist mayor in 1940, and got permission to borrow the Bell of La Demajagua for a student memorial act, without disclosing their true purpose. They took the three-hundred-pound relic to Havana by train, escorted by a soldier and three municipal officials. Ovares and Guevara joined them in Matanzas, and the delegation arrived at the Havana train station at 9:00 A.M. on November 3, 1947. They were greeted by a large crowd that followed the bell, which was in a Packard convertible, during a more than two-hour procession to the university. After laudatory speeches by Ovares, Castro, and others, announcing a grand rally two days later, the relic was exhibited in the Hall of Martyrs. Ovares then announced that the bell "would once again ring liberty" to "repudiate the present government and define the actual position of the university." Castro added that the students would come before the bell to "rescue the political dignity" of the university. The Communist newspaper *Hoy* published Ovares's lengthy declarations but omitted Castro's statements.[51]

The Manzanillo delegates, feeling deceived, met the next day with President Grau to assure that their heirloom had been loaned to the FEU only to commemorate the death of student martyrs and "never as a banner for backing political or other types of acts." That night UIR opponents Eufemio Fernández, twenty-three-year-old Tony Santiago Ruiz, and two comrades, aided by two university policemen, surreptitiously extracted the bell from the Hall of Martyrs and hid it in a closet in Santiago's home, around the corner from the Ovares residence. On the morning of

November 6, where the Bell of La Demajagua had been deposited there was a sign that read: "The bequeathed relics are not for politics. They are venerated." FEU leaders Ovares and Guevara filed a grievance against the rector and the university authorities at the Ninth Police Station. UIR members Fidel Castro, Rafael del Pino Siero, Pedro Mirassou Tarnío, Armando Galis-Menéndez, and Alfredo "El Chino" Esquivel Rodón went to the office of the National Police chief and blamed the theft on MSR leaders Rolando Masferrer, Eufemio Fernández, and Manolo de Castro.[52]

Fidel Castro then made the same accusation on the radio program of Guido García Inclán before going with del Pino to the Ovares residence. While the three were sitting on the porch with Alfredo Guevara discussing the situation, two cars screeched to a halt on the street in front of them. Del Pino grabbed his pistol as Eufemio Fernández and Tony Santiago emerged with handguns along with two other companions with machine guns. Fernández, who had heard the radio diatribe, insulted Castro and challenged him to "Come out, I'm going to kill you." Castro and del Pino froze, and Guevara turned pale. Ovares yelled at everyone to calm down and put away the guns, prompting his mother to emerge. She chided Santiago and asked him to leave. The situation was defused when Santiago told Fernández, "Let's go. We'll get them elsewhere." Del Pino argued with Castro for not responding to the insults. Ovares recalled that Castro, who wisely chose his battles, replied, "Don't be foolish, we were outgunned and they were trying to provoke an excuse to kill us."[53]

That night fifteen thousand people attended the campus rally. Fidel Castro was the third of seven speakers and the only one not identified in the press with an FEU title. The basic themes of most of the speeches were the denunciation of the disappearance of the Bell of La Demajagua, severe criticism of the Grau administration, and references to "Yankee imperialism." Ovares concluded the act by emphasizing the need to create a "vigorous anti-imperialist movement" and denounced the policies of the Cuban ambassador to the United Nations at that time, Guillermo Belt. He outlined the FEU's platform of "rescuing the national economy, fomenting the merchant marine, distribution of land and the participation of the workers in the profits of their work places," all tenets that Fidel Castro would later expound in *History Will Absolve Me*. The next morning Eufemio Fernández gave the bell to independence general Enrique Loynaz del Castillo, who left it at the Executive Mansion.[54]

In reprisal to this affront and to avenge Tro's death, the UIR went gunning for MSR leaders. Manolo de Castro and a friend were killed by two masked men on the night of February 22, 1948, in front of a movie theater. UIR triggerman Gustavo E. Ortiz Fáez, a twenty-eight-year-old agronomy student, was arrested two blocks away with a warm .45-caliber pistol and two ammunition clips. Manolo de Castro's nephew denounced four UIR members who had been recently shadowing his uncle. The suspects, Fidel Castro, twenty-seven-year-old Justo Fuentes Clavel, twenty-eight-year-old Armando Galis-Menéndez, and twenty-six-year-old Pedro Mirassou

Tarnío, were arrested three days later while traveling in a car on Malecón Boulevard. They purported to be on their way to the police station to surrender. The four were released after paraffin tests for gunpowder traces proved negative. Castro told the press that they were blamed for the murders because Masferrer wanted to make them victims of new attacks to gain absolute control of the university. Castro sarcastically exclaimed, "Had we known about the crime on time, we would have prevented it."[55]

Fidel Castro was not charged with murder after his future brother-in-law, Frank Díaz-Balart, provided an alibi. Masferrer stated that just before the assassination, Castro was seen a block and a half away in the Inglaterra Hotel. Police major Salabarría claimed that it was Fidel Castro who spotted Manolo de Castro and notified the gunmen at a nearby UIR hangout. UIR propaganda chief Vidal Morales concurred that Fidel Castro detected his MSR rival and "ran to inform other UIR members one block away on Prado." One historian places Fidel Castro "at the meeting of the UIR which agreed to undertake the attempt." UIR member El Chino Esquivel stated that Fidel Castro did not shoot Manolo de Castro "but knew of the planned attack." UIR cohort Pablo Acosta agrees with Esquivel's version. The FEU leadership signed a declaration condemning de Castro's murder and denounced "the climate of violence that prevails in the country with the satisfaction of the government." Ortiz was charged with two counts of murder and two counts of attempted murder after paraffin results proved positive. During the trial a wounded bystander positively identified Fidel Castro and Ortíz as the assassins wearing carnival masks covering half their faces. Although ballistics matched Ortíz's weapon to the crime, his godmother, First Lady Paulina Grau, obtained his release.[56]

After the murder of his rival, Fidel Castro went underground fearing a reprisal assassination. A developing international incident gave him the opportunity to leave the country temporarily. In early March, Argentine senator Diego Luis Molinari was in Havana attending an international conference. He met in his Hotel Nacional suite with law student and UIR member Santiago Touriño, who the previous month had been in Buenos Aires conferring with strongman Juan Perón. Molinari told Touriño that it was necessary for the Latin American student leaders to converge in Bogotá on April 10, coinciding with the Ninth Inter-American Conference, to back the territorial claims of the Argentine and Guatemalan delegations on the British colonies of the Falkland Islands and British Honduras (Belize). The Bogotá conference would replace the old Pan American Union with the proposed Organization of American States (OAS). The United States delegation was headed by Secretary of State George C. Marshall, who was concerned with Communist expansionism in Latin America during the cold war. According to the *Chicago Tribune* correspondent at the Pan American meeting, "The Communists were intent on breaking up the conference." FEU president Enrique Ovares stated, "It was the Peronists who were recruiting people to disrupt the conference. They thought that the United States was going to create a Marshall Plan for Latin America, which would lessen Perón's non-aligned position of regional influence."[57]

Touriño presented the plan to Ovares to create "a strong Latin American anti-imperialist position." Ovares recalled, "We were ideologically formed during an era when many Latin American leaders were anti-American and anti-imperialist. We had that mentality, unfortunately wrong, but it was prevalent at that moment." Aramís Taboada, FEU secretary of foreign relations, had organized a committee on behalf of Puerto Rican independence, in which he included Fidel Castro. The FEU leadership then agreed to participate in a congress against colonialism in Latin America, advocating Trujillo's overthrow, the independence of Puerto Rico, the relinquishing of the U.S. naval bases in Guantánamo and the Panama Canal, and denouncing British colonialism in the Western Hemisphere. Three student commissions were assigned to travel to various Latin American countries, divulge an FEU proclamation, and gather support for a student antiimperialist congress to coincide with the Pan American Conference in Bogotá.[58]

Taboada and El Chino Esquivel went to Guatemala, El Salvador, and Mexico. In Guatemala they were introduced to leftist president Juan José Arévalo, who backed their proposal. Pablo Acosta and Carlos Moreno traveled to Honduras, Nicaragua, and Costa Rica, and Fidel Castro, accompanied by UIR member Rafael del Pino, would go to Venezuela, Panama, and Colombia. Molinari's secretary, Carlos Iglesias Mónica, paid the travel expenses of the three commissions. Castro claimed, "The hostility of the United States toward the Peronist movement in Argentina made us instinctively see Perón and his followers in a rather favorable light." He asked Touriño that the Argentines provide him with diplomatic protection to leave the country safely. Through Ovares, Castro obtained five hundred pesos for expenses from *Bohemia* magazine editor Miguel Angel Quevedo and a letter of introduction for Rómulo Betancourt, who had passed the Venezuelan presidency to Rómulo Gallegos the previous month. In addition, Castro received from Dominican exile Juan Bosch a written recommendation for Betancourt. He was then detained on March 19 at the Rancho Boyeros airport for attempting to flee the country while under a judicial restraint order issued during the Manolo de Castro murder investigation. Taken before a judge, Castro claimed that his opponents were trying to obstruct his student activities, and his travel restrictions were lifted. Five days later he and del Pino, fearing that MSR policemen would kill them at the airport, were accompanied on a flight to Caracas by an Argentine diplomat.[59]

The FEU designated its president Ovares and secretary general Alfredo Guevara to attend the student congress. Ovares sent FEU delegate credentials to Castro and del Pino in Caracas at the bequest of Touriño so that they could participate in the congress. Castro was still auditing classes because he had not registered for that academic year while at Cayo Confites. Del Pino, a twenty-one-year-old machinist affiliated with the CTC since 1945 and with the Union of Electrical, Radio and Machine Workers of America (CIO) in New York since May 1946, pretended to be a student. They delivered the FEU proclamation to the Venezuelan government's newspaper *El País*, which published their photo on March 27. The two later met with the university student leadership, who agreed to send a delegation to Bogotá, and then saw Rómulo Betancourt, the head of the Venezuelan delegation to the Pan American Conference. The Cubans visited the home of president-elect Rómulo Gallegos, who was absent. An interview was arranged for the next day, but the Cubans "had to catch an early plane." Castro gave an apocryphal version in 1981: "We went to La Guaira where Rómulo Gallegos was and that is how we made that contact." He failed to mention his meeting with Betancourt, whom he tried to overthrow in the 1960s by arming Venezuelan Marxist guerrillas.[60]

Castro and del Pino proceeded to Panama, where they were interviewed at a radio station and student leaders promised to send representatives to the Bogotá meeting. The Cubans arrived by plane in the Colombian capital on March 31 and checked into the Claridge Hotel. Ovares and Guevara flew directly from Havana to Bogotá on April 1 and were met by a delegation of Colombian students, who left them at the San José boardinghouse. The next day the four Cubans went to the National University, where the rector introduced them to a group of students that included Liberals, leftists, and Communists. Castro later alleged that during the first organizational meeting he was chosen by the students to "continue in the role of organizer of the event." Ovares disclaimed this, saying that as president of the FEU, which had created the congress, and as the only representative of the World Student Congress that had met in Prague the previous year, he was elected to preside over it and Castro was named emissary to Jorge Eliécer Gaitán, leader of the Colombian Liberal Party. The students then approved a resolution condemning the Ninth Inter-American Conference scheduled for April 3.[61]

That day Fidel Castro wrote home giving lengthy details of his travels and indicating that after the conference he hoped to be invited by the Peronist government to Argentina for three months. The diplomatic delegations attending the Pan American Conference went to a performance in their honor on Saturday night, April 5, in the Colón Theater, hosted by Colombian president Mariano Ospina Pérez. Fidel Castro and del Pino appeared on the mezzanine and threw leaflets "printed in Cuba, of notable Communist political character." Castro admitted that their "little immature" actions led to their arrest. The authorities searched their hotel room and seized a letter of recommendation from Rómulo Betancourt, "various books of Communist disposition," photos of Gaitán, "and also a mysterious cablegram from Havana, of the 3 of April, in whose cipher (surely, ten), there's smell of tragedy." The Cubans were interrogated and booked at the Immigration Office of the National Police in La Capuchina and were released after they stated that their antiimperialist motives were not against Colombia "but against the United States." The chief of the Department of Security wrote in 1949: "Around these same days arrived in Bogotá the known Cuban Communists Fidel Alejandro Castro and Rafael del Pino; they provoked meetings of known leftist students in the University City, from which they frankly rejected all elements marked as rightist. They were taken with their papers to the Immigration Office and were interrogated: They came on holiday and propagandizing against colonialism in America; their papers confirmed this version and they were freed." Castro told a Colombian Marxist writer in 1981 that back then he was "attracted to the fundamental ideas of Marxism" and "was almost a Communist, but was not yet a Communist."[62]

Fidel Castro and del Pino, accompanied by Colombian students, went to a scheduled appointment with Gaitán on the afternoon of Monday, April 7, and requested that he address the inaugural session of the student antiimperialist conference. The Liberal leader gave them pamphlets with his speeches and agreed to meet them again two days later at 2:00 P.M. The following morning the first preparatory meeting for the student conference took place in the office of the Confederation of Colombian Workers. Those present included the four Cuban delegates, representatives from Venezuela, a Panamanian, and two Dominicans. The Argentine and Mexican students did not participate, and those gathered did not reach an agreement other than to meet again the next day. The chief of the Colombian Department of Security claimed that at the session Castro and del Pino "dictated conferences of revolutionary character and gave out instructions on the technique of a coup d'etat and the organization of a general strike." That night he ordered their arrest, but his agents were unable to find the Cubans, who never returned for the next meeting.[63]

The Guatemalan Communist heading his nation's university delegation claimed that a second meeting occurred on the morning of April 9 and ended around noon. Ovares stated that he and Guevara made the rounds of newspaper offices that morning seeking publicity for the student congress. At noon they joined some Colombian students and two Mexican delegates, Jorge Menvielle Porte-Petit and Manuel Vázquez, at the open-air Café Colombia, a block from Gaitán's office. Ovares stated that Menvielle, president of the Mexican FEU, was a Communist who later became his nation's ambassador to Moscow. The Mexicans were staying at the same San José boardinghouse as the two Cuban FEU leaders. Guevara agreed with this version, stating that the internal delegation had split into two groups that were going to converge just prior to the Gaitán meeting. Castro stated that he and del Pino "left our hotel to go sightseeing and have lunch before going to our meeting with Gaitán that afternoon." He later claimed that they ate lunch at the hotel, where they waited for the scheduled appointment. Two days later a report by the secret police, who had been tailing Castro since his detention, indicated that he was seen near Gaitán's office at 1:00 P.M.[64]

Ovares disputes this account as erroneous because he was the one who was near Gaitán's office and Castro had not arrived yet. He stated, "I told my companions that I was going to pick up the film I had left developing at the Kodak store next to Gaitán's office building. While at their sidewalk counter, the shooting started right in front of me. Everyone noticed me because I was a foreigner dressed differently, wearing a suit and fedora." As Gaitán stepped out for lunch with friends, he was shot four times in the upper back and head by Juan Roa Sierra. The assassin was quickly disarmed and arrested by a policeman, but an angry mob beat him to death with shoe-shine boxes taken from street urchins. Roa's half-naked body was dragged through the streets and dumped at the gate of the Presidential Palace. Thus started the Bogotazo, a devastating riot that cost more than three hundred lives, gutted thirty-five major buildings, and sparked Colombia's ten-year civil war. The Inter-American Conference hall was invaded by rioters, forcing the session to adjourn.[65]

Ovares and Guevara quickly returned to their boardinghouse. Castro affirmed that after leaving his hotel, he and del Pino briefly spoke with Ovares and Guevara outside their lodging. They discussed joining the Colombian students at the university. A drunken mob, brandishing machetes and carrying looted objects, rushed by around 2:00 P.M., headed for a mutinous police station commanded by a Liberal police chief. Fidel Castro, depicted by Guevara as "restless, impassioned," exclaimed that he was going to join the rioters. He described himself in those days as "quixotic, romantic, a dreamer, with very little political know-how but with a tremendous thirst for knowledge and a great impatience for action." Guevara and Ovares decided not to participate.[66]

Castro and del Pino went to the Police Third Division Station, where rifles were distributed to the growing mob. Castro entered a dormitory and put on a pair of boots, a military cape, and a cap. The Cubans joined a squadron being mustered in the courtyard, and each received a Mauser rifle and sixteen bullets. They then followed a street crowd going to the Presidential Palace and en route were fired at from inside the San Bartolomé Convent. Del Pino later falsely bragged that he and Castro had killed some priests. Ambassador Guillermo Belt, head of the Cuban OAS delegation, recorded the comment in his report to the Ministry of State in Havana. Ovares and Guevara did not see Castro and del Pino again until about 4:00 P.M., when, shouldering rifles, they stopped by the boardinghouse but failed to convince Ovares and Guevara to join the rabble. Guevara affirmed that he was frightened by what he termed "a disorganized riot . . . based on vengeance and hate and not a revolutionary process."[67]

Castro, del Pino, and five other insurgents decided to support the students holding the national radio station, who were besieged by the army. On the way there, Castro was afflicted by what he called "revolutionary fever" as he climbed a bench in front of the Ministry of War building, clutching a rifle, and harangued a group of soldiers to join the revolution. A squad exiting the building shot at him. Castro then fled in a commandeered bus, but del Pino was briefly detained, although he was released after he claimed to be a U.S. Army sergeant and World War II veteran belonging to Secretary Marshall's retinue. While on the bus, Castro noticed that his wallet with all his money had been stolen. When they got within two blocks of the radio station, the insurgents saw that it was being attacked by a cavalry unit, and they headed for the university. The disorganization on campus prompted Castro to go with a crowd to the nearby Police Eleventh Division Station, which had already fallen to the rebels. Castro claimed that he was appointed assistant to a police major, whom he accompanied in a jeep to the Liberal Party headquarters. After consultations, they returned to the police station. When Castro noticed that the major was "in a state of indecision and disinclined to proceed," he walked to the Police Fifth Division Station, where four hundred insurrectionists were being organized. Castro was assigned to a defense position at a second-floor window to await an imminent attack. He stayed at his post until dawn, occasionally gazing at passing looters who were carrying everything from a piano to a refrigerator.[68]

The next day, April 10, a government radio broadcast attributed the revolt to "foreign agents under the direction of Moscow" intent on wrecking the Pan American Conference and discrediting inter-Americanism. When Ovares heard the news flash at the boardinghouse that "President Ospina was ordering the arrest of Cuban Communist students who were linked to the assassination," he and Guevara went to the Cuban Embassy. They searched for Castro and del Pino at the Claridge Hotel, where the manager wanted them evicted. That morning Castro was sent with a platoon to guard the hill behind the Fifth Division headquarters. Returning to the police station at 4:00 P.M., he joined a patrol going to neutralize a sniper firing from a church steeple. Castro stated that after the mission was accomplished, he returned to the Fifth Division building to spend the night.[69]

Fidel Castro claimed that he found del Pino at the police station on Sunday morning, April 11, after the radio announced a peace agreement between the Liberals and the government. Castro called the accord "a great betrayal" of the populace. At noon the two Cubans relinquished their weapons and Castro acknowledged, "I had used only four of the sixteen bullets I had." They picked up their belongings at the Claridge Hotel and were informed that they were being sought for being "those responsible for everything." The two UIR members then went to the San José boardinghouse, where shortly before the 6:00 P.M. curfew Castro got into a political argument with the conservative owner and got thrown out. He and del Pino went to the Argentine Embassy, but the Peronists refused to grant asylum to the wanted fugitives. The Cubans went to the Granada Hotel looking for the Argentine Carlos Iglesias Mónica, the financier of the student congress, who was with Senator Molinari, a Pan American Conference delegate. "Some mess you've gotten me into," Iglesias said to Castro as he hurried to his Cadillac. The two Cubans climbed into the parked car with curfew-exempt diplomatic plates, while Castro pleaded, "You've got to get me out of here! You must get me out of here!" Iglesias drove them to the Cuban Embassy. Ambassador Guillermo Belt initially refused to help his four compatriots, saying that the Colombian authorities would arrest them at the airport, but later he changed his mind. President Grau then sent a military plane to retrieve the youths, which carried the newsreel cameraman Eduardo "Guayo" Hernández Suárez, who had filmed the Orfila gun battle. That night the fugitives slept in the home of Cuban consul Carlos Tabernilla Dolz.[70]

The next morning Guayo borrowed a Cuban embassy car and, accompanied by the Cuban students and Mexican FEU president Jorge Menvielle Porte-Petit, filmed them standing in a rubble-strewn street. Guevara stated that they posed in different places, "always in the area that was the most calm," and that the newsreel became "an event" in Cuba. According to Ovares, the Cuban Embassy alleged that the four Cubans were members of a touring theatrical troupe whose passports had burned in a hotel fire. While the Colombian authorities were watching the Cuban military plane, the Cuban youths, the two Mexican students, and Guayo departed on a Cuban transport plane without seats, which had taken cattle to a Bogotá livestock exposition. The seven passengers arrived in Havana five hours later, on April 13. Castro admitted in 1960, "I escaped arrest with the help of Cuba's Ambassador to Washington, Dr. Guillermo Belt, who put me on a cargo plane." Although Castro omitted mentioning Belt during a 1981 interview, Ovares, who had publicly criticized Belt five months earlier, years later wrote in a newspaper article, "we owe him our lives."[71]

Fidel Castro stated in December 1960, before declaring himself a Marxist-Leninist, that the Communists had an active participation in the Bogotazo: "But the experience taught me a lot about the way the Communists operate. Communist students grabbed microphones at radio stations and shouted into them: 'People of Colombia! The Leftist revolution of America has started! Soldiers of Colombia! The army has joined us! You join us, too! The Leftist revolution of America is triumphant!' I saw how Communists tried to take over power during an uprising and I could not be sold on any of their promises." In 1981 Castro contradicted himself, saying, "the Communist movement had absolutely nothing to do with the uprising," and instead claimed that "a popular leader like Gaitán could have been assassinated by the CIA."[72]

The Communist newspaper *Hoy*, when reporting the Cuban participation in the Bogotazo, cited only Enrique Ovares and Alfredo Guevara and omitted mentioning Fidel Castro and Rafael del Pino. Castro reminisced in 1960: "Bogotá was a hellish storm center, but it was exciting. It was fun. I was a student in revolt against the old generation. I fought against the *status quo*. I was for democracy and real liberty for all of Latin America. I felt important." Masferrer's *Tiempo en Cuba* describes him as an adventurer "with a chapter dedicated to international brigandage." Castro and the MSR clashed again on July 6, 1948, when university police sergeant Oscar Fernández Caral was gunned down in the doorway of his home. Fernández Caral, a former anti-Machado revolutionary and Auténtico Party militant, had taken part in the Orfilia gun battle under Salabarría. Before dying from eight .45-caliber bullet wounds, he accused UIR leader José de Jesús Ginjaume of being one of his four aggressors. A witness, Reinaldo Aranda Castillo, identified Fidel Castro as a participant in the shooting after picking him out of a police mug-shot file. Castro visited Aranda the next morning and took him to a newspaper office, where the witness stated that he had erred in his identification. According to UIR propaganda chief Vidal Morales, "Fidel did not shoot. He cranked up other UIR members into killing Fernández Caral and showed them where he lived." *Tiempo en Cuba* blamed the murder on Ginjaume, del Pino, and "the rich boy Fidel Castro, chief of the *bonches* of blackmailers and grade thieves of the University, son of a feudal lord of the Marcané sugar mill." Castro and Ginjaume were charged with murder in Havana's Fourth District Criminal Court, but the case was dropped for lack of evidence.[73]

Two months later, on the first anniversary of Emilio Tro's death, the UIR tried to retaliate against recently elected congressman Rolando Masferrer. Fidel Castro, enraged by his constant ridicule in *Tiempo en Cuba*, led the hit team. Castro and UIR triggermen Rafael del Pino, Justo Fuentes, and Armando Galis-Menéndez tried cornering Masferrer at a café on Twelfth and Twenty-third streets, where he usually lunched near his residence. The representative noticed the four men whispering and furtively glancing at him. He approached Castro and warned that he never wanted to see them again in his habitual places. The group departed in del Pino's gray jeep, its doors emblazoned with the seal of the National Federation of Sugar Workers. That night, when Masferrer got home at 1:30 A.M., he spotted the jeep near his house and averted a UIR ambush. In the ensuing gun battle, Galis-Menéndez was wounded in the ankle and the four UIR members ran away. According to Rafael Díaz-Balart, Castro had been hiding on the porch of Masferrer's house and fled by jumping over various backyard fences. He squeezed inside a neighboring doghouse and from there could see the legs of the policemen searching for him. Castro then sought refuge in the third-floor apartment of ATOM leader Ernesto de la Fe. He was offered a spare bedroom but glanced around and insisted on sleeping on the kitchen floor. De la Fe recalled: "Fidel had noticed the balcony next to the kitchen, where I kept a plank for access to the roof next door. He was already looking for an exit, which is how he always thinks. That is why no one has killed him." Castro left the next evening.[74]

Fidel Castro stayed out of sight in Oriente, where on October 12, 1948, he married Mirta Díaz-Balart in Our Lady of Charity Catholic Church in Banes. His father did not attend the ceremony. Rafael Díaz-Balart recalled that "it was expected that

Masferrer would go to Banes to kill Fidel so, my father, who was a very good friend of the chief of the Rural Guard in Banes, Lieutenant Felipe Mirabal Mirabal, asked him to please avoid a shootout there, where Fidel and Mirta might get killed." Wedding presents were carefully searched outdoors for possible package bombs. Mirabal arranged an automobile escort for the couple to Camagüey, where they boarded a plane to the United States. The Castros received gifts of more than three thousand pesos in cash, including one thousand pesos from Gen. Fulgencio Batista, a friend of the bride's family, then exiled in Daytona Beach, Florida. The marriage gave Castro the social standing he formerly lacked. The newlyweds spent their first week in a Miami Beach luxury hotel and went by train to New York City. They lodged in a "furnished room" in an apartment building at 155 West Eighty-second Street where Rafael Díaz-Balart lived with his wife. "They stayed for a month," affirmed Díaz-Balart; "Fidel bought a 1946 Lincoln that all four of us rode to Miami, and the car kept breaking down on the way. My spouse and I flew to Havana, while Fidel and Mirta went with the vehicle on the ferry, arriving in early December."[75]

In Havana, Fidel Castro and his wife sold the car and lived in the Andino Hotel, near the university, where both continued their studies. Their only son, Fidel Angel, was born the following September 1. Castro admitted that his parents economically assisted him with a hefty monthly allowance until he got his law degree. Political activism took precedent over family responsibilities. He appeared in the newspapers again after a public incident on March 11, 1949. That night four inebriated U.S. sailors on port leave in Havana were arrested for desecrating the Central Park statue of liberator José Martí. One had urinated on its pedestal while the others scaled the monument. Student leaders immediately organized street protests. Rafael Díaz-Balart recalled that "the Communists invited us to throw stones at the American Embassy. Fidel and Baudilio Castellanos went, but I refused to go because I felt that the United States government was not responsible for the actions of a few drunken sailors." Castellanos, the son of a Marcané pharmacy owner, was a childhood friend of Fidel Castro and a UIR member. He was clubbed by the police who dispersed the rioters, and he appeared photographed in *Bohemia* magazine with his shirttail raised, showing a bruised back, while Castro and other publicity-seeking students looked on. Castellanos later claimed that Castro participated in Marxist studies offered by the Cuban Communist Party for University of Havana students. In contrast, Communist leader Carlos Rafael Rodríguez indicated that party dogma and rigidity kept Castro away. FEU president Enrique Ovares dismissed any link between Castro and the Communist students during his 1947–50 term. He said, "I was the one who had contacts and relations with the Communist Party and they in turn were helping me."[76]

Fidel Castro received a degree in civil and diplomatic law on October 13, 1950. He had "showed little interest in his legal studies, attending lectures only rarely" and "had missed exams in the two preceding years." Castro quickly passed them because some professors gave oral exams and, according to a U.S. Embassy report, university "standards are low and professional competence mediocre." He then joined the law firm Azpiazo, Castro & Resende with Jorge Azpiazo Núñez de Villavicencio and Rafael Resende Viges. Historians have described Castro as "a young lawyer without clients." A biographer wrote that Castro handled only "a couple of obscure cases" and had little interest in the profession. Castro's practice "languished," and the lack of income was supplanted by the steady parental allowance. His salary during his three-year law practice was under six thousand pesos, derived from winning two land property cases related to his father's estate. Fidel Castro's only prominent political case was on September 5, 1951, when he accused police major Rafael Casals Fernández and Lt. Rafael Salas Cañizares of the death of Ortodoxo activist Carlos Rodríguez, who had been clubbed on the head at a street demonstration seven months earlier. Each of the officers had to post a five-thousand-peso bail, and the case was dismissed the following year.[77]

Fidel Castro now channeled his political aspirations through the Ortodoxo Party, founded on May 16, 1947, by thirty-nine-year-old populist Eduardo Chibás Rivas and Auténtico dissidents disgusted with government corruption. Chibás described their doctrinal goals as "carrying out the liberation of Cuba, through economic independence, political liberty and social justice." His program, based on honest government, was vague about economic or social controls. The party's agrarian reform project called for the redistribution of large estates to landless peasants. Former senate president Eduardo Suárez Rivas indicated that "Chibás, a university dropout, never introduced a single legislative bill during his seven years in the Cuban Congress. Seven months before founding the Ortodoxo Party, he publicly vowed never to leave the Auténticos, but did so after Grau refused to support his presidential aspirations." A historian described Chibás as having a "wild character" and being "overzealous, prone to exaggerate and to make claims that he could not support." A *New York Times* reporter wrote, "To some, Chibas is a hero, a militant voice for democracy; to others, a clown, a demagogue, or worse." Chibás, "an inveterate anti-Communist," was labeled by Communist Party leader Juan Marinello Vidaurreta as "a demagogue allied with North American imperialism." Castro had joined the Ortodoxo Youth branch, in which he did not gain a leadership post, and later incorporated Chibás's political ideology into his own revolutionary rhetoric.[78]

Fidel Castro had been initially supported by Ortodoxo leader Emilio "Millo" Ochoa Ochoa during the spring 1948 reorganization of the party. Millo, seeking the financial and vote-delivery clout of Angel Castro, placed his son's name among twenty-one Oriente provincial delegates on the ballot for the Ortodoxo National Assembly. The national political parties ran their membership drives during the registration campaign a month before the primary elections. The municipal neighborhoods elected their parties' delegates to the municipal assembly. These nominees, in turn, would later elect the delegates to the National Assembly of their respective parties. According to Millo, Fidel Castro desired the influential Havana party ticket but did not campaign, and he lost the primaries. Millo had previously promoted the candidacy of his stepbrother Pedro Emilio Castro as Auténtico representative from Oriente, at the urging of Chano Penabaz. As a result, Angel Castro gave Millo his controlled votes in Birán and Barajagua, supported the campaign of Marino Medina for mayor of Mayarí, and donated two thousand pesos to the Auténticos. Fidel Castro later recalled having seen his father taking cash from his safe to give to politicians. Pedro Emilio Castro ran as Auténtico representative in Oriente Province in every election from 1940 through 1954 but never won.[79]

A week before the June 1, 1948, national elections, Castro was one of the introductory speakers for presidential candidate Chibás at an Ortodoxo rally in Santiago de Cuba. Chibás received only 16.42 percent of the national vote. After Carlos Prío won the election, Castro and other UIR members in the Ortodoxo Youth created a splinter group, Ortodoxo Radical Action (ARO), fomenting revolutionary means of achieving power. However, they were rejected by the passive election-oriented party leaders. The "uncontrollable" Castro was vetoed from the Ortodoxo radio program. According to Ortodoxo senator Carlos Márquez-Sterling, in the spring of 1950 Castro was nominated by Adolfo Otero on the electoral ticket as a delegate for the municipal assembly of the Cayo Hueso district in Havana, but the party snubbed his aspirations and Chibás dismissed him as a "gangster."[80]

After this rejection, Fidel Castro had his brother-in-law Rafael Díaz-Balart arrange an interview with Senator Fulgencio Batista at his Kuquine estate. They were greeted cordially by Batista in his library and talked for almost two hours, mostly about intellectual topics. Castro quipped, "I do not see here in your library Curzio Malaparte's book *The Technique of the Coup d'etat.*" Díaz-Balart claimed that "Batista laughed and said he would have to ask his librarian about it." Castro was trying to get him to theoretically talk about a coup d'état, but Batista avoided the issue. "At that time, Fidel favored the overthrow of Prío, even with a coup d'etat," alleged Díaz-Balart, who years later told a reporter that the conversation digressed to how Napoleon met his Waterloo. According to Díaz-Balart, his brother-in-law promised to send Batista a copy of Emil Ludwig's biography of Napoleon, but "Fidel never sent the book. He explained he didn't want to take the chance of having his meeting with Batista discovered—lest Eddie Chibás suspect a double-cross."[81]

Chibás was facing the most critical moment in his political career. He was being ridiculed after making unfounded graft accusations against Minister of Education Aureliano Sánchez Arango, whom he called "the most shameless and hypocritic traitor in Cuban history." Chibás, a bachelor, shot himself in the abdomen with a Colt

.38 revolver at the conclusion of his regular Sunday radio broadcast on August 5, 1951. On the ride to the hospital, he murmured twice: "I die for the revolution! I die for Cuba!" Ten days later, in spite of progressive recovery, he expired from internal hemorrhage after Dr. Pedro Iglesias Betancourt prescribed decoagulants to counter blood clots developing in his sutured colon. Chibás's opponents described his suicide as a fumbled publicity stunt to regain sympathy, since he did not aim for his head or heart.[82]

Fidel Castro tried to make political headway with the absence of Chibás and the subsequent schism in the Ortodoxo Party. He tried to shed his gangster reputation by denouncing political violence and Auténtico graft. On January 28, 1952, Castro wrote the article "I Accuse," published in *Alerta* newspaper, chastising President Prío for trading political favors for land deeds. A week before the Tenth of March Coup, Castro filed a writ in the court of accounts, published in *Alerta,* naming 2,120 persons receiving government sinecures. He blamed that corruption for spawning the revolutionary groups "whose ranks were filled with older action elements and youths driven by an erroneous concept of heroism and revolution. The government degenerated and sooner or later all those organizations lost their ideological and social content. The Orfila massacre started a war without quarter on both sides." Fidel Castro omitted mentioning his own UIR militancy. Auténtico senator Eduardo Suárez Rivas claimed that Castro acquired most of the details from *Alerta* editor Ramón Vasconcelos, a Batista ally.[83]

In consequence of Fidel Castro's projected political respectability, Manuel Bisbé Alberni, the Ortodoxo leader in the Chamber of Representatives, nominated him at a party municipal assembly for one of the two representative seats from Havana Province for the June 1952 elections. The nomination still had to be approved at the end of March by the provincial assembly and party leader Roberto Agramonte Pichardo. According to Luis Conte Agüero, Castro had been accused of having relied on electoral fraud within the party when challenging Félix Martín for the post of neighborhood delegate, but the allegation was deemed unfounded. Ortodoxo leader Carlos Márquez-Sterling stated that he and Buenaventura Dellundé Puyáns had agreed on March 9 to award the party ticket selected for Castro to another candidate. Castro's political frustrations culminated the next day with Batista's seizure of power.[84]

Fidel Castro's life had been a torturous trail of lofty ambitions. Early childhood traits—being a bully, deceitful, and resentful—and devious manipulation became hallmarks of his personality, as depicted in his fights with schoolmates and teachers, his expulsion from La Salle, the crafty Roosevelt letter, his deception of the Manzanillo City Council, and the increasingly distorted historical accounts he has given biographers. His out-of-wedlock birth, growing up under three different names, and being raised in elite religious boarding schools for more than a decade produced pain and contempt for the Cuban aristocracy that ostracized him. Castro began in 1946 a practice of killing his most threatening political opponents, which he continued for more than sixty years. He was a triggerman in the attempted murders of Leonel Gómez and Rolando Masferrer and was arrested and released for the homicides of Manolo de Castro and Oscar Fernández Caral. Years later Castro replied to accusations that he was a gangster by explaining, "Those who saw the murder of their comrades wanted to avenge them, and a regime that was unable to establish justice allowed such vengeance. The blame cannot be placed on the young men who, moved by natural yearning and the legend of a heroic era, longed for a revolution that had not taken place and at the time could not be started."[85]

As a result of Castro's mercurial character and unsavory reputation, he failed to win an FEU elected position. He denounced Communists in high school and opposed them in university electoral campaigns. Castro was ridiculed in the Communist press and shunned by party leaders because of his Jesuit formation. He pursued his quest for revolutionary internationalism at Cayo Confites and in the Bogotazo riot. After 1959 this interventionism became a cornerstone of Cuban foreign policy. Castro's anti-Americanism, inculcated by his father and Spanish Jesuits, expressed itself at the Bogotazo and during his stoning of the U.S. Embassy in Havana. His student activism on behalf of the "liberation" of the American territories of Puerto Rico, the Guantánamo naval base, and the Panama Canal became his lifelong foreign-policy objectives. Castro's homophobia was later reflected in his revolutionary penal code that established prison terms for those publicly flaunting homosexuality. Fidel Castro neglected a mediocre law practice to pursue a shaky political career that was derailed by Batista's Tenth of March Coup. He could now direct his revolutionary aspirations against a dictator.[86]

TWO

"There is nothing unusual going on"

Having hidden in the apartment of his half sister Lidia all day on March 10, 1952, Fidel Castro feared arrest by the newly appointed chief of police Rafael Salas Cañizares, against whom he had pending charges of manslaughter. During the next twenty-four hours Castro surreptitiously stayed in the Andino Hotel, where he formerly resided, and in the apartment of an Ortodoxo militant. He penned the article "Not a Revolution, a Claw Blow" denouncing the coup d'état and inviting "courageous Cubans to sacrifice and fight back! If our lives are lost, that is nothing." Castro failed to outline a combative strategy other than this reckless challenge to the populace. He sent a copy to *Alerta* newspaper, where his other articles against the Prío administration had been published, but it was rejected due to government censorship. Castro then sequestered himself with other Ortodoxo activists in a farm in Güines. A few days later a newspaper quoted police chief Salas Cañizares as saying that he was not going to take reprisals against Castro for the legal proceedings. A historian described Castro at this time as "a politician without a platform as well as a lawyer without clients."[1]

Fidel Castro resurfaced on Sunday, March 16, at an Ortodoxo rally at the tomb of Eduardo Chibás in Colón Cemetery. An activist read a document signed by vice-presidential candidate and party president Millo Ochoa and presidential candidate Roberto Agramonte calling for a "National Civic Front" to oppose the coup d'état with "all the active and passive forms of 'adequate resistance' authorized by the Constitution." Castro, frustrated with the party leadership's failure to raise a call to arms, climbed onto a crypt and ranted at the crowd for the overthrow of Batista by force. A week later he filed a brief before the Urgency Tribunal accusing the general of violating six Social Defense Code articles totaling a one-hundred-year sentence. Prío's agriculture minister Eduardo Suárez Rivas and Ortodoxo senator Pelayo Cuervo

Navarro had petitioned against the coup d'état before the Tribunal of Constitutional and Social Guarantees, but it ruled against them on April 4, declaring, "The revolution is a source of law." That same day a new 275-article constitutional code, under which freedoms of speech, assembly, and the press could be suspended for forty-five-day periods, went into effect. The death penalty was abolished for political crimes, and political prisoners were granted special privileges. Elections were to be held after eighteen months. An Ortodoxo leader pleaded, in vain, before the OAS in Washington, D.C., for an inter-American force to oust Batista, who chided him for resorting to foreign intervention.[2]

The Ortodoxos were divided over pursuing armed resistance or judicial recourse. A minority of discontented party youths began clandestinely organizing a unifying revolutionary movement. Ortodoxo representative and radio commentator José Pardo Llada tried to defy the press censorship that silenced his program. He drove 150 miles to Colón, Matanzas, with two companions to meet with the local Ortodoxo Party president, Héctor de Armas Laucira, who introduced them to party sympathizer Dr. Mario Muñoz Monroy. The thirty-nine-year-old physician had established his practice a decade earlier in his home clinic, which had a consultation room, a laboratory, and X-ray equipment. His thirty-one-year-old wife, Dinorah Algarra Peralta, served as his assistant. They had a seven-year-old daughter named Dinorah, and another daughter, María Teresa, was born four months later. The doctor piloted his own two-seat aircraft and operated a ham radio. He had offered his shortwave radio transmitter for Pardo Llada to denounce the government, but the visitors lost interest after confirming that the range of the equipment was less than a mile. When Castro heard of the aborted plan, he started his own contacts to acquire the unit.[3]

Castro's revolutionary nucleus germinated when he attended a rally at Colón Cemetery on May 1 in memory of his former client Carlos Rodríguez. The participants included Ortodoxo activists Abel B. Santamaría Cuadrado and his sister Haydée, Raúl Gómez García, Jesús "Chucho" Montané Oropesa, the attorney Melba Hernández Rodríguez, and Elda Pérez Mujica. The group was distributing the first five hundred issues of the clandestinely mimeographed four-page bulletin *Son los Mismos* (They Are the Same), claiming it to be the "Official Bulletin of the Ortodoxo Fraternity." It was edited by Gómez García, a twenty-four-year-old illusive poet and teacher at the private Baldor School. Haydée said that he "always seemed to be looking at flowers, or birds or something infinitely lovely, good or beautiful, and this was true of even the simplest situation. He never seemed to be aware of anything bad or ugly." Castro, introduced by Montané to some of the others, praised their work and solidarity and arranged to meet them again to discuss revolutionary strategy.[4]

Abel Santamaría, the son of Spanish immigrants, was a twenty-four-year-old bookkeeper for a Pontiac dealership. He had left his Las Villas rural home in 1947, after "frequent quarrels and fights at the sugar mill and in the store" where he worked, and gone to live with his cousin in Havana. Four years later his twenty-nine-year-old unmarried sister, Haydée, joined him in a one-bedroom apartment on O and Twenty-fifth streets in El Vedado. The columnist Georgie Anne Geyer, who years later interviewed Haydée, depicted her as "homely but noble-hearted." Haydée described herself as being "somewhat humpbacked." Abel was taking evening high school classes at the Instituto de Segunda Enseñanza, and his sister was unemployed. Their fellow conspirator Raúl Martínez Ararás recalled, "Since both of them were supposed to be studying, their father sent them a monthly stipend to pay the rent. Abel was a dreamer, a romanticist, very noble and well mannered to the point of being somewhat strange. I never knew him to have a girlfriend. He was infatuated with Fidel and followed him blindly. Haydée had a stronger character and she was very protective of her youngest brother." None of Abel's biographies mentions any romance during his lifetime. Haydée later claimed that her brother's political ideas were leftist and that he had read Lenin and Marx. Melba, on the other hand, recalled that Abel mostly read "his usual Machiavelli and books about Cuban history." Abel played with little lead toy soldiers that he identified with each movement member. Rebel leader Orlando Castro García, who lived on the fourth floor of their building, regarded Abel as an "immature person who saw everything through the eyes of Fidel." In early May, Fidel Castro dined at the Santamaría home and adhered to the *Son los Mismos* group. Montané later stated, "We, along with Abel Santamaría joined Fidel, the First of May of 52," when it was the rabble-rousing attorney who sought them out and easily usurped the group's leadership.[5]

The twenty-eight-year-old Montané was the personnel manager at General Motors Inter-American Corporation and lived in Santos Suárez with his wife and son. Two months later he held a similar job at the Compañía Cubana de Refrigeración Eléctrica. Montané, an Isle of Pines native, had attended the American Center School in Nueva Gerona from first through twelfth grades, and there he learned to speak English and had an American girlfriend. Rebel leader Gerardo Pérez-Puelles Valmaseda described Montané as being "totally meaningless, without any depth of character. I never knew why he was with us." Montané was mixing revolutionary activities with lust by pursuing an adulterous affair with Melba Hernández Rodríguez, a thirty-year-old mulatto customs attorney who had worked for the Prío government. Ortodoxo leader Millo Ochoa regarded Melba as "having a racial inferiority complex because she always tried to pass off as white." Raúl Martínez indicated that she had a reputation after having various romances with other Ortodoxo Party youths. Ortodoxo activist Manuel Suardíaz Fernández bluntly described her as "a trollop who liked younger men." Melba resided in a modern third-floor apartment on Jovellar Street in El Vedado with her conservative parents, who tolerated the political activism of their only daughter.[6]

Six days after meeting Fidel Castro, Montané and Abel accompanied him to the city of Colón. Héctor de Armas Laucira introduced them to Dr. Muñoz, who agreed to loan his radio transmitter for a university rally on May 8 commemorating the death of 1930s revolutionary Antonio Guiteras Holmes. Mrs. Muñoz heard Castro praising her husband's idealism and projecting a plan for a simultaneous uprising in all six provinces. Castro impressed her as being "very charismatic and speaking like if he was José Martí." Dinorah Muñoz stated that "Fidel easily convinced me, but I do not know how he fooled my husband who was so intelligent. Mario was not a Communist, he detested Batista and was motivated by patriotism." Castro instructed engineering student Héctor de Armas Errasti, son of the local Ortodoxo Party president, to take the twenty-five-pound transmitter by bus to Havana the day before the act. The morning of the rally, a *Prensa Libre* columnist published the broadcast kilocycles. The radio antenna was affixed to the roof of the university's Engineering School to broadcast the anti-Batista speeches. De Armas recalled that "in spite of the limited range of the shortwave radio, it was proclaimed at the rally that the live program was being heard throughout the island. This caused a lot of applause and cheering."[7]

Another event was held in the University of Havana on May 20 to commemorate the fiftieth anniversary of Cuban independence. The clandestine radio was transmitting the act from a Tamarindo Street location on the forty-meter band, but "the broadcast was barely heard." The police subsequently confiscated the equipment when, according to Montané, "The person who was operating the station went over to the enemy." The *Son los Mismos* group attended the campus rally that day, and Melba Hernández helped distribute leaflets. She recalled how, "later on, Fidel, with the critical spirit that characterizes him, proposed changing the name of the newspaper to *El Acusador* (The Accuser), since according to what he explained, there was a need for a more combatant newspaper." Only eight issues of *Son los Mismos* were published from May to July 29, 1952. The mimeograph machine was kept in the home of an Ortodoxo activist in El Vedado.[8]

The *Son los Mismos* group initially balked at Castro's idea of the new format and continued publishing their pamphlet while at the same time printing *El Acusador*. Montané declared, "It was very hard for us to abandon the publication of *Son los Mismos,*" but Abel eventually told Castro what they were doing behind his back. Raúl Gómez García became the editor of *El Acusador,* under the pseudonym "The Citizen." Abel was assistant editor, and Castro, using his middle name Alejandro, provided "political orientation." The first issue of *El Acusador* contained the rejected article "Not a Revolution, a Claw Blow," by "Alejandro," written the day after the coup. "The Citizen" mourned Chibás, and another note denounced that "the Ortodoxo leaders spent millions of pesos in their electoral campaigns, but are not capable of spending one single cent on the insurrection." *El Acusador* was sold for five cents to raise funds for their movement. The second issue included cartoons mocking

Batista, a nine-paragraph diatribe by "Alejandro" called "I Accuse," and what Castro entitled "Critical Assessment of the PPC," which concluded that "the moment is revolutionary, and not political.... A Revolutionary Party should have a revolutionary leadership, youthful and of popular origin that will save Cuba." On two occasions Héctor de Armas took fifty copies of *El Acusador* to Colón for distribution among the Ortodoxo Youth. He recalled that all the issues were void of Marxist rhetoric.[9]

The second printing of *El Acusador* was sold on August 16, 1952, during a ceremony at the tomb of Eduardo Chibás, on the first anniversary of his death. The copies were retrieved from the residence of Joaquín González Cuadra by Montané and future Moncada combatants Mario Chanes, Fernando Chenard, and Ulises Sarmiento Vargas, a seventeen-year-old coffin-maker apprentice. A scuffle ensued in the cemetery when an undercover agent tried to arrest the *El Acusador* vendors, who all except for Sarmiento slipped away. When Montané, Raúl Gómez García, Abel Santamaría, Juan Martínez Tinguao, Elda Pérez Mujica, and Melba Hernández arrived at the González residence to get more *El Acusador* issues, the Military Intelligence Service (SIM) arrested them for slander and illegal publication, impounding their mimeograph machine and a typewriter. González and the women were not detained, leading the others to speculate that he was a police collaborator. The next day Castro obtained their release from El Príncipe prison, and the group was acquitted a month later. As a consequence of the arrest, Gómez García was fired from his teaching position.[10]

The day after the cemetery gathering, Abel Santamaría sent an open letter to Pardo Llada describing his frustrations with Agramonte and other Ortodoxo Party leaders who were not espousing belligerent action against the military regime. Abel wrote that Agramonte "should not appear pale and nervous and wavering before the followers of Chibás . . . before a multitude that clamors for justice in any manner, he is too fragile." The lackluster Agramonte was a forty-eight-year-old corpulent and balding University of Havana philosophy professor nicknamed "Masa Boba" (Foolish Blob) by the students. The Ortodoxo Youth disavowed the irresolution of their leaders in a radical manifesto on June 25, 1952, stating, "We support the line of revolutionary action of fighting in the streets, and open warfare against the de facto government in order to create the necessary conditions for the Cuban people in a given moment to do away with the heavy burden that the government imposed on us on March 10. Batista today, like Machado yesterday, cannot be overthrown with little pieces of paper [manifestos]."[11]

The nucleus of Castro's movement expanded in early September after he met with radicals of the Ortodoxo Party Professional Section in a public accountant's office. They were summoned by Raúl Martínez Ararás, a thirty-four-year-old accountant, who stated, "We felt we had to do something to punish the crime committed on March tenth, but had no military or revolutionary background." Martínez, his two brothers, and his three sisters were raised in Colón, Matanzas, until their family moved to Havana in 1936. Their self-employed father died two years later, leaving forty-eight-year-old Rosaura Ararás alone to raise her brood. She was a woman with fortitude and patriotic sentiments. At the age of six, Rosaura saw the corpse of her uncle, Cuban War of Independence colonel Octavio Hernández, dumped on their front porch by the Spaniards who murdered him. The family then suffered for two years the vicissitudes of a Spanish *reconcentrado* internment camp.[12]

Influenced by his mother's strong determination and patriotism, Raúl Martínez developed political yearnings after being elected president of the School of Commerce Student Association. In 1945 he married Coralia "Nenita" Varela Pla in Miami Beach, Florida, where her parents resided. Martínez later taught Spanish at the Berlitz School in New York and Miami, while he and his wife periodically returned to the island. After the Batista coup, Martínez told Nenita, "We have to go back to do something for Cuba." Leaving their two children Raúl and Tatiana with her parents, the couple returned to Havana, and Martínez became an Ortodoxo Party activist. During his first meeting with Fidel Castro, some members of the Professional Accountants Association donated money to the cause. A new recruit from outside their party ranks was twenty-five-year-old Orlando Castro García, the assistant chief of the credit department of Sabatés, a subsidiary of Procter & Gamble. He left the movement a few months later after disagreeing with Fidel Castro's tactics but rejoined at the last moment, persuaded by his friend Martínez.[13]

Almost all of Fidel Castro's followers were Ortodoxo Youth rank and file, who were awed by his fiery oratory, Benito Mussolini-like stance and gesticulations, UIR reputation, and his self-aggrandizement stories about Cayo Confites and the Bogotazo. The overwhelming majority derived from a low social stratum and had an elementary-school education. Castro admitted seeking followers in the most humble peasant sectors and in the Havana working-class neighborhoods. He said in 1967 that 90 percent of his men were "laborers and farmers." Many were the products of broken homes and/or poverty, had a large number of siblings, or like Castro, were born out of wedlock. At least twenty-five rebels were raised without fathers. Their existence was a constant struggle in a society-conscious era. Their menial occupations included parking-lot attendants, delivery boys, street vendors, busboys, chauffeurs, and unskilled laborers. Castro searched for socially marginal people he could mold and who were "young, angry, lost, alienated, deracinated, and left behind." They were "totally obedient to him, and to him alone." The rebels were "almost entirely men of the lower middle class or working class. Few were students, and only a small minority had been to the university." Only 4 of the, eventually, 160 followers were university graduates: the attorney Melba Hernández, the physician Mario Muñoz, the dentist Pedro Aguilera, and the chemical engineer Manuel Suardíaz Fernández. Of the 137 insurgents whose ages are known, the average age was twenty-six, the same as that of Fidel Castro. Nine were in their teens, 96 were in their twenties, 27 in their thirties, and 5 over forty (see appendix 1). The Afro-Cuban composition of the group was limited to 2 blacks and 12 mulattos, partly because most biracial Cubans identified with Batista. According to the historian Carlos Moore, "None of the black Moncadistas was personally close to Castro before the assault, nor did any of them have any special relationship with him other than that which was necessary for carrying out the attack."[14]

The heterogeneous group included people with criminal records and what Raúl Martínez called a gang of "illiterate delinquents," who rarely worked and frequently loitered in the Ortodoxo Party headquarters. Their leader was twenty-year-old Antonio "Ñico" López Fernández, a thin, six-foot, six-inch-tall, part-time unskilled laborer at Havana's Central Market. He wanted Eduardo Chibás to create within the party a section to represent the unemployed, and he aspired to preside over it. Martínez described Ñico as "being raised on the streets without parental care. He was socially resentful and illiterate, but he always kept an immaculate appearance and wore a sport coat." Castro acknowledged that he individually chose his followers "on basic criteria" among the *humildes,* the lowly. He avoided the "middle class or intellectuals, whom he felt he could not trust as much." The intellectuals were more apt to challenge his ideas. Raúl Martínez and Angel Díaz-Francisco agreed that Castro's educational and political superiority over his followers allowed him to sift out those who did not meet his criteria or who disagreed with him. Bogotazo companion Enrique Ovares stated that "Fidel was never with anyone superior to him because he did not want to feel inferior. He needs to be in total control and wants only those who are unconditionally loyal to him." Martínez recalled that Castro stressed his views repeatedly, in long monologues, as if by doing so he would make them more credible. He was intent on recruiting "soldiers," and not the leadership of the Ortodoxo Party.[15]

Fidel Castro needed to prepare his fledgling troops, but since the FEU president had prohibited his entry on campus, he sent Ñico López on September 10, 1952, to ask student activists to allow his followers to join their paramilitary training sessions. The trainees included students, Ortodoxo Youths, and Auténtico partisans. Engineering student Pedro Miret recalled that Ñico "came on behalf of Fidel to see if we could train a small group that he had, since he lacked the means of training them." Miret introduced him to engineering students Léster Rodríguez Pérez, Abelardo "El Perico" Crespo Arias, and others, who conducted weapons handling and calisthenics on the sciences department roof and the FEU premises. Their instructor was thirty-two-year-old bachelor Isaac Santos Domínguez, alias "Professor Harriman," a U.S. Army World War II officer and commando trainer, a former Auténtico militant, and the owner of a gymnasium in Marianao.[16]

A participant named Carlos A. Bustillo Rodríguez, a twenty-six-year-old bachelor who managed a road-construction company, recalled, "we did not have target practice in the university. There was an old M-1 that we would take apart and assemble and Harriman would teach us the identification and handling of weapons. The sessions also tested the commitment and dedication of those involved." Another instructor was a former army officer who taught how to operate a mortar using a wooden model. "Harriman" organized a series of twelve physical exercises such as sit-ups, push-ups, and chin-ups, which were supervised by Héctor de Armas and Raúl Castro, a social sciences student. Bustillo estimated that fifteen hundred militants passed these tests. Fidel Castro believed that there were about "twelve hundred men." Léster Rodríguez exaggerated that there were "no less than 4,000 persons" and stated that the SIM infiltrated various agents into the training sessions.[17]

At the end of 1952 the Ortodoxo Party was fragmented by dissent and disarray. Disenchanted Ortodoxo youths were abandoning their ranks due to the party's passivity and their leaders' claim that they could still operate militantly without violence. Castro's nucleus was "engaged in extracting those comrades from the Ortodoxo Youth who favored an armed struggle and moved away from the bosom of the party." They recruited new affiliates at a University of Havana rally on November 27 commemorating eight medical-student martyrs of the Ten Years' War of independence who had been unjustly executed in 1871. One newcomer was twenty-four-year-old Reinaldo Boris Luis Santa Coloma, whom Montané introduced to Haydée Santamaría as a Santos Suárez neighbor and former bookkeeper at the Compañía Cubana de Refrigeración Eléctrica. Haydée, six years older than Boris, claimed that that is when their romance began. Boris had been dismissed from his job for trying to organize a labor syndicate and later worked at Sears. His mother, a widowed seamstress, had raised him and his schizophrenic older brother in Madruga, forty miles southeast of the capital. After the family moved to Havana, Boris was introduced in 1952 to thirty-eight-year-old Nereida Rodríguez in Fidel Castro's law office. She was an itinerant photographer for Foto Torras, selling pictures and cigarettes to nightclub patrons and the public at large. Soon thereafter, she and Boris began a love affair that produced their son, Boris Luis Rodríguez, on July 11, 1953. The son and his mother have been omitted from all revolutionary historical accounts.[18]

During one of his frequent trips to Madruga, Boris enlisted into the group his friends Orbeín Hernández Díaz, the secretary general of the local Ortodoxo Youth, and twenty-eight-year-old bachelor Manuel Suardíaz Fernández, the Ortodoxo delegate of the east neighborhood, whose brother was the party president in the city. Suardíaz described Boris as "a playboy" who was simultaneously "bedding with Nereida and Haydée." Suardíaz, a Jobabo sugar mill chemical engineer, had been fired after his arrest for organizing a work strike protesting the Tenth of March Coup. He believed that "the only way to overthrow Batista was by force. An electoral process would be a farce, like it had been in 1940. Our Madruga group contacted an infinity of Ortodoxo and Auténtico leaders who eagerly spoke of waging war against

Batista; but they never delivered. It was all a lie. This quest led us to Fidel Castro, who had a clear and concise idea of what to do."[19]

Castro expanded contacts with dissatisfied Ortodoxo Youths favoring armed insurrection. He advised them to gather secretly in small groups and prepare for a nationwide uprising. In November, at the party headquarters, Castro approached José "Pepe" Suárez Blanco, the unemployed Ortodoxo Youth secretary in Artemisa, Pinar del Río. He queried him on the political situation, and Suárez replied that the party's leadership was deploying "a phony fight." Castro replied, "We have to do something. These opposition politicians are deceiving us and they are deceiving all the people. The Auténticos nor even the Ortodoxos are going to resolve anything." Suárez agreed to organize a clandestine armed group with party militants in Artemisa, thirty-five miles southwest of Havana. His first recruits were Ramiro Valdés Menéndez, a twenty-one-year-old unemployed truck driver's helper, and Gerardo Granados Lara.[20]

Granados, a twenty-two-year-old clerk at La Filosofía clothing store, induced his relatives into the group. He was joined by his older brother Guillermo, a shoe salesman and father of two children, who until then had been affiliated with an Ortodoxo clandestine organization headed by Millo Ochoa. Their twenty-nine-year-old brother-in-law, Gregorio Careaga Medina, a funeral home employee and the father of two children, also adhered to the cause. Gerardo recalled, "I was not very happy with my family's involvement, but if they were active with another group, I had more faith in our movement." Ramiro Valdés recruited his future brother-in-law José Ponce Díaz, who with his brother operated a small print shop in their home. The Ponce brothers had previously mimeographed a student manifest denouncing the Batista coup, inadvertently using their business stationery, which led to their arrest. Ponce later complained that he was beaten by the Rural Guard and jailed for six weeks. The Artemisa recruits ceased all Ortodoxo Party activities and created the first operational cell with ten people.[21]

Fidel Castro went to Artemisa in December 1952 and met with six rebels in a bar. He returned a few days later for a nighttime meeting with group leaders in the empty Evolución Masonic Lodge. Gerardo Granados recalled that Castro "did not mention Communism or Socialism. He told us that we had to be prepared and wait until the rest of the country was organized. Cells were being created in every city in Cuba, and at a precise moment everyone would act. Our mission was to take Artemisa, which would be easy, since we were about sixty, against an outpost of twenty soldiers." Castro advised them not to keep membership lists and to compartmentalize in cells of ten so that in case of arrest, few people would be implicated.[22]

The Artemisa group proved to be the largest and most militant faction of the Moncada attackers. They held handgun target practice in nearby farms. Gerardo Granados admitted using "a .22-caliber pistol and a paper target. Each one would fire three or four shots, and I would pass up my turn so that others could shoot more and become enthusiastic. During all that practice I think I fired the handgun once or twice. Our cell did not train with rifles or shotguns." Mario Lazo Pérez and four friends went by bus to the farm of their comrade Ismael Ricondo Fernández to train with .22-caliber pistols. Julio Díaz González, a hardware-store clerk in Artemisa, supplied the ammunition. In nearby Pijirigua, Ortodoxo Youth leader Fidel Labrador García and other Artemisa youths practiced with .22-caliber rifles at two farms. In neighboring Guanajay, Abelardo García Ylls trained his cell on the farm of the rebel José Costa Velázquez. The Artemisa rebels went to the University of Havana a few times, gaining admittance to a room for secret training sessions by using the countersign "Socrates" when asked "Who is the Greek?" Abel Santamaría demonstrated for them the handling of an old machine gun, which on one occasion accidentally fired a few rounds that almost hit someone.[23]

Other revolutionary cells were organized in various neighborhoods and municipalities of Havana, including Marianao, La Ceiba, Puentes Grandes, Almendares, Cayo Hueso, San Lázaro, Santos Suárez, Lawton, and Arroyo Naranjo. Groups were also formed in the Havana Province towns of Santiago de las Vegas, Rancho Boyeros, and Calabazar. La Ceiba cell was headed by thirty-four-year-old Fernando Chenard Piña, a twice-married father of two girls, who worked at El Bodegón eatery. Chenard and a partner owned the Chen-Per photo studio in a back room of the store. He recruited into the movement their twenty-one-year-old assistant Miguel Oramas Alfonso and neighborhood Ortodoxo Youths. These included Mario Chanes de Armas, elected second-in-command of their clandestine cell; Pedro Marrero Aizpurúa, a twenty-six-year-old Tropical Beer truck driver; and Eduardo Montano Benítez, a thirty-three-year-old barber. Montano's family included tobacco sharecroppers in Pinar del Río who began migrating to Havana in late 1933 to enlist in the army. When Montano was twenty-one, he became a barber in his brother's salon in La Ceiba. He followed another brother into the Marianao police force in 1943 but quit a year later after realizing that he made twice as much on his barber's salary. His one-chair barbershop had a back room that the rebels dubbed "the conspiracy office." Montano lived in another room with his wife Santa and their three-year-old daughter Yolanda. He recruited his neighbor Giraldo Córdova Cardín, a twenty-two-year-old mulatto amateur boxer and Fontecha refinery laborer. Castro met only once with the entire eleven-member La Ceiba cell at Chenard's home for an hour. Montano remembered, "He praised our group, spoke about Ortodoxo politics and the desire to reinstate the 1940 Constitution. Fidel never mentioned Communism or Socialism." The La Ceiba cell held target practice at the nearby La Panchita quarry, shooting at a tin can with a .32-caliber pistol. The neighboring Marianao affiliates secretly met in the Lyceum hall. Their first target practices were held in December 1952 at local shooting galleries. Their leader,

Hugo Camejo Valdés, was a thirty-five-year-old brickyard laborer with a fifth-grade education who supported a wife and three children on his meager salary.[24]

The Marianao group would later be consigned mostly to Raúl Martínez, who got his twenty-six-year-old brother-in-law, Ernesto Tizol Aguilera, to join them in late 1952. Tizol, a Sears clerk and poultry grower, was married to Raul's youngest sister, Emma. They lived with her mother, Rosaura Ararás, on a rented farm in San Pedro del Cotorro, seven miles southeast of Havana. The property was used for rebel target practice with .22-caliber rifles. Rosaura asked her younger son, twenty-eight-year-old Mario, to join the conspiracy to safeguard Raúl. Mario, a tall, muscular, long-distance runner, was the antithesis of his accountant brother. After their father died when he was eight, Mario became rebellious and eventually left school to become a truck driver. He married young, had a son, and worked at his father-in-law's bakery in his native Colón. His temperament landed him in jail overnight when he disarmed and battered a verbally abusive Rural Guard corporal. Raúl and his sister Elvira administered the Thion Laboratory owned by forty-eight-year-old Dr. Filiberto Ramírez Corría. Raúl hired twenty-nine-year-old Oscar Alcalde Valls to manage the company books and induced him into the conspiracy. Alcalde was a utilities inspector for Batista's Ministry of the Treasury and also handled other business concerns. He became the treasurer for the clandestine group and used the Thion Laboratory bank account as a front for their finances. Alcalde joined the El Cerro Hunting Club to take rebels in groups of six to target practice, spending up to fifty pesos a session.[25]

The insurgent ranks expanded along with new marksmanship locations. Nine peasants from Nueva Paz municipality, fifty miles southeast of Havana, joined the growing movement. The Marianao cell went on Sundays by railroad to a 230-acre farm outside the town of Los Palos, Nueva Paz municipality, owned by Mario and Horacio Hidalgo-Gato González. Twenty-six-year-old Mario, an agricultural engineer, was an Ortodoxo Party political leader in Nueva Paz. Thirty-year-old Horacio, an attorney, recalled that during one training session their Afro-Cuban neighbor, Julio Piedra Villadroin, went to investigate the gunfire. Some local rebels accused him of being a Batista supporter and a snitch. According to one insurgent, "Some of our people wanted to kill him, because they thought he was going to denounce us anyway." Castro, who rarely attended training sessions, warned the intruder, "if one of those present is arrested you will pay with your life."[26]

Due to their lack of military weapons, Fidel Castro decided to usurp the armaments of other revolutionary groups. According to one activist, "Castro and [Abel] Santamaría supported infiltrating the ranks of the [National Civic] Front which would obtain the control of the arms they would acquire and after seizing them, independently initiate the insurrection and therefore compel everyone to follow them in the endeavor." Castro advised his followers to fraternize with militants of other groups. Abel and Montané spoke with Millo Ochoa, who acknowledged that he was conspiring with army officials, but they distrusted his frankness. Abel unsuccessfully tried to infiltrate the Auténticos to seize an arsenal stored in a yacht. Castro and his closest associates met in Melba Hernández's home on December 29 with Auténtico plotters and gave them a list of desired weapons, which were never delivered. Castro later explained that "when none of these [opposition] leaders showed that they had either the ability or the realization of the seriousness of purpose or the way to overthrow Batista, it was then that I finally worked out a strategy of my own."[27]

By early 1953 Castro had consolidated his "command staff." He admitted for the first time in 1985 that he, Abel, and Raúl Martínez were the executive nucleus of the movement who planned the most secret activities without telling the others. Fifteen years later Castro supplanted Martínez from his historic version with Renato M. Guitart Rosell, a member of the military committee. This latter group included Ernesto Tizol, Pedro Miret, and José Luis Tasende, a twenty-eight-year-old cheese factory worker and ATOM militant. The civil committee consisted of Dr. Mario Muñoz, Reinaldo Boris Luis, Chucho Montané, and Oscar Alcalde. Raúl Castro, the godfather of Tasende's daughter, was not part of the command staff and did not have a leadership role in the Moncada attack. He admitted that their organization lacked a name and they were only known as "The Movement" among Ortodoxo Youths in contact with them.[28]

Fidel Castro later stated that the movement leaders were leftists and claimed having in 1953 a "fairly complete Marxist-Leninist formation." Yet, he never expressed these ideas in *History Will Absolve Me* or the movement's "Manifesto to the Nation." Raúl Martínez indicated that of the 160 rebels, only Abel Santamaría, Víctor Escalona Benítez, Ñico López, and Raúl Castro sympathized with Marxist ideology, although they were not Communist Party affiliates or activists. Raúl Castro and thirty-nine-year-old sugar-mill worker Luciano González Camejo belonged to the PSP. Martínez affirmed: "During our meetings, when anyone spoke about Communism, Fidel would prohibit it to avoid confrontations. He limited the discussions to the overthrow of Batista and the restoration of the Constitution of 1940. Ninety-eight percent of the combatants were not Communists and over ninety percent were affiliated with the Ortodoxo Party." Melba Hernández declared that "in our ranks in that period there was never talk about communism, socialist or Marxist-Leninism as an ideology ... the problem of workers' exploitation was not discussed." Haydée Santamaría concurred: "I am not going to say that we went to Moncada to make a socialist revolution. We went there with the idea of making a change, so that better men might govern and so that men would not steal.... We went to Moncada as disciples of Martí." The rebels "had little ideology save hostility to Batista, though in most of the leaders the notion of revolution, patriotic and social, burned fiercely, if vaguely."[29]

The command staff started accruing funds for their organization. Raúl Martínez introduced Fidel Castro to Ortodoxo senator José M. Gutiérrez Planes, an old family friend, in Matanzas. After listening to their belligerent proposal, the senator sent them five hundred pesos a week later, the first donation to the revolution. Martínez also obtained money from other wealthy friends, including an advertising-firm owner who employed the rebel Gerardo Pérez-Puelles Valmaseda. In January 1953 Castro and Martínez visited the home of Ortodoxo sympathizers forty-two-year-old Dr. Orlando Fernández Ferrer and his twenty-seven-year-old spouse Natalia "Naty" Revuelta Clews, who lived with their four-year-old daughter Natalie. Orlando was a prominent cardiologist at the Centro Médico Quirúrgico clinic, earning approximately two thousand pesos monthly. The family lived in a two-story, four-bedroom chalet on the corner of Fourth and Fifteenth streets in El Vedado, with Orlando's doctor's office on the ground floor. Dr. Ricardo Martínez Serrera stated that his brother-in-law Orlando and Naty had first met Fidel Castro at the clinic when Eduardo Chibás was moribund. The Fernández family had three servants and frequented the parties at the exclusive Biltmore Country Club and the tournaments at the Vedado Tennis Club. Raúl Martínez recalled that "Fidel went into his theatrics in their living room, walking about and gesticulating while giving a speech." When the evening was over, the guests were told to come back in a few days. Raúl Martínez stated that when he returned, "Naty was alone and gave me two envelopes; one on behalf of the family with $100, and a personal one from her, which contained $200." An extramarital love affair soon flourished between Castro and Naty, who provided her mother's apartment on Eleventh Street "for meetings and hiding weapons in transit, and contributed generously to the movement from her own funds."[30]

Naty's maternal grandfather was an English sugar engineer who migrated to Cuba in 1894 and obtained the rank of colonel during the Cuban War of Independence. According to Martínez Serrera, her mother, Natalia Clews Alvarez, in the 1920s led a licentious life with many lovers. She married Manuel Revuelta in 1924 but after four years divorced the "irresponsible alcoholic" and sought a more reliable provider. Naty said that her mother "no longer believed in love" and had a fling with Julio Lobo, a wealthy Cuban Jew, before marrying Heberto Coll, a divorced employee of the American-owned Havana Electric Company. Naty, at the age of thirteen, was sent to Mount St. Joseph's Academy in Philadelphia and later completed her studies at the Ruston Academy in Havana in 1943. Martínez Serrara stated that Naty, during her late teens, attended the exclusive parties of the American-owned Cayuga Company in Havana. She then spent two years at Marjorie Webster Junior College in Washington, D.C., before returning to Cuba. Naty obtained employment at the U.S. Embassy in Havana translating into English intelligence reports about Cuban politics. She lost her job after indiscreetly revealing to her friends the sensitive content of her work. Naty then went to work for the Standard Oil Company as an executive secretary. She met Dr. Orlando Fernández Ferrer during her appendectomy surgery at the Centro Medico Quirúrgico. Their lavish wedding on June 19, 1948, was attended by numerous socialites, various Ortodoxo leaders, and the American ambassador.[31]

After Naty provided funds to Fidel Castro, he introduced her to engineering student Héctor de Armas, who was in charge of buying weapons. De Armas remembered that "Naty eventually gave me three or four checks for $500 which I cashed without difficulty." He purchased numerous .22-caliber rifles and hollow-point bullets at two Havana gun shops without arousing suspicion, because his uncle owned a traveling carnival shooting gallery. De Armas transported the weapons, in lots of five, on public buses. Ernesto Tizol acquired at another Havana store some Browning 16-gauge and Remington 12-gauge shotguns with ammunition. Some weapons were hidden in the El Vedado apartment of Naty's mother, and others were stored in the residences of Rosaura Ararás, José Luis Tasende, and Gildo Fleitas López. The latter was a balding, obese, thirty-four-year-old Ortodoxo activist who had been an office clerk at Belén High School when Castro attended there. He worked at the San Francisco de Sales Trade School and also administered the Molino Arrocero de Matanzas office in Havana. Fleitas persuaded his boss to hire Abel Santamaría as a bookkeeper and retain Fidel Castro as attorney.[32]

The rebels attended all patriotic anniversary rallies or protest marches that served as forums for diatribes against the Batista regime and for selecting new recruits. A demonstration was held by University of Havana students on January 15, 1953, after a bust of Communist student leader Julio Antonio Mella, unveiled five days earlier near the campus, was spattered with tar. Raúl del Mazo Sera, a former Joven Cuba militant, stated that students from within the university began shooting at the police, prompting a violent confrontation. Three policemen and two students, including twenty-one-year-old Rubén Batista Rubio, were wounded. When Castro arrived on campus, Isaac "Harriman" Santos asked him to fetch his group's weapons to confront the authorities. Castro instead told Héctor de Armas, "There is nothing to do here, let's go see Guido García Inclán and harangue on his radio program." Castro's failure to return prompted Harriman to call him a coward. Castro responded by slandering the bachelor Harriman, labeling him a homosexual and an agent provocateur.[33]

A few weeks later Castro published an article in *Bohemia* denouncing a police raid on the workshop of forty-one-year-old sculptor José Fidalgo Rodríguez, an Auténtico activist. Fernando Chenard, the La Ceiba cell leader, photographed the broken statuettes of José Martí that illustrated the article. The figurines were going to be sold for five pesos each to raise funds for Castro's movement. The authorities "said they found a small printing press in the rear of the shop for which the sculptor had no license." Fidalgo went underground, arriving three months later in New York City as a stowaway. On February 14 Rubén Batista Rubio died of a gunshot wound received the previous month during the university confrontation. The mourners who attended his interment in Colón Cemetery then marched back to the university along Twenty-third Street. Castro, Pedro Marrero, and Ñico López were in the crowd that attacked the home of fifty-four-year-old Luisa Margarita de la Cotera O'Bourke, the publisher of the progovernment tabloid *Who's Who in Cuba*. Her front yard contained an illuminated billboard with Batista's image and the phrase "The light that shines the most." Castro joined the others in throwing rocks at de la Cotera's house and overturning her car before the police dispersed them.[34]

Another organized attempt to overthrow the Batista government was led by Rafael García-Bárcena Gómez, a forty-six-year-old University of Havana philosophy professor. He had been on the faculty at the Superior War College until his dismissal after the Tenth of March Coup. García-Bárcena had belonged to the DEU of 1930, was an Auténtico Party founder, and had been part of the executive council of the new Ortodoxo Party in 1947. He created the Revolutionary Nationalist Movement (MNR) on May 20, 1952, diverting the majority of its militants from the Ortodoxo ranks. The professor believed that his former student officers would "stage a counter-coup—or more precisely a putsch—whereby Batista would be overthrown and a true revolutionary government installed under the 'provisional' presidency of García-Bárcena."[35]

Mario Llerena, of the MNR National Committee, later wrote that "García-Bárcena had been entertaining the idea of a putsch even before Batista erupted on the scene on 10 March 1952." Their leadership meetings were sometimes held in the apartment of Llerena, who explained that the MNR "lacked organized cadres, cells, anything of that sort. Its only structural body, the national committee, did very little beyond holding meeting after meeting, all of which consisted of endless, mostly theoretical discussions that circled mainly around the topic of what should be done in Cuba once Batista was overthrown." They conspired to assault Camp Columbia with armed students during the afternoon changing of the guard. Junior officers allied with García-Bárcena would then seize the garrison and the MNR would assume power. The plan was such an open secret that on February 13, 1953, the American Embassy in Havana described it to the Department of State and U.S. embassies in Mexico, Guatemala, the Dominican Republic, and Venezuela.[36]

The MNR rented a house opposite Post 13 of Camp Columbia, establishing a "private school" as a front. The uprising, set for March 8, was postponed until the afternoon of Easter Sunday, April 5. A few hours before the scheduled start, police and SIM agents arrested García-Bárcena and the MNR leadership in an apartment in Almendares and forty-six followers inside the "private school." García-Bárcena denied trying to take over the military base. Army chief of staff Gen. Francisco Tabernilla Dolz initially labeled the conspiracy "the work of a crazy poet," and he later said that the attackers "wanted to utilize knives to stab our advanced sentinels without calling attention with gun shots." This accusation would be repeated after the Moncada attack. The government ridiculed the plot as "The razor-nick coup." Llerena retrospectively affirmed, "To be truthful, the MNR was more a fluid state of mind than a real revolutionary movement."[37]

When García-Bárcena's plan was initially delayed, he met with Fidel Castro, Abel Santamaría, and Chucho Montané to say that he was conspiring with various army officers, that the scheme was fail-safe, and that the gates of Camp Columbia would be opened to him. Castro later stated, "Yet, at that moment, March 1953, we had not made our own plan. Still, in our eagerness to cooperate with whoever wanted to fight, we were willing to adhere to whoever took the first step, and he said he had solid contacts." Castro told García-Bárcena not to divulge his plan to others, but a few days later it was known by more than two hundred people. Castro recalled, "It was the most announced attack in the history of Cuba. Then, we decided not to participate. . . . The last thing that made us decide to assume our own plan was the failure of García-Bárcena."[38]

Fidel Castro's attempts to infiltrate other revolutionary groups and seize their armaments had by then floundered. Pedro Miret and Oscar Alcalde, through a third party, contacted a Spanish Republican exile, who promised to deliver ten Thompson machine guns for twenty-five hundred pesos. At the transaction location, Miret and Alcalde observed some suspicious men wearing identical blue sports shirts and who appeared to be secret police. Assuming their contact to be an informant, they fled the area. Shortly thereafter Castro told his closest collaborators, "I know where there is a place with more than one thousand rifles very well guarded, very well kept, and very well greased. They only need to be recuperated." Thus germinated the concept of attacking an army garrison. Some rebels argued that automatic weapons were needed for such an endeavor. "Not if we take them by surprise," insisted Castro; "it can be done with light weapons."[39]

Camp Columbia, the strongest national citadel with an airfield and an armored division, could not be seized easily. The guard had been doubled after the Easter Sunday attempt. Therefore, Fidel Castro and Pepe Suárez drove to Pinar del Río to scout the provincial military base. The plan was rejected due to the proximity of Havana, from which reinforcements would quickly arrive. Castro then decided to attack the Moncada fortress in Oriente, where the army was weaker. The province was the cradle of the wars of independence. Two decades earlier the revolutionary Antonio Guiteras Holmes had planned a simultaneous assault on the Moncada garrison and the San Luis Rural Guard outpost on April 29, 1933. Guiteras believed that the Oriente insurrection would culminate in a national general strike to overthrow President Gerardo Machado's government. Although the Moncada attack was aborted at the last moment, twenty-nine rebels shot their way into the San Luis garrison, which was occupied by nineteen soldiers. The insurgents soon fled when army reinforcements arrived. This fiasco gained the twenty-six-year-old Guiteras the fame that propelled him six months later to the post of secretary of the interior, war, and navy in the one-hundred-day revolutionary government of Ramón Grau.[40]

In preparing a similar plan, Castro relied on twenty-one-year-old Renato M. Guitart Rosell in Santiago de Cuba, who was a consignment agent for his father's shipping business. Renato had attended the local Dolores School and La Progresiva Presbyterian Business School in Matanzas. He had an inferiority complex due to his asthma and a facial disfigurement—a large red birthmark on his left cheek. Former Santiago de Cuba mayor Luis Casero indicated that "his condition worsened after cobalt treatment to cauterize it had shriveled his cheek and drooped the corner of his left eye. As a result, he developed an impulsive character and easily got into fights." Manuel Bartolomé, the twenty-seven-year-old director of the Bartolomé Funeral Home, described Renato as an introverted gun enthusiast with a rare and irascible character.[41]

Guitart was the Oriente Province foreign relations secretary of Acción Libertadora, a clandestine organization created in April 1952 by fifty-year-old Justo Carrillo Hernández, the former president of the BANFAIC. The group incorporated intellectuals and radical elements from Joven Cuba and the FEU as well as some Ortodoxo Youths. The organizing secretary of Acción Libertadora in Oriente was thirty-five-year-old Raúl del Mazo Serra, a founder of the Peasant Confederation and a first-base player with the Cuba Mining baseball team. Del Mazo stated that Acción Libertadora was created "with the purpose of making assassination attempts and placing bombs to achieve government control and combat by all means the order established." Membership included "36 ten-man cells." Carrillo wrote in 1993 that the group's objective, "even though it had its violent actions, was mainly to plan the economic and banking instability of the Batista government."[42]

Guitart had gone to Havana in January as part of a student guard at the hospital deathbed of Rubén Batista Rubio. He was introduced to Fidel Castro before returning home. Guitart then asked del Mazo to join forces with Castro's movement. Del Mazo balked, saying that there was no reason to dismember their Acción Libertadora cell to join Castro, whose organization lacked a name. As Guitart got closer to Castro he distanced himself from Acción Libertadora. His first task for Castro was procuring a diagram of the Moncada citadel. Guitart befriended a soldier, entered the garrison with him various times, and penciled a rough sketch noting the arsenal and machine-gun locations. He took a flight to Havana, gave a copy of the layout to Castro, and returned home with two suitcases full of weapons.[43]

Fidel Castro had by then decided that army uniforms were required for the Moncada attack. He discussed this with Calabazar cell leader Pedro Trigo López, a textile factory worker. Trigo suggested approaching his relative Florentino Fernández León, a twenty-six-year-old military hospital orderly in Jaimanitas. Florentino's father was an army lieutenant in charge of the Guanajay post and the godfather of the rebel Gerardo Granados Lara. Castro asked Trigo to tell the orderly that Ortodoxo leaders planning to overthrow Batista needed army uniforms. Florentino, living at his in-laws' farm in Calabazar, agreed to get uniforms, weapons, and ammunition and received two hundred pesos for initial purchases. The orderly bought surplus khaki uniforms from other soldiers, purporting to be reselling them for sixteen pesos to peasants as durable working clothes. This was a usual transaction for military personnel, who received two sets of uniforms every six months, to augment their salary. Other purchases of uniforms and caps were made in the El Zorro factory in Agua Dulce. Florentino pilfered from the hospital laundry most of the uniforms needed to attire the rebels. The first outfits were handed to Trigo, who stored them in his father-in-law's farm. Trigo then gave Florentino a note with Melba Hernández's address and delivery instructions. Castro eventually had Trigo introduce him to Florentino in an effort to acquire high-caliber rifles. The hospital orderly was able to purchase only various handguns on the black market, including for eighty pesos a Luger with two clips, which Castro took to the attack.[44]

To augment the rebel armament, Castro decided to buy a discontinued lot of some twenty Canadian Mosberg .22-caliber single-shot rifles for eighty pesos each from a Havana hardware store. From Naty Revuelta he sought three thousand pesos needed for these and other purchases, but she had already depleted more than six thousand pesos from her bank account. Castro then drove with Raúl Martínez in early April to his family estate. His invalid father, sitting on the porch reading a letter from his son Raúl, greeted them by saying, "What is Raúl doing in Paris that he is asking for $500 to return home?" Martínez recalled that Angel Castro "without even looking at Fidel, cursed and complained about his sons." It would be the last contact ever between father and son. Castro went into the kitchen, and his mother, Lina, the plantation administrator, soon drove up in a jeep wearing a holstered revolver. When the visitors left after 7:00 P.M., Castro pulled out of his shirt pocket a roll of bills his mother had given him and handed it to his companion, saying, "Count this and tell me how much there is." Martínez replied with disbelief, "Fidel, this is only $116. We need three thousand." Castro, ever making his blunders appear to be victories, answered, "we cannot complain, because she has given us more than the entire Ortodoxo Party leadership." To solve the financial problem, Naty Revuelta pawned her "sapphires, emeralds and diamonds" to pay for "the necessary weapons."[45]

After the required weapons and uniforms were amassed, the date for the Moncada assault was set to coincide with the carnival weekend starting July 24. Cuban separatist general Narciso López had prepared a similar uprising for June 24, 1848, during the Cienfuegos feast day. His followers, dressed in carnival costumes for the occasion, would attack and take over the garrison while the bulk of the troops patrolled the streets during the event. José Martí's February 24, 1895, independence revolt was also planned for carnival week. Batista had likewise chosen the weekend of the Havana carnival to stage his successful coup d'état. In Santiago de Cuba the two-week annual festivities began on the three Catholic holidays of Saint Christine, Saint James, and Saint Ann. Thousands of people converged on the city, with many dispersed residents traditionally returning for the celebration, which included drinking and dancing in the streets to the beat of conga music. All lodgings filled to capacity, forcing some visitors to sleep on hammocks in the park, in doorways, or on porches. The tourist influx would lessen suspicion for the slew of rebels converging on the city. The Moncada fortress would be taken by surprise at dawn, and its weapons would be distributed to the populace. Fidel Castro "expected to arm a mass of volunteers." The rebels would then replicate the 1895 invasion march of the liberator Antonio Maceo toward Havana, capturing all garrisons in their path.[46]

Castro decided on a simultaneous attack against the Rural Guard barracks in Bayamo, sixty-five miles northwest of Santiago de Cuba. He was conscious of the great historical significance in taking the city. The Ten Years' War for independence began there, and the first stanza of the Cuban national anthem calls on its residents to rush to combat under the proud gaze of the fatherland. Castro indicated that "the strategy would be complete with the blowing up of the bridges on the Cauto River to impede the transit of military supplies and troops by the Central Highway." Raúl Martínez affirmed that "Pedro Aguilera was going to bring a mining expert from Charco Redondo to destroy the highway and railroad bridges leading into Bayamo to deter troop movements to Santiago de Cuba." The Bayamo plan became operational in April, when Fidel Castro chose the steadfast Raúl Martínez over the irresolute Abel Santamaría to lead that endeavor. Martínez acknowledged that "Fidel feared betrayal or that I would not show up. He wanted to absolutely control everything. Fidel was worried because some rebels insisted on going to the regattas in Varadero and killing Batista, who would be a spectator there, which seemed more logical and easier than attacking the Moncada."[47]

Castro gave Martínez command of the Marianao cell led by Hugo Camejo. Since Martínez was unfamiliar with most of those militants, he requested that Orlando Castro García be allowed to return as his aide. The latter recalled that a few days before the attack, José Luis Tasende gazed at a newspaper stand on a Havana street corner and morbidly quipped, "Maybe after this is over the front pages will depict photos of us dead with our mouths full of ants." The rebel contact in Bayamo was thirty-eight-year-old Elio Rosete, a Canada Dry distributor and former Joven Cuba member. Raúl del Mazo had introduced Rosete to Renato Guitart, who coopted him into Castro's group. After Rosete met with Fidel Castro and Raúl Martínez in Havana, he adhered to their cause.[48]

In early May, Fidel Castro sent Oscar Alcalde and a companion by bus to Santiago de Cuba to observe the Moncada security measures. They lodged at a nearby boardinghouse and walked around the citadel at dawn to detect the guards' response. The strangers approached the two sentries at each of the four cardinal point entrances and asked for directions to their own boardinghouse. At Post 3, the gate closest to the arsenal, the soldiers pleasantly prolonged the conversation and shared their coffee with the spies. After the rebels returned to Havana and reported their findings, Raúl Martínez drove his 1949 Dodge to Oriente with Castro. Tizol followed in his 1950 Plymouth station wagon, stopping in Holguín to visit his father. He then caught up with his brother-in-law and Castro at the Plaza de Dolores in Santiago de Cuba. The trio accompanied Renato to Escandel Hill and the Puerto Boniato heights, looking to lease a safe house. They searched in other isolated suburbs until spotting a farmhouse eight miles east of Santiago, near the village of Siboney. The three-bedroom, white stucco dwelling, named Villa Blanca, had been built in 1945 and was partly hidden from the road by banana and mango trees. It was near Las Guásimas, the site of the first land battle of the 1898 Spanish-American War.[49]

The conspirators drove onto the two-acre grounds enclosed by a rustic barbed-wire fence. A red-tipped white picket gate matched the white walls and French red-tile roof of the uninhabited farmhouse. Tizol crossed the road to the farm of Angel "El Gallego" Núñez Jurjo, a recent immigrant from Spain. Núñez stated that the Villa Blanca proprietor, José Vázquez Rojas, lived in Santiago de Cuba and owned a service station on Victoriano Garzón and Céspedes avenues. Vázquez sold gasoline, auto parts, and Goodrich tires and also operated a fleet of jitneys from the city to Siboney Beach. Tizol went to see Vázquez and identified himself as "Alvarez," a poultry merchant. He claimed that he and his partner wanted to rent the farm as a transit point for locally bought chickens going to his Havana hatchery. Vázquez mentioned a poultry grower who was a mutual friend, but he turned down the lease offer. Tizol relayed the conversation to Castro and Raúl Martínez before the trio returned to Havana. A few days later Tizol took a flight back to Santiago de Cuba and persuaded the reluctant Vázquez to lease the property. He gave Vázquez his real name, offered their mutual friend as reference, and claimed that "Alvarez" (Abel) was his business partner, who would close the deal. Vázquez agreed to rent the farmhouse for six hundred pesos annually and accepted a one-hundred-peso deposit.[50]

Castro's group gained other adherents after MNR leader Rafael García-Bárcena was sentenced on May 21 to two years of imprisonment. Thirteen followers got lesser prison terms, while fifty-four others were acquitted. MNR militants Mario Dalmau and Jacinto García quickly joined Castro's group. MNR activist Angel Díaz-Francisco stated that "Abelardo Crespo, Gustavo Arcos, and Carlos González were MNR members who out of despair followed Castro at the last moment because the opposition leaders were in jail or in exile." Díaz-Francisco did not sympathize with Castro and rejected an invitation from Gildo Fleitas to participate in their activities. He indicated that Léster Rodríguez, Pedro Miret, and Raúl Castro had been involved in the MNR conspiracy.[51]

Twenty-one-year-old Raúl Castro, living in a student boardinghouse on a parental stipend, was unaware of the Moncada attack preparations. He had gone to Europe in February with a Cuban Socialist Youth delegation, which included his future sister-in-law Nilsa Espín and Alfredo Guevara Valdés, to attend the Fourth World Youth and Student Festival in Vienna. Raúl went behind the Iron Curtain to Bucharest and spent a month in Rumania, Budapest, and Prague. After nine days in Paris he traveled to Italy and sailed home on the *Andrea Gritti*. On the ship he befriended a Russian and two Guatemalan Communists. Upon docking in Havana on June 7, the Guatemalans told customs agents that they were in transit but tried to debark with their luggage, which revealed "subversive literature." Raúl, accompanying them, was also detained after similar material was found in his valises. The police charged them with possession of "a large quantity of Communist propaganda." Raúl also carried a four-page manuscript entitled "Education in Cuba," which he had presented at the Vienna conference, denouncing "a number of Cuban centers of education and political and labor organizations." The Guatemalan Embassy interceded on behalf of its citizens to gain their freedom, but Raúl was remitted to El Príncipe Prison to await a court hearing. After being released a few days later, he moved into a rented room with Pedro Miret. Raúl then joined the University Socialist Committee, which expelled him after the Moncada attack because the Communists were then dedicated to nonviolence. Raúl joined his brother's organization when José Luis Tasende requested his participation.[52]

The opposition political leaders too were secretly planing a revolt. Carlos Prío and Millo Ochoa gathered with Auténtico and Ortodoxo leaders at the Ritz Carlton Hotel in Montreal, Canada. They signed the Montreal Pact on June 2, appealing to patriotic unity and a return to constitutional and democratic order through a provisional government. The agreement, drafted by the legislators Eduardo Suárez Rivas and José Pardo Llada, condemned gangsterism and terrorism as a form of struggle. It publicly omitted reference to armed revolt, but according to Millo Ochoa, there was a secret clause under which the signers pledged to use the force of arms to overthrow Batista. Fidel Castro, a lightweight Ortodoxo aspirant, was not invited to Montreal, nor were the Communist PSP leaders, who favored an electoral solution. The new alliance took shape after an Ortodoxo leadership rift in January, when Ochoa and Pardo Llada announced that they would cooperate with the Auténticos against Batista. Roberto Agramonte, who espoused civic resistance, denounced the move as a betrayal of Ortodoxo principles. Other Ortodoxo leaders declared their intentions to run in the future elections promised by Batista. Former president Ramón Grau and his Auténtico faction opposed the pact because he was going to run for the presidency. Aureliano Sánchez Arango did not go to Montreal since he still distrusted the Ortodoxos after his feud with Chibás. He rejected Grau's electoral path and favored revolutionary action against Batista. The Montreal Pact was criticized in Cuba by other politicians who called the Auténticos the "heroes from afar."[53]

When Millo Ochoa returned to Havana, he spoke with his military adherents stationed in La Cabaña fortress and the garrisons in Santa Clara and Holguín, which included some of his relatives and brother Freemasons. He also met with former army officers ousted after the Tenth of March Coup. In mid-June cashiered colonel Urbano Matos Rodríguez met in Santiago de Cuba with his nephew Pvt. Ariel Matos Romero and requested a diagram of the Moncada fortress for the Montreal Pact conspirators. The twenty-year-old soldier told his uncle that he had three other military friends in the garrison who would join him in an uprising against Batista. When Private Matos supplied the requested document, depicting the machine-gun emplacements in Moncada, the former colonel told him, "When we are ready to attack, I will let you know so that you can inform your comrades."[54]

The Montreal Pact prompted numerous rumors of imminent Cuban revolts and invasions. Rolando Masferrer's newspaper *Tiempo*, which had superseded his magazine *Tiempo en Cuba*, reported on June 2 that the Montreal Pact participants had secretly agreed to have an insurrection by mid-July. The article stated that "Millo Ochoa and Pardo Llada demanded that the principal armed effort be made in the Province of Oriente." As a result, the Moncada was subjected to a combat drill. The *retén* (reserve) auxiliary guard in each company was assigned a defense sector. In mid-June the New York Spanish-language magazine *Visión* claimed that "Cuba is in the eve of a revolution. After June, the movement could be unleashed at any moment. But it will always be before September." The article depicted a map labeled "Prío's Plan of Invasion," tracing the expedition routes from Yucatán and Guatemala to Havana, Pinar del Río, and Oriente provinces. The report emphasized that "insurrections will explode with more intensity in Santiago de Cuba." The attack "will be the awaited fulminating spark that will explode the insurrections being prepared in different parts of the Republic." Former Auténtico senator Manuel Antonio de Varona Loredo claimed, "The Montreal Pact indicates that the days are counted for the hateful dictatorship of Fulgencio Batista."[55]

Visión quoted sources as saying that a few thousand mercenaries and volunteers were training in Mexico with Caribbean Legion instructors. Eufemio Fernández would lead one of the contingents. A fleet of twenty combat planes, including new F-47s, would be commanded by Aureliano Sánchez Arango, leader of the clandestine Triple A organization. A team of sappers was reported to be in Havana to blow the bridges that would isolate ten M-8 tanks and a motorized battery of 75-mm cannons in Camp Columbia. The oppositionists claimed to "maintain direct contacts with numerous members of the armed forces." The report concluded that the only way to depose Batista was "through a path stained with blood." The article included a photo of a smiling José Duarte Oropesa, a U.S. Army World War II veteran and Prío confidant, who was described as "an important axis in the invasion plans." *Alerta* newspaper headlined on June 18 that "The Conspirators of Montreal Purchased 8 Airplanes and Thousands of Guns." The U.S. Embassy in Havana, noting that *Visión* was circulating on newsstands in the capital, had earlier dispelled these invasion rumors to the Department of State, doubting "that a plot of this magnitude is contemplated" or "the ability of the opposition to organize and execute an amphibious military operation."[56]

The Cuban government took seriously these exaggerated accounts. On June 22 Batista acknowledged being aware of the preparations to overthrow him and that four months earlier he had received a copy of a Caribbean Legion plan drafted in Montreal. Presidential aide Col. Francisco Tabernilla Palmero responded to the *Visión* article with an interview in *Bohemia* magazine on July 5, exhibiting a 160-page document entitled "Invasion of Country XXVI: Cuba," allegedly written by the Caribbean Legion for returning Prío to power. The plan outlined acquiring thirty thousand rifles, thirty-six hundred carbines, six hundred .30-caliber machine guns, three hundred .60-caliber mortars, two hundred bazookas, eight steel ships weighing over three hundred tons, forty PT boats, ten thousand rubber boats, five thousand life vests, twenty-five fighter-bomber planes, twenty-five amphibious planes, two transmission-receiver plants, nineteen transmission-receiver radios, twenty-four walkie-talkies, medical equipment, and fuel for the planes and ships "to initiate the first phase of the invasion of country XXVI (Cuba)." This illusive strategy was larger than the 1961 Bay of Pigs invasion sponsored by the CIA for $45 million. It was an apparent effort to impress Prío into donating large sums to the Caribbean Legion.[57]

Two weeks later, *Alerta* announced that there were three ships in Honduras "full of arms and with a considerable expeditionary force ready to assault the Cuban coast." The newspaper warned that "insurrection is imminent, it will be produced maybe this same week." The U.S. Embassy in Havana, continuing to monitor these events closely, informed its government on July 10 that Ortodoxo leader Manuel Bisbé two days earlier had stated, "We will take up arms if the Government does not give us, before August, a political solution." The acting counselor of the embassy wrote that "many Cubans now feel that a violent solution is inevitable. The Communists are reportedly biding their time, hoping to stage a Bogotazo should an opportunity present itself." He was told three days later by a minor official of the Ministry of Information that Batista had received reliable information that an invasion from Guatemala with five hundred men would land on July 16.[58]

Meanwhile, the Moncada conspirators were finalizing their plans. Fidel Castro was concerned that his efforts would be moot if the Montreal Pact participants struck the first blow. Abel Santamaría was secretly ordered on June 16 to occupy the Siboney farmhouse, and his sister Haydée moved to the apartment of Melba Hernández. Abel hired a carpenter, who built a three-sided, roofless, wooden enclosure in the front yard, measuring twenty square yards, to shield their cars from view of the highway. A backyard dry well with a wooden lid was reinforced with cement to hide the weapons that would begin arriving in mid-July. Abel told the workers that it was meant for incinerating chickens that were dead on arrival. Other preparations were being accomplished by Renato Guitart, who rented a row house at 218 I Street in Sueño neighborhood for $30 monthly. He later drove to Bayamo, where he asked a former schoolmate, Fernando Fernández Catá, to help him locate a place for a poultry business. They spotted a "For Sale" sign on the Gran Casino Motel, three blocks from the army garrison. After Guitart returned to Santiago de Cuba and relayed the information to Havana, on July 11 he went to the San Pedro del Mar cabaret, where a newspaper reporter overheard him deriding Batista and boasting to his friends, "Do not be surprised if you soon see me with the stars of a colonel on my shoulders." Three days later Guitart met Raúl Martínez and Gerardo Pérez-Puelles at the Bayamo train station when they arrived from Havana. He introduced them as his "business partners" to Fernández Catá and motel proprietor Juan Manuel Martínez. The conspirators leased the building, with an option to buy, paying $165 for fifteen days.[59]

According to Raúl Martínez, Fidel Castro anguished over the predicament of his possible defeat at Moncada and a victory in Bayamo. That would propel his subordinate into an unexpected leadership position of historic proportions. One week before the attack, Castro gambled on proceeding with the Bayamo plan. Pérez-Puelles was ordered to take by train two suitcases with arms and uniforms to the Gran Casino. He went with La Ceiba cell member Pedro Marrero, who was traveling in another coach with a clandestine cargo destined for Santiago de Cuba. The couriers went separately for security reasons. During the trip, Pérez-Puelles noticed that a man, accompanied by two others, intently stared at him. He got nervous and went to inform Marrero of the situation, fearing that the trio could be undercover police agents. Pérez-Puelles returned to his seat and drew courage to approach the gazing stranger and ask if they were acquainted. He recalled that "they turned out to be three homosexuals on their way to the Santiago carnival who invited me to join them." At the Martí junction in Camagüey, Pérez-Puelles took a southern route to Bayamo and Marrero continued to Santiago de Cuba, delivered his secret cargo at Siboney, and then returned to Havana.[60]

Another covert shipment of arms and uniforms went from Havana to Siboney on July 14 with twenty-four-year-old bartender Elpidio C. Sosa González. Léster Rodríguez afterward picked up a trunk and two suitcases with weapons at the Gildo Fleitas home. He sent the trunk by railroad to his native Santiago de Cuba and went by bus with the other baggage. Rodríguez visited his parents and proceeded alone to the Palace of Justice, where the court clerk provided a tour of the new building. He made a mental note of the location of the elevators, the stairs, and the guard posts but was unable to inspect the roof, which later proved to be a costly mistake. Rodríguez then returned to Havana and informed Castro of his findings.[61]

Other preparations in Santiago de Cuba were being completed by Renato Guitart. He rented a second safe house at 8 Celda Street for twenty-five pesos and purchased Remington shotguns, .22-caliber rifles, shotgun shells, and .38-caliber bullets at two hardware stores. Guitart leased three refrigerators for the two rebel hideaways in the city and the Siboney farmhouse, where he also delivered a dresser. He and Abel reconnoitered the Saturnino Lora Civil Hospital, behind the Moncada fortress, and checked the garrison entrances and the changing of the guard. Abel then on July 19 rented a room in the Rex Hotel, a flophouse located above the Sears department store on Victoriano Garzón Avenue. He kept the quarters until the rebel force began arriving from Havana five days later.[62]

Back in the capital the last week of planning took on a hectic pace. Gildo Fleitas got arrested with Marianao cell leader Hugo Camejo, Melba Hernández, and Rafael Freyre Torres and Pedro Veliz Hernández, both twenty-two-year-old bricklayers from Marianao, when the car he was driving collided with another vehicle near Güines after target practice at Los Palos. The five were detained for three days after the police discovered their weapons. They were released after a court hearing was set for the following month. Raúl Martínez, who would lead the Marianao group at Bayamo, evacuated his mother and siblings from San Pedro del Cotorro to a safe apartment on Aguacate Street in Havana. The rebel command staff, finding itself desperately short of money, "issued checks on bank accounts lacking funds and bought innumerable refrigerators, televisions and home appliances on credit that later were sold at a lower price for cash." Oscar Alcalde overdrew the Thion Laboratory checking accounts in two banks and acquired a phony business loan to partly finance the revolt. Alcalde admitted that "during the days of the 23, 24, and 25 of July we issued many checks without funds." Masonic grand master Carlos Piñeiro del Cueto confirmed that Alcalde, the treasurer of the Padilla Lodge in Havana, stole all their funds. Alcalde also embezzled a few thousand pesos from the Reporters Association account. "The association was threatening disclosure," stated Raúl Martínez, "so he had no choice but to gamble on the Moncada venture."[63]

Newspaper accounts reported that Gildo Fleitas, the rice mill administrator, "forged checks of that company totaling several thousands of dollars" that were cashed by him and Raúl Castro. The departure day for the attack, July 24, was when "most checks were issued, being given to those responsible for cells to initiate the mobilization of the comrades going to Oriente." The leaders rationalized their misdeeds by claiming that the checks "would have been paid to the bank, had the movement triumphed" but knowing that restitution was not feasible if they were killed or arrested. Accountant Raúl Martínez estimated total expenses at around $35,000. Fidel Castro later testified in court that the amount spent on weapons alone was $16,480. The disbursements included buying army uniforms, weapons, and ammunition; fees for target practice; airline fares between Havana and Oriente; housing in Santiago de Cuba and Bayamo; salaries for the Siboney farmhouse carpenter and a handyman; train and bus fare to Oriente for the combatants; rental of automobiles used during the attack; travel expenses for gas, food, and lodging; and freight charges to transport most weapons and uniforms, some of which were sent by train in crates marked "Bird Feed."[64]

During the weekend prior to the Moncada attack, the SIM received word that a large shipment of Auténtico weapons had been delivered to an islet near Varadero Beach. A naval contingent, which was headed by Fulgencio Batista and thirty-three-year-old SIM chief Manuel Ugalde Carrillo, went to the deserted island and seized some wooden crates marked "Tampico, Mexico," which had been sent from the United States and contained hand grenades, shotguns, .45-caliber pistols, machine guns, and a barrel full of dynamite. The government kept the find a secret for a few days, hoping to capture those going to retrieve it. On July 25, on the eve of the Moncada attack, the Cuban ambassador to the United States told a Department of State official that "Prío was crazy (*loco*) in wanting to bring about a 'Bogotazo' in Cuba."[65]

A few days earlier, Minister of Information Ernesto de la Fe sent to Colonel Ugalde Carrillo a young mulatto confidant who had heard rumors of an impending attack on the Moncada fortress and that weapons and uniforms were being sent to El Caney. The investigation was assigned to thirty-two-year-old Lt. Armando Acosta Sánchez, who flew to Santiago de Cuba in a military plane with the informant. After the two checked into different hotels, Acosta met with SIM informant Senén Carabia Carrey, a forty-five-year-old photographer. Carabia provided his car to Acosta and gave him a list of places frequented by arms traffickers. "The similar names of El Caney and Siboney confused our informant," affirmed Acosta. "I concentrated my investigation in El Caney after inspecting the hotel register in Siboney Beach and being told by the manager that he knew all the guests."[66]

Meanwhile, on July 20, Abel obtained reservations at the Perla de Cuba Hotel in Santiago de Cuba for twenty-five "employees" contracted for his "chicken hatchery." Two days later Renato Guitart received a five-hundred-peso salary advance from his father to cover last-minute expenses, after having already spent four thousand pesos for the Moncada attack preparations. That same Wednesday night, Renato and Abel met Haydée Santamaría at the train terminal when she arrived from Havana with two suitcases packed with weapons, and they drove her to Siboney. The following morning Fidel Castro went to the home of Melba Hernández but did not find her. He told her mother, "When Melba returns, tell her to get ready because we are coming to pick her up for a safe mission." Castro requested that Melba's mother pack for her daughter "two or three changes of clothes in a little box, not in a suitcase." That night Melba learned of her destination when she left Havana by railroad for Santiago de Cuba with two valises containing arms and ammunition. She also carried a flower box containing a dismantled 16-gauge shotgun that did not fit in the luggage. Melba and Haydée were the only women participating in the insurrection. Their friend Elda Pérez Mujica excused herself by claiming that she had to care for her suddenly ill mother.[67]

Melba was met at the train station on the afternoon of July 24 by Abel, Guitart, and Elpidio Sosa, who took her to the Siboney farmhouse along with the last arms shipment that arrived in soap crates. Guitart had spent the morning renting forty folding beds from a furniture store, sending twenty-five to the I Street house and the rest to the Celda Street address. He bought on credit two ironing boards and irons, pillows and bedsheets, plastic water jugs, a case of condensed milk, cooking oil, two dozen eggs, and other victuals that were taken to Siboney. That same Friday, at 6:00 P.M., SIM investigator Lt. Armando Acosta entered the Moncada fortress, briefly stopping on the parade ground to salute the flag during retreat. The regimental chief, thirty-eight-year-old Col. Alberto del Río Chaviano, was summoned from his home, across the street from Post 5. The colonel, whose father was a peasant from Las Villas Province, had joined the army twenty years earlier and enrolled in officers' school in 1938. A decade later he was promoted to captain in Camagüey and later received command of the Rural Guard post in Palma Soriano. His promotion to colonel and Moncada command after the Tenth of March Coup was in part due to being General Tabernilla's brother-in-law. When Lieutenant Acosta explained his secret mission, the colonel retorted arrogantly: "How does Ugalde in Havana know what is going on here? I am in charge here and I know everything that happens. There is nothing unusual going on."[68]

The rebel attack being prepared eight miles away from the Moncada had been quickly mustered in three months, following García-Bárcena's arrest. Fidel Castro's early efforts to attract the masses through limited clandestine shortwave radio broadcasts and a mimeographed bulletin with scant distribution were insignificant and were abandoned after five months. Rebel propaganda, including *El Acusador*, was void of Marxist rhetoric. Unable to reach the masses, Castro then created his own group of humble minions willing to obey him unconditionally. He would later rely on the same loyalty concept to form a revolutionary government. Castro's followers were mostly drawn from the Ortodoxo Youth ranks because the divided party leadership lacked a combative plan against Batista. Almost all were intellectually inferior to Castro and had menial occupations, and many came from broken homes. Their limited weapons training provided more revolutionary enthusiasm than marksman expertise. To maintain the cohesiveness of the nascent group, political discussions were limited to overthrowing Batista, Ortodoxo ideology, and restoring the 1940 Constitution. Communism or socialism was never discussed, nor was it a motivating factor for the revolt.

The blueprint for the rebellion was drawn from the historic events drafted by Narciso López, José Martí, and Antonio Guiteras. Castro equipped his group in part by unscrupulously raising funds, believing that the end justified the means. His refusal to confront the police when challenged by Harriman at the university showed that he continued to choose his battles wisely. Castro's response to Harriman's challenge, using slander and character assassination, became his hallmark tactic against political opponents. He was under pressure to act before the announced invasion of the Caribbean Legion in conjunction with the Montreal Pact participants. Sensationalist newspaper headlines warned of an imminent insurrection in Santiago de Cuba. Fidel Castro, with the SIM nipping at his heels, was going to strike with hardware-store weaponry against the second-largest army garrison on the island, a feat never previously accomplished in the history of the republic.

THREE

"On Sunday, Cuba will be in flames"

Moisés "El Moro" Mafut Delgado, a thirty-one-year-old Ortodoxo militant and employee of the Compañía Lechera dairy in Havana, was awakened at 1:00 A.M. on Friday, July 24, by the knocking on his residence door in Poey neighborhood, Arroyo Naranjo. Mafut, who had to be at work in two hours, was surprised to see Fidel Castro, who told him to gather his cell members that morning. El Moro queried: "What, more target practice?" Castro responded, "No. On Sunday, Cuba will be in flames." Mafut was ordered to take only Armando Mestre Martínez, Juan Almeida Bosque, and Emilio Albentosa Chacón and to leave behind two others due to a shortage of weapons.[1]

At daybreak Mafut took a bus to the homes of Almeida and Mestre, both twenty-six-year-old Afro-Cubans. He was told that Almeida, the eldest of ten siblings, was working as a mason's helper in the Chinese Cemetery in El Vedado and that Mestre was laboring at the construction site of the Masonic Grand Lodge in Havana. Mafut located them, and the trio returned to Arroyo Naranjo, looking for Albentosa, a mulatto native of Santiago de Cuba, who was a construction worker with a fourth-grade education. When he could not be found, his roommate Samuel Guzmán substituted for him. Mafut and his three companions then arrived at Abel's apartment by bus at 4:00 P.M. and reported to Castro.[2]

Castro had spent all day with Oscar Alcalde completing last-minute details. They had picked up Pedro Trigo in Calabazar that morning but were unable to locate the Rancho Boyeros cell leader Filiberto Zamora. In Santiago de las Vegas they could not find twenty-six-year-old Anibal Celso Stakeman Gómez, and none of the dozen cell members went to Oriente. When Fidel Castro heard from Mafut that Albentosa was absent, he began to question Guzmán about his knowledge of firearms. After

Guzmán replied affirmatively to everything, Castro allowed him to participate. Mafut then received two personal checks from the rebel leader, one for more than a hundred pesos and another for just over thirty pesos. Castro falsely assured that the checks would not bounce and instructed El Moro to cover gasoline and food expenses and divide up the rest among the families of the four insurgents.[3]

The Arroyo Naranjo group was driven by Alcalde back to their neighborhood at 6:00 P.M. Near Mafut's residence, Albentosa was spotted on a street corner. The cell leader then ordered Guzmán to leave, due to the lack of weapons, and Albentosa rejoined the group. El Moro asked his wife to call his workplace the next day to say that he was still sick. He cashed the larger check with a local grocer and redeemed the other one at a dime store. After briefly stopping in their respective homes, the four rebels departed with Alcalde, who left them dining at a café in San Pedro del Cotorro while he went home to shower and bid farewell to his family.[4]

That Friday, without divulging his plan, Castro instructed the cell leaders to bring their groups to Havana. Transportation was arranged for nearly 160 insurgents to travel in excess of five hundred miles to Oriente. Most rebels assumed that they were going to the Santiago de Cuba carnival, which was being advertised in Havana newspapers. Almeida believed that it was in recompense for excelling in the training exercises. Lawton cell leader Gabriel Gil Alfonso, a thirty-year-old café employee, arrived with eight followers at Abel's apartment at 4:00 P.M. Gil, a former soldier whose brother was on active duty, had told Fidel Castro the previous night that he had twenty-three men. Due to insufficient arms, he was instructed to take only nine, one of whom got lost in transit.[5]

Although Léster Rodríguez claimed that Castro had 250 followers, some could not be located and others were not summoned because of a shortage of weapons. About 100 rebels traveled to Oriente in twenty automobiles; five had been rented for the weekend, a few were borrowed, and others belonged to their respective drivers. The rest of the attack force went by train or bus. Ernesto Tizol was ordered to pick up Afro-Cuban Teodulio "Lulo" Mitchell Barbán, a twenty-nine-year-old soda-truck driver from Palma Soriano recruited by the dentist Pedro Aguilera. Fidel Castro had called him to Havana on June 13 because he was in need of Mitchell's military expertise and long-distance driving skill. Mitchell, whose father was an army corporal, had enlisted in 1943 but was dismissed fifteen months later when all syphilitics were summarily discharged. Tizol and Mitchell arrived at Abel's apartment, where Aguilera and a large crowd awaited instructions, while Castro coordinated the departures. Tizol then proceeded to rent, for fifty pesos, a 1952 blue Buick, which Mitchell later drove to Oriente. The first rebel contingent left at 5:30 P.M., after Castro told Oscar Quintela Bonilla, a thirty-one-year-old textile factory worker, to take half of the Calabazar cell in a borrowed 1950 Dodge to the Celda Street house in Santiago de Cuba.[6]

The other rebel drivers were ordered to leave at intervals from various rendezvous points and go to various lodgings in Santiago de Cuba. Juan Ameijeiras Delgado departed in his Chevrolet taxi with five rebels whom he picked up at Fraternity Park in Havana. Chucho Montané, taking a two-week vacation from his new bookkeeping job at Bauer and Black Band-Aid Company, left from Abel's apartment in his gray 1949 Pontiac with five Lawton cell members. Montané stopped at his home to get money after three stores refused to cash two forty-peso checks that Castro provided for travel expenses. Driving all night, Chucho fell asleep at the wheel near Camagüey and veered off the pavement. After the men took a roadside nap, a dead battery delayed them for an hour, until a passing truck provided a push start.[7]

Madruga cell members Manuel Suardíaz Fernández, Orbeín Hernández Díaz, and Andrés García Zulueta arrived by bus at Abel's apartment on Friday evening. Their comrade Raúl Molina backed out at the last moment, purporting that he was going with another group to kill Batista at Varadero. Upon encountering Fidel Castro, the peasant García Zulueta gave him eight hundred pesos and stated that he would be returning home because he could not abandon his six children. Castro then instructed Reinaldo Boris Luis to drive the newcomers and two others to the Rex Hotel in Santiago de Cuba. Suardíaz recalled that when they rode by Madruga at 10:00 P.M., Boris told his passengers to duck down to avoid being recognized, although the town streets were deserted at that hour. La Ceiba cell members gathered at 4:00 P.M. in their neighborhood park. Fernando Chenard had told them to inform their families that they were going on a fishing expedition to Varadero for the weekend. Mario Chanes, sharing quarters with a friend in a cheap rooming house, left behind farewell letters for his parents, his brother, and his girlfriend. Chenard appeared at the park at 7:00 P.M. in a black Plymouth and departed for Santiago de Cuba with four comrades. He was the lone chauffeur since none of the others knew how to drive.[8]

The other La Ceiba cell members were sent to Abel's apartment, and from there truck driver Pedro Marrero drove four to the Siboney farmhouse in a rented 1953 Chevrolet. Three others—Mario Chanes, Miguel Oramas, and Francisco "Pancho" González Hernández—were taken to the apartment of Melba Hernández, where Fidel Castro gave them three suitcases stuffed with handguns, bullets, and uniforms. Chanes recalled that the heavy luggage had to be bound with rope to prevent it from popping open. He was told by Castro to carry them to the train station and wait there for further orders. Gildo Fleitas left at 9:15 P.M., driving his car with the poet Raúl Gómez García, Gerardo Sosa Hernández, and San Leopoldo cell members Israel Tápanes Vento, Reinaldo Benítez Nápoles, and Carlos González Seijas. The last two rebels resided in the same boardinghouse on San Rafael Street. Benítez worked in the fashionable El Encanto store as assistant cloth cutter. Tápanes was a janitor in a photography store, where he lived in a back room. Their San Leopoldo cell, which initially had eighteen members, had decreased to nine, and only three went to the attack. Fleitas decorated his vehicle with Fourth of September military flags, which he provided to Tizol and other drivers so that they could pretend to be Batista supporters and avoid arousing suspicion.[9]

Fidel Castro had gone to the Basarrate Street boardinghouse where Léster Rodríguez awaited with Pepe Ponce and seven Artemisa rebels. He gave them bus tickets to Santiago de Cuba and instructions on meeting someone "with a birthmark on his face" at the Rex Hotel. Castro then went to Naty Revuelta's home to retrieve her typed copies of the "Manifesto to the Nation," written by Raúl Gómez García on July 23, along with the phonograph records that he had instructed her to buy. These included the national anthem, the Cuban *Invasion Hymn*, Beethoven's *Eroica*, and other selections to be aired during the attack after seizing a radio station. Castro asked Naty to deliver the document to the news media, the American Embassy, and opposition leaders on Sunday morning.[10]

The "Manifesto to the Nation" is permeated with traditional Cuban revolutionary rhetoric for popular consumption. It displays the liberal reformist ideology and fervent nationalism of the 1933 revolution and the Ortodoxo Party. The word "revolution" appears thirty times in its twenty-nine paragraphs. The manifesto claims an ideological continuity with José Martí, on the centenary of his birth, with other independence leaders, with anti-Machado revolutionaries, and with Eduardo Chibás in their struggle against dictatorship and corruption. Their new revolution is depicted as a response to the Tenth of March Coup by the Youth of the Centenary, to bring forth "an illuminated Republic." The nine points outlined in the manifesto profess a break with the "corrupt past," void of "binds with foreign nations"; praises citizens and soldiers with probity; and favors diversification of agriculture, industrialization, social justice, and Latin American solidarity. The future revolution proposes uniting all virtuous citizens, "from the rural shack to the General Staff of the Armed Forces," for "the grand task of Cuban reconstruction." They would "build the New Republic, with all and for the good of all, in the love and fraternity of all Cubans." The document is void of the Communist rhetoric that would engulf the Cuban revolution after 1961.[11]

After Fidel Castro left Léster's boardinghouse, Tasende called Raúl Castro at 8:00 P.M. and requested his urgent presence there. Raúl, nursing a hangover from a party the previous night, met with Tasende and accompanied him to the railroad station. Upon arriving, they were approached in the terminal cafeteria by Mario Chanes, who stated, "Fidel sent me here with three suitcases to await someone who has not contacted me yet." Raúl replied, "Grab them quick, the train is leaving." Chanes and his companions raced with the heavy luggage to the platform and managed to board as the train was slowly pulling away with sixteen rebel passengers. At the train stop in Unión de Reyes, Matanzas, the peasant Rubén Gallardo left after telling his companions that he was "worried about what would happen to his family if he got killed." The next morning Raúl Castro learned of the attack plan from Tasende in the dining coach. His reaction was described in his diary: "My stomach is paralyzed and my appetite disappears, I knew the magnitude and strength of that objective due to having studied in Santiago de Cuba for various years." Raúl later told the press that he was unaware of their purpose until just prior to the assault.[12]

That evening twenty-eight rebels from Artemisa reached Havana by bus at different intervals. Some were told to await further instructions at La Rotonda bar in El Vedado. Fidel Castro arrived there later that night, gave Mario Lazo and his comrades bus tickets to Santiago de Cuba, and drove them to the terminal. Six cell members, including Gerardo Granados Lara and Ciro Redondo, met in Havana with Carlos Bustillo, who arranged their bus travel and accompanied them to Oriente. Granados affirmed, "At the last moment, I talked Ramiro Valdés into not letting Froilán Enríquez join us because his father had just died and he was caring for his grieving mother and sister." The six-man Guanajay cell, led by Alfredo Corcho Cinta, a thirty-four-year-old dairy worker, also arrived at the Havana bus terminal that night and received their fares to Santiago de Cuba.[13]

Fidel Castro, after leaving Mario Lazo's group at the bus station, returned to Abel's apartment and gave army orderly Florentino Fernández a key to the Celda Street house in Santiago de Cuba. Florentino had spent all day with Pedro Trigo buying ammunition in various Havana gun shops. Nine Calabazar insurgents, most of whom worked in the same local textile factory, went to Oriente in two cars. Florentino drove his compact 1952 Crosley automobile with Trigo, Julio Fernández Alfonso, and Juan Villegas. After the car broke down in Palma Soriano, a military jeep towed them to Santiago de Cuba, where it was left in a garage for repairs. Meanwhile, when Oscar Quintela's vehicle briefly stopped in Colón, Matanzas, the passenger Argelio Guzmán panicked and returned home. Their companion, José L. López Díaz, who had never driven before, took the wheel and had difficulty steering straight. While passing a truck, he almost hit an oncoming car, which had to swerve off the road. Quintela resumed driving for the rest of the trip, stopping at El Cobre, near Santiago de Cuba. The rebels visited the shrine of Cuba's patron saint, the Virgin of Charity, and bought souvenirs.[14]

Raúl Martínez, the leader of the Bayamo attack, left Havana in a rented Chevrolet with Marianao cell leader Hugo Camejo Valdés; Afro-Cuban Agustín "Thompson" Díaz Cartaya, a twenty-two-year-old street musician; Pablo "Machito" Agüero Guedes, a seventeen-year-old bricklayer apprentice; and Elio Rosete, their Bayamo contact. Two days earlier Rosete had taken a flight to Havana, where he learned of the Bayamo plan. Fidel Castro, perceiving his hesitancy, whispered to Martínez, "Don't let him out of your sight, I think he is scared." Driving beyond Holguín, Camejo took over as relief driver under a rainstorm. He soon dozed off and plunged the car into a canal. Thompson went for assistance while the others waited by the roadside. When he returned with a peasant driving a jeep, two soldiers in a Bayamo Public Works truck were pulling the vehicle out of the water. The engine started after some difficulty, and the rebels resumed their journey.[15]

Four Marianao cell members gathered on Friday at the Old Havana efficiency room of Antonio "El Gallego" López García, a plumber's helper and member of Guiteras Revolutionary Action (ARG). Ibrahim Sosa González, whose brother Elpidio was already at the Siboney farmhouse, arrived just prior to departure. He nervously claimed to have accidentally shot himself in the hand, which was swathed with a bloody handkerchief. Raúl Martínez believed that Sosa intentionally injured himself as an excuse for backing out. Mario Martínez, driving a rented 1948 Buick, picked them up at 9:30 p.m. He was accompanied by his wife Juanita Aruca and their five-year-old son Mario Junior, whom he had evacuated from their rented home in San Pedro del Cotorro. Mario left his family with his wife's parents in Colón, Matanzas, and continued on to Bayamo. The dentist Pedro Aguilera was then instructed by Castro to transport to Bayamo five Marianao cell members who were waiting at the Café Raúl in their neighborhood.[16]

Members of the Arroyo Naranjo cell, temporarily left at a San Pedro del Cotorro café by Oscar Alcalde, were retrieved by him at 10:00 p.m. and proceeded to Santiago de Cuba. They had breakfast in Ciego de Avila, Camagüey, where Moisés Mafut took over as driver. He later unintentionally sideswiped a milkman on a bicycle, with two large metal containers astride, who had been pedaling toward them on the roadside. When El Moro slowed down to assist the fallen man, Alcalde blurted out, "don't stop, keep going." At a cafeteria in Victoria de las Tunas, Mafut went to greet other rebels on their way to Santiago de Cuba, but Alcalde warned him not to speak to anyone. Mafut questioned what was going on, and Alcalde replied, "either we win, or they will kill us all. I can't tell you anything else."[17]

Back in Havana, Léster Rodríguez had left instructions on Friday evening for law student Angel "Patachula" Díaz-Francisco to drive his 1950 Oldsmobile to the El Vedado apartment of former UIR gang member Carlos A. Merille Acosta. There Patachula found medical student Jesús "Garabato" Blanco Alba and MNR members Gustavo Arcos and Abelardo Crespo. Arcos, a twenty-five-year-old night watchman at Cu-Mex Petroleum Company, was motivated "by the moral imperative of fighting by all means necessary to reestablish the 1940 Constitution." Patachula and Arcos had been individually told a week earlier by Léster and Pedro Miret that Aureliano Sánchez Arango's Triple A would disembark a cargo of weapons in Siboney for distribution among all the opposition organizations. They would then go to a nearby farm for target practice. No mention was made that Fidel Castro would be there. On the way to Oriente, Merille, the group leader, kept urging Díaz-Francisco to go faster. Since none of his companions knew how to operate the vehicle, Patachula was resentful that he had to drive five hundred miles to Santiago de Cuba while the others slept.[18]

That Friday night engineering student Héctor de Armas arrived with a rental car at Melba's apartment, where Naty Revuelta told him that Fidel Castro was waiting for him at La Rotonda bar in El Vedado. Before departing, she squeezed his upper arms and pleaded, "Héctor, take care of Fidel." Naty went home, and de Armas drove to the rendezvous point, where he picked up four rebels whom Castro told him to take to the Rex Hotel in Santiago de Cuba. De Armas received thirty-two pesos and two phonograph records for Abel containing the last speech of Eduardo Chibás and the *Invasion Hymn*. He later recalled, "When we left at 2:30 A.M., I found out that none of the passengers knew how to drive. I do not drink coffee, but that night I had to drink espresso in Holguín and Bayamo to keep from falling asleep."[19]

Fidel Castro then returned to Melba's apartment before leaving with the next-to-last group, chauffeured by Lulo Mitchell in a leased 1952 blue Buick. An hour later Ernesto Tizol departed in a rented 1949 Oldsmobile with Almendares cell members Orlando Cortés Gallardo, the watch repairman Eduardo Rodríguez Alemán, and the cobblers Víctor Escalona Benítez and Gilberto Barón Martínez. He purposely drove more slowly to assist possible stragglers. Escalona and the rebel Raúl de Aguiar were delegates of the Ortodoxo Havana municipal assembly. Twenty-five miles east of Havana, in Catalina de Güines, Tizol found Pedro Marrero arguing with two rebels wanting to return to Artemisa, and he tried, in vain, to dissuade the dissidents. During the trip Escalona, the thirty-six-year-old Almendares cell leader, undermined rebel morale by persistently questioning Tizol about their objective. Tizol later spotted Gildo Fleitas six miles outside Holguín, where his automobile was being repaired in a garage. Tizol waited until the vehicle was fixed and had Escalona switch cars with Raúl Gómez García.[20]

Shortly before departing for Oriente, Fidel Castro had Lulo Mitchell drive him to the home of thirty-one-year-old railroad worker Mario Dalmau de la Cruz in El Cerro. Dalmau was told to retrieve four Artemisa rebels at La Rotonda bar and drive them in his 1948 Chevrolet to La Mejor boardinghouse in Santiago de Cuba. Castro and Mitchell then went after midnight to Rancho Boyeros for Manuel Lorenzo Costa, a thirty-nine-year-old airport radio-telegraphist with Cubana Airlines. On the way there, Mitchell got a speeding ticket. Castro talked Lorenzo into joining them on a secret mission related to a radio transmission, apologizing for his ambiguity and ignorance of the technical terms. Castro afterward checked the Café Raúl in Marianao to ascertain that the local cell had left. He later stopped at his home in Marianao to get a book and a guayabera before leaving for Oriente at 2:00 A.M. Castro used a worthless check to buy fuel for the car.[21]

Fourteen miles southeast of Havana, Fidel Castro flagged down Pedro Aguilera's car with seven passengers. He had Nito Ortega switch over to his Buick to make the others more comfortable and less conspicuous during the long trip ahead. The rebel leader and his three companions reached Colón, Matanzas, at 7:00 A.M. and had breakfast at the Santiago-Habana Hotel. Castro walked alone to the home of Dr. Mario Muñoz, requested his immediate presence in Santiago de Cuba, and asked that he wait for him at the El Cobre crossroads. According to Mrs. Muñoz, Castro had earlier promised her husband an appointment as minister of health in a future revolutionary government. She bid a tearful farewell and begged, "If this is something dangerous, please think of your daughters. Let others fight." The physician responded, "rest assured that I will not take risks because of my daughters and you." Muñoz added that he was going to a medical convention in Havana and would call her from there. He left hidden at home three army uniforms and three .22-caliber rifles. The doctor then departed in his black Lincoln and picked up the bank teller Julio M. Reyes Cairo, the local Ortodoxo Youth secretary, who brought a revolver and two pistols. Concerned that the police might stop and search them, they left the weapons with a friend in Placetas, Las Villas.[22]

After Fidel Castro rejoined his travel companions, they continued driving to Santa Clara, where they stopped at 10:00 A.M. for an hour. The rebel leader bought eyeglasses to replace those he had misplaced in Melba's residence. Mitchell recalled that Lorenzo frequently bickered with Castro over the secrecy of their mission. The group had lunch in Camagüey at 3:00 P.M., and after refueling in Holguín, Mitchell sped past Montané and overtook Tizol outside Bayamo at 8:00 P.M. Castro signaled Tizol to stop and instructed him to go to the Siboney farmhouse and inform Abel that he would be there shortly. He then briefly met with Raúl Martínez in the Gran Casino Motel and synchronized timing and attack plans. Twenty-five miles outside Santiago de Cuba, Mitchell halted at a roadblock in front of the garrison in his native Palma Soriano. The sentry, an old army buddy, waved him on without searching the car.[23]

Santiago de Cuba, the second-largest city on the island, was founded on the eastern shore of Santiago Bay in 1514. Many of its 163,237 inhabitants were blacks and mulattoes. In 1898 the metropolis was the scene of the Spanish-American War's last naval and land battle, witnessing the surrender of the Spanish colonial army. The city's hilly terrain is webbed with narrow, winding streets. In late July, in the midst of sweltering summer heat, Santiago de Cuba was adorned for the traditional carnival week. People of different races, ages, and social classes mingled in merriment. Each neighborhood organized a parade ensemble. The most renowned competitors were Los Hoyos, El Tívoli, San Agustín, and Punta Blanca. They paraded down Paseo de José Martí Street to the reviewing stand facing the Moncada fortress. A prize was awarded by a jury judging the groups' organization, rhythm, and costumes. Food and beverage kiosks blaring music lined the parade route, next to stacks of beer kegs and slowly melting ice blocks. That year the regime prohibited using masks to avoid political assassinations or personal vendettas, which sometimes occurred during the festivities. Batista contributed twenty thousand pesos to the event to assure its success.[24]

On Saturday, July 25, with the festivities in full swing, the weary insurgents arrived in Santiago de Cuba after a cross-island journey of more than fifteen hours. Renato Guitart and Abel Santamaría met the rebels at the train and bus depots and directed them to the lodgings reserved in five locations: the house at 218 I Street, in Sueño neighborhood; an old residence at 8 Celda Street; the Rex Hotel on Victoriano Garzón Avenue, where seven rooms with extra folding beds were reserved; the two-story La Mejor boardinghouse facing the Rex Hotel; and the two-story, sixty-room La Perla de Cuba Hotel on Lorraine Street, opposite the train station, near the bay. Léster Rodríguez and eight Artemisa rebels arrived at noon at the Route 80 bus station, across from the Plaza de Marte Park, three blocks from the Moncada, and then found Renato and Abel at the Rex Hotel. The men walked to a nearby café to lunch on goat meat, rice, and beans. Léster was instructed to lodge part of his group at the hotel and take the others by bus to the I Street house. Guitart then received Pedro Miret and six Guanajay peasants at the same bus terminal, provided a seafood meal, and led them to I Street. Reinaldo Boris Luis, driving the first rebel car to reach the city, checked into the Rex Hotel at noon with his four companions. The rooms were equipped with electric fans, but Manuel Suardíaz found the heat unbearable. Montané arrived there in his Pontiac a few hours later with five Lawton cell members after being stopped by the city police for a traffic violation. At midafternoon Tasende's group reached the train station, where Abel and Renato walked them across the street to the reserved rooms at the La Perla de Cuba Hotel. Raúl Castro recalled staying "in some cubbyholes on the first floor, and while some waited with patience for their turn to clean up a bit, using the only washbowl on that floor, others laid down on the beds to rest awhile."[25]

That afternoon Moncada chief Col. Alberto del Río Chaviano was gazing at the carnival activities from his third-floor office window. He summoned sixty-three-year-old Lt. Col. Angel González Alfonso, second-in-command of the regiment, and said, "Gonzalito, I am going to the carnival. If SIM Lieutenant Armando Acosta needs any troops for his secret investigation while I am not here, provide whatever he requests." González Alfonso, who joined the army in 1912 to escape his Havana neighborhood and "see the world," replied, "I have been thinking about that. If there is going to be an attack against the garrison, they will probably be dressed in carnival costumes, and will most likely split into two groups in front of the main entrance. One half will attack the reviewing stand across the street, where you will be sitting with the governor and other government officials, and the other half of their force will charge Post 2, trying to capture the machine gun emplacement. I think that you should not attend the carnival tonight, and we should move that machine gun at the main gate up to the parade ground in front of the Guard Corps." The colonel responded, "Yes, you are right, make the changes, and do not worry about me, I am not going to the festivities."[26]

Lieutenant Acosta's mission prompted precautionary defense measures at Moncada, the *retén* auxiliary guard was increased, and hearsay spread among the troops. That afternoon Pvt. José Ferrá Mulet was detailed with a group of soldiers from the Fusilier Company to load bullets into .30-caliber machine-gun canvas belts. Ferrá was told that an invasion landing was expected in the Manzanillo area. Pvt. Rafael Morales Gros was surprised by the defensive preparations being made by the Fusilier Company and the machine-gun emplacement near the Guard Corps. He heard rumors that revolutionaries disguised in uniform would attack the carnival participants to provoke the populace to rise against the armed forces. Cpl. Eugenio Alcolea Ramírez was informed by a quartermaster sergeant that evening that "Millo Ochoa is in Siboney and is thinking of attacking the Moncada garrison." Alcolea in retrospect believed that Colonel del Río Chaviano, whom he described as "usually careless," should have taken the warning more seriously.[27]

Meanwhile, scores of rebels continued pouring into the city without arousing suspicion. Carlos Bustillo and six Artemisa companions were met at the bus depot at 5:00 P.M. by Abel, who took them to the Celda Street residence. Thirty minutes later an Artemisa contingent with Mario Lazo arrived and were led by Guitart to the same locale. Guitart then went home and told his father not to await his return from the carnival. Oscar Alcalde had driven to Celda Street earlier with the Arroyo Naranjo cell. Since Florentino Fernández had not yet appeared with the key, Emilio Albentosa suggested visiting his family's residence on Bayamo Street. They found his mother nursing a few broken ribs from a fall in the bathtub that morning. Alcalde briefly departed and found Abel at the Rex Hotel, and Abel then retrieved those at Albentosa's home at 7:00 P.M. and drove them to Celda Street. Albentosa, desiring to stay longer with his ailing mother, asked Abel to return for him later. Guitart appeared at the I Street house after 7:30 P.M. with sandwiches and juice drinks, promising to return in three hours. That evening the twenty-five rebels at the La Perla de Cuba Hotel ate a chicken-and-rice dinner. Mario Chanes was left with only a nickel after paying for his meal.[28]

Twenty rebels at the Rex Hotel consumed chicken and rice, fried bananas, and salad. The bill for $48.05, which included desserts, coffee, mineral water, three beers, and nine cigars, was charged to Abel's room account. Héctor de Armas left one of his passengers there and took three others to La Mejor boardinghouse across the street. They were joined at 7:00 P.M. by Fernando Chenard and four La Ceiba cell members and half an hour later by Mario Dalmau and four Artemisa travel companions. Angel Díaz-Francisco then drove with his passengers to the dwelling, where he shared a room with Abelardo Crespo. He stored his suitcase there and went out to eat. The carnival parades on Victoriano Garzón Avenue filed past the boardinghouse, prompting some rebels to join the merriment, although Abel had ordered them to avoid the festivities and to turn in early.[29]

Among the rebels arriving at the Celda Street house was Oscar Quintela, who drove up with three Calabazar cell members. Florentino Fernández and his three companions arrived there on foot after leaving their car in a garage for repairs. The rebels took turns showering, and the lack of a mirror prompted Juan Almeida to shave Florentino and Alcalde with a straight razor. Julio Trigo, a twenty-six-year-old traveling salesman afflicted with tuberculosis for a decade, began coughing up blood after taking a cold shower. When Abel arrived to take them to dinner, he ordered Trigo to return to Havana by bus. Florentino, the military orderly, injected Trigo with a syringe containing a drug acquired at a nearby pharmacy. The group went to a Chinese restaurant at 8:00 P.M. for a fried-rice dinner before accompanying Trigo to the bus station at the Plaza de Marte Park. Trigo agreed to return home, but after his friends left, he joined the carnival festivities.[30]

The Moncada regimental chief also joined the merriment. Lieutenant Colonel González Alfonso recalled, "He did not abide by our agreement and even danced among the multitude." Del Río Chaviano was accompanied by Maj. Florentino E. Rosell Leyva, chief of the Army Corps of Engineers, who had arrived in the city that day to inaugurate a public beach in Siboney. The colonel congratulated the carnival queen at the reviewing stand. While the ceremony was being broadcast live, the rebels in the Siboney farmhouse listened to it on the radio. Melba quipped, "What a great moment to strike at del Río Chaviano." González Alfonso was standing by the .30-caliber machine gun in front of the Guard Corps when the colonel returned, boasting, "You see, nothing happened, and nothing is going to occur." The lieutenant colonel chided him, "you are going to get killed one of these days. Someone in that mob is going to stab and murder you." Del Río Chaviano insisted, "nothing is going to happen, do not be silly." González Alfonso then went to his boardinghouse room. A local businessman wrote in his memoirs, "That night no one remembered the political crisis, the usurpation of power by Batista, nor the flight of Prío. Santiago de Cuba celebrated the feast of its Patron Saint with the overflowing happiness awaited and longed for during the whole year."[31]

The citizenry was unaware that the attackers were conscious of the political situation that they hoped to change soon. The rebel shuttle between Santiago de Cuba and the Siboney farmhouse started after 10:00 P.M. with Abel driving his 1952 green-and-white Oldsmobile, Guitart in his 1950 black Mercury, and Héctor de Armas in a rental car. At the various gathering points they instructed the other rebel drivers to follow them to an undisclosed location. Those at La Mejor boardinghouse were among the first to leave. Eduardo Montano recalled staying there only a few hours and not eating dinner. Angel Díaz-Francisco was standing in front of the building watching the carnival parade when a shuttle leader ordered him to follow in his car.

"I am going to go upstairs and get my suitcase," he replied. "You do not need it, come on," he was told. "Anyway, I have to go get something," he insisted. "Forget it, we are coming right back, let's go!" Patachula, a diabetic, did not want to admit that he needed to retrieve his syringe and insulin in case he stayed out overnight; he was concerned that he would be rejected due to his medical condition. Díaz-Francisco quickly followed the lead car to Siboney with his four trip companions. The twenty-five rebels at the Rex Hotel departed without paying the bill for their seven rooms. The rebels in the I Street house were retrieved at 11:30 P.M. Renato and another driver transported the Celda Street dwelling occupants to Siboney after midnight. The transfer of more than 120 men during five hours did not arouse suspicion due to the carnival throng. The three rebels staying behind were Julio Trigo, Emilio Albentosa, and Ramón Callao. Julio Trigo had been ordered back to Havana due to illness, and the forgotten Albentosa waited at his mother's house for his friends to return. Callao had a nervous breakdown in the Rex Hotel and remained in his room without eating.[32]

The first rebel vehicles, driven by Ernesto Tizol and Pedro Marrero, reached the Siboney estate directly from Havana at 8:00 P.M. A yellow lightbulb at the gate marked the entrance in the darkness. Tizol told Melba and Haydée that he had brought gifts for them and in jest gave them Fourth of September flags. An hour later Fidel Castro and his companions reached Santiago de Cuba and stopped for espresso in a Plaza de Marte Park cafeteria. His driver, the former soldier Lulo Mitchell, suddenly realized that the nearby Moncada fortress, where he had been previously stationed, was the target. "Excuse me, doctor," he asked Castro. "What kind of weapons do we have?" The revolutionary lawyer misleadingly replied, "Do not worry. We have everything." Castro's entourage arrived at Villa Blanca after 10:00 P.M. "Halt, who goes there?" harked rebel sentry Chucho Montané. "Silence, it's me," replied Castro, as he entered the dwelling to oversee preparations. In the crowded house an ebullient José Luis Tasende greeted Gerardo Granados, saying, "We will meet again in victory." Artemisa peasant Fidel Labrador spotted military hospital orderly Florentino Fernández and, fearing betrayal, told Melba, "He is the son of the Guanajay lieutenant." Labrador was informed that Florentino had provided the army uniforms. The damp and wrinkled outfits, withdrawn from a false ceiling, were being ironed by Melba and Haydée. Guitart, who longed for the rank of revolutionary colonel, was the first one to don a uniform. The weapons, wrapped in bundles in a backyard dry well, were retrieved at midnight by Abel, Tizol, Miret, and Suardíaz as Orbeín Hernández held a lantern overhead and Elpidio Sosa stood guard. The arms were sorted out in a back room. Miret, Tizol, and Mitchell loaded the five-cartridge shotguns. A potpourri of about thirty handguns was placed in orderly rows on a table top, the rifles were propped against the wall, and the ammunition boxes were stacked in a corner.[33]

The total weaponry used at Moncada and Bayamo consisted of forty 12- and 16-gauge shotguns, costing fifty-eight hundred pesos; thirty-five .22-caliber Mosberg and Remington rifles, bought for eighty pesos each; sixty handguns of various models; twenty-four rifles of different caliber, including eight 1898 Krag-Jorgensen rifles, three 1892 .44-caliber Winchester sawed-off rifles, and a .30-caliber 1903 model Springfield rifle; a .30-caliber M1 Garand rifle with a folding metal stock; and a malfunctioning .45-caliber submachine gun. The last three weapons, the best in the lot, had been taken by Guitart from Acción Libertadora. Thirty-year-old house painter René Bedia Morales was disheartened when he recognized the same armament used during training. He told Pedro Trigo, "It looks like this is going to be with 22-caliber bullets."[34]

At 1:15 A.M. Fidel Castro ordered everyone except the sentinels to sleep on the mattresses strewn on the floor. The stifling summer heat inside the crowded house and nervous expectation prevented most rebels from sleeping. Many stayed up all night chatting in whispers. The only edibles available were some mangoes, crackers, and "three large buckets of milk from a neighboring dairy farmer." Castro returned to Santiago de Cuba with Abel and Pedro Trigo looking for Luis Conte Agüero, a popular Ortodoxo radio commentator, to harangue the masses by radio during the attack. Abel dropped off Castro and Trigo in downtown Céspedes Park at 2:00 A.M. and proceeded to El Cobre to find Dr. Mario Muñoz. Trigo waited on a park bench while Castro walked to the Conte Agüero home on Estrada Palma Street. Luis's sixty-six-year-old mother stated that he had moved to Havana weeks earlier. The rebel leader returned to the park, where Trigo had found Gildo Fleitas and his five companions, who, after not locating Abel at La Mejor boardinghouse, had joined the public festivities. Abel appeared shortly thereafter, followed by Dr. Muñoz and Julio Reyes in their car. Castro climbed into Muñoz's Lincoln and told Fleitas to take Trigo and follow him back to Siboney. The physician, noticing that it was after midnight, commented that it was his forty-first birthday and wondered how many more years he would live. Castro replied, "Do not worry, you will live many more." The three cars arrived at the Siboney farmhouse at 4:00 A.M.[35]

The rebel leader immediately ordered the allotment of weapons and uniforms. Some rebels squabbled over the shirts with sergeant's stripes and the larger-caliber weapons. Castro had them return everything for redistribution. The mismatched uniforms did not properly fit many rebels. Gerardo Granados recalled, "At first there was much confusion in sorting out the uniforms. Since Ciro Redondo and I were clothing store employees, we helped with the distribution. We would look at the length and waist size of each pair of pants and then gave it to the person we chose out of the crowd." Mario Chanes, Miguel Oramas, and Pancho González assisted in handing out uniforms and caps. As the supply dwindled, nineteen-year-old Jaime "El Catalán" Costa Chávez, who had a twenty-eight-inch waist, received a pair of size-38 cavalry knickers that exposed his lower legs. Israel Tápanes rolled up his uniform pant cuffs above his nonregulation brown shoes. Fidel Castro got the largest uniform available, but it was too short for him. The barber Eduardo Montano, issued an extra-large outfit, stated that there were not sufficient uniforms for everyone and that a few rebels went in their civilian clothes.[36]

The deficient weapons and meager ammunition were distributed by José Luis Tasende and three others. Pepe Suárez obtained the only automatic weapon available, a .45-caliber submachine gun. Suardíaz indicated that the weapon was inoperable due to jammed recoil springs. When Tápanes received a rifle, he also requested a pistol but was told that each combatant could have only one weapon. Juan Almeida recalled how his "heart froze" when he got a .22-caliber rifle and stated that he had to massage his chest to renew his heart's normal rhythm. Severino "Vero" Rosell remembered, "the total armament I carried was a .38-caliber pistol with one magazine and around twenty single bullets." Mario Chanes went to the attack with "a .32-caliber pistol and a fistful of bullets in my pocket." Ciro Redondo got a .38-caliber revolver. Marcos "El Curro" Martí Rodríguez "carried an old .44-caliber revolver with only 4 or 5 bullets." After Eduardo Montano received a .22-caliber rifle with sixteen bullets, he heard "someone warning not to waste bullets." Díaz-Francisco confirmed that no one had more than twenty bullets. This austere rationing contrasted with Castro's claim that they had "collected some 10,000 bullets of different caliber," for an average of sixty rounds per attacker. For some rebels who never attended target practice, it was the first time they ever handled a weapon. Alejandro Ferrás test-fired his .45-caliber pistol toward the ceiling. The report caused a general pandemonium, awakening some and frightening others into thinking that they were under attack.[37]

Military hospital orderly Florentino Fernández received a dozen bullets and an antique .44-caliber Winchester sawed-off rifle. He had no idea how to use it and later admitted being a "poor marksman" with little knowledge of arms. As the weapons were being distributed, Lulo Mitchell kept staring at the only Springfield rifle, knowing that it was the best in the lot since he had used the same model in the army. Castro allowed him to get it along with two .30-caliber five-bullet clips. Lulo then saw the baby-faced Raúl Castro and asked Antonio Ferrás, "What is this boy doing here?" "He is Fidel's brother," said Antonio. "Oh! Well," said Mitchell, "in that case it's different."[38]

After the weapons and uniforms were handed out, Raúl Gómez García recited a poem he had written for the occasion and read the "Manifesto to the Nation." Castro then stood on a soda crate and harangued the crowd on their "historic destiny." Vero Rosell recalled, "Fidel told us that the assault on the 'Moncada' would be produced by surprise and that, probably, there would not be any bloodshed." Castro explained that wearing army uniforms would facilitate entry into the garrison and stressed, "It will be a surprise attack that will not last more than ten minutes." He tacked a rough sketch of the Moncada on the wall and explained that a vanguard of six men would disarm the two sentries on Post 3. The rebel motorcade would then enter the citadel, with each vehicle stopping at a corresponding stairway leading to the barracks. A dozen attackers with shotguns would rush into each of the five dormitories and surprise fewer than ninety soldiers asleep in each building wing, keeping them covered while the others tied them up. The rebel leader assured, "We might not even have to fire one shot." Someone asked, "What if the doors to the dormitories are locked?" Castro replied, "We will just have to shoot off the lock." To avoid mistaking each other as soldiers, the password would be "Who lives?" and the countersign "Chibás."[39]

According to the plan, if the attackers met resistance, they would fire a fusillade to drive the soldiers from the barracks onto the rear patio. Their comrades occupying the Saturnino Lora Civil Hospital behind the citadel would pin them down in a crossfire. Six rebel snipers on the roof of the nearby three-story Palace of Justice would neutralize any further hostility. After taking the communications room, they would transmit the national anthem, combat hymns, their own statement, and a recording of Eduardo Chibás's final commentary. Castro purported that Luis Conte Agüero would support them by haranguing the populace during the attack from a seized radio station, although he had failed to contact the Ortodoxo leader. Díaz-Francisco recalled someone asking "What do we do if the Air Force attacks?" Fidel Castro deceitfully claimed, "Don't worry, some pilots have agreed to give us air cover with a few planes based in Camagüey." While responding to other questions, Castro called Mitchell, told him to raise his Springfield rifle, and said to the crowd, "You see this rifle? Shoot anyone that you see with this army regulation weapon." The astonished Mitchell exclaimed, "Well, doctor, what about me?" Castro replied, "The problem is that you do not advance too far so that you then have to back up."[40]

Haydée Santamaría heard Fidel Castro say that if they "succeeded taking the citadel they would hand over the arms to the populace and resist in Santiago until it was possible." Castro told the gathering that Raúl Martínez and his companions would simultaneously take the Bayamo barracks. They would arm the Bayamo citizenry, who would join the rebel advance in seizing garrison by garrison across the island until reaching Havana and overthrowing Batista. Raúl Castro gave a contradictory account after his capture, stating that he was unaware if it was a national plan and knew nothing of the Bayamo attack. Fidel Castro alleged five months later, "our triumph would have meant the immediate ascent to power of the Ortodoxos, first provisionally and later through general elections." Vero Rosell recalled Fidel saying that "all of us were willing to fight and to die, although our sacrifice would not be in vain." Another combatant heard Castro say, "If we win, tomorrow will fulfill what Martí aspired to. If we don't, the gesture will have set an example for the people of

Cuba." Granados and Montano listened as Castro ended his tirade by stating, "All of you are now sergeants," but he did not choose a rank for himself. Abel then spoke of "dying willingly for Cuba" and repeated the order to leave behind all identification documents. The gathering sang in a low tone the national anthem, whose first stanza concludes, "To die for the fatherland is to live." As Castro stepped off the soda crate, he placed both his hands on Carlos Bustillo's shoulders and asked him if he knew Santiago de Cuba. "No," responded a puzzled Bustillo. "Then, you are dead," replied the rebel leader. Former MNR member Gustavo Arcos, who had been unaware that Fidel Castro was leading a revolt, asked him if this was an isolated plan or a coordinated national effort. Castro replied, "We will emulate what Carlos Manuel de Céspedes did in 1868. His premature uprising forced all the other conspiratorial groups to support him. Everybody who is willing will join us." Castro then asked Fernando Chenard to take "a historic photo." Gerardo Granados, Suardíaz, Bustillo, and others posed together, but according to Suardíaz, "I turned my face away but luckily there was no flash magnesium and the photo could not be taken. Otherwise, it would have been used to arrest us later."[41]

A skeptical Suardíaz remembered that "Fidel said the people of Oriente would join us, but I do not know who he was counting on, because the ones I saw were only thinking of partying and drinking rum." A few rebels openly argued that the arms were insufficient for the endeavor. Montano and Díaz-Francisco heard Castro trying to restore calm by falsely reassuring them that the garrison would easily fall because soldiers who were part of the conspiracy awaited to join them. Suardíaz heard Castro say that navy vessels in the bay would participate in the revolt. Fidel Castro later reiterated in *History Will Absolve Me* that "The Navy did not fight against us, and it would undoubtedly have come over to our side later" and that the army would not have fought against a people in revolt. Montano afterward claimed, "That was Fidel's first treachery. He could not even be honest with those who were risking their lives." Díaz-Francisco later commented, "The more Castro vacillated, the sooner I was convinced that he was lying. No one understood the plan. Fidel Castro had read about military tactics, and he used his imagination greatly when describing the attack, but it was not a plausible scheme." Alfredo Corcho Cinta remarked, "I'm going to go. But I know they're going to snare me like a little bird." Dr. Mario Muñoz, who had put on an army uniform, was among those who complained that it was a suicide mission. According to Díaz-Francisco and Héctor de Armas, Muñoz argued with Fidel Castro and refused to go as a combatant. He removed his gun belt, changed into his physician's frock coat, and committed himself only to his medical capabilities. De Armas later repeated this version to Muñoz's wife, adding that the doctor told him, "What this man has done is a trick, this is not what I thought." Castro offered everyone three bottles of rum to brighten their gloom, but many were in no mood for a celebration.[42]

The dissenters included the entire six-man Almendares cell headed by Víctor Escalona. To avoid arguing in front of the others, Castro led them into the kitchen, where they stated that the plan "was madness, that it could not be achieved." Díaz-Francisco felt that Castro was taking them into a slaughter to gain personal recognition and discussed the matter with his travel companions. Patachula stated that his group, along with agronomy student Manuel Vázquez Tió, did not like the plan and refused to go. Manuel Lorenzo confronted Castro and demanded to know why he had been taken to Oriente. Castro replied that his mission was to "operate the transmitter of the Moncada garrison to send messages once that fortress was taken." When Lorenzo balked, Castro accused him of being deceitful. Unable to persuade the dissidents, the rebel leader ordered the Almendares cell detained in a room. Chucho Montané, Fernando Chenard, and Mario Chanes stood guard outside the door. Raúl Castro then told Carlos Bustillo, "I want you to come with me, grab your shotgun, because there is a group of comrades who do not want to participate." Díaz-Francisco, Manuel Lorenzo, Jesús Blanco Alba, Carlos Merille Acosta, Manuel Vázquez Tió, Abelardo Crespo Arias, and Gustavo Arcos Bergnes were confined in another area. Díaz-Francisco claimed that after some meditation, Crespo and Arcos told him that they would join the attack. After failing to deter them, Patachula asserted, "Well, I am staying." Arcos disagreed with this version, saying that he and Crespo never opposed Castro's plan, even though "the majority of us were not prepared, everything depended on the surprise factor, so that the Trojan Horse could enter." He acknowledged that Patachula tried to dissuade them from going.[43]

Carlos Bustillo did not blame the dissidents for backing out since "Fidel's speech should have been stimulating, but instead, it was depressing. We all knew there was no possible victory because Fidel had said so. The assembly we had in Siboney was a massive immolation of a group of people as a protest of the Cuban youth against the event of the Tenth of March Coup. It was suicidal, like the followers of Jim Jones in Jonestown, Guyana." Suardíaz recalled that Castro's address was "very mediocre. We were waiting for a speech that would make our blood boil, as he had done previously, but it did not happen." Juan Almeida commented on the dissidents in 1984: "under the actual conditions, I would have had them shot by firing squad."[44]

Castro selected a squad to storm Post 3 dressed as sergeants. He ordered Abel to seize the Civil Hospital with nineteen rebels. Léster Rodríguez would command the six snipers on the Palace of Justice rooftop. Fidel told the two women to wait in Villa Blanca until the rebels returned. The overprotective Haydée insisted on accompanying her younger brother Abel. Melba recalled that when she asked to join in, Dr. Muñoz "solved the great problem we presented Fidel" by offering to take them as his assistants. Moments before departing, the rebel leader asked Díaz-Francisco to change his mind, but the law student refused, saying that he had been called to Oriente under false pretenses. When Castro requested to use his car, Díaz-Francisco responded that he was immediately leaving in it. Castro then asked him to wait to depart until everyone else was gone. The rebels exited the farmhouse through a side door, formed into a double line, and piled into the vehicles as they were driven up. Léster Rodríguez, who had fallen asleep in a rocking chair, remembered, "When Melba woke me up, the rest of the comrades were already in the car." Díaz-Francisco, who had an aggressive reputation, was taunted by Reinaldo Boris Luis "for being scared." Threats were exchanged between them as others stepped in to break up the disagreement. Díaz-Francisco quickly departed in his Oldsmobile, joined by Manuel Vázquez, Carlos Merille, and Jesús Blanco.[45]

Sixteen automobiles left Siboney that Sunday at about 5:00 A.M. and traveled on a two-lane dirt road eight miles to Santiago de Cuba. The first two cars, Abel's 1952 Oldsmobile and Ameijeiras's Chevrolet taxi, headed for the Civil Hospital. Dalmau's 1948 Chevrolet was in third place, going to the Palace of Justice. Pedro Marrero was next in Guitart's 1950 black Mercury with the vanguard that would take Post 3. As Fidel Castro was stepping into his rented 1952 Buick, he told Fernando Chenard to follow him and instructed that everyone else should line up behind them. Mario Chanes was heading toward Chenard's vehicle when a rebel clutching a .22-caliber rifle asked him, "How does this work?" Chanes replied, "Don't ask me." The other automobiles in the caravan were driven by Reinaldo Boris Luis, Ernesto Tizol, Chucho Montané, Oscar Alcalde, Ricardo Santana, Ciro Redondo, Gildo Fleitas, Héctor de Armas, Oscar Quintela, and Dr. Muñoz, who was in his black Lincoln.[46]

Boris's overloaded car, with rebels sitting on each other's laps, blew out a worn rear tire after a quarter-mile. Tizol stopped to pick up Boris and Vicente Chávez. Díaz-Francisco drove by and saw Montané, who had stopped to help, standing on the roadside. Montané later told the press, "I did not take part in the assault because, before the car arrived, I had trouble with one of the tires and since there was no spare, I had to remain where I was until we later fled into the mountains." Alcalde halted to get Ulises Sarmiento and Gerardo Sosa. "Stay here, we are coming back to get you," Tizol told about a dozen rebels, including Tomás "Tocororo" Rodríguez, Manuel Isla, Orbeín Hernández, and Manuel Suardíaz, who hid in the woods. Tizol initially claimed that he picked up the eight stranded rebels, packing sixteen people into his Oldsmobile. He later said, "We were ten or twelve in the car. The caravan was greatly dispersed and this confused us a bit. Upon reaching the iron one-lane bridge over the San Juan River, we had to let pass an approaching jeep with hunters. This forced us to halt, and therefore we were able to regroup and continue in order."[47]

When Fidel Castro's vehicle halted by the bridge, Gustavo Arcos asked him, "Is there action in Bayamo at this time also?" Castro replied, "By now, Bayamo has been taken." When the cars renewed their march, the red dust blowing on the Siboney highway was so thick that Pedro Trigo could barely see two yards ahead. The rebel caravan followed the Siboney highway into Santiago de Cuba, taking Roosevelt Avenue and later the four-lane Victoriano Garzón Avenue. The lead cars, driven by Abel and Ameijeiras, turned right onto Central Highway, one block past the Palace of Justice. They went left on Trinidad Street, parallel to the Civil Hospital, and pulled up to its main entrance. Dalmau had lagged behind, missing the right turn toward the courthouse and continuing on Victoriano Garzón Avenue. Léster Rodríguez told him to make a U-turn at the Plaza de Marte Park and directed him back to the Palace of Justice. Pedro Marrero and the vanguard veered right onto Moncada Street and sighted the garrison two blocks away. In Castro's car Arcos prayed silently.[48]

Moncada Street is about one hundred yards in length from Victoriano Garzón Avenue to the Post 3 side gate. On the intersection with Victoriano Garzón Avenue stood the home of medical lieutenant Rolando Pérez Sainz de la Peña, surrounded by a vacant lot. Halfway down the left side of Moncada Street, on the corner of Tenth of March Street, stood the Joaquín Castillo Duany Military Hospital. Its rear emergency entrance faced the back of the Palace of Justice. Opposite the military hospital, on the right flank of Moncada Street, was the Private Bernal Figueredo military housing project, a square block of sixteen wooden bungalows. These were occupied by sergeants and their families and had twenty-eight-inch-high concrete fencing separating the front yard from the sidewalk. Nine new concrete three-bedroom houses next to the military hospital, between the Tenth of March Street and Trinidad Street, had been raffled to sergeants who were heads of households.

The Moncada fortress occupied a 13.5-acre irregular rectangle compound ringed by a battlement cement wall. Built in 1859 as a colonial prison, within twenty years it was turned into a Spanish citadel. Afro-Cuban independence general Guillermo Moncada was imprisoned there in 1893. Nearly a decade later the new Cuban republic posted a Rural Guard squadron in it and named the fortress after its former patriot prisoner. The garrison was destroyed by fire in December 1937 and rebuilt nine months later to its present proportions. It stands on a hillside with its forward ramparts on the parade ground higher than those protecting the rear and side perimeters. There are four entrances on each of the cardinal points, containing two sentry boxes with gun slits and a chain drawn across them. These entrances comprised the major defensive positions, along with cylindrical watch towers on each corner and Post 1, located on the sidewalk in front of the Guard Corps, to the center right of the main building. Post 1 was protected by an M1917A1 .30-caliber water-cooled machine gun, placed there the previous night by order of Lieutenant Colonel González Alfonso. The automatic weapon could sweep the parade ground and its three surrounding gates: the main entrance at Post 2; the left side entrance at Post 3 on Moncada Street; and the right side entrance at Post 5, facing the regimental chief's home. This house, with an outward appearance of a modest wood-frame dwelling, had inner walls of reinforced concrete twelve inches thick. The Post 4 entrance at the rear of the garrison, protected by another machine gun, faced the back of the Civil Hospital.[49]

The light-yellow, three-story main building, wedged into a hillside, lay on a row of chambers housing the general quartermaster, the post exchange, four company kitchens, the Rural Guard Squadron communications room, other subaltern services, and the Guard Corps office. This office contained desks for the corporal and the sergeant of the guard and the Officer of the Day. Next door was a dormitory for the Guard Corps personnel shift. Behind both rooms were detention cells. In the center of the main edifice a passageway led up to the rear patio and Post 4. Six frontal stairways with eighteen steps reaching the first floor accessed the doorways to six building wings. They contained, from left to right, the administrative offices section, the Service Company, the Headquarters Company, the Infantry Company, the Fusilier Company, and the Rural Guard barracks.

To the immediate right of each dormitory entrance was the first sergeant's office and across from it the bedroom and office of the company lieutenant. Beyond this area was the recreation room, with the company barbershop to its left and the quartermaster room to its right. There were two bilateral doorways at the rear of the recreation room leading to a large dormitory. Inside, between the length of both entrances, was the four-and-one-half-foot-high gun cabinet, with four sliding glass doors, capable of storing more than one hundred rifles. The barracks had a red-tile floor and contained four rows of bunks, two in the center facing away from each other, and rows along opposite walls separated by four-foot-wide walkways. At the rear of the dormitory were the toilets on the left side and the shower room to the right.

The six entrances to the main building, designed for a quick evacuation onto the parade ground, were connected by a balcony across the length of the structure. A central tower complex had offices on the second floor and the regimental command staff headquarters on the third floor. Parallel to the Rural Guard barracks, near Post 5, was the one-story Mariana Grajales theater. Nearby was a small shrine to Saint Barbara, patron saint of artillerymen and a deity of the Santeria Afro-Cuban religion. Behind the theater was the power plant and a structure containing the mechanic repair shop, dual gasoline pumps, and a stable for two dozen transport mules. To the right of Post 4 was a small-arms target range, enclosed by a concrete fence twelve feet wide with a fifteen-foot-high rear retaining wall. The targets were positioned in front of a stack of sandbags. To the left of Post 4 was a three-story building containing the Enlisted Men's Club on the ground floor, the Officers' Club above it, and the Regimental Intelligence Service (SIR) office on top. Behind it was a courtyard with a horseshoe-shaped walkway adorned with five trees.

On duty at the fortress were 374 men of the First Regiment Antonio Maceo and 26 soldiers of the Rural Guard Eleventh Squadron. The command structure consisted of a colonel, a lieutenant colonel, a major, 24 officers, 87 sergeants and corporals, and 288 privates. Many personnel resided in the city with their families or in boardinghouses, others lived in the twenty-five homes of the adjacent military housing project, and the rest occupied the barracks. Their total armament consisted of 2 Browning M2 .50-caliber machine guns, 2 M1917A1 .30-caliber machine guns, 10 Thompson .45-caliber submachine guns, 865 Springfield .30-caliber rifles, 471 Colt .45-caliber revolvers, and 500 bayonets.[50]

As the rebel motorcade approached Post 3 on Moncada Street at 5:20 A.M., the fewer than 300 soldiers in the garrison were mostly asleep. The sentries for the 6:00 A.M. shift were getting ready for breakfast. Warnings and rumors of an imminent attack had been dismissed by the overconfident garrison commander but continued to worry some of the troops. Some precautions had been taken by subalterns, including the repositioning of a machine gun and incrementing the *retén* auxiliary guard. Gen. Fulgencio Batista was five hundred miles away that morning at the Varadero national regatta. The annual event was traditionally attended by the head of state, and it had been announced that Batista would present the winner's trophy cup. It would have been simpler for the 160 rebels to assassinate Batista at Varadero. They would have easily blended in with the spectators and at a given signal attacked Batista outdoors. Instead, Castro appeared to be emulating the historically significant planned uprisings of Narciso López in 1848, José Martí in 1895, and Antonio Guiteras in 1933. His scheme for a simultaneous revolt in all of the provinces, copied from Martí's plan that initiated the 1895 Cuban War of Independence, was hurriedly compressed to two cities in Oriente. Castro was trying to give fruition to the "unfulfilled revolution" concept preached by Chibás and the UIR. All day the rebel leader kept making references to patriotic figures and living a historic moment.

Fidel Castro did successfully manage to transport a large rebel force surreptitiously across the island, although some vehicles had no relief drivers, there were traffic mishaps and breakdowns, and poor coordination almost made a few miss their rides. All the rebels except a few cell leaders were misled about their purpose for going to Oriente. Some insurgents were not invited to participate due to the shortage of weapons, and others deserted during departure. The entire Santiago de las Vegas cell failed to go because of bad planning. A few rebels went to the attack without army uniforms because of a deficient supply, and the disguises did not properly fit those who wore the uniforms. Others lacked training with the weapons they received for combat, and some had never handled a weapon. The attackers, with inadequate arms and scant ammunition, were warned not to waste bullets. Castro resorted to deception to get recalcitrant followers to participate in battle. This prompted a dozen rebels to defect, and others, such as Dr. Muñoz, Bustillo, and Corcho, felt that they had little chance of survival. Castro hoped that their premature action would prompt other revolutionary groups to rise up behind him. The furtive possibility of victory now awaited beyond the massive citadel walls.

FOUR

"Shoot at those wearing tennis shoes"

The rebel caravan approached the Moncada fortress at 5:20 A.M., thirty-seven minutes before sunrise. The vanguard was unaware that some vehicles had been diverted when Ernesto Tizol veered off course onto Las Américas Avenue instead of proceeding on Victoriano Garzón Avenue. This delayed a large contingent from reaching their objective. Fidel Castro later admitted that of the ninety rebels traveling to Post 3, only sixty to seventy arrived. Luis Conte Agüero estimated the number of participants at forty-five. When Tizol reached Quintero Heights in the suburbs, his companions heard the distant echoes of gunfire. They all fled the city except Reinaldo Boris Luis, who headed for the Moncada. Oscar Quintela and the Calabazar cell, following Tizol's automobile, never made it to the garrison. Pedro Trigo, military orderly Florentino Fernández, and former soldier Lulo Mitchell were among those led astray. Oscar Alcalde, who with Tizol stopped to pick up those stranded on the Siboney highway, also got lost and arrived late. Dr. Mario Muñoz, driving the last vehicle, had to make a U-turn on Central Highway to find his way to the Civil Hospital. Castro acknowledged, "It was extremely difficult to re-establish contact with them." Haydée Santamaría indicated that "the ones who were sidetracked . . . kept circling Santiago de Cuba again and again."[1]

"Tizol got scared at the last moment and pretended to be lost," said his brother-in-law, Bayamo rebel leader Raúl Martínez Ararás. Tizol later admitted, "I learned of the whole plan, that is, which positions would be taken, the places where the attack would occur, when Fidel explained it a few moments before leaving for combat on the dawn of July 26." Martínez quipped, "Tizol had driven around Santiago de Cuba various times. He rented the Siboney farmhouse and knew the direct route to the Vázquez gas station and the Moncada. It was impossible for him to get lost."

Angel Díaz-Francisco, a defector, was later blamed in revolutionary accounts for diverting the caravan while leaving Santiago de Cuba. Díaz-Francisco was still on Victoriano Garzón Avenue, headed for Central Highway, when he saw the first two rebel cars turn toward the Civil Hospital.[2]

The vanguard car, driven by Pedro Marrero, was adorned with military Fourth of September flags, and a photo of General Batista was taped to the windshield to make it appear "official." As the vehicle turned onto Moncada Street, Fidel Castro, driving directly behind, stopped his Buick to provide leeway and slipped his eyeglasses into his shirt pocket. When Marrero got halfway down the street, two perimeter patrol soldiers, part of a 6:00 P.M. to 6:00 A.M. watch reinforcement unit dubbed the Cossack Guard, coincidentally emerged from Tenth of March Street. An additional two-man roving patrol was circling the outer wall on the opposite side of the fortress. Cpl. Argelio Guerra was making the rounds alone, supervising both surveillance teams. The two sentinels who spotted the approaching vehicles, Pvts. Alfonso Silva Domínguez and Luis Triay, called "Cara de Chivo" (Goat Face), were walking in the middle of the street between the military hospital and the new housing project. They wore white steel helmets, military-police armbands, white leggings, white cartridge belts, holstered .45-caliber pistols, and shouldered .45-caliber Thompson machine guns. As the caravan drew near, Silva ported his weapon and loudly ordered them to halt. The reply was "Make way for General Batista." Silva issued another warning but hesitated to shoot because the passengers wore army uniforms. The *Havana Post* later reported, "The assailants had not taken into account the detail that at that hour the only authorized entrance into the Army Post was through the central gate, and this slip-up aroused the suspicion of the small guard patrol." Guard duty at each Moncada entrance consisted of a sentinel and an auxiliary armed with Springfield rifles. They were joined after 6:00 P.M. until dawn by a corporal of the Cossack Guard. The sentries would be substituted after a two-hour shift by another team that was nearby resting on cots. The process was repeated four times, in three turns, during an entire day until the changing of the guard at noon.[3]

Inside the Moncada, thirty-two-year-old Cpl. Eugenio Alcolea Ramírez, of the Fusilier Company, was making the security rounds after returning from the carnival at midnight. He was substituting for a corporal who inspected the machine-gun emplacements and the exterior roving patrols. As Alcolea passed by Post 3, he saw Cpl. Isidro C. Izquierdo Rodríguez of the Cossack Guard sitting on the second step of the nearby stairway. Izquierdo was holding across his lap a Springfield rifle without the firing bolt mechanism. Many soldiers habitually kept the bolts in their pockets or tucked behind the buckles of their web belts because the weapons were stored without them. Alcolea briefly chatted with Izquierdo, who had recently been transferred from the Guantánamo Rural Guard post to the Service Company, before going behind the main building to check the other guard posts.[4]

Moments after Alcolea departed Post 3, the lead car driven by Pedro Marrero stopped ten yards away. The sentinel, eighteen-year-old Pvt. Orlando Molina Amores, told Marrero that all vehicles had to enter through the main gate. Molina and his auxiliary, Pvt. Walfrido Monzón, who had been on duty during the 4:00 to 6:00 A.M. shift, were quickly disarmed by the rebels. Cpl. Isidro Izquierdo hurried toward Post 3 to investigate the commotion. He noticed that the intruders wore ill-fitting uniforms and civilian belts and shoes and that they lacked military haircuts, signifying that they were impostors. Vanguard rebel José Luis Tasende wore a belt buckle with a prominent "J" adornment. When the corporal saw that the guards had been overpowered, he pushed the alarm button in the sentry box, setting off a loud and continuous electric bell at all four entrances. Izquierdo was then shot with small-caliber bullets in the stomach. As he spun around, two shots hit him in the left armpit and another on the nape. Pvt. Efraín Galano Liranza, rushing to assist Izquierdo, was hit in the abdomen with a large-caliber bullet that went out his lower back. He stumbled back into the main building passageway, where he went into shock while sitting on the ground with his back against the wall. The gate chain was dropped, and all the occupants of the first car ran into the compound, instead of driving in, leaving their abandoned vehicle partly blocking the caravan from penetrating the citadel. One intruder picked up Izquierdo's rifle, which was rendered useless without the firing bolt that was in the corporal's pocket.[5]

Ninety yards away, on the sidewalk in front of the Fusilier Company, nineteen-year-old Pvt. José Ferrá Mulet was on reinforced guard duty overlooking the three entrances to the parade ground. During the commotion at Post 3, he saw that the two sentinels were disarmed and forced to lie on the ground face down. Afro-Cuban 2nd Lt. Cándido Garrido Wilson, the chief of the guard, ran out of the nearby Guard Corps office after hearing gunshots. He saw the frightened Ferrá working the bolt action on his Springfield and yelled at him, "Have you gone crazy?" The teenager pointed toward Post 3 and replied, "No, look, we are under attack." Hours later Ferrá went to inspect the rebel automobile and noticed that its engine was still running, a front wheel was pressed against the curb, and there were traces of blood inside.[6]

Thirty yards behind the lead car, the Cossack Guards who ordered it to halt were facing Post 3 with their backs toward the rest of the caravan. Fidel Castro, driving up behind them, told an interviewer years later, "I had two intentions: one, to protect those who had taken the post; second, to take the weapons of the Cossack Guards. I believe that if we had continued along with the other cars ignoring the guards, we would have taken the garrison." Castro halted and ordered Gustavo Arcos, sitting behind him, to detain a lone soldier who was walking on the sidewalk to their left in front of the military hospital. Pvt. Luis E. Frómeta Naranjo of the Rural Guard had just exited a bus on Garzón Avenue and was carrying his lunch in a grease-stained brown paper bag. He suspiciously glanced at the caravan while heading for Post 3.

Arcos believed that "the soldier was distrustful because it is not logical for a military unit to enter a garrison in civilian automobiles." Arcos thrust his head out the rear-door window and shouted at him to halt. Frómeta stopped and instinctively reached for his holstered revolver. Israel Tápanes, sitting near Arcos, was trembling so furiously that he had to hold his jaw with both hands to control his chattering teeth. Upon hearing Arcos, the two military policemen in front turned toward him. Arcos had one foot on the ground when Castro accelerated the car in an attempt to run over the Cossack Guards. He slipped and fell to his knees, balanced on his left arm, while aiming a Colt pistol with his right hand. As Frómeta drew his weapon, Arcos shot him "two or three times in the torso." Arcos stated that when he fired, shots had just been heard coming from Post 3. Military policeman Silva indicated that he first heard the gunfire at the garrison entrance.[7]

As Silva jerked the firing lever on his Thompson machine gun, he was shot at from various vehicles. He fired a burst over Fidel Castro's vehicle, which hit army residence number eleven on the street corner facing the military hospital entrance. Silva did not aim directly at the automobile, fearing "shooting at whom I thought were soldiers, since there was the possibility that it could be a mistake, and I might be facing a court martial, like my brother awaited at that moment." Castro reacted by further accelerating while turning a hard left, colliding with the curb and stalling the engine. Sgt. Carlos Rojas Ortiz exited his military housing residence, on his way to the Moncada, when he was shot at from the third vehicle, but he escaped unscathed.[8]

"Shoot, damn it, shoot," yelled Silva as his partner fumbled with his weapon. "I can't, it's jammed," replied the nervous Triay. Snatching the machine gun and dropping to the ground, Silva noticed that Triay had not cocked the firing lever. He recalled, "Cara de Chivo was not familiar with the machine gun. That day he was substituting for Private Diocles Martínez Bles." After Silva discharged a thirty-round clip, the two military policemen hastily crawled along the side of the military hospital to its rear utility door. "Check inside while I cover out here," ordered Silva. Triay encountered forty-three-year-old Lt. Juan Piña Martínez with three or four men in the hospital corridor and quickly retreated, fearing that they might be with the attackers. Rushing back outside, Triay hastily fired a badly aimed burst at someone hiding behind a garbage can. "You idiot, it's me," shouted Silva; "I ought to kill you!" Triay told him that Piña and others were inside, and they decided to confront them. "Whose side are you on?" asked Silva as he and his partner leveled their machine guns at Piña's retinue. "I am with Batista," affirmed Piña; "we are here to defend this position from the attackers."[9]

Silva's machine-gun burst rudely awakened Sgt. Eulalio "El Mulo" González Amador, his wife Angelina, and their baby daughter. It stitched a row of holes across the upper wooden wall of their living room, killing their parrot on its perch. The forty-year-old González scrambled out of bed and peeked through the front window curtain at the uniformed attackers. He thought they were Camp Columbia soldiers leading a coup d'état until seeing one with two-tone shoes. Melba Hernández later affirmed that "Boris had a new pair of shoes of that type." Other rebels wore nonmilitary footwear, including Raúl Castro, who had new yellow shoes. El Mulo went to comfort his crying infant and found her covered with splinters splayed from her crib headboard by a hail of bullets. González had his wife and daughter lie on the floor, placed a mattress over them, dressed in civilian clothes, and grabbed his .45-caliber pistol. He departed through the back door and entered the fortress through Post 2. The González home, situated in the crossfire, was hit ninety-two times.[10]

Across the street from the González residence, Private Frómeta had just been shot by Gustavo Arcos. According to the *Havana Post*, as Frómeta "fell to the ground, they pumped bullets into him, then left him there. Another carload of revolutionists followed them. Some of its occupants got out and kicked him savagely, wounding him again and firing at him . . . Frómeta suffered 24 bullet wounds, injuries to the right lung, the liver, the groin and one leg." The gunfire and Frómeta's cries alerted Roberto Ferrándiz Millán, a policeman convalescing from hernia surgery in the military hospital. As Ferrándiz peered out from the second-story window toward Post 3, he was shot in the back of the head by the attackers.[11]

Meanwhile, the second rebel objective, the Palace of Justice, was attained by Léster Rodríguez with Raúl Castro, Mario Dalmau de la Cruz, Angel Sánchez Pérez, José Martínez Alvarez, and Abelardo García Ylls. On the sidewalk they seized Afro-Cuban Cpl. Carlos Chauvín, the regimental chief's chauffeur, on his way to the garrison. "What is happening?" asked the startled soldier. "Batista has fallen!" responded Raúl Castro. The concierge who answered the courthouse doorbell was taken hostage. Léster recalled, "That's when we started hearing the shots from our companions and the soldiers." Two custodians and the fifty-year-old policeman Genaro Quintana Riverí were rounded up. The intruders found Pvts. Juan Trujillo and Eulogio Triana Manzo of the Rural Guard sleeping in their underwear on cots in different basement rooms. They were herded along with the other detainees onto the elevator and taken to the third floor while Abelardo García remained guarding the front door. To reach the roof, the rebels had to ascend a narrow stairway. Raúl broke the lock on the roof door with the butt of a handgun. According to Léster, "The retaining wall around the roof was fairly tall and made it difficult to shoot at the citadel." Raúl later stated, "we found it was impossible to fire on the army post, because it was necessary to expose too much of the body, due to the height of the roof." The seven hostages, guarded by Mario Dalmau, were kept face down on the roof.[12]

By that time most of Abel Santamaría's contingent had arrived at the Saturnino Lora Civil Hospital (hereafter referred to as the Civil Hospital). The 670-bed provincial public institution was staffed by sixty-two employees, including eighteen physicians. To the left of the vestibule the main building contained the emergency room and four private rooms for paying clients who were avoiding the public wards. To its right were two administrative offices, maternity and delivery rooms, and the pathology section. Open-air corridors inside the hospital led to a central grassy patio surrounded by eight individual medical wards, the veterans' dormitory, the infant ward, and the surgery room. Directly behind the latter was the cancer ward. There were outdoor concrete benches next to the entrances of all the structures except the last two. The veterans' and infant wards had adjacent green plots. The outer hospital perimeter had a long narrow edifice on its left serving as the Nursing School and the student-nurse dormitory. The opposite side included wards for obstetrics, X-ray, doctors' dormitory, contagious diseases, indigents, detainees, and mental patients. Beyond the nursing school were the garage and maintenance facilities. The rear building, facing Los Libertadores Avenue and Moncada's Post 4, contained the employees' quarters, a laundry, a kitchen, a pantry, and a medical dispensary with a doorway leading to the street. The Nursing School annually enrolled up to twenty-two student nurses. The hospital director, Dr. Norberto Machirán Ortiz, and the military supervisor, medical captain Mario Porro Varela, were absent when the rebels arrived just before dawn.[13]

The invaders disarmed the policeman José Sosa Jurado and hospital night watchman René Domingo Osorio, detained the doorkeeper Miguel Núñez Cinta, and wounded the policeman Humberto Barzaga Vázquez. Dr. Mauricio León Orúe, the twenty-eight-year-old night-shift supervisor, heard the assailants shouting subversive slogans when entering, which prompted some hospital employees and nurses to lock themselves inside offices and linen closets. The nurse Amalia Díaz Conde and a group of student nurses who had been working the night shift hid in the Nursing School bathroom. Abel assigned Horacio Matheu Orihuela, Tomás Alvarez Breto, and Gerardo Alvarez Alvarez to guard the vestibule in a prone position. He led thirteen others to the rear windows of the laundry, the kitchen, and the pantry facing Post 4, and from there they fired at the garrison. While passing by the detainees' ward, the rebels shot at the military orderly Pvt. José W. Fonseca Martínez, who managed to flee even though he had "a bullet in his foot and another shot deprived him of two fingers on his left hand."[14]

The last rebel vehicle headed for the Civil Hospital. The black Lincoln driven by Dr. Mario Muñoz and carrying Julio Reyes Cairo, Melba Hernández, Haydée Santamaría, and Raúl Gómez García had been diverted by the vehicles straying from the rebel caravan. According to Haydée, they were lost for "five or ten minutes" and debated about "how crazy it was to go on at that point" as they heard the shooting intensify. Melba recalled finally arriving at the Civil Hospital "under a terrible hail of bullets." Muñoz went to the emergency room, broke the glass door on the medicine cabinet, and seized medical instruments and stimulant drugs. He offered a sedative to a woman who fainted after being taken hostage. Haydée had

Dr. León Orúe point out the linen closet where they could obtain white uniforms. A group of student nurses sleeping in their dormitory awakened amid the ensuing hostilities. Emma Pérez peeked into the corridor, saw Dr. Muñoz pass by wearing a physician's coat, and asked what was happening. "Batista has been killed," he replied. Muñoz and his companions then went to the rear of the hospital looking for Abel, who told them to remain with the rebels guarding the entrance. When maintenance man Francisco Anglada showed up for work, he was challenged by the rebels. He was allowed to enter after stating that he had to fire up the kitchen steam boilers. Anglada was invited to join the revolt, but he alleged to be ignorant of using weapons. The employee "felt very bad, nervous" and scurried to hide in the first ward, where the nurses told the patients to crawl under their beds.[15]

Also seeking safety in the Civil Hospital were 2nd Lt. Pedro V. Feraud Mejías, a drill instructor with the Fusilier Company, and his thirty-three-year-old brother, Cpl. Mauricio Feraud Mejías. They headed for the garrison after hearing the gunfire from their nearby home. Approaching the hospital entrance, the lieutenant was shot in the left temple by rebels firing from the vestibule. Mauricio was dragging his fallen brother behind a parked car when a shotgun blast shattered his left forearm. He crawled away and flagged down a milk truck, which took him to the nearby emergency clinic. A nurse who pleaded to have Lieutenant Feraud taken into the hospital for treatment later stated that Haydée Santamaría told her to leave him there. Haydée denied the accusation, saying that she and Raúl Gómez García went to pull Feraud inside but were unable to budge him. She alleged placing her hand over Feraud's heart but could not tell if he was dead or alive. Returning inside, Haydée asked Dr. León Orúe to render assistance, but he refused to go outside. Haydée said that she "looked him square in the face and told him he was no doctor," and they "exchanged some bitter words." Dr. Liam Chomat Fetué then crawled out and pronounced Feraud dead. Thirty-five years later León Orúe twice refused to talk to the author regarding these events.[16]

Shortly thereafter Julio Trigo, the rebel ordered home after a tuberculosis recurrence, appeared at the Civil Hospital seeking medical attention. Trigo, coughing up blood onto his white guayabera, was treated by Dr. Muñoz and left to rest in private room number eight. Muñoz then attended Julio Reyes, whose face was nicked by glass shreds when a bullet shattered an emergency room window. Nurse María Luisa Palma, fearing that a round might explode a tall oxygen tank near the window, had three rebels carefully lay it on the floor. Upon hearing the commotion, Trigo went to the emergency room, grabbed Reyes's shotgun, and joined Melba, Haydée, Raúl Gómez García, and Tomás Alvarez Breto guarding the entrance. The hospital telephone, located in a corner of the vestibule, continuously rang. When Dr. Chomat tried to answer it, the rebels yelled at him to get back into the emergency room. Student nurse Violeta Moisés stated in 1967 that when she attempted to telephone her family,

"Haydée pulled out a pistol" and prevented her from calling. A patient named Crespo witnessed the encounter. Emilia Jiménez, a forty-two-year-old employee, telephoned the hospital a few times but was told by Haydée not to come to work. Three student nurses heard Haydée haranguing her comrades: "Be careful, save bullets; shoot, protect yourselves behind the column!" Melba and Haydée admitted in 1959 that they "assisted passing out bullet boxes and loading rifles." Police corporal Pedro H. Pompa Castañeda then entered the vestibule with a Thompson machine gun and approached Horacio Matheu. Melba later acknowledged that she and Haydée screamed, "Shoot him!," prompting both men to fire at each other. This version is contradicted by Pompa's death certificate, which indicates that he died of a single shot to the back of the head. Nurse Palma stated that when she went to assist both men, Haydée impeded her. Matheu, grazed on the head, was taken to room eight, which was occupied by slightly wounded rebels Gerardo Alvarez Alvarez and Tomás Alvarez Breto.[17]

The hospital occupiers then challenged another person seeking the safety of the vestibule. Roberto Sánchez López, a member of the National Police Marching Band, was returning to the garrison dressed in mufti. The 120-man ensemble, temporarily lodged in the Moncada while they participated in the carnival parade, was scheduled to leave at dawn. After Sánchez identified himself to the rebel sentries, he was placed in detention in the emergency room along with SIM agent Angel Esteban Garay. The other white-uniformed police musicians whom Sánchez was going to join had been piling up their instrument cases on the Moncada parade ground since 5:00 A.M. At that precise moment fifty-year-old José Tobío, the Route 80 bus line administrator, was visited in his downtown office by Sgt. Amarante Pagés Portuondo. The sergeant inquired about the bus scheduled to transport twenty-five police musicians to Holguín for a municipal park concert. When Tobío stated that the assigned chauffeur was absent, Pagés asked him to conduct the thirty-seven-passenger vehicle to the Moncada, where a military driver would take over.[18]

Pagés returned to the garrison on his military Harley-Davidson motorcycle, followed by Tobío in bus number 929. At Post 2 the sentry jotted down on the entry sheet the bus identification and time of arrival. Tobío then drove up the middle of the parade ground, turned left at the Antonio Maceo monument, and parked facing Post 3. Suddenly a soldier boarded the bus shouting "Go on, it's for real!" Tobío replied, "What's for real?" and leaned over the steering wheel for a closer view. The windshield was suddenly shattered by a bullet that sprayed glass shreds into the driver's face. "Don't jump, I am pulling back," yelled Tobío, but the soldier was shot while exiting the vehicle. The rebels Mario Lazo and Pepe Suárez, twenty-five to thirty yards away, saw the musicians in formation trying to board the bus. The driver tried backing away as the attackers concentrated their fire on his vehicle, which ended up facing broadside to Post 3. Tobío closed the bus door, yanked the emergency brake, and lay down on the aisle floor.[19]

Meanwhile the rebel motorcade remained stranded in the middle of Moncada Street after Fidel Castro's Buick hit the curb. When the rebel leader, who was next in line to drive through Post 3, failed to do so and abandoned his automobile, the insurgents behind him followed suit. They did not enter the garrison and instead sought cover behind the concrete fences in the front yards of the military housing project. Jesús Montané, who initially admitted not participating in the attack, later stated, "Many comrades who did not know the topography of the Moncada, mistakenly entered the houses bordering the garrison, thinking they were part of the fortress." Castro acknowledged that since the military dwellings had the same color and design, some rebels believed themselves to be already inside the Moncada. Artemisa buddies Gelasio Fernández Martínez and Julio Díaz exited the third vehicle and occupied the front yard of wood-frame house number seven on the corner of Moncada and Trinidad streets, facing Post 3. Rural Guard 1st Sgt. Ramón V. Silveiro Enríquez suddenly emerged from the doorway. Fernández warned Díaz, "Look, he is trying to get the drop on us, shoot him." Díaz, aiming at moving targets inside the fortress, replied, "You shoot him, I can not." As Silveiro stood on the porch, while his frightened family watched from inside, Fernández killed him with a 12-gauge shotgun blast to the chest.[20]

The occupants in the third car of the motorcade bailed out upon hearing the gunfire and the electric bell alarm. Mario Chanes remained behind a fender firing "a fistful of bullets" at the citadel with his pistol. Eduardo Montano, huddled next to Chanes, recalled, "There was no objective to shoot at, other than the walls of the garrison. I fired my .22 rifle a few times but could not see the soldiers inside shooting at us." Ciro Redondo, driving the fourth automobile, jumped out with Fidel Labrador, Guillermo Granados, and other Artemisa cell members. Vero Rosell, in the fifth vehicle, remembered, "A good stretch before arriving we heard the start of the shooting. That warned us that the surprise factor had not functioned. When passing by the post they fired a grouped volley at us. We got out unscathed, jumped from the car and positioned ourselves behind the sedan. From there we started shooting against everything that moved through the windows and hallways of the garrison." Gerardo Granados, in the seventh or eighth car, recalled, "We were supposed to stop in front of a barracks, according to the plan, but I did not see it. The chain across the entrance was something unexpected. Upon hearing the first sporadic shots, everyone spontaneously got out of the cars, although no orders to do so were given. We lingered in the street behind the vehicles until the machine gun in the garrison fired upon us. Then the car no longer provided sufficient protection and we dove behind the concrete fences."[21]

Héctor de Armas was driving the twelfth automobile carrying Carlos Bustillo, Generoso Llanes, and the three Ferrás brothers. After turning onto Moncada Street and seeing the caravan immobilized by the shootout, de Armas parked close to the left sidewalk and sought cover. He reported, "I was disoriented. I did not know where the entrance to the garrison was, or if we were inside the compound. There was no coordination; it was anything goes." The Ferrás trio bailed out and sought cover in the yard of the home of medical lieutenant Rolando Pérez Sainz de la Peña, on the corner of Victoriano Garzón Avenue and Moncada Street. Suddenly, Rural Guard Cpl. Nemesio A. Traba Montero exited from a public bus nearby, revolver in hand, and asked them, "What's going on? How can I help?" Alejandro Ferrás, intimidated by the corporal's towering size and armed presence, fired two .22-caliber bullets into his lower back.[22]

Other rebel vehicles had stopped on the same side of the street in front of the Joaquín Castillo Duany Military Hospital, which they considered a target. The two-story structure, built into a hillside, had a semicircular driveway leading to the glass doors of the lobby. A rear ramp, facing the back of the Palace of Justice, accessed the emergency entrance. The left wing of the ground floor contained the administrative offices and consultation rooms. The right wing held the contagious diseases ward, the respiratory illnesses ward with a rear-patio utility door, and the quarters for the day officer and the night watchman. An inner stairway led to a mezzanine flanked by a sixty-bed ward for military personnel and a forty-bed ward for their relatives. The upper floor also contained a venereal ward, a surgical room, two smaller chambers, the commissary, and the kitchen.[23]

A few minutes before the attackers arrived, forty-two-year-old medical lieutenant Rolando Pérez Sainz de la Peña had reported to his day-watch shift. As he switched on the light in the employees' dormitory, it awoke medical lieutenant Erik G. Juan Pita, who chided him to turn it off. The night-shift orderlies, Pvts. José Joaquín Vázquez and Gerardo Hernández Font, remained asleep. Dr. Pérez had undressed and was lying in bed smoking a cigarette when he heard the first shot fired at 5:20 A.M. The four men in the room quickly got out of bed. Dr. Juan Pita saw that "the elderly Vázquez went to the window without wearing his eyeglasses, squinting his vision into focus." Israel Tápanes, emerging from Fidel Castro's Buick, spotted a figure on the first-floor, right-corner window of the military hospital. He inadvertently fired his rifle close to the head of Castro, who pressed his hand against his painful, ringing ear. The .22-caliber hollow-point bullet struck the hospital orderly between the eyes.[24]

These fragmentation projectiles had been prohibited in warfare by the Hague Convention of 1899. Héctor de Armas confirmed buying the lethal bullets for the attack, and the rebel Gelasio Fernández Martínez acknowledged using them. A pro-rebel journalist later indicated that "Raúl and his men had .22 rifles loaded with hollow-point shells." Dr. Pérez emphasized, "I was stunned when I saw the x-rays taken of the wounded soldiers. The hollow-point bullets had disintegrated into dozens of pieces. Many could not be removed because they did not appear on the negative." The physician was sitting on the floor of the employees' dormitory lacing his shoes when the Cossack Guards bolted in. One tore the window screen open with his machine-gun muzzle and riddled someone on the sidewalk carrying a shotgun. The military policeman blurted, "Look, he has white pants under his uniform," and he assumed it was a National Police Marching Band outfit. "The police band is leading an insurrection," exclaimed his partner. "That is impossible," replied Pérez; "the musicians do not have weapons."[25]

Three blocks from the military hospital, Cpl. Norberto Batista Seguí was sipping a beer at a carnival kiosk. The hefty twenty-eight-year-old Afro-Cuban bachelor, assigned to the juridical service of the army general staff, assumed that the gunshots were the traditional fireworks of La Polar brewery. He was startled by a mob fleeing the garrison area and queried a passerby. "The world is coming to an end," replied the frightened man. The corporal headed for the Moncada in his civilian clothes. He avoided the skirmish on Moncada Street by entering the military hospital through the back door. Norberto Batista encountered the orderly Sgt. José Lemes González, who requested assistance in carrying the mortally wounded Vázquez to the emergency room. Lemes exclaimed, "There is a dead sergeant sprawled on the front sidewalk, but I have never seen him before, maybe you can recognize him." Batista Seguí went out to retrieve the attacker's shotgun and bandolier and began firing out a hospital window at the rebels entrenched in the military housing yards.[26]

Moments later, as Corporal Batista bent over to remove shotgun shells from the bandolier at his feet, he noticed a stream of blood spurting from a wound on his left shoulder. Lt. Pedro Morejón Valdés, arriving at the hospital in mufti from a nearby boardinghouse, took Batista's shotgun and sent him to the emergency room for treatment. The corporal, stopping in the receiving room to telephone regimental headquarters, was suddenly hit by a .22-caliber bullet fired from the street. Batista collapsed as the round penetrated the left side of his abdomen and erratically arched rightward, through the fatty waist tissue, to within three centimeters of his spine. Someone dragged him into a room strewn with other casualties, where he heard Lt. Juan Piña shouting "Long live the Tenth of March, long live General Batista!"[27]

The military hospital entrance glass doors were blasted away by the insurgents Ciro Redondo and Guillermo Elizalde Sotolongo. When Batista Seguí saw them enter the casualties room, "defiantly pointing their weapons at those on the floor," he closed his eyes and played dead. A group of attackers advanced into a hallway, where Dr. Pérez, peering from the employees' dormitory, saw one aiming a shotgun at him. As the physician ducked back in, a shotgun blast barely missed his head as he slammed the door. Cpl. Erico Verdecia, one of the two watchmen sleeping in the room across the hall, exited with a .45-caliber pistol and fired at the intruders. Pvt. José D. Agüero, a patient who against hospital regulations had kept a pistol under his pillow, also came out shooting and was joined by the second watchman.

The rebels who entered the building, surprised by this unexpected resistance, retreated outside, where Fidel Castro was desperately trying to regroup his followers. Castro said that he spent "five or six minutes" attempting to get his men out of the military hospital.[28]

After the attackers fled from the military hospital, the medical day officer, Dr. Juan Pita, emerged from the employees' dormitory into the first-floor corridor, where a throng of patients clamored for weapons. Unable to find the master keys, he ordered breaking down the doors of the surgery room and the gun closet. The patients grabbed the Springfield rifles reserved for the hospital commissary guards and began shooting from the second-floor windows. Return fire from the street dropped wall plaster onto the bed of sleeping eighty-one-year-old Manuel de Cárdenas Armenteros, a retired Liberation Army major. He admonished his roommates for playing practical jokes, before realizing that they were in peril.[29]

In front of the military hospital, Mario Chanes, who emerged from the third vehicle, saw that no one in his car or from Fidel Castro's Buick was able to enter the garrison. He and Mario Lazo estimated that only "five or six" rebels from the vanguard automobile, which was left blocking the Post 3 entrance, actually penetrated the Moncada fortress. In *History Will Absolve Me,* Castro claims that among that group, Ramiro Valdés, José Suárez, and Jesús Montané "managed to enter a barracks and hold nearly fifty soldiers prisoner for a short time." Montané, who when arrested stated that he remained at Siboney with a flat tire and did not participate in the attack, later perpetuated this myth to gain revolutionary stature. Valdés and Suárez afterward gave apocryphal and contradictory versions that tend to discredit their claims. Military accounts confirm that a few attackers rushed behind the first stairway to their left, where under the balcony, in front of the regimental quartermaster office, were scattered cots occupied by three relief sentinels and visiting members of the National Police Marching Band from Havana. The intruders did not harm any of the men lying down and were unable to enter the quartermaster room of any of the barracks in the upper balcony.[30]

The five rebels known to have penetrated the Moncada, including Pedro Marrero, José Luis Tasende, and Artemisa natives Carmelo Noa, Flores Betancourt, and Rigoberto Corcho, rushed into the administrative wing hallway, at the top of the first stairway, looking for the arsenal depicted on their map. Truck driver Marrero was described by Mario Chanes as "extremely brave and above all very audacious." Tasende, renowned as a person "determined in taking the initiative," had been with the ATOM revolutionary organization and had cooperated in the 1947 Cayo Confites expedition. Noa and Betancourt were ex-convicts; the former had served six months in prison for attempted murder, and the latter as a teenager had been sentenced to a year in reform school for various crimes. Inside, the intruders encountered five doorways. On the left was the operations and training section office and behind it the military courtroom. Both rooms had windows facing Trinidad Street. On the right side of the hallway was the newly remodeled, two-chair officers' barbershop and behind it the police adjutant office. The barbershop and the operations and training section office had windows overlooking the parade ground. A right rear hallway door led to an outer cement patio. The courtyard had a central stairway leading to the lower chambers and a kitchen. To its right were the open windows of the Service Company barracks. To its left, directly behind the exit, was a row of chambers containing the judicial service of the army general staff office, the paymaster's office, the veterinary office, and the communications room.[31]

In the administrative wing corridor, police corporal Doris Mesa González, a thirty-four-year-old member of the National Police Marching Band, was sleeping on a cot when awakened by what he assumed were carnival firecrackers. As he strapped on his .38-caliber holstered revolver, the rebels entered and shouted, "Drop it, or you are dead." A Private Ruiz was also taken prisoner. Mesa, yielding his weapon, pleaded that he was a musician and not a soldier. He was allowed to scurry to the nearby paymaster's office, where he found three unarmed soldiers and another firing a Springfield rifle through the wooden Venetian blinds toward Trinidad Street. A shotgun blast from outside sprayed splinters into the room. "Damn, look what happened to me," clamored the sniper, dropping his weapon and showing the others his bloody face, neck, and chest riddled with buckshot.[32]

The rebel intruders in their haste were unable to find the arsenal, which unbeknownst to them was the regimental quartermaster room located directly below the barbershop, with its entrance behind the first stairway. Renato Guitart had failed to note on his one-dimensional sketch the existence of the lower chambers. Had he been with the vanguard, he would have led them directly to the arsenal. This crucial mistake makes it highly unlikely that Guitart entered the fortress. Some rebels claimed that Guitart and Pepe Suárez penetrated the Moncada, but in a letter that Suárez sent to Renato's parents years later, he said that they were at Post 3 firing into the garrison at around 6:00 A.M. when "Suddenly I saw that Renato jumped violently to the right and fell bleeding abundantly from his head. Seeing that he was immobile, I realized he was dead." Fidel Labrador also witnessed Renato fall outside the Moncada. Another insurgent version stated that Renato stayed at Post 3 as the vanguard entered the garrison, and while he was defending that position, "the fatal bullet hit Renato's head." After the rebel vanguard failed to locate the arsenal, two of them assumed a prone position in the administrative wing corridor, shooting through the front and back doorways. Two others occupied the barbershop and the operations and training section office, from whose windows they had a commanding firing position over the soldiers on the parade ground. Another rebel in the police adjutant office shot into the rear courtyard and through the open windows of the Service Company barracks.[33]

Inside the dormitory the soldiers sustained numerous casualties as the rebel fusillade sprayed through the side windows. The National Police Marching Band had temporarily filled all the empty bunks of the men out on patrol. Police corporal Manuel Miras Mierez was killed in bed by small-caliber rounds that hit his left armpit, side, and back. His fellow musicians Sgt. Alberto Pagés and Pvt. Luis Bayona were wounded in their sleep. The soldiers scrambled for the Springfield rifles kept inside a locked wooden cabinet against the dormitory wall. Pvt. Eusebio Baró Melodio smashed its sliding glass doors and began distributing weapons. He was assisted by mulatto teenager Víctor Manuel "Baracoita" Hernández, a Ceiba del Agua Institute orphan who lived in the barracks, shined shoes, and did odd jobs in the citadel while waiting for an enlistment vacancy. Pvt. Urbano Sánchez Abalos was shot in the back of the head while reaching into the gun cabinet. In the darkness, haste, and confusion, Pvt. Clemente Godó Estenóz accidentally shot himself in the foot. Twenty-one-year-old Pvt. Armando F. Oliva López, confined to his bunk with an infected leg, awakened when showered by the cabinet's broken glass. As he rolled off his bed, Private Baró crumpled with a bullet through his right eye, and Baracoita fell wounded next to him. Taking Baró's weapon, Oliva crawled to his locker, got dressed, grabbed his rifle bolt and ammunition belt, and went out the rear barracks door.[34]

The gunfire and shouts of "Viva la revolución!" prompted Afro-Cuban quartermaster captain Juan de Dios Ruiz Herrera, the Superior Officer of the Day, to go toward Post 3. Ruiz ducked into the nearby regimental quartermaster office when a stranger aimed a weapon at him. The Officer of the Day, fifty-year-old 2nd Lt. Andrés D. Morales Alvarez, exited the Service Company barracks and, as he was descending the stairs, was hit in the abdomen by two hollow-point bullets. Morales was also shot in the thigh, the buttocks, and the back of his foot while running for cover. His nephews, Pvts. Rafael and Orlando Morales Gros, sons of the regimental inspector general, were sleeping next door in the Headquarters Company wing when awakened by the hostilities. They were soon joined by another member of their company, twenty-seven-year-old Pvt. Justo Ramón Martija, who in the officers' dining room heard the initial shots as he finished serving a breakfast of fried eggs, bread, and beer to the National Police Marching Band members.[35]

Lt. Manuel Piña Martínez appeared in their dormitory and called for twenty volunteers to occupy the three-story apartment building facing Post 2. According to Pvt. Martija, "only ten soldiers stepped forward, including Orlando and Rafael Morales, Pvt. Diocles Martínez Bles, Sgt. Mauricio Castillo and myself. The rest were too scared to leave the barracks." As they ran across the parade ground, Private Martínez, still tipsy from the carnival festivities, was slightly wounded on the hand by a bullet. The platoon dominated the roof of the apartment building for the remainder of the battle, and from there they had a commanding view of the parade ground and its surroundings. Pvt. José Ferrá, a member of the squad, said that had the attackers seized that position, "it would have been a headache" for the army.[36]

When the skirmish started, city policeman Evelio Xenis López, a twenty-four-year-old former Rural Guard soldier assigned to the SIR, was walking on Moncada Street in civilian clothes. He entered through Post 3, retrieved a Springfield rifle dropped by a sentry, and cautiously crawled up the administrative wing stairway. As Xenis peered over the top landing into the hallway, a .22-caliber bullet hit him under the right clavicle. He retreated into the quartermaster room behind the stairway and did not feel pain as he wadded a handkerchief between the wound and his shirt. Inside was forty-five-year-old Cpl. Eugenio García and eight soldiers on *retén* auxiliary guard. Xenis joined the soldiers who were shooting out the Trinidad Street windows at the rebels entrenched in the new military housing project. After quartermaster sergeant major Luis Oliva arrived, he looked out the window where Corporal García had been standing and was hit in the forehead with a .22-caliber bullet. Captain Ruiz, Sgt. Braulio J. Curuneaux, and Sergeant Bravo were busy loading .30-caliber, five-bullet clips into ammunition belts that held ninety rounds. The captain later had Corporal García accompany him to distribute twenty loaded belts to the soldiers outside.[37]

As the first shots rang out in Post 3, Cpl. Néstor Reyes Martín was entering the rear door of the Headquarters Company barracks with a cup of coffee he had gotten from the dining hall. The twenty-one-year-old had been assigned that night to the company's eight-man *retén* auxiliary guard, supporting the regular night watch. Reyes recalled, "I ran to the foot of my bunk, grabbed my Springfield and ammo belt, and banged the rifle stock against a row of bunk railings to awaken the others." He quickly mustered a squad and hurried to his assigned sector, covering the garrison wall from Post 3 to the watchtower on the front corner. After reaching the sidewalk in front of the main edifice, Reyes began running in a zigzag pattern toward Post 3. His followers took the safer passageway under the balcony behind the columns. "I could hear the bullets ricocheting at my feet and on the walls," recalled Reyes; "I never even thought that I might get wounded or killed, believing that it was not an attack, but rather some drunken soldiers."[38]

As the corporal approached Post 3 with his Springfield rifle, he noticed that the chain across the gate was down on one end. He remembered, "Next to the entrance of the sentry box nearest the stairway, Cpl. Isidro Izquierdo lay on his side, unconscious, without his weapon, bathed in blood. I slung my rifle on my shoulder and when I hooked the chain back up, I was hit by buckshot on my right thigh and a bullet fired from the barbershop window bent the shell casings inside my ammo belt." Reyes was thrown to the ground, his rifle barrel hitting him under the chin and the bolt snapping off his upper front tooth. He was sprawled in a daze between both sentry boxes when someone in a military uniform wearing tennis shoes dashed across the street from the yard of one house to the other. A dead rebel was later found wearing black high-top tennis shoes. "Shoot at those wearing tennis shoes," yelled Reyes; "they are wearing tennis shoes."[39]

Reyes then saw two vehicles, one brown and one black, race down Moncada Street toward Post 3 and turn left on Trinidad Street, heading for the Civil Hospital. The last car was Dr. Muñoz's black Lincoln. As the automobiles rounded the corner, their occupants fired at Reyes on the ground, hitting his left leg with a shotgun blast and a .22-caliber round. He recalled, "I could feel the warm blood seeping out of the wounds in my legs, but I was not in pain. I lacked the strength to raise my arms, much less to shoot my rifle." Reyes then noticed Pvt. Poliano Drago Grajales and another unarmed, frightened soldier peering from the sentry box gun slits opposite where Corporal Izquierdo lay dead. He ordered them to get out and fight with his weapon. The *Diario de la Marina* reported that when Reyes "could not handle the rifle he offered his body as a shield for his fellows."[40]

When the shooting started, a corporal turned on the lights in the Fusilier Company barracks and shouted, "We are under attack." Pvt. Ernesto Cuello Silveira, a twenty-one-year-old recent boot camp graduate, assumed that it was a prank and remained in his bunk. Turning sideways to resume sleeping, he was startled out of bed when the corporal smashed the gun cabinet glass doors with a rifle butt. Cuello and twenty-year-old Pvt. Luis H. Hodelín Angulo, in the next bunk, hurriedly dressed and pushed bolts and five-bullet clips into their Springfield rifles. Exiting the barracks and pivoting to the right, they ran along the balcony toward the gunfire. As Cuello and Hodelín passed the officers' barbershop windows, a corporal shouted, "Look out, that's where the enemy is." Hodelín suddenly collapsed on the balcony when hit in the chest by a small-caliber bullet fired from inside. Another shot shattered the stock of Cuello's rifle. Cuello thirty-five years later recalled, "That Springfield saved my life and I will never forget its serial number, 152034." Cuello quickly dragged his fallen comrade backward into the Service Company dormitory.[41]

Thirty-two-year-old Sgt. José H. Virués Moraga had returned to the Fusilier Company barracks around 3:00 A.M. because he was unable to find a vacant hotel room in which to sleep with a woman he had met at the carnival. Two hours later he awoke to the gunfire and ran outside shirtless, chomping on a cigar, while the rest of his company scrambled to evacuate the building. The last soldier to leave the dormitory was twenty-four-year-old Pvt. José H. Olivares Pérez, who had gone to bed two hours earlier after doing guard duty at Post 4. He slept through the initial commotion and was awakened when twenty-eight-year-old Pvt. Jesús R. Sánchez Pruna lifted and shook the end of his metal bunk and shouted, "Get up, we are under attack." Olivares recalled looking around and seeing that "there was not a soul in the barracks and it looked like a tornado had entered. All the bedding was scattered around, the lockers were wide open with upturned drawers on the floor, bullets and canteens strewn on the ground. Everyone had run outside." Olivares noticed that the tipsy Sánchez Pruna, who had gone to the carnival dressed in drag, was still wearing lipstick. He rushed to the gun cabinet; grabbed his rifle, which was the only one left there; inserted the firing bolt from his locker; and dressed in a green jumpsuit before emerging from the barracks. Sánchez Pruna had already left and was ascending the administrative wing stairway with his weapon. He hesitated shooting at a uniformed man in the hallway, unsure if he was friend or foe. "Why are soldiers killing each other?" he asked seconds before being hit above the right eye by a small-caliber bullet. Sánchez Pruna fell backward down the steps and was carried behind the stairway by his comrades.[42]

Meanwhile, Lt. Ismael Valdés Cabrera and Pvt. Manuel I. Alvarez Morgado were completing the night shift in the communications room, where two other soldiers on the same watch were sleeping on cots. Upon hearing the fusillade, the thirty-two-year-old lieutenant ordered the radio-telegraphist to immediately notify army staff headquarters in Havana that the Moncada was under attack. In his haste, Alvarez forgot to use the secret emergency code, sending the message via a routine transmission. The receiving officer in the capital, perceiving this violation of regulations, telephoned Moncada regimental headquarters to confirm the news. Lieutenant Valdés ordered Private Alvarez not to leave the telephone switchboard as he went out to organize their perimeter defense. However, Alvarez asked the messenger to cover for him and went to retrieve his rifle from the Headquarters Company barracks. While crossing the patio, Alvarez was hit by a .22-caliber bullet piercing the cartridge belt suspender below his left shoulder. While turning to flee, he was felled by a bullet in his lower back. At the doorway of the adjacent paymaster's office, Cpl. Gerardo Hechavarría Granados was hit in the neck by a small round as he reported for duty. Unable to gain entry, he remained with his back pressed against the door for the remainder of the conflict.[43]

Meanwhile, the rebels in the back of the Civil Hospital maintained a concentrated fire on Post 4 and the rear area of the Moncada. Pvt. Antonio H. Rodríguez Pérez, a twenty-six-year-old peasant from Camagüey, was sleeping on one of three cots inside a sentinel relief tent near Post 4. He was awakened by a Private Santana shouting "Get up, we are fighting!" Rodríguez replied, "Those are fireworks, leave me alone." Santana insisted, "Wake up, we are fighting, it is true." The sentinel and the auxiliary on Post 4, Afro-Cuban Pvts. Lázaro "Tirilo" Tejadilla Suárez and Argeo Sarmiento Moreno, were both immediately wounded by shots fired from the Civil Hospital. Rodríguez and another private went into the left sentry box and returned fire through the gun slits. Pvt. Publio Labañino and another soldier occupied the opposite sentry box, and two more were shooting from behind a sandbag barrier below the chain across the gate. Lt. Eugenio Rizo Viel later joined them in firing at the rear windows of the Civil Hospital.[44]

Abel Santamaría and the thirteen rebels firing from the Civil Hospital laundry room wounded Cpl. José "Pancho Villa" Llanes León in the right lung and abdomen while he was in the watchtower on the corner of Los Libertadores Avenue and Trinidad Street. The same snipers mortally wounded Afro-Cuban Pvt. Pedro "Piatano" Guilarte, a former camp cook in his fifties, as he left the Enlisted Mens' Club, where he worked as a janitor. Pvt. Felino Miró Ríos was then hit in the left eyebrow and chest while exiting the rear door of the Rural Guard barracks. He belonged to the Rural Guard Fourteenth Squadron in Palma Soriano, temporarily assigned to the Moncada during the carnival weekend to reinforce the public-order patrols. A bus on Trinidad Street got caught in the crossfire, and fare collector Alicia Castillo Ramírez was hit twice on the right arm and once on the side. The teenager Hebrecinio Pacheco was gravely wounded by a stray bullet while walking on Victoriano Garzón Avenue. Six blocks south of the garrison, erratic fire hit eighteen-year-old Pedro Angel López in a lung and twenty-eight-year-old Gisel Chaprón was killed by a bullet to the head as both men stood on a street corner. Stray bullets also wounded ten-year-old Migdalia Toledano on the leg, and eighty-three-year-old Felipa Castillo was hit on the knee while kneeling on the street to pray.[45]

The initial shooting awakened forty-year-old Lt. Angel S. Machado Rofe in the third-floor officers' room. He hurried one flight down to the aide-de-camp's office, where moments later Adj. Capt. Manuel E. Aguila Gil telephoned from home inquiring about the situation. Machado stated that Post 3 was under siege but that Post 5 was accessible. Aguila Gil arrived shortly thereafter, assumed command of the regimental headquarters office, and ordered Machado to assist him. Lt. Manuel Arpa Ceballo soon joined them and from the third-floor rear window sniped on the rebels in the Civil Hospital. Colonel del Río Chaviano later called his office, and Machado said that Post 5 was clear for entry.[46]

When the attack began, Sgt. Bernabé González started operating the M1917A1 .30-caliber water-cooled machine gun in front of the Guard Corps post covering the parade ground. The sergeant, assisted by Cpl. Generoso Martiniano and others, fired a burst into the air to disperse the police musicians in his line of fire before directing his aim at the side entrance. Rebel accounts admitted that when this machine gun "started to sweep with its burst the area of Post 3, where the vanguard group had penetrated, it impeded any further entrance or exit through that place." The weapon, equipped with a 250-round canvas belt, had a rate of fire of 400 to 600 rounds per minute and an effective range of eleven hundred yards. It riddled the insurgent vehicles, shattered windshields and headlights, punctured radiators and tires, gouged the asphalt pavement, and splintered the trees in the military housing project. Cpl. Néstor Reyes, prostrate at Post 3 with both legs severely wounded, saw Lt. Manuel Piña Martínez taking a turn at firing the machine gun. The staccato bursts suddenly ceased when the ammunition belt jammed. Reyes recalled that

"Sergeant Jonás López Betancourt, working very calmly under a hail of bullets, disassembled and fixed the weapon. There were over a dozen prone men around the machine gun and behind the Maceo monument, shooting toward Post 3 over my head." The corporal suddenly felt someone grab him by the hair, pull him out of the line of fire, and drag him halfway into the left sentry box. He stated, "My pants were weighed down by a great amount of blood and although my vision was cloudy, I recognized Sergeant Braulio Curuneaux as the person who came to my aid." Curuneaux exclaimed that there were too many casualties and that he was going to get medical assistance. Reyes recalled, "He ran out through Post 3 toward the military hospital, spraying lead from one side to the other."[47]

The disorganized rebels were unable to breach Post 3. Pedro Miret commented, "A group of us was two yards from the entrance of the post, with our backs stuck to the wall.... Other comrades were entrenched behind the automobiles that we had left parked on the narrow street in front and on the sidewalk opposite to ours." Pepe Ponce, pinned down behind his vehicle, imprudently tried moving forward. He later related, "I advanced decidedly toward the second car that was to my right. For an instant I was out in the open. Suddenly I felt a strong impact on my right shoulder, and the left hand, which knocked me to the ground. In brief seconds I had the hand horribly swollen, [and] blood was flowing profusely from my shoulder." Héctor de Armas saw "a tall rebel wounded in the shoulder desperately walking back and forth with an anguished look. He did not know what to do." Ponce fled and intercepted a taxi with a passenger. "Take me to Siboney," he demanded, but the driver replied, "I do not have enough gasoline to get there." Ponce insisted, "It does not matter, we will put some in." The driver left Ponce at the Colonia Española Clinic, saying, "stay here so they can assist you." Dr. René Eldidy, who treated Ponce, stated that the wound was caused by a .22-caliber bullet grazing the back of his hand and shattering a few bones.[48]

Ponce had been mistakenly shot by another rebel. Marino Collazo Cordero affirmed that "there was some confusion between our own selves for wearing uniforms similar to the soldiers of Batista." Gustavo Arcos seems to have also been wounded by friendly fire. After stumbling out of Castro's car, he sought cover behind a bus on Moncada Street, and from there he fired his Colt pistol at the garrison. A soldier wearing a Rural Guard hat appeared on a distant house patio firing a handgun. Arcos shot at him a few times but was unsure if the man fled or fell. He saw other rebels looking for their friends and cell leaders for orientation. Arcos, facing the garrison, was glancing about for a recognizable face when a bullet knocked him to the pavement and paralyzed his right leg. He described "being shot in the lower back, in an upward trajectory, by someone who was crouching, and the bullet coming out the right front." Arcos saw various rebels pass him by without offering assistance. Finally his friend Abelardo Crespo, still clutching a carbine, tried carrying him away. Ciro Redondo assisted in placing Arcos onto the backseat of a car. Moments later, as Crespo returned to the sidewalk, a .22-caliber bullet fired from behind punctured his lung. The insurgents Mario Chanes and Angel Díaz-Francisco confirmed that Crespo's wound was caused by a rebel bullet. Chanes received a slight bullet wound of unknown origin on his index finger. The *Diario de la Marina* reported that Reinaldo Benítez Nápoles was "wounded by buckshot on a leg." The rebels were using that type of ammunition.[49]

Benítez, still shooting from behind a garden wall, had his wound attended by Rolando Guerrero Bello, who tied a handkerchief tourniquet around his thigh. Guerrero indicated that from fifteen yards away he shot a soldier, who was dressed only in a shirt and underwear and was advancing hunched over with a Springfield rifle. Israel Tápanes claimed to see another soldier with a Springfield rifle and an unbuttoned shirt going to the garrison. When the man ignored an order to halt, Tápanes alleged that he killed him with a bullet to the chest and took his weapon. These rebel accounts do not factually correspond with information on the three military personnel killed outside the Moncada, none of whom carried a rifle. The Springfields were secured in the barracks and not taken home overnight.[50]

In a neighboring yard of the military housing project, Gerardo Granados was behind a concrete fence returning fire at the silhouettes in the fortress windows. Next to him the exuberant Marcos Martí repeatedly sprang up fearlessly to discharge his revolver. "Get your head down, you are going to get killed," Gerardo admonished the teenager. His brother Guillermo Granados was wounded while advancing toward the citadel and ducked behind a concrete patio fence next to Marino Collazo. As both rebels were shooting at the Moncada, Guillermo was killed by a bullet to the head that flung him backward. Collazo, bleeding from a round that grazed his skull, immediately fled. Two other rebel combatants, the brothers Manuel and Virginio Gómez, were killed alongside the Moncada walls while attempting to enter the fortress.[51]

Gerardo Granados saw Fidel Castro "in the middle of the street with a Luger pistol in his hand. I did not see Fidel shooting, but I assume he did. Fidel stayed in the street the whole time, giving instructions to someone, but I did not see who it was." The rebel Carlos Bustillo recalled being shot at from the dark upper windows of the military hospital across the street. He fired his shotgun toward a shadowy figure with a pistol on the upper floor trying to shoot Castro in the back. The rebel leader tried to drive his Buick forward, but it would not start. He then ran under fire toward Post 3. Bustillo affirmed, "Fidel was behind the left sentry box and Héctor de Armas and I were in back of the opposite one. Fidel and a group with him could not enter the garrison because of the machine gun fire pouring out through the entrance. The only thing we could do was stick close to the wall until Fidel ordered the retreat." De Armas stated that he did not remember seeing Castro during the attack. The rebel Moisés Mafut said that it was impossible for the rebel leader to have penetrated the fortress because "those who entered were killed inside." Despite these rebel assertions, the hagiographer Robert Taber wrote eight years later that Fidel Castro went into the Moncada and "appeared briefly in the barracks." Castro has never described in detail his Moncada combat role.[52]

The skirmish awakened Lt. Teodoro Rico Boué, the thirty-nine-year-old aide-de-camp of Colonel del Río Chaviano, who resided with his family in a rented house behind the colonel's home. He quickly slipped into a military jumpsuit, grabbed a Belgian pistol, and headed for the garrison. Rico stated that as he crossed the street toward Post 5, Colonel del Río emerged from his house and told him to investigate the brouhaha. The lieutenant alleged that the colonel entered the citadel shortly thereafter and went up to his office. Pvt. José Ferrá Mulet, positioned near the Guard Corps, recalled seeing the regimental chief enter through Post 5 carrying a dangling web belt with a holstered pistol soon after the firefight began. Colonel del Río Chaviano stated that he reached his office "three or four minutes" after the shooting started. The whereabouts of the camp commander during the battle remains in dispute. Bureau of Investigations chief Col. Orlando Piedra wrote in his memoirs that del Río Chaviano "was at a bacchanalia" during the attack. Cpl. Eugenio Alcolea heard that the regimental chief was at a Rancho Club party in Quintero Heights. Pvts. Alfonso Silva, Antonio Rodríguez Pérez, and Justo Ramón Martija agreed that the colonel arrived after 6:00 A.M. Pvt. José Olivares stated that "thirty or forty minutes" after the attack started, he yelled at a shadowy figure in uniform who was "as if on a leisurely walk" entering through Post 5: "Hey, *comemierda,* they are going to kill you." Olivares, who had been stationed at Moncada only a month, was apologetic when the stranger who then ran past him turned out to be Colonel del Río Chaviano. His superior replied, "Forget it. You saved my life." Maj. Rafael Morales Alvarez, who publicly voiced disdain of del Río Chaviano, admitted that when he arrived at headquarters the regimental chief was already there.[53]

Major Morales, the forty-nine-year-old bibulous inspector general of the regiment, had joined the army in 1923. He resided with his wife on Pedrera Street, near the Plaza de Marte Park, and had sixteen relatives in the armed forces and the police force. Morales awoke that morning to the staccato of the Moncada machine gun. He telephoned regimental headquarters, where Lt. Manuel A. Pupo reported that Post 3 had been overrun by attackers. Driving toward the Moncada in his jeep, Morales saw a group of men in army uniforms at the Civil Hospital entrance. He stopped to question them and was surprised when these assumed subordinates shot at him. The major sped away and entered the fortress through the main gate. In the third-floor headquarters Morales found Colonel del Río Chaviano "lying down between the wall and a desk that protected him with the telephone on the floor, asking Havana for reinforcements." Morales was ordered to assume the citadel's defense since the operations chief Maj. Andrés Pérez-Chaumont Altuzarra was absent. Pvt. Ariel

Matos regarded Colonel del Río Chaviano as a "coward" because "he did not fight or take command of his regiment to direct the counterattack."[54]

Police major José Izquierdo Rodríguez appeared in the office asking for his brother. Morales replied, "I do not know, this is all very confusing." The forty-eight-year-old Izquierdo had gone home at 4:30 A.M. after supervising the police patrols. Awakened by the raging gunfire, he telephoned the Moncada and was told that soldiers were fighting each other. Izquierdo drove to the police station at Santa Rita and Rabí streets, but when he called again the situation was still unclear. He then mustered a squad armed with 1898 Krag-Jorgensen rifles and led them into the garrison through Post 2. Izquierdo recalled that when he later approached Post 3, he found "a man sitting on the ground, leaning against the sentry box. I got closer and recognized my brother. He was soft and hot. I think he had just died. I took him to a cot and placed a pillow under his head. He was not assigned to guard duty that night: he was doing a favor for the sergeant on that shift."[55]

After Izquierdo left regimental headquarters, Major Morales went searching for his sons and his brother, 2nd Lt. Andrés D. Morales Alvarez, the Officer of the Day. He found the lieutenant lying wounded in a bunk of the Service Company barracks next to eight dead soldiers. The major had his brother, Corporal Izquierdo, and other casualties transported to the military hospital in his jeep. Unaware of the extent of rebel penetration and assuming that he and his men were fighting against soldiers leading a coup d'état, Major Morales occupied the central passageway area under the main building. He assembled the soldiers running in disarray and gathered the officers to prepare a defense. Morales organized groups into strategic dominant positions and distributed personnel to their assigned sectors. Major Morales then slowly approached the skirmish area shouting "Viva Batista!" and advanced upon a favorable response until he was able to determine that the invaders were contained in the administrative wing. The officer then gave Capt. Juan de Dios Ruiz Herrera command of the .30-caliber machine gun in front of the Guard Corps that was sweeping Post 3 and instructed others to effect a condensed fire on the Civil Hospital rear windows. Pvt. José Olivares was ordered to join a group that fired at enemy positions in the Civil Hospital from the rear bathroom windows of the Fusilier Company barracks. He fired about ten bullets "that injured no one."[56]

Olivares and the military personnel had no inkling of the purpose or identity of their foes. Some thought that the absent Major Pérez-Chaumont was behind the attack. Pvt. Ariel Matos, who six weeks earlier had given a map of the Moncada to the Montreal conspirators, wondered why the attackers had not provided him with the agreed advance warning. The first indication of who the insurgents were occurred after Afro-Cuban Lt. Marcelo Otaño Cookerman captured a man in uniform in the military housing project who was shooting at the garrison. Pvt. José Ferrá saw the shirtless Otaño entering through Post 2 at a trot while grasping the prisoner by the hair with his left hand and pointing a pistol at the man with his other hand. The captive quickly implicated Fidel Castro and revealed the details of their attack plan.[57]

By that time the hostilities had awakened Lt. Col. Angel González Alfonso, who had been expecting an attack the previous night. The owner of the boardinghouse where he lived said that the Moncada soldiers were fighting each other. A navy ambulance soon arrived to retrieve a naval officer residing there, but the officer instead drove his own car to the naval station and ceded the emergency vehicle to González and Lt. Eladio Carrillo Morales. As the ambulance headed for Post 3 on Moncada Street, soldiers in the military hospital frantically gestured to its occupants not to proceed further. González and Carrillo entered the hospital, where moments later two disoriented rebels appearing at the rear door were arrested. Shortly thereafter a jeep brought Lt. Andrés Morales and some wounded companions to the emergency entrance. The officer told a surgeon to first attend the others injured. "It is only a little wound," said Morales, pointing to the .22-caliber punctures in his stomach. He was operated on that evening but died hours later from perforations in his liver and spleen causing massive internal hemorrhage. After Morales arrived, Lieutenant Colonel González rode the jeep back to the garrison, leaving Lieutenant Carrillo in charge of the hospital's defense. The soldiers in the military hospital who tried exiting through the front door were kept in check by the rebels Abelardo Crespo, Ramiro Valdés, and Ciro Redondo, who were shooting from behind a garden wall across the street.[58]

The military hospital director, forty-two-year-old medical captain Edmundo Tamayo Silveira, arrived at the rear entrance around 5:45 A.M., and medical lieutenant Roberto P. Mas Renedo entered soon afterward. Tamayo went to the morgue with medical lieutenant Pedro Hernández Vilaret to view the casualties and exclaimed, "Look, they killed Corporal Batista!" Recognizing the voice, Norberto Batista, playing dead after the attackers entered the hospital, responded, "No doctor, they have not killed me yet." Tamayo, before remaining all day in the surgery room with Dr. Rolando Pérez, telephoned the nearby Los Angeles Clinic and requested that they take Corporal Batista and three other urgent military casualties. He also ordered medical lieutenant Erik Juan Pita to accompany them to the clinic in an ambulance.[59]

In the Los Angeles Clinic, a three-story, 150-bed facility two blocks from the Moncada, twenty-eight-year-old medical intern Roberto Villalón Virgilí was about to finish a twenty-four-hour shift at 7:00 A.M. Awakened by the shooting, he gazed from a third-floor dormitory window at the commotion outside. Villalón promptly telephoned clinic director Dr. José Antonio Ortiz Rodríguez at home and then ordered the nurses to summon for duty all the staff physicians. The anesthesiologist Fernando Pedro Fornaris, who had returned home at 5:00 A.M. after a party, was called to work. His vehicle was stopped near the Plaza de Marte Park by armed soldiers. Although the thirty-eight-year-old Fornaris identified himself and his mission, the soldiers blocked his path and kept their weapons aimed at him. Fornaris then drove to his sister-in-law's house in Vista Alegre and telephoned the clinic to explain his predicament. He proceeded to work after being informed that the rear entrance was clear. The call to duty was also answered by Dr. Eduardo García Ferrer, who went in his car to pick up his son, the intern Eduardo García-Ferrer Méndez. Soon after they arrived, two fleeing rebels pursued by the police burst into the clinic and were directed to the rear exit by some employees. The cops giving chase mistakenly seized a male nurse, who was quickly released after Dr. Villalón identified him.[60]

The ambulance carrying Corporal Batista screeched to a halt at the entrance to the Los Angeles Clinic. Military policeman Alfonso Silva jumped out of the vehicle and dispersed a gawking crowd by firing a 30-round Thompson machine-gun clip into the air. The corporal was wheeled in a gurney into an elevator, but halfway to the second-floor surgery room an electrical blackout occurred. The elevator then had to be manually lowered to the ground floor. Since the clinic orderlies were unable to carry the heavyset Batista up the stairs, he had to proceed on foot in spite of his wounds. He then had to wait until the lights were restored before being submitted to surgery. Private Silva departed in the ambulance, stopping on the corner of Victoriano Garzón Avenue and Moncada Street to assist Cpl. Nemesio Traba, who had been shot twice in the lower back. Silva recalled, "When I reached Traba, he was already dead. His holster was empty; they had taken his .45-caliber revolver. We left the corpse there and I returned to the military hospital."[61]

In the Los Angeles Clinic, Rafael Parladé, the main operating-room surgeon, assisted by the physicians Roberto Villalón Virgilí and Héctor L. Ortiz Fernández (the son of the clinic administrator) and the anesthesiologist Fernando Fornaris, first attended Pvt. Efraín Galano Liranza. Dr. Ortiz Fernández recalled that "a large-caliber bullet had penetrated to the left of his navel, leaving a huge exit hole in his lower back." The soldier died on the operating table after the doctors finished drying and suturing his intestines. Parladé and his assistants then attended Pvt. Pedro Guilarte, whose liver had been shattered by a hollow-point bullet, but Guilarte died three days later. Dr. Ortiz afterward went into the auxiliary operating room with the physician Francisco Pérez Acosta to assist Cpl. José Llanes León, shot in the right lung and abdomen. Dr. Ortiz sutured his intestines but was unable to remove the .22-caliber bullet fragments from his lung. The physician then helped the surgeon Eduardo García Ferrer and his son operate on Cpl. Norberto Batista, who had a .22-caliber bullet lodged near his spine and another one in his shoulder. A platoon of armed soldiers looking for wounded rebels suddenly burst into the surgery room. Dr. Ortiz felt the muzzle of a machine gun pressed against his back, while another intruder pulled the ether mask off the patient's face. "It is Corporal Batista, he is one of ours," confirmed a soldier before the squad moved on.[62]

Government personnel in Santiago de Cuba and its suburbs hurried to the defense of the Moncada. The police and military were obligated to report to their assigned units or to the nearest post during a national emergency. One of the few exceptions was Capt. Armando Romaguera, director of the National Police Marching Band from Havana, who immediately fled the city and was detained in Palma Soriano for unauthorized travel. Army lieutenant Mario Martínez Arbona and sergeant René Caso Pérez, Havana residents attending the carnival, quickly reported to the Moncada. The policeman Patricio "El Chino" Moreno Rubio, a former army veterinary assistant living near the fortress, rushed there in civilian clothes at the sound of gunfire. He was hit by a shotgun blast in the legs and groin while entering Post 3. The wounded man then put up a fierce resistance with his service revolver.[63]

The policeman Horacio Martínez Verdecia had returned home at 3:00 A.M. after his carnival patrol shift. His mother-in-law awakened him and told him that the Moncada soldiers were fighting among themselves. Horacio, a former Moncada army sergeant until March 1952, dressed in civilian clothes and took a bus to the vicinity of Post 5, where an old army buddy let him in. He reported to Lt. Cándido Martínez in the Guard Corps post and changed into a military uniform. Horacio grabbed a rifle and joined a platoon under Sgt. Mario Galano Rodríguez. Confronting the intruders in the administrative wing, Horacio shouted during a lull in the fight, "Give up, you do not have a chance." They replied, "Surrender, Batista has been killed in Havana," and then resumed firing.[64]

The shootout was a wake-up call to the Moncada soldiers residing in nearby Sueño neighborhood. Pvt. Angel Pupo Miranda, a thirty-four-year-old communications radio repairman, resided with his wife and daughter five blocks from the citadel. Pupo recalled, "I thought it was rare that the machine gun was firing at that hour. Since I did not have a telephone, I went next door and woke up Private Lázaro, the communications room telephone operator, who was half drunk from the previous night's celebration." Pupo called their superior, Lt. Ismael Valdés, who replied, "Do not come near here, the garrison is under attack. They already killed Alvarez Morgado, and I am substituting for him." Disregarding the advice, Pupo and Lázaro felt duty bound to enter through Post 5 and went to their Service Company barracks. Pupo retrieved his rifle from the gun cabinet and saw his friend Eusebio Baró Melodio sprawled dead, while the unarmed police musicians cowered under the beds. He heard the gruff voice of Sgt. El Mulo González defiantly cursing the attackers and haranguing the others to fight on. Pupo called Lieutenant Valdés from the barracks phone to report his location. He was ordered to proceed cautiously to the communications room, where he was stationed at a window facing Trinidad Street. Lieutenant Valdés had to leave his post around 6:00 A.M. when a bullet snapped an electric cable and knocked out the Moncada lights. Valdés ran to the emergency generator room on the opposite side of the compound, kicked in the door, and renewed the current to the radio transmitter. He then found a camp electrician, who restored power to the fortress within an hour.[65]

Lieutenant Valdés had positioned Pvt. Armando Oliva and two other soldiers behind the crenelated wall on Trinidad Street facing the Palace of Justice. Oliva saw a person shooting from a third-floor courthouse window and fired at someone hiding behind a roof air vent. Two men suddenly appeared on a side street running toward the Moncada. One wore a sergeant major's uniform, and the other was a civilian in a guayabera brandishing a Luger. They began scaling the fortress wall at its lowest inclined point, behind the communications room, where it was only three feet high. Oliva started engaging his Springfield bolt action to shoot the intruders when Lieutenant Valdés yelled not to fire since he recognized the civilian as forty-six-year-old Waldo Pérez Almaguer, the governor of Oriente Province. Once inside, Pérez requested a rifle, and Valdés directed him to the regimental quartermaster office. The lieutenant then felt a shotgun blast near his feet and bolted for cover. The governor encountered Pvt. Jesús Sánchez Pruna in death throes in front of the quartermaster door, and the private expired in his arms. Pérez then served as a stretcher bearer, taking the wounded to the military hospital during the rest of the morning. Santiago de Cuba mayor Maximino Torres Sánchez arrived shortly thereafter to defend the citadel.[66]

The sound of gunfire in the citadel also awoke Capt. Rosendo Abreu Jiménez in his Sueño neighborhood residence. The forty-three-year-old mulatto officer had been transferred in January to Santa Clara due to a personal feud with Colonel del Río Chaviano. He had driven his 1952 Cadillac convertible to Santiago de Cuba three days earlier for a five-day family furlough. Abreu had been dancing with his wife in the streets until 4:00 A.M. before returning home. When he telephoned regimental headquarters, a nervous voice told him, "There are snipers shooting at us from all angles." While Captain Abreu was donning his uniform, his friend Senén Carabia Carrey drove up to inquire about the shooting. Carabia, a photographer and SIM confidant, was outfitted in colorful carnival clothes, facial greasepaint, and a straw hat. Police sergeant Godofredo Camps, a neighbor, also went to Abreu's house. The captain had Carabia drive him and Camps to the naval headquarters at Punta Blanca. Carabia then proceeded to Post 2, where, after being denied admission into the garrison, he remained watching the machine gun near the Guard Corps firing on the rebel positions.[67]

The M1917A1 .30-caliber, water-cooled machine gun was soon redeployed by Sgt. José Hidalezio Virués Moraga and a group of soldiers trying to neutralize the intruders in the administrative wing. They quickly disassembled the ninety-three-pound weapon, carried it across the parade ground, and remounted it on its tripod opposite the location where the five vanguard rebels were holding out. Virués felt "two or three" bullets zing past him before he discharged a burst at a forty-five degree angle toward the upper floor. The rebels stopped firing as the machine-gun bullets gouged the building's concrete facade, perforated the metal railings on the stairway and balcony, and splintered the wooden Venetian blinds on the windows of the barbershop and the operations and training section office. During a lull in the fighting, the attackers waved a white handkerchief from the barbershop window and shouted that they wanted to surrender to an officer. Sgt. Braulio Curuneaux began climbing the blood-drenched stairway toward the administrative wing, but before he reached the top, a .22-caliber bullet fired diagonally from the barbershop nicked his nose. Curuneaux bellowed, "I am wounded" and quickly retreated. "Move out of the way," yelled Virués. "Now we are really going to show them." As the machine gun renewed its staccato firing, the rebels assumed a prone position to avoid the bullets that flew overhead and tore into the upper wall.[68]

Private Olivares, who had been shooting at the Civil Hospital from the rear of his company dormitory, was ordered with a group of soldiers to retrieve a Browning M2 .50-caliber antiaircraft machine gun from their barracks quartermaster room and position it on the parade ground between Posts 2 and 5 next to a Public Works flatbed truck. Olivares and Afro-Cuban Private Salas carried the forty-four-pound tripod while Corporal Silveira and a group of volunteers wrestled with the sixty-two-inch, eighty-four-pound gun to set it up. The five-foot-high antiaircraft tripod, designed for a standing gunner, could not be swiveled horizontally and therefore never went into action. Some of its crew members then lit cigarettes, which provided targets for a rebel sniper in a front yard of the military housing. Olivares, flat on the ground as the sniper bullets kicked up dirt around him, looked for the muzzle flash of the shooter. He was unable to detect it because the .22-caliber rifle had barely left a trace.[69]

Across the parade ground José Tobío cowered on the floor of the public bus he had driven into the citadel to pick up the police musicians. He heard someone try to open the vehicle door and shout "Let's get this bus out of here." Just then Capt. Juan de Dios Ruiz exited the regimental quartermaster room and ordered Lt. Teodoro Rico Boué to "throw these hand grenades in there to get them out," referring to the rebels entrenched inside. Tobío, assuming that his vehicle door was going to be blown open, rushed out. He was intercepted by the policeman Enrique Despaigne Noret, who, shoving a Thompson machine-gun barrel against Tobío's abdomen, blamed him for bringing in the enemy. Tobío blurted, "I am the Route 80 administrator and brought the bus for the musicians when the driver did not show up." A civilian named Arencibia, who accompanied Despaigne, recognized Tobío, who was allowed to proceed to safer ground. "What is going on here?" Tobío asked the veterinary Lt. Horacio York Botella, who replied, "I do not know, there is a lot of confusion."[70]

Lieutenant Rico, clutching a few grenades, crept along the balcony toward the administrative wing with a backup team. Sergeant Virués, still pouring machine-gun bursts in that direction, was ordered to cease fire. He estimated having fired nearly the entire belt of 250 rounds at the building during fifteen minutes. The five attackers inside were isolated and leaderless. The military desertions that Fidel Castro predicted had not occurred, and no other rebels had penetrated the citadel to assist them. The stealthily advancing squad was discomfited, however, when the wounded Pvt. Angel L. Duvallón-Gilbert Cuello, sprawled in a pool of his own blood on the balcony below the barbershop window, began shouting for assistance. He had earlier been hit by rebel shotgun blasts to both legs as he approached the hallway entrance. Cpl. Eugenio Alcolea, a member of the backup team, feared that the cries for help would reveal their position and threatened to kill Duvallón-Gilbert if he did not shut up. Lieutenant Rico then lobbed three fragmentation grenades through the barbershop windows and the administration wing doorway. The explosions mortally wounded Rigoberto Corcho López, and José Luis Tasende received shrapnel in both thighs and his lower left leg. The rebel Héctor de Armas, crouching in the yard of a nearby military house, regarded the grenade detonations as ominous signs of defeat.[71]

Rico's stealth team included Sgt. Miguel Benítez, a tall and husky camp electrician. Upon reaching the barbershop windows, Benítez heaved his shoulder against the wooden shutters and led the way inside. Corporal Alcolea, Pvt. Luis Enrique Naranjo, and other soldiers armed with handguns followed him through the window into the empty room. When they opened the barbershop door to the inner hallway, Tasende fired a shotgun blast from a prone position in the opposite doorway, hitting Naranjo in the legs. Alcolea was wounded on the right calf, and another pellet shattered the metatarsal of his small toe. The corporal saw his assailant jump out of the operations and training section office window onto Trinidad Street. Naranjo was yanked back into the barbershop by his comrades, who slammed the door shut and quickly applied tourniquets to his lower extremities.[72]

Moments later Corporal Alcolea, with blood sloshing in his right shoe around his numb foot, cautiously reopened the door and stepped into the hallway holding a .45-caliber pistol. He slowly advanced to the right with his back against the wall, toward the entrance of the police adjutant office. Alcolea noticed a shadow behind the doorjamb and fired his pistol overhead at a forty-five-degree angle into the upper wall of the police adjutant office. "Do not kill me, I give up," exclaimed Pedro Marrero. The corporal ordered him to throw down his weapon and come out with his hands up. The uninjured Marrero dropped his shotgun and stepped into the hallway with his arms raised. Alcolea noticed that the sergeant's stripes on his uniform were sewn with white thread, instead of the regulation brown color, indicating that he was an impostor. When the corporal escorted Marrero outside, Lt. Juan Piña, followed by an angry mob, snatched the prisoner. Marrero was felled by a blow to his crown with a handgun butt. Lieutenant Piña then charged into the administrative wing hallway firing his weapon, and a bullet ricocheting off a granite column wounded his leg. Private Olivares indicated that three of the five rebels who were in the building surrendered. He later stated that "the soldiers pummeled them with rifle butts even though there were officers saying, 'Do not kill them, do not kill them.' No one could stop the infuriated soldiers. They killed them with rifle-butt blows." Olivares went into the administrative wing hallway and in front of the doorway to the judicial office saw sprawled on the floor an attacker with the back of his head blown away. He then entered the Service Company barracks, where more than eight dead soldiers in bunks were draped with bedsheets. Olivares reeled back and dropped his rifle upon uncovering Pvt. Jesús Sánchez Pruna, who had awakened him that morning.[73]

The rebel José Luis Tasende, who had jumped through the open window of the operations and training section office onto Trinidad Street, was limping along the sidewalk next to the Moncada wall toward Los Libertadores Avenue. At the intersection Pvt. Mónico García, a camp cook, assumed that Tasende was a sergeant and offered to assist him. García gave him a piggyback ride for two blocks to the Emergency Hospital. While the practitioner Darío Larrea was cleaning Tasende's shrapnel wounds and bandaging his leg, police corporal José Ortiz Quintero started filling out the customary incident report. Tasende was evasive when asked his name and assigned unit. Outside the room the policeman conveyed to Private García his suspicion that the wounded man was one of the attackers. They notified regimental headquarters, and an SIR retinue whisked Tasende to the garrison. The prisoner was interrogated in the regimental headquarters, where he was photographed huddled in a corner with bare feet, blood-splattered pants, his right leg bandaged, and his wrists tied together.[74]

The defeat of the rebel vanguard brought the Moncada interior perimeter under control. The wounded soldiers were collected and transferred to the military hospital. Pvt. Néstor Reyes recalled being evacuated from Post 3 on a makeshift bed-frame stretcher assisted by Gov. Waldo Pérez Almaguer. Major Morales then focused on neutralizing the gunfire from the Civil Hospital. Lt. Claudio Morales García ordered a squad from the Fusilier Company to position a Browning M2 .50-caliber machine gun near Post 4. Lt. Marcelo Otaño Cookerman remembered that one of their best marksmen, Cpl. Juan Silva Domínguez, was incarcerated in the Guard Corps awaiting a court-martial for killing two outlaws in La Maya. Otaño released some eight detainees, including a sailor. Silva joined Pvt. Isidro Ferrer, Cpl. José Gerardo Rosabal Rosales, and Sgt. Braulio Curuneaux in discharging the .50-caliber machine gun at rebel positions in the rear of the Civil Hospital. The 128-pound weapon had a cyclic rate of fire of 550 rounds per minute. The bursts gouged out chunks of the rear wall, splintered windows, and destroyed the kitchen boiler plumbing in the pantry. Otaño then led Sgt. Diógenes Heredia and a different crew to operate a Browning M2 .50-caliber machine gun on the second-story roof of the Officers' Club. They fired in a straight trajectory at the rebels on top of the Palace of Justice. Upon hearing the loud machine-gun clatter, the policeman Genaro Quintana Riverí, a hostage on the courthouse rooftop, told his captors that resistance was useless.[75]

Léster Rodríguez agreed. Raúl Castro recalled, "Then we decided to descend again. In a short time, three or four policemen and a civilian armed with a pistol arrived. We opened the door. They entered and were also disarmed. We stayed there a little longer, until we realized that the attack had failed and left the premises." Léster later falsely claimed that they had seized fifteen policemen while leaving. The prisoners were locked in a courthouse holding cell. Léster took a bus to his parents' house in the city and incinerated his uniform. His father arranged for a chauffeur to take him to Palma Soriano. Raúl Castro followed the railroad tracks going north, determined to walk the forty miles to his father's Birán plantation. The four other rebels departed by automobile for the suburbs.[76]

The combatants outside Post 3 began a disorganized retreat after their ammunition ran out. A Civil Hospital janitor indicated that the "intense stage of combat was prolonged until about six in the morning." There are conflicting rebel estimates regarding the duration of the battle. Marta Rojas erroneously claimed that it was "two hours and forty minutes." According to Castro biographer Tad Szulc, "The entire action was over in less than a half hour." Eduardo Montano and Moisés Mafut estimated that the shooting ended in half an hour. Carlos Bustillo believed that it lasted twenty minutes. Mario Chanes stated that after the machine-gun fire impeded entry through Post 3, the attackers remained only "eight or nine minutes." Gerardo Granados calculated that the skirmish and the retreat lasted thirty to forty minutes. When the rebels started dispersing, he heard Fidel Castro shouting "Retreat, retreat!" on various occasions. Mario Lazo remembered, "The comrade who was next to me told me they ordered a retreat, but I didn't pay attention to him; I thought he had become cowardly. Later on, I saw the cars leaving." Carlos González Seijas, who had arrived with Castro, recalled, "The cars had retreated and I found myself alone in a place I did not know." González, who had kept his blue pants under his uniform, ditched his shotgun and bought a red shirt for two pesos in a grocery store a few blocks away. He rode a bus to a friend's home in Maffo and hid there for five days before returning to Havana.[77]

The fleeing rebels, many of whom had never driven a car, could not find their drivers. Most of their vehicles on Moncada Street, riddled during the crossfire, had shattered windshields, perforated radiators, and flat tires. After Eduardo Montano heard Castro order the retreat, he was unable to locate his cell leader, Fernando Chenard, the only one in their automobile who could drive. Ramiro Valdés departed in a car with a flat tire. He was accompanied by Reinaldo Boris Luis and Gustavo Arcos, who lay wounded on the backseat. Gerardo Granados saw Valdés weave in reverse at high speed and then slam with a loud crunch into Fidel Castro's Buick. Granados lingered outside Post 3 until the last moment looking for his brother Guillermo, unaware that he lay dead in the yard of a military house.[78]

The wounded Abelardo Crespo was carried by Jaime Costa to an automobile driven by Ciro Redondo and slipped in through a window because the door was jammed. The novelist Robert Merle described this version in 1965, but after Costa went into exile four years later, subsequent rebel accounts credited Fidel Castro with assisting Crespo into the vehicle. Crespo added to the myth in 1973: "When Fidel saw me [wounded] he immediately got out of his automobile and ceded me his seat." The roar of Redondo's car engine prompted a swarm of desperate rebels to rush the vehicle. Those squeezing in with the other three were Mario Chanes, Pepe Suárez, Emilio Hernández Cruz, Severino Rosell, Gerardo Granados, and the slightly wounded Marino Collazo. Castro then dove in through the open front passenger door onto the laps of Chanes and Costa, but he quickly exited after being unable to wedge in his entire body. Israel Tápanes counted "five men in the back seat and four in the front" before he and the wounded Reinaldo Benítez wriggled in. Eduardo Montano then straddled the rear-door window frame, with only one leg inside the vehicle. Chucho Montané alleged that he fled in this vehicle, but four of its occupants denied that he was with them. As they pulled away, Granados saw his friend Julio Díaz on the street and had Redondo stop to retrieve him. Costa recalled seeing Rosell hunched on the floor while repeatedly mashing the accelerator with his hand. During the disarray someone accidentally fired a bullet through the roof of the car. Pepe Suárez panicked when he saw a carload of soldiers giving chase and fired a pistol at them. A fellow passenger shouted, "Do not shoot, those are our guys," after recognizing Ricardo Santana at the wheel of the vehicle behind them.[79]

Santana, a nineteen-year-old Artemisa taxi driver, had earlier ditched his antique Spanish pistol and seized the service revolver of Cpl. Nemesio Traba, who was sprawled dead on the corner of Victoriano Garzón Avenue and Moncada Street. As he was returning to his rented 1952 Studebaker, which had been fifth in the caravan, Oscar Alcalde, who had found his way to the Moncada after being led astray by Tizol, drove up to the same corner with Armando Mestre, Juan Almeida, Gerardo Sosa, Ulises Sarmiento, and Moisés Mafut. The latter recalled that as they followed Alcalde on foot toward Post 3, "many rebels were fleeing back beyond us. More than twenty minutes had already passed since the start of hostilities. No one in my group fired a shot. I assure you." Alcalde later purported that he arrived in the third vehicle and gunned down a lieutenant leading a group of soldiers down the street. Calabazar cell leader Pedro Trigo, who had also ended up in Quintero Heights, stated that he arrived at Moncada while the retreat was in progress and then took a bus to Havana. Mafut saw Fidel Castro getting into Santana's Studebaker, the windshield and top half of the steering wheel of which were blown away. He thought to himself, "If the chief is leaving, so am I," and he bolted into the vehicle. Others crammed inside included Mestre, Almeida, Rosendo Menéndez, the brothers Roberto and Orlando Galán, and Alcalde, who abandoned his own car to accompany Castro. The nine passengers sped past Ramiro Valdés near the entrance to Vista Alegre, overcoming Ciro Redondo's crowded vehicle on the Siboney highway. Mario Lazo's car stopped at a traffic light while fleeing the city. He recalled that "a drunken individual climbed on the hood of the automobile. We got out and threatened him, so that he would get off, but he didn't want to." The rebels proceeded with the merrymaker sprawled on the hood until they forcibly removed him upon reaching the San Juan River bridge. A witness to the incident was seized and taken back to Siboney for interrogation. The frightened man lived near the farmhouse and claimed not to know anything.[80]

When the rebels started dispersing, Héctor de Armas and Carlos Bustillo were shielding themselves behind Alamo trees on Moncada Street. They abandoned their rental vehicle, weapons, and army shirts. After walking a few blocks in their T-shirts and khaki pants, they saw a woman standing on a porch and nonchalantly entered her home. The strangers stated that they were tourists from Havana attending the carnival. Bustillo, who had friends in the city, asked the lady for the address of the Almeida family residence and received a phone-book location and directions to Vista Alegre. Bustillo recalled, "She was very intrigued and said that we were lucky to have gone into her house, because both of her neighbors were in the army." The woman gave him a shirt belonging to her sleeping husband. Bustillo requested permission to use the bathroom, flushed down the toilet the shotgun shells from his pockets, and hurriedly departed with his companion.[81]

Other combatants left stranded included Pedro Miret, Fidel Labrador, Gildo Fleitas, Fernando Chenard and his assistant Miguel Oramas, and three others on the patios of the new military houses near Post 3. Although Fidel Castro later claimed that these "expert marksmen" were ordered to cover the retreat, Miret admitted that they "became separated" from the main force. Chenard allegedly went to warn those in the Palace of Justice, unaware of their earlier departure, and was supposedly captured en route. Fidel Labrador, firing from behind a concrete patio fence, was shot diagonally in the right eye by a bullet that clipped his ear. Miret, assuming that his comrade was dead, was startled when Labrador asked to be taken to a hospital. In the adjacent yard of Sgt. Carlos Rojas Ortiz, Oramas fell dead from bullets fired from the garrison. Inside the Rojas home, "women and children threw themselves on the floor in one of the rooms, while the bullets sprayed its walls." Next door Sgt. Julián Fajardo Mendoza, a fifty-two-year-old file clerk in the military hospital, his wife, and their son and three daughters huddled in a bedroom. They heard the attackers yelling "Viva Chibás!" and unsuccessfully trying to kick in their outward-opening rear door. Two rebels forced open a kitchen window, ransacked the rear bedroom, and tossed civilian clothes to comrades in the backyard. Soldiers in the military hospital across the street who saw the attackers inside the Fajardo home assumed that the family had been massacred and spread that rumor. Miret, on a neighboring patio, felt "a profound impression of moral fatigue." Three years later he admitted to Mario Llerena that "Castro abandoned the field, leaving wounded and exposed men behind." The historian Hugh Thomas concurred that Castro retreated, "leaving behind some wounded and some others to be captured."[82]

The isolated rebels decided to surrender. Lt. Juan Piña, who had returned to the military hospital with a wounded leg, received a telephone call there from Capt. Juan de Dios Ruiz at Moncada indicating that three attackers in the Fajardo yard were waving a white handkerchief. Piña passed the information to military policeman Alfonso Silva, who had been guarding the military hospital main entrance, and ordered him to go with another soldier to detain them. While the two cautiously proceeded on Moncada Street toward the Fajardo home, they encountered Miret, Labrador, and a shirtless companion, with their arms raised, walking toward them. Private Silva handed the prisoners over to Lieutenant Piña inside the military hospital and resumed his post outside. Dr. Erik Juan Pita recalled that the soldiers immediately trounced the trio. He witnessed Miret being violently kicked in the groin and Pvt. Luis Aguila Cuevas karate-chopping him on the head so forcefully that he broke his hand. Miret later falsely claimed that the head wound was caused by a rifle-butt blow. Alcalde grossly exaggerated by saying that Miret had been "shot in the head." Labrador claimed that he was unconscious after being wounded and recovered his senses four days later.[83]

During the hospital melee, Sgt. René Feraud Mejías arrived through the rear entrance, searching for his two brothers who had been shot in front of the Civil Hospital. The sergeant went berserk upon hearing that Pedro was dead and Mauricio was wounded. From the second-floor mezzanine he saw the rebels being beaten below. Feraud grabbed a Springfield rifle, engaged the bolt action, and screamed for everyone to get away from the prisoners so that he could avenge his brother's death. Dr. Juan Pita remembered, "While Feraud was aiming down at us and the crowd continued to punch the rebels, Dr. Tamayo and I managed to get them into a room for protection." Miret gave contradictory accounts, first alleging that after he was "wounded" outside he recovered his senses in the military hospital. He later provided a more heroic version of how, upon entering the hospital, the soldiers were fearful of him and stepped out of his way.[84]

After the outer Post 3 perimeter was neutralized, the Moncada dead and wounded, including the rebel intruders, were transferred to the military hospital. Army squads systematically searched the military housing project. The patios were littered with scores of discarded uniforms and caps. A search team broke down the front door of Sgt. Julián Fajardo's home. Inside they discovered a pair of sweat-stained army uniforms on the kitchen floor and two men hiding under the beds in a rear dormitory. The strangers claimed to live there but suspiciously wore civilian clothes three sizes too small. When the Fajardo family was asked to identify them, twenty-year-old Julián Junior pointed at one of the rebels and exclaimed, "Hey, those are my clothes!" As the intruders were being led away, the youth reached into a detainee's guayabera pocket and retrieved the two peso bills he had left there the previous night. Nine-year-old Ana María Fajardo saw in her backyard the corpse of the corpulent Gildo Fleitas, shot through the side, lying behind a fifty-five-gallon water drum. That shocking image has haunted her with nightmares for more than fifty years.[85]

When the skirmish ceased around Post 3, the rebels in the Civil Hospital realized that something was amiss as no other gunfire was heard except the shots directed at them. Haydée, accompanied by Melba, went to the rear of the hospital to consult with her brother. He was indecisive, expecting reinforcements to appear, and opted to continue fighting. The women returned to the vestibule. Melba suggested hiding with a friend who lived in the city, but Haydée refused to leave her brother behind. They then went back to see Abel, who told Haydée that "there was now no doubt that the garrison was not in the hands of our comrades, something had failed." Abel hurried to the entrance, informed his companions, "we are running out of bullets," and had a whispered conversation with Dr. Muñoz. He was not sure about their next move. Muñoz suggested that they might escape capture by donning hospital gowns and dressings to disguise themselves as patients. Dr. Mauricio León Orúe "showed them where the patients' gowns were stored." Haydée then saw her brother hiding some rifles in the patio concrete flowerbeds and asked him what they should do. He replied, "Each one can do what they want because everything here has ended, we stopped combating five minutes ago and we are losing time." Haydée recalled how she reproached him, saying, "something has to be done, you have to give an order, you are the chief here." Abel responded, "Now, what I do believe is that we have to prepare ourselves to meet our death." Haydée stated that she and Melba "refused to accept that." After further arguing, the domineering older sister told her brother to take off his uniform and put on a hospital gown. The irresolute Abel replied, "Bring it to me. From this moment on I do everything that you want." Dr. Muñoz asked a student nurse for a white bedsheet to hang from the rooftop as a sign of surrender, but this was never done. Muñoz panicked and tore off his coat pocket embroidered with his name. Dr. Liam Chomat suggested putting it back on to identify him as a physician. Unable to sew it back on, Muñoz wrote his name with blue ink on adhesive tape and stuck it on his vestment. He then asked student nurse Josefina Milet Alavo for the key to the morgue, which had a side exit. When his escape attempt was thwarted by the wrong key, Muñoz hid in a female patient's private room.[86]

After the rebels stopped firing from the Civil Hospital, Colonel del Río Chaviano ordered police major José Izquierdo to occupy it with his force. Major Morales simultaneously deployed a platoon pincer movement on the building. He told Lt. Manuel

Piña to take a squad of nineteen men west on Victoriano Garzón Avenue and circle behind the Los Angeles Clinic toward the main entrance of the Civil Hospital. Lt. Mario Martínez Arbona led a ten-man squad, including Pvt. Justo Ramón Martija, that carried out a similar maneuver on Paseo de José Martí Street on the opposite side of the Civil Hospital. Major Izquierdo and ten cops advanced through the center on Trinidad Street. They were the first to enter the empty hospital vestibule, where they found the corpse of police corporal Pedro Pompa with his weapon shattered by a bullet. The policemen occupied the deserted central patio and found on a bench the phonograph records for airing during the attack. SIM agent Angel Esteban Garay, who had been held hostage, told them that there were weapons and uniforms abandoned in the rear area. Major Izquierdo interrogated a few employees, who were too scared to denounce the ruse. Someone approached Izquierdo, pointed to Abel in bed with a bandaged head, and said, "He is one." Melba Hernández later accused SIM confidant Senén Carabia of denouncing the rebels. Carabia had earlier entered the Civil Hospital disguised as a milkman to reconnoiter inside.[87]

Lieutenants Martínez and Piña went into the hospital behind Izquierdo's squad, leaving part of their units guarding the outside. The combined force searched all the wards, asking patients their names and comparing them to those appearing on the bed charts. If the data did not match, the individual was detained. Raúl Gómez García gave nineteen-year-old janitor Bienvenido Sánchez his wristwatch, a black leather billfold with money, and a pistol, along with a note that Gómez's mother received in the mail three days later, which said, "Taken prisoner, your son." A slightly wounded Gerardo Alvarez wrote his mother a five-line message, which read in part, "If I do not see you again, forgive me." He gave it to Sánchez along with a ring that was a gift from his daughter. Both rebels hid under a rubbish pile in the garage until an elderly employee denounced them. Another insurgent was discovered under a pile of kindling next to the boilers. The wounded Horacio Matheu and Tomás Alvarez were removed on stretchers and taken in a jeep to the garrison. In their room the authorities found hospital orderly Alberto Robaina, who had taken a tranquilizer, asleep under a bed. Robaina was being led outside when a staff member obtained his release. The hospital corridors were patrolled by soldiers verifying the identification of all patients and employees. Isabel Mafobrio Prieto indicated that Dr. Muñoz was seized in her private room "at eight something." Melba stated that the rebels stopped shooting at 8:00 A.M. and the soldiers entered the hospital thirty minutes later.[88]

Nineteen insurgents were herded into the central patio, without the women or Ramón Pez Ferro, a small and thin nineteen-year-old mulatto from Artemisa. He wore the pants he had kept under his army uniform and a civilian shirt purloined from the laundry. An aged black retired army patient, Tomás Sánchez, saved Pez by pretending that he was a visiting grandson. The teenager, who was in the veterans' ward at the rear of the hospital, acknowledged that he was unsure of what was happening and was unable to witness any arrests. Pez was allowed to leave the building but was later detained at his grandmother's house in Havana after sending a telegram to his family in Artemisa. The rest of the rebels captured in the hospital, ringed by the police squad, were escorted on foot, with their hands behind their heads, into the Moncada through Post 4. Dr. Muñoz, lagging behind and flanked by two soldiers, loudly protested that he should be treated with respect since he was a physician and not a combatant. Muñoz kept trying to justify his actions and to reason with those who were in no mood to listen to him. "We came because of an ideal," he said. Muñoz was confronted at the intersecting walkways in the Moncada rear patio by an angry soldier. Pvt. Antonio Rodríguez Pérez saw Major Izquierdo trying to protect the physician. When the aggressor pulled out a pistol, Muñoz raised his right arm in reflex, as if to stop the bullet. The shot tore through his forearm and deltoid muscle, lodging in his chest. Another bullet was fired into his left temple. Izquierdo falsely told a Cuban government reporter in 1968 that he was not present when Muñoz was gunned down.[89]

The Civil Hospital military supervisor, medical captain Mario Porro Varela, went there with a detachment at 10:30 A.M. to nab the rebel women who had evaded capture. Their participation apparently had been divulged by rebels under interrogation. Inside the hospital a lady whose child was a patient denounced Melba and Haydée. The rebel women never explained why they remained in the Civil Hospital for more than two hours after their companions were led away, nor did they depart when the female visitors were allowed to leave. When Porro arrived, Melba and Haydée ran to the infant ward and pounded on the screen door. They told Nurse Camelia Rodríguez that they were in the revolution and needed to hide. The nurse initially balked, fearing for the safety of some fifty infants, but then relented "because of their despair and insistence." The rebel women pretended to be new mothers by holding infants feeding on baby bottles. Rodríguez stated in 1967 that Melba and Haydée were quickly recognized as impostors "because mothers back then did not wear slacks."[90]

Melba later stated that after 10:00 A.M., "we were taken in an automobile to the garrison," but she has changed her story frequently in accordance with Haydée's repeated fabrications. Haydée claimed that while walking to the Moncada they witnessed the murder of Dr. Muñoz on Trinidad Street, although it had occurred much earlier inside the garrison. Melba purported that she saw when Muñoz "was shot in the back," but his death certificate describes frontal wounds. Muñoz's widow, Dinorah Algarra, later asked both women about her husband's participation and fate. She recalled that "Haydée only told me about the [civil] hospital but did not give me great details." The rebel women actually saw little after their arrest because they were immediately confined in the recreation room of the second-floor Officers' Club. Haydée admitted once that they were kept separate from the others. A *Havana Post* reporter who interviewed both women three days later wrote that they denied "any participation in the assault on the Army post and demanded that paraffin tests be applied to their hands to show that they had not used firearms. They said they were grateful for the treatment they had received at the hands of the officers of the Moncada Army post and the heads of the Municipal jail of Santiago."[91]

The surprise assault on the Moncada was a total failure due to deficient rebel leadership, bad planning and strategy, and tactical human errors. This was due to the fact that the rebel leaders lacked military cognition and were unable to command their scattered cell members in combat. Fidel Castro neglected appointing adjutants or couriers to relay his field orders to his followers in the Civil Hospital and the Palace of Justice. As a result, he had little control of his disarrayed troops, his combat role was minimal, and Castro initially wasted precious time extricating a strayed group from the military hospital. Abel Santamaría demonstrated irresoluteness in the Civil Hospital. He was unable to perceive the unfolding events, he failed to evacuate his force by erroneously awaiting for imaginary reinforcements, and his foreboding of doom prompted him to succumb to the directives of his domineering older sister. Military committee member Ernesto Tizol deserted and veered off course a third of the insurgents who never reached their objective. Raúl Castro, a subordinate of Léster Rodríguez, was not part of the leadership, and his group was unable to go fully into action due to the high retaining wall on the Palace of Justice roof. The cell leaders erred when they acted as chauffeurs since combat-unit commanders should rely on designated drivers. The vehicles remained exposed in the crossfire during the attack, and more than half were left behind. Most of the drivers could not be located during the retreat, and many rebels did not know how to drive. In the ensuing pandemonium, Fidel Castro abandoned more than a dozen dead and wounded men on the field.

The attack plan, unknown to the cell leaders until an hour before the assault, had numerous flaws. These included failing to note the precise location of the rebels' major objective–the regimental quartermaster arsenal; being unaware of the prohibited nighttime entry through Post 3; not knowing about the locked exits in the Civil Hospital; and overlooking the impossibility of shooting at the garrison from the Palace of Justice roof. The rebels could have gained commanding firing power over the parade ground and all the entrances to the barracks had they placed snipers on the roof of the three-story apartment building facing Post 2. They could then have quickly silenced the machine gun that impeded entry through Post 3 and kept in check the soldiers exiting the barracks. The rebels' scant ammunition and light weapons were no match against the army's machine guns, large-caliber rifles, and grenades, making it impossible to resist for long. The rebel units lacked walkie-talkies and ended up operating separately without coordination or communication with each other at Post 3, the Palace of Justice, and the Civil Hospital. The cell leaders were not given instructions on what to do other than penetrating the garrison and occupying the barracks and the arsenal. Even if the attackers had seized the regimental quartermaster room, with contained surplus weapons and accoutrements, it could not have prevented the soldiers from arming themselves with hundreds of rifles stored in the gun cabinets in the barracks. Topographical disorientation resulted in unnecessarily attacking the army residential complex and the military hospital. The rebels had no concept of a combat goal other than shooting at the garrison or at any stranger wearing a military uniform and carrying a Springfield rifle. The use of army disguises created much confusion among the rebels of different cells, and they were unable to distinguish between friend and foe. Fidel Castro neglected taking medical supplies or drawing up contingency plans in case of failure.

Tactical human errors greatly contributed to rebel defeat. The initial encounter with the roving military-police patrol was coincidental, but Fidel Castro blundered in ordering their detention, prompting a shootout. He should have ignored them, as did the vanguard driver, and proceeded into the citadel. Castro, by prematurely exiting his car, precipitated the rebels in the caravan to follow suit and disperse. Members of the insurgent vanguard, after removing the chain across Post 3, failed to drive into the garrison as planned and therefore to be followed by the other cars; instead they left their vehicle partly blocking the entrance. Friendly fire wounded at least four rebels, and it will never be known if it also killed other insurgents disguised as soldiers.

Fidel Castro expected the Moncada and Bayamo attacks to prompt the radical Auténticos and Ortodoxos to follow his lead. Yet, the insurgents failed to get their revolutionary message on the airwaves. There was no effort to simultaneously seize a radio station after Luis Conte Agüero was not located and broadcasting technician Manuel Lorenzo refused to participate. The populace did not respond because they considered the disturbance a local feud between two military factions. The rebels were surprised by the stiff military resistance. Castro's assurance of a brief and bloodless surprise victory, as well as the purported air cover and naval assistance, failed to materialize. Rumors of a possible attack had reinforced the Moncada's security measures. Lt. Col. Angel González Alfonso had positioned a machine gun on the parade ground covering the entrances. *Retén* auxiliary patrols had been mobilized. Scores of soldiers, police, and civilians entered the Moncada under fire to participate in its defense.

The results of the attack were best described by Santiago de Cuba entrepreneur Enrique Canto Bory, the future national treasurer of Castro's 26 of July Movement: "Fidel, in spite of his apparent failure, had gained his major and maybe, his only objective, attacking the Moncada. His name was now in the national sphere, having gone from anonymity to being a determining figure in the political game. This was also his major ambition. He did not care that to achieve it so many sacrifices had to be made and so much blood was spilled." Fidel Castro also attained international recognition for the first time when the New York Times and the global cable news agencies identified him as a "leader of the Ortodoxo Party" who commanded the revolt. Years later New York Times correspondent and Castro hagiographer Herbert Matthews called the Moncada plan "a mad, hopeless, suicidal adventure."[92]

According to Fidel Castro's brother-in-law Rafael Díaz-Balart, "The Moncada attack was a coup d'état by Fidel Castro against the opposition leadership consolidating under the Montreal Pact." Millo Ochoa indicated that under the Montreal Pact the Ortodoxos and Auténticos were planning a simultaneous military uprising in all the provinces. After the Moncada attack, Ochoa and Prío were notified by their conspiratorial military contacts "not to count on them because soldiers had been murdered in their hospital beds." Ochoa acknowledged that his secretary, Juan Orta, had told Castro of their insurrectional plan.[93]

Raúl Chibás Rivas, a Montreal Pact opponent and Ortodoxo leader, stated that Fidel Castro never divulged his plan and stressed that it was necessary for the Ortodoxos to take action. Chibás said: "He thought that Prío and the Auténticos were going to act first. I warned him that an isolated incident, like the March 1935 strike, had consolidated Batista in power. Castro believed that if he revolted first, the Auténticos who were better prepared, would have to follow suit behind his leadership." Former president Carlos Prío described the attack as "a folly." The magistrate Adolfo Nieto Piñeiro-Osorio, who presided over the sedition trial, affirmed, "The only thing Fidel wanted to do was to abort a revolutionary movement planned by Carlos Prío and Aureliano Sánchez Arango in Montreal. By attacking the Moncada, he wanted to place himself in first place as the leader, even though he was repudiated by all the political groups in the country, as was shown in the Montreal conference, because they knew his background." Ramón Vasconcelos editorialized in Alerta, "Cuban blood has run abundantly because of political hatreds and personal ambitions! . . . Sending a handful of fools to their death is an abominable crime. . . . May Cubans never again kill other Cubans for political passions that with wisdom and mutual tolerance would have a satisfactory solution." The government casualties included fifteen soldiers and three policemen dead or mortally wounded and twenty-three soldiers and five policemen wounded. Nine rebels were killed and eleven were wounded in combat.[94]

The insurgents followed Fidel Castro to the Moncada due to various motivating factors. The most predominant were Ortodoxo Party idealism and camaraderie, the restoration of the 1940 Constitution, and a visceral hatred for Batista and the military coup that disrupted the political process. No one claimed to be fighting for socialism or the creation of a Communist state. They believed that their patriotic duty was the redemption of their democratic republic, and many saw themselves as emulating the founding fathers who had fought for Cuban independence in the previous century. A few rebels were motivated by a sense of adventure or, like Renato Guitart, the ambition to become a colonel overnight. Ironically, the 1933 revolution had immediately ascended Batista from sergeant to colonel. Fidel Castro deviously manipulated the yearnings and frustrations of his lesser-educated followers for his own political ambition. When his promises and expectations of popular support and easy victory failed to materialize, the rebels found themselves fleeing in disarray for their lives.

The La Demajagua Bell, which rang the start of the Ten Years' War of independence in 1868, arrives in Havana on November 3, 1947. It is escorted by, from left to right, Fidel Castro, Enrique Ovares, Alfredo "El Chino" Esquivel, and Gustavo Ortiz Faez, grasping the relic. Three months later Castro and Ortiz were implicated in the murder of student leader "Manolo" de Castro. Courtesy of Enrique Ovares

Rebels at target practice on the Hidalgo-Gato farm in Nueva Paz in 1953. Standing, from left to right: Antonio "Ñico" López, Abel Santamaría, Fidel Castro, unidentified person, and José Luis Tasende. Below: Horacio Hidalgo-Gato, left, and Ernesto Tizol. Courtesy of Mario Hidalgo-Gato

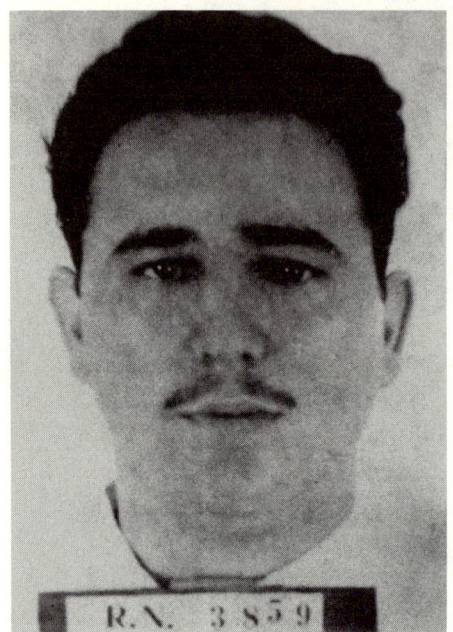

Fidel Castro. Author's collection

Raúl Castro. Author's collection

Renato Guitart. Courtesy of José Pujol

Eduardo Montano. Author's collection

Mario Chanes. Courtesy of Orlando Castro García

Mario MartínezArarás. Courtesy of Raúl Martínez Araras

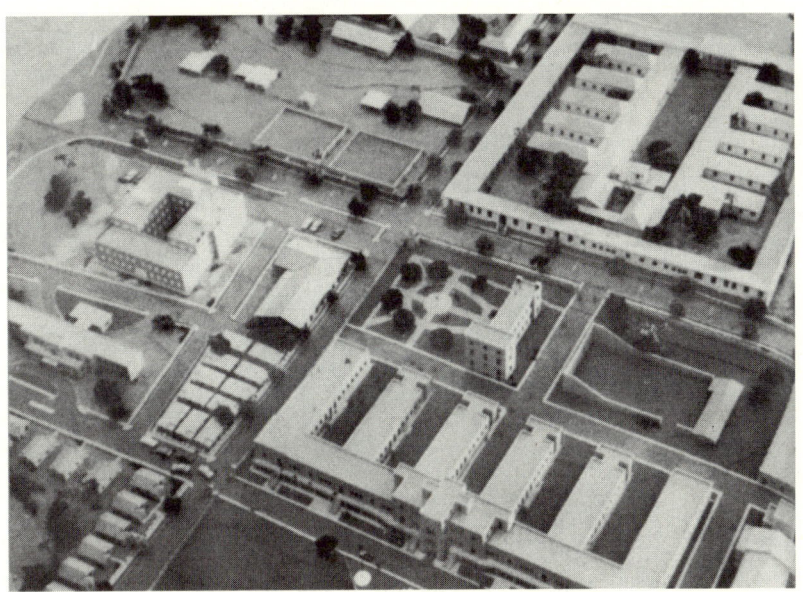

Mockup of the scene of the action: the Moncada garrison is in the lower center. The administrative offices wing occupied by the rebels is on its far left, followed by the barracks of the Service Company, the Headquarters Company, the Infantry Company, the Fusilier Company, and the Rural Guard barracks. To the left rear is the Officers' Club building and adjacent horseshoe-shaped park. The small-arms target range and its high retaining wall, where captured rebels were executed, is to its right rear. Behind the fortress is the Civil Hospital, occupied by twenty-two rebels. On the lower left corner is the military housing project on both sides of the street. Five vehicles (others are not shown) are lined up outside Post 3, consisted of the main thrust of the attack. To their left is the Military Hospital, with a half-circle emergency entrance driveway in back. Behind it is the Palace of Justice, seized by six rebel snipers. Courtesy of Orlando Castro García

Post 3 side entrance. A chain hangs across the sentry boxes. The flag is at half-staff after the attack. The colonel's residence is in the background center, beyond Post 5. Courtesy of El Mundo

The Post 2 main entrance viewed from the third-floor regimental headquarters. A bust of Gen. Antonio Maceo is on the left, at the end of the driveway that divides the parade ground. The rebels neglected seizing the rooftop of the three-story apartment building on the upper left, which would have provided snipers with a commanding view of the parade ground and all the entrances to the barracks. Courtesy of Orlando Castro García

The Post 3 side entrance viewed from the third-floor regimental headquarters. Below, right, is the upper balcony and the stairways leading to the Service Company barracks, foreground, and the administrative offices wing. Outside, on the left, are the clapboard sergeants' residences overrun by the rebels, who fired at the garrison from behind the white garden fences. Courtesy of Orlando Castro García

The upper-floor administrative offices wing mistakenly occupied by the rebels. Below are the barred windows of the quartermaster depot that was their objective. Above them are the open windows of the officers' barbershop. The upper far-left window is of the Operations and Training Office. The quartermaster entrance overlooked by the rebels was behind the stairway. The pockmarks on the walls were made by a .30-caliber machine gun manned by Sgt. José Virués attempting to flush out the intruders. Courtesy of the Havana Post

The Officers' Club building and adjacent park, on the left, as viewed from the Palace of Justice. The Regimental Intelligence Service Office is on the third floor, from where some rebel prisoners were threatened with being thrown off. On the right are the rear of the barracks separated by courtyards. The gabled building on the right background is the movie theater. Courtesy of Orlando Castro García

Three of the nine new military houses on Moncada Street, near Post 3, built in 1952. From left to right are the homes of Sergeants Julián Fajardo, Carlos Rojas, and Raúl Cárdenas. The rebels fired at the garrison from behind the concrete fences and broke into the Fajardo residence. The Military Hospital is on the far left, and the back of the Palace of Justice is on the rear right. Courtesy of Beralia Oliva

The Palace of Justice, from where six rebel snipers fired at the garrison. Their trial was later held in the third-floor Plenary Hall. Courtesy of José Pujol

The Bayamo garrison entrance. Courtesy of Orlando Castro García

In the rear patio adjacent to the administrative offices wing, Lt. Angel Machado, on the right, with cap, looks at the executed rebels strewn about to depict phony combat. On the left, the doorways of the paymaster, veterinary, and communications offices. The garrison park is in the background. Courtesy of Diario de la Marina

The Moncado courtyard between the administrative wing on the right and the Service Company barracks on the left. Cpl. Juan Bautista Corrales looks down at the executed rebels scattered about to simulate death in combat. Behind him are the two open windows of the Police Adjutant Office, from where the rebels fired diagonally into the three partially opened dormitory windows on the left. Courtesy of Orlando Castro García

Fourteen of the nineteen government casualties. Left to right: Cpl. Nemesio Traba, Policeman Roberto Ferrándiz, Pvt. José Vázquez, Sgt. Ramón Silveiro, Pvt. Jesús Sánchez Pruna, Cpl. Isidro Izquierdo, Policeman Pedro Pompa, Pvt. Felino Miró, Pvt. Urbano Sánchez, Sgt. Luis Oliva, Pvt. Eusebio Baró, Lt. Pedro Feraud, Police Sgt. Gerónimo Suárez, and Pvt. Efraín Galano. Courtesy of Diario de la Marina

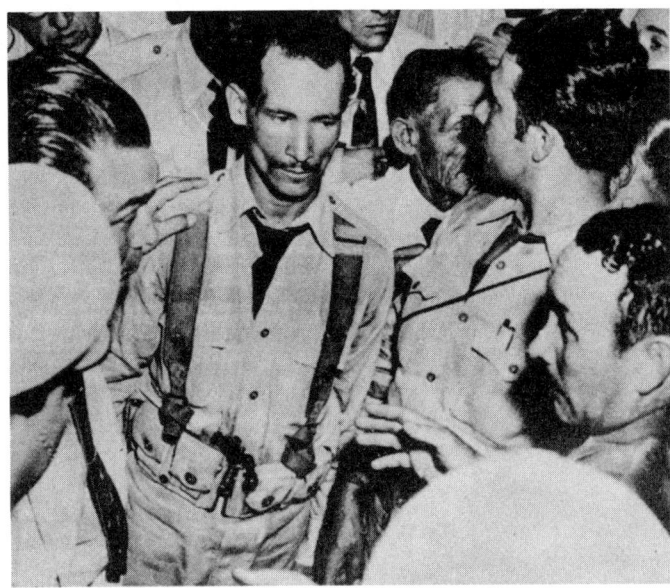

Gen. Fulgencio Batista, left, congratulates the two MPs who first fired on the attackers: Luis "Cara de Chivo" Triay (with Springfield rifle bolt tucked in his web belt) and Alfonso Silva, looking to his right. Col. Alberto del Río Chaviano, on far right, addresses Batista. Courtesy of Alfonso Silva

The Morales family had sixteen relatives in the armed forces and the police. From left to right: Andrés (killed at Moncada), Rafael, Ramón, Emilio, and Horacio Morales Alvarez and their parents, Andrés Morales and Micaela Alvarez. Courtesy of Orlando Morales Gros

Pvt. Antonio H. Rodríguez Pérez, right, and his brothers José Luis, left, and Gregorio. The Moncada regiment included many family members. Courtesy of Antonio H. Rodríguez Pérez

Pvt. Armando Oliva López and Beralia Fajardo on their wedding day, October 1, 1955. In the background is one of the sergeants' residences in the Moncada military housing project and the concrete garden walls from where the rebels fired at the garrison. Oliva's squad captured Fidel Castro, and the Fajardo home was penetrated by the rebels during the Moncada attack. Courtesy of Beralia Oliva

Pvt. José Ferrá Mulet. His pistol grip is adorned with the flags of Cuba and the Fourth of September. Courtesy of José Ferrá Mulet

Pvt. José Humberto Olivares. Courtesy of José Humberto Olivares

Pvt. Justo Ramón Martija. Courtesy of Justo Ramón Martija

A brooding Fidel Castro in the Santiago de Cuba vivac jail after his surrender, August 1, 1953. A beard would later hide his double chin. To his right, Maj. Rafael Morales Alvarez. Behind him is the major's son, Pvt. Rafael Morales Gros. Courtesy of Orlando Morales Gros

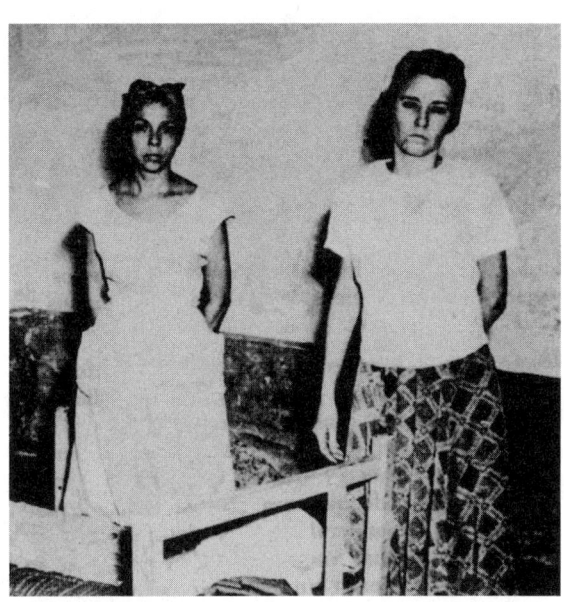

Melba Hernández, left, and Haydée Santamaría, in the Santiago de Cuba vivac *jail, after changing clothes. Courtesy of* El Mundo

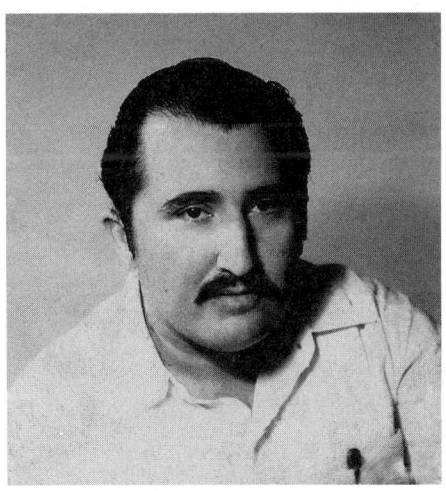

Manuel Bartolomé, director of the Bartolomé Funeral Home in Santiago de Cuba, retrieved all the rebel corpses after the Moncada attack and saw no signs of torture or dismemberment. Courtesy of Manuel Bartolomé

José "Pepín" Pujol (right) and his brother Juan (on motorcycle, left) stood for hours across the street from the Moncada, at their Harley-Davidson dealership, listening to the shots being fired inside the garrison and watching the military patrols racing in and out. Courtesy of José Pujol

Bayamo rebel leader Orlando Castro García, on July 27, 1953, and the vehicle that took him to a Sierra Maestra mountain hideout after the attack. Courtesy of Orlando Castro García

Rebels exiled in Mexico City in 1954. From left to right: Calixto García, Ibrahim Sosa, Severino Rosell, and Bayamo attack leaders Gerardo Pérez-Puelles, Raúl Martínez Ararás, and Orlando Castro García. The last three severed relations with Fidel Castro in 1955. Courtesy of Orlando Castro García

Rebels at a Mexico City reception in 1954. From left to right: Ibrahim Sosa, Carlos Bustillo, Orlando Castro García, Léster Rodríguez (led the Palace of Justice raid), Reinaldo Castro, and Héctor de Armas. Courtesy of Orlando Castro García

The author with former sergeant Eulalio "El Mulo" González at his Miami residence in 1975. Author's collection

Former adversaries Moncada private Ariel Matos and Bayamo rebel leader Orlando Castro García reconciled on July 26, 2004, on the María Elvira Confronta program, WDLP TV, Miami. The author was a special guest on the show. Author's collection

FIVE

"We are going into history"

Gerardo Pérez-Puelles, a twenty-five-year-old advertising agent with a high school education and no military experience, was the combat strategist of the Bayamo attack. A week prior to July 26 he arrived in Bayamo, population 20,178, via railroad to finalize the assault plan envisioned by Fidel Castro. Pérez-Puelles was met at the station by Fernando Fernández Catá, the unsuspecting school chum of Renato Guitart, who drove him to the rebel headquarters at the Gran Casino Motel. The building, an old rectangular masonry structure with a flat roof, was boldly emblazoned along the length of its facade: "Gran Casino - Lodging." Two "For Sale" signs had been painted on the lower right wall corners at the intersection of Zenea Street and Augusto Márquez Avenue. The foyer contained six small rooms on the right, each with its own discreet street exit, and a bar in the rear. The motel usually charged hourly rates for romantic trysts. The elderly proprietor, Juan Manuel Martínez, had rented the building to the rebels with an option to buy. He would daily, but unannounced, visit Pérez-Puelles to chat about closing the deal.[1]

Orlando Castro García arrived by train from Havana on Friday morning, July 24, to conclude attack preparations. He brought three suitcases with weapons, ammunition, and army uniforms that had been stored in his apartment. Pérez-Puelles assisted in taking the luggage by taxi to the motel and locking it in a closet. The two men discussed the arrival schedule of their comrades and how to get them inside without arousing suspicion from the landlord or the authorities. They then had lunch at a downtown restaurant and afterward rested on a bench in Céspedes Park. Orlando was startled when he heard someone calling out his name. It was the local salesman of Sabatés, the Havana firm where Orlando was the assistant chief of the credit department. The vendor produced a few credit request forms and asked for an authorization signature. The abashed rebel quickly signed the papers without reading them and pleaded that his presence there be kept secret from the home office because he was enjoying an unauthorized holiday. The conspirators then encountered the Bayamo police chief, Afro-Cuban Capt. Adolfo Fernández, to whom Pérez-Puelles had previously expressed an interest in buying a local farm for their poultry enterprise. Pérez-Puelles introduced Orlando Castro to the official and gave him a few cigars as a token of friendship. In reality, the rebels were trying to detect any sign of suspicion from the authorities.[2]

That afternoon Pérez-Puelles climbed the aqueduct tower along the Bayamo River, behind the army garrison, and photographed the area while Orlando Castro waited below. They had the film quickly developed at a downtown studio and returned to the Gran Casino to discuss the attack strategy. Both men spent the evening of July 24 in the motel loading weapons while clad in their underwear to ward off the stifling summer heat. At 8:00 P.M. a jeep screeched to a halt outside with its headlight high beams shining through the slits in the front door planks. "Open up, it's the Rural Guard," shouted someone banging on the door. The rebels quickly grabbed pistols, fearing that the photographs they took of the garrison had prompted an investigation. As Orlando hid behind the door ready to shoot, Pérez-Puelles opened it and was temporarily blinded by the bright headlights. Their apprehension turned to chagrin when Fernández Catá gloated in the doorway, "Hey, I really fooled you guys." Pérez-Puelles slipped his weapon to Orlando, who covertly put away the handguns. They admonished the prankster not to pull that stunt again.[3]

The next morning, July 25, Orlando and Pérez-Puelles bought a ham shank, a few cognac bottles, and refreshments for their comrades expected that evening. At 10:30 A.M. they took a taxi to the railroad station and met Ramiro Sánchez Domínguez and Rolando Rodríguez, who brought the rest of the arms and uniforms in two suitcases they had received from Raúl Martínez Araras. Pérez-Puelles, who was raised in the same Old Havana neighborhood as both men, had recently recruited them. The rebel group leaders had been instructed not to enter the motel until after dark. When Mario Martínez Araras and his five companions arrived at 1:00 P.M., they drove back to a Cauto Cristo outdoor bar and grill for lunch. Chucho Montané, heading for Santiago de Cuba with five Lawton rebels, also stopped there to eat. The groups joined tables and ordered a round of drinks after finding the food grill closed. After the Lawton insurgents departed, Ñico López played the guitar and Adalberto Ruanes accompanied him on the harmonica until 5:00 P.M.[4]

The dentist Pedro Aguilera also arrived early in Bayamo, driving a car decorated with Fourth of September flags. He left five rebels at the park, went to have dinner at his home in Palma Soriano in order to establish an alibi, and returned just prior to the attack. His companions, pretending to be tourists, rented a horse-drawn carriage for a city tour. They later went to a pool hall until dark and afterward discreetly entered the Gran Casino in pairs every ten minutes. Raúl Martínez arrived around 7:00 P.M. with four followers, including Elio Rosete, their Bayamo contact, who was scheduled to play a crucial role in their plan. He found everyone already inside and assigned four men to each of the six rooms, ordering them to rest. Martínez split them up to avoid conglomeration and hubbub in the foyer.[5]

At 8:30 P.M. Fidel Castro and his companions drove up to the Bayamo bus station on Central Highway, where Andrés García Díaz awaited to guide them to the Gran Casino. Castro went into a back room and remained standing with Raúl Martínez and Orlando Castro. He was assured that everyone had arrived but did not call them out of their rooms because he wanted to keep the excitement down and was pressed for time to reach Santiago de Cuba. Fidel Castro asked if there had been any problems, and Martínez replied, "The owner of the place has been coming every night to snoop around. I sent Gerardo out to distract him, but I am concerned that he will return tonight." The Bayamo rebel leaders were instructed to say that they were an SIM unit doing a secret investigation in the city. The question of rank arose for the first time. Orlando Castro recalled that "Fidel appointed Raúl Martínez as a colonel and I would be the Bayamo civil administrator once the city was taken." Orlando then asked Fidel Castro, "What is your rank?" and he responded, "No, I do not have any rank." They agreed that the attack would take place at the Moncada at 5:00 A.M. and in Bayamo twenty minutes later. Martínez described this exchange as "brief and superficial," and when it ended, Fidel Castro asserted, "We are going into history." Martínez replied, "Don't you think we are going into our graves?" The trio synchronized their watches before the rebel leader departed for Santiago de Cuba. Rolando Rodríguez was then instructed to rent a downtown hotel room and inform the night clerk that he was waiting for a telephone call from his family. If the Moncada assault was postponed, someone would call and say "We cannot go to Bayamo today" to cancel the plans. Rodríguez was to return to the motel just prior to the attack.[6]

After Fidel Castro departed, the insurgents were individually called to a dimly lit back room and fitted out by Pérez-Puelles and Orlando Castro. The weapons were as inadequate as those of the Moncada combatants: .22-caliber rifles, shotguns, and two unusable .38-caliber pistols that had arrived from Havana with 9-mm bullets. The ammunition was also distributed sparingly, with Pérez-Puelles receiving about twenty shotgun shells. The Bayamo rebels, like their Siboney counterparts, wore ill-fitting uniforms. Pedro Aguilera wore an oversized outfit with black-and-white shoes. Adalberto Ruanes had to roll up his uniform pant cuffs and shirt sleeves. The slender Pérez-Puelles, who was six feet, two inches tall, said that he "felt ridiculous in clothes that were too short and tight" and kept his civilian shirt underneath. Some rebels quickly removed their uniforms and were admonished by Orlando Castro to put them back on. The rebels were then gathered in the foyer, where Pérez-Puelles circulated his photos of the garrison and explained the combat strategy. Raúl Martínez told them that Fidel Castro and a larger group were simultaneously attacking the Moncada.[7]

The Bayamo attack plan had been drafted by Fidel Castro with information provided by Elio Rosete, the only Bayamo conspirator who had been inside the garrison on various occasions. His role was to accompany Raúl Martínez, dressed in a sergeant's uniform, to the entrance. The rebel leader would say that he had been to the Santiago de Cuba carnival and needed a place to stay. It was a common military practice to board personnel from other districts overnight, and this would not arouse suspicion, especially with Rosete vouching for him. The sentries would then be disarmed and a rebel contingent would rush in and seize the sergeant of the guard. Half of the group would capture whatever soldiers were sleeping in the dormitories, while the others would neutralize the rear-gate sentinels and let in the remaining insurgents waiting out back. After seizing the garrison, they would attack the police station. Pedro Aguilera would then drive to Charco Redondo and get the miners, who would dynamite the road bridges between Bayamo and Holguín. This would impede the Holguín army regiment from advancing on Bayamo and Santiago de Cuba. Rosete later admitted that "the plan was bound to fail. The .22-caliber rifles were no match against army weapons. It had a very strong psychological effect." He then begged for a chance to visit his pregnant wife and his son at home briefly, claiming that it might be the last time he would see them. Due to his constant whining, which Martínez deemed bad for the group's morale, he was allowed to leave. "I will be back in a few minutes," promised Rosete.[8]

The prevailing tension inside the Gran Casino was heightened by the sporadic knocks on the door from couples wanting to use the facility. Although signs had been posted announcing that the motel was closed for remodeling, some people insisted that they did not mind the disorder, and these were turned away on various occasions. The situation worsened after 11:00 P.M. when the proprietor Juan Manuel Martínez returned to sleep in the building. Orlando Castro recalled that "when the old man saw Raúl in uniform he jested, 'Hello, general.'" Martínez took the owner into a back room and stated that they were an investigative unit from Camp Columbia rooting out local corruption and that they were going to arrest some bandits in uniform. The landlord agreed, exclaiming that some soldiers were indeed crooks and adding, "seeing as how things are fine here, I am going home." Orlando then retorted, "Now you cannot leave. Had you not come, you would not have this problem." The elderly man, confined to a rocking chair, was later chided for repeatedly guzzling a bottle of cognac.[9]

The attack plan had to be altered when Elio Rosete did not return by midnight. It would exclude the frontal approach and focus on entering surreptitiously through the back gate. Ñico López then received a pair of wire cutters and was assigned the task of breeching the barbed-wire fence at the rear of the garrison. Rosete gave a conflicting account: "I did not go to the attack because they did not want me to. It seems they felt something was going to go wrong and they wanted someone who knew the area well to help them solve any problem that might occur later." The all-night vigil discouraged others who had second thoughts about the possibility of success. Seventeen-year-old Pablo "Machito" Agüero Guedes told Raúl Martínez at 2:30 A.M. that Marianao cell leader Hugo Camejo, Andrés García Díaz, and his stepbrother Pedro Véliz had just fled through the side door of their room but that he refused to go with them because he was a man of principles. The rebel leader, worried that more desertions would abort his mission, gathered the remaining twenty-one insurgents in the foyer to watch them closely. He ordered his brother Mario to guard the entrance with a rifle while Orlando Castro covered the back door with a shotgun.[10]

Another alarming situation developed when a vehicle on the side street of the motel constantly blared its horn. Some rebels feared that it might be a signal initiating a police raid, but they then saw that Mario Martínez's car, which he had earlier used for an errand, was blocking the road. Mario went to move the car halfway clad in pants, a T-shirt, and barefoot, pretending to have been awakened so as not to arouse suspicion. The rebels then noticed that the army sentry at the Public Works Department depository across the street, who usually had coffee with the motel owner at daybreak, kept glancing over at the building. Raúl Martínez and Pérez-Puelles took turns standing on a chair to peek at him through the lintel window. Martínez recalled, "We were unsure of what to do with the soldier, whether to ignore or detain him. The drunken proprietor, who was very cooperative, suggested calling him over so that we could seize him." The rebels decided to disregard the sentry.[11]

Most of the rebels remained awake due to anxiety and stress, but Gerardo Pérez-Puelles, Ramiro Sánchez, Agustín "Thompson" Díaz Cartaya, and Calixto García Martínez fell soundly asleep, with the latter snoring loudly. Raúl Martínez recalled, "Just prior to leaving, we had a hard time awakening Thompson, who was a heavy sleeper." He then gathered the remaining force and gave a brief patriotic speech, stressing that no matter what happened, they had to fulfill their mission. The rebel leader announced that if they were defeated, the remnants should regroup on the opposite bank of the Bayamo River behind the garrison until knowing what transpired in Santiago de Cuba. Martínez concluded by saying, "Well, lads, it is 4:45. The moment has arrived. Let's go! Some are missing, but we cannot wait. Forward!" Orlando Castro recalled that as the attackers exited through the side doors and climbed into their four vehicles, "we made so much noise leaving the motel, that we must have awakened the whole block. I was surprised that the sentry across the street did not come over to investigate." The drunken proprietor remained behind saying that he would straighten up the place.[12]

The Carlos Manuel de Céspedes garrison, headquarters of the Rural Guard Thirteenth Squadron, was built in 1903. It had a crenelated rubble masonry wall on its facade and east side, parallel to a dirt road. A chain-link fence enclosed the back, which had a rear gate, and the west side along the Bayamo River. To the immediate right of the entrance was the enlisted men's club, a neoclassic-style rubble masonry building constructed in 1935. In the center of the compound stood the U-shaped wooden barracks. Further back were three parallel structures containing the kitchen, the garage, and the stable. There was a vacant lot behind the garrison, used as the kitchen garbage dump, which was enclosed by a four-foot-high, five-strand barbed-wire fence. The main entrance was kept closed at night while the sentries stood guard inside. Forty-five soldiers were assigned to the squadron, only a dozen of whom were present. Eight were asleep in the wooden barracks, three were on guard duty, and the kitchen auxiliary, Pvt. Dionisio Jorge García, had been up since 4:00 A.M. brewing coffee. The other troops were either sleeping at home or on duty at the guard posts at Veguitas, Río Cauto, Mabay, Santa Rita, Jiguaní, Baire, and Cauto Cristo. Some of these posts lacked quarters, as did the soldiers stationed at sugar mills in the region, and the guards slept in private residences. Rebel leaders Raúl Martínez, Gerardo Pérez-Puelles, and Orlando Castro admitted being unaware of the lack of military strength in Bayamo and assuming that they faced superior numbers. When the author told Martínez Ararás that there were only twelve soldiers in the barracks, he exclaimed, "Had we known that, we could have taken over the garrison with only our fists!"[13]

The rebel caravan that departed the Gran Casino drove three blocks and turned left on General García Street, stopping on the dirt road next to the rear vacant lot of the garrison. Raúl Martínez and Gerardo Pérez-Puelles were among those in the first vehicle; Pedro Aguilera followed behind with another group; Mario Martínez drove the third automobile with four companions; and Orlando Castro was one of the passengers in the last car. While walking toward the rear barbed-wire fence, Raúl Martínez requested from Ñico López the wire-cutter tool assigned to him. Ñico had left it at the motel, prompting an unexpected delay as the men cautiously surmounted the prickly obstacle. As the intruders crossed the vacant lot in the darkness, they stumbled on piles of firewood and hundreds of discarded tin cans littering the ground. A startled dog began barking, and more than a dozen horses in the stable started neighing and snorting. The rebels then discovered that the rear chain-link fence postern, kept open during the daytime, was padlocked at night. The back gate sentry, Pvt. Juan P. Navarro Molina, at that moment had been ordered out of the kitchen and back to his post by corporal of the guard Indalecio Estrada Calderón. Upon hearing the commotion, Navarro called out, "Who is out there? What is going on?" The rebel Antonio "El Gallego" López García immediately opened fire. He described how "Soldiers and Texan horses inside the garrison started a hurly-burly. We made a condensed fire with our weapons that certainly were too light."[14]

Private Navarro was hit in the arm and exclaimed, "Brother, I've been winged!" as Corporal Estrada went to assist him. Estrada saw strangers wearing army uniforms and lacking regulation hats advancing toward the back gate. He initially assumed that they were soldiers and wondered why they were not using the main entrance. The corporal yelled at them to stop, dropped to one knee, and took aim with his Thompson .45-caliber machine gun. The attackers replied with shouts to surrender and a volley of lead that whizzed by the corporal's head and slammed into the stable behind him. Estrada sought cover behind the stable wall, emptied his machine gun clip in three bursts, and went to get more ammunition. His bullets stitched the ground near the rebels and gouged holes in their lead vehicle. Estrada wrongly estimated that only two or three insurgents were able to cross the barbed-wire fence and take cover behind the wood stacks. Raúl Martínez stated that most of his men passed the first obstacle but were not able to breach the chain-link fence without the wire cutter. The rebel leader, commanding twenty-one closely grouped insurgents in a narrow field, ordered them to take positions behind the kindling piles and to shoot at those in the garrison.[15]

The eight soldiers in the barracks, awakened by the shooting, began firing their Springfield rifles through the dormitory windows and shouted at their adversaries, "What is happening? What is going on?" Raúl Martínez ordered a brief cease-fire so that his response could be heard: "Surrender, Batista has fallen." In retrospect, Orlando Castro thought that it was absurd to expect that the fortified and better-equipped military men would passively surrender after being attacked. The soldiers renewed their rifle fire, and Corporal Estrada, positioned between the stable and a jeep in front of the garage, opened up again with his machine gun. Martínez ducked behind a kindling pile when he felt a stream of large-caliber bullets spraying dirt around him. Orlando Castro would later recall the chilling effect of listening to the pinging sound of their .22 rifles against the loud report of the Springfield rifles and the machine-gun staccato.[16]

Pérez-Puelles, firing a 12-gauge shotgun while kneeling on his left leg, was situated between Raúl Martínez and Ramiro Sánchez. Five minutes into the fight, he felt a blow on his thigh and, assuming that Sánchez had accidentally kicked him, snarled at him to move over. Pérez-Puelles then noticed blood stains on his trousers and later remembered being "hit in front of the left thigh by a .30-caliber bullet that went out the back. It was a clean shot that did not hit the femur or the artery. Since I was not feeling pain or bleeding profusely, I continued shooting and told Raúl I was wounded." He was the only rebel combat casualty. Martínez indicated that the darkness was the major reason that none of his followers died in battle. Corporal Estrada's horse was killed by three bullets. Thirty years later Orlando Castro recalled that his most unforgettable sight was the frightened horses racing back and forth across the line of fire.[17]

Pérez-Puelles expended his twenty shotgun shells within fifteen minutes after being wounded. Raúl Martínez had by then emptied the two ammunition chargers for his .22-caliber rifle and decided not to waste the bullets in his .45-caliber Commander pistol. He told Pérez-Puelles, "There is nothing more we can do here. This got screwed up, we have been discovered, there was no surprise, and they are going to kill us all here." He then gave the order to withdraw. A few rebels got injured on the barbed-wire fence during their hasty retreat. At that moment Pvt. Antonio T. Blanco Rodríguez, the camp cook, arrived at the citadel and was shot in the neck by a .22-caliber bullet that exited through his mouth. Martínez estimated that the skirmish lasted ten to twenty minutes. Pérez-Puelles calculated its duration from fifteen to twenty minutes. Other rebel accounts claimed that the encounter began at 5:10 A.M. and ended ten minutes later. Corporal Estrada believed that the fight went on for ten or fifteen minutes, without any insurgent deaths. He estimated firing about thirty shots, while the soldiers spent some two hundred bullets. Estrada stressed that if the rebels had not crossed the garbage dump and instead had entered on the opposite side by the river, "they could have taken the garrison without firing a shot." Pérez-Puelles reminisced, "That was militarily a disaster. We are alive by a miracle."[18]

Pérez-Puelles threw his arm over Raúl Martínez's shoulders and hobbled back to their automobile. His childhood friends Rolando Rodríguez and Ramiro Sánchez climbed in, followed by José Testa Zaragoza. They drove a few blocks to the bank of the Bayamo River, where they abandoned their bullet-riddled car because it would attract attention. The five forded the shallow river and hid in a wooded area. Martínez was dismayed that no one followed instructions to regroup on the opposite side of the river. Moments later Testa opted to depart on his own against the wishes of his comrades, who pleaded for greater safety together. The twenty-nine-year-old flower vendor with a primary education decided to seek relatives in Holguín.[19]

Testa appeared distraught as he stopped on a Bayamo street corner, realizing that he was penniless, and pondered his next move. He shed and neatly folded his white guayabera. After walking a few blocks, he stopped a man going to work, indicated that he needed money to solve a problem, and sold his shirt for eighty cents. Testa, in a sleeveless T-shirt, headed for the bus station to buy a ticket to Holguín. His suspicious appearance prompted a woman to call the authorities. When a soldier ordered Testa to halt, he fled into a foundry but was seized by his pursuer, who escorted him to the garrison. Testa insisted that his brother Guillermo, who was in the army, could vouch for him. His captors held him until the arrival of Lt. Juan A. Roselló Pando, commander of the Rural Guard Thirteenth Squadron, who entered the garrison when the skirmish ended. Six years later Corporal Estrada testified before a revolutionary tribunal that after Lieutenant Roselló interrogated Testa, he ordered Pvt. Juan Pérez Castañeda to kill Testa. When the soldier refused, the same order was given to Pvt. Filiberto Rodríguez, who also balked. An enraged Roselló purportedly shouted, "Coward. This is how it's done," and he allegedly emptied his .38-caliber revolver into Testa's chest.[20]

When the rebels retreated from the garrison, Mario Martínez got into his rental Buick and frantically searched his pockets for the missing ignition key. He abandoned the car, ran a few blocks to a bus terminal, and crouched behind the last seat of an empty Rivas Line omnibus. An alert driver notified the Rural Guard. Mario, previously jailed for assaulting a Rural Guard in his native Colón, resisted arrest. He was struck on the head with a pistol butt and taken to the garrison. Dr. Aurelio Martínez Pimienta, who was called to assist the wounded soldiers, treated Mario's injury and tied a bandage around his head. Manuel Tamayo, who lived next to the garrison, claimed that he and his friend Delio Sosa Aguilar looked into the compound at about 8:00 A.M. and saw a light-haired prisoner bleeding at the mouth. They then heard two shots fired and saw the man, drenched in blood, fall to the ground. Another neighbor gave a different account, claiming that the detainee was killed with rifle-butt blows to the head. The bodies of Mario and Testa were laid out inside the barracks to simulate death in combat.[21]

After the rebels were routed, Pedro Aguilera, Thompson Díaz Cartaya, and El Gallego López García jumped over a wooden fence adjacent to the garrison and into the backyard of a house on General García Street. Its inhabitant, fifty-five-year-old José Desiderio Corona Fernández, opened the back door and queried the uniformed intruders. "Some prisoners have escaped" was the answer. "Prisoners? You are crazy," replied Corona. Sensing the imminent danger to himself, his wife, his seven children, and the strangers, he allowed them inside. The rebels removed their uniforms, bathed, and wore the clothes that they had kept underneath. El Gallego López quickly departed alone. Meanwhile, the Corona family shredded the uniforms, buried the pieces inside large flower pots, and discarded the spare bullets in the toilet. Aguilera received a guayabera and a pair of shoes, having lost one of his own while fleeing. At his request, the family accompanied him and Thompson to the train station, where they obtained passage to Havana via Santiago de Cuba. Díaz Cartaya returned to Marianao and was quickly detained as a possible suspect. He was released that same afternoon when a friend, 2nd Lt. Julio M. Sed Arias, mistakenly vouched for his whereabouts on Saturday night. Thompson was rearrested three hours later when a police bulletin confirmed that his wallet was found in the Gran Casino. A paraffin test on his hands proved that he had recently fired a weapon. El Gallego López, after leaving the Corona residence, got into a rebel car with Ñico López, Calixto García, and Armando Arencibia. El Gallego stated, "Ñico took the vehicle without knowing how to drive. He did not work the clutch right and the car started jerking. After a few blocks we went into a ditch in the street. We could not continue in the car and proceeded on foot." The four rebel vehicles were later impounded by the authorities.[22]

News of the attack reached police sergeant Gerónimo R. Suárez Camejo while he was having breakfast at the Vista Alegre café. The forty-two-year-old officer had been the Santiago de Cuba chief of transit until his recent transfer to Bayamo. He was substituting that day for police chief Adolfo Fernández, who had gone to the Santiago de Cuba carnival. Suárez Camejo got into the front passenger seat of his jeep and told the driver to head for the garrison. When they reached the intersection of José Martí and Santa Isabel streets at 5:50 A.M., their vehicle was spotted by Ñico López and his three companions in the nearby San Juan Park. Ñico, leaning against a monument to steadily aim his 12-gauge shotgun, wantonly murdered Suárez Camejo. The driver sought cover in a nearby house while the four rebels ran to the city limits and hid in a thicket.[23]

While fleeing from the garrison, Orlando Castro heard someone calling his name. Pivoting, he leveled his shotgun at a man in uniform. "Don't shoot, Castro. I am with you," replied Enrique Cámara Pérez. "Okay, let's go," said Orlando; "we have to get out of here." They stopped two blocks away, in front of the Calás Cafetería, where a half-dozen clients, including some uniformed bus-line employees, were sipping espresso and speculating about the gunfire. Juan Olazábal Garcés, a mulatto foster son of motel proprietor Juan Manuel Martínez, emerged from his nearby home buttoning his shirt. "What is going on here?" he asked. "I am in the best disposition to help," he said to the insurgents, assuming that they were soldiers. Orlando snapped back, "You want to help the army?" When Olazábal hesitantly started to reply, "Well . . .," "the rebel leader raised his voice, "Do you really want to help the army?," to which the puzzled young man replied, "Well, no, not me." Orlando tried to incite an insurrection by haranguing the patrons, proclaiming that the "revolution" was in progress and the tyrant Batista was being overthrown. He recalled, "No one said anything. They looked at me like if I was crazy."[24]

Olazábal, noticing that Orlando Castro was startled when a military jeep raced by, warned them to leave quickly. The rebels were indecisive about what to do. Olazábal pointed to a parked milk truck and told them to take it. The frightened milkman, José Collada Alonso, returning with an empty carrying case, was hesitant to leave. Orlando asked Cámara if he knew how to drive. Receiving a negative reply, he responded, "I also do not know how to drive." Olazábal then seized the initiative and said, "Make the milkman take you. Don't you have a rifle with you?" The two rebels boarded the milk truck and told the driver to whisk them away. Collada started bawling, made references to his family, and nervously careened the vehicle onto the sidewalk. He then stopped at every intersection, asking if he had driven far enough. Orlando insisted on leaving the downtown area and reaching the Manzanillo highway. Cámara threatened the milkman, who got hysterical, although Orlando managed to calm him down for ten minutes until he left them at the Lallanilla farm in the suburbs.[25]

The two rebels made their way into the countryside, arriving at noon at a peasant's hut, where they received lunch and changed into work clothes. Orlando had the farmer mail for him a terse letter to his family in Havana, signed with a pseudonym, assuring that he was fine. Before the guests departed two hours later, the man's wife had the fugitives kneel and pray with her in front of a small altar crowded with images of saints. She assured them, "You will be safe. God is watching over you." The insurgents discarded their weapons and walked for more than an hour through the woods contiguous to the highway. Cámara flagged down a bus to Manzanillo, thirty-one miles west of Bayamo, from which location he took public transport to Santiago de Cuba the next day and then continued on another bus to Camagüey. Orlando stated that because his companion was mulatto he easily blended with the majority of the province's population. Cámara panhandled and hitchhiked back to Marianao within a few days. He was later detained and taken to SIM headquarters for questioning. Cámara gave a false explanation for his infected and swollen hand, which had been injured on the garrison's barbed-wire fence when he was fleeing, but was incarcerated after a paraffin test proved positive. He and Díaz Cartaya later signed confessions implicating themselves in the revolt.[26]

After Cámara departed, Orlando Castro waited an hour before boarding another bus to Manzanillo. He removed his wristwatch, an item not used by peasants; discarded the wristband; and put the watch face in his pocket to avoid attracting attention. The vehicle was stopped and searched twice by the military, while the rebel in peasant clothes fretted over the strong smell of gunpowder on his hands. After arriving in Manzanillo at 8:00 P.M., he asked a taxi driver to take him to the home of Nelson Bécquer, the local salesman of Sabatés products and a former Ortodoxo city councilman until the Batista coup. Orlando was erroneously left at the residence of patriarch Gustavo Bécquer, on Pedro Figueredo Street, who refused to let him stay there shortly before the 9:00 P.M. curfew, saying, "You have come to the wrong place. My son is hiding and this house is under surveillance by the police because he is an Ortodoxo activist." Orlando walked to a cafeteria a few blocks away and bought ice cream. After hearing the final curfew call, he boarded a local bus that pulled into its garage terminal five minutes later. The fugitive, pretending to be a peasant looking for work, was allowed by the garage owner to sleep in the parked bus. He remained awake most of the night, fearful and tense, listening to the military jeeps circulating the area. At daylight Orlando was awakened by the clinking of milk bottles in a passing delivery wagon. He headed for the railroad station to hop a freight but found the place swarming with military police from the local naval station. At a grocery store he bought a soda and obtained directions to the storefront residence of "Chicho" Bejar, the local Sabatés distributor. Awakening Bejar at 7:00 A.M., the unkempt stranger identified himself as the Sabatés assistant credit manager from Havana. Bejar, assuming that he was a bum, replied, "We are closed, come back later" and began closing the door. Orlando stuck his foot in the jamb and desperately pleaded, "I need to enter, please." He then heard Bejar's wife, Rafaela, say, "let him in."[27]

The fugitive bathed, got clean clothes, and had breakfast. That night Nelson Bécquer, who had been searching for the insurgent, arrived with a friend and took him to the home of a bakery owner José Ramón Piñeiro on Merchán Street. The next morning Piñeiro drove Orlando Castro to the Cayo Espino hamlet at the foothills of the Sierra Maestra and snapped a photograph of him as a memento. The rebel was left with José "Pepín" Silano, a peasant huckster in his fifties, who led him on foot all night to his mountaintop *bohío*. During the next few weeks Orlando slept in a hammock in the shack's loft until covert arrangements were made for his return to Havana. Piñeiro forwarded to Orlando a radio and newspapers detailing the July 26th attacks. Reading and hearing of the many deaths caused "a great impression" on the fugitive rebel. Piñeiro later gave Orlando a conductor's uniform from La Cubana bus line as a disguise and drove him from Cayo Espino to the bus stop at Yara. The bus driver, involved in the plot, sat Orlando beside him. When the vehicle stopped at the Holguín roadblock, the phony conductor tried to muffle his nervousness by voluntarily assisting the soldiers who began searching the passengers' luggage. When he reached Havana, Orlando learned that his home had been raided by the SIM and that his mother's house was under surveillance. He then obtained asylum in the Argentine Embassy.[28]

While fleeing Bayamo, Rolando "Wiki" San Román de las Llamas and Adalberto Ruanes were chased across a bridge by soldiers shooting at them. Wiki, a twenty-four-year-old oyster vendor, jumped over the railing and landed knee-deep in the embankment mud. His corpse later appeared in a SIM photograph; he was lying in a field with his left hand holding the barrel of a shotgun resting on his shoulder. Ruanes encountered Juan Olazábal, who asked him, "Are you with those who came from Havana?" After receiving an affirmative reply, Olazábal briefly hid Ruanes in his home and provided a change of clothes. The fugitive was afterward taken by Triple A militants to the Cauto Cristo farm of Ortodoxo activist Leopoldo Gómez Ochoa, and from there he later returned to Marianao. Another insurgent, Angel Guerra Díaz, a twenty-two-year-old flower vendor, vanished without a trace after the Bayamo attack.[29]

On the city outskirts Ñico López and his three companions were hiding in the woods when a light airplane buzzed low overhead. Ñico, assuming that the pilot was Dr. Mario Muñoz bringing news from Santiago de Cuba, enthusiastically signaled the aircraft. El Gallego López chided him, "Ñico, you are crazy, they are going to see us." Around noon the rebels met a black man on horseback and followed him home for a drink of water. Ñico, El Gallego, and Arencibia entered the *bohío*, while Calixto García kept watch outside. When the rebels proposed exchanging their weapons for civilian clothes, their host told them to wait there while he returned to the woods to search for a lost wristwatch. After the rider departed, Calixto García told his comrades that through another room window he saw a portrait of Fulgencio Batista. The group immediately fled, believing that the stranger was summoning the authorities.[30]

The four fugitives were walking in the woods adjacent to the highway when they encountered another man, to whom Ñico sold his wristwatch for ten pesos. The stranger provided directions to the Santa Ana rice mill farm, where the rebels obtained soiled peasant clothes, ditched their weapons, and boarded a bus to Camagüey. The vehicle was searched in Holguín at a roadblock facing the army garrison. The unassuming El Gallego and Arencibia did not arouse suspicion, but Ñico and Calixto García, lacking identification papers, were among those removed for questioning. Both men claimed to be returning to Camagüey after being told at the rice mill to reapply for work in a month. Their story and shabby appearance fooled a lieutenant into releasing them. In Camagüey, El Gallego located a relative employed with a bus line, and this person provided the group with tickets to Havana.[31]

The three deserters from the Gran Casino—Hugo Camejo, Andrés García, and his stepbrother Pedro Véliz—went by bus to Manzanillo to find García's relatives in nearby Campechuela. They were arrested upon arriving in Manzanillo and held in the army garrison garage, along with a dozen other suspects, for a routine identification check. The detainees were interrogated by squadron chief Lt. Domingo Suárez Espinosa and Sgt. Abraham de la Paz. The following night their identities were verified by a National Police bulletin authorizing their release. As the trio was leaving, an arrest order arrived from the Bureau of Investigations in Havana, which had obtained a list of all the Marianao cell members that had been provided by the brother of a rebel. That same Monday night the three prisoners were informed that they were being taken before a judge for a preliminary hearing. Sergeant de la Paz, accompanied by six soldiers, carried a coiled rope. The squad departed with García and Camejo in one jeep and Véliz in another. The vehicles traveled fifteen miles to a sugarcane field next to the Veguitas Cemetery. García later accused Sergeant de la Paz and Private Noriega of beating the manacled prisoners with rifle butts into unconsciousness. The rebels, with ropes noosed around their necks, were dragged behind a jeep to a field and left for dead.[32]

García recalled that upon regaining his senses that afternoon, he "was in terrible pain and with a rope that strongly tightened my neck. It seems, the way it was left [knotted] and by my being the one who was tied to its end, it was not able to strangle me." He tried detecting signs of life on the corpses of his two companions before crawling to a nearby cane field. Someone noticed him going over the embankment fence and notified the Rural Guard, but he managed to get away. The next morning García obtained milk at the Ciro León dairy farm, forded the Buey River, and was aided by the peasant Bernardo Amaya López, who concealed him in a cane field and nursed him back to health. García later gave Amaya various letters to mail to his family, but the frightened man secretly burned them. García remained hidden for a few weeks until a priest arranged his surrender. His stepbrother Pedro Véliz and Hugo Camejo were buried together in the same pine box in Veguitas Cemetery.[33]

Other insurgents fled from Bayamo toward Santiago de Cuba. Rafael Freyre Torres and his companions were hiding in the woods along Central Highway on Sunday afternoon when a truck loaded with soldiers appeared in the distance. Freyre, a twenty-two-year-old bricklayer with a fourth-grade education, believed that they were Moncada rebel allies coming to join them. He went to signal the vehicle and identified himself. His concealed comrades quickly fled upon hearing gunfire. Freyre's cadaver was later found at the Ceja de Limones farm, six miles outside of Bayamo, along with dead rebels Lázaro Hernández Arroyo, Pablo Agüero Guedes, and Luciano González Camejo. The bodies were removed to Bayamo in the Casate funeral home hearse. All four, along with Mario Martínez and José Testa, who were murdered in the garrison, were buried in Bayamo Cemetery. The deserter Elio Rosete had a local barber, Robert Paneque, purchase the six burial plots at city hall.[34]

The last group of fugitives, including Raúl Martínez, Gerardo Pérez-Puelles, Rolando Rodríguez, and Ramiro Sánchez, wandered in the woods after fleeing the garrison and crossing the Bayamo River. At the *bohío* of Fernando Viñas Batista, Pérez-Puelles received the only medicinal remedy available, sulphate used on castrated animals, which he applied on his wounded thigh. The blood flow was stemmed with an herbal astringent remedy concocted by the peasant's wife. Raúl Martínez asked Viñas to find Rosete and obtain four sets of clothes and a syringe with penicillin. At the Rosete residence the peasant was told by a maid that the family had gone to Veguitas. Viñas acquired the needed items elsewhere and returned home at 6:30 P.M. to say that the Moncada attack had failed and that in both cities there were many dead rebels. Martínez decided to seek help from his wife's uncle, the attorney Antonio Varela, residing in Manzanillo. He asked Viñas to write to his mother in Havana indicating that the group was safe. The rebels departed at 8:00 P.M., determined to walk all night and rest during the daytime to avoid detection. Viñas guided them to the Manzanillo highway, and as they bid farewell, Pérez-Puelles gave him a handgun as a token of gratitude.[35]

The wounded Pérez-Puelles slowed the group's pace as they crossed the pastures contiguous to the Manzanillo highway. The next morning they encountered a black peasant named Marino Tornés, who was felling coconut trees at the San Antonio farm. Raúl Martínez requested that he locate his relative in Manzanillo. Tornés later returned with a newspaper, canned milk, cheese, and other edibles, saying that the frightened uncle refused to receive them. He also indicated that three rebels had been recently strangled nearby. Pérez-Puelles was shocked when he saw in the newspaper a photograph of José Testa, who initially fled with them, depicted as having died in combat.[36]

Pérez-Puelles suggested going to Las Mil Una farm, owned by his uncle Inocencio Valmaseda and located north of the Cauto River. Ramiro Sánchez, who as a Boy Scout had studied astronomy, led the group that night by following the North Star. The next day the fugitives reached the *bohío* of a peasant, who slaughtered a hog to feed them. He later accompanied them on the Cauto Embarcadero skiff ferry across the Cauto River. Another farmer obtained more penicillin for Pérez-Puelles and guided the rebels to their destination. The fugitives slept one night at the Valmaseda farm, discarded their weapons, and received clothes, provisions, and money before leaving in two groups. Rodríguez and Sánchez went to Camagüey and eventually arrived in Havana. Raúl Martínez and Pérez-Puelles were taken on horseback to the Omaja train station, where they bought passage to Victoria de las Tunas. They continued by bus to Camagüey, where the rebel leader was horrified by a newspaper article identifying his brother Mario among the dead in Bayamo. Both men took another bus to a friend's home in Santa Clara, where Martínez notified his family by messenger. His wife knew that he was involved in clandestine activities but was unaware of the details.[37]

Nenita Varela had been visiting friends on July 26 before returning to their El Vedado apartment at 9:00 P.M. A neighbor stopped by to say that her spouse had participated in the Oriente uprising. After a restless night, Nenita tried seeking refuge with an uncle the next day but was turned away. She then went to the safe house on Aguacate Street where her in-laws were hiding. That afternoon the Martínez family saw in the late edition of *El Crisol* newspaper a closeup photograph of Mario's cadaver. Nenita, fearing for her husband's fate and the inevitable police investigation, spent the next few days hiding at the home of his aunt. Meanwhile, SIM agents who searched her residence were unable to find any incriminating evidence. The building superintendent saw them carrying away pillowcases stuffed with housewares. He later sent word to Nenita when it was safe to return home. After Raúl Martínez returned to Havana with Pérez-Puelles, he secretly met his wife in a movie theater. Both fugitives, assisted by Juan Orta, Millo Ochoa's secretary, obtained asylum in the Argentine Embassy. They departed with Orlando Castro on September 13 for exile in Costa Rica. Ortodoxo representative José Pardo Llada, who also sought refuge in the embassy, went to Buenos Aires with a special invitation from the strongman Juan Domingo Perón.[38]

A few hours after the Bayamo attack, motel owner Juan Manuel Martínez, his adopted son Juan Olazábal, taxi driver Sergio González Machado, and Fernando Fernández Catá were rounded up and taken to the garrison for interrogation. Olazábal was soon released. The Bayamo police chief, Capt. Adolfo Fernández, who had unwittingly met with the rebel leaders two days before the attack, was relieved of his post and placed under arrest in the Moncada garrison on Monday, July 27. That afternoon former mayor and Ortodoxo representative Alberto

Saumell Soto was arrested at the Bayamo bus station while waiting to travel to the capital, along with Havana resident José Velasco Montalvo, who was carrying a .38-caliber revolver without a permit. No further arrests linked to the revolt were made in the city.[39]

The last detention related to the Bayamo attack occurred in early August at Holguín when nineteen-year-old Manuel J. Norman García-Iñiguez was removed from a bus headed for Havana and held in the Calixto García garrison. The teenager, born and raised in England, had been living with relatives near Bayamo during the previous year. The authorities believed that his Boy Scout trousers were part of a stolen army uniform. Other "incriminating evidence" discovered in his suitcase included a Boy Scout knife and a hand-drawn street map of Bayamo in a loose-leaf folder. Norman also did not know some of the answers to the questions being asked, prompting the authorities to believe that he was being evasive. The youth was not ill-treated during the few days that he stayed in the barracks with the soldiers while his alibi was verified. He stated that he was the great-grandson of General García, after whom the military base was named, and joked that if he were to stay any longer he "might as well join the army." Upon his release, an officer wrote a safe-conduct note on the back of his bus ticket, which got him through another checkpoint in Santa Clara.[40]

The Bayamo strategy drafted by Fidel Castro was described by Raúl Martínez as being "theoretical, improvised, and without depth." Martínez still believes that the plan would have succeeded if Rosete had abided by his assigned role of bluffing their way into the garrison. Fidel Castro never indicated what to do once Bayamo was taken, other than to blow up the bridges over the Cauto River and await his orders. The bridges, located nine and eighteen miles north of Bayamo, were guarded by lone sentries and could have been easily destroyed without attacking the military post. Bayamo was an ineffective target since its seizure could not impede troop reinforcements from being airlifted to Moncada. In contrast to that at Santiago de Cuba, there was no plan to seize a radio station and harangue the Bayamo populace. There was no alternative strategy if Moncada failed and Bayamo were taken. Martínez stated that under such a scenario it would have been suicidal to hold the city.

Fidel Castro was concerned that his own revolutionary role would diminish if he lost at Moncada and that the seemingly easier Bayamo victory would catapult Raúl Martínez to historical fame. He did make the right choice in having Martínez lead the Bayamo attack instead of the indeterminate Abel Santamaría. The latter vacillated in the Civil Hospital after the Moncada defeat, failed to evacuate his force, and relegated himself to the orders of his older sister Haydée. Martínez wisely chose Orlando Castro as his second-in-command rather than Marianao cell leader Hugo Camejo, who deserted at the last moment. Martínez demonstrated leadership under fire while commanding a score of attackers. He faced the same problem as Fidel

Castro after ordering the retreat—his raw recruits fled in disarray and forgot their orders to regroup on the opposite bank of the Bayamo River. In contrast to those in Santiago de Cuba, the Bayamo rebels suffered only one wounded rebel, had no incidents of friendly fire, and suffered no combat deaths.

Orlando Castro believes that the Bayamo plan was a folly. He thinks that the attackers should have seized the camp commander at home and forced him to lead their way into the garrison. Orlando indicated that the Bayamo police station could have been easily taken the same way without firing a shot. He stated, "We were acting like an amateur chess player who does not think beyond each move." Orlando Castro declared that his only goal as Bayamo city administrator under a revolutionary government was to provide shoes to all barefoot children. He hoped that their revolt would serve as a detonator to free Cuba from tyranny and affirmed that he "was led to believe that after overthrowing the Batista regime, Fidel Castro would not be the leading national figure and political power would be handed over to the Ortodoxos and other traditional opposition parties."[41]

The assault on the Bayamo garrison was a disaster comparable to the Moncada attack. In both camps the insurgents were novices highly motivated by youthful idealism and contemplating only immediate victory. Four rebels deserted in Bayamo, and twelve backed out in Siboney. The surprise attack element was lost in both cities. Inadequate rebel intelligence failed to note that the Bayamo garrison rear gate was locked at night, while their comrades in Santiago de Cuba were unaware that Post 3 was closed until 6:00 a.m. Ñico López forgot to take the wire cutter to breach the back fence, and the vanguard car at Moncada was left blocking the Post 3 entrance. Likewise, neither rebel group had an accurate estimate of the number of troops in both garrisons. Their inferior weapons and ammunition shortened the length of combat and impeded victory. In both cities the rebels lacked medical supplies, and most of their vehicles were abandoned during their flight. The Bayamo insurgents acted with undue excess after their defeat by killing a police sergeant and wounding a soldier arriving at the garrison. The military chief in Bayamo was as ruthless as his counterpart in Moncada in sanctioning the murder of the prisoners. The attackers who survived in both cities fled into the countryside and were assisted by peasants and Ortodoxo activists. Although Fidel Castro expected the revolt to inspire a popular uprising, this failed to materialize in Oriente, despite defiantly shouted revolutionary slogans and Orlando Castro's patriotic street-corner harangue at dawn.

SIX

"That savagery cannot be blamed on Batista"

In Havana the only person aware of the impending attack was Fidel Castro's paramour Naty Revuelta. He had assigned her to distribute the "Manifesto to the Nation" to reporters and the American Embassy and to warn Ortodoxo Party leaders of their imminent peril. Leaving her home at dawn on Sunday, July 26, Naty delivered the document to Pelayo Cuervo Navarro, Roberto Agramonte Pichardo, and Raúl Chibás Rivas, indicating that Castro was leading an insurrection in Oriente and suggesting that they should hide. Naty then relayed the same message to elderly statesman Cosme de la Torriente but was unable to locate Miguel Angel Quevedo, the publisher of *Bohemia* magazine, who was out of town. She next gave the manifesto to Raúl Rivero, editor of *Diario Nacional,* and at the home of Sergio Carbó, editor of *Prensa Libre,* she left the document with his son-in-law Humberto Medrano. Naty then returned home to await news of the insurrection. The manifesto was not delivered to the closed U.S. Embassy and was not published due to the press censorship decreed that Sunday night.[1]

That morning Ortodoxo leader Millo Ochoa was awakened in his Havana residence by a machine-gun muzzle pressing against his head. The maid had inadvertently opened the door to SIM colonel Irenaldo García Baez and his agents, who took Ochoa to their Camp Columbia headquarters. Millo was questioned regarding his return from Santiago de Cuba the previous night on the 6:00 P.M. Cubana flight. Communist Party leader Juan Marinello Vidaurreta had been on the same plane and told Ochoa that he had been in Santiago de Cuba with other comrades celebrating the birthday of Blas Roca Calderío. The *Havana Post* reported, "Four Communists arrested in Holguín claimed they had come to Santiago de Cuba to attend a celebration in honor of Blas Roca, which had been suspended and had been on their way home via Holguín, where they were arrested Sunday." This sounded highly suspicious because Roca, a Manzanillo native, lived in Havana. Government agents perceived this coincidence as part of a cold-war Communist conspiracy against the Batista regime. The SIM immediately closed the offices of the Communist newspaper *Hoy*. The party leadership circumvented censorship ten days later by publishing an official statement denouncing the Moncada attack in the *New York Daily Worker*: "We repudiate the putschist method, peculiar to bourgeois political factions, of the action in Santiago de Cuba and Bayamo, which was an adventuristic attempt to take both military headquarters. The heroism displayed by the participants in this action is false and sterile, as it is guided by mistaken bourgeois conceptions."[2]

SIM agents also targeted Auténtico activists. Ignacio A. Fiterre Rivera, a thirty-eight-year-old mathematics professor at La Víbora Institute and member of the clandestine Triple A organization directive, got careless that Sunday morning. He had been underground since the aborted Easter Sunday insurrection, after the authorities erroneously accused him of being the link between Triple A chief Aureliano Sánchez Arango and MNR leader Rafael García-Bárcena. Fiterre was detained by SIM agents at home while picking up his children for an outing. Ramiro Arango Alsina, a twenty-nine-year-old attorney who attended the Montreal Conference as an Auténtico observer, was at the Casino Español beach resort that morning. He sought refuge in a friend's home after being told by telephone that his residence was surrounded by the police. Arango surrendered to the SIM a few weeks later. Two months earlier, on May 27, 1953, a U.S. State Department memorandum had described Arango as "a man who has been thrown out of his own country's foreign service for dishonesty, and a man who is strongly suspected of trafficking with our enemies, the Communists."[3]

Scores of renowned revolutionaries and political opponents were detained throughout the island, especially those who had attended the Montreal Conference. Many were released within a few hours, including five former military officers and two former Havana police chiefs, when their alibis excluded them from the uprising. In Palma Soriano, Oriente, the former mayor, the Ortodoxo Party president and the youth leader, Prío's former undersecretary of defense, and fourteen others were interrogated in the Rural Guard barracks. In Manzanillo the Rural Guard chief had the leading political opponents arrested for questioning and released them that afternoon. In the city of Camagüey, Auténtico leaders Manuel Antonio de Varona Loredo and his brother Roberto were detained at the airport shortly after flying in from Havana and then were promptly freed. In Santa Cruz del Sur opposition spokesmen, labor leaders, and some Communists were held for five hours. In Las Villas Province the authorities protected public buildings and foreign properties and occupied the Santa Clara Institute but made no arrests. In Matanzas Province more than sixty persons were arrested, including the ex-governor, the deposed mayor, Prío's minister of labor Arturo Hernández Tellaheche, and other activists, some of whom were taken to SIM headquarters in Havana. In the town of Los Palos, Nueva Paz municipality, Mario Hidalgo-Gato González was detained after the Rural Guard discovered the rebel target range at his farm. Fifteen paper targets were found with the shooting records and signatures of Hidalgo-Gato and eleven rebels. In Pinar del Río Province the army regimental chief, unaware of the large rebel contingent from Artemisa that went to Santiago de Cuba, made no arrests and assured that there was peace.[4]

Soon after the attack in Santiago de Cuba, some news reporters headed for Moncada. Marta Rojas Rodríguez, a twenty-three-year-old local freelance reporter, was covering the carnival for *Bohemia* magazine. She was accompanied by part-time photographer Francisco "Panchito" Cano, a police lieutenant assigned to the Moncada's Bureau of Press and Radio. They entered the Los Angeles Clinic at 6:20 A.M. and from a second-floor window viewed the fortress for thirty minutes. Cano and Rojas then walked to Post 2, where they encountered other journalists. These included two *Diario de Cuba* reporters and a photographer, who began taking pictures. A sergeant threw the photographer's camera on the ground and locked the trio in a Guard Corps detention cell. They were released fifteen minutes later by Colonel del Río Chaviano.[5]

After the garrison was secured, the regimental chief had radio communications relay a message to every military post in Oriente Province alerting them to possible attack. He sent out platoons to scour the city, especially the railway and bus terminals, the airport, hospitals, clinics, and lodgings. Patrols were assigned to check pedestrian identification at all major urban intersections and along Central Highway. Anyone found wounded was to be immediately remitted to the Moncada. Colonel del Río Chaviano sent twenty soldiers to occupy the telephone exchange and the electric company, and to investigate the situation at Naval Headquarters in Punta Blanca. José Tobío, who had earlier driven a bus into the Moncada to pick up the National Police Marching Band, offered to take a platoon as an excuse to leave the citadel.[6]

Tobío drove the troops downtown in his bullet-riddled bus, leaving a squad to occupy the telephone company. He was then ordered to wait one block from the Naval Headquarters while another squad went to investigate there. Maj. Gumersindo Fernández Febles, the second-in-command at the naval base, denied entry to the soldiers because he feared that they might be part of a coup d'état, and he refused to send reinforcements to Moncada. Pvt. Ernesto Cuello Silveira recalled doing a visual inspection of the naval facility before being ordered back to camp. The apprehensive Fernández Febles was arrested by his subordinates, who asked Naval Headquarters in Havana for permission to submit him to a summary court-martial. The high command defused the situation by replying that "Fernández Febles had been retired from the Service five days earlier, although his retirement had not yet been published."[7]

Tobío returned with the soldiers to the Moncada, parked his bus outside the gate, and accompanied the officers to regimental headquarters. Private Cuello was summoned to Colonel del Río Chaviano's office, where he saw him sitting on the floor behind his desk with his back against the wall and three telephones in front of him. Cuello, who spoke English, was instructed by the colonel to telephone American consul Henry Story and say that the situation was under control and that the military expected the cooperation of the United States government. After Cuello relayed the message and received a positive reply, the regimental chief hugged him and those in the office applauded, assuming that they had gained the crucial backing of the American authorities. The consul telephoned the American Embassy in Havana at 11:30 A.M. to report that "firing continued fairly heavily until 8:00 A.M. with desultory shots still being heard." He called back a few hours later to confirm "unusual activity at Siboney" and all civilian "traffic prevented from entering or leaving the city." Tobío, waiting outside the colonel's office with blood dribbling from facial lacerations received at the start of the attack, was confronted by two armed soldiers who ordered him to raise his hands and identify himself. "Don't touch him, that's my boss," retorted bus terminal ticket clerk Ibis Fonseca, peering from an office door. She was one of the colonel's paramours and had gone to Moncada to inquire about her employer's fate. Tobío received a clean shirt and Mercurochrome to dab his cuts. He departed for home unaware of the reprisals being taken against the rebel prisoners, which constituted the random shots heard by the American consul during three and one-half hours.[8]

Some soldiers affected by the death of relatives or close friends clamored for vengeance. The Moncada regiment was closely interrelated through family ties. Maj. Rafael Morales Alvarez had sixteen relatives in the service when his brother Andrés was killed in the attack. The dead included the brothers of Feraud, Izquierdo, and Pompa. The wounded Cpl. Norberto Batista Seguí had two brothers, Luis Manuel and Juan, serving at Moncada, and their father was an army retiree. The father of the wounded Pvt. Lázaro Tejadilla was an army sergeant. The authorities were appalled at the nature of the sneak attack, the forty-nine government casualties, and the personal tragedies, including that of the pregnant widow of Pvt. Eusebio Baró Melodio, who was left with eight children.[9]

The rank and file of the army, enlisted under four-year contracts, consisted mostly of peasants without land or education and the urban unemployed, with barely primary schooling. They were humble, family men who were disciplined and loyal. Afro-Cubans constituted approximately one-third of the army officers, and a higher percentage of blacks and mulattoes existed in the lower ranks. The number of biracial soldiers was greater at Moncada, which was located in the predominantly Afro-Cuban province of Oriente. A strong solidarity flourished among those who wore the revered military uniform. They admired General Batista because he was one of their own: a multiracial former cane cutter, railroad brakeman, and barber who had risen through the ranks into the highest national office. Batista, in turn, used his own heritage to appeal for Afro-Cuban support. Col. Ramón M. Barquín López, imprisoned in 1956 for conspiring against Batista, wrote of his former troops: "For the illiterate soldier, of rural origins, the Republic ended in the limits of the garrison and loyalty was unconditionally constrained to the immediate chief. The blind subordination to his commander was the guarantee of conserving the comfort he enjoyed and the basis for obtaining betterments in the future. In other words, they became soldiers without forging in each one a citizen consciousness. The total dependence fatally engendered the unconditional submission."[10]

Some officers and soldiers at Moncada belonged to Masonic lodges and as a result were usually more ethical and circumspect than others. Capt. Juan de Dios Ruiz Herrera was a thirty-third-degree Freemason, while Maj. Rafael Morales Alvarez and police major José Izquierdo Rodríguez were lodge officials. The three remained in Cuba after 1959, and the Castro regime, recognizing their merit in battle and nonparticipation in atrocities, never prosecuted them. In contrast, Colonel del Río Chaviano was blackballed from joining a Masonic lodge at Palma Soriano. The Afro-Cuban lieutenant Antonio Ochoa Ferrer, his confidant, stated that del Río Chaviano's "problem" was "being a playboy." Lt. Carlos Lazo Cuba, Cpl. Norberto Batista Seguí, Pvts. Rafael and Orlando Morales Gros, Ariel Matos, Osvaldo Toledo Niebla, and other soldiers described their former commanding officer as a hedonist who indulged in orgies. They also claimed that the colonel received payoffs from brothels, casinos, and illegal lottery bankers. Col. Orlando Piedra, chief of the Bureau of Investigations, wrote in his memoirs that del Río Chaviano later continued his bacchanalia in a Havana hotel.[11]

The regimental chief got part of the Casa Granda Hotel's casino franchise from its owners. According to Corporal Batista Seguí, casino administrator Ernesto Vargas Machuca had to make regular large payoffs to Colonel del Río Chaviano. The cash was picked up by the SIR chief Capt. Agustín "Bebo" Lavastida Alvarez. The SIR also had an agent in mufti as a bouncer in the casino. Other large payoffs were received from the Club Aponte; El Maracas, which was half-owned by the colonel; and other casinos. The exclusive brothels of Lola Bragaña, Amada, and María Soto also had to submit their quotas. Colonel del Río Chaviano had his two closest aides, Lts. Teodoro Rico Boué and Antonio Ochoa Ferrer, collecting the graft in the city, while Pvt. Roberto Lescano Lescano, Lavastida's assistant, retrieved it from the regional outposts. The corruption was nationwide, "from top to bottom," according to Afro-Cuban Capt. Rosendo Abreu Jiménez. "It was well organized and I was part of it. If a general you work for gives you an envelope with money, you are not going to question where it came from." The officer commanding a rural post had to collect local bribes for the squadron chief, who in turn had to give a portion to the regimental colonel. All eight regimental chiefs then answered to the army chief of staff Maj. Gen. Francisco Tabernilla Dolz.[12]

The soldiers knew of this deeply rooted corruption, which had been endemic in most Latin American countries since colonial times. Lt. Vicente Camps Ruiz, a forty-year-old officer who enlisted in 1934, exclaimed, "I was an illiterate peasant who became an army officer. To me, anyone who wore a military uniform was my brother. We had good comrades, but also some who brought disgrace. There were more good than bad, but the populace only wanted to look at the rotten side of the apple. There was a lot of negligence in army headquarters; those who were closest to Batista were the first to betray him. On the other hand, the relatives of the rebel martyrs of Moncada, instead of blessing Fidel, they should hate him because he is the one who tricked them into going there to get killed."[13]

Sgt. Eulalio "El Mulo" González, with more than twenty years in the army, exclaimed, "I did not invent the revolutions of the Fourth of September or the Tenth of March. I had been in the service all my life. I do not think the Moncada soldiers were to blame for those revolutionary events occurring in Havana. The rebels came to assassinate us in our homes and I was not going to stand by with my arms folded. What can you ask of a soldier whose brother has just been murdered? If a soldier got violent, it was provoked by the killing of his relatives. I am glad that many attackers died because that group later gave my country away to Russia." Pvt. José Olivares concurred, "The nineteen soldiers and policemen killed on July 26 were the first martyrs of the struggle against Communism in Cuba."[14]

The violence bewildered the Santiago de Cuba citizenry. Some believed that the fracas involved a group of drunken soldiers who were returning to the barracks after the carnival and then fired on those trying to arrest them. Fidel Castro later acknowledged that "Santiago thought our attack was only a local disturbance between two factions of soldiers." The businessman Enrique Canto recalled that "the populace remained calm, indifferent to everything that happened. They were upset that the carnival festivities had been suspended and called crazy those who had launched the attack against the garrison without any possibility of success."[15]

Some rebel detainees quickly implicated Fidel Castro and revealed the location of the Siboney farmhouse, prompting Colonel del Río Chaviano to dispatch Lt. Angel Machado Rofe with a squad of soldiers in three jeeps. They arrived at Villa Blanca about 10:00 A.M. and discovered an abandoned car outside. The deserted house was strewn with civilian clothing, army uniforms, weapons, ammunition, and many personal documents. These included Melba Hernández's attorney identification, bus ticket stubs from Havana and Artemisa, and greeting cards from La Perla de Cuba Hotel. The Moncada chief sent Sgt. El Mulo González with a squad in a pickup truck to retrieve Maj. Florentino E. Rosell Leyva, chief of the Army Corps of Engineers, from the Rancho Club motel in Quintero Heights. Rosell stated that after arriving at regimental headquarters, he helped "write down the names and personal information of those arrested on the street." Lt. Jesús Yanez Pelletier, the thirty-six-year-old military supervisor of the Boniato Provincial Prison, joined Rosell in questioning Osvaldo Socarrás Martínez, a thirty-two-year old mulatto parking-lot attendant, who was captured in the Civil Hospital. Socarrás described the Siboney farmhouse and the landmarks he saw during his ride to Santiago de Cuba. Rosell instructed Yanez to take the prisoner under guard to Siboney and verify his account.[16]

At the farmhouse Yanez found Lt. Horacio York, who gave him a satchel containing the rebel identity cards and three books: *Pluma en Ristre*, by Pablo de la Torriente Brau, property of Oscar Alcalde; José Ingenieros's *Las Fuerzas Morales*, dedicated by Naty Revuelta to "My incomparable Fidel"; and a Spanish-language volume of the *Selected Works of Lenin*, published in Moscow in 1948, which "belonged to Abel and his signature could be seen on the first page." SIR chief Bebo Lavastida showed the latter book and other evidence of what he described as a Communist conspiracy to the United States consul at Santiago de Cuba, who replied that "Fidel Castro was not a Communist." Lavastida commented that "because some people disliked Batista, they said the army had planted this evidence and that we were making up stories." According to the reporter Ray Brennan, army officers told the American tourists who had sought shelter at the consulate, "The Communists are trying to take over our government and ruin our country. We must take stern steps or we, too, will be behind an Iron Curtain. We feel that you understand."[17]

Returning to regimental headquarters with his prisoner, Yanez encountered Maj. Andrés Pérez-Chaumont Altuzarra, who had entered Moncada at 11:00 A.M. dressed in mufti. He claimed having been delayed after an unknown assailant shot at him as he left his Ciudamar Beach mansion. The major's automobile windshield had a bullet hole, but Yanez and many soldiers believed that it was a result of a cowardly act staged as an excuse for not going to the garrison during the battle. Pérez-Chaumont, a reputedly corrupt aristocratic playboy, was designated by Colonel del Río Chaviano as chief of operations in search of the fleeing rebels. The major then relieved Yanez of his prisoner. As Osvaldo Socarrás was being removed from regimental headquarters, his fate was silently signaled to his escort when Pérez-Chaumont motioned his index finger across his throat. The major then ordered numerous squads into jeeps and trucks and the equestrian Rural Guard to patrol the El Caney and the Siboney highways. The army requisitioned the abandoned rebel vehicles and some jitneys to bolster their patrols.[18]

Among the first rebels to flee Santiago de Cuba were the dissidents Angel "Patachula" Díaz-Francisco and his three companions. They stopped twenty-five miles away in Palma Soriano to buy gasoline and oil. Díaz-Francisco, worried about lapsing into a diabetic coma, unsuccessfully tried purchasing insulin and a syringe, to replace the dosage left in his suitcase at the Rex Hotel. Driving along Central Highway toward

Havana, the fugitives came upon a fork in the road where an armored vehicle was parked on the curb. Two soldiers were erecting a makeshift barrier with wooden crates blocking a bridge entrance. "Shall we take the other fork?" Díaz-Francisco asked his friends. "No, we might get lost, run the barricade," someone replied. As the speeding Oldsmobile rammed through the obstruction, the sentries fired shots that pierced the trunk. Patachula, who had remained awake for two days because none of his passengers knew how to drive, kept nodding at the wheel. Manuel Vázquez, repeatedly slapping his face to keep him alert, shouted, "Look out, we are going to crash!" When the Oldsmobile skidded to a stop, its hood had slipped undamaged under the rear of a tractor-trailer truck. Upon reaching Holguín, 123 miles from Santiago de Cuba, they were forced to stop by an army tank with armed soldiers positioned behind it blocking the road.[19]

The other Siboney rebel deserters had run away in various directions. Radio operator Manuel Lorenzo Costa went to the home of his aunt Rosa Dau in Santiago de Cuba and surrendered a month later. The four Almendares cell members led by Víctor Escalona agreed to disperse and regroup at noon in the downtown square. Eduardo Rodríguez Alemán stated, "At twelve sharp Víctor met with us in Céspedes Park in front of the Casa Granda Hotel and the city hall here in Santiago. From there, we departed by different routes to escape because we knew the attack had failed." Rodríguez and Orlando Cortés Gallardo, lacking funds for transportation, walked along Central Highway until they were detained at the Puerto Boniato checkpoint. Both were escorted to Moncada for lacking identification documents. Escalona and Gilberto Barón Martínez made it beyond Bayamo on the road to Manzanillo before being arrested that afternoon. Their military captors forced them to dig their own graves before executing them.[20]

Ernesto Tizol, who led the rebel caravan astray, discarded his uniform and weapon at Quintero Heights and with Vicente Chávez boarded a bus to Holguín. Tizol remained at his father's residence while Chávez arrived in Havana at dawn the next day and went directly to work. Military orderly Florentino Fernández León, driving behind Tizol, also quickly left Santiago de Cuba but was intercepted at a roadblock in Palma Soriano. He was detained in the local garrison for lacking a military travel permit. It took three days to confirm his identity through the Second Regimental District Headquarters in Holguín and for a travel pass to be issued. Florentino was able to resume his duties at the Jaimanitas military post without immediately arousing suspicion because his time card was falsified and the other orderlies covered for him.[21]

Palma Soriano native Lulo Mitchell had been sidetracked to Quintero Heights before the attack began. He returned to Villa Blanca to retrieve his guayabera and then took a jitney home. At the Palma Soriano military checkpoint he was recognized by his old army buddy Cpl. Narciso D. Sánchez Domínguez and allowed to proceed. Mitchell felt safe until three days later, when Lt. Luis Magín Hernández and four soldiers detained him in a café at 7:00 A.M. and escorted him in a jeep to the local garrison for interrogation. He was disrobed and examined for wounds and rifle-butt abrasions on his shoulders, then queried about the group of strangers he was seen driving with on Saturday. Mitchell claimed that he had been their temporary chauffeur and that Corporal Sánchez, whom he saw in Palma Soriano on Sunday morning, could vouch for him. He was released after his story was verified. On August 4 he left for Havana, where he obtained employment in a garage.[22]

The rebels who fled from the Palace of Justice—Mario Dalmau, José R. Martínez, Angel Sánchez, and Abelardo García—undressed in their moving car and threw their uniforms out the windows as they fled Santiago de Cuba. They proceeded in their underwear for two miles to Ciudamar Beach and stole four sets of clothes from unsuspecting bathers. Martínez suggested returning to the city to find Alfredo Díaz Cominches, whom he had befriended nine months earlier when both were hospital patients in Havana. Dalmau left his black Chevrolet at a car wash to remove the telltale red dust of the Siboney highway. The group approached twenty-four-year-old Antonio Bartolomé, director of the Bartolomé Funeral Home, and asked for directions. He led them to the home of Micaela Cominches, Alfredo's mother, on San Felix Street. Her son-in-law Rubén Pérez Proenza obtained clothes for the fugitives, and her nephew, José Méndez Cominches, had Ortodoxo Youth activist Enrique Rubio Llerena hide them in the homes of party militants. Dalmau then retrieved his Chevrolet from the car wash but got lost and ended up back at the Palace of Justice. He abandoned the automobile and took a taxi to the railway station.[23]

Ramiro Valdés drove away from Moncada Street in a car with a flat tire that thumped harder with each passing block. The wounded Gustavo Arcos lay in the backseat held by Reinaldo Boris Luis. The vehicle was ditched in Vista Alegre when the tire finally shredded off the rim. Arcos was left on the porch of the nearby Pellicier residence by his fleeing companions. When a young lady answered his knock, Arcos stuck his foot in the doorjamb, thwarting her attempt to slam the door. The woman shrieked, "We are not involved in politics." Arcos pleaded, "Are you a Christian?" He later recalled that it was the "saving phrase" because she then let him in and offered assistance. A maid helped the wounded rebel into civilian clothes. Arcos, recalling that his family doctor Alejandro Posada Recio had moved to Santiago de Cuba, asked his host to telephone him. The fifty-eight-year-old Colombian-born physician, director of the Colonia Española Clinic, had lived in Cuba for more than thirty years. Posada went in his Dodge to retrieve Arcos and returned before 7:00 A.M. to the clinic, where he encountered six wounded people, including the rebel José Ponce, awaiting treatment. Ponce, shot in the hand, claimed to be a soldier from Havana. Dr. René Eldidy arrived shortly thereafter and assisted Dr. Posada, Posada's son Dr. Alejandro Posada Gómez, and Posada's son-in-law Dr. Guillermo Holy in performing surgery. Arcos had a shattered appendix and a spinal lesion that left him with a sciatica limp. The thirty-two-year-old Eldidy then attended to Ponce, whose left hand had a few broken bones from a small-caliber bullet.[24]

Some wounded soldiers were also being treated in the clinic before being transferred to the military hospital later that day. Pvt. Miguel Mariano Ruiz, wearing civilian clothes when he was shot, was wheeled in a stretcher next to Ponce, who was still in military uniform. When asked if he was a soldier, Ponce replied, "No, I am one of the attackers." According to the *Havana Post*, "Ruiz tried to overcome him with his own hands, causing such terror in his opponent that he began to scream and call for help." Ponce ran down the hall to tell Dr. Posada, "A wounded soldier has threatened to kill me. He has a revolver." Posada disarmed Ruiz just as six soldiers searching all the hospitals arrived to arrest the injured rebels. Posada and Dr. Vicente Guach Ovieto intervened, stressing that both men were dying. Ponce credited this brave action with saving their lives.[25]

Other insurgents managed to escape the city safely. The three Ferrás brothers were assisted by an aunt residing in Santiago de Cuba; her son quickly drove them to Holguín, where the trio boarded a bus to the capital. The entire Calabazar cell managed to return to Havana within forty-eight hours and sustained only one loss, Julio Trigo, captured in the Civil Hospital. Oscar Quintela returned the 1950 Dodge borrowed by Fidel Castro to its original location, locked the doors, and left the keys in the glove box. The owner of the vehicle, after learning of the attack and fearing arrest, went into exile. Quintela, Pedro Trigo, Pedro Gutiérrez, and René Bedia were interrogated by the police a few days later. Gutiérrez had gone to Guanabo Beach on Monday and claimed that his suntan was a result of having spent the weekend there. All except Bedia, who implicated himself, were quickly released after providing credible excuses.[26]

Fidel Castro, fleeing in a Studebaker with eight others, stopped on the Siboney highway where Boris Luis's automobile had been abandoned with a flat tire. A dozen forgotten insurgents emerged from the road embankment. Castro flagged down an approaching rebel car and ordered half the stragglers into it and then took the rest with him back to Siboney. Manuel Suardíaz recalled boarding Castro's vehicle about thirty minutes after being left behind. When he asked what had happened, Castro tersely replied that the attack had failed. Upon arriving at the farmhouse, their companion Moisés Mafut quickly shed his uniform and kept on the clothes he had left underneath. He saw Boris Luis arrive and frantically search for his girlfriend Haydée and her companion Melba. Boris went back to find them and was taken prisoner. No one else made an attempt to rescue the women.[27]

The overloaded car driven by Ciro Redondo "at an incredible speed" inadvertently overshot the Siboney farmhouse. When they passed a previously unseen agricultural checkpoint, Mario Chanes realized that they were lost. He warned his twelve companions not to fire at the inspectors who were playing dominoes outdoors.

Redondo doubled back and located Villa Blanca after seeing the other vehicles outside. Gerardo Granados recalled that once inside, "Some went to the bathroom, others were running around taking off their uniforms and looking for their clothes. Fidel was already there when we arrived, and he was asking everyone if they had seen his brother Raúl." Granados found Oscar Alcalde, Pepe Suárez, and Fidel Castro in a bedroom and overheard the latter exclaim, "They have killed Raúl! They have killed Raúl!" Castro uttered other incoherent words before blurting, "This has failed, I am going to kill myself," and he put a pistol to his temple. Granados snatched the weapon from him, assisted by the two other rebels. "I do not know if he really meant to kill himself or if he was faking," stated Granados, "but we acted instinctively under those circumstances."[28]

Manuel Suardíaz remembered "a terrible disorder because nothing had been planned in case of failure." When Abelardo Crespo arrived at the farmhouse with a .22-caliber slug in his lung, Suardíaz and Orbeín Hernández laid him out on a mattress in the living room, using a wooden soda crate as a makeshift pillow. Suardíaz then noticed that the rebels lacked a first-aid kit. The only relief available for Crespo was a handkerchief, soaked in a cold water pitcher from the refrigerator, that was pressed against his wound. Granados recalled that Crespo "was complaining a lot, but there was nothing we could do for him. We had to leave him there and I felt a lot of pity for him." Crespo claimed in 1973 that after he fainted, Fidel Castro left him behind believing that he was dead. During the pandemonium, someone threw a shotgun on the ground and the discharge hit Nito Ortega above the ankle. Chanes stated that Castro told the injured rebels to remain there until he could send them medical assistance. Reinaldo Benítez, wounded on the leg by buckshot, refused to stay.[29]

Mario Lazo, a passenger in the last vehicle to arrive at the farmhouse, found forty-five other rebels there. He stated that they pondered two options: "to return to the city and hide and wait for new orientations, or that of taking to the mountains." Fidel Castro suggested regrouping and attacking the small El Caney army outpost. Chanes recalled that Mafut told Castro, "You are crazy. We should take to the hills because the outpost is on the alert for us." Mafut, Ciro Redondo, José Antonio Labrador, and Marcos Martí departed carrying Nito Ortega, who was in agony, to a *bohío* a few hundred yards away for assistance. Mafut recalled, "The only relief available was to place his leg in a tub of water." Jaime Costa remembered the big argument over whether to head for the hills or return to Santiago de Cuba, with Fidel Castro favoring the latter. Costa stated, "I grabbed the first pair of pants and a shirt, saying that I was leaving for the hills because I did not know the city. Someone yelled that the army was approaching and a group ran out the back door, some still in their underwear carrying their clothes, and jumped over the fence."[30]

Costa and Chanes agree that they were in Villa Blanca for thirty minutes. By that time more than half of the group had lost faith in Fidel Castro's leadership, and only nineteen decided to follow him. Artemisa native Julio Díaz headed for the hills with his friend Gerardo Granados, but after a short distance he returned to the farmhouse to retrieve a forgotten item. Granados waited for him but later saw Díaz signaling that he was going with Ciro Redondo. Oscar Alcalde, walking next to Granados, commented, "Fidel is the one we have to protect now."[31]

Manuel Suardíaz remained at Villa Blanca sifting for his own clothes among the dozens of piles scattered throughout the house. After an extensive search, he found his pants and grabbed someone else's guayabera. Suardíaz and his Madruga friend Orbeín Hernández walked on the highway toward Siboney Beach, hoping to flee in a stolen boat. Upon encountering Gerardo Sosa and Manuel Isla, the group signaled a passing jitney. Suardíaz faked a regional accent to request a ride to Santiago de Cuba. The driver became nervous when they had him stop to pick up Ulises Sarmiento. When they arrived at the Plaza de Marte Park, Suardíaz paid all their fares. He bought a pack of cigarettes and coffee for himself and his comrades and had only two pesos left. Suardíaz advised the group to split up around 8:00 A.M. Isla, who departed alone, was later captured and killed. Suardíaz walked with Hernández to the bus terminal and gave the ticket vendor his seventy-five-peso watch as a guarantee to repay for two three-peso passages to Victoria de las Tunas. He recalled fervently praying to all the saints each time the bus was stopped at roadblocks, which was frequently. They reached a friend's home, and the two rebels returned to Madruga by bus a few days later without arousing suspicion.[32]

Back in Santiago de Cuba, Lawton cell leader Gabriel Gil sought refuge in a barbershop on Pedrera Street with twenty-three-year-old Ismael Ricondo, whose right hand was mangled by a bullet. Gil obtained a guayabera and argued with Ricondo about their options. He decided to leave the city while his companion, in excruciating pain, sought medical assistance. At 11:00 A.M. Gil approached a Central Highway checkpoint manned by two soldiers, where he found Gerardo Sosa and Ulises Sarmiento. The three furtively retreated and spent their combined eight cents on crackers. At another army roadblock, on the El Cobre highway, the trio claimed to be making a pilgrimage to the Virgin of Charity shrine. A sentry let them proceed before noticing that Gil had stained his guayabera with Ricondo's blood. The group was led to El Cobre outpost, where Gil, proclaiming his innocence, stressed that he was a former soldier and that his brother was on active duty. He then saw Cpl. Julio Corbea Monteagudo, who had served with him in La Cabaña, and told the officer in charge that he knew Corbea. "Yes, I know him," the corporal admitted, "but I have not seen him in years and I do not know of his activities." The three suspects were sent to Moncada for interrogation.[33]

Ismael Ricondo had gone to the Casa de Socorro First Aid Clinic on Trocha Street, where he was detained with Guillermo Elizalde by a military search patrol, and from there they were taken to the garrison. The *Diario de la Marina* reported that Ricondo was arrested "after having a grave wound on his hand treated." The rebel Gelasio Fernández Martínez, Ricondo's brother-in-law, found refuge that afternoon in the home of Rubén Pérez Proenza, who had asked him on the street if he was from Pinar del Río. Fernández requested that the Good Samaritan inquire about Ismael at the clinic, where the admission record indicated his prior presence. Ricondo apparently confessed his participation and was killed in Moncada. Elizalde, giving a convincing excuse for his slight injury and claiming to be from Santa Clara, was remanded for trial. The rebel Manuel Rojo Pérez, a forty-nine-year-old peasant mortally wounded in the abdomen, was taken to the Civil Hospital, where he died days later. Anyone on the street acting suspicious or mouthing off to the authorities ended up in the Moncada holding cells. Three tourists with criminal records were killed while, probably, resisting arrest and were mistakenly identified as rebels in the press. Soldiers firing on rebels fleeing through a neighborhood accidentally killed forty-eight-year-old José Casamayor Caballero as he went to assist his eleven-year-old son Baudilio Casamayor Martínez, who had fallen wounded on the street.[34]

When the attackers retreated from the garrison, Isidro Peñalver O'Reilly, a thirty-year-old mulatto from Havana, discarded his military apparel for the civilian clothes he had kept underneath, but his own pants resembled khaki material. He walked to the Plaza de Marte Park and sat on a bench near the Route 80 bus station, lacking funds to buy passage. At noon he was joined by his cell member Humberto Valdés Casañas, a twenty-two-year-old mulatto parking-lot attendant. Valdés publicly gestured the secret sign of distress of the Caballero de la Luz para-Masonic fraternity, which was acknowledged by a black taxi driver. The rebels received the address of a fraternal brother who could aid them, but before reaching there, a lieutenant mistook Peñalver's pants for an army uniform and detained them. At Moncada a captain assumed that they could not be rebels because most Afro-Cubans supported Batista.[35]

After their release, Peñalver and Valdés headed for the address provided by the taxi driver. Walking past the Provincial Palace, Isidro's suspicious pants prompted a soldier to take both men before Gov. Waldo Pérez Almaguer. The rebels explained their predicament and requested a safe-conduct pass, but the skeptical governor sent them back to Moncada for it. This time they were questioned for three hours by SIR chief Bebo Lavastida, who locked them in the Guard Corps cells. The other detainees included about twenty innocent suspects; the rebels Gabriel Gil, Gerardo Sosa, Ulises Sarmiento, Orlando Cortés, Eduardo Rodríguez, and four others; and two informants. Cortés and Rodríguez told reporters that they had been tricked by Fidel Castro into going to Santiago de Cuba and that when informed in Siboney of the planned attack, they and Víctor Escalona, whose whereabouts were unknown to them, had left on foot. Gil was summoned to the third-floor SIR office for interrogation. While there, two soldiers escorted Fernando Chenard to a sofa. Gil was taken outside to the roof of the Officers' Club building and forced to stand at the ledge with other detainees. Lavastida had him peer down at rebel bodies sprawled on the sidewalk and told them that those rebels had been thrown off for not talking. Chenard was then brought out to identify the prisoners, but as he walked by each one he repeated, "I do not know this man." Gil and the others, who insisted that they were carnival tourists, were led back to the holding cells. Chenard's name later appeared on the list of combat dead.[36]

Back at the Siboney farmhouse, the wounded Abelardo Crespo awoke to find everyone gone. He changed into civilian clothes, pressed a towel against his wound, and staggered across the road to the farm of Angel "El Gallego" Núñez. According to Mario Chanes, Crespo said that he had been stabbed during a fight. Núñez summoned jitney driver Julio "Mongolé" Duany and instructed that he take Crespo to Doctor Aguilera at the Centro Gallego Clinic in Vista Alegre. When they reached the clinic, Crespo was placed under an oxygen tent and given intravenous plasma. He pulled the needle from his arm when he heard soldiers enter the clinic and was seized while escaping out a window. Crespo insisted during interrogation at Moncada that he was wounded at the Plaza de Marte Park during the carnival festivities. In 1973 he claimed that he fainted during the questioning and awoke in a military hospital bed next to Pedro Miret, Fidel Labrador, and the mortally wounded Rigoberto Corcho.[37]

Meanwhile, Moisés Mafut and his companions, nursing the wounded Nito Ortega in a peasant's *bohío* near Villa Blanca, decided to leave when they saw a truck approaching on the Siboney highway. The peasant promised to take care of Ortega and directed them toward the coast, opposite the direction of Fidel Castro's route. Mafut, Julio Díaz, José Labrador, Ciro Redondo, and Marcos Martí climbed the southeastern hills toward the ocean reefs. They rested at Sardinero after hiding their weapons in a dry well. Mafut followed a strong breeze to a cliff overlooking the Siboney highway. The weary Díaz had to be assisted during their descent until reaching the woods along the highway. El Moro decided to search for potable water and followed the road to Siboney Beach while the others remained hidden. He recalled, "Behind a large rock I heard voices. I took out my revolver and approached slowly until I saw a pickup truck. A man, two women, and some children in bathing suits had a large water container. I was invited to drink some and then asked for more to take back, and they gave me six bottles of mineral water. I put two in my back pockets and cradled the others in my arms during my return."[38]

In the meantime, his four companions had gotten a ride from fishermen in a jeep to Las Múcaras hamlet at 9:00 A.M. The strangers told Ricardo Prada that they had attended the carnival but were lost after being separated from a friend. The peasant invited them into his *bohío*, and his wife provided coffee. Meanwhile, Mafut was crossing a nearby barbed-wire fence when some youngsters demanded that he pay ten cents for trespassing. When he drew his gun to scare them away, one kid stated, "There are some people inside who are probably your companions." El Moro then rejoined his comrades in the *bohío*. A few hours later Prada was informed by his stepson that a pickup truck with soldiers was speeding toward them. The rebels admitted their role in the Moncada assault and begged their host to assist them. Prada went outside and told the inquiring Corporal Sellén that he had not seen any strangers in the area. Sellén replied that he would take his squad up to Rivero and thoroughly search on their way back. Mafut informed his companions, "We are dead if we stay here." When Redondo suggested selling his gold chain, El Moro replied, "We do not need to risk selling it, I have about sixty pesos. If we can make it back to Albentosa's home in the city, we are safe." Prada's wife pointed to a nearby grocery store where the Santiago de Cuba jitneys transported beach-goers. Mafut and José Labrador departed after Redondo opted to stay with Julio Díaz and Marcos Martí. El Moro ditched his revolver when he saw an army pickup truck on the Siboney highway, but it sped past him. Labrador, lagging behind, was detained near the Prada home. He was heard confessing to his captors before being taken away in a commandeered passing car. Labrador and another corpulent rebel were later found dead along the Siboney highway.[39]

When El Moro reached Los Criollos food mart, a jitney driver was loudly heralding his return trip to Santiago de Cuba. The man turned to the rebel and told him, "Hey, sir, with you my fare is complete and we can go now." Mafut bought a cigarette pack before squeezing next to the driver in the crowded automobile. He recalled, "As we were leaving, a platoon of about fifteen soldiers appeared on both sides of the road and I got very nervous. A heavyset sergeant told us to get out and while we stood by the car the driver said, 'There is no problem, I always bring these people to the beach.'" As the passengers were reboarding, the sergeant spoke with the clerk who had sold cigarettes to Mafut. He then shouted at the driver to halt and ran toward the vehicle. Mafut believed that he had been denounced and feared imminent doom, but the sergeant told the driver, "Wait, so that you can take refreshments to the soldiers in the farmhouse." While loading a soda case into the trunk, the sergeant cursed the rebels who had "gone to the Moncada to kill soldiers." When the jitney halted at a roadblock in front of Villa Blanca, the chauffeur declared that "the sergeant who already searched us sends a case of sodas for you." During the trip to the city, the driver praised the bravery of the attackers, but Mafut kept silent until paying his fare near Albentosa's home. El Moro returned to Havana by bus the next day, and Albentosa followed by train two days later.[40]

When Mafut and Labrador did not return, Julio Díaz, Ciro Redondo, and Marcos Martí left the Prada home with a note for jitney driver Julio Duany to help them. Díaz went back to the Prada home shortly thereafter and was hidden nearby in Las Múcaras cave. On the Siboney highway Redondo and Martí encountered thirteen-year-old Arturo "Turín" Campanal, who took them home after they pleaded for assistance. His father, Spanish Republican civil war veteran Arturo González del Río, who went by the alias "Arturo Campanal," provided the rebels a change of clothes and a knife. He concealed them that afternoon in Dead Man's cave, located fifty yards behind his property. Both men continued to wonder about the fate of their comrades.[41]

The eighteen rebels captured in the Civil Hospital were herded into the two holding cells of the Moncada Guard Corps room after 8:30 A.M. Inside was thirty-five-year-old José Manuel Villa Romero, the former Santiago de Cuba police major and militant of the clandestine Triple A, who had been arrested at home ninety minutes earlier. After the shooting began, he went in his van with another Triple A member to the Civil Hospital entrance to appraise the situation before returning to his residence. His presence there made him a prime suspect. Villa knew of the impending attack because a few days earlier Renato Guitart had requested information about the garrison and its most vulnerable points. Guitart asked the former police chief if he would be willing to cooperate in case something occurred. Villa replied that he could not act without orders from Triple A military chief Jorge Agostini Villasana nor loan the few weapons in his possession. After Villa entered the Moncada holding cell, he asked 2nd Lt. Cándido Garrido Wilson, the chief of the guard, to record in the prisoners' logbook that he had been detained at home. When Lt. Manuel Piña Martínez arrived with Abel Santamaría and four other prisoners, he cursed Villa and engaged his Springfield rifle bolt action to shoot him. Abel declared, "That man did not come with us." Piña relaxed after Lieutenant Garrido confirmed this.[42]

Over the next two hours the prisoners were escorted to the third-floor regimental headquarters office for interrogation by SIR chief Bebo Lavastida, Lt. Antonio Ochoa, and other officers. The rebels readily confessed their role, with some giving political justification for their actions. According to Pvt. José Olivares, anyone who proved positive on the paraffin test "and had no reason to be in the Moncada or its surroundings, was done for." Small groups of attackers, with their hands tied behind their backs, were then led to the rear small-arms target range and riddled with a .30-caliber machine gun placed there for that purpose. A few soldiers, at the orders of Lts. Luis S. Gamboa Alarcón and Antonio Barquet Aguiar, participated in the target-range massacre. Pvt. Ariel Matos saw Lieutenant Barquet riddling "two or three" prisoners with a Thompson machine gun. Matos stated, "I was not pleased to see that in the target range were soldiers that I knew had not fought, who did not fire a shot defending the garrison, but were then killing those people." Pvt. José Olivares was invited by a soldier from his company to participate, but he refused, saying, "I will not kill a man who is bound." When Maj. Florentino Rosell, who had been interviewing prisoners at regimental headquarters, was recently asked about the prisoner executions, he replied, "I do not know anything about that."[43]

Lt. Teodoro Rico Boué was accused by the novelist Robert Merle of "directing with fervor the execution of the prisoners." Rico emphasized thirty-five years later, "that is history, true or false, that is history." Pvt. Angel Pupo Miranda affirmed that

Rico was later in charge of having dead rebels removed in the garrison's butcher-shop van and dumped in the countryside. Pvt. José Olivares, standing guard at Post 2, saw the lieutenant make at least three trips at dawn in a Studebaker military truck, transporting cadavers from the countryside into the garrison for identification purposes. Pvts. Justo Ramón Martija and Ariel Matos confirmed that Rico and Sgt. René Caso Pérez participated in the execution of the rebel prisoners. Martija witnessed José Luis Tasende, wounded on the leg by grenade shrapnel, being carried by four soldiers to the target range without resisting or saying a word. Tasende was dropped on the ground and shot through the head by Pvt. Manuel Avila Sánchez with a Springfield rifle. Martija stated, "What happened to Tasende bothered me, because he was wounded. I did not care about the fate of the other prisoners." Pvt. José Olivares saw another rebel prisoner also being carried by a group of soldiers to the firing range with his mangled lower leg flopping loosely in the air. The detainee was screaming, "Don't kill me! Don't kill me! I am innocent, I did not participate in the attack. Fidel Castro shot me." This was apparently Nito Ortega, left behind at Siboney when accidentally wounded by a dropped shotgun. Civilians and reporters outside the garrison who heard the sporadic shots assumed that a few barricaded attackers continued to resist. As a result, some newspapers reported that the battle did not end until 10:30 A.M. Castro erroneously claims in *History Will Absolve Me* that the prisoner massacre did not commence until after 3:00 P.M., when Inspector General Martín Díaz Tamayo arrived from Havana with orders from Batista to kill ten rebels for each dead soldier.[44]

That false accusation, as well as Batista's complicity in the massacre, was disavowed by Oriente governor Waldo Pérez Almaguer and magistrate Adolfo Nieto Piñeiro-Osorio, who later presided over the rebels' trial. Pérez Almaguer, who resigned from his post three weeks later, told *La Calle* newspaper in 1955 that he witnessed the execution of thirty rebel attackers ordered by Colonel del Río Chaviano. "That savagery cannot be blamed on Batista," he emphasized. Nieto explained, "Most of the soldiers in Moncada were related to each other. The reaction of personal vengeance was such that someone whose relative died in the attack would kill whoever they took prisoner without asking permission from anyone. That is all there was to it." Lt. Teodoro Rico concurred, "You could say that power to command was in suspense.... There was an unhinging, a stagnation of the military leadership." The outraged soldiers "went looking for vengeance."[45]

The sporadic shots emanating from the target range throughout the morning during the execution of the prisoners were heard by twenty-three-year-old José "Pepín" Pujol Soler and his brother Juan. They owned Pujol Motors, a dealership of Austin and Hillman automobiles and Harley-Davidson motorcycles, on the corner of Paseo de José Martí Street and Los Libertadores Avenue, across from Moncada garrison. Pepín and his wife Aurora "Chia" Venero were awakened that morning by the shootout but initially believed that it was in celebration of the Korean War armistice. When the milkman arrived, he told them that Gen. José Pedraza and his followers were attacking the Moncada garrison. Pepín and his brother went to their shop at 9:30 A.M. and stood for hours on the corner listening to the disturbance inside the fortress and watching jeeps crowded with soldiers racing about and taking detainees from the city and the countryside to the garrison.[46]

The Siboney farmhouse was occupied at 2:00 P.M. by Maj. Andrés Pérez-Chaumont, Lts. Teodoro Rico, Antonio Ochoa, Claudio Morales García, Manuel Arpa Ceballo, and some forty soldiers. Lt. Angel Machado was relieved of duty and returned to Moncada. Pérez-Chaumont interrogated the neighbor El Gallego Núñez, who was escorted to the garrison for further questioning. Villa Blanca owner José Vázquez went into hiding until Tuesday, when he was incarcerated for three days. Pérez-Chaumont later reported to Colonel del Río Chaviano that twenty-one rebels were killed in the countryside that day "due to an encounter with an army patrol." The major told U.S. vice consul Arthur W. Feldman that "there were about eight unidentified slain men who were not Cubans and who were short, dark, and hairy." That afternoon Cols. Marcelo and Carlos Tabernilla Palmero arrived at San Pedrito airport in Santiago de Cuba piloting two C-46 planes from Cuba Aeropostal. They delivered a large quantity of ammunition, machine guns, four 75-mm cannons, and twenty-four artillerymen from La Cabaña fortress to reinforce the Moncada garrison. They returned with the aircraft to Havana that night. Also arriving in Oriente from SIM headquarters in Havana was a team from the technical department to photograph and fingerprint the dead attackers and the prisoners.[47]

The detainees being processed at Moncada included the four rebel dissidents who had been arrested in Holguín and arrived under escort at 5:00 P.M. Angel Díaz-Francisco and his companions claimed that they had been to the carnival and departed upon hearing the gunfire that caused the bullet holes in their car trunk. As Patachula limped up the stairs to the third-floor regimental headquarters, a soldier knocked him down and dragged him the rest of the way. Another private, noticing his childhood surgical scars, stated, "This one is an old war dog, look at the bullet wounds on his left leg." While Díaz-Francisco awaited questioning with a dozen other suspects, someone whispered to him, "Blame Gildo Fleitas for everything." "Why Gildo?" he asked. The answer was, "Because he is dead." Patachula refused to lie and later stated, "I was not beaten or pressured during two interrogation sessions, which convinced me we were going to be killed." Díaz-Francisco and his three companions were subjected to paraffin tests that proved negative, and then they were led downstairs. Carlos Merille asked permission to urinate and told the others, "you better relieve yourselves now so that they won't say later that you pissed in your pants in front of the firing squad." Those in need did so on a patio barracks wall before they were placed in a Guard Corps cell.[48]

That afternoon the newsmen who had waited at Post 2 all morning were told by Adj. Capt. Manuel Aguila Gil that an interview with the regimental chief was scheduled for later that day. Colonel del Río Chaviano then prepared the Moncada garrison for a tour. Cpl. Eugenio Alcolea stated, "When the colonel saw all the dead bodies in the target range, it was ordered that they be scattered around outside so that it would look like they died in combat." Pvt. Armando Oliva indicated that the cadavers, clad in their underwear, had to be dressed again since angry soldiers had stripped off the army uniforms. Thirty-three dead rebels were outfitted carelessly: some had their vestments inside out; ten had mismatched khaki apparel and white hospital-patient outfits; eleven cadavers had uniforms without perforations, which did not conform with their wounds; a few were left shirtless; and others were shoeless. Pvt. José Olivares acknowledged that after the corpses were "dressed in uniform, the dead had clothing without bullet holes." Lt. Jesús Yanez Pelletier confirmed that the cadavers were then strewn inside Moncada and behind the military hospital to simulate a battleground. Some, such as the heavyset Gildo Fleitas, "who died in one place were thrown in another." Beralia Fajardo had seen the cadaver of a "very obese" rebel in her backyard right after the shootout, but the body later appeared in a *Bohemia* photograph on the grassy knoll behind the military hospital along with four others. It was near the corpses of Renato Guitart and Dr. Mario Muñoz, still in his white physician's outfit and with a large bloodstain on his chest.[49]

Around 5:00 P.M. some fifteen civilians, including newsmen, photographers, civic leaders, and lawyers representing detainees, were escorted to regimental headquarters. They were shown the revolutionary proclamations and phonograph records retrieved from the Civil Hospital. Lt. Teodoro Rico gave the reporters a two-hour tour, starting at Post 3, where three attackers lay dead. The entourage then saw five bodies in the barbershop. Another twenty dead insurgents lay in the administrative wing and on the rear patio. The reporters saw buzzards circling low overhead. Colonel del Río Chaviano joined the newsmen at 6:00 P.M. and allowed them to film a newsreel and take numerous photographs, which later appeared in the press. One picture depicted the body of Raúl Gómez García, who was captured in the Civil Hospital, sprawled by a doorway of the Moncada rear patio next to a weapon.[50]

The regimental chief addressed the reporters in a radio interview, which was broadcast later that night. This interview was partially published in the *Havana Post*, which falsely stated, "The barracks had been attacked from two different angles. He [del Río Chaviano] said 50 or 60 men dressed in Army uniforms and armed with grenades, machine-guns and rifles . . . had taken up strong positions from which they could only be dislodged, first, and later put to flight by use of hand grenades. He said 30 or 40 of the attackers had been killed in that operation, while 15 soldiers were killed. I want to make it clear, he said, that most of the deaths among the armed forces occurred in the Military Hospital, where the assailants knifed sick soldiers confined there." Del Río Chaviano said that "ten members of the Army were assassinated in the Military Hospital," and he blamed former president Prío, as "intellectual author" of the attack, and the Montreal Conference participants. Afro-Cuban Cpl. Elio Rizo Carbonell was photographed by reporters displaying an eighteen-inch butcher knife purportedly used by the attackers to slay the military hospital patients.[51]

There had been a news blackout all day in Havana, where rumors abounded of "something" happening in Santiago de Cuba. The station Cadena Oriental de Radio had ceased transmitting the Santiago de Cuba carnival and switched to a musical program. Television channels broadcast images of Batista presenting a trophy cup to the winning team of the Varadero national regatta. After Batista returned to Camp Columbia at 4:30 P.M., the news censorship ended when the minister of information Ernesto de la Fe read an official statement saying that "elements in accord with ex-President Prío tried today in Santiago de Cuba a new crazy attempt to commit an outrage against the regime and against the public order . . . in the hope of an impossible return" to power. No further details were forthcoming until the nightly extra editions of *Alerta* and *El Crisol* reported the Moncada and Bayamo attacks with a partial list of casualties.[52]

In Havana that evening the Council of Ministers held an extraordinary session to approve decrees suspending ten articles of the Constitutional Code of April 4, 1952, for a period of ninety days. These included articles 26 through 29, protecting detainees and the principles of habeas corpus; article 30, providing the right to freedom of movement; article 32, guaranteeing the inviolability of communications; article 33, recognizing freedom of expression without prior censorship; and articles 36, 37, and 71, safeguarding the rights of petition, public gathering, and labor strikes, respectively. As a result mail, telephone, and telegraph communications were subject to government restraint and official censors were assigned to all newspapers and magazines except the English-language daily *Havana Post*. The U.S. Embassy informed the U.S. Department of State that American wire service correspondents circumvented censorship by telephoning "their Miami or New York offices without interference."[53]

The judicial process of the Moncada attack was set in motion after 10:00 P.M. when instruction judge Leoncio Despaigne Grave de Peralta of the Northern District of Santiago de Cuba, his secretary Ciro Sánchez del Campo, and medical examiners Manuel Prieto Aragón and Carlos M. Padrón Ferrer were summoned to the garrison. An instruction judge collected evidence, took depositions, and prepared a written summary for the prosecutor, who then determined probable cause. According to law, no corpse could be moved until the medical examiners had issued a death certificate. The investigative team was taken to the Officers' Club, where fourteen defenders were in their coffins. Lt. Rafael Canet Comas had called the Bartolomé Funeral Home two hours earlier requesting identical caskets for all officers, noncommissioned officers, soldiers, and policemen. The physicians had the dead soldiers undressed to verify their wounds. They then examined the rebel corpses in the administrative wing hallway, the barbershop, and Post 3. The judge and doctors were led to the grassy knoll behind the military hospital where five attackers lay dead. Prieto found on Dr. Mario Muñoz his Colón Medical Association membership card and notified the local Medical Association to call his family. He then recognized nearby the remains of Renato Guitart.[54]

Judge Despaigne had medical captain Edmundo Tamayo and medical lieutenant Erik Juan Pita transfer four wounded rebels from the military hospital to the Civil Hospital two hours later. The judicial team then visited the homes of the dead second lieutenants Pedro Feraud and Andrés Morales, where traditional all-night wakes were in progress, before completing their work after midnight. Judge Despaigne filed a brief affirming the political motivation of the violent crimes, which came under the jurisdiction of the Urgency Tribunal. These special courts, established in 1938, dealt with national security cases, civilian attacks on the military, terrorism, and violent political crimes. There were four criminal courts and one for civil cases in Santiago de Cuba. During the hottest months of July and August, half of the criminal courts went into recess, and the two remaining in session were called the first and second vacation courts. Either of these functioning courts could serve as an Urgency Tribunal. The second vacation court, acting as an Urgency Tribunal, handled all interim matters until the four criminal courts resumed their normal schedule on September 1. The Cuban legal system was void of trial transcripts. The Urgency Tribunal administered a verbal process without an appeal. Attorneys presented witness testimony without prior deposition before three magistrates. In an Urgency Tribunal, any prior confession to the authorities was void; only the statement to the instruction judge was valid.[55]

The second vacation court of the Urgency Tribunal met on Monday at 8:00 A.M. in the Palace of Justice. It was composed of the magistrates Manuel Urrutia Lleó, presiding; Mario Vázquez Martínez; and Evelio Morales Castillo. Urrutia summoned forensic physicians Manuel Prieto Aragón, Carlos Padrón Ferrer, José Ramón Cabrales Arjona, and Alipio Rodríguez López. The fifty-one-year-old Urrutia, a Las Villas native, had been appointed as a municipal judge in Oriente in 1928. The tribunal, court secretary Raúl Mascaró Yarini, and the physicians conducted the forensic examinations on some of the dead rebels. Dr. Prieto recalled that behind the military hospital they found one more corpse, totaling six, but the soldiers argued that it had not been added overnight. The last body was that of Manuel "El Niño" Cala Reyes, a fifty-year-old former army sergeant, former member of ARG, and Cayo Confites filibuster. The policeman Horacio Martínez Verdecia described Cala as "an expert marksman with a notorious reputation as a gun-slinging gangster." Manuel Bartolomé remembered him as "a professional revolutionary who did not agree with any government, but he was old and exhausted. There was no need to kill him. He was not involved in anything." Cala had been shot through the interior left forearm and behind the right ear by a soldier early that morning near the municipal slaughterhouse on Calzada de Crombet. His body was then dumped on the grassy knoll behind the military hospital.[56]

Judge Urrutia and his retinue stopped by the Moncada detention cells at 10:00 A.M. and assured twenty-one prisoners not to worry now that the tribunal was handling the situation. The detainees, lacking food and sleeping on the floor, were promised better conditions. Urrutia jotted down their names and addresses and obtained the immediate release of former police major José Villa Romero on his own recognizance. The magistrates then took depositions from doctors, nurses, and other witnesses in the Civil Hospital. Colonel del Río Chaviano sent the judges a statement of "facts" regarding the Moncada attack. He blamed "elements directed by Carlos Prío Socarrás, Aureliano Sánchez Arango, Eufemio Fernández, a someone named Fidel Castro, who frequents Havana and Santiago de Cuba, Juan Marinello Vidaurreta, Blas Roca, Emilio Ochoa, and other chiefs and leaders of the Communist, Auténtico, and Ortodoxo Parties." Since some rebel weapons were Canadian Mosberg .22 rifles, del Río Chaviano wrote in his report, "Almost all the arms are from Montreal, Canada, which can be justified with the wrappers and boxes of shells that contained the ammunition, being evident that the Montreal meeting was an insurrectional agreement to attack our Fatherland's territory with Cubans and foreigners." The colonel falsely claimed that when the rebels "surreptitiously entered the military hospital, knife in hand, they opened the abdomen of three patients." He also lied when stating that there were four to five hundred assailants, that the attack lasted more than four hours, that many of the dead and captured wore brick-colored rubber gloves to avoid gunpowder traces, and that those who penetrated the garrison used hand grenades. The Urgency Tribunal got another report the next day, authorized by the regimental chief and signed by Adj. Capt. Manuel Aguila, alleging that the confiscated evidence included "modern instruments of war coming from Canada ... 40 hand grenades ... 2 sharpened knives, with which two hospitalized soldiers were assassinated ... 4 pants and 6 blue police jackets, one with major insignias ... 2 blue police shirts, with major insignias ... all belonging to ex–Santiago de Cuba Police Major José M. Villa Romero." Mention of the last items, taken from Villa Romero's home, was meant to frame him.[57]

On Monday morning three innocent civilians were implicated in the uprising. Mario Burman Corman, a Jewish, twenty-eight-year-old, Havana hardware-store owner, had been on a cross-country business trip accompanied by his paramour Lázara Sarah Pérez Cuesta, a twenty-eight-year-old employee of the Ministry of Labor, and his chauffeur, Oscar Gras Escalona. The night before the attack they went to Club 300, across from Céspedes Park, and later checked into the nearby Casa

Granda Hotel. The next morning the trio found that a bullet had pierced their car radiator and exited through the trunk. Burman reported it to police captain Bonifacio Haza Grasso, who instructed him to get a safe-conduct pass from the military authorities. When the visitors arrived at Moncada, an investigation revealed cutlery samples in the vehicle and a large amount of money and checks in Burman's possession. Capt. Bebo Lavastida interrogated each individually at SIR headquarters. Lázara claimed that she suffered great mental duress under questioning. She was later informed that her paraffin test had proved positive, even though she had not handled a weapon. Suspected of being a rebel conspirator and financier, Burman, along with his chauffeur, was placed in a cell with rebel suspects while Lázara was kept in a second-floor room of the main building with Melba and Haydée.[58]

Melba recalled looking out the window at the military exequies on the parade ground that began at 11:00 A.M. that Monday. The troops were formed in front of a row of sixteen flag-draped caskets propped between metal folding chairs. The National Police Marching Band played the Fourth of September hymn, and Adjutant Captain Aguila Gil read a presidential decree listing all the fatalities in ascending rank. As the artillery fired a twenty-one-gun salute, army inspector general Martín Díaz Tamayo, who flew in from Havana that morning with Cols. Fermín Cowley Gallegos and Antonio Blanco Rico, pinned the Medal of Military Merit with the Red Ribbon of Valor on each coffin's flag. Also present were Gov. Waldo Pérez Almaguer, Mayor Maximino Torres Sánchez, and the families of the fallen. The assembly heard on loudspeakers General Batista's forty-five-minute speech from Camp Columbia, which was broadcast live on radio and television. Batista stated that the Moncada attackers "silently knifed the sentries at the gates of the garrison," they "assassinated patients in their hospital beds," and they had "Communist documents, Soviet propaganda and books of Lenin." He added, "It is positively true that the Communist action is against the national interest. The people of Cuba and the Army, which is part of that people, are contrary to Communism and will not permit it to proliferate in our land." Batista pointed out that, in contrast, during the Tenth of March Coup no shots were fired and no blood was spilled when he took over Camp Columbia in a "fraternal returning to our home," calling his regime "humane, revolutionary and democratic."[59]

Afterward the funeral cortege departed from Moncada with two artillery limbers and all the local hearses available, including three Cadillacs from the Bartolomé Funeral Home and one borrowed from the Manuel Sigas Funeral Home in Palma Soriano. The Havana Police Marching Band, stepping in unison and playing Chopin's funeral march as well as other dirges, led the way to the Armed Forces Mausoleum in Santa Ifigenia Cemetery. The remains of their comrade Cpl. Manuel Miras Mierez were flown to Havana for interment. The coffin with Sgt. Ramón Silveiro was sent to Camajuaní, Las Villas. The rest were buried with honors in Santiago de Cuba, including police sergeant Gerónimo Suárez Camejo, killed in Bayamo. Inspector General Díaz Tamayo pronounced the eulogy and then visited the wounded in the military hospital.[60]

Those hospitalized included Pvt. Saturnino Ramírez Santiesteban, who had been shot in a lung and was under an oxygen tent. A relative stayed constantly at his side until he expired five days later. Cpl. Néstor Reyes, Pvt. Miguel Mariano Ruiz, and Baracoita Hernández, the orphan teenager waiting to join the army, were all in the same room. Cpl. Eugenio Alcolea lay in a bed with his foot in a cast. Next to him was Pvt. Luis Enrique Naranjo, shot in the legs. Both were wounded in the barbershop during the final resistance. In the same ward was Lt. Juan Piña, hit on the leg by a ricochet bullet, and Pvts. Luis Bayona, Emilio Reyes, and Lázaro Tejadilla. That afternoon the gravely wounded privates Luis Frómeta, Daniel Lavastida, and Luis Hodelín and the policeman Patricio Moreno were flown in a C-47 transport to the military hospital in Havana. SIM lieutenant Armando Acosta accompanied them, carrying identification documents found in the Siboney farmhouse. Col. Manuel Ugalde Carrillo, SIM chief, then flew to Santiago de Cuba for one day to inspect the crime scene and collect the cards with fingerprints taken from the dead insurgents and civilians. Sgt. Carlos A. Delgado Martínez, who was returning to Havana as part of General Díaz Tamayo's retinue, recalled seeing "the cadavers of eight or ten rebels strewn on a barracks patio, their heads swollen as big as pumpkins."[61]

That Monday afternoon René Guitart claimed the body of his son Renato after appearing at Moncada with customs administrator Mariano Velázquez, a friend of Colonel del Río Chaviano. They were accompanied by Chamber of Commerce president Fernando Ojeda Sancho and José Medina Puig, president of the Rotary Club where René Guitart was a member. Renato had been shot in the buttocks and the right side of the forehead with a large-caliber projectile that exited behind his left ear. According to Medina, his father identified him by the gold chain around his neck, since his swollen, bloody face was unrecognizable. The corpse was retrieved by Antonio Bartolomé, of the Bartolomé Funeral Home, at the request of Velázquez. It was forwarded to Santa Ifigenia Cemetery at 4:00 p.m. and interred in the family crypt. Bartolomé was also contracted by the local Medical Association to provide a coffin for Dr. Muñoz. The services selected for both rebels cost three hundred pesos each, well above the average price of one hundred pesos.[62]

Manuel Bartolomé received a telephone call that night from Santiago de Cuba mayor Maximino Torres, who asked him to remove the unclaimed rebel bodies still in the garrison. Bartolomé responded, "You have called the wrong person because we do not have the municipal contract for paupers' burials." The mayor said that the assigned funeral home, which received six pesos per indigent transaction, lacked the thirty-three coffins needed. Bartolomé replied that his enterprise did not carry cheap coffins and therefore could not handle the large task at such a meager cost. Torres begged Bartolomé to do it as a personal favor, due to their long-standing friendship, and promised an equitable payment. The mayor then asked that all the rebel dead be removed that night. Bartolomé and his assistant Emilio Luna worked all night taking wooden coffins in a van to the garrison and placing the bodies in them. They stacked them up on the parade ground before going home at dawn on Tuesday, permeated with the stench of death. The coffins were later taken in a flatbed truck from Expreso Alvarez Company to Santa Ifigenia Cemetery. Dr. Muñoz's widow, who had arrived from Colón, Matanzas, with her father-in-law, attended her husband's burial in the Rosillo family vault at 11:30 A.M. According to Dr. Prieto, the forensic team examined the remainder of the corpses at the cemetery all day Tuesday and Wednesday morning. Twenty-three of the thirty-three rebel cadavers examined had been shot in the head at close range. One body, wearing high-top tennis shoes, was riddled with twenty bullet wounds. When the doctors finished their work, the rebel coffins were stacked into eleven graves in the paupers' yard of the cemetery. Two years later the remains were transferred to a plot purchased by René Guitart.[63]

After the Moncada attack was suppressed, warnings were quickly relayed from regimental headquarters to the surrounding military outposts. Lt. Vicente Camps had been assigned two days earlier to the fifteen-man garrison in San Luis, seventeen miles north of Santiago de Cuba. He responded to the fugitive alert by establishing a highway roadblock and a covert watch on the railroad tracks between San Luis and the town of Dos Caminos. Early on Monday morning Raúl Castro was walking toward San Luis on the railroad tracks, having slept in a cane field in El Cristo the previous night. He had bought bread and water in Dos Caminos before stepping into the trap manned by police sergeant Emilio Bóveda González, Corporal Canet, and the policeman Victoriano Pellicier. Bóveda drove the suspect to the San Luis post because he lacked identification, while the two other policemen remained at their post.[64]

When Lieutenant Camps interrogated Raúl Castro around 8:00 A.M., Raúl claimed to be Ramón González, a brother of the leader of Batista's PAP Party in Marcané. He stated that he had attended the Santiago de Cuba carnival and was returning home to Cueto, near Marcané. Camps recalled, "Raúl lacked documentation and only had a forty-cent coin in his pocket. I became suspicious when he could not satisfactorily explain why he had not bought a round-trip ticket to attend the carnival. He then claimed that he had gone to Santiago de Cuba in a car with two friends that he named." Camps had the detainee undress so that he could check for wounds and closely examine his shoulders for traces of rifle-butt abrasions. "Although he claimed to be a peasant, I noticed that he wore jockey briefs, an undergarment not used by peasants because of their similarity to female panties. I then knew that he was a city dweller," recalled the lieutenant. Raúl's hands were shaking when he was left in a detention cell while his identity was verified.[65]

Lieutenant Camps telephoned the army chief in Alto Cedro, who replied that the person who supposedly drove Raúl to Santiago de Cuba had sold his car a month before and that the other alleged companion was convalescing with a fractured leg. Camps was given a description of Ramón González, whom Raúl Castro claimed to be, and it did not match his appearance. When the suspect was confronted with this information and the fact that neither of the two friends he mentioned had gone with him, he quickly admitted his real identity and confessed his participation. A paraffin test indicated that he had not fired a weapon. The next day Camps and two corporals escorted the prisoner to the Palma Soriano garrison, where he remained for three days before being transferred to the Santiago de Cuba *vivac* city jail, a colonial structure built in 1845. Camps then told Raúl, "Look, your brother got killed," and he gave him the progovernment *Ataja* newspaper headlined "Fidel Castro Dead." The article stated that "with all certainty, among the civilians not identified who died in the Moncada garrison attack, fell the leader of the attackers, Fidel Castro." According to Camps, the distraught youth blurted out, "He died like he wanted to. He was a big rogue." Camps asked, "Why do you say that?" Raúl replied, "Because he betrayed us. He said we were going to join some soldiers at Moncada for a coup d'etat. I did not kill anyone."[66]

After arriving in Santiago de Cuba, Raúl Castro stated to the reporters of Cadena Oriental de Radio and the *Havana Post*:

> I arrived in Santiago de Cuba on Saturday night for the purpose of taking part in the assault on the Moncada army post. I left Havana, where I live at No. 214 Neptuno St., on Friday, on the invitation of my brother Fidel, who had not explained to me the plans to take part in that attack until we arrived at the El Siboney estate. There we were told that we were going to take the Moncada Army post and how it was to be done, but everything turned out different (they had been deceived and told that the soldiers and officers were against the government and would support them). My brother assured us that there would be no murders, but when we arrived at the Civil hospital some did occur. I entered the building of the Santiago Court of Appeals, with five other comrades, to take it and prevent the armed forces from taking up positions there and firing on the attackers....
>
> At the El Siboney estate we were given the army uniforms we were to use and the weapons. We had no plans on what should be done in Cuba. I was an Ortodoxoist and I say "was" because Ortodoxoism no longer exists. Once the plan had failed, I got rid of the army uniform I was wearing and descended the hill beside the Court of Appeals, leaving the city and making for Dos Caminos, where I was arrested and taken to San Luis. Both in the San Luis and Moncada army posts we were well treated.[67]

On Tuesday morning, July 28, the army evacuated the residents around Siboney to isolate the fugitives. Julio Díaz González was sleeping in an abandoned *bohío* when its owner returned to retrieve a few belongings. The startled dweller notified a navy corporal, who arrested the rebel. Díaz voluntarily stated to the press, "I came to Santiago Saturday for the carnivals. When we arrived we were taken to a house on the Siboney highway. We were dressed in army uniforms, almost at pistol point. I was arrested on the same estate. I have not been struck. I was deceived when I was brought here. They told us that the soldiers of the army post would support us and come over to our side and that we would then go from army post to army post until we reached Havana."[68]

That morning the rebel José R. Martínez departed Santiago de Cuba in a car with Micaela Cominches, her husband, and their two children and was taken to the Panamanian Embassy in Havana, where he received asylum. His two comrades Angel Sánchez and Abelardo García had been moved from the Díaz home by Max E. Figueroa Araújo and his sister María Antonia, the organizer of the Ortodoxo Party women's section in Santiago de Cuba. Sánchez stayed with Oriente University professor Quinidio Armaignac, who applied a painful chemical formula on his hands to remove gunpowder traces. He remained in Santiago de Cuba until August 31, when he returned by bus to Havana with false identification and also obtained asylum in the Panamanian Embassy.[69]

On that same Tuesday morning, all the detainees in Moncada were transferred to the *vivac* city jail. A soldier asked the elegantly dressed Lázara Pérez Cuesta, "Are you the attorney who wanted to be First Lady?" She replied, "Look, I do not know these people." Her custodian responded, "If you are innocent, do not worry, you will be freed." Soon after arriving at the jail, Angel Díaz-Francisco began having diabetic coma symptoms. Medical student Jesús Blanco Alba took his pulse and asked him what was wrong, but an embarrassed Patachula claimed not to know. A doctor examined Díaz-Francisco, injected a dose of insulin, and had him transferred to the Civil Hospital prison ward that afternoon. Patachula joined the rebels Pedro Miret, who had a bruised forehead; Abelardo Crespo, shot in a lung; Fidel Labrador, who had lost an eye; and the comatose Rigoberto Corcho, wounded on the arm, forehead, and spine during the barbershop siege. Corcho died the next day moaning "Mama, mama."[70]

At the *vivac*, Haydée Santamaría and Melba Hernández, who was in no mood that day to celebrate her thirty-second birthday, denied to the press any link to the Auténticos or Communists. As they walked past the holding cells, Haydée told Melba, "Look good. If Abel is not here then they killed him." Haydée admitted in her 1967 memoirs that she had been looking for Fidel Castro, her brother Abel, and her boyfriend Boris Luis, not knowing what their fate was. In an interview six years later Haydée stated that at 9:00 P.M. on July 26 she heard shots in the Moncada and assumed that was when Abel was killed. These statements contradicted her previous accusations that the soldiers had shown her Abels gouged-out eye and the castrated organs of Boris immediately after their arrest. Haydée's memoirs also fail to substantiate the charge in *History Will Absolve Me* that the soldiers "burned her arms with lighted cigarettes" or Fidel Castro's statement to the reporter Kurt Singer in 1960 that soldiers "burned her arms with hot irons, trying to force her to talk." This torture falsehood has been omitted from all other accounts, including those that give credence to other aspects of the Black Legend. Weeks after the attack, while in Boniato Provincial Prison, Haydée and Melba admitted to their codefendant Ignacio Fiterre that they had exaggerated the mutilation story, although Haydée insisted that her boyfriend had been tortured. Fiterre affirmed, "Some captured rebels were beaten but I was never touched. The soldiers did not have time for organized torture, what they did was simply murder them."[71]

Herbert Matthews wrote that the eye-gouging story is "one of the enduring myths of the Moncada episode" and that although Fidel Castro learned "that it was not true" after he left prison, "the story has never been expunged" from subsequent printings of *History Will Absolve Me*. Two Cuban-American authors, supporters of the revolution, admitted that propaganda stating that the women witnessed torture is false and the accounts of ripping out eyes and castrations in *History Will Absolve Me* never occurred. Rebel leader Raúl Martínez Araras stated that his brother and other captured insurgents were murdered, but he discredited the theory of systematic torture and mutilation. Funeral director Manuel Bartolomé, who retrieved the rebel dead from Moncada and the Siboney farmhouse, including Abel Santamaría, affirmed, "I did not see any corpses showing signs of torture or missing eyes. Besides, the city had a very capable team of forensic physicians who would have voiced alarm if any evidence of torture existed. The revolutionaries created a black legend."[72]

The horrific Black Legend was unwittingly fueled by Sgt. Eulalio "El Mulo" González. Weeks after the attack, while El Mulo was on a bus to Boniato Provincial Prison, an acquaintance teased him, "I thought that you were dead after seeing your house full of bullet holes and looking like a sieve." González loudly boasted, "If I ever catch the Mau Maus who did that, I am going to rip out their eyeballs and tongues." Among the bus passengers was an elderly female dressed in black. When she got off the bus with González at the penitentiary, he learned that she was visiting her daughter Haydée Santamaría. The horrified woman repeated what González said, giving birth to the torture legend. The tale was propagated by Fidel Castro, in *History Will Absolve Me*, who emphasized, "In the annals of evil, distinction is due to Sergeant Eulalio González, known as the 'Tiger' of the Moncada Barracks. This man felt no qualms even in bragging about his unspeakable deeds. It was he who with his own hands murdered our comrade Abel Santamaría." Castro gave González a ferocious portrayal by changing his lifelong moniker, "The Mule," which he got while working with the mule transport team at La Cabaña fortress.[73]

Former police major José Villa Romero falsely declared in *Granma* newspaper in 1973 that he saw Sergeant González hold Abel Santamaría in a headlock in a Moncada cell and then order a Private Batista to stick a bayonet in his eye. Haydée previously said that her brother's eye had been poked out in the Civil Hospital and that she was pushed away by the soldiers while attempting to assist him. Lt. Ismael Valdés saw Abel unscathed at 3:00 P.M. sitting on a regimental headquarters chair. Eight hours later Lt. Jesús Yanez Pelletier noticed a truck in front of the quartermaster room being loaded with a tripod machine gun and rifles. There were two automobiles parked near the Gen. Antonio Maceo monument on the parade ground. One vehicle had just brought a prisoner from Holguín. Yanez peered into the other one and saw five young men, bound and gagged with heavy ropes; four were sitting on the backseat, and one was kneeling in the rear foot well. The lieutenant recalled, "One of them looked at me in a special way, like saying, remember this, they are going to kill me. His gaze, his eyes, are fixed in my soul, I will never forget it." He then heard Major Pérez-Chaumont tell a subaltern to ask Colonel del Río Chaviano if he wanted to include the Holguín prisoner with the others. "Tell him I do not want to make two trips," said the officer.[74]

The six prisoners, including Abel, Boris Luis, and Fernando Chenard, were taken to the Siboney farmhouse, where Angel Núñez, a neighbor, heard rifle and machine-gun fire at 1:00 A.M. Their corpses appeared in the Villa Blanca backyard the next morning. The SIM photographed each one marked with a numbered paper. In 1981 these images of Luis and Chenard were published in the book entitled *Moncada: La Acción*, and they do not depict signs of torture or mutilation. Abel's evidence photo has been omitted from all Cuban publications because it would contradict the Black Legend. Years later Yanez told Haydée of the prisoner incident and she showed him family photos of Abel. Yanez positively identified as her brother the detainee with the forlorn look in the car. Funeral director Manuel Bartolomé was called at noon the next day by Mayor Maximino Torres to dispose of the rebel dead at Siboney. Bartolomé found a body dangling on the Villa Blanca barbed-wire fence and the others scattered throughout the backyard. None had indications of torture or missing organs. After placing them in coffins, his assistant drove them to El Caney Cemetery. SIR chief Bebo Lavastida falsely claimed that Abel led "fifteen or twenty" rebels into the Moncada administrative wing and that they were all killed with hand grenades.[75]

The SIR overestimated the number of attackers and only guessed at how many had fled. They believed that Fidel Castro was in the Gran Piedra mountain range with fifty men. In jeeps the soldiers continued patrolling the dirt roads leading to El Caney and Siboney, while rebel corpses appeared in the countryside in lesser numbers. On Tuesday another body appeared on the Villa Blanca grounds and Guanajay bus driver Miguel A. Ravelo Ravelo was found shot to death in El Caney. Ravelo had gone to Santiago de Cuba with friends to enjoy the festivities. On Monday at noon he had appeared at the Route 80 bus station and showed his company identity card to obtain free return passage. Ticket clerk Ibis Fonseca, Colonel del Río Chaviano's paramour, upon hearing that he was from the same region as many of the insurgents, had notified a passing policeman. Ravelo's suitcase was searched, revealing a blood-stained shirt and T-shirt. He was taken away in a jeep by soldiers and afterward killed. Lt. Angel Machado later retrieved his suitcase from the terminal. Fonseca's boss, José Tobío, learned of the incident when he returned from lunch. A former member of the Joven Cuba revolutionary organization, he later gave a rebel passage to Havana and had him accompanied by an employee. Tobío hid another insurgent in an empty cistern while the soldiers searched the terminal.[76]

On Tuesday, at 5:00 A.M., Artemisa native Gregorio Careaga walked into Maffo and found a place to eat. He was detained by Sgt. Vicente Alonso Cruz and a squad of soldiers after being denounced by a customer. Careaga, who may have admitted his role in the attack, was murdered that morning and interred in the local cemetery. Cayo Hueso cell members Raúl de Aguiar, Armando Valle, and Andrés Valdés reached the Castro family plantation in Birán, where older brother Ramón supplied food and hid them in a cane field. When they insisted on leaving for Havana, Ramón provided funds for their trip. The trio was subsequently arrested at the Alto Cedro train station and escorted to the Rural Guard Fourteenth Squadron barracks. At midnight they were taken to the Los Cayos farm in Barrancas, near the Cauto River. Sgt. Eliodoro Montes de Oca Mayea, chief of the Central Miranda post; Cpl. Pedro A. Maceo Martí; and the lieutenant-in-chief of the Alto Cedro post killed them and dumped their bodies in a dry well.[77]

On Wednesday, July 29, a dead rebel was found in Las Piedras farm near Santiago de Cuba, and three others were killed in the Palmira farm in Bayamo. Six bodies were discovered on the road to the Gran Piedra, by the Carpintero River margin, in a wooded terrain of the San Enrique farm in Damajayabo. The medical examiners estimated that death occurred twenty-four hours earlier. Six more dead insurgents appeared on Thursday afternoon on the Daiquiri highway embankment in El Conuco, Damajayabo, having died the previous day. The twelve corpses found in Damajayabo showed signs of being shot in the head execution style.[78]

The rumors of the rebel massacre and news accounts of unidentified bodies found along the highways distressed the magistrate José M. Subirats de Quesada, president of the Cuban-Haitian Cultural Association. On Tuesday morning he called a meeting of the Santiago de Cuba civic leaders, held in the Provincial Palace of Gov. Waldo Pérez Almaguer, to find a peaceful resolution. Those present included fifty-year-old Felipe Salcines Morlote, rector of the University of Oriente; fifty-year-old Luis Savigne Pavón, grand senior warden of the Masonic Grand Lodge of Cuba and venerable master of the Armonía Lodge in Santiago de Cuba; Carlos Dellundé, editor of *Oriente* newspaper; university professor Francisco Ibarra Martínez; and a dozen others. After discussing various alternatives, they used the governor's telephone to call Catholic cardinal Manuel Arteaga in Havana. His secretary Raúl A. del Valle claimed that Arteaga was unavailable due to a migraine headache. Subirats then phoned a friend, presidential secretary Andrés Domingo Morales del Castillo, a Santiago de Cuba native, and irately asked, "What is happening? Do all of you have the intention of reviving the Machado era again with all these killings?" Morales del Castillo gave a noncommital reply, prompting Savigne to contact Masonic grand master Carlos Piñeiro del Cueto in Havana to explain the situation.[79]

Piñeiro then wrote a memorandum to General Batista regarding his telephone conversation and handed it to Morales del Castillo that afternoon in the Presidential Palace. "When I happen to see the president, I will give it to him," responded Batista's secretary. "No," stressed Piñeiro, "we have to see him quickly because this is an urgent matter." Morales del Castillo snapped back, "No one sees the president when they feel like it, it is his excellency who arranges his visits." After a heated exchange, Piñeiro went to the office of public health minister Dr. Carlos Salas Humara, whose wife, Lilia Fernández Miranda, was Batista's sister-in-law. Piñeiro, on legal retainer for the ministry, explained the situation to Salas Humara, who promised to inform the president. The Masonic grand master went home around 5:00 P.M.[80]

Two hours later Piñeiro received a call from Salas Humara urgently beckoning him to his residence, where Batista was waiting. There, Piñeiro expressed to Batista the grievances of the Santiago de Cuba civic leaders, criticized the excesses of Colonel del Río Chaviano, and pleaded for the lives of the prisoners and those willing to surrender. Batista, in the role of benevolent dictator, replied, "Yes, you are right, those young men have done the wrong things but they should not be killed, they should be taken before the tribunals." He then ordered his assistant Angel "El Viejo" Alonso Elliot to call Moncada immediately. Piñeiro overheard Batista insulting del Río Chaviano and making him responsible with his own life for any further deaths. Twenty-one years later, when the author said to Colonel del Río Chaviano, "Fidel is alive because you gave the order not to harm him," the colonel replied, "No, not me. That was the president who could do it. I think that was well done at that moment." General Batista confirmed in his memoirs, "Orders were given not to kill him." Pvt. Rafael Morales Gros, son of the regimental inspector general, stated that "there was a specific order from the President of the Republic not to kill anyone else." Batista then solicited the names of the rebel prisoners and those wanting to surrender. Piñeiro returned to the Grand Lodge at about 8:00 P.M., telephoned the request to Savigne, and described the latest developments. Savigne returned Piñeiro's call after midnight and dictated a roster, starting with Gustavo Arcos and Fidel and Raúl Castro. The list was forwarded to Batista the next day by way of Minister Salas Humara.[81]

Meanwhile, in Havana the rebel leader's wife, Mirta Díaz-Balart, had been desperately seeking intercession to safeguard her husband's life. Her father, the minister of transportation, refused to intervene. Her brother Rafael, vice minister of the interior, responded, "Fidel got himself into that mess, he should figure a way to get out of it." He later assured the press that the events in Santiago de Cuba "were part of a vast plan directed to commit a crime against the families of government members." Mirta then sought out an old school friend, the attorney Rolando Amador Hernández, and requested that he go to Oriente, fly over the countryside in a helicopter with a loudspeaker, and call on Castro to surrender. She said that Cardinal Arteaga had agreed to send his personal secretary Raúl A. del Valle to Camp Columbia and plead for her husband's life. Del Valle later told her that the authorities were uncooperative. Arteaga visited General Tabernilla on Wednesday "to say that if the Government would guarantee not to kill Fidel Castro when they captured him, his wife would reveal his hiding place." The government declined his offer, claiming that "it might not be respected by the soldiers and out of fear that Castro might resist capture." The next day, July 30, Mirta departed for Santiago de Cuba to search for her husband.[82]

The situation was being closely monitored by the American Embassy in Havana, which had a keen interest in the arrest of Communist leaders. They informed the U.S. Department of State that "Fidel Castro participated in the Cayo Confites expedition and has been accused of 'gangsterism' as a University student and of several murders." Ambassador Willard L. Beaulac sent his public affairs officer, forty-two-year-old Dr. Jacob Canter to Santiago de Cuba by bus at noon on July 26. Canter later submitted a report stating that all vehicles were stopped at military roadblocks in Oriente Province at Victoria de las Tunas, Holguín, Bayamo, Baire, Contramaestre, Palma Soriano, El Cobre, at the entrance to Santiago de Cuba, and at the bus station. At each stop, the passengers were ordered to disembark, their baggage was searched, and the men were frisked for firearms. Canter stayed at the Casa Granda Hotel that night and visited the University of Oriente the next morning. He was told by professors that persons living near Moncada heard cries of "Don't kill me!" coming from the fortress. Canter was informed that "the captured assailants had been shot down in cold blood and that the wounded assailants had also been liquidated." Canter went to the U.S. naval base at Guantánamo the next day before returning to Havana on Friday by train. To his surprise, "The train was not stopped at any point, nor searched by the military."[83]

An embassy dispatch to the U.S. Department of State on Tuesday, July 28, read: "The attack indicates considerable preparation and determination on the part of the opposition, as well as a similar determination on the part of the Armed Forces to defend themselves. While the Government has shown its ability to defend itself against attacks of this type, the fact that men were willing to die in the attempt to capture the military garrison at Santiago de Cuba is bound to impress the mass of Cubans. The suspension of Constitutional Guarantees will probably increase the Government's unpopularity."[84]

The embassy later confidentially got further details from forty-one-year-old Conrad Allain, the Cuban Ministry of Information official assigned to gather data at Santiago de Cuba. The minister of information Ernesto de la Fe Pérez, who had warned the SIM about a possible attack against Moncada, told Batista that Colonel del Río Chaviano "should be tried by court martial for breach of duty for not taking the appropriate defensive measures." Batista replied, "You take care of your ministry, because I know a lot about this." The minister of information offered his resignation, but Batista refused to accept it. De la Fe stated in 1990, "Chaviano's conduct toward those defeated was incorrect, condemnable, and unmilitary. It went against all regulations of war everywhere."[85]

The next day a commission of the Joint Committee of Civic Institutions of Santiago de Cuba, known as the Fuerzas Vivas, visited Catholic archbishop Enrique Pérez Serantes. The commission included Magistrate Subirats; Rector Salcines; thirty-nine-year-old Mariano Roca Gutiérrez, president of the Lions Club; José Medina Puig, president of the Rotary Club and venerable master of the Libertad Masonic Lodge; and others. Pérez Serantes, a sixty-nine-year-old Galician Spaniard, warmly greeted them and jested with Medina, "If the Pope sees me welcoming a Freemason, he will dismiss me." The commission suggested that Pérez Serantes meet with Colonel del Río Chaviano and plead for an end to the bloodshed. While the civic leaders waited in his office, Pérez Serantes went to see the garrison commander. Colonel del Río Chaviano denied that the army was murdering prisoners and claimed that the fugitives were clashing with their pursuers, resulting in combat deaths. The colonel stated that he would respect the lives of those surrendering for trial. He advised the archbishop to go to the countryside to find Fidel Castro and bring him in. It was the only way to save his life, claimed the regimental chief, because if there was a confrontation with the troops, he likely would not survive. Returning to the rectory, the prelate relayed the information to the civic leaders. Medina affirmed, "The only way to compromise the colonel to keep his word is to make it known publicly, otherwise it will not have any effect." Someone suggested sending a pastoral letter to the news media. Pérez Serantes replied, "My secretary is not here and I do not know how to use the typewriter." Medina began typing as the archbishop dictated the document. The prelate signed it and affixed the Church seal, and those present took copies to the newspapers, the radio stations, and the cable office, which relayed it to the press in Havana.[86]

Pérez Serantes met that evening with forty-three-year-old bachelor businessman Enrique Canto Bory, founder and president of Catholic Action in Oriente Province, to discuss the possibility of searching for the rebels in the countryside. Canto replied that it would enhance the prestige of the archbishop and the Church because the citizenry was appalled by the brutal repression. The upper classes, who did not sympathize with the government, would feel consternation if he refused to mediate. Canto added, "If you want me to accompany you, I will gladly do it. You know I am at your disposal." After his departure, Pérez Serantes summoned Subirats and Salcines to visit Colonel del Río Chaviano at home. The regimental chief stated that he had conveyed a message of pacification to the news media that afternoon. The colonel promised to suspend the search patrols to facilitate the surrender of the fugitives and ordered a 1:00 A.M. curfew on the city.[87]

On Thursday morning Canto was summoned again to the archbishop's palace, where Pérez Serantes met with more than a dozen civic leaders who were motivated by the published pastoral letter, the colonel's communiqué guaranteeing the prisoners' lives, and the prelate's acceptance to find Fidel Castro. Magistrate Subirats volunteered for the search party, indicating that his presence would ameliorate any possible danger. Thirty-five-year-old businessman Teófilo Babún Selman offered the use of his plane for the archbishop to fly over the countryside with a loudspeaker. Others expressed their own zany ideas for finding the rebel leader. Female civic leaders also got involved that day. The Lyceum Society board of directors, presided over by Corina Mestre de Arango, visited Colonel del Río Chaviano's wife, María del Carmen Palmero, and asked her to intercede in the matter. They also telephoned First Lady Marta Fernández Miranda with the same proposition and received promises of cooperation from both women. That evening Pérez Serantes called Canto to his office and confided, "In reality no one knows where Fidel is. No one gives a lead where to find him. I have spoken to Chaviano again and he has again offered me a safe-conduct to find him and turn him over to the authorities. I do not know if all of this included a plan of his to detain him, or I think that maybe he has received superior orders from the presidency. It is possible that national public opinion and the foreign press, could have forced Batista to take the determination." Canto agreed, adding that the Vista Alegre bourgeoisie had greater sympathy for the rebel plight while the workers remained neutral, possibly because the Cuban Workers Confederation (CTC) secretary general Eusebio Mujal Barniol, a former Auténtico senator, was a Batista supporter.[88]

While they spoke, Maj. Andrés Pérez-Chaumont and the paymaster Capt. Manuel F. Alonso Lemus visited the archbishop, who asked Canto to wait outside. After privately meeting with the officers, Pérez Serantes asked his friend to reenter the room. The archbishop introduced Canto as the person willing to accompany him to find Fidel Castro. The major smiled sarcastically and asked Canto if he was not afraid of searching for the "murderers" in the countryside. Canto responded, "I am willing to go where the archbishop goes, in whose company no harm can occur." Pérez-Chaumont claimed that the dead bodies appearing along the highways were the results of armed encounters between the army and the "criminals" who attacked Moncada. When the officers departed, Pérez Serantes informed Canto that the major confidentially supported the humanitarian gesture of sparing Castro's life if he was presented to the authorities. Pérez-Chaumont stated that he could not guarantee anything if there was a confrontation with the troops. "Our soldiers, he said, are very nervous. They have a great desire of avenging those who, without logical or moral reason, attacked the garrison and killed some of their comrades." The archbishop added that the officers were concerned that the rebels might take him and the search party as hostages to break out of the army's encirclement.[89]

The indiscriminate killing of prisoners by a group of vengeful soldiers ceased after Batista reproached Colonel del Río Chaviano. Corporal Alcolea recalled that mimeographed flyers were posted on the Guard Corps wall proclaiming: "Respect the lives of the insurgents as if it were the life of the chief of the regiment." Although sixty-one revolutionaries died, Fidel Castro claimed that more than seventy were killed, and José Ponce inflated the amount to "99 combatants dead." A few rebels surrendered after the publication of the pastoral letter guaranteeing their lives. Raúl del Mazo Serra, organizer of Acción Libertadora, appeared at Moncada's Post 5 to turn himself in after hiding since Sunday. He was surprised when told to return the next day because SIR chief Bebo Lavastida was absent. The following morning del Mazo was interrogated in regimental headquarters and locked in a Guard Corps holding cell. Among the prisoners was Gustavo Ameijeiras Romo, who was charged with aiding the attackers after arriving from Havana to claim the body of his half brother Juan Ameijeiras Delgado. The dentist Pedro Aguilera was persuaded by his parents to surrender. Ernesto Tizol, after hiding at his father's home in Holguín, turned himself in after the truce. He was wrought with guilt for deserting his comrades on the way to the Moncada attack. His father arranged his surrender on Friday, July 31, through a priest and the venerable master of a local Masonic lodge. Tizol was escorted to Moncada, where he gave a full confession to Captain Lavastida. The next day Mauro Suárez Suárez was arrested and erroneously accused of participating in the Bayamo attack.[90]

The disorganized rebel retreat was, like the attack, catastrophic. Although many rebels went into combat believing Fidel Castro's claim that some Moncada soldiers would join them, this turned out to be false. Raúl Castro stated after his arrest that the rebels had no plan for what should be done in Cuba. The Communist Party was technically correct in accusing Castro of leading a bourgeois putsch instead of a revolution. Castro had not prepared the groundwork with the Cuban masses for a traditional revolution but had instead based his actions on a dissatisfied youth faction of the Ortodoxo Party. He told his followers that the government would have collapsed into his grasp by one blow had the Moncada attack succeeded. That would have constituted a putsch, similar to Adolf Hitler's 1923 beer-hall putsch in Germany, and the Cuban Communists rightly accused Castro of using "Putschist methods."

The rebels had no contingency plan in case of failure and lacked medical supplies for the wounded at Villa Blanca and in Bayamo. Leaving behind all their personal documentation in both cities was a tactical error that later allowed the SIM to identify many of them quickly. The fugitives, abandoned to fate in a province in which their appearance and idiom made them identifiable strangers, could survive only with the assistance of Ortodoxo militants and Good Samaritans. The Catholic Church, the Freemasons, and civic leaders played decisive roles in interceding on behalf of the rebels because of the ghastly impression caused by the deadly reprisals. As a result, Raúl Castro and Julio Díaz told the media after their arrest that they had not been beaten and were "well treated" by their captors.

The government, responding to the Montreal Conference propaganda and conspiracy rumors, detained scores of opposition leaders nationwide. Colonel del Río Chaviano blamed Auténticos, Ortodoxos, and Communists for leading an insurrection planned in Montreal. The regimental chief was guilty of disregarding stronger security measures under warnings of a possible pending attack, avoiding combat, and condoning the massacre of rebel detainees and innocent civilians. It was the largest slaughter of prisoners in the history of the republic and violated the rules of war under the four 1949 Geneva Conventions, of which Cuba is a signatory nation, prohibiting the inhumane treatment of noncombatants. These were defined as civilians, prisoners, and enemy soldiers wounded in battle. The rules specify that noncombatants cannot be executed or treated cruelly.

Colonel del Río Chaviano, to cover up the murder of prisoners and his own ineptitude, falsified his report to the tribunal and fabricated the story that his sentinels had their throats slit and hospital patients were stabbed to death in their beds. Batista unwittingly repeated these apocryphal accounts during his speech to the nation on July 27 and claimed to be defending the country against Communist action. The threat of Communist involvement in the attack and cold-war fears prompted the United States Embassy to gather information and forward their own assessment to the U.S. Department of State. The initial report was superficial and speculative, failing to determine rebel strength and motives properly and focusing instead on the government repression and atrocities.

Fidel Castro's Black Legend of systematic torture, the burning of Haydée's arms with lit cigarettes and hot irons, eye gouging, castration, and dismemberment does not hold up to the impartial testimony of funeral director Manuel Bartolomé or revolutionary leaders Raúl Martínez Araras and Ignacio Fiterre, and it is not sustained by forensic photographs or death certificates. The manhunt headed by a faction of vengeful officers had a devastating effect on the insurgents. More than half of those returning to the Siboney farmhouse lost faith in their leader and left him. The nineteen who followed Castro after the Moncada attack lacked the will to continue fighting, wanted to avoid a confrontation with the army, had no plans or supplies to start a guerrilla war, and desperately sought safety in the nearby wooded hills.

SEVEN

"You do not kill ideas"

Fidel Castro and nineteen followers fled the Siboney farmhouse on Sunday at around 7:00 A.M., thirty minutes after arriving there. They crossed the Siboney highway heading in a northeastern direction, toward Ocaña Heights. Castro stated years later that "our objective was to go to the mountains to carry out irregular warfare in the mountains." According to the participants Mario Chanes, Eduardo Montano, Gerardo Granados, and Jaime Costa, there was no plan for guerrilla operations; they wanted only to avoid a military encirclement. The rebels crossed the Angel Núñez farm and regrouped two hundred yards further at Moya Hill. Castro tore up his driver's license and told the others to discard all identification documents. Emilio Hernández, his feet galled by new shoes, decided to return to Santiago de Cuba. He flagged down a truck, which was later stopped at a military roadblock. Hernández was escorted to the Siboney farmhouse, where his corpse was later found.[1]

The rest of the fugitives hiked for ninety minutes before sighting a *bohío* in the hilly woodlands. Castro ordered Jesús Montané, Rosendo Menéndez, and Mario Lazo to search it. Its owner, Leocadia "Chicha" García Garzón, a black woman in her eighties, soon appeared with her daughter Tomasa and daughter-in-law Justina. She proposed going to find her grandson to assist them, but the intruders were hesitant. Chicha, sensing their distrust, produced an 1895 letter signed by Cuban independence general Antonio Maceo and identifying her as a patriot messenger. The octogenarian began brewing coffee for the trio, while Montané and Menéndez went to summon the others. Castro, wearing military pants and a knitted, short-sleeved, white sports shirt, tinkered in vain with a broken radio to tune in the news. The insurgents, constantly fearing betrayal, left after sipping coffee and obtaining cigarettes. A grateful Gerardo Granados recalled giving Justina "all the money I had, which was three pesos and eighty cents, and asked her to take it, since we would not be needing it." Some rebels, unfit for the strenuous hike, lingered behind the rest, especially the pudgy and asthmatic Montané, who was burdened by flat feet. Granados remembered that Armando Mestre, a robust Afro-Cuban, "was almost carrying Montané, who was leaning heavily on him." Eduardo Montano quipped, "Montané was worse off than the wounded." Reinaldo Benítez, hobbling on a wounded leg, was aided by Israel Tápanes and Lazo.[2]

At 9:00 A.M. Chicha's twenty-three-year-old grandson, Esmérido Rivera Ruá, returned home after fetching water from a river and heard of the recent events. The peasant took a nap but was soon awakened by dogs barking at the troops scouting the area. Fearing retribution against his family for assisting the escapees, he went to alert them to leave the area. As Esmérido approached the fugitive encampment on a nearby rocky bank of the Carpintero River, Jaime Costa aimed a gun at him. The frightened man quickly raised his hands, identified himself, and warned of the approaching danger. Fidel Castro asked the peasant to guide them to the Gran Piedra mountain, but Esmérido replied that it was a dangerous route and instead took them along the river's edge toward Ocaña Heights. After a few miles the group stopped under a honeyberry tree to gather its yield while Castro climbed a guava tree to pick fruit and reconnoiter the area. Esmérido led them for ninety minutes in a northeastern direction up to the Gran Piedra highway bridge over the Carpintero River. Before departing, he gave Castro a pack of cigarettes and shook hands with all the rebels. Armando Mestre begged the peasant not to betray them. On his return home, Esmérido was questioned by the soldiers but claimed not to have seen anyone.[3]

As the rebels continued following the riverbank, a female voice pleaded not to proceed because her daughter was bathing. Oscar Alcalde chuckled, "Don't worry, we will look the other way." That afternoon the fugitives reached La Pelá cane field, owned by the Salmón family, and stopped to rest. Castro replayed the suicide scene he had acted out at Villa Blanca earlier. Chanes heard him say, "The revolution is lost, my brother has been killed, and I should shoot myself." As the rebel leader pulled out his pistol, Chanes grabbed it from him and said, "You are crazy. How can you say that?" Forty years later Chanes commented in retrospect, "Time has shown that instead of studying law, Fidel should have been an actor." An hour later the escapees sighted a *bohío* at Caballería Hill in Ocaña Heights. Castro sent as scouts the only two dark-skinned insurgents, Mestre and Juan Almeida, who could blend in with the local blacks. After signaling that no one was home, they were joined by Roberto "Bolo" Galán and Mario Lazo in searching the shack for food. The rebels found only salt, a chunk of yam, coffee, and a water container. Chanes recalled that "Pepe Suárez saw four piglets outside and fired a bullet at one, which then ran away." Felipe Rigel Boris, the forty-five-year-old Afro-Cuban tenant, who had been sitting under a nearby tree, protested their intrusion. Some rebels laughed when the man stuttered in fear. When they failed to coerce him into forfeiting a piglet, Pepe Suárez snarled, "find a rope to hang him right now." Castro then managed to convince the stubborn Rigel to help them find a hog. The peasant led them to a nearby six-dwelling hamlet occupied by his relatives, who were squatters on the Juraguá Iron Company lands. The region had abounded during the early nineteenth century with coffee plantations owned by wealthy French refugees from Haiti. The ravages of the Cuban wars of independence (1868–98) had left only the charred ruins of their mansions and overgrown trails.[4]

The fugitives were introduced to Justino Rigel Boris, who provided a guayabera for Alcalde and gave Castro a pair of medium-size pants that were altered to fit him. Efigenia Despaigne and her sister Basilia washed, ironed, and sewed the tattered rebel garments and tended Benítez's wound. Gilberto Despaigne slaughtered a pig, and by sundown the insurgents were eating pork fricassee, beechnuts, and yams. Castro expressed his gratitude by giving Justino a pistol. Chanes saw the peasant "grab the weapon with his thumb and forefinger, not knowing what to do with it." Justino later discarded the firearm and Castro's torn khaki pants. Montano conjectured, "I do not know if they helped us motivated by fear or to quickly get rid of us. Every time we appeared, people were frightened." Oscar Alcalde stated that "the peasants saw us with distrust and if they did not denounce us, they also did not provide aid. The revolutionary consciousness was not yet mature." Jaime Costa reminisced, "All those peasants interviewed in 1967 who said that they gladly helped us, except for two or three, they did so out of fear because we were armed. Nobody did it voluntarily. We were scared and without food."[5]

Before dinner ended, news arrived of an approaching Rural Guard detachment, and Castro asked his host to lead them to the Escandel region. Mario Lazo hurriedly crammed the pork and yam leftovers into a large tin can, which he placed in a jute sack. Felipe and Justino Rigel and their cousin Felipe Despaigne guided the group up a wooded, rocky hillside in a northwestern direction. Castro soon sent Despaigne back due to his continuous nervous cough. As the rebels groped their way through the darkness, along steep slopes littered with loose rocks, Chucho Montané tumbled into a ravine, landed on a thorny bush, and lost his eyeglasses. He tearfully told his companions to leave him there. Costa replied, "horses get shot when they break a leg. If you do not continue, I am going to kill you, because you are going to denounce our position." After Montané was pulled out with a cane pole, the group bedded down in a dell at 11:00 P.M. Justino warned some insurgents who lit cigarettes not to smoke "because there are lights below and the dogs bark." He then pointed out the distant glare of the Santiago de Cuba skyline. Before departing with his brother, Justino advised the fugitives to keep to the right of a nearby barbed-wire fence until they heard roosters crowing. They would then be at El Café farm, and from there the road led to Escandel Hill. The rebels moved a few hundred yards further up the slope, establishing a four-man perimeter watch at 1:00 A.M. while the rest slept. Granados recalled, "I dozed with my legs between a tree to prevent from rolling down the hillside in the darkness."[6]

At dawn on Monday, July 27, the eighteen rebels wearily moved on. Lazo said that they camouflaged their heads with foliage upon hearing an aircraft approaching. The regimental plane, a de Havilland DHC-2 Beaver piloted by 2nd Lt. Randolfo Cossío, was reconnoitering the coast of Siboney and Daiquiri searching for the escapees and Prío's invasion force recently heralded in *Visión* magazine. The fugitives, after a four-hour march, spotted a few *bohíos* in the distance at the bottom of a precipice and began a precarious descent. They approached Eduardo Despaigne, a young Afro-Cuban peasant with polio-withered legs, who was scooting on a trundle board while planting lettuce. He was frightened by their rifles and expressed amazement that they had descended the steep cliff without injury. Despaigne provided coffee and crackers and distracted himself by playing a three-string instrument. Castro chided him, "Boy, do not play, many brothers have died." Mario Chanes and others shaved with Despaigne's razor. Jaime Costa recalled, "To gain his confidence, we promised the crippled man a wheel chair." Mario Lazo stated that Castro gave Despaigne a note instructing him to write for assistance to radio commentator Guido García Inclán, who penned the charity column "¡Arriba Corazones!" in *Bohemia*. Fourteen years later the paraplegic, still without a wheelchair, stated that Castro was going to give him the note but instead kept it in his pocket and told him, "When we triumph, present yourself." Despaigne told the rebels that the only neighbor with a radio was Feliciano Heredia and pointed toward El Café farm. The escapees reached the Heredia residence around 11:30 A.M. Feliciano's wife provided water and tuned in a battery radio, which broadcast Batista's speech denouncing the previous day's events. Montano reminisced, "I barely heard the radio because it had very bad reception. Fidel is the one who listened to all of it." Chanes recalled that "the news gave the names of thirty-three dead rebels. We commented that the prisoners were being murdered, since our estimated combat losses were no more than eight." Listed among the battle casualties was Emilio Hernández, who had abandoned their group near Siboney.[7]

The fugitives ventured further into the countryside, where Lazo and Menéndez approached the *bohío* of Pedro Despaigne Vinent and Tomasa Tejeda. Despaigne recalled that "they asked if I could cook food, that they were eighteen." His son Agustín was sent to scout for army patrols and quickly returned after seeing them nearby. Despaigne then agreed to feed the group if they did not stay in his house. Castro gave the boy a twenty-peso bill to buy condensed milk, crackers, and cigarettes and told him to bring back the change in single denominations. Agustín returned with the full amount because his father insisted on paying for everything. The group ate at 3:00 P.M. in the nearby Arroyo Seco del Café clearing and departed after a few hours. When they reached the summit of a hill thirty minutes later, the insurgents rested while Chanes and two others returned to Despaigne's home to fetch water.[8]

Fidel Castro led his followers for an hour in the opposite direction of the Gran Piedra. A torrential downpour compelled them to seek shelter in a cave. An hour later the disoriented rebels unwittingly headed back on the same route, walking on rocks to avoid leaving footprints. Lazo recalled, "we were lost often, sometimes we would march for a while and again come out in the same place where we had left. This I personally proved by making a mark on a small tree." Granados, with Almeida in agreement, told Castro, "We want to go to a specific place and instead are needlessly going in circles. If you insist on leading us, we will take another route." The rebel leader replied, "We should all stick together. Which way do you want to go?" Someone said, "this way," pointing in another direction, and Castro followed them. Granados believed that "Fidel wanted to stay in that area so that he could later return to Santiago de Cuba where he had friends." At midnight the insurgents encamped on the rocky Alto de la Redonda hillside. Granados recalled asking Lazo to swap weapons because "Mario had a pistol without a trigger guard and I wanted to trade him my rifle for it, since it would be easier to conceal, but he balked at the suggestion."[9]

Lazo placed the loaded pistol next to him when he went to sleep. He initially stated that it "discharged when a sentry stepped on it," firing a bullet that penetrated under his right armpit and exited though his back. Lazo recalled how he "remained tranquil on the ground, laying as I was, not feeling pain. Everyone was alarmed and upon seeing me on the ground bleeding they thought I was dead. Fidel said that it was very sad having to leave a companion buried there. I responded that no one had to be buried, that I was all right." Lazo later stated that the pistol might have discharged when he rolled over on it. Chanes dismissed Lazo's account as an embellishment, stating, "Lazo was standing next to me when he dropped his pistol and collapsed from being shot. I immediately applied my handkerchief to his wound. No one mentioned leaving him buried there. That is an exaggeration." Since there were no medical supplies, the only relief Lazo received was gulping two cans of condensed milk.[10]

Granados recalled that on Tuesday morning, July 28, "Fidel said we should split into smaller groups to make our escape easier. I asked who wanted to go with me, and Jaime Costa responded affirmatively. We stayed awhile after the others left and grabbed a discarded wicker bag full of bullets. It was an assortment of rounds that we later sorted out and threw away the calibers we did not need." Artemisa natives Ricardo Santana and the Galán brothers backtracked to Siboney Beach. Castro then ordered those slowing him down to return unarmed to Santiago de Cuba to seek medical attention for Lazo and Benítez. The wounded men were accompanied by Severino Rosell, Rosendo Menéndez, Israel Tápanes, and Jesús Montané, who departed wearing foliage camouflage due to the increase of army surveillance flights. After walking for three hours in a heavy rainfall, they arrived back at the Despaigne *bohío*. The peasant's wife Tomasa treated Lazo's wound with medicinal herbs, sugar, and a tobacco-leaf plug, which stemmed the bleeding. She also washed his guayabera and mended the bullet hole. The fugitives hid in a nearby cave while the peasant woman prepared their lunch. They departed that afternoon, during a lull in the rain, with a jute sack containing a few chunks of bread, crackers, and a can of condensed milk. Montané gave his car keys to Tomasa as a memento, and she still had them fourteen years later. The six insurgents headed west toward Santiago de Cuba until bedding down under a pigpen eave after midnight.[11]

The group hiked on Wednesday morning for three hours under an intermittent rain. When they approached a *bohío*, its frightened inhabitant refused to let them in. The strangers requested and received directions to La Dorotea dairy farm, owned by Benjamín Arza and his wife Barbara Balart, the aunt of Mirta Díaz-Balart. After receiving refuge at the farm, Lazo and Rosell bickered with their companions about returning safely to Santiago de Cuba and decided to remain on the Arza property. Montané, Menéndez, Tápanes, and Benítez departed and walked a few miles in a southwestern direction until reaching the residence of Domingo Badell and Mercedes Silva on the Siboney highway, halfway between the Moncada garrison and Villa Blanca. They were treated to breakfast, and Benítez received medical assistance before the four split up. Montané and Menéndez were arrested on the Siboney highway near Santiago de Cuba after a "hysterical woman" denounced them to two passing motorcycle officers. Tápanes and Benítez were captured in a dry dell near the Badell home by an army patrol. The four detainees were sent to the Moncada garrison for interrogation by SIR chief Bebo Lavastida.[12]

Tápanes told reporters, "They arrested me when I had almost arrived at Santiago de Cuba, for I was on my way to give myself up. I was taken to the Army Post under duress and did not participate in the assault on it. I have been offered cigarettes and everything we needed." Menéndez then provided his version of the events: "I was brought here under false pretenses by some friends of Fidel Castro and others who lived around Artemisa. I was not put into uniform nor did I take part in the assault. I have been well treated. My relatives need have no fear for me." Reinaldo Benítez followed suit, claiming, "No, I am not directly acquainted with Fidel Castro, for I have never seen him, but Tápanes told me we were going to the carnival. I received my wound as I turned a corner in the car during the shooting. I fell to the ground and realized I was wounded. I stayed there but immediately another car came and picked me up, making off in the direction of the jungle."[13]

Jesús Montané declared "that he had surrendered voluntarily to a patrol on the Sevilla highway. He said he was taken to the Moncada Army Post at 10:00 A.M." He emphasized, "I did not take part in the assault because, before the car arrived, I had trouble with one of the tires and, since there was no spare, I had to remain where I was until we later fled into the mountains." Montané concluded, "In justice I can say that I have not been beaten at any time . . . I came to Santiago on the invitation of a friend, together with five others, without knowing what was in store for us and believing that we had come only for target practice." Montané changed his story in 1959, claiming that he was insulted, slapped, threatened with death, and subjected to "mental tortures, but I always denied my participation in the attack."[14]

The next morning the four prisoners were transferred from the garrison to the *vivac* city jail and subjected to paraffin tests on their hands. The Urgency Tribunal then indicted forty-three detainees in Santiago de Cuba; Millo Ochoa and Juan Marinello Vidaurreta, who were imprisoned in Havana; former president Carlos Prío and his minister of state Aureliano Sánchez Arango, who were in exile; and Fidel Castro and other escapees. Havana Bar Association president José Miró Cardona instructed the attorney Humberto Sorí Marín to obtain legal assistance from the Santiago de Cuba Bar Association for those implicated who were lawyers.[15]

After the eighteen rebels split up on Tuesday morning, Fidel Castro was left with Oscar Alcalde, Juan Almeida, Mario Chanes, Pancho González, Armando Mestre, Eduardo Montano, and José Suárez. According to Chanes, they spent all day "walking up and down hills," backtracking in a southeasterly direction. He stated that they did not encounter any peasants and were unable to find any food or water. The group was slowed down by those afflicted with diarrhea after overindulging on mangoes the previous night. On Wednesday morning, after being drenched by torrential rain, the rebels were spotted near an abandoned strip mine by 2nd Lt. Randolfo Cossío while he was piloting a regimental aircraft. Cossío radioed the information to Moncada, prompting Capt. Bebo Lavastida and sixty soldiers to converge on the nearby Soledad farm mining pit, which was operated by José Rodríguez, known as "Pepe Secundino." The soldiers found a group of miners loading mineral rock onto trucks that were parked 350 yards downhill from the escapees. The foreman vouched for the identity of the laborers. As the army patrol was leaving, a lieutenant told a sergeant, "The plane made a mistake, damn. He saw the miners and communicated they were the attackers."[16]

After the incident, the miner Alfonso Feal Despaigne, a forty-six-year-old squatter, left for home during a rainstorm. While walking along a curve in the road, he encountered the eight fugitives. Chanes recalled that Feal warned them, "Boys, do not continue. Up ahead, at the mine, there is a jeep with soldiers. They are going to kill you." The peasant agreed to assist them if they did not enter the *bohío* where his wife had just given birth to their eleventh son. He was concerned that she would be frightened and die of shock. Feal, accompanied by his ten-year-old son General and a younger boy, took the rebels up a hillside. Castro asked the miner to send the boys for food and a pair of trousers, but Feal insisted on going himself. Chanes requested a jute sack and a pair of peasant, rope-soled sandals. The miner soon returned with the requested items plus a bag of crackers, a bottle with coffee, and a pair of pants too short for Castro. Feal continued leading the fugitives in a northeasterly direction toward the Gran Piedra mountain range. Chanes kept glancing back at the Santiago de Cuba lights fading in the distance as they walked uphill until 8:00 P.M. Before returning home, Feal advised the rebels to keep traveling upward in a straight line. The insurgents went beyond Tierra Colorada and changed course various times to evade distant flickering lights that they assumed were army patrols. They eventually bedded down on palm fronds under a mango tree.[17]

When the rebels awoke at dawn on Thursday, July 30, they saw a boy on the road leading a cow by a rope. After the boy indicated that his family lived nearby, Castro asked him to get his father. Chanes recalled, "we were greatly surprised at seeing Feal arrive. We had walked in a circle and ended up back behind his home." Castro told the miner, "Excuse my returning to your home, I am asking you to get me away from here." The disoriented fugitives were only two miles northwest of Felipe Rigel's *bohío*, where they had been three days earlier. Feal hid them in the bushes while he scouted the area from a treetop. He then took the rebels to Los Chivos Cave on a hill crest near the Soledad farm mining pit. After returning home, Feal heard the news that Colonel del Río Chaviano had promised Archbishop Pérez Serantes to safeguard the lives of surrendering fugitives. The peasant then carried a few bottles with coffee and water and eight codfish sandwiches to the cave. He informed the rebels of the latest news and insisted that they stay there. A reporter who interviewed Feal years later stated that "he chatted with three of them, one of whom asked him about the possibility of taking them to Santiago de Cuba in a mineral truck."[18]

René Celeiro, a truck driver on the route from the mine to the city wharf, remembered that Feal "proposed to me that I take Fidel to Santiago de Cuba, as if he worked on the truck with me, disguised as a trucker's assistant. Fidel and two others did not want to surrender and wanted to leave surreptitiously. It was impossible because the soldiers were everywhere, searching all the vehicles that went out." Chanes and Montano were unaware that the rebel leader was secretly negotiating his own escape. Castro had given them the name and address of a woman who owned a pharmacy in Santiago de Cuba and who could help them get away. This was apparently Dr. Ana Rosa Sánchez, whom the widower Fidel Pino Santos was wooing and for whom he had bought the business. Feal sought his boss, Pino, the rebel leader's namesake and his father's benefactor, and explained the situation. Pino agreed to go to Santiago de Cuba and have the archbishop intercede. According to Celeiro, Feal feared that the army might return with the prelate and endanger his household in a crossfire with the rebels. Feal fled with his family to Santiago de Cuba in Pino's vehicle. When he did not return by 5:00 P.M., Castro led the rebels away from the area. Celeiro stated that "Fidel saw from the mountain top when Feal evacuated his family with their belongings. Fearing betrayal, he left with his followers and later ended up in Las Delicias farm, owned by my cousins." According to Enrique Canto, Pino notified Pérez

Serantes that Fidel Castro and seven companions were hiding in a cave near Sevilla; that one of them was black; that another one, Oscar Alcalde, was in an extreme state of exhaustion; and that "the rebels wanted to surrender in his presence."[19]

Among the escapees still at large that Thursday were Artemisa natives Ciro Redondo and Marcos "El Curro" Martí, who had been hiding in Dead Man's Cave for four days while receiving covert assistance from the Campanal family. Arturo Campanal had taken his brood to Santiago de Cuba the previous morning to safeguard them. He consulted with his friend Vicente Castelló, a fifty-seven-year-old in the coffee business, who agreed to transport Redondo and Martí to his farm in a coffee truck. Castelló's forty-three-year-old wife, Amelia Fajardo, recalled that the Campanal family then stayed "during three or four difficult days" at her home in Sueño neighborhood.[20]

On Thursday morning a dozen soldiers acting on a tip from a local alcoholic nicknamed "Carburo," arrived at Dead Man's Cave. When Redondo saw them enter the cave, he shouted his willingness to surrender. Pvt. Farik Babún Serret heard Marcos "El Curro" Martí yell, "do not give yourself up to those rogues." The teenage rebel, who three months earlier had been arrested in Artemisa for slapping a Rural Guard at a dance hall, refused an order to raise his hands and cursed at the soldiers. In 1982 Babún stated, falsely, that a soldier "shot Martí in the back." Yet, El Curro's forensic certificate indicates that bullets hit him in the chest, right shoulder, and through the heart. Redondo was sent to the El Caney *vivac* jail, and his companion was interred in El Caney Cemetery in the same tomb as Reinaldo Boris Luis, near sixteen unmarked rebel graves. Another Artemisa native, Ramiro Valdés, who abandoned his car with a flat tire in Vista Alegre after the attack, was arrested on Friday by the army in the Santiago de Cuba suburb of La Calera while on the El Morro highway. In the *vivac* city jail he told the press that he had been invited to the carnival but upon arriving was transferred to the Siboney farmhouse. Valdés indicated that after being taken to Moncada he "fled to the hills toward Morro Castle," and he "assured not knowing Fidel Castro or the other detainees."[21]

These events, along with Fidel Pino's message, prompted in Archbishop Pérez Serantes the urgency to save rebel lives. On Friday, July 31, at 9:00 A.M. he telephoned Enrique Canto at work and requested that Canto accompany him to retrieve Fidel Castro and his companions from the cave in which they were hiding. Although the archbishop insisted on discretion, Canto informed his brother of their plans. Shortly thereafter three jeeps stopped in front of Canto's La Francia department store, the second largest of its kind in the city. Pérez Serantes was in the first vehicle with Magistrate José Subirats de Quesada and the businessman Manuel Cuadrado Barrueco at the wheel. The second jeep was driven by Cuadrado's father-in-law, Fidel Pino Santos, accompanied by grocery retailer Antonio Guerra Cisneros. Canto got into the last vehicle driven by the archbishop's chauffeur, Oscar Anglada.[22]

The caravan took the Siboney highway to the Sevilla hamlet, where an army patrol led by a black lieutenant was deployed at a gas station. Pérez Serantes informed the officer of his mission and continued with his retinue up a winding, narrow road. At a prearranged roadside location, a large *guásima* tree, Alfonso Feal appeared shortly thereafter with his seventeen-year-old son. He stated that they had searched all morning further up the hill for the fugitives. Pérez Serantes ordered his driver to proceed slowly, as he stood grasping the top of the windshield while calling on the insurgents to come out. Assuming that the jeep might be mistaken for a military vehicle, the archbishop walked alone on the road so that his white cassock would be clearly visible to the rebels.[23]

Canto, accompanying Feal's son onto a wooded trail, found a freshly discarded mango peel. He called out Castro's name but heard only his own echo in reply. Canto was then joined by another Feal youngster at an abandoned dry coffee bed. After returning to the *guásima* tree, the search party ate sardines that Anglada had bought in Sevilla to observe the archbishop's Friday meat abstinence. The soldiers had suspected that the food was destined for the rebels. At 2:00 p.m. Canto asked Feal's sons to search again for Castro, believing that the younger one knew his location, but the boys returned at sundown with only a handful of .22-caliber hollow-point bullets. Pérez Serantes headed back to Santiago de Cuba, assuming that if the rebels had not heard their calls, they would be informed of his mission by the local peasants. He stopped at various *bohíos* to distribute medals of the Virgin of Charity, Cuba's patron saint. Some peasants cried as the archbishop left, fearing army reprisals because the fugitives were in the area. The prelate again spoke with the black lieutenant in Sevilla before returning home. Canto told the archbishop that he would see him at the six o'clock mass the next morning.[24]

Pérez Serantes was annoyed when he met that night at Moncada with Colonel del Río Chaviano and Lt. Col. González Alfonso. He stated, "Well, gentlemen, my mission has ended. I have been unable to find Fidel." The archbishop admitted that the rebels, who were supposed to surrender to him near El Cilindro farm in Sevilla, never appeared. After Pérez Serantes left regimental headquarters, the officers discussed renewing the search patrols that had been suspended during the archbishop's mission. "Colonel," said González Alfonso, "do not send Pérez-Chaumont, who is unfamiliar with the area; send a Rural Guard squad that knows the territory." Del Río Chaviano summoned Capt. José C. Tandrón Femenías, chief of the Rural Guard Eleventh Squadron, and ordered that he "assign an officer with a patrol to go on a search mission tomorrow morning."[25]

Meanwhile, after the insurgents fled Los Chivos Cave on Thursday evening, according to Chanes, Fidel Castro "was indecisive on what course to follow. Sometimes he went one way and then would lead us in the opposite direction. We were lost. When Almeida and Mestre started falling behind, a despondent Fidel accused them of attempting to leave the group, but they denied it." That night the escapees slept in a cattle pasture. The next morning a discussion ensued in which Almeida complained about their irresoluteness. Chanes proposed remaining in the mountains instead of returning to the city, and everyone agreed. When the archbishop and Feal searched for them that day above Los Chivos Cave, the rebels had descended to the Aguada de Yaba dell. Chanes remembered, "We were looking for food and water when we came upon some rain puddles that contained larvae. Everyone drank from them to avoid dying of thirst." In the afternoon they plucked all the fruit from a honeyberry tree, eating some and saving the rest in a jute sack. At six o'clock that evening the rebels sighted a column of smoke in the distance. They headed toward the *bohío* of Luis Piña, a youthful squatter on the 100-acre Mampriváa property. Piña worked as a dairy hand on the 430-acre Las Delicias farm, which was owned by the Leizán family and bordered on the north side with Mampriváa.[26]

Chanes recalled that they encountered Piña walking on a trail and that he led them to his *bohío*. The shirtless Castro identified himself as "Alejandro" and asked the peasant if he knew about the Moncada attack. After a positive reply, he inquired if he knew the fate of the leader's brother but got a negative answer. Castro requested food, and Piña provided the fugitives with rice-and-beans dinner leftovers simmering in a kettle over an open pit. The rebel leader then queried about the strength of the local Ortodoxo Party, admitting that they belonged to the Ortodoxo Youth. When Castro inquired about their location, he was told that they were within earshot of the Siboney highway, less than three miles northwest of Villa Blanca. During the previous six days Castro had never led his men beyond a five-mile radius from the Siboney farmhouse. Montano believed that Castro's secret agenda was to remain in the area. Fidel Castro had been the Belén High School Explorers' leader and had frequently visited El Caney and Siboney Beach while a student at Santiago de Cuba. It was suspicious that he would be so disoriented in familiar territory. The rebels distanced themselves from Piña to discuss their situation. The peasant overheard Pepe Suárez say, "If he tries to leave we have to kill him." Castro overruled him, stressing that the young man could help them.[27]

When Fidel Castro asked Piña for more food, he led the group downhill in the darkness to Las Delicias farm. The peasant indicated that soldiers were quartered in the dimly lit houses seen half a mile away. Las Delicias dairy farm contained a family dwelling and a smaller adjacent ranch-hand bunkhouse. In the main house lived Manuel Leizán, his fifty-four-year-old wife Manuela Montero, their sons Juan and Alfredo, their twenty-three-year-old daughter Carmen, and Josefita, an adopted black girl. The bunkhouse was occupied by their twenty-six-year-old cousin Manuel Montero Moscoso, who had emigrated from Spain in February, and two farmhands. While the rebels waited by a cattle trail, Piña knocked on the house door and asked for Manuel "Lelín" Leizán Montero. The patriarch replied that his oldest son was in

Santiago de Cuba and summoned Juan, who listened to Piña and said, "wait until the women go to bed because they are very excitable." The peasant returned to where he had left the rebels, but they were gone. After he whistled loudly, they emerged from various places. Piña chided Castro for being distrustful, and Castro apologized and asked for the requested food. He was informed that they would have to wait until the women were asleep. Castro then asked to meet the farm owner, prompting the peasant to go back to the house for instructions.[28]

Juan Leizán told Piña that only one person should come forward to meet him. The farmhand departed with a seven-pound can of Miño sausages, bread, crackers, and a liter of milk. Three rebels gulped the entire contents of the milk bottle among themselves, prompting Castro to scold them for not sharing with the others. Piña announced that whoever was their leader should go back with him to speak to his boss. "I am the one who is going," replied Castro, and at Piña's request he left his pistol behind. At the rendezvous site Piña found Juan hiding behind a barn post. The "almost naked" Castro shook hands with Leizán, and they spoke in whispers. Piña stood closely behind the stranger. Leizán recalled that the rebel leader "asked if there was consternation in the country, and what did the people, the newspapers, and the radio say about the Moncada attack. I gave him the work shirt that I had on because he told me he wanted peasant clothes. He asked if I had a younger brother to acquire other clothes." Castro replaced the small trousers provided by Feal with a pair that he got from Lelín's cousin Manuel Montero, but these also were too short for him.[29]

When Leizán met the other rebels, he informed them that Raúl Castro had been jailed and that the captured fugitives were being spared. He questioned the group regarding their location the previous day and stated that Pérez Serantes had been in the area with some civilians to mediate their surrender. Castro then took aside Almeida, Chanes, González, Mestre, and Montano and asked them to surrender. Chanes recalled, "Our initial reaction was unanimous: we did not risk our lives to get this far to just surrender now." Castro exercised his attorney's power of persuasion on his recalcitrant followers. According to Chanes and Montano, he told the five that if they turned themselves in and declared that their leader was hiding in Siboney Beach, he would be able to escape, leave the country, and return with an armed expedition to save the revolution. Chanes remembered that after a heated discussion, "Fidel convinced us that if we had sacrificed ourselves attacking the Moncada, we now had to sacrifice ourselves again to save the revolution and its leader." Montano reminisced, "We had spent a week under tremendous weariness, barely eating, and drinking dirty water wherever we found it." Chanes heard Castro tell Leizán to ask the archbishop to return the next morning for those who were going to turn themselves in. Alcalde stated that Leizán "agreed to meet with the civic and religious institutions. Resistance was becoming each time more impossible in the condition that we were in." The fugitives went back to Piña's *bohío* at 2:00 A.M. and slept on the floor. The shack measured fifteen feet long by ten feet wide and had a central partition. Fidel Castro, Oscar Alcalde, and Pepe Suárez stayed in the front section, and the other five were in the rear.[30]

A few hours later, just before dawn on Saturday, August 1, a military truck arrived at the Moncada Guard Corps post. Lt. Manuel Piña Martínez was in charge of mustering a force to pursue escapees believed to be hiding in the Sevilla area. A crowd of volunteers gathered around the truck requesting to go. Piña randomly chose fifteen men, who quickly climbed aboard. One of them, Pvt. Armando Oliva López, recalled, "As the lieutenant was getting into the passenger's side of the cab, a messenger brought a last minute order from regimental headquarters, requiring Piña's presence upstairs." Moments later Sub-Lt. Pedro Sarría Tartabul descended the stairs, informed the driver that he was replacing Piña, and summoned his orderly, thirty-nine-year-old Cpl. Julio Corbea Monteagudo. Private Oliva believed that the switch was because Piña might be motivated to avenge his comrades. Sarría was a forty-nine-year-old Afro-Cuban with more than twenty years in the service, mostly spent as a sergeant in the military marching band. His precarious economic situation, due to raising six children, had led him to decline retirement. As a result, he had been automatically promoted to sublieutenant file clerk in regimental headquarters. Sarría was a peaceful, unassuming person who spent his idle hours at his desk reading and eating crackers before being reassigned to the Rural Guard. He was described by Sgt. Julián Fajardo, who knew him from the time they were both privates, as a "good, honest, serious person." Sarría acknowledged fifteen years later that he was ordered by Capt. José Tandrón Femenías to pick up some fugitives at El Cilindro farm.[31]

When the truck with Sarría's squad departed at about 5:00 A.M., another search party, which included Pvt. Rafael Morales Gros, was mustered by Lt. Luis S. Gamboa Alarcón. At dawn the regimental De Havilland Beaver plane flew low over the area where the rebels were hiding. Thousands of leaflets were dropped announcing the archbishop's mediation and guaranteeing the lives of the fugitives if they surrendered. Sarría went to El Cilindro farm, half a mile from the village of Sevilla, which had access to the Mamprivá property directly behind it. Pérez Serantes had told Colonel del Río Chaviano the previous night that he had been searching for Fidel Castro in that area. At 5:30 A.M. Juan Leizán arrived in his jeep at the home of his oldest brother, "Lelín," in Sueño neighborhood, near Moncada. He told him of what had transpired and indicated that the rebels wanted to surrender not at night but during the day. Lelín's wife, Berta González, accompanied her husband and Juan to the home of her sister-in-law Leida Sarabia, who presided over the Catholic Teachers' Association. The group found Pérez Serantes officiating the 6:00 A.M. mass in the archbishopric chapel. Enrique Canto was kneeling in a rear pew when Sarabia asked him to step outside. She said, "There is a group of young men who want to surrender to the authorities under the mediation of monsignor Pérez Serantes. They are in the farm of my relatives Leizán. He is here and wants to speak with you."[32]

Canto recalled Juan Leizán saying, "It is necessary that you go quickly. I have five hidden in my farm. They are very afraid of being discovered by the army and we are also fearful they could be detained in our farm. You know how the soldiers act." Canto asked, "Will we have to go into the woods to find them like yesterday?" "No," replied Juan, "you will find them in a ravine after the first curve of the Siboney highway past our home. It is necessary that you do not waste time. They are in an extremely dangerous place." Juan Leizán then took Berta and Leida to their homes and sped back to Las Delicias with Lelín to inform the rebels that the archbishop was on his way. The mass was nearly over when Canto returned to the chapel. Pérez Serantes later invited him to breakfast, but Canto explained the urgency of going to the Leizán farm. As they boarded a jeep driven by Oscar Anglada at 6:30 A.M., they were approached by Juan Emilio Friguls García, a reporter for the Havana *Diario de la Marina* and Catholic Youth member. "You come at a good time," said the archbishop; "climb quickly into the jeep, we are going to find Fidel."[33]

Arriving at El Cilindro farm at daybreak, Sublieutenant Sarría and his troops discovered that the owner, Francisco Sotelo Piña, was at his other ranch in Sigua. His son Francisco provided coffee and a guide nicknamed "Camagüey." Julio Piña, a cousin of Juan Leizán living in the El Cilindro bunkhouse, informed the platoon that some strangers had been sighted around the *bohío* of Luis Piña, and he pointed northward. The army truck returned to Moncada while Sarría ordered three soldiers to stay at the farmhouse and continued with the rest. They went into the hills, traversing tall guinea grass that sometimes reached their chest, looking for the *bohío*.[34]

Inside the *bohío*, Luis Piña awoke the fugitives shortly after 7:00 A.M. The five who were going to surrender bid farewell to the others. Montano recalled that Fidel Castro ordered them to go unarmed and to say that their leader had previously left them. They walked down a trail toward the Siboney highway with Piña following behind part of the way. When the rebels saw the embankment fence, they continued on their own. As the jeep with Pérez Serantes and the reporter approached El Cilindro farm at 7:10 A.M., they were signaled by Juan Leizán, who nervously informed them to proceed a little further up the road and stop on a curve and then stated, "Up ahead are eight who are waiting to turn themselves in." The group advanced as instructed and waited awhile. The area seemed deserted. When no one appeared, Pérez Serantes exclaimed, "another deceit just like yesterday." Canto pleaded that he make himself visible by walking along the highway, and the cleric complied.[35]

Meanwhile, Sublieutenant Sarría and his subordinates continued advancing into the countryside for an hour until sighting Piña's *bohío* on a hillock. The officer positioned his force into a half-circle, three-pronged formation with its flanks spread out more than two hundred yards wide, with each soldier at about twenty-yard intervals.

Sarría ordered Cpl. Julio Corbea to proceed with five men and search the shack. Corbea, carrying a Thompson .45-caliber machine gun, silently moved through the center toward the summit with Cpl. Pedro E. Suárez González and Pvts. Armando Oliva López, Luis Manuel Batista Seguí, Leonardo Cala Cala, and another soldier. Sarría, Private Rodríguez, and two other men went around the bottom right side of the hill. Three soldiers circled the left flank to meet up with Sarría at the rear and cut off any attempted escape. Stopping at a barbed-wire fence near the summit, Corbea told Private Cala to advance quietly and peek through the *bohío* wall slats. The soldier then signaled back with three fingers the number of persons inside and, rubbing them across the back of his other hand and shaking his index finger, indicated that none of them was black. This meant that those inside were probably not from the area since most of the local peasants were Afro-Cubans.[36]

Corporal Corbea whispered to twenty-two-year-old Afro-Cuban Private Batista Seguí to approach the entrance while he covered him. Corbea stood aside with his machine gun ready as Batista Seguí kicked in the palm-frond door. Oscar Alcalde was rudely awakened when the door fell on him. The soldier shouted, "Come out with your hands on your head!" Alcalde responded, "we are good people." The corporal fired a burst into the air to intimidate the fugitives and signal the other soldiers flanking the bottom of the hill. Private Oliva recalled, "A nickel-plated pistol with mother-of-pearl handles was thrown out the door at ground level. Batista Seguí tucked it behind his belt buckle, while Fidel and another rebel walked out in their underwear with their arms raised." Batista Seguí went inside and brought out Pepe Suárez. Oliva perceived the trio as "frightened and pathetic." Batista Seguí, whose brother lay critically wounded in the Los Angeles Clinic, picked out the tallest one and said, "You are Fidel Castro, the one responsible for all of this." Castro replied, "No, I am not, my name is Francisco González Calderín," adding, "Fidel was here a few days ago, but we have not seen him since." According to the novelist Robert Merle, "Fidel noticed that his own hands were shaking and that one of his forehead veins throbbed and pulsated."[37]

Doubting Castro's words, Batista Seguí began working his Springfield rifle bolt action, determined to kill him, and exclaimed, "You son of a bitch, my brother is dying because of you!" Alcalde thought, "this is the end of everything," made the Masonic sign of distress, and exclaimed, "I am a Mason." He hoped that one of the soldiers might belong to the brotherhood and assist him. Just as Batista Seguí was leveling his weapon at Castro, Sarría deflected it upward with his left forearm and with his right hand grabbed the pistol from the soldier's waistband. He loudly reproached, "You do not kill ideas," a famous phrase from the writings of Argentine educator-politician Domingo Sarmiento. Alcalde identified himself to Sarría as a Freemason, although the lieutenant was not a member of the fraternity, and told him where the other weapons were hidden. Alcalde later stated that the soldiers' "first intention was to shoot us right there," except for the lieutenant's intervention. He called Sarría "the father of the revolution, because without him Fidel would have surely been killed." Sarría asked his captives, "Where are the others?" and one replied, "The other five went in that direction toward the highway to give up to monsignor Pérez Serantes, who is coming soon." Private Oliva wondered how Sarría already knew how many rebels to find. Castro, Alcalde, and Suárez were ordered to sit on the ground while two soldiers went into the *bohío* and confiscated "eight rifles, two pistols laying on the ground, and two jute sacks full of ammunition for said arms." Corporal Corbea, Privates Oliva and Batista Seguí, along with another soldier stayed in front of the hut with the prisoners while Sublieutenant Sarría fanned out the other troops in a defensive perimeter, in case of a rescue attack. Private Oliva helped Castro into a pair of jeans and tied his wrists in front with a rope as the two other prisoners were secured likewise. During the interrogation process, Sarría ran his fingers through Fidel Castro's curly hair to detect kinkiness because the deep tan he had acquired while on the run projected a mulatto appearance. Surprised by Sarría's gentle manner, Castro asked to speak to him privately. When the lieutenant took him aside, the rebel leader admitted his true identity and was told not to tell anyone else. "Let's go," ordered Sarría, "we have to find the others."[38]

The remaining five rebels had by then reached the Siboney highway. Mario Chanes, leading the group, saw Archbishop Pérez Serantes on the road near a jeep. As he placed his foot on the lower strand of the barbed-wire fence by the embankment, Chanes heard a rifle shot and dropped to the ground. Newspaper reporter Friguls crawled under the jeep. The two soldiers who stayed at the neighboring farm had spotted the rebels and fired into the air to intimidate them and to alert Sarría's squad. Enrique Canto saw a soldier running across the farm, while the other one hurried along the highway yelling insults at the fugitives and calling them murderers and bandits. Pérez Serantes later described how he "instinctively ran toward them, yelling and waving to the soldiers that the firing must stop." He shouted that he had orders from the colonel that the prisoners were to be turned over to him. Canto recalled that Armando Mestre begged the archbishop, "Father priest do not leave my side." Chanes claimed that the only comment he remembered was one soldier telling the other upon seeing Mestre, "Look, a black revolutionary, when he should be either a *batistiano* or a Communist." Afro-Cuban soldiers later taunted the two black rebels for trying to overthrow Batista, with whom they racially identified. Canto told the rebels to raise their hands, and they promptly did so while drawing closer around the prelate. As the two soldiers advanced, Pérez Serantes continued claiming custody of the group. Canto heard a soldier say that he was not going to hand them over, "not even to a priest, nor to a monk, or nobody, they are killers, criminals, who murdered our comrades," and the soldier continued firing into the air to attract Sublieutenant Sarría and the others, who were some six hundred yards away. The gunfire prompted Sarría's squad to spread out and drop to the ground. Castro stated that he "believed it was a pretext of the soldiers to shoot us and I remained standing."[39]

Meanwhile, thirty-six-year-old Gerardo Abascal Berenguer, the honorary Mexican consul in Santiago de Cuba, approached in his car from his summer villa in Siboney headed for his family's coffee and cocoa export business in the city. He stopped upon hearing the shots and saw his friend Canto, who told him that Fidel Castro was in the nearby hills about to surrender. Pérez Serantes approached the vehicle and instructed Canto to "try to go to Santiago de Cuba and find an officer in the garrison. I believe that with these soldiers here a tragedy might occur." As Abascal took Canto to the city, they agreed that it would probably be difficult to enter Moncada. The driver suggested that they telephone the garrison from the home of their mutual friend and chief prosecutor Francisco Mendieta Hechavarría, who resided in the Vista Alegre suburb. Mendieta, a member of Canto's Rotary Club, was awakened and promptly telephoned the private number at regimental headquarters. He and Canto spoke with Maj. Andrés Pérez-Chaumont, who assured the safety of the prisoners and vowed to send a group of officers to the Leizán farm immediately.[40]

Back at Las Delicias farm, as Castro and his two companions approached the Siboney highway escorted by the soldiers, Sarría sent a message to Manuel Leizán requesting transportation. According to Private Oliva, while they waited on the farmhouse porch, a woman gave each prisoner a glass of milk. Juan Leizán arrived shortly thereafter behind the wheel of his family's 200 CV Chevrolet flatbed truck. Sarría ordered all the soldiers with the prisoners except Castro into the rear. Leizán remembered, "When I saw that Sarría made a distinction with that young man, that he put into the cab, next to his side and mine, I said, 'God, this man knows this young man is the chief'; who could have told him?" Pvt. Luis Batista Seguí continued to insist that the man was Fidel Castro, but the corporal ordered him to shut up. The jeep with Pérez Serantes was traveling behind the truck. The prisoners were bunched into the middle of the cargo area while the soldiers sat around the edge with their legs dangling over the side. The rebel Mario Chanes saw Private Batista Seguí smoking and requested a cigarette. Another soldier replied, "You got nerve. Don't you know his brother was gravely wounded during the attack?" Chanes recalled that Batista Seguí, "nearly in tears," gave him a cigarette. He stated that at no time were the prisoners offended or mistreated.[41]

Just before reaching the village of Sevilla, Abascal and Canto appeared driving from the opposite direction. The prelate's jeep stopped to pick up Canto, who told his friends of his conversation with Major Pérez-Chaumont, while Abascal continued to his office. When the caravan reached the Tree of Peace, the Spanish-American War armistice memorial at the city limits, Pérez-Chaumont, coming from Moncada in a jeep, stopped them. He ordered Sublieutenant Sarría to have the truck follow him into the city. Castro's "official history" claims that Pérez-Chaumont tried to take custody of the prisoners to kill them and that Sarría disobeyed him. Lt. Col. González Alfonso acknowledged, "Fidel was saved because Colonel del Río Chaviano gave the order that he be taken to the *vivac* city jail, instead of the garrison, where he would have been killed by the relatives of the dead soldiers." Montano admitted, "Pérez Serantes told us that they took us to the *vivac* precisely to avoid going to the Moncada garrison, because the soldiers still wanted to avenge what occurred."[42]

The threat against their lives was greater than they imagined. Lt. Antonio Ochoa admitted that he conspired with Capt. Bebo Lavastida and Lt. Manuel Arpa Ceballo to kill Fidel Castro upon his capture. The three officers were in separate jeeps with their retinues looking for fugitives at Siboney Beach that morning. A passing milkman informed them that Sublieutenant Sarría had just detained Castro and a group of rebels and was headed back to the city with a priest. The three jeeps hastily departed at such high rates of speed that Lieutenant Arpa's vehicle flipped on a turn and he broke his clavicle. Ochoa recalled, "We did not even stop, leaving him there, to see if we could catch them on the way before they reached Santiago. We were going to knock off Sarría, the priest, Fidel, and those with him, except the soldiers." He added that "Lavastida would have fixed that well," to make it appear that the deaths occurred when the prisoners had attempted to escape. When they arrived at the *vivac* late, Colonel del Río told Ochoa, "Nothing can be done to this man, it is an order from President Batista."[43]

The truck with the prisoners had stopped at the *vivac* city jail entrance at 8:45 A.M. Some soldiers jumped off and fired their Springfield rifles into the air to disperse the gathering onlookers. According to Canto, Major Pérez-Chaumont approached the archbishop's jeep and told them, "Here comes Fidel. Nothing is going to happen to him." On their way back to the rectory, Canto told the prelate that the news media should be informed of Castro's arrest to avoid any possible reprisals. Canto then stopped by the offices of the *Oriente* evening newspaper and CMKR radio station before returning to his store. Pérez Serantes was later approached at the rectory by Temístocles Fuentes Rivera and Orlando Benítez Hernández, radical Afro-Cuban student leaders sought by the authorities, whom he accompanied to the *vivac* to surrender. Three months earlier the duo had kidnapped a taxi driver, who drove them near National Police Headquarters on Intendente Hill, where they detonated a bomb. Fuentes, a former MNR member, saw Sgt. René Feraud Mejías, whose one brother was killed and another maimed in the attack, arrive waving a handgun and threatening to kill Castro. Feraud was disarmed and led away.[44]

Fidel Castro sat down on the *vivac* floor at the end of a hallway flanked by Pvts. Armando Oliva and Luis Batista Seguí. The prisoners in the cells on opposite sides of the corridor, including Raúl Castro, shouted out his name. "You see," Batista Seguí told Oliva, "I was right. This is Fidel Castro." The rebel leader told them, "The truth is, I did not think that the army would treat me this good. You have behaved very well, and I would like to have the names of everyone in the search patrol so that in the future I can demonstrate my gratitude." Oliva replied, "We are not authorized to do so, you will have to ask Sublieutenant Sarría." The guards were told to take Castro upstairs where his wife, mother, and sister Emma awaited. Mirta Díaz-Balart wailed and cried as she embraced her husband, who reassured her that he was all right. Five minutes later the custodians were ordered to take him back downstairs, where shortly thereafter Maj. Rafael Morales, Colonel del Río Chaviano, and police major José Izquierdo interrogated Castro for two hours in the warden's office. Two military stenographers transcribed his confession into a fourteen-page document. Chanes stated that Major Izquierdo, whose brother was killed at Post 3, later stopped by their cell and shook hands with Fidel Castro and the other prisoners captured that day. Chanes recalled, "He was a gentleman. That man behaved in a way that we possibly would not have done in his place." Major Morales also visited all the prisoners and inquired about their welfare. His teenage son, Pvt. Orlando Morales, recalled fifty-two years later, "My father gave me a five-peso bill and told me to go to the pharmacy and buy Kotex for Melba Hernández. I had never heard of that and did not know what it was used for."[45]

At noon, after a two-hour wait, the press entered the *vivac* jail to photograph and interview the rebel prisoners. Carlos Selva Yero, a twenty-nine-year-old CMKR Radio reporter, was lugging a thirty-pound Revere reel-to-reel tape recorder. When Castro saw the photographers, he strategically stood in front of a portrait of the liberator José Martí, just as Batista had done at Camp Columbia during the Tenth of March Coup. He was quickly flanked by Colonel del Río Chaviano and Majors Morales and Pérez-Chaumont. Castro addressed the news media uninterrupted for twenty minutes. He "pronounced a programmatic speech in which he said he had not gone to Moncada to kill soldiers, but to initiate a Revolution: 'The Revolution that the people long for'—he said. Fidel Castro narrated his activities from the tenth of March onwards and emphasized that the movement he led did not have complicity with the political past and that his only mentor was José Martí." Castro denounced Batista as "the main enemy of the army and of the soldiers." Pvt. Rafael Morales Gros heard him say, "I regret a thousand times the bullet that in one opportunity should have taken my life so that I may not be going through this difficult time." César A. Marín, a *Prensa Universal* reporter, recalled Castro stating that "a shot escaped from one of our men precipitated the shooting much before anticipated." The rebel leader also said that 120 men had taken part in the attack in Santiago de Cuba and 28 in the uprising at Bayamo.[46]

Fidel Castro was quoted in *Bohemia* magazine as saying that "after six days of continuous walking in the forest, he comprehended that resistance was useless, and he surrendered to the soldiers." Two years later Castro gave a different version in a

Bohemia article by claiming, "Let it be said once for all—because much trouble has been made due to my arrest—that I never surrendered to the army." When questioned by the reporters regarding the actual combat, Castro replied that "both sides behaved well, each one fighting for its respective ideals with dignity. The only thing to regret is the deaths that occurred." Selva recorded Castro as saying that he "respected the memory of those soldiers who died fulfilling what they considered their duty." When the interview ended, Colonel del Río Chaviano told Selva to take his tape recorder and reel to Moncada. Lt. Jesús Yanez Pelletier was present when the colonel had Fidel Castro's statement edited from twenty minutes down to eight before returning it to the reporter. It was then broadcast at 3:00 P.M. by Cadena Oriental de Radio and quoted in the Havana newspaper *El Crisol*. The events of that day were also reported internationally by the Associated Press correspondent in the city, who erroneously described Castro as a "30-year-old student leader at the University of Havana."[47]

The rebel leader's eloquent address and media attention angered Lt. Angel Machado. He asked Lieutenant Yanez in the *vivac* receiving room if he had knowledge of medicine. After he received an affirmative reply, Machado requested that he find "a poison that can be put into food, to liquidate this guy without any problems." Machado suggested that Yanez, who was the Boniato Provincial Prison military supervisor, put Castro in solitary confinement and cover his cell floor with water and grain salt used for making ice cream. The prisoner would then contract pneumonia from sleeping on the cold wetness. "That way, we can say that Castro arrived ill, and kill him off with the poison," concluded Machado. Yanez believed that Machado was acting under orders from Colonel del Río Chaviano, but Machado admitted in 1974 that it was his own idea. Yanez stated to the press thirty-five years later, "When I got to the prison . . . I took all the precautions so they would not kill that man inside there, because I would be the only one responsible for that. It was also not in my convictions to take the life of someone who was fighting for what he believed was the truth." Yanez was discharged from the army "for the good of the service" a few weeks later.[48]

The forty-nine rebel prisoners in the *vivac* were taken to the Boniato Provincial Prison in paddy wagons that Saturday at 7:00 P.M. Maj. Rafael Morales escorted Castro to a 1950 Buick driven by Lieutenant Yanez, who heard Castro tell the officer, "I greatly lament the death of your brother." As Morales opened the front passenger door for the rebel leader, he courteously stated, "After you, doctor." He then instructed Yanez to switch his holstered gun to his left hip, so that the prisoner would not be sitting next to it, as they occupied the front seat. The two female detainees, Melba Hernández and Haydée Santamaría, squeezed into the backseat between the major's sons, Pvts. Rafael and Orlando Morales. The caravan was led by a jeep with a .30-caliber machine gun manned by Pvt. Ariel Matos, while another armed jeep covered the rear. No one spoke in Castro's vehicle during the trip. At the penitentiary entrance, Fidel Castro sat on a concrete bench as the captured rebels filed past. He then asked Major Morales why so many of his comrades were missing. Morales stated that those present were all of the detainees given to him. Castro was unaware that rebel casualties amounted to sixty-one dead, fifty-one prisoners, and forty-eight fugitives.[49]

In the penitentiary, medical examiner José Ramón Cabrales administered paraffin tests to detect gunpowder traces on the rebels' hands. The doctor stated that when he arrived, "Fidel was in a separate cell and the rest of the combatants were together." All the prisoners submitted to paraffin impressions except Castro, who stated, "Me? It will not be done to me; put that it is positive because I did shoot. The paraffin does not have to be applied to me. Find me a weapon and you will see how I continue to shoot." This braggadocio seemed an excuse to avoid evidence that could prove that he did not use a firearm during the attack. It would have been to Castro's credit, as confessed rebel leader, to submit to a paraffin test that would have provided positive results.[50]

After the capture of Fidel Castro and his seven companions, all military search operations ceased. On August 7 Artemisa native Marino Collazo, grazed on the forehead by a bullet during the battle, surrendered and implicated himself. That same day Bayamo rebel Pedro Aguilera gave up in his native Palma Soriano and fifty-year-old Luis Casero Guillén, former Santiago de Cuba Auténtico mayor, was at the airport awaiting a flight to Havana when he was arrested for supposedly being an "intellectual author" of the attack. Four days later Calabazar rebel Florentino Hernández Enríquez and Rafael Núñez Leyva, a twenty-nine-year-old peasant from San Felipe, Oriente, were detained in Santiago de Cuba. That same day Colonel del Río Chaviano rescinded the military curfew on the city. A week after Castro's arrest, a Bayamo priest, Alfredo Lamadrid, asked Archbishop Pérez Serantes to mediate the surrender of Andrés García, the rebel deserter who survived strangulation. The archbishop called Enrique Canto one morning to meet him at the rectory, where he awaited with the socialite Concha Ramsden and her daughter Miriam Bueno. Canto was asked to join them on an eighty-mile trip to Veguitas and return with a wounded rebel who wanted to give up. The group departed at 10:00 A.M. in an automobile driven by Mrs. Ramsden, with the archbishop riding up front and Canto next to the young lady in the backseat. Canto's memoirs indicate that during the trip Pérez Serantes expressed doubts about Fidel Castro's personality. They discussed his gangster era and his involvement in the Manolo de Castro murder. Miriam, who knew the rebel leader from her student days in Santiago de Cuba, described him as "impulsive, eloquent, imposing, conceited, and resentful, whose home environment had influenced his character, making him introverted at times, and on other occasions euphoric in his determinations." Canto, who secretly sympathized with the rebels, kept quiet.[51]

In Bayamo they located Father Lamadrid, who led them in a jeep driven by José Escala, the president of the Manzanillo Catholic Youth, to a *bohío* near Veguitas. Andrés García was found there and assisted into the backseat of Ramsden's car. The fugitive was weak from a shoulder wound that had been treated with medicinal herbs and hardly spoke during the trip to Santiago de Cuba. When the archbishop told him that God had helped him, García smiled and opened his shirt to reveal Santeria prayers written on his chest by peasants. Upon reaching the city, Canto did not want to enter Moncada with the others and asked to be left a block away. García was handed over to the military, who guaranteed his safety.[52]

On August 1, the day of Fidel Castro's capture, the Council of Ministers in Havana, on a motion presented by national defense minister Nicolás Pérez Hernández, proposed that the highest military decoration, the Cross of Honor, be awarded to the First Regiment in a solemn ceremony at the Moncada the next day. Fulgencio Batista arrived at the San Pedrito Airport in Santiago de Cuba in his modified C-47 aircraft, *Guáimaro*, on Sunday, August 2, at 11:15 A.M. He was accompanied by Cols. Francisco Tabernilla Palmero, Manuel Ugalde Carrillo, Orlando Piedra Negueruela, and Antonio Blanco Rico, along with other officials. The troops were reviewed on the Moncada parade ground, and Batista pinned the Cross of Honor on the First Regiment banner. The newly minted Cross of Maceo Medal was awarded to most officers and the soldiers who participated in combat. The monthly salaries of the latter were augmented by four pesos. Batista appeared on the main building balcony at 11:45 A.M., surrounded by the garrison's general staff and Gov. Waldo Pérez Almaguer. He was wildly cheered and applauded by the troops before pronouncing a speech. Batista referred to the rebels as "traitors who assassinate patriots in the back" and who "decimate the sick in their beds in the military hospital." He erroneously stated that no one from Oriente Province participated in the attack, unaware that at least seven rebels were from the region.[53]

After the ceremony, Batista met in the regimental headquarters office with the widows, orphans, and relatives of those killed in action and promised that they would never be abandoned. The children—five girls and four boys older than fourteen, and twenty-three girls and fourteen boys under fourteen—received scholarships to attend the Ceiba del Agua Institute. Batista had founded the school in 1936 to educate the orphans of military personnel, peasants, and laborers. The general then visited eleven wounded soldiers in the military hospital. A patient tried to get out from under an oxygen tent and exclaimed in a weak voice, "At your orders until death, mister president!" Photos of Batista shaking hands with the injured were published in the press. In the Los Angeles Clinic the convalescing Cpl. Norberto Batista asked, "President, if I do not die, I would like to see you again." Col. Ugalde Carrillo was ordered to make the arrangements. Batista then presented floral offerings at the armed-forces pantheon in the Santa Ifigenia Cemetery. A mass was held in the cathedral that Sunday for all those who lost their lives as a result of Moncada and Bayamo attacks.[54]

A few days later Enrique Canto was asked by Mrs. Hernández, a university professor, to transport Léster Rodríguez, the Palace of Justice rebel leader, from his hideout in Palma Soriano to Santiago de Cuba. She stressed that he had been a member of the Catholic Youth and that Paquita Sáenz had offered shelter for him. Canto asked the dentist José Antonio Roca, president of the Jesuit alumni of Santiago de Cuba and Fidel Castro's former classmate, to pick up Rodríguez. Roca drove to Palma Soriano, retrieved the fugitive, and provided refuge. A University of Havana professor then took Rodríguez to the Mexican Embassy in the capital, where he obtained asylum.[55]

Other insurgents escaping arrest included the five who split away from Fidel Castro's group on Tuesday morning. Gerardo Granados and Jaime Costa hid during the day in the countryside and walked at night in a northern direction. They requested food at the *bohío* of Mariano Echevarría, whose wife cooked a chicken-and-rice dinner for them. Granados recalled that the woman was so nervous that she did not fully pluck the fowl before cooking it. When the rebels departed, they left behind a .22-caliber rifle as a token of appreciation. At the Cujabo farm in El Cristo, Granados and Costa remained in the woods assisted by an elderly overseer who provided their meals. After a month, twenty-eight-year-old Higinio "Nino" Díaz Landrían drove them individually in a jeep to Santiago de Cuba, where Rubén Pérez Proenza hid Granados in the home of the dentist Zenaida Zambrano and Costa went to the residence of Eladio Rodríguez for two months. Pérez Proenza asked Enrique Canto to intercede with the wealthy Babún brothers in aiding Granados and Costa to leave the country. Teófilo Babún Selman sent them in one of his ships to Puerto Cortés, Honduras.[56]

The last three rebel escapees, Artemisa natives Ricardo Santana and Orlando and Roberto Galán, made their way to Aguadores, on the bank of the San Juan River near Santiago de Cuba, and found refuge among the peasants. Santana spent four months in the home of Leopoldo Gómez Ochoa in Cauto Cristo, near Bayamo. He returned to the Siboney area, staying with a peasant until December 1954, before leaving for Mexican exile the next month. The Galán brothers remained in Oriente Province working as charcoal vendors for two years. Severino Rosell and Mario Lazo, who was recuperating from a bullet wound in his armpit, hid at the Benjamín Arza farm for a month. On August 29 they were taken in a milk truck to a refuge in Santiago de Cuba. Three days later Lazo went to stay in the home of thirty-four-year-old attorney Lucas Morán Arce, and Rosell went to the Punta de Sal beach house of José Espín Vivar, whose daughter Nilsa had been a delegate with Raúl Castro to the Socialist Youth International Congress in Vienna the previous spring. Rosell pretended to be a vacationing nephew. He later went to Havana, obtained asylum in the Uruguayan Embassy, and then left for Costa Rica.[57]

The Morán family told the neighbors that Lazo was a cousin from Guantánamo who was receiving medical treatment in Santiago de Cuba. He remained in the Morán residence until September 20, when his host arranged to leave him in the home of Ortodoxo activist sisters Nayibe and Ibis Atala Medina. Morán was a defense attorney in the Moncada trial scheduled to start the next day. Enrique Canto was contacted to assist Lazo in leaving the city, but the fugitive refused to go because he had fallen in love with Ibis, whom he later married. The rebel Gustavo Arcos, convalescing in the Colonia Española Clinic, was pleasantly surprised when prior to his trial he received a visit from Ibis and the audacious Lazo.[58]

After fleeing Santiago de Cuba, Florentino Fernández León, the military orderly who acquired uniforms for the attackers, faced a perilous situation. He became suspect when the army paymaster in Palma Soriano billed his counterpart in Camp Columbia regimental headquarters for boarding him during the three days he was held there for not having a travel pass. Florentino's paymaster checked his falsified work records and responded that the orderly had never left Jaimanitas. The Palma Soriano post commander then telephoned Camp Columbia and confirmed that Florentino had been detained there July 26–29 for being absent without leave. The SIM in Havana pursued the investigation and discovered that Florentino had been buying large quantities of uniforms from other soldiers. They searched his house and found on a closet floor the scrap of paper that Pedro Trigo had given him containing Melba Hernández's name, address, and phone number. Florentino was interrogated, failed to give convincing responses, and was locked in solitary confinement facing treason charges. He decided that his only salvation was feigning insanity and began screaming and acting wild in his cell, prompting his transfer to the psychiatric section of the military hospital. Florentino refused to eat, and when visited by his wife and parents, he pretended not to know them. He went to the extreme of eating his own excrement to feign insanity. The 1950s era was one of electroshock therapy, and Florentino was subjected to such treatment eight times in eight months, until he was discharged from the army for mental incompetence.[59]

In late August some of the political leaders detained by the SIM in La Cabaña, including Millo Ochoa, Arturo Hernández Tellaheche, and Ignacio Fiterre Rivera, along with the telegraphist René Betancourt Castillo, were escorted by Maj. Rafael Morales on a military transport flight to Oriente. At the San Pedrito Airport, SIR chief Bebo Lavastida demanded the detainees, but Morales would not release them unless Colonel del Río Chaviano signed a prisoner receipt. When they arrived at the Moncada, Millo told Hernández, "Let's sit at the back of the cell so that we do not hear the insults," as passing soldiers taunted them with obscenities. The captives were later escorted to the Boniato Provincial Prison. Seven remaining opposition leaders held in Havana were transferred from La Cabaña by plane to the same penitentiary the day before the trial started.[60]

The Boniato Provincial Prison was built in 1947 amid scenic hills covered with palm trees. One hundred yards behind its two-story administration building were five symmetrical, two-story cell blocks separated by patios. Each unit was divided into parallel tiers. The right wing of the first cell block contained the infirmary, where Fidel Castro was kept in a single cell facing the hallway. A guard sat on a chair next to the door. The clinic had a dental office where the codefendant and dentist Pedro Aguilera attended Castro on a few occasions. In *History Will Absolve Me,* the rebel leader claims that he was prohibited by the prison authorities from receiving documents to prepare his defense. The codefendant Raúl del Mazo stated that the attorney Baudilio Castellanos García provided Castro with copies of all the legal briefs and accusations filed against the defendants, including military and police reports. Mario Chanes said that a prison hospital employee passed messages and notes between Fidel Castro and his followers. Castro's tier contained the cells of opposition political leaders, including Luis Casero, Sergio Mejías, Oscar Alvarado, Ignacio Fiterre, Ramiro Arango, the Communists Lázaro Peña and Joaquín Ordoqui, and twenty-nine others. Millo Ochoa and Arturo Hernández Tellaheche shared quarters. Chanes recalled that the Communists' cell was dubbed the "Soviet Embassy" by some prisoners. To pass the time, Arango, who had a law degree from the Sorbonne University in Paris, taught French to other prisoners. He recalled, "Peña and Ordoqui were my best students, because the others did not give a damn." Arango confirmed that they were not harassed or mistreated by the correctional guards.[61]

The left wing of the first cell block contained units housing seventy combatants and suspected rebels. Acción Libertadora members Raúl del Mazo and José F. Pila Teleño shared a cell with Raúl Castro, Reinaldo Benítez, Isidro Peñalver, and Santiago de Cuba student leader Temístocles Fuentes. Chanes was with Eduardo Montano, Pancho González, and another rebel. Luis Casero used a shaving basin across from Fidel Castro's cell. Thirty-one years later Casero reminisced, "While I shaved, the shirtless Fidel would hang his arms out the cell bars and ask me questions about the merchant marine. I was surprised by his intelligent rapport about things that he had no knowledge of. In those conversations I also saw his lies, his conceit, his egotism, his dictatorial spirit, and his belittling what others thought."[62]

Yet, after Casero was released from prison two months later, U.S. Vice Consul Arthur W. Feldman reported to the American Embassy in Havana that Casero "had long conversations with Mr. Fidel Castro in jail and has come away with the impression that Mr. Castro is an idealist and an intellectual." Embassy officials forwarded this information to the U.S. Department of State with the caveat that they were "not prepared to go along with Sr. Casero's opinion that the leader of the attack, Fidel Castro, is strictly an idealist. The Embassy's impression of Fidel Castro is that he is an extremely ambitious and ruthless opportunist, obviously not adverse to violence when it serves his purpose." U.S. policy toward the Batista regime as outlined by Robert

F. Woodward, the deputy assistant secretary of state for inter-American affairs, was "to see the return of constitutional government in Cuba, the removal of censorship and the restoration of constitutional guarantees." Woodward was also concerned about "the increasing influence of communists in the Cuban labor movement."[63]

The political prisoners in Boniato Provincial Prison were later joined by Angel Díaz-Francisco, who had been confined in the Civil Hospital prisoners' ward due to his daily insulin treatments. After Patachula arrived, Juan Almeida asked him to admit in court, along with a large group of rebels, that he had participated in the attack. Díaz-Francisco, who had left Siboney with other dissidents, refused to do so. He acknowledged that Raúl Castro was a prankster in prison, stating, "In the morning he would wake me up by reflecting the sun into my eyes with a mirror."[64]

The detainees' visits were initially restricted. On one occasion prison supervisor Lieutenant Yanez Pelletier received superior instructions to allow a family visit for Mario Burman, a Jewish hardware-store owner and Havanan. The newspapers had erroneously identified his paramour Lázara Pérez as his spouse and published her photograph in a *vivac* jail cell with Melba and Haydée. Moments before going to see his relatives in the military supervisor's office, Burman confided to his cell mate Luis Casero that he was worried about their reaction. Yanez recalled that when Burman entered the room, his mother slapped him and shouted in a heavy Yiddish accent, "Your wife is this one with me. How dare you say that you are married to the woman that you brought here?" The lieutenant, after repeatedly telling the indignant woman to calm down, asked her to leave the room.[65]

Another unusual incident occurred when the eccentric *batistiana* Luisa Margarita de la Cotera appeared at the penitentiary to see Millo Ochoa. When told that the prisoners were not allowed visitors, Ochoa recalled that "she threatened the warden with telephoning '*Mi Chino Lindo*,' which is how she affectionately called Batista, and was immediately brought in." De la Cotera asked Ochoa how Fidel Castro was being treated, and he replied, "I am told that he is in a bare cell." According to Millo, the next day "she returned with a bundle of clothing, underwear, pajamas, socks, bed sheets, and even a folding cot for Fidel, but was told that it was not necessary. It was not odd behavior for Margarita, who always defended the underdog." Six months earlier Fidel Castro had been with the street mob that stoned de la Cotera's home and overturned her car.[66]

In order to get the visiting restrictions rescinded, Fidel Castro ordered a protest, which was organized by Ernesto Tizol, Oscar Alcalde, and Juan Almeida. When breakfast arrived, the rebels declared a hunger strike. The new military supervisor replacing Yanez, 2nd Lt. Miguel D. Rosabal, tried coercing them with a goon squad brandishing truncheons, but no one budged in spite of the threats and insults. Rosabal had all the prisoners stand in the hall and ordered those not participating in the protest to take a step forward. Mario Chanes recalled that the Communists and civilians wrongly implicated in the attack did not join their protest. Rosabal and Warden Augusto B. Taboada Bernal then conferred with Castro and agreed to their demands: visits would be allowed; the three prisoners needing medical attention would be returned to the Civil Hospital; inmates would be permitted onto the sun patio; and money could be deposited in the prisoners' canteen accounts so that they could purchase victuals.[67]

Fiterre stated that the penitentiary food was awful and that "Fidel ate what was brought for everyone so that he could not be singled out in an attempt to poison him." Chanes, a bakery employee, said that the bread was the only good, edible item. One night the detainees awoke amid general vomiting and diarrhea after being served spoiled meat. Although some rebels claimed that it was an attempt to poison them, Casero acknowledged that the soldiers and the prison administrator had also eaten the same food and gotten sick. According to Haydée, the politician "big shots from Havana . . . all had food brought in!" The three female inmates were not subjected to the chow. They were escorted daily to the quarters of Warden Taboada, whose wife Blanquita cooked their meals. Millo Ochoa recalled that he and Haydée would sometimes play dominoes with Lieutenant Rosabal in an empty cell but that Melba always refused to join them. The local Bar Association sent the prisoners "clothing, medicine and food." Ernesto Tizol was the administrator of the provisions' commission. All rebel prisoners donated 20 percent of their canteen accounts for buying food to be shared by everyone. Those who smoked received an equitable ration of cigarettes. A hot plate was used for cooking egg omelets and steaks. Raúl Castro and Oscar Alcalde headed a cultural commission. They read excerpts from the *Works of José Martí* and the *Chronicles of the Cuban War of Independence*, with a follow-up question-and-answer period. The books were donated by Prof. Augusto Pila Teleño, whose brother José was incarcerated with the attackers.[68]

After the daily 5:00 P.M. meal, when the cells stayed open for a few hours, the festive committee organized entertainment. Juan Almeida and Andrés García, who had survived strangulation in Bayamo, would sometimes sing a duet. Chucho Montané served as sentinel when any of the three women prisoners used the bathroom or showers at the end of the hall. The toilets without partitions were in one room, and the showers were in an area directly across from them. These facilities were reserved for the political prisoners on that penitentiary wing. Melba Hernández, Haydée Santamaría, and Lázara Pérez shared a cell near the bathroom, with canvas draped across the bars facing the hallway to allow privacy. Haydée later reminisced, "I never regarded prison as a painful experience. In Boniato it was great because it was very militant." Thirty minutes before the 9:00 P.M. lockdown, Fidel Castro would head for the shower room. As he passed the other cells, his comrades would salute him. When del Mazo first saw that show of discipline, he asked someone what the name of their organization was. "We are Fidel's Commandos," replied a combatant.[69]

Although Fidel Castro's movement had no name, its sixty-one martyrs constituted the greatest number produced by any group challenging Batista. While most oppositionists viewed Castro as a revolutionary hero, the American Embassy regarded him as "an extremely ambitious and ruthless opportunist, obviously not adverse to violence when it serves his purpose." This ominous warning was lost or ignored five years later when the U.S. Department of State and the CIA changed its Cuba policy to favor Castro's guerrillas and concluded that "Batista must leave Cuba."[70]

Despite Castro's future claim that he meant to initiate irregular warfare in the mountains if the Moncada attack failed, four companions fleeing with him acknowledged that that was not their objective. No preparations were made for such an endeavor. The rebels lacked survival equipment and medical supplies for their accompanying wounded; were frequently drenched by tropical downpours; were tormented by fear, hunger, and thirst; and suffered from exhaustion and diarrhea. Most of them were not in physical shape for the strenuous week-long hike in the mountainous wilderness. After only forty-eight hours Castro dispersed his eighteen followers and discarded most of their ammunition, showing no desire to operate as a guerrilla unit. Castro, a former youth scout familiar with the region, never ventured beyond a five-mile radius from the Siboney farmhouse. At times he appeared to his followers as being indecisive, disoriented, and despondent over what course to follow. He was apparently buying time for revengeful passions to subside and the military murder spree to cease.

During the week on the run, Fidel Castro did not play the role of a hero but rather masterfully manipulated the events in order to maximize their benefits to himself in opposing the Batista regime. He twice faked attempted suicide and later boastfully rejected a paraffin test to sustain his honor and stature. Castro stayed behind while sending others to search empty huts, dismissed the wounded who slowed him down, and persuaded five of his final seven companions to surrender. He reduced his followers to only two in order to enhance his possibility of returning covertly to Santiago de Cuba and leaving the country. The rebel leader secretly negotiated his own escape in a mining truck without telling his companions. Castro was thinking only of his own survival, a trait that he had previously displayed during his UIR days, at Cayo Confites, at the Bogotazo, and immediately after the Tenth of March Coup. Meanwhile, civic institutions organized a campaign to guarantee his life. Archbishop Enrique Pérez Serantes played a leading role in mediating the surrender and safety of the escapees.

The main reason Fidel Castro survived was good luck. Captain Lavastida's patrol barely missed capturing the fugitives at the Soledad farm mining pit before the cease-fire went into effect. Lavastida, who had orchestrated the execution of prisoners, undoubtedly would not have otherwise spared the rebel leader. Castro was assisted by peasants who did not betray him to the authorities. Colonel del Río Chaviano, after being threatened by General Batista against harming Castro, ordered the trustworthy Sublieutenant Sarría to pick up the last fugitives and deliver them to the city jail instead of to the Moncada garrison. Castro initially lied to his captors about his identity. His closest call came when Sarría intervened just as Private Batista Seguí was about to shoot him. Lieutenant Yanez later rejected suggestions to poison Castro in jail.

The incarcerated rebels regarded their political-prisoner status as a militant experience. Castro and his followers never complained of mistreatment and carried out a successful strike to achieve their demands. All their needs were supplied by the local Bar Association and other supporters. Although Fidel Castro was kept in a separate cell, he was in frequent communication with his codefendants and received copies of the judicial documentation to prepare his defense. It was going to be the greatest career challenge facing the youthful attorney, who had not practiced in a courtroom in nearly two years.

EIGHT

"*A leader is born*"

The Urgency Tribunal indicted 122 defendants in Case 37 of 1953 to stand trial for the July 26 insurrection. Fifty-one of the 99 rebel survivors were captured and remanded for trial. Six indicted rebels remained hiding. The other 65 defendants implicated throughout the island were mostly political leaders and opposition activists not involved in the rebellion. Fifteen of them, including Carlos Prío, Aureliano Sánchez Arango, José Pardo Llada, and Communist leader Blas Roca Calderío, were underground or in exile and never went to court. The Urgency Tribunal could not grant the imprisoned defendants bail because of the suspension of constitutional guarantees. Under those circumstances, bail approval rested solely with the supreme court prosecutor Elpidio García Tudurí, head of all the district chief prosecutors. This post, similar to that of the U.S. attorney general, was appointed by and responded directly to the chief of state. Therefore, when the constitutional guarantees were not in force, the supreme court prosecutor, answering to Batista, decided who was eligible for bail. The lower courts were overruled in this matter.[1]

When members of the Urgency Tribunal returned from vacation on September 1, some investigative reports awaiting them were incomplete. The further gathering of this evidence postponed the proceedings for three weeks. On the first day of the trial, Monday, September 21, the army deployed at dawn a defensive cordon around the Palace of Justice in Santiago de Cuba. All available military personnel were summoned to duty. Army jeeps with mounted .30-caliber machine guns patrolled the six miles of highway to the Boniato Provincial Prison with soldiers posted at strategic points of the road. Capt. Pedro A. Rodríguez Medrano and Lts. Vicente Camps and Luis Figueroa were in charge of the defendants' custody. Camps, who had arrested Raúl Castro in San Luis, had been transferred to Santiago de Cuba three days earlier.

The 101 incarcerated defendants were transported to the courthouse in three buses, each carrying four soldiers. Jeeps rode in front and at the rear of each bus. Fidel Castro rode in the lead jeep with Lieutenant Camps and three guards. Before departing, the codefendant Ignacio Fiterre saw that "a soldier clamped the handcuffs on Fidel down to the bone, but he did not complain." The political opposition leaders and three female defendants went unshackled in a bus with other, manacled prisoners. After arriving at the Palace of Justice, the detainees were led to the third-floor library, where they waited until called into the courtroom.[2]

The Cuban Civil Code of Justice was based on the Napoleonic Code practiced then in most European and Latin American countries. Its trial procedure differed from the "common law" tradition of the United Kingdom Commonwealth and the United States. Instead of being adjudged by a jury of peers, the verdict was determined by a panel of three magistrates. This was similar to a bench trial in the United States, except that the determination was derived by majority or unanimous vote. The Case 37 magistrates were Adolfo Nieto Piñeiro-Osorio, presiding the tribunal; Ricardo Díaz Olivera; and Juan F. Mejías Valdivieso. Nieto had graduated from the University of Havana Law School in 1921, at the age of twenty-one, and had been on the bench twenty-five years. Díaz, who headed the civil case court, had thirty years of experience. He was substituting for the magistrate Rafael Arango Bustamante, who withdrew because he was related to the defendant Aureliano Sánchez Arango. Mejías, a judge since 1928, told reporters, "This is the most difficult case the Cuban Justice Tribunals have encountered. It is also the most important of all that have been known in political matters." Chief prosecutor Francisco Mendieta Hechavarría represented the government. He was born in the town of Cauto Embarcadero in 1900, and his father and uncle had been colonels in the Cuban Liberation Army during the War of Independence. Mendieta, an Auténtico Party sympathizer, had been appointed as a prosecutor in 1937. His son, nineteen-year-old Francisco Mendieta Tamayo, a vacationing University of Havana law student, attended the trial "motivated by pure curiosity" and sat near the tribunal.[3]

On Monday, September 21, at 10:30 A.M. the three judges entered the plenary hall, the largest courtroom available. The white-walled, rectangular chamber was packed with family members and friends of the accused, including Fidel Castro's wife, brother-in-law Waldo, mother, and sisters. The prosecutor's son recalled that the public benches were full and the back of the courtroom was dense with standing spectators and newsmen who spilled into the hallway. Judge Mejías estimated the civilians present at "300 or 400 people." Judge Nieto recalled, "No one was denied admission. Fidel was the last to enter the courtroom, as if he was Napoleon Bonaparte, waving, arrogant, and looking at everybody over his shoulder." Soldiers with Springfield rifles stood at the doorways and surrounded the handcuffed prisoners. Nieto then asked the chief custodian if he had previously escorted prisoners to the Palace of Justice.

After a negative reply, the magistrate insisted, "Don't you know that the defendants cannot be brought before the tribunal in handcuffs?" After another negative reply, Nieto ordered the guards to "immediately remove their shackles and withdraw all the weapons from the courtroom." The defendant Mario Chanes heard Nieto chiding their escort and thought that the judge "undoubtedly behaved well." Judge Nieto then learned that everyone entering the building, including the defense attorneys, was being frisked. He went to the main entrance and admonished the guards: "Let this be the first and last time you shakedown a lawyer in the course of his duties. If I receive another complaint, I will tell the colonel to dismiss you from this post." While Nieto was gone, law student Mendieta Tamayo, who later joined the guerrillas and presided over a revolutionary tribunal in 1959, heard a soldier next to him say loud enough for Castro to hear, "Look at him, so tough when he attacked the garrison, and now he is shitting in his pants with fear." The prosecutor's son saw Castro turn to look at the soldier, not respond, and face the front again.[4]

The proceedings started fifteen minutes later when tribunal secretary Raúl Mascaró Yarini called the roll of the 122 defendants, with 98 responding that they were present. There were 24 absentees. Three of them—the rebels Angel Díaz-Francisco, Gustavo Arcos, and Abelardo Crespo—remained hospitalized. The other 21, including 6 rebels, were declared fugitives. Rafael "Pilin" Mendoza Guanche, a forty-nine-year-old veteran of the ABC revolutionary group and Conservative Party activist, was living in the United States when he read in a newspaper of his indictment. Mendoza was described by the U.S. Embassy in Havana as a "friend and confidant of ex-President Carlos Prío, [who] left the country on August 9, 1953." The defendants were charged with promoting and carrying out an armed uprising against the state, which violated two clauses of article 148 of the Social Defense Code. The charges against all the defendants had been formulated from the summary report drafted by the Urgency Tribunal's vacation court, presided over by Manuel Urrutia Lleó. Mascaró then read aloud the July 30 military report from regimental chief Col. Alberto del Río Chaviano, which contained some distorted accounts of the attack.[5]

In accordance with due process of law, after the accused heard the charges, they were called to testify on their own behalf. Fidel Castro immediately interrupted the proceedings by demanding to represent himself, but he was told by the court to await his turn. Judge Nieto then warned the defense attorneys and the defendants that "they could not make political propaganda in their statements." The first to take the stand was Roberto García Ibáñez, an Ortodoxo representative from Oriente. He stated that on July 26 he was at home and believed the detonations to be part of the carnival fireworks. García testified that he was arrested on August 13 and denied being associated with the attack leaders. Ramiro Arango Alsina then declared that he had been to Montreal twice that year as a tourist. On one occasion he met and spoke with some of the Montreal Pact delegates, but he falsely denied his participation in the conference. After their testimony, the attorneys García and Arango requested and received permission to assume their own defenses. They donned attorney robes provided by the local Bar Association and joined the lawyers at the defense platform to the right of the tribunal. Arango admitted thirty-five years later that, prior to the trial, "we planned everything we were going to testify in court."[6]

Fidel Castro later admitted, "All of us knew that we had to turn the trial into a tribunal for Batista's cruel dictatorship." He was the third defendant called to the stand and confirmed his prior declaration of being the chief of the movement. According to Judge Nieto, Castro "initiated a political speech before the public, with all the audacity that characterizes him." The magistrate admonished him, "Limit yourself to answering the prosecutor's questions. You are not here as a public figure, you are one of the accused of a substantiated serious charge." Prosecutor Mendieta bluntly asked, "Who instigated the attack?" Castro replied, "I was the real and effective leader, but the intellectual author was José Martí." Mendieta then asked, "Why did you not attack Camp Columbia, where the bulk of the armed forces are, instead of the Moncada garrison?" Castro responded, "We did not have the necessary weapons for that. We did not want to shed blood, we wanted to take the Moncada garrison by surprise. Unfortunately, it did not occur that way." Nieto stated that Castro also blamed their failure on the map erroneously depicting the arsenal entrance and committed perjury by testifying that Renato Guitart was the only local resident participating in the revolt.[7]

The rebel leader then gave an inaccurate history of his organization, to protect unindicted members, and "denied that the Communist Party had organized the movement." When asked if his group was Communist-inspired, since Abel Santamaría's volume of *The Selected Works of Lenin* was seized in the Siboney farmhouse, Castro retorted, "we read all kinds of books. People who do not read books on socialism, communism, as well as fascism and Nazism, are ignorant." He stressed that they had resorted to violence "as the only solution to the present national problem" because his hourly radio program and newspaper articles were censored after the Tenth of March Coup. Fidel Castro disavowed receiving any money or armaments from former president Prío or the Montreal Pact participants. He again committed perjury by denying that he or his followers forged checks. He claimed having spent $16,480 on weapons in Havana gun shops whose owners had nothing to do with their plans. Castro said that he could prove that the money came from codefendants and other comrades killed in the attack. When asked by the prosecutor who would have governed if they had succeeded, the rebel leader replied that it would have been "a revolutionary government in Oriente, integrated by chosen persons," whom he refused to identify. Responding to a question from Judge Nieto, Castro confirmed that neither the Ortodoxo Party nor any other political group organized the movement. "We are the Youth of the Centenary," he acclaimed proudly and then concluded by saying that he admired the brave Moncada soldiers who died fighting.[8]

Most of the twenty-four defense attorneys then briefly questioned Fidel Castro on the stand, attempting to disassociate their clients from the movement. After being interrogated for two hours, Castro petitioned the bench to assume his own defense and was allowed to wear an attorney's robe and occupy a seat at the defense section. The Havana Bar Association had assigned the defense of Castro and Melba Hernández to the attorney Jorge Paglieri Cordero, president of the Santiago de Cuba Bar Association and a law professor at the University of Oriente. Paglieri represented both of the accused until Castro began defending himself. Melba, who continued with Paglieri because she did not represent herself, was described by the rebel Manuel Suardíaz as "a worthless attorney."[9]

The fourth defendant taking the stand was former Auténtico senator and Prío's minister of labor Arturo Hernández Tellaheche, who testified that he was arrested on July 26 at his Camagüey home. He claimed that his activities were limited to finding a political solution to the Cuban problem. Luis Casero Guillén, Prío's minister of public works and Auténtico Party vice-presidential candidate in 1952, was then sworn in. Casero, the former Santiago de Cuba mayor, stated that he had abandoned politics after the Batista coup and was a life-insurance salesman. Both defendants were represented by José F. Valls Tamayo. The court then adjourned at 12:20 P.M. until 9:00 A.M. the following day.[10]

On Tuesday morning the proceedings were delayed for twenty minutes. Millo Ochoa remembered seeing the eccentric *batistiana* Luisa Margarita de la Cotera, who attended all the trial sessions, "distributing flyers with Batista's photograph and mine, which read on top 'Batista Is Peace,' and on the bottom 'Millo Is Love. President and Vice President.' The soldiers were flabbergasted when she handed it to them." The tribunal secretary again called the roll of the defendants and repeated the charges against them. Prosecutor Mendieta began interrogating the opposition politicians regarding their participation in the Montreal Conference and their acquaintance with Fidel Castro. The first witness was Millo Ochoa, the former senate secretary, who as president of the Ortodoxo Party was accused of being the intellectual author of the insurrection and the alleged link between Castro and the Montreal group. Ochoa reiterated that the opposition leaders who met in Canada drafted a public political plan void of covert activity. He said that he attended the conference "because he considered it the only means of avoiding bloodshed." Ochoa denied Communist participation in the Montreal meeting. He gave a detailed account of his whereabouts during his stay in Santiago de Cuba on July 24 and 25. On the last evening he had seen the codefendant Roberto García Ibáñez at his home before taking a flight back to Havana. Millo was represented by Ortodoxo attorney Juan José García Benítez, who had been mayor of Holguín and Auténtico representative from Oriente.[11]

The next witness summoned by the court was José Manuel Gutiérrez Planes, a former Ortodoxo senator from Matanzas and signer of the Montreal Pact. He denied the charges against him and disavowed influencing his party members who joined the rebellion. Gutiérrez did not mention his donation of five hundred pesos to the rebel movement. The physician Oscar Alvarado González, a former Auténtico representative from Las Villas, testified that "he was a friend of Fidel Castro but did not agree with his ideas and had not taken any part in the uprising." The *Havana Post* reported that forty-four-year-old Aracelio Azcuy Cruz, an Auténtico participant in the Montreal Conference, "manifested his sympathy and respect for the rebelliousness of the young men, but [said] that he had nothing to do with this movement, and that he was in Santiago de Cuba airing problems related to his profession as an attorney." Sergio Mejías Pérez, former president of the Chamber of Representatives, Prío's minister of communications, and Auténtico senator from Matanzas, testified that he was not involved in the insurrection.[12]

The first of the Communist defendants was then summoned. Joaquín Ordoqui, leader of the PSP, testified that "he was not invited to the Montreal Conference and that the political line of his party was independent and supported the 1940 Constitution. He said he was arrested in Havana on the day of the revolt and that no member of his party was killed or wounded in Oriente." Ordoqui added that the party's paper, *Hoy,* published their criterion that "problems could not be solved through sporadic deeds." Another PSP leader, Lázaro Peña, then made similar renunciation statements. Both were represented by the attorney Luis Pérez Rey. The Communists denounced the Moncada attack as a "bourgeois putsch" and publicly adhered to a conciliatory course after *Hoy* was closed down by the government. They called the rebels a "little group of young men, well-intentioned but influenced by the putschist line, [who] made a frustrated assault against the military barracks in Santiago de Cuba, hoping to take possession of this important position and launch an attack from there against Camp Columbia in Havana." Two Cuban-American historians wrote, "Cuban Communists were widely considered staunch *batistianos,* and very few persons could imagine Juan Marinello, Blas Roca, Fabio Grobart or other aging theoreticians taking part in a real insurrection. Like their comrades in Latin America, Cuban Communists were as comfortably bourgeois as the members of the oligarchy with whom they were always on the best of terms."[13]

The next defendant called to the stand was Aida Pelayo Pelayo, a forty-two-year-old public-school teacher, leader of the Women's Civic Front of the Martí Centenary, and secretary of ARG. She had been detained in Havana on July 26 and sent to the *vivac* city jail on September 6. Pelayo was confronted with a checkbook and other documents found in her residence linking her to the movement's finances. She claimed that the evidence was planted because of her Auténtico political activities. Cecilio T. Benítez León then testified that he was arrested in Nuevitas, Camagüey, because of bloodstains on his pants. He stated that he was illiterate and therefore had no interest in politics. The magistrates then called to the stand Ignacio Fiterre Rivera, a directorate member of the clandestine Triple A organization, who said that he was a mathematics professor and curator at the University of Havana's Astronomy Museum, and not a politician. He admitted being a personal friend of Aureliano Sánchez Arango but denied any conspiratorial participation with the insurgents.[14]

Fiterre was defended by fifty-three-year-old attorney Andrés Silva Adán, who also represented the next witness, René Betancourt Castillo, an Auténtico militant and telegraphist. Betancourt owned a store that sold radio broadcasting equipment. He denied having a secret rebel code and explained that he had made his last transmission on July 26 at 7:00 P.M. His attorney declared years later that his client, who was married to Silva's cousin, "was really compromised" in the affair. Silva also represented three Nueva Paz peasants: Guillermo Elizalde, who had blasted open the door of the military hospital and had been arrested at the Emergency Hospital; Rolando Guerrero, who told his comrades that he had shot a soldier outside Post 3; and Genaro Hernández. Silva later stated, "I knew they had participated, but it was my duty to defend them. I asked Castro on the stand if my clients had participated in the attack and he denied it." Castro again committed perjury to avoid implicating rebels against whom there was little or no evidence. Judge Nieto then called a ten-minute recess.[15]

The trial resumed with the testimony of former Santiago de Cuba police chief José Villa Romero, accused of giving the rebels the Moncada layout map, information about its security, and police uniforms. During his interrogation, the longest of the day, Villa pointed to a corporal in the courtroom who had seen him at his residence during the attack. The *Havana Post* summarized his testimony by saying that "he was arrested at his home and added that he is always arrested when there is any political abnormality because of his personal friendship with Mireya Prío and her husband. He said he is interested only in his [sausage] business." The next witness was Leonel Gómez Pérez, an Auténtico activist and former UIR member, whom Fidel Castro tried to assassinate in 1946. He said he was arrested on July 30 and described his whereabouts four days earlier. Gómez added that he belonged to a commission designated by former president Grau to resolve the Cuban electoral problem.[16]

The tribunal then summoned four defendants implicated in the Bayamo attack. Juan Manuel Martínez, the elderly owner of the Gran Casino Motel, swore to being unaware of the insurrectional plans and leasing the place to Renato Guitart under the recommendation of Fernando Fernández Catá. Afterward, Fernández Catá testified that Renato told him that the building would be used for a business venture and that he trusted him because they were childhood friends. Sergio González Machado, the taxi driver who dropped off some of the rebels after the attack, declared that he thought they were soldiers and therefore did not consider their destination unusual. There was a stir among those in the courtroom when Andrés García Díaz was called to the witness chair. García, his stepbrother Hugo Camejo, and Pedro Véliz had deserted the Bayamo combatants hours before the attack. He readily confessed his participation, giving an account of their capture in Manzanillo and detailing the murder of his companions by the soldiers. He described his narrow escape after being dragged behind a jeep with a rope noosed around his neck. During cross-examination, Fidel Castro questioned García in detail, trying to implicate the perpetrators and their commanding officer. He queried, "Do you see before you in this court any of the soldiers who tortured you and murdered your friends?" Before García could answer, the prosecutor raised an objection, which was sustained by the tribunal. "Then," Castro told the court, "write down everything denounced here so that in its proper moment charges can be filed for murder and tortures against the persons alluded." Judge Nieto later justified his action, saying, "I had to overrule Fidel because he was not abiding by the charges in question and instead wanted to level accusations against the military. As a lawyer, he knew very well that matter required another legal process that had to be initiated outside of the trial in progress." The magistrate ordered the court secretary to note the accusations and adjourned until Thursday at 8:00 A.M. The codefendant Ignacio Fiterre was so impressed with Castro's oratory that he turned to Sergio Mejías and quipped, "A leader is born." That weekend Fidel Castro wrote to his parents for the first time since his arrest to assure them that he and Raúl were "well treated, we do not need anything," and he promised to write more frequently.[17]

On Thursday morning, September 24, a packed courtroom waited anxiously for the arrival of the prisoners. After a brief delay, Lieutenant Camps gave the tribunal a letter from Colonel del Río Chaviano stating that many of his troops had been transferred to Holguín for Batista's visit. Therefore, he was unable to muster a detachment to escort the defendants nor to guard the Palace of Justice. Judge Nieto postponed the trial until Saturday. The next day Nieto sent a confidential message to the defendants, by way of the prison doctor, which was relayed to Fiterre and others. The message said that Colonel del Río Chaviano was furious with the accusations made in court by Fidel Castro. The regimental chief had said that he would not appear in court to testify, that he was not going to be ridiculed by Castro under cross-examination, and that the rebel leader should not return to the courtroom or he would kill him. Advised of the situation, Castro insisted on going to trial. After a long discussion with Fiterre and other codefendants, Castro told them, "Do whatever you want." The physician then signed a medical certificate claiming that Fidel Castro was ill and could not attend the trial.[18]

The judicial proceedings resumed on Saturday at 8:00 A.M. with the usual roll call. Those in the plenary hall responded "present," while the defendants not answering three consecutive calls were pronounced "absent" by Secretary Mascaró. When Fidel Castro was called, there was a prolonged silence. The court clerk looked inquisitively at Judge Nieto, who motioned him to proceed. Public defender Baudilio Castellanos, representing Raúl Castro and more than thirty other defendants, raised an objection and demanded to know why the rebel leader was not present. The president of the tribunal sent for Lieutenant Camps, who, following orders, handed the court a letter from the regimental chief. It claimed that Fidel Castro was sick and as proof enclosed the medical certificate signed by the prison physician. Melba Hernández then stood up and asked Nieto for permission to speak. "Doctor Fidel Castro is not sick, I have brought a letter from him," she said, withdrawing a folded paper from her bosom as she approached the bench. It was a letter from Castro stating that he was not ill and was being held capriciously. He demanded that the court appoint a physician to verify his good health and that his letter be made public, with copies forwarded to the Havana Bar Association and the supreme court. Castro appealed to the tribunal to guarantee safeguards for his life because he feared being killed. His letter concluded, "The performance of the court until now and the prestige of its magistrates accredit it as one of the most honorable in the Republic, which is why I expound these considerations in blind faith in its vigorous action." The codefendant Fiterre stated, "Fidel was saving his political reputation with that letter and at the same time trying to stop any attempt on his life."[19]

After including the letter in the court record, the tribunal president ordered a twenty-minute recess to discuss with his two associates whether to declare a mistrial for all the defendants or to grant Fidel Castro a separate trial. Nieto recalled that "we unanimously thought that the military authorities would indefinitely delay bringing Fidel to trial because the accused was assuming the role of accuser. Therefore, any further postponement would prejudice innocent defendants imprisoned without bond, such as Luis Casero, Arturo Hernández Tellaheche, and Millo Ochoa, whom I believed were not involved." When the judges reconvened, they separated Castro from the case, granted him a new trial, and instructed that all the demands in his letter be fulfilled.[20]

The trial resumed with the testimony of José Vázquez Rojas, who admitted leasing his Siboney farmhouse to Ernesto Tizol for fifty pesos monthly and giving the keys to "business administrator" Abel Santamaría, but without knowledge of their plans. José A. Batista Lotti then declared that he was at a Masonic lodge meeting in Holguín on the morning of July 26 and did not participate in the revolt. Silverio E. Brito Oquendo denied on the stand that he had recruited anyone in Palma Soriano for the attack, indicating that he saw Fidel Castro for the first time in court. The defendant Ramón Campos Delgado professed his innocence, and forty-year-old Bayamo native Eriberto Sánchez Tamayo denied that he participated in a subversive campaign. Manuel Lorenzo Costa admitted under oath going with Fidel Castro to Oriente but stressed that he had refused to participate in seizing the Moncada radio transmitter. He said that after remaining in the Siboney farmhouse, he went to the home of his aunt Rosa Dau in the city.[21]

The next defendant called to testify was José Luis González Ruiz, from Quemado de Güines, Las Villas, who stated that he went to Santiago de Cuba on vacation and was detained as he left the city on a bus. He was represented by Lucas Morán Arce, who hid the combatant Mario Lazo in his home for two weeks. Moto Mendel Weis and Luis Pérez Cabrejas followed, denying that they knew Fidel Castro and refuting the accusations against them. Orlando Castro García described eighteen-year-old Mendel as being "a small, blond, Jewish schizophrenic weighing less than ninety pounds." Carlos C. Hall, the American Embassy counselor, later described Mendel to the U.S. Department of State as a "young punk" who "had served time in a Federal reformatory in Florida for check forgery" and had been "implicated in various frauds here in Habana. . . . Also, that his sister, known as 'Rosa la Polaca,' is one of the most notorious prostitutes in Habana." Documentary evidence was presented showing that on July 26 Mendel was confined in the National Insane Asylum at Mazorra, Havana Province, and that he was released two days later. The next witnesses taking the stand were six Communist activists: Bernardo Hernández Hernández and Juan M. Llosas Perera were represented by the attorney Rafael A. Cisneros Ponteau; José A. Cabrera, Antonio Pérez Mujica, Armando Díaz Castelar, and Rolando Hevia were defended by José M. Pérez Lamy, an old Communist militant. The PSP militants disavowed the charges against them, abiding by the previous denunciations of their leaders Ordoqui and Peña. They claimed that on the day of the attack "they were in Santiago along with other companions because they were celebrating the birthday of 'comrade' Blas Roca." According to Mario Chanes, Pérez Mujica was too scared to admit that he had been shot and wounded when arrested.[22]

Anibal Quesada Granados then testified that he had gone to Santiago de Cuba with his family for the carnival and was arrested three days after the attack even though he was a retired policeman. "I am a member of the PAU, headed by the illustrious President Fulgencio Batista," said the sixty-four-year-old witness. Judge Nieto interrupted him to admonish, "I do not want speeches, be concrete." Quesada responded that he would not have gone to the Moncada attack had he been invited because he was "one-hundred percent *batistiano*." Then Mario Burman Corman, owner of the Burman Hardware Store in Havana; his paramour Lázara Pérez Cuesta; and their chauffeur Oscar Gras Escalona testified that they were wrongly implicated after their car was disabled by a bullet. All three were represented by the attorney Domingo Estrada de Beatón, who charged one thousand pesos for their defense. The prosecutor asked Lázara only one question: "Did you come here to attack the Moncada garrison?" "No," she replied. The next defendant, Ramón Serrano Alfonso, also refuted the charges against him. His lawyer was Raúl Villalvilla, an Ortodoxo, former Santiago de Cuba alderman, and law partner of Baudilio Castellanos, renowned for defending Joven Cuba revolutionaries and poor peasants free of charge. A ten-minute recess was called at 10:20 A.M.[23]

When the proceedings resumed shortly thereafter, Vicente Chávez Fernández, who had fled with Tizol and did not participate in the Moncada attack, falsely stated that he was not home on the July 26 weekend because as a bachelor he often went away on weekends. He stressed that it would have been impossible for him to be at work early on Monday morning if he had been in Santiago de Cuba during the attack the previous day. Under further questioning from Prosecutor Mendieta, Chávez admitted knowing the rebel Reinaldo Boris Luis, who was killed in the revolt, because they worked for the same company. The tribunal then summoned José Pila Teleño and Raúl del Mazo, members of Acción Libertadora in Santiago de Cuba, who disavowed any participation in the insurrection. Pedro Aguilera, who lost his shoe while fleeing the Bayamo garrison, falsely stated that he was in Havana during the disorder in Oriente. He claimed to travel often between the capital and his hometown of Palma Soriano due to his dental practice. Humberto Lamothe Coronado and Angel Eros Sánchez then subsequently testified about their noninvolvement. Eros, a twenty-five-year-old textile worker and member of García-Bárcena's MNR in Guanajay, was honeymooning in Santiago de Cuba when detained. The next defendant, forty-seven-year-old carpenter Florentino Hernández Enríquez, convincingly stressed that after being arrested in Calabazar he was coerced into signing a confession. He was being truthful when swearing that he did not participate in the attack because his vehicle got lost on the way to Moncada.[24]

The court then heard the testimony of Fernando Limia Rodríguez, an Auténtico politician and former Santiago de Cuba municipality employee, who denied taking part in the events. The next witness, Abelardo del Pozo García, a forty-six-year-old peasant from Santiago de Cuba, had been visiting his brother in Ciego de Ávila, Camagüey. He was arrested upon returning home on September 15 after a long stay in Havana, where the police alleged that he was hiding after leading a Moncada assault team. Then Luis A. Frías and Rafael "Onay" Valdés Calvo, a photographer in Santiago de las Vegas, disavowed any link to the insurrection. The only evidence against Onay was a group photo of the Santiago de las Vegas cell, where he appeared with Fidel Castro, Abel Santamaría, Ernesto Tizol, and eleven others. Afterward, Bayamo rebel Agustín "Thompson" Díaz Cartaya denied his role, stating that the SIM detained him in Marianao because he was not home on the July 26 weekend. He could not explain why his wallet was found in the Gran Casino Motel or the positive results of his paraffin test. The next four rebel witnesses—Ramón Pez Ferro, Marino Collazo Cordero, Ramón Callao Díaz, and Generoso Llanes Machado—all denied being insurgents. Although some had confessed after their arrest, it was inadmissible evidence before the Urgency Tribunal.[25]

The secretary of the tribunal then called to the stand Eduardo Rodríguez Alemán and Orlando Cortés Gallardo, two rebel dissidents who admitted their roles to the news media after their arrest. They were represented by thirty-year-old attorney Luis

Gómez Domínguez, a member of the National Assembly of the Ortodoxo Party, who had been hired by Eduardo's brother in Sagua la Grande. Rodríguez related on the stand the events in the Siboney farmhouse until his Almendares cell withdrew from what they deemed a foolhardy adventure. Cortés corroborated Rodríguez's account, verifying that Fidel Castro had them held in a room under armed guard until the rebels departed for Moncada. He also detailed how his cell split up and regrouped in Santiago de Cuba, and how some later met tragic consequences. Dissident rebel Manuel Vázquez Tió was then summoned to testify. He acknowledged being a University of Havana agronomy student who had gone to the Santiago de Cuba carnival with his friends Angel "Patachula" Díaz-Francisco, Jesús Blanco Alba, and Carlos Merille Acosta but falsely denied any involvement. They were represented by public defender Baudilio Castellanos. Patachula testified that he left Santiago de Cuba with his companions early that Sunday morning and had no notion of the bullet holes in the trunk of his car until they were detained at the roadblock in Holguín.[26]

Prosecutor Mendieta then responded affirmatively to various defense motions requesting the provisional release of eleven political leaders who had testified and Bayamo motel owner Juan Manuel Martínez, since no evidence linked them to the charges. While the tribunal recessed for ten minutes, supreme court prosecutor Elpidio García Tudurí, monitoring the case from Havana, telephoned Mendieta with a list of defendants approved for bail on their own recognizance. When the trial resumed, provisional liberty was granted to those dozen people, who "were warned, however, that their arrest would be ordered and they would be kept in prison if they failed to attend any of the sessions of the court." The proceedings were then adjourned until Monday, September 28.[27]

That weekend Mirta Díaz-Balart visited Judge Nieto at his home to plead for her husband's life and safety. One of Fidel Castro's sisters had previously visited the magistrate's residence and made a similar petition. Nieto recalled Mirta saying, "All I want is that they do not kill him. I do not care what sentence you impose on him, even one hundred years, whatever you wish. You know how things are done here, later an arrangement will be made and an amnesty given, and he will definitively not complete his sentence before being freed." The judge reiterated that the court would provide all guarantees that Fidel Castro and the other defendants would not be harmed. On Sunday court-designated physicians Juan Martorell García and Aurelio Portuondo examined the rebel leader in his cell and certified that, other than a nervous disorder, he was in perfect health. In spite of this, Warden Augusto Taboada sent the court a letter dated September 28 and claiming that Castro "is not presented in trial, due to continued illness and not being discharged by the prison doctor."[28]

The fourth session of Case 37 started Monday, September 28, at 8:00 A.M. Bayamo rebel Enrique Cámara reaffirmed his previous confession at SIM headquarters after being arrested in Marianao. René Bedia testified that he was detained after returning to Calabazar and implicated himself due to death threats. The rest of the Calabazar cell avoided prosecution, with the exception of the codefendant Florentino Hernández, who denied involvement; army orderly Florentino Fernández, held in a military prison for treason; and Julio Trigo, killed in Santiago de Cuba. Gustavo Ameijeiras Romo then took the stand to allege that he had gone to Oriente after being notified that his half brother Juan Ameijeiras Delgado was killed in the attack, and that he was arrested while claiming the body.[29]

The next witnesses called before the tribunal were the seven rebels arrested with Fidel Castro at Las Delicias farm. All of them acknowledged their participation in the attack, although none admitted having killed anyone or having engaged in a commanding role. Eduardo Montano affirmed being conscious of his actions, which were motivated by the principles of José Martí, to restore a democratic constitutional process. Mario Chanes recalled, "What else could I say? It would have been ridiculous for me to claim that I had gone to the carnival when I was captured in the countryside with Fidel. Besides, I had no witnesses to testify to the contrary." Ciro Redondo then gave the court an account of his role in the attack and how he was captured with Marcos Martí on July 30 while hiding in a cave. José Ponce and Ramiro Valdés subsequently admitted their participation. Julio Díaz, arrested in a farmhouse where he had sought refuge, insisted in court that he was innocent of the charges against him. Oscar Alcalde, the check bouncer captured with Fidel Castro, admitted contributing thirty-four hundred pesos to the movement. Ernesto Tizol, who fled on the way to the Moncada and later surrendered in Holguín, recognized his participation in the insurrection, claiming to have joined because of personal conviction. Tizol said that he distributed the weapons prior to the attack and that Siboney farmhouse owner José Vázquez Rojas was unaware of their plans when he signed the rental agreement.[30]

The secretary of the tribunal then called in succession those four rebels captured on the El Caney highway on July 29 who had admitted to the press their participation. Rosendo Menéndez gave his version of the events, and Israel Tápanes followed with self-incriminating testimony. Jesús Montané acknowledged his involvement in the movement and named its leaders. Reinaldo Benítez hobbled up to the witness stand on crutches and confessed being wounded in the leg during the attack. The two rebels who surrendered in the Moncada military housing were summoned before the bench. Pedro Miret spent nearly an hour describing what happened after they were taken to the military hospital. He claimed that on two occasions someone injected twenty cubic centimeters of air into his veins and gave him a dose of camphor, leaving him for dead. Fidel Labrador then admitted being wounded in the eye during combat and ending up with Miret in the military hospital. The court proceedings ended at 12:15 P.M., after Raúl Castro made a last-minute appeal to the tribunal for the safety of his brother. All the defendants were returned to the Boniato Provincial Prison, and the dozen who were granted provisional liberty were processed and released. Although they did not make statements to an awaiting group of reporters, a *Bohemia* magazine photographer took a dozen pictures, which Marta Rojas published with her report.[31]

The fifth session of the trial began on Tuesday, September 29. The first three rebel defendants testifying had been captured on July 26 on the highway to El Cobre. Gerardo Sosa and Ulises Sarmiento denied any complicity and purported having gone to Santiago de Cuba for the festivities. Both stated that they were arrested at a roadblock for being with Gabriel Gil, who had a bloodstained guayabera. When Gil was summoned to the stand, he confessed his participation but did not implicate the others.[32]

After a brief recess, Haydée Santamaría was sworn under oath. She testified that her only purpose for going to Oriente was to visit her brother Abel at the Siboney farmhouse. Haydée stated that after Melba Hernández arrived they were told about the impending attack. She alleged that they both went along as "nurses," although neither had medical experience, and did not handle weapons. Haydée claimed that her companions were beaten and tortured but acknowledged not seeing this happen. She did not state under oath her subsequent allegation that she had been shown by the soldiers her brother's gouged-out eye or the castrated organs of her boyfriend on the day of her arrest. Haydée did not denounce any personal mistreatment while under detention, nor did she claim that the soldiers "burned her arms with lighted cigarettes," as written in *History Will Absolve Me*. She denied that Melba or she had prevented Civil Hospital staff from aiding 2nd Lt. Pedro Feraud after he was gunned down outside the entrance. Haydée later acknowledged that her "testimony wasn't very long. I had planned what I was going to say, but that isn't what came out." Melba was then summoned to the witness stand. She gave an account of the events in the Civil Hospital, claiming that she and Haydée served as "nurses" for the combatants. Melba disavowed allegations that she was seen armed and helping the rebels load their weapons. She testified that the revolutionaries disguised themselves as patients to avoid capture but were denounced by someone. Melba also declared that she, like Haydée, was unaware of the attack plan until the final moment.[33]

The last defendant called to testify was Raúl Castro, who admitted joining the movement out of personal convictions. He said he "was not a leader but a mere participant who was assigned the task of taking over the courthouse to prevent its occupation by the military." Although Lester Rodríguez had been in charge of seizing the building, Raúl avoided implicating his friend, who escaped arrest. The forty-eight rebels present had all testified on their own behalf, but the *Havana Post* reported that only "23 of them pleaded guilty to the attack on the Santiago de Cuba Army Post and two to that on the Bayamo Army Post." Fidel Castro and two other wounded rebels, Abelardo Crespo Arias and Gustavo Arcos, were to be tried later, along with Gerardo Poll Cabrera, a railroad worker implicated in the revolt. In the second phase of the trial, which started after all the defendants had testified, the prosecutor would present his case and summon state witnesses, including military personnel, crime-lab technicians, physicians who treated the casualties, and other material witnesses.[34]

According to medical lieutenant Erik Juan Pita, Cpl. Eugenio Alcolea, and Pvt. Alfonso Silva, all military deponents, prior to their court appearance, were summoned by Colonel del Río Chaviano to his office to go over their testimony with him. The first prosecution witness was Lt. Col. Angel González Alfonso, who described how he assumed the defense of the military hospital upon arriving there at 6:00 A.M. and confirmed that one patient and an orderly were killed by the rebels. Maj. Rafael Morales was then sworn in and detailed his participation in commanding the defense of the garrison. Capt. Juan de Dios Ruiz testified that he was the Superior Officer of the Day on July 26, that he heard gunfire and subversive shouts, and that one of the attackers pointed a machine gun at him but did not shoot. He said that a sergeant next to him was killed and that soldiers were gunned down as they rose from their beds. Police major José Izquierdo Rodríguez was called to the witness stand and affirmed during his testimony that his brother Isidro was killed at Post 3 after activating the alarm. The next witness was SIR chief Capt. Agustín "Bebo" Lavastida, who gave a brief statement about the weapons used by the rebels. Then Lt. Mario Martínez Arbona said that he had gone to Santiago de Cuba from Havana to participate in the festivities. According to Martínez, he led a squad to the Civil Hospital when the attack subsided but did not encounter any rebels. Sgt. José Cigues Morales provided the tribunal with his version of the events. The prosecutor then presented the testimony of Sgts. José Virués, Diógenes Heredia, and Bernabé González, who manned the machine guns during the assault.[35]

The next prosecution witness was Cpl. Generoso Martiniano, who told of his participation in repelling the attack. Manuel Pérez Rodríguez of the National Secret Police verified the information he presented after the insurrection. Judicial police investigator Eduardo Riveiro Suárez "confirmed his report, declaring that some of the defendants had nothing to do with the revolt." The last witness was Zoila Romero Díaz, represented by defense attorney Villalvilla, who claimed that she was with Leonel Gómez the entire weekend of July 26. The trial was then adjourned until the next day.[36]

Case 37 started its sixth session at 9:00 A.M. on September 30. Medical captain Edmundo Tamayo Silveira, the military hospital director, was the first witness. He recalled entering the hospital at about 5:45 A.M. and remaining in the operating room tending the wounded until midnight. Tamayo described the various wounds he diagnosed on the soldiers. Under cross-examination from some defense attorneys, he admitted that none of the casualties had stab wounds. Adj. Capt. Manuel Aguila Gil then testified that he stayed at his regimental headquarters post, answering the telephone and relaying instructions, and therefore did not see the fighting. Military physicians Rolando Pérez Sainz de la Peña and Mario Porro Varela confirmed that all of the government casualties had received gunshot wounds. Police captain Bonifacio Haza Grasso followed, giving his version of the events. Fifteen lieutenants and three sergeants then testified regarding their personal participation in the events. Lt. Horacio York contradicted Colonel del Río Chaviano's official report by testifying that the attackers "did not possess or use hand grenades." Lt. Teodoro Rico, on the other hand, swore that the rebels had thrown two grenades at him, although he did not clarify if they were merely lobbing back the ones he had thrown into the administrative wing. Judge Nieto then ordered a recess at 10:20 A.M.[37]

The proceedings continued twenty minutes later with the testimony of medical captain Mario Porro Varela, the Civil Hospital military supervisor. He said that Colonel del Río Chaviano ordered him to occupy the Civil Hospital with a detachment and that inside they captured only Haydée Santamaría and Melba Hernández since the other rebels had previously been taken away. Prosecutor Mendieta then summoned Amalia Díaz Conde, a Civil Hospital night-shift nurse. She recalled hearing the commotion as the rebels entered wearing military uniforms and had initially assumed that they were soldiers pursuing burglars hiding in the building. Díaz stated that she and the student nurses on her shift "hid with fear in the Nursing School bathroom and did not come out until hours after the tragedy had ended." The court proceedings then adjourned at 11:30 A.M. until the following morning.[38]

The seventh session of Case 37 started at 8:00 A.M. on Thursday, October 1. It "opened with the filing of a writ by the defense counsels of all the defendants against whom no evidence has been presented, asking for their provisional release." The prosecution then called to the witness stand other nurses and student nurses who were in the Civil Hospital on July 26. Idelisa Balgán Fresco stated that she hid in a room the entire time, and Delia Hernández testified that she was unable to assist Lieutenant Feraud and the policeman Pompa due to the intensity of the firefight in the vestibule. Camelia Rodríguez, assigned to the infant ward, declared that two unarmed women pleaded their way inside and pretended to be employees by trying to placate the crying children. The prosecutor asked her if she could identify the females, and Rodríguez pointed to Melba and Haydée. The nurses Josefina Milet Alavo, María Antonia Márquez, and Herminia Delgado Cortez were also called to the stand. Márquez stated that she did not leave the contagious ward during the fracas, while Delgado testified that the frightened women in the maternity ward asked her to remain there the entire time.[39]

Medical lieutenants Erik Juan Pita and Roberto Mas Renedo then gave accounts of their roles in the military hospital the day of the attack. Both declared that none of the death certificates or casualty reports that they had signed mentioned knife wounds. Maj. Andrés Pérez-Chaumont testified that after arriving at Moncada that day, the regimental chief ordered him to lead a contingent of fifty soldiers, who chased the attackers fleeing to the Siboney countryside. He falsely claimed that his troops killed in combat twenty-one insurgents and that none of them were executed after being captured. The prosecution subsequently called Lt. Juan López Alvarez and five corporals, who gave details of their participation in the Moncada defense. Police corporal Doris Mesa González, a marching band musician, stated that he was sleeping on a cot in the administrative wing hallway when the attack began and that he and another soldier scurried to safety. The tribunal then summoned those assigned to the military patrols on July 26. Pvts. Rafael González, Francisco Cruz, Alfonso Silva, Luis Triay, and Cristino Oliva took the stand to give their versions of what occurred that morning. Afterward, Judge Nieto called the first recess of the day at 10:25 A.M. and resumed the trial twenty-five minutes later.[40]

The next prosecution witness was Dr. Mauricio León Orúe, the Civil Hospital night-shift supervisor on July 26. He described how the attackers seized the building and killed 2nd Lt. Pedro Feraud. Dr. León said that one of the rebel females asked him where the linen closet was located because they needed white uniforms. Prosecutor Mendieta asked him if he could identify the woman in the courtroom. Dr. León pointed to Haydée Santamaría in the defendants' section and remarked that he did not see her armed during the uprising. He described the attitude of both rebel women during the revolt as "humanitarian." Bayamo garrison chief Lt. Juan Roselló Pando was then called to testify. He admitted not being at his post during the attack and provided an inaccurate account of the aftermath and subsequent investigations. He accused Bayamo civil defendants Juan Manuel Martínez and Fernando Fernández Catá of being rebel accomplices. The *Diario de la Marina* reported, "This witness was subject to intense interrogation by the prosecutor and the defense attorneys, as well as the tribunal, his declarations being of great importance." Sgt. Buenaventura Capote testified that in Bayamo two attackers were killed and two sentries were wounded.[41]

The prosecution then called Sgt. Vicente Alfonso Cruz of the Maffo outpost, who stated that his squad killed the fugitive Gregorio Careaga outside of town during armed resistance. Pvt. Lázaro Tejadilla took the stand but remembered little other than being wounded at Post 4. Vicente Rigual, a Santiago de Cuba police detective, substantiated his investigative report filed after the attack. Various attorneys questioned him about the direct participation of their clients, and he replied that many of them were innocent. Eight character witnesses for the defense were then summoned before the tribunal. Miguel Corral, president of the Cuban Federation of Radio Amateurs, declared that René Betancourt Castillo was not using for revolutionary activities the shortwave transmitter seized in his house. Gerardo Castro Martínez, the de facto mayor of Santiago de las Vegas, confirmed that local photographer Rafael Valdés Calvo was with him on July 26. Two character witnesses testified in favor of some accused Bayamo civilians. Four other witnesses also vouched for the innocence of some defendants. The thirty-seventh witness of the day was the policeman Alfredo Acosta, who was at Moncada during the attack. Tribunal secretary Mascaró then called Col. Alberto del Río Chaviano to take the stand. The regimental chief was absent, and Judge Nieto decided to terminate the proceedings at 12:30 p.m. until the next day. The *Havana Post* reported, "Meanwhile, the public prosecutor is studying the petition of the defense counsels for the release of their clients."[42]

The trial resumed at 8:30 a.m. on Friday, October 2. The first witness called was Lt. Ismael Valdés Cabrera, who was in the communications room during the assault. He narrated the events he saw and confirmed that Pvt. Manuel Alvarez Morgado was killed after running out onto the patio. The policeman Horacio Martínez Verdecia then related that he rushed from his home to Moncada and entered through Post 5 after being told that the garrison was under siege. The next witness was Dr. Liam Chomat Fetué, who stated that he "did not see that Haydée Santamaría or Melba Hernández were armed nor were they haranguing their companions to fight against the armed forces of the republic." Chomat claimed that he observed "shooting into the air to intimidate the population to stay in their homes." Hospital night watchman René Domingo Osorio declared that he was disarmed by the insurgents. The policeman Victoriano Hernández, a patient in the Civil Hospital, detailed what he saw. The policeman Ramón Díaz Quintero testified about the events that transpired when the attack started.[43]

The prosecution then presented the testimonies of the policeman and two custodians who had been on duty in the Palace of Justice on July 26. The next group of witnesses included six corporals and four privates wounded in Santiago de Cuba, who had been examined by forensic physicians Dr. José R. Cabrales Arjona and Dr. Alipio Rodríguez López. The doctors reported that some were permanently crippled and others had wounds that healed in ten to sixty days. Cpl. Mauricio Feraud Mejías declared that when he and his brother Pedro neared the Civil Hospital entrance, a group of rebels mortally wounded his brother and caused disabling injuries to his arm. Feraud added that he "witnessed when the accused, Misses Santamaría and Hernández, pistol in hand, prevented a nurse of the hospital from picking up his brother and he from the pavement."[44]

Cpl. Carlos Chauvín, the regimental chief's driver, recounted in court how he was seized by the rebels outside the Palace of Justice and forced inside. Sgt. José González, a military hospital orderly, then provided his version of the events. Colonel del Río Chaviano unexpectedly entered the courtroom, and Judge Nieto allowed him to testify immediately. The regimental chief spoke extensively about the Moncada attack, purporting that it lasted two and a half hours, and explained the measures he had ordered to protect the garrison. He described the rebel weaponry, assuring that there were hand grenades and many types of arms, including some that fired hollow-point bullets. A reporter wrote, "Colonel del Río Chaviano limited himself exclusively to the facts, without making concrete accusations." The colonel did not comment on his previous allegations that the sentries on Post 3 and hospital patients had been knifed to death; rather he stated simply that they "were murdered." Bayamo corporal Indalecio Estrada Calderón then described how he repelled the attack with a machine gun at the rear gate of the base. Prosecutor Mendieta summoned two military ballistics experts, who affirmed that all the rebel weapons were operational and that they could be bought along with corresponding ammunition in any gun shop. A fifteen-minute recess followed before fifteen character witnesses testified on behalf of ten defendants. The trial was then adjourned at 12:15 P.M. until the next day.[45]

The ninth session of Case 37 started on Saturday, October 3, after a slight delay. As an observer described, "The hearing opened at 9:20 A.M., when the defendant Isidro Peñalver was taken to the Civil Hospital for medical attention. The rest of the accused and their defending counsels were present." Four appraisers declared that the damages caused in the Santiago de Cuba and Bayamo attacks on July 26 were estimated at twenty-four hundred pesos. The policeman José Sosa Jurado subsequently stated that he was disarmed when the attackers arrived at the Civil Hospital and that he saw police corporal Pedro Pompa and Lieutenant Feraud gunned down. A corporal and three privates gave their versions of what transpired inside the Moncada during the assault. The two soldiers seized while sleeping in the Palace of Justice then presented their testimonies.[46]

Nine character witnesses were summoned to the stand on behalf of four defendants. Afterward, medical lieutenant Erik Juan Pita was recalled to review all the death certificates he issued, none of which indicated stab wounds. Two forensic physicians then diagnosed five wounded soldiers before the tribunal, describing their injuries. The trial recessed at 10:25 A.M. and continued twenty-five minutes later with the testimonies of three other wounded soldiers. The policeman Primitivo Magariño recounted his participation in the events. The defense then summoned nine other character witnesses, who declared on behalf of seven accused. When the trial adjourned at 12:15 P.M., a total of 202 witnesses along with 99 defendants had taken the stand.[47]

On Monday, October 5, the proceedings started at 9:45 A.M. with the public prosecutor and the defense counsels refusing to call further witnesses, thereby avoiding redundancy and prolongation of the trial. Prosecutor Mendieta affirmed his provisional conclusions and petitioned the bench for the conditional release of fifty-eight defendants, who along with the thirteen previously exonerated totaled seventy-one exonerated (see appendix 3).[48] The prosecutor maintained the accusations against the other defendants. Mendieta summarized the government's case, declaring:

What purpose impelled the accused who are being tried to commit such deeds? By the word of their leaders we know they invoked the doctrine of Martí to, by way of violence, establish liberty in Cuba; I do not believe, nevertheless, that Martí inspired war between brothers. Neither did Christ encourage fratricidal wars. Martí preached war, but not between Cubans, but rather against the foreign yoke. I believe we should not invoke Martí in these matters.

I, as representative of the Public Ministry, and society, do not find justification for the actions of the accused; because the government that they, having triumphed, would have made, would not have been of order, but of chaos. Their ambitions would have brought disagreement between them and as a consequence of those disputes brought the greatest harm to the national economy with bloodshed and grief for the Cuban family.

I asked the leaders of this Movement . . . , I asked them, I mean, that, with what political prestige they counted on, so that this skeptical populace would follow them?; I was told that neither did the muleteer [Antonio] Maceo or the attorney [Carlos Manuel de] Céspedes who were well-known men when a nation followed them. But it is because that muleteer had already fought in the Ten Years' War and had protested in Baraguá, and his civic example had stirred the Cubans. But . . . finally, they considered themselves with that prestige. I understand they were mistaken; taking sorrow to their own homes, those of their friends and of the soldiers. What has this Movement brought about? That hate be incremented between Cubans. And that should not occur between noble and generous Cubans. We have seen the greatest proof of the nobleness of this nation in this trial, on one side and on the other.[49]

Mendieta "went on to demand under Article 148 of the Social Defense Code, 20 years imprisonment for each of the remaining 31, with an additional third of the term for the leaders." Article 148 had two clauses: "Anyone who promotes an armed uprising against the *constitutional* [author's emphasis] powers of the state will be imprisoned for three to ten years"; and "The penalty will be from five to twenty years if the insurrection is carried out." Castro had cited the same article in March 1952 when he petitioned the Havana Urgency Tribunal to process Batista for violating the Social Defense Code. Seventeen defense lawyers subsequently briefly addressed the tribunal in support of the prosecutor's petition. Afro-Cuban attorney Gerardo Hernández Vera adhered to the dismissal motion and argued successfully for Abelardo del Pozo García, whose name was added to those of the seventy-one previously acquitted. Judge Nieto then informed the attorneys of those clients whose charges were dismissed by the prosecutor that they were free to leave. The remainder represented defendants who were greatly implicated or had already admitted their culpability.[50]

The attorney José M. Badell Romero, a poet known for expressing his judicial arguments in verse, made a passionate plea for Manuel Lorenzo Costa. Badell stressed that since his client had remained in Villa Blanca and not consummated the act, article 159, granting absolution to anyone withdrawing at the last moment, was applicable to him. The court then recessed at 10:35 A.M. and reconvened fifteen minutes later. Elizardo Díaz Lorenzo spoke on behalf of confessed participants Fidel Labrador and Julio Díaz. Then Héctor Canciano Labory pleaded for José Ponce, who was wounded on the shoulder and hand outside Post 3. Similar absolution contentions were made by the attorney Luis Gómez Domínguez, who insisted that articles 157 and 159 should be implemented for his clients, Eduardo Rodríguez and Orlando Cortés, because they had remained at Siboney. Judge Nieto ordered another fifteen-minute recess at 11:20 A.M. to consider the earlier prosecutorial motion. Upon reconvening, "the court ordered the provisional release of 58 defendants, as requested by the prosecutor, with the proviso that they must attend the remaining session of the trial." The hearing then adjourned until the next day.[51]

The eleventh and final session of Case 37 began at 9:20 A.M. on Tuesday, October 6, after legal motions were submitted by the lawyers of Ignacio Fiterre and René Betancourt. Fiterre had been rearrested by the SIR on other pending charges after his release from Boniato Provincial Prison the previous afternoon. The attorney Jorge Paglieri, representing Melba Hernández, "maintained that the prosecution had been unable to show that she was at the scene of the events, armed and prepared for combat. He spoke for over an hour and when he had finished, the court recessed briefly." Paglieri "was congratulated by all his companions who stated that he had offered a class in Criminal Law, classifying it as formidable." After a brief recess, the judicial proceeding continued at 10:35 A.M., with public defender Baudilio Castellanos addressing the tribunal. Twenty-one of his forty-five defendants had been released. All the rest except for one had already admitted participating in the revolt.[52]

Castellanos said that "the court had given evidence of high civil responsibility in its handling of the case and praised the attitude of the public prosecutor for his spirit of justice and responsibility." He added that the charges against the remaining defendants should not be based on a single article of the Social Defense Code for everyone but should differentiate the roles of leaders and participants. He went on to relate historical events that had occurred in Cuba and other countries during their struggle against oppressive regimes. Castellanos narrated his version of the Moncada attack based on the judicial documentary evidence. He claimed that some of the rebels' statements of culpability to the instruction judge should be voided because they had been coerced and that the paraffin tests were illegal since they were not authorized by a magistrate. The public defender then pleaded for the acquittal of Calabazar rebel Florentino Hernández, who claimed innocence, although he was in one of the vehicles that got lost on the way to Post 3. Castellanos's defense lasted over two hours, ending with a plea for the release of Haydée Santamaría, whom he said had suffered enough with the deaths of her brother and her boyfriend. Prosecutor Mendieta then asked the tribunal for permission to rebut what he called the twisted concepts expressed by some of the defense attorneys. The lawyers agreed to this request, believing that he had acted strictly according to the law during the course of the trial.[53]

The court recessed again at 12:30 p.m. and then continued twenty minutes later, "when it awaited the arrival of one of the accused, who had been released and been arrested the night before as a result of a disagreement with the police." Cecilio Benítez León had gotten drunk celebrating his freedom after two months of imprisonment and caused a public nuisance that landed him back in the *vivac* jail. Twenty-five minutes later, when Benítez was brought in, Judge Nieto asked all the defendants to rise and then passed sentence: thirteen years of imprisonment for confessed leaders Pedro Miret, Oscar Alcalde, Ernesto Tizol, and Raúl Castro; ten years for Juan Almeida, Fidel Labrador, Jesús Montané, Israel Tápanes, Reinaldo Benítez, Julio Díaz, Ramiro Valdés, José Ponce, Ciro Redondo, Eduardo Montano, José Suárez, Mario Chanes, Armando Mestre, Francisco González, René Bedia, Agustín Díaz, Enrique Cámara, Gabriel Gil, Andrés García, and Rosendo Menéndez; three years for the dissidents Manuel Lorenzo, Eduardo Rodríguez, and Orlando Cortés; and seven months for Melba Hernández and Haydée Santamaría, "since it was never proven that they handled weapons." Calabazar rebel Florentino Hernández was adjudged not guilty, and the rest of the seventy-one defendants previously conditionally released were acquitted. Nieto later explained his sentencing decision: "The Civil Defense Code established that when a revolution was carried out against a Constitutional government, the penalty was up to thirty years incarceration, but if it was initiated against any other form of government, such as a coup-produced regime, the maximum term was reduced to fifteen years." The 1940 Constitution had abolished the death penalty and set a maximum of thirty years imprisonment for any crime. Likewise, Batista's Constitutional Code of April 4, 1952, followed the same precepts.[54]

Nineteen insurgents were found not guilty due to a lack of evidence and their false testimonies. Judge Nieto stated, "Some of the guilty went free because several investigative reports of the army contradicted those of the police. But you can rest assured that no one innocent was convicted." The *New York Times* reported, "The revolt leaders also were ordered to pay an indemnity to the families of the armed forces killed in the revolt ranging from $2,000 to $5,000 and life pensions to soldiers and policemen who have been completely disabled by wounds." The court ruled that the men be sent to the military prison in La Cabaña fortress, to avoid incarceration with common criminals. The two women, destined for the National Women's Prison in Guanajay, Pinar del Río, would also receive political prisoner status. Amid the courtroom hubbub, Judge Nieto rang his desk bell and declared the trial concluded. The local *Diario de Cuba* indicated that none of those sentenced showed any displeasure with the penalty imposed and noted that the press received "the enthusiastic support of the tribunal, the prosecutor and the attorneys." The sixty acquitted defendants not under provisional liberty were returned on the buses to the Boniato Provincial Prison with the rest of the prisoners to gather their belongings and await the written orders granting their freedom.[55]

After being released from prison, Ignacio Fiterre was flown under armed escort to SIM headquarters in Camp Columbia. He recalled, "Captain Agustín Lavastida's wife was on the plane and after I chatted with her she ordered the removal of my handcuffs. Before landing, I told her that I lived near the military airfield, and I would like to briefly stop by my house to see my family. She then told the sergeant in charge of the guard to take me there before going to SIM headquarters." Fiterre had his escorts take him home in a taxi he hired instead of waiting for the SIM transport vehicle. From there he telephoned Batista's minister of justice, César Camacho, an old family friend, and explained his predicament. "Since there were no charges pending against me, I believe they were going to take me to SIM offices and torture me into telling where Aureliano Sánchez Arango was hiding. Once I let others know I was in Havana, I was released the next day due to influences," affirmed Fiterre.[56]

Rebel dissident Angel Díaz-Francisco and his parents stayed in Santiago de Cuba at the Imperial Hotel for a few days waiting to reclaim his confiscated 1950 Oldsmobile. His codefendant Manuel Vázquez Tió also lodged there. The hotel administrator told Patachula that the three sensuous young women lounging in the lobby were prostitutes and SIM informants. "I do not care who they work for," said Vázquez, "I have been incarcerated too long, and I am going to have fun with them."[57]

Ramiro Arango and Leonel Gómez went to the Casa Granda Hotel before returning to Havana by bus. Arango's French wife convinced him to move to Paris. U.S. vice consul Arthur W. Feldman informed his embassy in Havana, "There have been no public demonstrations in favor of the accused and the sentiment which immediately after July 26 was in favor of the Army has veered to the opposite.... The city has returned somewhat to a normal outward appearance with few soldiers and police seen about."[58]

On October 12 Minister of the Interior Ramón Hermida Antorcha ordered that the twenty-seven male defendants destined for La Cabaña be transferred from the Boniato Provincial Prison to the National Men's Prison on the Isle of Pines. The order specified that they be segregated from the common criminals confined there. The detainees, including the two women, were taken the next day in a military plane to the Isle of Pines. The DC-3 then flew the females to the Camp Columbia military airport, where a car transported them to the National Women's Prison. Fidel Castro remained in the Boniato Provincial Prison after being granted a separate trial. He was placed in a cell with Fidel Labrador, who was being fitted with a glass eye by Dr. Luis Velazco. Three other defendants awaited trial: Gerardo Poll Cabrera and the wounded rebels Gustavo Arcos and Abelardo Crespo.[59]

The government's roundup of defendants had cast a wide net and snared sixty-five innocent people, including many opposition political leaders, illiterate peasants, a Batista supporter, and a schizophrenic delinquent. Magistrate Mejías considered the case the most important political trial in the history of the republic. The judicial process, under a nonconstitutional regime, was equitable and impartial. The three judges hearing the case had excellent reputations, and each had more than twenty-five years of experience on the bench. The defendants received a speedy trial according to law. The proceedings were open to the news media and hundreds of public spectators, including family and friends of the defendants. The only possible government influence, due to the suspension of constitutional guarantees, was the control of bail eligibility by the supreme court prosecutor, who responded to Batista.

Fidel Castro was allowed to assume his own defense. He donned a lawyer's robe and sat with the defense team, thereby raising his stature within the context of the trial. He, and not his crime, was thrust into the spotlight, especially after he raised in court formal accusations of murder against the military. When Colonel del Río Chaviano tried to silence Castro temporarily by claiming that he could not be escorted to trial due to illness, the court granted the rebel leader a new proceeding and guaranteed his personal safety. Castro praised the tribunal and its performance as highly honorable. The leading public defender, Baudilio Castellanos, a future Castro government official, complimented the tribunal and the prosecutor for their "spirit of justice and responsibility." The prosecutor did not attempt to frame any defendant, and all the defense attorneys agreed that he had acted strictly according to law. None of the accused or their defense attorneys ever complained of trial irregularities or unjust sentences. The death penalty was not applicable by law. Most of the convicted rebels received ten-year terms and not the maximum penalty of fifteen years. The sentence amounted to about six months in prison for each of the nineteen soldiers and policemen killed in the attacks.

Fidel Castro repeatedly committed perjury to protect his followers after failing to convince them all to plead guilty. Fewer than half of the rebel defendants admitted their culpability in court, most of them having previously made incriminating statements. Haydée Santamaría, Ramiro Arango, and others accused rehearsed their testimonies before taking the stand. Raúl Castro truthfully acknowledged not being a leader and having a minor role in the affair. No innocent defendants were convicted, and nineteen rebels were acquitted after giving false testimony about their participation. Some opposition figures also lied under oath to avoid being implicated with the rebels. Likewise, Colonel del Río Chaviano, Major Pérez-Chaumont, Lieutenant Rico, and other corrupt officers perjured themselves regarding their roles and the execution of prisoners.

Colonel del Río Chaviano's exaggerated official report to the tribunal was in part not supported by testimony. His claim that soldiers had been stabbed to death was disproved by medical military witnesses. The defense attorneys did not substantiate the Black Legend of prisoner torture, mutilation, and dismemberment when questioning the forensic examiners and military doctors on the stand. In spite of this evidence presented in court, both pro- and antigovernment myths persist today. Militarily, the attacks in both cities were disastrous but of no material consequence, causing only twenty-four hundred pesos in damages. The Bayamo assault received lesser significance during the trial because only four of the twenty-five rebel participants and four local innocent civilians were charged. Three of the Bayamo rebels had already admitted their roles.

The attackers who confessed told the prosecutor that they were emulating the heroes of the Cuban War of Independence to establish liberty on the island. They were the "Youth of the Centenary" nationalists, disassociated from the Montreal Pact, political parties, or Communist ideology. The Communists, in turn, denounced the revolt as a "bourgeois putsch" and did not support Castro until seven months before he seized power in 1959. By then the prosecutor's ominous forewarning in his closing statement became a reality. The revolutionary government established a chaotic order that destroyed the very fabric of Cuban society.

During the trial Fidel Castro began to achieve the prestige and stature that he had been unable to gain prior to and with the failed garrison attacks. He emerged, however, as the leader of the only belligerent action carried out against Batista. This overshadowed his past as a UIR triggerman. Castro portrayed himself and his movement as victims of a dictatorship's brutal oppression and persecution. In his prison cell the rebel chief prepared for what would become his revolutionary legacy, his edited and now renowned self-defense speech titled *History Will Absolve Me*.

NINE

"History definitively, will say it all"

On October 13 the Santiago de Cuba news media announced that the trial of Fidel Castro and two codefendants would be held in three days. The public proceedings were again heralded on the morning of Friday, October 16, in the local newspaper *Diario de Cuba*. The Urgency Tribunal held a special session in the Saturnino Lora Civil Hospital because the wounded Abelardo Crespo could not be moved from his bed. Castro and Gerardo Poll Cabrera, a Santa Clara railroad worker falsely implicated in the revolt by a coworker, were included in this judicial process. The last rebel defendant, Gustavo Arcos, was in the Colonia Española Clinic with a spinal-cord lesion and would be tried later. At 9:00 A.M. the rebel leader arrived at the hospital in an automobile escorted by Capt. Pedro Rodríguez Medrano and Lt. Vicente Camps. He was the last to enter a nursing-school classroom that had been accommodated for the trial. Military policemen stood guard at both doors, which remained open to allow a mild tropical breeze to circulate.[1]

To the right of the main entrance, the magistrates Adolfo Nieto Piñeiro-Osorio, Ricardo Díaz Olivera, and Juan F. Mejías Valdivieso sat behind a desk. An adjacent table and chairs were occupied by chief prosecutor Francisco Mendieta and tribunal secretary Raúl Mascaró. Castro shared a mahogany desk with defense attorneys Baudilio Castellanos and Marcial Rodríguez Gutiérrez. Abelardo Crespo, recovering from a .22 bullet in his lung, was propped up on a nearby hospital bed. Six newspaper reporters, including Marta Rojas, occupied folding wooden chairs. Captain Rodríguez and Lieutenant Camps remained in the room. Judge Nieto stated that no one was turned away from the public proceedings. Judge Mejías pointed out that the spectators included his daughter Irma Mejías, a recent law-school graduate; patients; nurses; hospital employees; and many other citizens, some of whom were standing in the hallway.[2]

Judge Nieto instructed Castro on the charges of promoting and carrying out an armed uprising against the state and told him to answer the prosecutor's questions. The *Havana Post* reported, "Fidel Castro testified that he had organized and led the insurrectionary movement which assaulted the army posts of Bayamo and Santiago." When the prosecutor concluded his interrogation, the two defense attorneys questioned the defendant regarding the culpability of their clients. Castro denied their participation, even though he had driven Crespo to Post 3 during the attack. He denounced the murder of prisoners but also made positive statements about the military. According to the *Havana Post*, "He praised the chivalrous conduct of the army lieutenants who arrested him and his brother, declaring that they had helped to redeem the honor of the Cuban Army." Castro then asked for and received permission from the court to act as his own counsel, and he donned a lawyer's black robe.[3]

Mendieta then summoned the military and medical witnesses who had appeared in the first trial, including twenty-one wounded soldiers and policemen. The reporter Marta Rojas wrote, "Everyone said the same thing they had stated in the previous trial, including [Col. Alberto del Río] Chaviano, whom Fidel, as an attorney, did not ask any questions and ignored, although he did interrogate Major Andrés Pérez-Chaumont." Castro decided not to cross-examine Colonel del Río Chaviano, after having accused him of murdering and torturing rebel prisoners, due to fear of reprisal. The colonel had previously told Judge Nieto that if he were ridiculed by Castro on the stand he would kill him, and the magistrate had secretly relayed the message to the defendants.[4]

Judge Nieto called the three defendants to testify on their own behalf. Abelardo Crespo declared in a weak voice from his bed that he went to Santiago de Cuba to visit his girlfriend Romelia Pérez and that he was not involved in the attack. He falsely claimed that on the morning of July 26 he was walking on Victoriano Garzón Avenue, by the Plaza de Marte Park, when he was shot. The court called the physician Arturo de Feria Mora and the radiologist Fernando Blanc Corbín for their diagnoses of Crespo's wound. Crespo still had a .22-caliber projectile lodged in his lung.[5]

Gerardo Poll Cabrera then denied the prosecutor's charges. The only evidence against him was a letter from coworker Pablo Nager Rodríguez to Santa Clara military chief Col. Pilar García, under the pseudonym "Luis Perdomo." Nager wrote that he had heard Poll admit being in the Moncada attack. The *Havana Post* reported, "Both Fidel Castro and several other witnesses denied that Poll had participated in the movement. Some of the witnesses established his alibi." At the conclusion of the testimony, the prosecutor presented his final statement. Mendieta asked the tribunal for "the liberty and acquittal of the accused Gerardo Poll Cabrera, and as for the two other accused, give them the punishment specified in section B of article 148 of the Social Defense Code, increasing it by a third for Doctor Fidel Castro Ruz for being the leader of the movement. Nothing more." The prosecutor demanded a twenty-six-year prison sentence for Castro instead of the maximum thirty-year term. The attorney Marcial Rodríguez Gutiérrez then subscribed to Mendieta's petition for the acquittal of his client. Baudilio Castellanos again solicited freedom for Abelardo Crespo, although he knew him to be an attacker. Fidel Castro afterward began his closing statement by saying, "Perhaps few times has an attorney had to practice his trade in such difficult circumstances. ... Difficult for many reasons, first, because I am the accused and second, because I am the comrade of a group of young men having confessed a crime ... that I also committed. The attorney always asks the absolution of his defendants, but, how can I ask for mine when my companions are in prison in the Isle of Pines?"[6]

For the next two hours Castro presented a defense speech that later would be expanded and revised into a published pamphlet entitled *History Will Absolve Me*, which became the manifesto of the Cuban Revolution. The rebel leader attempted to justify the attacks on the Moncada and Bayamo garrisons by claiming that he was carrying out the ideals of Cuban liberator José Martí. His defense speech was void of Marxist ideology. Judge Nieto stated that Castro's lengthy monologue was basically a condemnation of Batista's Tenth of March Coup and an indictment of the army's brutality against the attackers. He affirmed that "Castro spoke at length without being interrupted. Some of the points mentioned in *History Will Absolve Me*, such as the agrarian reform and other social questions, Fidel spoke about them, but everything else was written later." Lieutenant Camps agreed with Judge Nieto's view that Castro was not dogmatically Marxist in his discourse and did not speak long enough to include everything mentioned in the pamphlet. Anyone timing a reading of *History Will Absolve Me* will discover that it is impossible for Castro to have pronounced the speech in just two hours.[7]

The rebel leader also denounced his prison conditions and his removal from the first trial on the third day. He lashed out at the perceived unconstitutionality of the charges against him, claiming that the government could not judge him since the coup had violated the Cuban Constitution of 1940. Castro justified his actions by claiming that the right to revolt was valid under the constitution's article 40. He described the planning and the attack, and he credited the encounter with the military patrol as being the decisive factor for its failure. Judge Nieto affirmed, "Fidel talked about two hours. Some of the things he said were not true, others had nothing to do with the accusations against him, nor were they related to the law. It was a form of political expression, trying to call attention, and demagoguery. We did not cut him off, because we wanted the defendants to fully express themselves, so they would not say we tried to coerce them." Castro claimed in 1960 that he "gave a three-hour speech in court." According to the December 27, 1953, issue of *Bohemia*, Fidel Castro concluded by saying, "Gentlemen of the court, in gratitude for your generosity, honorableness and justice, I am going to finish. I am not asking for my liberty. You count on the backing of the people of Cuba, although you condemn us. The silence of today does not matter. History definitively, will say it all."[8]

Marta Rojas alleged decades later that the final paragraph of Castro's closing statement had been modified by the Batista government censors, forgetting that press censorship had been lifted on October 24. Her earliest version of Castro's speech, transcribed into a 179-page manuscript from her trial notes, has Castro declaring: "In conclusion, my pardon, in the name of my companions, for all those who did not have consideration for our fallen brothers. For the Tribunal that fulfills its duty, my respect. I am not asking for my liberty. You count on the backing of the people of Cuba, although you condemn us. The silence of today does not matter. History definitively, will say it all." When the pamphlet *History Will Absolve Me* was published, this last paragraph was changed to read: "In regards to me, I know that prison will be hard like it has never been for anyone, full of threats, of vile and cowardly rage, but I do not fear it, like I do not fear the fury of the miserable tyrant who took the lives of seventy of my brothers. Condemn me, it does not matter, history will absolve me."[9]

The latter, melodramatic ending bears a strong resemblance to Adolf Hitler's final speech before a German tribunal in 1924 following the Munich beer-hall putsch: "The judges of this state may go right ahead and convict us for our actions at that time, but History, acting as the goddess of a higher truth and a higher justice, will one day smilingly tear up this verdict, acquitting us of all guilt and blame." Both conclusions, by Hitler and Castro, inspired by a defeated putsch, are substantially the same. They express an equal sentiment, a singular idea, and the same objectivity. Judge Nieto and Lieutenant Camps agreed that Castro's conclusion was more like the *Bohemia* version and that he never articulated what was to become his revolutionary signature phrase "history will absolve me."[10]

After Castro ended his tirade, the magistrates whispered among themselves, shuffled through some papers, and pronounced judgment. Gerardo Poll was acquitted, Abelardo Crespo got a ten-year term, and Fidel Castro received a fifteen-year sentence. Judge Nieto indicated that he gave Castro the maximum term allotted by law: "The Civil Defense Code established that when a revolution was carried out against a Constitutional government, the penalty was up to thirty years incarceration, but if it was initiated against any other form of government, such as a coup-produced regime, the maximum term was reduced to fifteen years, which is what Fidel received. Although the prosecutor asked for a twenty-six-year sentence for Fidel Castro, because the Batista government was unconstitutional, we had to abide by the fifteen-year maximum sentence law."[11]

The trial lasted six hours and was over by 3:00 P.M. Castro then approached the bench and shook hands with the three magistrates. He asked Nieto if the safest route to the penitentiary was by train or airplane. After pondering a moment, Nieto replied that "the best thing they can do is take you in an airplane, because if you do not arrive, it can only mean you were thrown overboard, but on a train, anything can happen." Castro was handcuffed by Lieutenant Camps, who along with Captain Rodríguez drove him back to Boniato Provincial Prison.[12]

The next day, October 17, the new U.S. ambassador Arthur Gardner presented his credentials to General Batista. Cooperation pledges were exchanged during the ceremonial speeches. The Batista regime upheld "its firm position of opposition to Communism and its penetration in this hemisphere." It vowed to fulfill all the inter-American resolutions against such subversive intrusion and that it was against "any Communist action in this continent." Earl T. Crain, the embassy's acting counselor, wrote to the U.S. Department of State that the statement placed "the Cuban Government squarely on the side of the United States in its dispute with the Communist-ridden regime in Guatemala."[13]

Cuban Communist leader Juan Marinello Vidaurreta appeared on October 23 before the last session of the Urgency Tribunal. It was held in the Colonia Española Clinic to accommodate the wounded rebel Gustavo Arcos, Ortodoxo leader Luis Conte Agüero, and Camagüey Auténticos Santiago Noriega Plaza, José A. Núñez Carballo, and Roberto de Varona Loredo. The defendants were escorted by Lieutenant Camps. Gustavo Arcos, in a wheelchair because of a spinal injury, was represented by the attorney Carlos Peña-Jústiz Arrieta. He admitted his role in the attack while all the other defendants denied any involvement. Arcos received a ten-year sentence, and the five political leaders were acquitted. The court ruled that he should stay in the clinic until he had recovered completely and then be transferred to La Cabaña prison in Havana. Case 37 remained open for about a dozen indicted fugitives. Years later Judge Juan Mejías told a revolutionary government historian that "no member of the military nor the government went to see us to impose any criteria," a fact that was confirmed by Judge Nieto. On October 24 the constitutional guarantees suspended on July 26 were restored.[14]

The Constitutional Statutes established by the Batista regime on April 4, 1952, title 4, article 26, guaranteed that political prisoners be kept in special segregated sections, did not have to work, and were not subjected to penal regulations for common criminals, such as wearing prison uniforms. The twenty-nine rebels convicted in the first trial had been flown out of Oriente on October 13 in a DC-3 military transport that landed in the Nueva Gerona airport on the Isle of Pines. The circular-shaped island, with a two-hundred-mile circumference, lies fifty-six miles south of the Havana provincial coast. The prisoners were met by Lt. Pedro "Perico" Rodríguez Coto, chief of the prison's internal order, who accompanied them on the bus trip to the penitentiary. The warden, Maj. Juan M. Capote Fiallo, also headed the Rural Guard Fifty-seventh Squadron stationed on the island. After the prisoners were dropped off, the aircraft continued to Camp Columbia in Havana. There,

Melba Hernández and Haydée Santamaría were transferred to a SIM automobile that left them at the National Women's Prison in Guanajay, Pinar del Río, built in 1948. They were received by the administrator Dr. Carmelina Guanche, a 1930s feminist leader, who immediately telephoned their families to inform them of the women's safe arrival. The rebel women were kept apart from the common criminals in a large storage room outfitted with their own sleeping quarters, bathroom, dining room, and kitchen for cooking their own meals. They received visits from family and friends and were allowed unrestricted books, newspapers, and magazines and a radio.[15]

Fidel Castro and Fidel Labrador, who was fitted with a glass eye after being wounded during the attack, arrived at the Isle of Pines on October 17 in a military transport plane. The penitentiary was built in 1931 to house five thousand men, and its architectural design was copied from the Illinois state prison at Joliet. It contained four five-story circular buildings in a quadrangle, with ninety-three double-man cells per tier. The dining hall, a two-story round building, was located in the center of the four cell units. The rear area of the quadrangle had two square one-story pavilions, with four inner patios, containing the hospital and the segregation cells. Twenty yards behind it, separated by a chain-link fence, were the prison power plant and three storage sheds.[16]

The political prisoners lived in a hospital ward near the first pavilion. It was a rectangular room measuring 120 feet in length by 24 feet wide, with single beds aligned on both sides. Breakfast was served at 5:30 A.M., lunch at 11:00 A.M., and dinner at 5:00 P.M. The rebels had access to an enclosed outdoor patio until the 9:00 P.M. prisoner count. Underneath a patio awning two wooden tables with benches, facing a blackboard, served for holding classes and eating meals. The inmates organized the "Abel Santamaría Ideological Academy" for discussions and studies. Their dormitory contained two bookcases with more than six hundred volumes, comprising the "Raúl Gómez García Library." The men played cards, chess, Ping-Pong, and volleyball for recreation. According to Mario Chanes, they had radios and could have obtained a television upon request. Since the ceiling lights were permanently on, the prisoners could sleep or read at their leisure, but they had to keep silent after 10:00 P.M. Castro told a reporter in 1960, "I organized a school for fellow political prisoners, where we developed undying loyalties and friendship."[17]

The rebels declined prison food and prepared their own meals on a hot plate. Friends and relatives provided money, books, and victuals, including local fruits and vegetables. On the first and third Sundays of each month, the political prisoners received visits from family; friends; priests; nuns; opposition political leaders such as Guido García Inclán, who went several times; and a delegation of Havana professors headed by Judge Waldo Medina. Mario Chanes stated that each political prisoner also had a monthly nine-hour conjugal visit in an isolated *bohío* within the penitentiary grounds. According to Eduardo Montano, Warden Capote allowed special visits for his spouse Santa and Fidel Castro's wife and their children when they jointly arrived from Havana during a weekday. Castro was never visited by his paramour Naty Revuelta, who initially wrote to him via his mother. He responded to Naty on November 7, 1953, that he loved her "very much" and would take his memories of her to his grave. In their secret correspondence she pledged her eternal devotion to him.[18]

Fidel Castro spent his time reading mostly world history and political doctrines, including Karl Marx's *The Eighteenth Brumaire of Louis Bonaparte*, *The Civil Wars in France*, and *Capital*, the latter of which he lost interest in after reading the first seventy-six pages, and Lenin's *The State and Revolution*. He referred to both Communist authors as "model revolutionaries." Castro also showed a keen interest in a study of Roosevelt's New Deal on social reforms. In a December 19 letter to an Ortodoxo activist, the twenty-seven-year-old Castro boasted, "What tremendous school this prison is! Here, I have rounded out my view of the world and determined the meaning of my life. I don't know if it will be long or short, fruitful or in vain, but my dedication to sacrifice and struggle has been reaffirmed." Montano said that Castro entertained them with stories about his role in the Cayo Confites expedition and the Bogotazo. During their political discussions, Montano "first heard Fidel talking like an Old Guard Communist, repeatedly denouncing Yankee imperialism. Our library had more books on Communism than anything else." He recalled, "If you spoke against Socialism, Fidel branded you a traitor to the revolution. From then on, Fidel was dictatorial. You could not discuss anything with him because his word was sacred. Fidel would ostracize you for having different beliefs. When I noticed that tendency, I no longer followed him after leaving prison."[19]

Seeking public support, Castro wrote to Ortodoxo leader and radio commentator Luis Conte Agüero on December 12, 1953, asking why no one was denouncing "the atrocious tortures and the mass murder" of the captured rebels. He requested that his friend be the spokesman of "this honorable cause, since you have more than enough intelligence, more than enough valor and more than enough grandeur." The rebel leader asked Conte Agüero to announce that the political prisoners would refuse a special Christmas Day dinner to fast in mourning. He was annoyed that the Ortodoxo Party Directive Council had discussed whether the events of July 26 were a revolution or a putsch, as denounced by the Communists. Castro stressed, "Had our revolutionary effort triumphed, it was our purpose to place power in the hands of the most fervent Ortodoxos." Seeking the party's support, after Raúl Castro had declared when arrested that "Ortodoxoism no longer exists," Castro asked Conte Agüero to show his letter to Ortodoxo president Roberto Agramonte. He instructed that Conte Agüero "express to him that our sentiments are full of loyalty to the most pure ideals of Eduardo Chibás; that those who fell in Santiago de Cuba are militants of the Party that he founded; and that with him they learned to die when the fatherland needs the heroic immolation to raise the faith of the people." Castro also pleaded that his friend exhort *Bohemia* editor Miguel Angel Quevedo to support their denunciations. Conte Agüero became the voice of the political prisoners, reading Castro's letters on his *Cadena Oriental de Radio* program, which mobilized public opinion into a movement for general political amnesty. In all of his prison correspondence to Conte Agüero, Castro highly praised him and nurtured his vanity.[20]

Fidel Castro lamented in a New Year's Day letter to Conte Agüero that the Moncada martyrs were hardly remembered while most of the populace was merry-making. Venting his eternal contempt for the wealthy class, he wrote, "What do our homeland's pain and the people's mourning matter to the rich and fatuous who fill the halls? For them, we are unthinking youths, disturbers of the existing social paradise, and there will be no lack of stupid ones who think we envy them and aspire to the same miserable existence of idleness and crawling that they enjoy today." His letter concluded, "There is nothing greater than the stubbornness of a man who believes in his ideas and his truth. He is invincible, and all the power on earth is of no avail against him."[21]

That belief was put to the test on the morning of February 12, 1954, when the political prisoners were removed from the patio and locked in their pavilion. Hours later they heard a commotion outside. Juan Almeida, standing on the shoulders of a comrade, peered out the barred windows high on the dormitory wall and observed that Fulgencio Batista and his retinue had just arrived. The general was attending the formal inauguration of the prison power plant, which had been repaired to run at full capacity. Mario Chanes recalled that the rebels agreed by majority vote to sing what later became known as the "26 of July Hymn." A few, fearing reprisals, voted against it. As Batista was leaving, the revolutionaries, about sixty yards distant, defiantly sang loudly enough for him to hear them. Col. Orlando Piedra, accompanying Batista, upbraided Warden Capote for being lax with the political prisoners. The next afternoon Lieutenant Rodríguez Coto placed Fidel Castro, Ramiro Valdés, Oscar Alcalde, Ernesto Tizol, and Israel Tápanes in the adjacent solitary-confinement pavilion. The trustee in charge of the cell block was the notorious Salustiano "Cebolla" Rodríguez, a squat, barrel-chested, common criminal serving various life terms for murders committed in and out of prison.[22]

The following day the guards found in the rebels' dormitory a copy of the revolutionary hymn signed by its composer, Thompson Díaz Cartaya, who was also sent to segregation. Cebolla told him, "So you are the author of that piece of shit. Well, now you're going to sing it for us." Díaz Cartaya refused, became aggressive, and threatened the trustee. That night Cebolla, Lieutenant Rodríguez Coto, and four guards returned and assaulted Thompson. Fidel Castro accused Warden Capote of ordering the attack. This was an isolated incident, since Castro and the other twenty-nine political prisoners never complained of abuses; nor did they ever stage a protest hunger strike there as they did in Boniato Provincial Prison. Upon arriving at the Isle of Pines, Fidel Castro had written to his brother Ramón, "The persons running this prison are much more decent and educated than those in Boniato." Pedro Miret stated, "To the authorities, we seemed like very quiet prisoners, so they left us alone."[23]

A week later the five insurgents in segregation returned to their ward. Fidel Castro was confined to four months in solitary and kept in a separate room in the hospital building. He read ten to fourteen hours a day, wrote, smoked cigarettes, and listened to the radio. Castro told a reporter that he also spent this time "memorizing an English dictionary." Three times a week he was allowed into a yard by himself, where he communicated with his comrades by throwing cloth or rubber balls with notes back and forth between patios. Fidel Castro also cooked his own meals with food and delicacies sent to him, according to a letter he wrote on April 4, 1954, to a friend: "I'm going to dine on spaghetti with squid, Italian bonbons and fresh coffee and then smoke a four-inch H. Upmann cigar," he boasted. "Aren't you jealous? They look after me; they take very good care of me." The day before, Castro had appeared for the first of five hearings before the Nueva Gerona Court, where the political prisoners had testified between October 1953 and January 1954, accusing the army of killing the rebel detainees after the attack. Castro explained in a letter to Conte Agüero that they had filed three murder and torture cases in the Instruction Court of Northern Santiago de Cuba against Batista, Tabernilla, Ugalde Carrillo, and Díaz Tamayo for killing the prisoners. The legal motions named as executors Col. Alberto del Río Chaviano and other officers and soldiers. Castro had filed other charges "for continuous violations of individual rights."[24]

In April 1954 the rebel leader began transcribing the defense speech he had pronounced before the Urgency Tribunal six months earlier; this was eventually published as *History Will Absolve Me*. Its basic contention was outlined in a letter he wrote on December 12, 1953, to Conte Agüero and which his wife Mirta smuggled out of prison. The document repeated Castro's denunciations of the Batista coup and elaborated on the crimes committed against the Moncada and Bayamo prisoners. Castro asked his friend to "Make up a manifesto to the people following the content of this letter, sign it with my name, and give it to Mirta. She will try to get it published in *Alma Mater*." Conte Agüero was to take the letter to *Bohemia* publisher Miguel Angel Quevedo and to former ABC organization leader Jorge Mañach Robato, a renowned writer and José Martí's biographer. Conte Agüero recalled that "Fidel wanted Mañach to perfect it, as his way of being obsequious with Mañach, but I did not take the letter to Mañach because I did not want to implicate others in clandestine activities." Conte Agüero edited the document and released it as a typed letter, dated January 6, 1954, called the "Manifesto to the Nation" under Fidel Castro's name. Its brief foreword said, "The Cuban Patriotic League issues the following

Manifesto because of its great historical significance. You should copy it and distribute it between your friends and try to have them do the same." The letter was clandestinely circulated in Havana with a limited distribution. Judge Adolfo Nieto described it as "a mimeographed subversive document, differing from other versions of *History Will Absolve Me* that were published later." Prosecutor Francisco Mendieta also read the missive and told his son that it had been "substantially changed" from what Castro said in court.[25]

The Castro letter was printed in pamphlet form and titled *Message to Suffering Cuba*, with a photo of José Martí on the cover. It appeared after Haydée and Melba were freed upon completing their seven-month sentences. Writing to Melba on April 17, 1954, Castro told her that "Mirta will tell you of a way to communicate with me every day if you want," alluding to a jailer who was serving as a courier. Castro instructed Melba to meet in Mexico City with Raúl Martínez Ararás and Léster Rodríguez to commemorate the first July 26 anniversary. When Martínez Ararás heard that Fidel Castro had decided to organize a political "Moncada Veterans Movement," he objected because "There was a group of us in exile who fought in Bayamo, and not in Moncada, who believed that name would exclude us, and we suggested it should be called the 26 of July Movement." When his third child was born two years later, Martínez Ararás named her Ana, in memory of Saint Ann's Day on July 26.[26]

Fidel Castro also stressed in the letter to Melba not to neglect propaganda, "for it is the soul of any struggle. Ours should have its own style and be adapted to the circumstances. Mirta will tell you about a pamphlet of decisive importance because of its ideological content, and tremendous accusations to which I would like you to pay the closest attention." The manifesto had reached few people, and Castro wanted something on a larger scale before the November presidential election, in which former president Ramón Grau San Martín, endorsed by the Communists, was challenging Batista. *History Will Absolve Me* was finished in June, written in minute longhand on onionskin paper. Mario Chanes stated that Fidel Castro penned it while isolated from the other prisoners. The manuscript was smuggled out of prison and typed by Melba and her father, with production coordinated by Castro's half sister Lidia and Luis Conte Agüero. On June 18, in a letter to Haydée and Melba, Castro ordered the distribution of one hundred thousand copies throughout the island within four months, stressing, "The document is of decisive importance: it contains our program and our ideology, without which nothing great may be expected, and a denunciation of the crimes. These haven't been publicized enough, and we must do this as our first duty to those who died." According to Melba, only twenty thousand issues of *History Will Absolve Me* were initially printed. Herbert Matthews acknowledged that the pamphlet had no impact and disappeared from circulation. A second edition was printed during the fifth anniversary of the Moncada attack, when the Sierra Maestra campaign was in full swing after the Eisenhower administration had imposed an arms embargo on the Batista regime.[27]

The authenticity of *History Will Absolve Me* has been disputed. The final published version mentions only five revolutionary laws, not the six referred to in the letter sent by Fidel Castro to Luis Conte Agüero on December 12, 1953. The document proposes political and social solutions borrowed in large part from the 1930s nationalist program of the ABC organization and the ideologies of the Auténtico and Ortodoxo parties. All three groups had espoused the nationalization of the United States–owned telephone and electric companies, which made Castro's similar demand, the most radical aspect of *History Will Absolve Me*, appear trite. The pamphlet is void of the shrill anti-American denunciations that after 1959 became integral parts of Castro's speeches. It expresses a desire to expand the rural and urban bourgeoisie while continuing private ownership of the means of production, which contradicted socialist ideology. Theodore Draper describes *History Will Absolve Me* as "little more than an anthology of familiar ills and cures, long the staples of Cuban politics, especially as practiced by the late Eduardo Chibás." Mexican-American historian Ramón Eduardo Ruiz called it "a potpourri of middle-class panaceas, quasi-Marxist remedies, and paternalistic attitudes." Luis Conte Agüero, who wrote the prologue to the first English-language version, alleged that Castro received from *Bohemia* reporter Marta Rojas and another newspaperman the notes they took at his trial. Conte Agüero defined *History Will Absolve Me* as practically a Christian-Democrat ideological document that "contains no reference to Karl Marx or any Marxist or Socialist writers." Castro completed the document with quotes from the books and references he had in prison. Conte Agüero confirmed that "*History Will Absolve Me* is not textual in relation to what Fidel said at the trial. The judicial proceedings were not recorded and the reporters who were there did not write in shorthand, but wrote rapidly."[28]

It would have been almost impossible for Castro during his trial to quote verbatim historic documents and the words of over a dozen renowned thinkers and political theorists, including John of Salisbury, St. Thomas Aquinas, Martin Luther, John Althusius, John Milton, John Locke, Jean-Jacques Rousseau, Thomas Paine, the French Declaration of the Rights of Man, and the United States Declaration of Independence, all referred to in *History Will Absolve Me*. The text also cites numerous specific civil and criminal codes whose lengths are beyond memorization. This further suggests that the document was written with ample research material. Mario Llerena, an MNR member, who three years later wrote the "Manifesto-Program of the 26 of July Movement" entitled *Our Reason*, claimed that a new version of *History Will Absolve Me* was printed in March 1959 and that this was an amalgam of the prison manuscript and the economic thesis of *Our Reason*. Former revolutionary Teresa Casuso wrote in 1961, "The fact is that what was published after the victory is not what Fidel Castro originally said at that private trial . . . the document now being circulated has been altered to include statements which describe subsequent events, but which Fidel never made at the trial." Magistrate Adolfo Nieto and the attorney Ramiro Arango Alsina, a codefendant acquitted in Case 37, believed that Mañach revised the final version of *History Will Absolve Me,* in spite of Conte Agüero's assertion to the contrary. Castro had been corresponding with Mañach, whom he addressed as "Dearest friend," and probably insisted that he review the document.[29]

Fidel Castro's prison letters sometimes reflected an authoritarian and resentful attitude that eventually caused some of his closest supporters, including Raúl Martínez Ararás, to abandon the movement. In an April 2, 1954, letter Castro renounced traditional party politics, exclaiming, "Politics is such a hoax! In my experience, even with the best men and the best parties, it is unbearable . . . I was a player in that circus; like Archimedes, I searched for the pivot on which to move my world. Deep in my heart I hated it all; I thought I saw hypocrisy and mediocrity everywhere, and time has shown I was right." Affirming his belief that Cuban society had to be obliterated, in a letter to a friend on March 23, 1954, Castro praised French revolutionist Robespierre for being "hard, inflexible and severe. . . . A few months of terror [in France] were needed to end the terror which had lasted for centuries. Cuba needs many Robespierres." Castro affirmed in another letter two weeks later, "frankly, how pleased I would be to turn this country upside down! I am sure that all the people could be happy—and, for them, I would be ready to incur the hatred and ill will of a few thousand, including some of my relatives, half of my acquaintances, two thirds of my professional colleagues, and four fifths of my former schoolmates." In a Machiavellian manner he then advised Melba Hernández in a letter of April 17, "Use a lot of sleight of hand and smiles with everybody. We must follow the same tactic we employed in our trial: defend our points of view without raising hackles. There will be plenty of time later to crush all the cockroaches together."[30]

A general political amnesty was decreed in May 1954, excluding the July 26 participants, as a goodwill gesture toward the scheduled November elections. All other political prisoners were freed, including MNR leader Rafael García-Bárcena. Three months later government decree 1580 granted amnesty to soldiers accused of crimes committed in relation to the Moncada and Bayamo attacks. Luis Conte Agüero, who spent one hundred days of a six-month sentence in solitary confinement in the Isle of Pines Penitentiary for violation of the Public Order Law, was pardoned by Batista just prior to the general amnesty. He recalled, "I was not able to speak to Castro in prison. One day I saw him at a distance out in the yard going to the visiting room and I yelled at him from my cell window. Recognizing my voice, he stopped and waved back."[31]

Castro complained to Conte Agüero on June 19, 1954, that "the attitude of the Bar Association has been very weak. . . . The FEU with its group interests and its cliques has behaved very badly." Fidel Castro wrote another letter that same day to the movement leaders who were free, ordering them to "strictly follow the decisions made here and do so with the zeal and discipline imposed on you by duty and with the responsibilities of your positions. You know I have always taken a hard line on these matters, and I mean to do so again today." Those who would not follow the rules "must be expelled without any further thought, just as the cowards who back out when the time comes must be executed." Fidel Castro instructed Melba and Haydée the following month that their immediate task was to build their ranks instead of organizing revolutionary cells. He wanted to "mobilize public opinion in our favor, to spread our ideas and win the people's backing. Our revolutionary program is the most complete, our line of action the clearest and our history the most sacrificial. We have the right to the people's faith—without which, I repeat a thousand times, there can be no revolution."[32]

When Castro completed his four-month solitary punishment on June 27, two incarcerated midshipmen were assigned to his cell. One was an Afro-Cuban nicknamed "Pata de Plancha" due to his large, wide feet, who served as the rebel leader's cook. Two weeks later *Bohemia* published an interview with Castro titled "With the Political Prisoners in the Isle of Pines," which portrayed him in seven photos in his cell and accompanied in the prison library by his wife Mirta, their son Fidelito, and his brother Raúl. The rebel leader wore an elegant suit and tie. There was also a group photograph of the twenty-seven political prisoners on the patio, without Fidel Castro, Gustavo Arcos, and Manuel Lorenzo Costa. The latter, the radio technician who refused to join the attack, was confined separately at his own request. In another picture Castro appeared reading a *Bohemia* report on the overthrow of the leftist Guatemalan government of Jacobo Arbenz, engineered by the U.S. Central Intelligence Agency (CIA). Yet, in none of his prison writings did Castro comment about this or any other world revolutionary events. The focus of his politics was on the internal Cuban situation.[33]

Eight days after appearing in *Bohemia* with his smiling family, Castro heard a radio news bulletin that minister of the interior Ramón Hermida had fired Mirta Díaz-Balart. This may have been provoked by the magazine article or because she had earlier attended a tribute to Luis Conte Agüero in a Havana theater and read a statement from her husband calling Batista a tyrant and a despot. Castro wrote to Mirta that he could not fathom under any circumstances her employment in the ministry, and he told her to file a defamation lawsuit against Hermida because "your name is at stake." Castro also wrote to Conte Agüero, saying that the incident "is a plot against me: the most ruin, the most cowardly, the most indecent, the most vile and intolerable." He exclaimed that Mirta was too smart to "have been seduced at any time by her family to figure in a government payroll, no matter how hard her economic situation." Castro asked Conte Agüero to talk to his brother-in-law Rafael Díaz-Balart, vice minister of the interior, and discover his role in the matter. Castro vented his homophobia: "Only an effeminate like Hermida, in the last stages of sexual degeneration, could turn to such proceeds of inconceivable indecency and lack of manhood." He stated that he did not want to become a murderer after leaving prison but that he would like to challenge his brother-in-law to a duel because "the prestige of my wife and my honor as a revolutionary are at stake."[34]

Four days later a letter from his half sister Lidia confirmed that Mirta previously had a sinecure with the Batista regime and that she was filing for divorce. The next day, addressing Lidia as "my dear and loyal sister," Castro excused himself for being brief because he did not feel like writing and simply stated, "Do not worry about me; you know I have a heart of steel and I shall be dignified until the last day of my life. Nothing has been lost!" Mirta's divorce was provoked by the receipt of a love letter her husband had sent to his paramour Naty Revuelta. Mirta got the envelope intended for Naty after prison censor Miguel Rives switched them. The offended spouse telephoned Naty to demand her letter, which was forwarded unopened. Teresa Casuso admitted that the love affair continued through prison correspondence and that "Discovery of one of the letters almost caused the lady to be divorced." Castro had previously assured his wife that his relationship with Naty was over, and this new evidence left Mirta feeling deceived and manipulated. Castro assigned former Ortodoxo senators Pelayo Cuervo Navarro and José Manuel Gutiérrez Planes to handle his divorce, while Mirta retained Aramís Taboada, her husband's law-school friend. The marriage was legally dissolved the following year, and Mirta later wed Ortodoxo politician Emilio Núñez Blanco, with whom she had two daughters. The rebel leader, who remained sensitive about his divorce, refused to talk about it to television interviewer Barbara Walters in 1977, and years later he told his biographer Tad Szulc that he "ignores what happened."[35]

On July 26, 1954, the first anniversary of the Moncada and Bayamo attacks, thousands of leaflets titled *To the People of Cuba* and signed by the Centennial Youth were distributed in Havana. That same day Melba and Haydée headed a demonstration in Colón Cemetery that was disbanded by the police. That afternoon Fidel Castro received a surprise twenty-minute visit in his cell from interior minister Hermida and his assistants Gastón Godoy and Marino López Blanco, who inquired about his treatment. Castro had previously been visited by Col. Dámaso Sogo Hernández, who let Batista into Camp Columbia during the Tenth of March Coup. Sogo, accompanied by his staff, gave Castro a cigar and offered him a book. Fidel Castro claimed that Hermida blamed Rafael Díaz-Balart for the press release announcing that Mirta had been fired from her government job. Díaz-Balart later confronted Hermida in Batista's office and chided him for visiting the "assassin of soldiers" on the Moncada attack anniversary instead of going "to visit the widows and orphans of the dead soldiers." Prison conditions improved for the political prisoners after the Hermida meeting. Castro wrote in August that Raúl had joined him in a larger cell with patio access and that they slept with the lights out and awoke at their leisure. In addition they had "plenty of water, electric light, food and clean clothes."[36]

Fidel Castro constantly denounced the "illegality and unconstitutionality" of the November elections, but on October 25 he wrote to his half sister Lidia that he had stayed up until 1:30 A.M. listening to the radio broadcast of the campaign speech of her brother Pedro Emilio in Santiago de Cuba. Not wanting to alienate Lidia, his closest family supporter, the rebel leader lauded, "I heard Pedro Emilio; he did not do it badly; I consider that he has some possibilities of success." His half brother failed in his Auténtico Party bid for the Chamber of Representatives. Fidel Castro was surprised to hear his name chanted by the crowd when former president Grau San Martín spoke at the political rally. Grau responded to the crowd by saying that when elected, he would decree an amnesty to include the "Moncada lads." Twenty-four hours before the national elections on November 1 Grau withdrew from the race, claiming fraud, and this denied Batista his desired political legitimacy. Batista's single candidacy won with 1,262,587 votes from six progovernment coalition parties.[37]

Trying to "arouse the nation against Batista when he is about to assume power on February 24," Fidel Castro wrote on January 1, 1955, to Ñico López and Calixto García Martínez, Bayamo combatants exiled in Central America. He exhorted them to return to Cuba and turn themselves in so that the trial would have to be reopened and then would stir public opinion. He suggested, "This would be a tremendous psychological blow, especially since everyone is calling for amnesty. The presentation of evidence would once again be the center of public attention, and a perfect opportunity for expounding our ideas." Hoping that other rebels would also surrender, Castro told López and García to "tell all the exiled comrades you think should know about this plan, but make sure it appears as your own idea; I don't want to put any moral pressure on them." The illiterate Ñico López was dissuaded by his parents from turning himself in. None of the forty-eight insurgents who escaped capture adhered to Castro's plea for surrender.[38]

On January 28, 1955, the 54 senators and 114 representatives elected in November held their congressional inaugural session. The Council of Ministers, which had replaced the Cuban Congress since the Tenth of March Coup, was abolished and the 1940 Constitution was reinstated. Castro's principal revolutionary goal of fighting to restore the former constitutional system was now moot. On February 24 Fulgencio Batista and Rafael Guas Inclán, the leader of the Liberal Party, were sworn in as president and vice president, respectively, of the republic. That day a proclamation called "A Public Appeal," signed by thirty-six political activists of various political persuasions, not including the Communists, appeared in the press exhorting, "we address public opinion to demand liberty for the political prisoners and guarantees for the return of all those in exile, with no qualification or exclusions which might affect the peaceful coexistence we all seek." Batista declared to the reporter Marta Rojas on inaugural day, "I applaud the laws governing pardon... I would not be averse to approving an act of pardon passed by the Congress if it would bring the nation long-term peace." On March 10, the third anniversary of the coup d'état, the political opposition introduced an amnesty bill in Congress. Arturo Hernández Tellaheche, acquitted in Case 37, presented it in the senate, and house minority leader Juan Amador Rodríguez proposed it in the Chamber of Representatives.[39]

The amnesty bill was approved by the Chamber of Representatives on May 2, 1955. It was ratified by the senate the next day, and Batista signed it on May 6, with the condition that it take effect on May 15, as a goodwill gesture to Mother's Day. It became the 113th amnesty law approved by the republic since 1902. Rafael Díaz-Balart, the former vice minister of the interior, had been elected to the Cuban Congress, where he became house majority leader and majority caucus chairman. Following party discipline, he voted in favor of the amnesty bill but gave a dissenting opinion on the floor. Díaz-Balart said that "an amnesty should be an instrument of pacification and fraternity" and forewarned that his former brother-in-law, "Fidel Castro[,] and his group only want one thing: Power; but total power. And they want to attain it by violent means, so that total power will permit them to definitively destroy all vestiges of constitution and law in Cuba to install the most cruel, the most barbaric tyranny."[40]

The political prisoners walked out of the Isle of Pines Penitentiary at noon on Sunday, May 15, 1955, greeted by a crowd of reporters, family, and friends, including Melba Hernández and Haydée Santamaría. Fidel Castro served twenty-one months and fifteen days of a fifteen-year sentence set to expire on July 31, 1968. He bid farewell to Lt. Roger Pérez Díaz, chief of the Rural Guard Squadron, saying, "I do not see the army as an enemy but as an adversary. I have the highest respect for those who deserve it." The rebel leader was driven to the home of Chucho Montané and held a press conference that evening in the Isle of Pines Hotel in Nueva Gerona, releasing a communiqué entitled "Manifesto to the People of Cuba." He told the reporters, "We did not go to Moncada to fight against the soldiers. We went to combat one man, one date, one idea. We have nothing against the Cuban army, and for those brave ones who fell in the arid land of the Santiago garrison, we feel admiration and respect. In regards to my plans I should say that I do not aspire to anything, absolutely nothing." That night the revolutionaries left on the ferryboat *El Pinero* for the mainland port of Batabanó. Arriving at dawn, Castro was interviewed by a reporter from Radio Cadena Habana and stated that he would stay in Cuba to fight the government, denouncing its errors and unmasking gangsters and thieves. The rebels traveled by train to Havana, where a crowd of supporters greeted them at 7:45 A.M. in the Central Train Station. Fidel Castro was hoisted onto the shoulders of a mob that sang the national anthem. The Moncada attack had now made him more famous than ever.[41]

Castro went to live with his half sister Lidia in her Vedado apartment. There, accompanied by Ortodoxo leaders Raúl Chibás Rivas, Roberto Agramonte Pichardo, and Max Lesnik Menéndez, he was interviewed by *Bohemia* reporter Agustín Alles Soberón. Castro claimed that the amnesty was the result of "the extraordinary popular mobilization, [and] masterly support by the Cuban press." When asked about the events of July 26 and his future plans, Castro, who sought the backing of the Ortodoxo leadership, minimized his revolutionary rhetoric: "Someday that story will be told, at its proper time. Meanwhile, we must look to the future. An army must not turn its rifles to shoot at the past. We will not do what is convenient for the government, that is, engage in conspiratorial activities, but we will do what is beneficial for the fatherland; that is, to work tirelessly for the union of all moral forces of the country under the flag of Chibás' thought. For that endeavor I am thinking of staying in Cuba, struggling openly, for we are not men of hate or resentment, as some suppose." Concerned that Fidel Castro might form a new political party and decimate Ortodoxo ranks, the party leadership offered him the presidency of Havana Province. Castro turned it down but declared that he was still a member of the party.[42]

Castro also received in Lidia's apartment a visit from Bayamo rebel leader Raúl Martínez Ararás, who had been exiled in Mexico City until the amnesty. "When I arrived, I was told that Fidel was asleep. After a two-hour wait, he emerged from the bedroom, followed by Naty Revuelta," recalled Martínez Ararás. He spoke to Castro on behalf of a group of July 26 combatants who wanted to create a movement with a balanced leadership because they would not accept a *caudillo* (political boss) autocracy. Castro rejected their conditions, and two months later Martínez Ararás, Orlando Castro García, Carlos Bustillo Rodríguez, Gerardo Granados Lara, and Pedro Trigo López—all having evaded capture after the attack—joined the Radical Liberation Movement (MRL) headed by Amalio Fiallo, opting for electoral, instead of revolutionary, change.[43]

The freed rebels had a strong ally in the newspaper *La Calle*, subtitled "The Journal of the Cuban Revolution," which had an initial distribution of seven thousand issues in April 1955. It was edited by Luis Orlando Rodríguez, an Ortodoxo militant and former revolutionary triggerman during the Machado regime, who was married to a wealthy socialite. The day before the amnesty, *La Calle*'s sensationalist headline proclaimed that there was a plan to murder Fidel Castro upon his release. Col. Alberto del Río Chaviano reacted to the amnesty of the Moncada attackers with a letter published in *Bohemia* on May 22, giving his own twisted version of what happened and calling the rebels "criminals full of hate." Castro replied a week later in the same magazine with "Chaviano, You Lie!," reiterating the contentions in *History Will Absolve Me* regarding the crimes perpetrated against the prisoners. He also accused the "miserable provocateur" of controlling illicit business, vice, and contraband in Oriente. He dared Auténtico representative Waldo Pérez Almaguer, former governor of Oriente, who entered the Moncada during the battle, to reveal everything he knew about the murder of the detainees since he enjoyed congressional immunity. Responding to Castro's article, the pro-Batista newspaper *Ataja*, which had proclaimed that the rebel leader had been killed during the Moncada attack, ran the editorial "Fidel Castro Is a Murderer" on May 29 and lauded the army. The next day Castro again lashed out against Colonel del Río Chaviano in *La Calle*, with the front-page headline "Chaviano, the Provocateur."[44]

Pérez Almaguer answered Fidel Castro's challenge with an exclusive interview, which appeared in *La Calle* on June 3, headlined "I Saw More than 30 Revolutionaries Executed - The Massacre Commenced When Chaviano Arrived - Batista Cannot Be Blamed for That Savagery." The following day President Batista declared at a rally that his tolerance was being interpreted by bullies and braggarts as a sign of weakness and said, "Let not the attacks made against us be repeated by some who have received amnesty, because I do not want them to provoke our men anymore. And let it not be said afterward that force was out of our hands, for the men and women of the ruling parties have brains, hearts, and also hands." Castro regarded this statement as a personal challenge and escalated the war of words to provoke the government into taking harsh measures. On June 7 he published in *La Calle* the article "Murderers' Hands," expressing that Batista's followers "have hands, but I do not believe they have brains or hearts . . . I do not want to assume that Batista is a coward, but I am sure that he is vain, conceited, dishonest and mistaken." He then admonished the president, "Do not offend or humiliate the people any more with words, speeches and deeds that wound Cuban sensibility. Remember that 'tyranny foments the virtues that sooner or later destroy it.'"[45]

Two days later Castro escalated the verbal war in *La Calle* with the article "Stupids," denouncing an attack on Juan Manuel Márquez, the Ortodoxo president of the Marianao municipality. He blamed the government for "beating defenseless citizens" during the previous three years and declared that "hundreds, thousands of Cubans have had to suffer this barbarous affront. . . . What monstrous sentiments are stored in the minds of these barbarians that in such a way trample human dignity." That night, when Castro went to appear on a weekly Channel 11 television program, he was banned from participating for seven weeks. Two days later a telegram from the minister of communications prohibited the TV station and Union Radio from including Castro in their programs.[46]

Castro, who was unemployed, continued going to his office in *La Calle* each afternoon to type an article for the next day's edition, staying until the proofs had gone to press each night. On June 11 he wrote "Against Terror and Crime," denouncing the murder of the revolutionary Jorge Agostini Villasana and seven bombings that occurred the previous night. "To set off bombs, then, can only be the work of scoundrels without conscience who want to serve the government instead of fighting it," the article read. Efigenio Ameijeiras, whose brother Juan was killed at Moncada and brother Gustavo was a codefendant in Case 37, admitted that even before the amnesty he and other rebel supporters "started planting bombs," which they continued doing until Batista fled. Haydée Santamaría later admitted that she was also detonating bombs in her "undercover work" and ordering others to do the same. Castro was being hypocritical, since during the later guerrilla campaign he never denounced hundreds of bombings perpetrated by his followers and those who died while placing explosives were revered as revolutionary martyrs. The next night the National Directorate of the 26 of July Movement was organized in Havana by Fidel Castro, Pedro Miret, Chucho Montané, Melba Hernández, Haydée Santamaría, Pepe Suárez, Pedro Aguilera, Ñico López, and newcomers Faustino Pérez, Armando Hart, and Luis Bonito. All of them had already demonstrated blind obedience to the rebel leader.[47]

The government responded to what it considered insults and diatribes by closing down *La Calle* on June 16, alleging that "in all its editions it attacks and criticizes, with Communist tactics, not only government officials, but anyone who is serious, stable and constructive." Fidel Castro's unpublished article "One Cannot Live Here Anymore" complained of receiving anonymous telephone death threats against him and his brother. The next day Raúl Castro obtained asylum in the Mexican Embassy, after being charged with exploding a bomb in the Tosca movie theater. He departed for Mexico on June 24. Fifty-three days after leaving prison, on the afternoon of July 7, Fidel Castro went to the airport with a Mexican tourist visa and bade farewell to his sisters Lidia and Emma, his son Fidelito, and Naty Revuelta, who was pregnant with his child. He left behind a public statement, which said in part, "I am leaving Cuba because all doors of peaceful struggle have been closed to me."[48]

Fidel Castro and his followers had received a just and impartial trial under an independent judicial system permitted by the Batista regime. The magistrates resisted the machinations of Colonel del Río Chaviano and disregarded his phony official report. Castro's separate trial was announced with anticipation in the local news media. The proceedings, although in cramped quarters, were open to the public and covered by six newspaper reporters. Castro was permitted to assume his own defense and question witnesses without restrictions. He counterbalanced his accusations against corrupt officers by praising the lieutenants who arrested him and his brother. Castro was astute in opting not to interrogate Colonel del Río Chaviano in order to avoid a confrontation. He once again committed perjury when stating that the codefendant Abelardo Crespo, whom he drove to Moncada, did not participate in the attack. Although the prosecutor requested a twenty-six-year sentence for Castro, the tribunal strictly abided by the law when condemning him to only fifteen years.

The rebel leader's closing statement, later expanded and revised for publication as *History Will Absolve Me*, was presented without coercion or interruption. When the government censorship was lifted eight days afterward, the press ignored the rambling monologue. Ten weeks later *Bohemia* quoted only the closing paragraph, finding no reason to publish other aspects of the defense speech that had been transcribed by their reporter Marta Rojas. *History Will Absolve Me* was later converted into a revolutionary platform that was propagandized to perpetrate a fraud on the Cuban people. Castro eventually turned his references to agrarian reform and limited nationalization of foreign enterprises into a base for the intervention and confiscation of all private property on the island.

The political prisoners served their sentences under humane conditions with special privileges. They were kept segregated from common criminals, did not wear prison uniforms, and were exempt from labor. The rebels enjoyed conjugal and special visits, interviews with news reporters, and recreation, and they had uncensored reading material, including Communist books. They also had radios; maintained secret correspondence; received delivered groceries; cooked their own meals; were provided a special Christmas dinner, although they rejected it; and even had a chance to demonstrate defiantly against Batista.

While serving time, Fidel Castro prepared the groundwork for a traditional revolution. He devoured Communist works and tried to indoctrinate his followers during political discussions. Until then, as he wrote to Luis Conte Agüero on December 12, 1953, his struggle had been carried out by Ortodoxo Party militants, as a "heroic immolation to raise the faith of the people," and their purpose had been "to place power in the hands of the most fervent Ortodoxos." In contrast, he expressed contempt for traditional party politics, which he suppressed after taking over. In July 1954 Castro ordered Melba and Haydée to start organizing the ranks of the nascent 26 of July Movement, encompassing all social levels. Fidel Castro now began expressing stronger anti-American and pro-Communist sentiments to his inner circle, but he would not publicly proclaim being a Marxist-Leninist until December 1961. The Communist Party, in turn, did not sign the proclamation calling for the release of the political prisoners. Castro's deceptive character led his wife to divorce him after she accepted a sinecure from the Batista government. He demanded strict loyalty from his followers and threatened to execute "the cowards who back out." Castro rejected sharing political power with other revolutionaries and prepared his own continuity of one-man rule in Cuba. The rebel leader was on a course that, according to his own words, would turn Cuba "upside down."

Batista, confident in his electoral victory, felt magnanimous and for purely political purposes approved pardons passed by Congress, in spite of the opposition by the armed forces. The rebels served only twenty-two months in prison, amounting to fewer than five weeks for each of the nineteen soldiers and policemen killed in the attack. The Bayamo rebel leadership and the other attackers who wanted to create a democratic political movement broke with Castro a month after he left prison.

Fidel Castro then organized the core of his new revolutionary movement with cohorts who unquestioningly obeyed him. With their help he achieved complete control in 1959 over 6.5 million, mostly literate people living in a developing island economy. He then transformed the nation into an anti-American Communist outpost of the Soviet Union at the height of the cold war to assure his perpetual hold on power.[49]

TEN

The "Grand Task of Cuban Reconstruction"

Fidel Castro's early life had strong parallels with that of Nicaraguan rebel Augusto César Sandino (1895–1934). The latter was born out of wedlock to a teenaged peasant woman servant who lived on his father's plantation. Sandino bore his illiterate mother's last name and lived in her hut until his early adolescence, when his father welcomed him into his household. The Nicaraguan resolved his arguments with a gun and had to flee abroad after shooting and wounding a man. Castro likewise traveled abroad after the murder of Manolo de Castro and the attempted assassination of Rolando Masferrer. Sandino developed a hatred for Americans, and his nationalist philosophy was centered on anti-Americanism. He created the red-and-black flag for his movement, later copied by Castro. Sandino's initial assault on the Ocotal barracks, on July 16, 1927, was similar to the Moncada attack. He retreated into the mountains with his decimated force, but instead of surrendering, he initiated a guerrilla war that lasted six years. Castro would later emulate the same irregular warfare strategy.

The Moncada and Bayamo attacks gave birth to Fidel Castro's revolution. The plan was a patchwork of ideas adapted from Cuban historic events. Narciso López had similarly prepared an 1848 uprising during the Cienfuegos carnival, when his disguised followers would attack the local garrison. Carnival week had also coincided with José Martí's 1895 independence revolt and Batista's 1952 coup. An aborted attack on the Moncada garrison in April 1933 had catapulted twenty-six-year-old Antonio Guiteras to revolutionary prominence. The attack on the Bayamo garrison, void of strategic military importance, had greater historic significance. The city was the cradle of the 1868 Ten Years' War for independence. Castro's illusive design to march across the island once the Moncada had fallen, taking garrison after garrison, was borrowed from the 1895 invasion march accomplished by independence generals Máximo Gómez and Antonio Maceo. After Batista fled, Fidel Castro led a triumphant one-week caravan from Santiago de Cuba to Havana instead of flying directly to the capital. He was conscious of playing a historic role, as exemplified by his statement to Raúl Martínez Ararás hours before the July 26 revolt that they were "going into history."[1]

The July 26 uprising was a botched, amateurish effort rather than a well-executed plan capable of mobilizing popular support and overthrowing a dictatorship. Castro failed in his initial attempts to rally a nationwide following because of limited propaganda methods. He was able only to attract a small, radical, and mostly uneducated youth group within the divided Ortodoxo Party. Castro and his "command staff" were hindered by their lack of military cognition. As a result, the assault strategy was elementary and did not have a contingency option. Rebel intelligence was unable to determine the military strength or the proper entries at both garrisons, neglected occupying an apartment building roof that overlooked the Moncada parade ground and barracks entrances, and failed to determine the exact location of the Moncada arsenal. Hasty preparations, designed to upstage the Montreal Pact and the announced invasion by the Caribbean Legion, hindered the procurement of medical supplies, walkie-talkies, adequate weapons, and sufficient ammunition and uniforms for all the insurgents. The shortage of firearms excluded some Arroyo Naranjo rebels from going to the attack, and faulty coordination left behind the entire Rancho Boyeros and Santiago de las Vegas cells. A financial deficit was resolved by issuing worthless checks and embezzling business and Masonic-lodge accounts. The initial plan of simultaneous uprisings in all six provinces, as José Martí had attempted in February 1895, was quickly narrowed to only two cities in Oriente Province. During the 1956 Granma expedition Castro again scheduled an island-wide insurrection, but only his Santiago de Cuba followers revolted, and they were quickly suppressed.

Fidel Castro's leadership was deficient due to his micromanagement. He abandoned, at the last moment, the plan to seize a Santiago de Cuba radio station and harangue the populace during the attack. According to Raúl Martínez Ararás, no similar event was devised for Bayamo. The failure to notify the citizenry of the unfolding events and the confusion created when both sides wore the same uniforms led the masses to misperceive the shootout as a feud between military factions. The rebel disguises prompted confusion and friendly fire that wounded at least four attackers and possibly killed others. Castro did not appoint adjutants or couriers to relay his orders and lost control of his men on the field. He initially wasted precious time trying in vain to regroup his scattered forces, which diminished his own combat role at the most crucial moment. Those close to Castro at Post 3 do not recall seeing him firing a weapon. After his capture, the rebel leader was the only prisoner who refused to take a paraffin test that would have certified his use of a handgun. His brother Raúl tested negative for paraffin, indicating that he did not have a combat role. Some attackers stated that they found no target to fire at during the skirmish other than the Moncada walls and windows. The rebel Moisés Mafut assured that no one in his late-arriving group fired a shot. It is possible that Fidel Castro was also unable to discern a plausible target at which to shoot. When Castro ordered a retreat from Post 3 after less than thirty minutes, he failed to notify his followers at the courthouse and in the Civil Hospital, leaving behind two rebel women and more than a dozen dead and wounded men. Castro repeated this tactic during the Granma expedition, when at the Alegría de Pio skirmish he again abandoned his men on the field of battle. On July 26, the attackers and military violated the conventional rules of warfare. The rebels used hollow-point bullets and disguised themselves in army uniforms, and unscrupulous officers responded with inhumane treatment of prisoners and their execution.

The July 26 attackers were motivated by youthful idealism, democratic patriotism to restore the 1940 Constitution, and Ortodoxo Party ideology. No one expressed Socialist goals or a desire to establish a Communist state. Fidel Castro misled the insurgents regarding their final destination. As a result, more than a dozen rebels deserted during the departure for Oriente and at Santiago de Cuba and Bayamo. Castro further deceived his followers into participating in battle by purporting that Luis Conte Agüero would harangue the citizenry by radio during the assault and by claiming that some Moncada soldiers and air force pilots awaited to provide easy victory. Fidel Castro unexpectedly encountered his younger brother Raúl at the Siboney farmhouse just hours prior to leaving for Moncada. Raúl Castro did not have a leadership role and went to Oriente at the invitation of a friend two days before the assault. The rebel leader assigned his sibling to the least dangerous position at the courthouse rooftop with the sniper team.

Tactical human errors accelerated the rebels' defeat. Ernesto Tizol, the military strategist, deserted while driving to Moncada, deviating a third of the insurgent caravan and preventing it from reaching its objective. There was no coordination or communication between the insurgents firing on the garrison at Post 3 and those in the Palace of Justice and the Civil Hospital. The three groups arrived at their destinations at different intervals instead of simultaneously. Abel Santamaría exhibited irresoluteness and poor leadership in the Civil Hospital. He was the only rebel commander who failed to evacuate his force, and under stress he relinquished decision making to his domineering older sister. The cell leaders received only last-minute instructions to follow the vanguard vehicle entering the Moncada garrison and rush the barracks. They had little control over their scattered men and afterward could not be found to drive the getaway vehicles. The rebel force was not trained to carry out commando tactics, teamwork, or orderly retreat, and these deficiencies resulted in disarray at Post 3. Some had barely attended the target practice sessions, and others were unfamiliar with the firearms assigned to them. A few of the men, including the obese Gildo Fleitas and Chucho Montané, were not physically fit for the rigor of combat or the subsequent flight into the mountains.

After the Moncada attack failed, fewer than half of the insurgents who retreated to the Siboney farmhouse continued following Fidel Castro. He split up the group two days later, showing no desire to carry out guerrilla warfare in the hills where they had sought refuge. Instead, during that week Castro never went beyond a five-mile radius from the starting point, convinced the others to surrender, and secretly tried to negotiate his own safety. The brutal repression unleashed by the Moncada and Bayamo army commanders allowed the rebel leader to turn his military defeat into a political victory. The murder of more than fifty rebel prisoners and innocent civilians during four days prompted the intercession of the Catholic Church, the Freemasons, and civic organizations. Castro survived by a combination of sheer luck, orders from Batista not to harm him, Lieutenant Sarría's timely intervention, and Lieutenant Yanez's refusal to poison him.

The fifty-one indicted rebels received impartial due process and a speedy trial that was open to the public. None of the defendants have ever complained of judicial improprieties or unjust sentences. Castro and his followers repeatedly perjured themselves to win the acquittal of nineteen comrades. The rebel leader was allowed to assume his own defense, cross-examine witnesses, and present a closing statement without censure or interruption. The attackers did not face the death penalty, and the maximum sentence allotted was fifteen years.

Castro's apparent motivation in proceeding with the doomed attacks on July 26 was to achieve international recognition as the first rebel leader who employed military action against General Batista. It would have been simpler and less bloody to kill the dictator that day at the Varadero national regatta. No Cuban head of state had ever been assassinated, and this would have propelled the successful triggermen into immortality while greatly diminishing Fidel Castro's revolutionary mystique. It is impossible to predict how the Cuban people would have reacted to Batista's death in 1953. The inevitable chaos would have been of great concern to the United States. The American Embassy in Havana, prompted by cold-war fears, investigated possible Communist involvement in the insurrection and the effect that the army's brutal response had on the population. The embassy's assessment given to the U.S. Department of State described Fidel Castro as "an extremely ambitious and ruthless opportunist, obviously not adverse to violence when it serves his purpose." This ominous warning was lost or ignored five years later when the U.S. Department of State changed its Cuba policy in favor of the rebels.

The Cuban Communist leadership stated in July 1953 that Fidel Castro had carried out a "bourgeois putsch." Castro's actions had strong similarities to Adolf

Hitler's 1923 Munich beer-hall putsch. Both incidents lacked popular support, and each failed to overthrow a government with one blow. Hitler had hoped that his putsch in Bavaria would prompt a march on Berlin to bring down the Weimar government, emulating Benito Mussolini's march on Rome the previous year. Castro was going to descend on Havana after taking Moncada. When Hitler seized the Bavarian triumvirate at the beer-hall meeting, he put a revolver to his temple and threatened to kill them and himself if they did not join him. Similarly, after the Moncada attack failed, Castro twice pretended that he was going to shoot himself in the head, in order to regain the respect and sympathy of his followers. Before leaving the beer hall, Hitler stated, "If I am not victorious by tomorrow afternoon, I am a dead man." Likewise, before departing on the Granma expedition from Mexico, Castro told the reporter Benjamin de la Vega, "In 1956 we will be heroes or martyrs."

Hitler and his followers marched from the beer hall to the center of Munich and ignominiously fled after a brief gun battle with the police. This produced the first sixteen Nazi martyrs whose deaths were used to great success for propaganda purposes. The martyrs of the July 26 attacks were used by Castro to foment his revolutionary stature. Castro wrote to Melba Hernández that propaganda "is the soul of any struggle. Ours should have its own style and be adapted to the circumstances." Hitler, like Castro at Moncada, was not wounded during the shootout, quickly escaped in a car, left his men behind, and was arrested days later while hiding in a house. Both men used the judicial process for political purposes to present themselves as national redeemers. Each received a lenient sentence: Hitler served nine months of a five-year term, and Castro was imprisoned twenty-two months of a fifteen-year sentence. Castro's final statement to the magistrates, alluding to his historic destiny, contained nearly the same conclusion as that in *Mein Kampf*. Castro and Hitler spent their short times in prison mulling over their mistakes, penning their revolutionary legacies, and convinced that their struggles were just beginning. Both men eventually achieved totalitarian power in their respective nations. Hitler brought war and ruin upon Germany, and Castro nearly prompted nuclear war during the Cuban Missile Crisis.

Fidel Castro achieved a significant milestone on his road to power after he organized in Mexico the Granma expedition, which landed at Oriente Province on December 2, 1956, eighteen months after he received amnesty. The eighty-two expeditionaries included only twenty of the ninety-nine Moncada and Bayamo attack survivors. The 26 of July Movement waged a guerrilla war in the mountains and an urban terror campaign with assassinations, kidnappings of scores of U.S. citizens and an Argentinian racing driver, hundreds of indiscriminate bombings in public places, and various airline hijackings. The Batista regime responded with brutal repression that was criticized in the American news media, especially the *New York Times*, and in the U.S. Congress. As a result, the Eisenhower administration imposed an arms embargo in March 1958 that demoralized large segments of the Cuban army fighting the rebels.[2]

The Cuban Communist Party, which had opposed Castro's movement, adhered to the revolution that summer. On December 17, 1958, American ambassador Earl E. T. Smith, under direct orders from the U.S. Department of State, informed President Batista that "the United States will no longer support the present Government of Cuba." Thereafter some Cuban army officers secretly began to aid or negotiate with the rebels. Former Moncada garrison chief Alberto del Río Chaviano had been promoted to general and commanded the army in central Las Villas Province. He conspired with Gen. Francisco Tabernilla Dolz and other officers to overthrow Batista. After the plot was discovered, they were dismissed from the service and went into exile. Batista fled on New Year's Day in 1959, and Judge Manuel Urrutia Lleó, who presided over the second vacation court of the Urgency Tribunal in Santiago de Cuba gathering evidence after the Moncada attack, became provisional president of the revolutionary government.[3]

The 26 of July Movement seized power after Batista's departure. The foreboding of the prosecutor Francisco Mendieta's closing statement regarding the rebel goals came true: "Their ambitions would have brought disagreement between them and as a consequence of those disputes brought the greatest harm to the national economy with bloodshed and grief for the Cuban family." The rebels quickly established kangaroo courts that sent thousands of *batistianos* and "counter-revolutionaries" to the firing squad. Fidel Castro, in Stalinist fashion, then purged from the ranks of his movement anyone not responding with blind obedience. Scores of revolutionary leaders, including the commandants Pedro Díaz Lanz, Huber Matos Benítez, Humberto Sorí Marín, Aldo Vera Serafín, Jorge Sotús, Ramón Guin, Rolando Cubela, William Morgan, and Eloy Gutiérrez Menoyo and provisional president Manuel Urrutia Lleó, were imprisoned, executed, or went into exile. Moncada and Bayamo veterans Gustavo Arcos Bergnes, Orlando Castro García, Moisés Mafut Delgado, Manuel Suardíaz Fernández, Jaime Costa Chávez, and Mario Chanes de Armas—the last two also Granma expeditionaries—received prison terms of up to thirty years for being "counter-revolutionaries." Nine of the Moncada trial defense attorneys went into exile, and two of them were imprisoned by the Castro regime.

Castro achieved his goal expressed in a 1954 prison letter, "to turn this country upside down!" He destroyed the society under which he had suffered stigma and rejection. Castro created a new privileged class from the *nomenklatura* of devoted political followers. He made sure that a situation such as the Moncada attack would not be repeated against him. He imposed population controls with neighborhood watch groups called Committees for the Defense of the Revolutions (CDR) and internal passports for travel between provinces. Private enterprise was abolished in Cuba, making it impossible for anyone to purchase the large quantities of hunting weapons and ammunition used during the July 26 uprising. Under Castro, state security agents have rounded up dissidents throughout Cuba to impede public protests when foreign dignitaries visited the island, reminiscent of Batista's detention of opposition leaders after the Moncada attack. Circulation of the 1997 dissenting document titled "The Fatherland Belongs to All" netted its four authors jail terms of up to five years. In contrast, Castro and his followers spent only twenty-two months in prison for an attack that killed nineteen soldiers and policemen.

Once in power, Fidel Castro did not grant his opponents the same impartial due process of law that he received under the Batista regime, and he rescinded the privileges he enjoyed as a political prisoner. Habeas corpus no longer exists in Cuba, and dissidents are tried behind closed doors. The brutal and repressive conditions of Castro's jails, their "political rehabilitation" plans, and the murder of prisoners have been denounced for decades before the United Nations Human Rights Commission and by human rights organizations, including Amnesty International and Americas Watch. The death penalty, abolished under the 1940 Constitution, was reinstated during the Sierra Maestra campaign and implemented with firing squads. Thousands of "counter-revolutionaries" have been shot for a variety of charges, from conspiracy against the powers of the state to a boat hijacking in April 2003. The hijackers were arrested, tried, and executed within one week.

When Fidel Castro steered the revolution onto the longest totalitarian path by one ruler in history, twenty-seven of the ninety-nine surviving July 26 veterans became dissidents. Castro temporarily allotted powerful governmental positions to only a few of his most trusted Moncada followers. By 1980 only Juan Almeida, Pedro Miret, and Ramiro Valdés were members of the governing politburo headed by Fidel and Raúl Castro, the latter serving as minister of the armed forces. Valdés was dismissed from his repressive post as minister of the interior in 1986 and from the politburo by 1992. He reappeared at public ceremonies in Artemisa during the fiftieth anniversary of the Moncada attack. The following year, his son, Ramiro Valdés Puentes, defected to the United States. In 2006, Valdés was named minister of communications and information science. Calixto García Martínez, the former pharmacy bicycle messenger, became an army division general. Jesús Montané, the former GM personnel manager, was shifted to various Central Committee department posts and was private secretary to Castro before his death in May 7, 1999. His son Sergio Montané López, a government diplomat, deserted in 1994 to join his aunt Mireya in Puerto Rico. Montané's grandson Yotuhel followed suit the following year. Moncada veterans in lesser bureaucratic positions included Haydée Santamaría, a Council of State member, who committed suicide on July 26, 1980. Oscar Alcalde, who embezzled funds for the Moncada attack, in 1983 served briefly as president of the national People's Savings Bank. He passed away in Havana in January 1993. His son Emilo Alcalde Sánchez, born in 1962, studied at the VGIK Soviet

State Film School in Moscow from 1986 to 1991. He then resided in Bogotá, Colombia, until settling in Miami in 1998. Israel Tápanes, the former photography store janitor, was Communications Section chief of the Central Committee Communications and Transportation Department until his death in May 1990. Humberto Valdés Casañas, previously a parking-lot attendant, was vice minister for development of the urban transportation in 1979. Agustín "Thompson" Díaz Cartaya, the Marianao street musician, was assigned to the arts and spectacles section of the Ministry of Culture. Pedro Trigo, who had worked in a textile factory, was an official of the Department of Revolutionary Orientation in 1980. His son, Julio Trigo Crespo, left on the 1980 Mariel boat lift and died of AIDS in Miami on July 28, 1998. Abelardo "El Perico" Crespo Arias was appointed national chief of the firefighters corps. Mario Lazo, a peasant laborer, became administrative director of the Institute of History of the Communist Movement and the Cuban Socialist Revolution in 1981. Other Moncada rebels were sent abroad to secondary diplomatic posts: Léster Rodríguez to Jordan; Ernesto Tizol and Oscar Quintela to Czechoslovakia; Melba Hernández to Vietnam; Carlos González Seijas to Leningrad; and Ramón Pez Ferro to Turkey.

The Moncada military fortress was converted to an educational institution on January 28, 1960, following the 1948 Costa Rican model of turning army garrisons into schools. Nineteen days earlier Castro had personally driven the bulldozer that demolished the crenelated fortress walls. In 1978 he turned half of the Moncada into the 26 of July Historical Museum to display revolutionary memorabilia. He ordered the massive perimeter walls rebuilt to their original specifications. The facade of a building wing was chipped or riddled with machine-gun fire to simulate phony rebel combat. Today the museum is open daily and charges an admission fee.

The nearby Civil Hospital, occupied by Abel Santamaría and twenty-four rebels, was demolished in the mid-1960s, and the grounds became the Abel Santamaría Historic Park in 1973. The nursing-school building used for Castro's trial was preserved and turned into the Abel Santamaría Museum. The park contains a huge granite-cube monument on a tall column with Santamaría's image equal in proportion to that of Cuban-independence apostle José Martí. Another side of the cube contains a stanza from the Cuban national anthem: "To die for the fatherland is to live." The Palace of Justice, occupied by rebel snipers during the Moncada attack, was still used as a provincial courthouse in 2006. The *vivac* city jail, where the insurgents were initially held, was converted to the Historic Municipal Archive in 1999. Eight miles away the Siboney farmhouse that served as rebel headquarters became a tourist attraction in 1965. All of these buildings and the park have been declared national historic monuments.

In contrast, the Bayamo garrison and the Gran Casino Motel gathering point were demolished in the early 1960s to prevent them from becoming revolutionary relics. In similar fashion, the yacht *Corinthia*, which carried a fateful Auténtico organization expedition to Oriente in 1957, was scuttled by rebel commandant Manuel

The "Grand Task of Cuban Reconstruction"   257

Piñeiro at the Santiago de Cuba naval base in January 1959. Bayamo attack leaders Raúl Martínez Ararás, Gerardo Pérez-Puelles Valmaseda, and Orlando Castro García had broken with Castro in 1955 when he assumed authoritarian leadership of the 26 of July Movement. The first two were in exile by 1960, and the latter was imprisoned the following year with a thirty-year sentence. To supplant them, Ñico López, a martyr of the 1956 Granma expedition, was mythically elevated to leadership proportions. In Bayamo the former garrison grounds were converted in 1978 to the Ñico López Park, where López's bust is displayed on a pedestal. The facade of the post was rebuilt, and the small enlisted-men's club became a history museum. In the latter a portrait of the illiterate López appears in equal dimensions next to one of Carlos Manuel de Céspedes, the father of Cuban independence. The Bayamo site has been considered so trivial that it was omitted from many Cuba travel handbooks, including Fodor's. In 2004 it was the last place related to the July 26 revolt to be declared a national monument. The National Men's Prison on the Isle of Pines was closed in June 1967. In May 1973 the penitentiary was declared a national monument and the pavilion where the Moncada attackers lived became a museum. The home of Jesús "Chucho" Montané in nearby Nueva Gerona was also turned into a museum. The storage room where Melba and Haydée served their sentences at the National Women's Prison in Guanajay became a historic museum on July 21, 1983.

The revolutionary promises of 1953 were never instituted. The five projected laws outlined in *History Will Absolve Me* were ignored: the 1940 Constitution was not restored; landowners were not indemnified for confiscated property; workers were not given "thirty percent of the profits of all the large industrial, mercantile and mining enterprises, including the sugar mills"; the planters did not share in "fifty-five percent of the sugar production"; and the money from confiscated ill-gotten gains did not "subsidize retirement funds for workers." Cuba did not become a "bulwark of liberty," nor was its economy diversified with industrialization. Castro had clamored for a time "when we no longer buy tanks, bombers and guns for this country" but instead turned the island into the largest military arsenal in Latin America while pursuing the revolutionary interventions that he had begun in April 1959. The threat of a U.S. attack vanished after the 1962 Kennedy-Khrushchev understanding, and their noninvasion pledge has been upheld by all American presidents and has never been abrogated. While the "Manifesto to the Nation" claimed that "The revolution declares itself free of binds with foreign nations," Castro received subsidies from the Soviet Union estimated at $65 billion until 1990 and owes more than $35 billion to other countries. In addition, a Soviet combat brigade was stationed on the island for three decades, more than five hundred thousand Cuban troops served as Soviet proxies in African civil wars during fifteen years, and a Russian electronic listening post operated at Lourdes, Cuba, from 1964 until 2001; the latter, a twenty-eight-square-mile base, housed some fifteen hundred Russian engineers, technicians, and soldiers.

The Moncada Manifesto called for only one national flag and one anthem, in reproof of Batista's Fourth of September flag and hymn, but when the rebels achieved power, their red-and-black flag and the "26 of July Hymn" became parallel national symbols. Because the grievances outlined in the document were never abolished, Cuba continued to experience governmental economic mismanagement; decrease in industrial production in favor of the primary tourism sector, which has grown 1,000 percent since 1990; workers' discontent; the experimental dollarization of the economy during 1993–2004; persecution and imprisonment of dissidents; prohibition of opposition political parties; the dissolution of the 1940 Constitution; and authoritarian power by an "ambitious Chief of State and his main cohorts." In spite of the promises of freedom and democracy made in the Moncada Manifesto and *History Will Absolve Me,* the Cuban people have been subjected to a totalitarian continuity that still exists. The manifesto's projected "grand task of Cuban reconstruction" failed. There are children in Bayamo who remain shoeless, in spite of Orlando Castro's main goal as revolutionary city administrator to provide them with footwear. More than half a century after the July 26 uprising, the democratic goals professed by the revolutionaries, for which sixty-one of them gave their lives, have not been fulfilled.

ABBREVIATIONS USED IN THE APPENDIXES

Code

(A) Acquitted in court.
(B) Attacked the Bayamo garrison.
(C) Captured in the Granma expedition.
(D) Disembarked in Granma expedition.
(E) Went into exile or became a dissident after 1959.
(G) Killed in the Granma expedition.
(H) Occupied Saturnino Lora Hospital.
(I) Imprisoned in Cuba after 1959.
(L) Political leader.
(M) Killed in the Sierra Maestra campaign.
(O) Castro government official.
(P) Occupied the Palace of Justice.
(S) Killed in underground campaign.
(T) Indicted, did not go to trial.
(W) Wounded in action on July 26.
(X) Member PSP Communist Party.

Education

P- Primary
S- Secondary
U- University, or grades 1 thru 12

APPENDIX 1

Rebel Participants in the 26 of July 1953 Insurrection

Convicted	Code	Sentence	Age	Grade	Occupation	Residence
1) Oscar Alcalde Valls		13 years	30	U	bookkeeper	Cotorro
2) Juan Almeida	(D,O)	10 years	26	3	laborer	Arroyo N.
3) Gustavo Arcos	(I,W)	10 years	25	P	watchman	Havana
4) René Bedia Morales	(G)	10 years	30	P	house painter	Calabazar
5) Reinaldo Benítez	(C,W)	10 years	25	P	cloth cutter	San Leopoldo
6) Enrique Cámara	(B,C)	10 years	23	S	cobbler	Marianao
7) Fidel Castro Ruz	(D,O)	15 years	26	U	attorney	Marianao
8) Raúl Castro Ruz	(D,O,P)	13 years	21	U	student	Havana
9) Mario Chanes	(C,I)	10 years	27	S	bakery assistant	La Ceiba
10) Orlando Cortés		3 years	20	P		Almendares
11) Abelardo Crespo	(O,W)	10 years	28	U	student	Havana
12) Agustín Díaz	(B)	10 years	22	S	street musician	Marianao
13) Julio Díaz González	(D,M)	10 years	22	P	store clerk	Artemisa
14) Andrés García Díaz	(B)	10 years	22	S	store clerk	Marianao
15) Gabriel Gil Alfonso	(C)	10 years	30	P	café employee	Lawton
16) Francisco González	(C)	10 years	25	S	commerce	La Ceiba
17) Melba Hernández	(H,O)	7 months	32	U	attorney	Vedado
18) Fidel Labrador	(W)	10 years	28	P	peasant	Artemisa
19) Manuel Lorenzo	(E)	3 years	39	S	telegraphist	Rancho B.
20) Rosendo Menéndez		10 years	22	P	railroad worker	Artemisa
21) Armando Mestre	(G)	10 years	26	S	laborer	Arroyo N.
22) Pedro Miret Prieto	(O)	13 years	25	U	student	Santiago
23) Jesús Montané	(C,O)	10 years	29	S	office clerk	Santos Suárez
24) Eduardo Montano		10 years	34	P	barber	La Ceiba
25) José Ponce Díaz	(C,O,W)	10 years	25	5	typographer	Artemisa
26) Ciro Redondo	(D,M)	10 years	21	P	store clerk	Artemisa
27) Eduardo Rodríguez		3 years	31	S	watch repair	El Cerro
28) Haydée Santamaría	(H)	7 months	30	S	unemployed	Havana

Convicted	Code	Sentence	Age	Grade	Occupation	Residence
29) José Suárez Blanco		10 years	25	S	unemployed	Artemisa
30) Israel Tápanes		10 years	26	P	janitor	San Leopoldo
31) Ernesto Tizol		13 years	26	S	poultry grower	Cotorro
32) Ramiro Valdés	(D,O)	10 years	21	P	unemployed	Artemisa

Rebel Participants in the Insurrection of July 26, 1953 263

Fugitives or acquitted	Code	Age	Grade	Occupation	Residence
1) Orestes Abad	(B)				Marianao
2) Pedro C. Aguilera	(A,B)	27	U	dentist	Palma Soriano
3) Emilio Albentosa Chacón	(D)		4	laborer	Arroyo N.
4) Armando Arencibia	(B)	25	P		Marianao
5) Jesús Blanco Alba	(A,E)			student	Havana
6) Carlos Bustillo Rodríguez	(E)	27	S	business manager	Jaimanitas
7) Ramón Callao Díaz	(A)	23	S	pharmacy clerk	Artemisa
8) Orlando V. Castro García	(B,E,I)	25	U	credit manager	Vedado
9) Reinaldo Castro	(S)	32	P	carpenter	El Cerro
10) Vicente Chávez	(A,S)	26	S	refrigeration	San Lázaro
11) Marino Collazo Cordero	(A,O,W)	30	P	laborer	Artemisa
12) Félix Córdoba Alonso					Almendares
13) Jaime Costa Chávez	(C,E,I)	19	P	peasant	Guanajay
14) Mario Dalmau de la Cruz	(P,T)	31	P		El Cerro
15) Héctor de Armas Errasti	(E)	23	U	student	Colón
16) Angel L. Díaz-Francisco	(A,E)	24	U	student	Mariano
17) Guillermo Elizalde	(A,W)	23	P	carpenter	Nueva Paz
18) Julio C. Fernández					Calabazar
19) Florentino Fernández	(O)	26		hospital orderly	Calabazar
20) Gelasio Fernández		26	P	peasant	Artemisa
21) Alejandro Ferrás Pellicer			S		Cayo Hueso
22) Antonio Ferrás Pellicer			S	typographer	Cayo Hueso
23) Armelio Ferrás Pellicer		30	S		Cayo Hueso
24) Orlando Galán	(T)			peasant	Artemisa
25) Roberto Galán				peasant	Artemisa
26) Rubén Gallardo			P	peasant	Nueva Paz
27) Abelardo García Ylls	(P)				Guanajay
28) Calixto García Martínez	(B,D,O)	21		bicycle messenger	Marianao
29) Carlos González Seijas					San Leopoldo
30) Ernesto González					Lawton
31) Gerardo Granados Lara	(E,T)	22	S	clothing store clerk	Artemisa
32) Rolando Guerrero Bello	(A)		P	peasant	Nueva Paz
33) Pedro Gutiérrez Santos			P	textile worker	Calabazar
34) Florentino Hernández	(A)	47	P	carpenter	Calabazar
35) Genaro Hernández	(A)		P	peasant	Nueva Paz
36) Orbeín Hernández Díaz					Madruga
37) Mario Lazo Pérez	(W)	24	P	peasant	Artemisa
38) Generoso R. Llanes	(A)	38	1	maintenance man	Jaimanitas
39) Antonio López	(B,G,T)	20	3	market porter	Marianao
40) Antonio López García	(B,C,T)		P	plumber's helper	Havana
41) José L. López Díaz					Calabazar
42) Moisés Mafut Delgado	(E,I)	31	2	milkman	Arroyo N.
43) José R. Martínez Alvarez	(G,P)	25	5	tanner	Guanajay

Fugitives or acquitted	Code	Age	Grade	Occupation	Residence
44) Raúl MartínezArarás	(B,E)	34	U	accountant	Vedado
45) Carlos A. Merille Acosta	(A)	25	S		Havana
46) Teodulio Mitchell Barbán		29	P	truck driver	Palma Soriano
47) Ramón Montes Cuba					Almendares
48) Isidro Peñalver O'Reilly	(A)	30	P	repairman	Cayo Hueso
49) Gerardo Pérez-Puelles	(B,E,W)	25	U	advertising agent	Havana
50) Ramón Pez Ferro	(A,H,O)	19	S	student	Artemisa
51) Angel Pla Picette		30		chauffeur	Cayo Hueso
52) Oscar Quintela Bonilla	(O)	31	6	textile worker	Calabazar
53) Léster Rodríguez Pérez	(P,O)	26	U	student	Santiago
54) Rolando Rodríguez	(B,E)	25	S		Havana
55) Tomás D. Rodríguez	(A,E)	19	P	peasant	Nueva Paz
56) Severino Rosell González	(O,T)	24	P	café employee	Artemisa
57) Adalberto Ruanes Alvarez	(B)		P		Marianao
58) Angel M. Sánchez Pérez	(O,P)	31		commerce	Guanajay
59) Ramiro Sánchez	(B)	21	S	commerce	Havana
60) Ricardo Santana		22	P	taxi driver	Artemisa
61) Ulises Sarmiento Vargas	(A)	17		carpenter	Marianao
62) Gerardo Sosa Hernández	(A)	24			Havana
63) Manuel Suardíaz	(E,I)	28	U	chemical engineer	Madruga
64) Pedro Trigo López	(O)	25	P	textile worker	Calabazar
65) Humberto Valdés	(A,S)	22	8	parking valet	Cayo Hueso
66) Manuel Vázquez Tió	(A)				Havana
67) Juan Villegas					Calabazar

Rebel Participants in the Insurrection of July 26, 1953

Killed	Code	Age	Grade	Occupation	Residence
1) Pablo Agüero Guedes	(B)	17	6	bricklayer	Marianao
2) Reemberto A. Alemán	(H)	24	9	putty-layer	Lawton
3) Gerardo A. Alvarez	(H)	27	6	small farmer	Havana
4) Tomás Alvarez Breto	(H)	28	3	laborer	Artemisa
5) Juan M. Ameijeiras	(H)	20	P	taxi driver	Havana
6) Gilberto E. Barón		22	P	cobbler	Almendares
7) Antonio Betancourt	(H)	20	P	butcher	Artemisa
8) Flores Betancourt		23	P	stonecutter	Artemisa
9) Hugo Camejo Valdés	(B)	35	5	brickyard laborer	Marianao
10) Gregorio Careaga Medina		29	P	funeral home	Artemisa
11) Pablo Cartas Rodríguez	(H)	21	S	busboy	Havana
12) Fernando Chenard Piña		34	S	photographer	La Ceiba
13) Alfredo Corcho Cinta		34	4	dairy worker	Guanajay
14) Rigoberto Corcho López		21	6	store clerk	Artemisa
15) Giraldo Córdova Cardín		22	5	refinery laborer	La Ceiba
16) José F. Costa Velázquez	(H)	29	6	truck loader	Guanajay
17) Raúl R. de Aguiar		30	S	unemployed	Cayo Hueso
18) Juan Domínguez Díaz	(H)	22	4	furniture maker	Lawton
19) Víctor Escalona Benítez		36	P	cobbler	Almendares
20) Gildo M. Fleitas López		34	S	office clerk	La Ceiba
21) Rafael Freyre Torres	(B)	22	4	bricklayer	Marianao
22) Jacinto García Espinosa		28	P	stevedore	El Cerro
23) Raúl Gómez García	(H)	24	U	teacher	Santos Suárez
24) Manuel Gómez Reyes		41	4	janitor	La Ceiba
25) Virginio Gómez Reyes		40	5	janitor	La Ceiba
26) Luciano González	(B)	39	4	shoe salesman	Marianao
27) Guillermo Granados Lara		29	4	shoe salesman	Artemisa
28) Angel Guerra Díaz	(B)	22	5	flower vendor	Marianao
29) Renato M. Guitart Rosell		21	S	consignment agent	Santiago
30) Emilio Hernández Cruz		20	P	carpenter	Artemisa
31) Lázaro Hernández	(B)	18	6	laborer	Marianao
32) Manuel E. Isla Pérez		20	P	peasant	Nueva Paz
33) José A. Labrador Díaz		26	P	peasant	Artemisa
34) Reinaldo Boris Luis		24	S	bookkeeper	Santos Suárez
35) José J. Madera Fernández		17	6	factory worker	Cayo Hueso
36) Pedro Marrero Aizpurúa		26	P	truck driver	La Ceiba
37) Marcos Martí Rodríguez		18	3	peasant	Artemisa
38) Mario Martínez Araras	(B)	28	S	truck driver	Colón
39) Horacio Matheu	(H)	24	6	putty-layer	Lawton
40) José W. Matheu Orihuela	(H)	23	6	putty-layer	Lawton
41) Roberto Mederos	(H)	24	6	bookstore	Havana
42) Ramón R. Méndez	(H)	24	11	food sales	Lawton

Killed	Code	Age	Grade	Occupation	Residence
43) Mario Muñoz Monroy	(H)	41	U	physician	Colón
44) Carmelo Noa Gil		27	5	dairy worker	Artemisa
45) Miguel A. Oramas		21	10	photo developer	La Ceiba
46) Oscar A. Ortega Lora		24	S	dental assistant	Palma Soriano
47) Julio M. Reyes Cairo	(H)	23	8	bank teller	Colón
48) Ismael Ricondo		23	S	peasant	Artemisa
49) Félix Rivero Vasallo		26	3	bartender	Luyano
50) Manuel M. Rojo Pérez		49	6	peasant	Nueva Paz
51) Manuel Saíz Sánchez	(H)	18	P	carpenter	Lawton
52) Rolando San Román	(B)	24	P	oyster vendor	Marianao
53) Abel B. Santamaría	(H)	25	11	bookkeeper	Havana
54) Osvaldo Socarrás	(H)	32	P	parking valet	Havana
55) Elpidio C. Sosa González		24	8	bartender	Marianao
56) José L. Tasende		28	8	factory worker	La Ceiba
57) José Testa Zaragoza	(B)	29	P	flower vendor	Marianao
58) Julio Trigo López	(H)	26	P	traveling salesman	Calabazar
59) Andrés Valdés Fuentes		24	5	baker	Cayo Hueso
60) Armando Valle López		23	8	furniture maker	Cayo Hueso
61) Pedro Véliz Hernández	(B)	22	S	bricklayer	Marianao

APPENDIX 2

Military Casualties

Killed in Santiago de Cuba
	Location
1) Pvt. Manuel I. Alvarez Morgado	Moncada courtyard
2) Pvt. Eusebio A. Baró Melodio	Inside Service Company
3) Second Lt. Pedro V. Feraud Mejías	Civil hospital
4) Policeman Roberto Ferrándiz Millán	Military hospital
5) Pvt. Efraín Galano Liranza	Post 3
6) Pvt. Pedro Guilarte	Outside Enlisted Mens' Club
7) Corporal Isidro C. Izquierdo Rodríguez	Post 3
8) PMB Corporal Manuel Miras Mierez	Inside Service Company
9) Pvt. Felino Miró Ríos	Behind Rural Guard barracks
10) Second Lt. Andrés D. Morales Alvarez	Moncada balcony
11) Sergeant Luis Oliva	Inside quartermaster room
12) Policeman Pedro H. Pompa Castañeda	Civil hospital
13) Pvt. Saturnino Ramírez Santiesteban	Mortally wounded in a lung
14) Pvt. Urbano Sánchez Abalos	Inside Service Company
15) Pvt. Jesús R. Sánchez Pruna	Administrative wing stairway
16) First Sergeant Ramón V. Silveiro Enríquez	Home
17) Corporal Nemesio A. Traba Montero	Corner of Garzón Ave.
18) Pvt. José Joaquín Vázquez	Military hospital

Killed in Bayamo
19) Police Sgt. Gerónimo R. Suárez Camejo	In his jeep on the street

Wounded in Santiago de Cuba
	Location
1) Pvt. Luis Cosme Aguila Cuevas	Inside military hospital
2) Corporal Eugenio Alcolea Ramírez	Barbershop
3) Policeman Humberto Barzaga Vázquez	Inside civil hospital
4) Corporal Norberto Batista Seguí	Inside military hospital
5) PMB Luis Bayona	Inside Service Company

Wounded (*cont.*)

6) Pvt. Angel L. Duvallón-Gilbert Cuello	Administrative wing balcony
7) Corporal Mauricio Feraud Mejías	Civil hospital
8) Pvt. José W. Fonseca Martínez	Inside civil hospital
9) Pvt. Luis E. Frómeta Naranjo	Outside military hospital
10) Pvt. Clemente Godó Estenóz	Inside Service Company
11) Corporal Gerardo Hechavarría Granados	Rear courtyard
12) Enlistee Víctor Manuel Hernández	Inside Company barracks
13) Pvt. Alberto Hernández Rodríguez	
14) Pvt. Luis H. Hodelín Angulo	Administrative wing balcony
15) Pvt. Daniel Lavastida Martínez	
16) Corporal José P. Llanes León	Central highway sentry box
17) Pvt. Diocles Martínez Bles	Crossing the parade ground
18) Policeman Patricio Moreno Rubio	Administrative wing stairway
19) Pvt. Luis Enrique Naranjo	Barbershop
20) PMB Sergeant Alberto Pagés	Inside Service Company
21) Second Lieutenant Juan E. Piña Martínez	Inside administrative wing
22) Pvt. Pedro Porto Chacón	
23) Corporal Nestor Reyes Martín	Post 3
24) Pvt. Emilio Reyes Rodríguez	
25) Pvt. Miguel Mariano Ruiz	Corner of Victoriano Garzón
26) Pvt. Argeo Sarmiento Moreno	Post 4
27) Pvt. Lázaro Tejadilla Suárez	Post 4
28) Policeman Evelio Xenis López	Administrative wing stairway

Wounded in Bayamo

29) Pvt. Antonio T. Blanco Rodríguez	Inside the garrison
30) Pvt. Juan P. Navarro Molina	Inside the garrison

Civilian Casualties

Killed in Santiago de Cuba

	Age
1) Manuel *El Niño* Cala Reyes	50
2) José Casamayor Caballero	48
3) Gisel Chaprón	28
4) Rubén Cordero Sánchez	
5) Eduardo A. Hernández Ravella	32
6) Armando Miranda Montes de Oca	45
7) Miguel A. Ravelo Ravelo	
8) Pedro Romero Fonseca	30
9) Francisco Viera Milián	43

Wounded in Santiago de Cuba

1) Julio Aguila	27
2) Baudilio Casamayor Martínez	11

Civilian Casualties (*cont.*)

3) Alicia Castillo Ramírez
4) Felipa Castillo   83
5) Pedro Angel López   18
6) Hebrecinio Pacheco   14
7) Migdalia Toledano   10

APPENDIX 3

Civilians acquitted in Case 37

Name	Code
1) Oscar Alvarado González	(L)
2) Gustavo Ameijeiras Romo	(S)
3) Ramiro Arango Alsina	(E,L)
4) Luis Arrastía Navarrete	
5) Aracelio Azcuy Cruz	(E,L)
6) José A. Batista Lotti	
7) Cecilio T. Benítez León	
8) René Betancourt Castillo	
9) Silverio E. Brito Oquendo	
10) Mario Burman Corman	(E)
11) José A. Cabrera	(X)
12) Ramón Campa Delgado	
13) Luis Casero Guillén	(E,L)
14) Benjamín de Yurre	(E,T)
15) Raúl del Mazo Serra	(E,I)
16) Abelardo del Pozo García	
17) Armando Díaz Castelar	(X)
18) Angel Eros Sánchez	
19) Fernando Fernández Catá	(E)
20) Ignacio A. Fiterre Rivera	(E,L)
21) Luis A. Frías	
22) Roberto García Ibáñez	(L)
23) Leonel A. Gómez Pérez	(E)
24) Anibal González	
25) José L. González Ruiz	
26) Sergio González Machado	(S,T)
27) Oscar Gras Escalona	
28) José M. Gutiérrez Planes	(E,L)

Name	Code
29) Arturo Hernández Tellaheche	(E,I,L)
30) Bernardo Hernández Hernández	(X)
31) Rolando Hevia Ruiz	(X)
32) Humberto Lamothe Coronado	(G)
33) Fernando Limia Rodríguez	
34) Juan M. Llosas Perera	(X)
35) Porfirio Loynaz Hechavarría-Cordovés	
36) Juan Marinello Vidaurreta	(X)
37) Juan Manuel Márquez Rodríguez	(G,T)
38) Juan Manuel Martínez	
39) Sergio Mejías Pérez	(E,L)
40) Moto Mendel Weis	
41) Rafael Mendoza Guanche	(E,T)
42) Rafael Núñez Leyva	
43) Emilio Ochoa Ochoa	(E,L)
44) Joaquín Ordoqui Mesa	(I,L,X)
45) José Pardo Llada	(E,L,T)
46) Aida Pelayo Pelayo	
47) Lázaro Peña González	(L,X)
48) Antonio Pérez Mujica	(X)
49) Lázara Pérez Cuesta	(E)
50) Luis Pérez Cabrejas	
51) José F. Pila Teleño	(E)
52) Gerardo Poll Cabrera	
53) José Ponte	(T)
54) Carlos Prío Socarrás	(E,L,T)
55) Anibal Quesada Granados	
56) Blas Roca Calderío	(O,T,X)
57) Antonio San Román de las Llamas	
58) Aureliano Sánchez Arango	(E,L,T)
59) Eriberto Sánchez Tamayo	
60) Ramón Serrano Alfonso	
61) Mauro Suárez Suárez	
62) Angel Valdés Rodríguez	
63) Rafael Valdés Calvo	
64) José Vázquez Rojas	
65) José Villa Romero	

See Appendix 1 for the names of the thirty-two rebels convicted, the nineteen rebels acquitted for lack of evidence, and the six rebels who were indicted but did not go to trial.

APPENDIX 4

Defense Attorneys and their Case 37 Clients

Attorney	Code	Defendant
1. Rubén Alonso Alvarez	(E)	Oscar Alvarado, Aracelio Azcuy, José Gutiérrez Planes, Humberto Lamothe, Sergio Mejías and Rafael Valdés.
2. José M. Badell Romero		Manuel Lorenzo Costa.
3. Héctor Canciano Labory		Luis Arrastía and José Ponce.
4. Conrado Castell Cordero	(E)	Aida Pelayo Pelayo.
5. Baudilio Castellanos García	(O)	Oscar Alcalde, Juan Almeida, Gustavo Ameijeiras, René Bedia, Cecilio Benítez, Reinaldo Benítez, Jesús Blanco, Ramón Callao, Enrique Cámara, Raúl Castro, Mario Chanes, Marino Collazo, Luis Conte Agüero, Abelardo Crespo, Angel Díaz-Francisco, Agustín Díaz Cartaya, Andrés García Díaz, Gabriel Gil, Francisco González Hernández, Florentino Hernández, Generoso Llanes, Porfirio Loynaz, Moto Mendel Weis, Rosendo Menéndez, Carlos Merille, Armando Mestre, Pedro Miret, Jesús Montané, Eduardo Montano Benítez, Rafael Núñez Leyva, Isidro Peñalver, Luis Pérez Cabrejas, Ciro Redondo, Tomás D. Rodríguez, Antonio San Román de las Llamas, Haydée Santamaría, Ulises Sarmiento, Gerardo Sosa, José Suárez Blanco, Mauro Suárez, Israel Tápanes, Ernesto Tizol, Angel Valdés Rodríguez, Humberto Valdés Casañas, Ramiro Valdés and Manuel Vázquez Tió.

Attorney	Code	Defendant
6. Rafael A. Cisneros Ponteau	(O)	Bernardo Hernández and Juan M. Llosa.
7. Elizardo Díaz Lorenzo		Julio Díaz, Fidel Labrador and Ramón Pez Ferro.
8. Eduardo Eljaiek Eldidi		Angel Eros and Fernando Fernández Catá.
9. Domingo Estrada de Beatón	(E)	Mario Burman, Lázara Pérez Cuesta and Oscar Gras.
10. Juan José García Benítez		Emilio Ochoa.
11. Recaredo García Fernández		Pedro Aguilera, José Batista Lotti, Silverio Brito, Raúl del Mazo and José Villa Romero.
12. Luis A. Gómez Domínguez	(E,I)	Orlando Cortés Gallardo and Eduardo Rodríguez Alemán.
13. Gerardo Hernández Vera		Abelardo del Pozo and Anibal Quesada.
14. Lucas Morán Arce	(E)	José L. González Ruiz.
15. Jorge Nariño Brauet	(E)	José Vázquez Rojas.
16. Jorge Paglieri Cardero	(E)	Melba Hernández.
17. Carlos Peña-Jústiz Arrieta	(I)	Gustavo Arcos, Ramón Campos Delgado, José Pila Teleño and Eriberto Sánchez Tamayo.
18. José Miguel Pérez Lamy		José A. Cabrera, Armando Díaz, Rolando Hevia and Antonio Pérez Mujica.
19. Luis Pérez Rey		Lázaro Peña, Joaquín Ordoqui and Juan Marinello.
20. Marcial Rodríguez Gutiérrez		Gerardo Poll Cabrera.
21. Roberto Rosillo Rodríguez		Vicente Chávez, Sergio González and Fernando Limia.
22. Andrés Silva Adán	(E)	René Betancourt, Guillermo Elizalde, Genaro Hernández Martínez, Rolando Guerrero and Ignacio Fiterre.
23. José F. Valls Tamayo	(E,I)	Luis Casero Guillén and Arturo Hernández Tellaheche.
24. Raúl Villalvilla Carbonell		Leonel Gómez, Juan Manuel Martínez and Ramón Serrano.

Defendants who assumed their own defense: Ramiro Arango Alsina, Fidel Castro Ruz and Roberto García Ibáñez.

APPENDIX 5

Manifesto to the Nation

Before the pathetic and sorrowful sight of a Republic under the capricious will of only one man rises the national spirit from the most profound souls of dignified men.[1] It rises to continue the unfinished revolution that Céspedes initiated in 1868, Martí continued in 1895, and Guiteras and Chibás actualized in the republic era. In the probity of the men of Cuba is based the triumph of the Cuban Revolution.

Before the defiant arrogance of the dictatorship and the conciliabulum and the ridiculous compromise of the leading politicians, the unbreakable probity of the Cuban people rises in the unanimous decision to reconquer its Constitution, its essential liberties and its inalienable rights, trampled without respite by the treacherous usurpation.

Before the chaos in which the Nation has fallen by the insistence of the most ambitious of all Cubans and the heartless interests of his followers, the Cuban youth, who love liberty and respect the decorum of free men, rises vibrantly in a gesture of immortal rebelliousness, breaking the insane pact with the concept of the past and with the present of grief and deceit.

Before the tragedy of Cuba, contemplated calmly by political leaders without honor, rises in this decisive hour, arrogant and potent, the youth of the Centenary, which does not maintain another interest that is not the decided longing of honoring with sacrifice and triumph, the unrealized dream of Martí.

In the name of the relentless struggles that have marked summits of glory in the history of Cuba, comes the new Revolution, rich in men without blemish, to renovate once and for all the unbearable situation which the ambitious and the improvised have submerged the country and, grasping the roots of the Cuban national sentiment, to the preaching of its greatest men and embraced to the flag of the solitary star, comes to declare before the honor and the probity of the Cuban people.

In the probity of the men of Cuba lies the triumph of the Cuban revolution. The revolution of Céspedes, of Agramonte . . . of Maceo . . . of Martí . . . of Mella and of Guiteras, of Trejo and of Chibás. The Revolution that has not triumphed yet. By the dignity and the decorum of the men of Cuba, this Revolution will triumph.

The Martí Centenary culminates its historic cycle that has marked the continuing progression and retrogression of the political and moral realms of the Republic: the bloody and virile fight for liberty and independence; the civic struggle among Cubans to reach political and economic stability; the unfortunate process of the foreign intervention; the dictatorships of 1929-33 and of 1934-44; the unrelenting struggle of heroes and martyrs to make a better Cuba.

The purpose of finding the true course was dawning in the Cuban life; the consciousness of the citizenry was in a state of giving its best fruit, conquered by the sacrifice of the life of one of its most famous statesmen and by the mandate of his admonishing voice; when, at the command of the most ambitious of all Cubans, a ridiculous minority seized the country, dissipating illusory promises and deceptive propaganda. Their purpose was to make the sensible people believe that treacherous coup in the heart of the institutions, was capable of engendering social progress, peace and work.

To the collar of blood and infamy, of unmeasured lust and plunder of the national treasury, that was linked to the name of the new ruler, was linked to the large chain of violations against Cuba: institutionalization of the "coup d'etat" to secure regimes of force; bribery of the Congress and of the puppet presidents; physical destitution of various Presidents; imposition of castes and privileges; dissolution of the Congress; illegitimate appointments of persons in the Judiciary; destitution of Councilmen and Mayors; physical trampling and abuses of peaceful citizens, and the placing of an inglorious flag next to the most glorious flag.

The present grew in excess, a short time after the treacherous coup, the calamities, the anguish, the eviction and hunger that are unmistakable signs of the ambitious Chief of State and his main cohorts. The harsh paralyzation of the popular desire by the abuse of force, brought as a consequence the gravest situation engendered by a Cuban political event in any era: the industrial production decreases; the discontent of the workers or expulsion from their work centers; persecution and imprisonment of students for their civic protest against the Regime; isolation and division of the political parties; sudden disappearance of money in the street; flight of the frightened capital; imprisoned those who dared to publicly protest the trampling of the Republic; dissolution of the Civil Code and death of the Constitution and its rights. On the conscience of the author of all of this falls the contempt of free men and the cutting edge of the sword of justice.

In the chaos sprung on our people, wounded, but never dead, fell other tardy ambitions. Those who could not make of the country what they promised a thousand times when they were in power . . . those that, not having drowned the serene expression of liberty, also did not contribute to make it just and eternal for our country, to pull out of the roots of our history the tragic unaccustomed coup; they then came as apostles, trying in vain to reconquer past glories. Another idea can not triumph in the spirit and the conscience of the people that is not the total disappearance of this latent state, of this infected chaos that we have been subjected to not only those guilty of the dawn coup against the national institutions, but those who have been able to calmly watch the crime. It is not honest or just to attempt against the heart of the Republic, nor is it just or honest to climb on her to let the others attempt.

Before the political situation of Cuba are rejoicing the wretched dictator and his cohorts who have climbed on the head of the people in their anxious eagerness to loot. Before the pathetic situation of Cuba the venal politicians are associating to create the new pantomime. Fossils of Cuban politics publicly expound the most retrograde ideas, the most useless thoughts while the people's longing, which is never wrong, awaits the clarion call of alert, the defense of its most sacred rights, of its tricolor flag and of the eternal idea for which the most illustrious and disinterested citizens have died.

For defending these rights, for raising that flag, for conquering that idea, the present youth has its knees in the ground, youth of the Centenary, historic pinnacle of the Cuban

Revolution, epoch of Martiism sacrifice and magnitude. To conquer it, the youth has its watchful eye at the entrance of the men of truth, of agile mind, giant spirit, who knew how to give it all for a Cuba worthy of the spontaneous blood of its sons, live in the consolidation of its inevitable destiny for the supreme dream of the Apostle.

Those who disregarded the lovers of liberty to carry out the coup d'etat, arise against them in this decisive hour, arrogant and potent, the Youth of the Centenary, echo of the honorable yesterday, cradle of a better future. Those who did not count with that honest and studious youth, capable of writing with sacrifice and triumph its best homage to Marti, do not know that in the hearts of all Cubans is the valor and the probity of the Fatherland and that we will place it in victory in the lofty palm fields. The justice of the people in this glorious year should be there. In 1853 with the birth of an illuminated man, began the Cuban Revolution; in 1953 it will end with the birth of an illuminated Republic.

A. The Revolution declares that it does not pursue hate or useless blood, but to save the probity of Cuba in its crucial year. Surging from the most genuine layers of national valor, the revolution of the Cuban people is born, with the vanguard of a youth longing for a New Cuba, clean of past errors and small ambitions. It is the revolution emanating from the men and new procedures prepared with the unredeemed power and the decision of those who dedicate their lives to an ideal.

   The Revolution declares that it is the meditated front of insistence; pulling out once and for all the binds that link us to the corrupt past and all the myths that presently keep us in bitterness and pain.

B. The revolution declares itself free of binds with foreign nations and also free of influence and of the appetite of politicians and of self-styled personages. The revolution is a virile entity, and the men who have organized it and who represent it pact with the sacred will of the people to conquer the future that it deserves. The revolution is the decisive fight of the populace against all those who have deceived them.

C. The Revolution declares that it respects the integrity of free citizens and of the men in uniform who have not betrayed the national heart, nor have submitted their glorious flag nor have abjured their Constitution.

   It salutes in this decisive hour all Cubans with probity, where ever they may be, and joyously embraces those who are decided to seek shelter on its arc of triumph.

D. The Revolution declared its energy and rigor against those who have only had energy and rigor to snatch from the people its sacred rights and institutions, violating liberty and sovereignty at a cost of the pain and anguish of the sons of Cuba.

E. The Revolution declares its firm decision to situate Cuba at the level of economic well-being and prosperity that would assure its rich subsoil, its geographic location, its diversified agriculture, and its industrialization, which have been exploited by illegitimate and spurious governments, by unmeasured ambitions and of culpable interest.

F. The Revolution declares that it recognizes and bases itself in the ideals of Martí, contained in his speeches, in the foundations of the Cuban Revolutionary Party and in the Manifest of Montecristi; and makes its own the Revolutionary Programs of the Joven Cuba, A.B.C. Radical and the Partido del Pueblo Cubano (Ortodoxo).

G. The Revolution declares its respect for the free sister nations of America who have known to conquest, at the cost of bloody sacrifices, the position of economic liberty and social justice that is the index of our century. And it vows, in this decisive hour, that the Cuban clarion call be one more star in the conquest of the Latin American ideals and interests, latent in the blood of our nations and the thoughts of our most illustrious men.
H. The Revolution declares its eagerness and decision to renovate, completely and totally, the national economic means, with the implantation of the most urgent measures to resolve the crisis and distribute honest work and equitable money to all the Cuban homes, a decision that is one and indivisible in the hearts of the men that defend it.
I. The Revolution declares its respect for the workers and students as accredited masses in the defense of the inalienable and legitimate rights of the Cuban populace throughout all of history, and it assures them and all the people, the implantation of a total and definitive social justice based in the economic and industrial advancement under a synchronized and perfect plan, fruit of thoughtful and meticulous study.
J. The Revolution declares its absolute and reverent respect for the Constitution given to the people in 1940 and reestablishes it as the official Code of Laws. It declares that the only flag is the tricolor of the solitary star and it elevates it as always, glorious and firm, to the din of combat, and that there is no other hymn than the Cuban national, renown throughout the world by the vibrant stanza: That to die for the fatherland is to live!
K. The Revolution declares its love and its confidence in the virtue, in the honor and decorum man and expresses its intention of utilizing all those who really are valuable, in function of those forces of the spirit, in the grand task of Cuban reconstruction. These men exist in all the places and institutions of Cuba, from the rural shack to the General Staff of the Armed Forces; and the watchful eye of the Revolution will situate them in the position of service that Cuba asks of them. This is not a revolution of castes.

Cuba embraces those who know how to love and build, and despises those who hate and destroy. We will build the New Republic, with all and for the good of all, in the love and fraternity of all Cubans.

The Revolution declares itself definitive, gathering the incommensurable sacrifice of the past generations, the unbreakable will of the present generations, and the life and well-being of the future generations.

In the name of the Martyrs.
In the name of the sacred rights of the Fatherland.

For the honor of the Centennial.
The Cuban Revolution

July 23, 1953

Translated by the author from Dirección Política de las FAR, *Moncada: Antecedentes y preparativos, 223–27.*

APPENDIX 6

Letter from Cuba, July 26, 2003

Gustavo Arcos Bergnes, Secretary General of the Cuban Committee for Human Rights

Cuban television is broadcasting nightly shots of an empty hospital room. It is spacious and clean, and has big windows. We are shown this room because 50 years ago today, Fidel Castro was held prisoner here.

After the failed attack on 26 July 1953, at the Moncada barracks in Santiago de Cuba where the troops of the dictator Fulgencio Batista were stationed, Castro and about 100 other surviving assailants (myself among them) were tried for sedition and sentenced to up to 15 years in prison.

Castro's sentence was 15 years, although he was given amnesty, along with the rest of us, after 21 months. He was never again jailed. He came to power in the 1959 revolution and has since become He Who Sends Others to Jail.

For me, 1953 was not the last time: in the mid-1960s, when I was Cuba's ambassador to Belgium, I expressed frustration with the Castro government, was recalled and sentenced to ten years, of which I served three. In the 1980s I planned to escape from Cuba and was jailed for seven more years.

Four months ago, 75 brave Cuban dissidents were rounded up and two weeks later sentenced to prison terms of up to 28 years. Unlike us so-called Moncadistas, today's dissidents did not use violence. Their "weapons" were typewriters, cameras, radios and tape recorders.

They are writers, doctors, lawyers, economists, teachers, peasants and human rights activists who believed, naively, that their ruler would at least tolerate the Universal Declaration of Human Rights, of which Cuba is a signatory, instead of jailing people for distributing it.

Lately, I have been reflecting, after 50 years, on the tragic contrast between Castro, inmate, and Castro, prison warden.

Prisoner Castro, a lawyer, had three months between his arrest and his October 1953 trial to prepare his own defense. Warden Castro allows today's dissidents their first glimpses of their lawyers minutes before their trials, if at all.

Their quarters do not resemble Inmate Castro's bright and spacious hospital room of 1953: most are in cells full of rats and mosquitoes; in many, the tap for drinking water juts from the wall just above the hole in the floor the prisoners use as a toilet. When they have family visits, every three months, they come out in handcuffs, some in shackles.

Because we used violence, the Moncadistas would not have been considered prisoners of conscience by today's humanitarian groups. Nonetheless, Batista gave us special treatment as political prisoners: we were given our own section of the Isle of Pines prison so that we were not held together with common criminals.

Today's dissidents, who were declared prisoners of conscience by Amnesty International, have been tossed in with murderers and rapists. The poets Raúl Rivero and Manuel Vázquez Portal, to mention the best documented cases, share wards with some of the most violent alumni of what Castro himself once called "genuine universities of delinquency."

Back in 1953, two women from our group took their meals at the table of the prison chief; a relative of one of the inmates bought a butchery on the Isle of Pines and prisoners were allowed cooking facilities.

The food in the jails today is another story: many of the 75 dissidents are sick (some are denied medicines brought by spouses) and one has had a heart attack. Family members report frightening weight loss after only four months of detention.

I am an old man now - 76, the same age as Castro - and there is not much more harm that the warden can inflict on me for speaking out. (Although there is no doubt in my mind that my younger brother, Sebastian, died in prison in 1997 because of deliberate lack of medical attention.)

I have no reason to expect that Castro will show his political prisoners the magnanimity that he himself benefitted from 50 years ago, or that he too will give them amnesty. I hope to be proved wrong. It would be the only fitting way to mark the anniversary.

NOTES

Preface

1. "El gobierno debe ser sereno y justo, pero enérgico" (Batista quoted in *Diario de la Marina*, July 28, 1953, 1).
2. Fulgencio Batista, *Cuba Betrayed* (New York: Vantage Press, 1962), 35-36.
3. Mario Riera Hernández, *Cuba libre 1895-1958* (Miami: Colonial Press, 1968), 193.
4. Batista, *Cuba Betrayed*, 35-36; Daniel Efrain Raimundo, *Habla el Coronel Orlando Piedra* (Miami: Ediciones Universal, 1994), 174, 177.
5. Roberto Fernández Miranda, *Mis relaciones con el General Batista* (Miami: Ediciones Universal, 1999), 137.
6. Jules Dubois, *Fidel Castro: Rebel-Liberator or Dictator?* (Indianapolis: Bobbs-Merrill, 1959), 38.
7. Robert Taber, *M-26: The Biography of a Revolution* (New York: Lyle Stuart, 1961), 12, 27, 34-44.
8. Robert Merle, *Moncada: Premier combat de Fidel Castro* (Paris: Robert Laffont, 1965), 351-52; Autores varios, *Mártires del Moncada* (Havana: Ediciones Revolución, 1965), 337, 349, 413.
9. Herbert Matthews, *Fidel Castro* (New York: Simon and Schuster, 1969), 65; K. S. Karol, *Guerrillas in Power: The Course of the Cuban Revolution* (New York: Hill & Wang, 1970), 133-34; Ernst Halperin, *Fidel Castro's Road to Power: Cuban Politics from Machado to Moncada* (Cambridge: MIT Center for International Studies, 1970), 82-91.
10. Hugh Thomas, *Cuba: The Pursuit of Freedom* (New York: Harper & Row, 1971), 843.
11. Rolando E. Bonachea and Nelson P. Valdés, eds., *Revolutionary Struggle 1947-1958: Volume I of the Selected Works of Fidel Castro* (Cambridge, MA: MIT Press, 1972), 47-56.
12. Dirección Política de las FAR, Sección de Historia, *Moncada: Antecedentes y preparativos* (Havana: FAR, 1972); ibid., *Moncada: La acción* (Havana: Editora Política, 1981); ibid., *Moncada: Motor de la Revolución* (Havana: Editora Política, 1983).
13. Ramón L. Bonachea and Marta San Martín, *The Cuban Insurrection 1952-1959* (New Brunswick, NJ: Transaction Books, 1974), 16, 19-20, 23.
14. Herbert Matthews, *Revolution in Cuba: An Essay in Understanding* (New York: Charles Scribner's Sons, 1975), 49.

15. Lionel Martin, *The Early Fidel: Roots of Castro's Communism* (Secaucus, N.J.: Lyle Stuart, 1978), 119–20, 124, 132.

16. Tad Szulc, *Fidel: A Critical Portrait* (New York: William Morrow and Co., 1986), 158.

17. Peter G. Bourne, *Fidel: A Biography of Fidel Castro* (New York: Dodd, Mead & Company, 1986).

18. Robert Quirk, *Fidel Castro* (New York: W. W. Norton & Company, 1993), 51–55.

19. Gladys Marel García-Pérez, *Insurrection & Revolution: Armed Struggle in Cuba, 1952–1959* (Boulder, Colo.: L. Rienner Publishers, 1998).

20. Leycester Coltman, *The Real Fidel Castro* (New Haven, Conn.: Yale University Press, 2003), 62, 65, 76, 82–85, 88.

Introduction

1. Armando Hart, *Aldabonazo: Inside the Cuban Revolutionary Underground 1952-58* (New York: Pathfinder, 2004), 76.

2. Pedro A. García, "El pequeño motor que echó a andar el motor grande," *Granma*, July 25, 2000.

3. Grupo Cubano de Investigaciones Economicas, *Un estudio sobre Cuba* ([Coral Gables, Fla.:] University of Miami Press, 1963), 933–64.

Chapter 1—Growing Up under Three Different Names

1. In 1942 the Cuban Congress passed a law reorganizing the armed forces. The rank of major general was created for the chief of staff of the army, Manuel López Migoya, and for those who previously held the position. As a result, Fulgencio Batista was promoted from retired colonel to retired major general. Batista's Unitary Action Party (PAU) was reorganized in December 1952 as the Progressive Action Party (PAP). See Rafael Díaz-Balart Gutiérrez, personal interview, Miami, Fla., March 9, 1988; Katiuska Blanco, *Todo el tiempo de los cedros: Paisaje familiar de Fidel Castro Ruz* (Havana: Casa Editorial Abril, 2003), 290.

2. Edmund A. Chester, *A Sergeant Named Batista* (New York: Henry Holt and Company, 1954), 225; Guillermo Alonso Pujol, "Ante la historia," *Bohemia*, October 5, 1952, 62.

3. Dirección Política de las FAR, *Moncada*, 28–30; Pedro A. Barrera Pérez, "Por qué el ejército no derrotó a Castro," *Bohemia Libre* (Caracas), July 16 and 28, 1961; Chester, *Sergeant Named Batista*, 229–30; Francis L. McCarthy, "Historia de una revolución," *Bohemia*, March 30, 1952, 68; Batista, *Cuba Betrayed*, 240; *El Mundo*, July 10, 1952, 1; "10 de marzo de 1952: Una fecha negra en la historia," *Bohemia*, March 8, 1959, 71.

4. McCarthy, "Historia de una revolución," 68; Dirección Política de las FAR, *Moncada*, 39; Col. Orlando Piedra Negueruela, personal interview, Miami, Fla., October 24, 1974.

5. Luis Casero Guillén, personal interview, Miami, Fla., August 9, 1984; Eduardo Suárez Rivas, personal interview, Miami Beach, Fla., May 13, 1974; Luis G. Wangüemart, "Como cae un gobierno," *Carteles*, March 16, 1952, 41; Enrique Serpa, "Los últimos instantes de Carlos Prío en el Palacio Presidencial," *Bohemia*, March 16, 1952, 82; Vicente León, "Lo que pasó realmente en Palacio el 10 de marzo," *Carteles*, August 12, 1956, 59; Thomas, *Cuba*, 781.

6. *El Mundo*, March 12, 1952, 1; U.S. Department of State, *Foreign Relations of the United States 1952–1954, Volume IV, The American Republics* (Washington, D.C.: U.S. Government Printing Office, 1983), 868–72.

7. Two days after the coup, the Republican Party participated in the government. Within a year they were joined by the Liberal and Democratic parties. See *El Mundo,* March 11, 1952, 1, 9; Batista, *Cuba Betrayed,* 32; Juan Amador Rodríguez, "Si el pueblo derrota a Batista acepteremos a su decisión," *Bohemia,* April 27, 1952, 58; "La nueva oficialidad del Ejército," *Bohemia,* March 30, 1952, 56–59, 69; "Jefes de regimientos de las provincias," *Bohemia,* April 20, 1952, 48–49; Gonzalo Zorrilla, "Los nuevos jefes de la Marina," *Carteles,* April 13, 1952, 42–44.

8. Rafael Estenger, "La doble cara del golpe de estado," *Bohemia,* March 16, 1952, 49; *El Mundo,* March 11, 1952, 16; *El Mundo,* March 13 and 14, 1952, 1; Thomas, *Cuba,* 785.

9. Thomas, *Cuba,* 821, erroneously places Castro at the university on March 10 distributing weapons. See Angel Díaz-Francisco, personal interview, Miami, Fla., March 3, 1988; Gustavo Arcos Bergnes, telephone interview, Havana, Cuba, May 6, 1997; Mario Chanes de Armas, personal interview, Miami, Fla., August 12, 1993; Rolando Masferrer Rojas, personal interview, Miami, Fla., August 1, 1975; *El Mundo,* March 11, 1952, 9; Thomas, *Cuba,* 783.

10. René Rodríguez Cruz later fought in the Sierra Maestra campaign. After the revolution seized power in 1959, he directed the firing squads and was photographed shooting the coup de grácе into the victims' heads. In November 1982, while presiding over the Cuban Institute of Friendship with the Peoples (ICAP), he was indicted by a federal court in Miami, Case 82-643-Cr-JE, on seven counts of narcotics trafficking. Rodríguez Cruz committed suicide in October 1990. See Pablo Alfonso, "Fallece en Cuba presidente del ICAP," *El Nuevo Herald* (Miami), October 16, 1990, 1; Mario Mencia, *El grito del Moncada* (Havana: Editora Política, 1986), 147; Díaz-Francisco, interview; "Relato del comandante Miret: Un Grupo Verdaderamente Heroico," *Verde Olivo,* July 29, 1962, 6; José Duarte Oropesa, *Historiología Cubana* (Miami: Ediciones Universal, 1974), 3:227.

11. The journalist Lee Lockwood perceived in 1966 that Fidel Castro was still "biased about America." See Lee Lockwood, *Castro's Cuba, Cuba's Fidel* (New York: Macmillan, 1967), 26; Serge Raffi, *Castro el Desleal* (Madrid: Aguilar, 2004), 15–17; Frei Betto, *Fidel y la religión* (Santo Domingo: Editorial alfa y omega, 1985), 92; Blanco, *Todo el tiempo,* 16; Georgie Anne Geyer, *Guerrilla Prince: The Untold Story of Fidel Castro* (Boston: Little, Brown and Company, 1991), 19–20; Quirk, *Fidel Castro,* 7–8; Coltman, *Real Fidel Castro,* 1; Thomas, *Cuba,* 803.

12. Blanco, *Todo el tiempo,* 37, 41–44, 80, 498–99, 503; Nathaniel Weyl, *Red Star over Cuba: The Russian Assault on the Western Hemisphere* (New York: Devin-Adair Company, 1960), 40–41; Szulc, *Fidel,* 101; Bourne, *Fidel,* 15; Bonachea and Valdés, *Revolutionary Struggle,* 3–4; Geyer, *Guerrilla Prince,* 21–23; Quirk, *Fidel Castro,* 8.

13. Fidel Castro stated that his father owned eight hundred hectares and rented another ten thousand, which is the total equivalent of twenty-six thousand acres. See Blanco, *Todo el tiempo,* 45, 64–67, 73, 78, 90; Betto, *Fidel y la religión,* 92–93, 96, 98; Szulc, *Fidel,* 103–4; Thomas, *Cuba,* 805; Coltman, *Real Fidel Castro,* 5; Luis Conte Agüero, *Los dos rostros de Fidel Castro* (Mexico City: Editorial Jus, 1960), 22–23.

14. Betto, *Fidel y la religión,* 96–97, 100–102, 106; Blanco, *Todo el tiempo,* 168–69; Juana Castro, "My Brother Is a Tyrant and He Must Go," *Life,* August 28, 1964, 27.

15. Dr. Emilio Núñez Portuondo was the father-in-law of Mirta Díaz-Balart after she divorced Fidel Castro and married Emilio Núñez Blanco. When Angel Castro died on October 21, 1956, his estate was worth five hundred thousand dollars. See Coltman, *Real Fidel Castro,* 3; Geyer, *Guerrilla Prince,* 23; Thomas, *Cuba,* 807; Quirk, *Fidel Castro,* 9; Mario Llerena, *The Unsuspected Revolution: The Birth and Rise of Castroism* (Ithaca, N.Y.: Cornell University

Press, 1978), 202; Weyl, *Red Star over Cuba,* 42; Carlos Franqui, *Vida, aventuras y desastres de un hombre llamado Castro* (Mexico City: Planeta, 1989), 17-18; Bourne, *Fidel,* 16; Lockwood, *Castro's Cuba,* 16.

16. Raúl Castro was born in June 3, 1931. On February 25, 1943, two months before Lina Ruz married Angel Castro, she was legally inscribed by her father in the Cueto courthouse in Mayarí municipality. He swore that she was born in Cueto on July 23, 1908. In spite of this legal document, a baptismal certificate stating that Lina was born in Guane, Pinar del Río, on September 23, 1903, is cited in Blanco, *Todo el tiempo,* 481-83. Blanco omits Lina's birthplace from a 1951 legal document cited on page 516, but it appears as Mayarí municipality on other documents reproduced on pages 521, 523, and 526. Her hagiography of the Castro family erroneously has María Argota (1890-1984) estranged from her husband before Lina's children are all born in the plantation main house. Fidel Castro was not affected by his father's death in 1956, nor did he mention it to his friends. According to Teresa Casuso, *Cuba and Castro* (New York: Random House, 1961), "Apparently there was some hidden wound relating to his childhood which had never healed" (131). The Dominican Juan Bosch, long acquainted with Castro, claimed that his illegitimacy later had traumatic effects. See "República Dominicana: Entre la terquedad y la ambición," *Bohemia Libre* (New York), October 13, 1963, 7; Blanco, *Todo el tiempo,* 45, 76-77, 84, 113, 507; Betto, *Fidel y la religión,* 104, 108-10, 117; Serge Raffy, *Castro el Desleal* (Buenos Aires: Aguilar, 2004), 23-25; Alina Fernández, *Castro's Daughter: An Exile's Memoir of Cuba* (New York: St. Martin's Griffin, 1999), 5, 7.

17. Fidel Castro's baptismal certificate is reproduced in Raffy, *Castro el Deslea,* 615. Castro misled Frei Betto by saying that he was baptized when he was between five and six years old. An exclusive interview detailing his childhood covers a chapter in Carlos Franqui, *Diary of the Cuban Revolution* (New York: Viking, 1980). Castro's family history also appears in *New York Times,* November 18, 1979, sec. 6, p. 63. See Betto, *Fidel y la religión,* 101, 107-8, 120, 125; Bourne, *Fidel,* 21; Raffy, *Castro el Desleal,* 13; Blanco, *Todo el tiempo,* 133, 142; Thomas, *Cuba,* 807-8; Szulc, *Fidel,* 111.

18. Juana Castro was born on May 6, 1933, and her sister Emma on January 2, 1935. On December 20, 2005, the author showed this book manuscript to Juana Castro Ruz at her Mini-Price Pharmacy in Miami and requested an interview. She claimed to be writing her own memoirs and asked that I call back a few days later. When I did so, Ms. Castro informed me that she was busy and would telephone me in the future. On December 29 a mutual friend, Salvador Lew, telephoned Ms. Castro, praised this work, and asked her to meet with me. During a subsequent telephone call with the author, she agreed to an interview and asked to be called back the following day. Ms. Castro never again spoke with me and did not return numerous calls that I placed to her during the next three weeks. See Franqui, *Vida,* 29; Raffy, *Castro el Desleal,* 39; Blanco, *Todo el tiempo,* 113, 132, 147, 150; Coltman, *Real Fidel Castro,* 7; Bourne, *Fidel,* 24; Brian Latell, *After Fidel: The Inside Story of Castro's Regime and Cuba's Next Leader* (New York: Palgrave Macmillan, 2005), 58.

19. Franqui, *Vida,* 29; Raffy, *Castro el Desleal,* 39; Blanco, *Todo el tiempo,* 153-57; Betto, *Fidel y la religión,* 126, 128, 138.

20. Latell, *After Fidel,* 41; Blanko, *Todo el tiempo,* 134, 187-88, 207, 507; Betto, *Fidel y la religión,* 104.

21. According to Lt. Carlos Lazo Cuba, who was imprisoned in 1959 with Felipe Mirabal Mirabal and Narciso Campos Pontigo (September 3, 1898-April 1970), the latter was released

from the Santiago de Cuba *vivac* jail in early January 1959 by three rebel captains under Raúl Castro's orders and allowed to obtain asylum in the Brazilian Embassy in Havana. Campos settled in New York, where he passed away. Mirabal was sentenced to death by firing squad on September 17, 1959, but the penalty was never enforced. He died of cancer in the Combinado del Este prison on January 4, 1984. According to Lazo, Mirabal assured him that Campos was indeed Raúl Castro's father. Lt. Antonio Ochoa Ferrer also attributed Raúl Castro's paternity to Campos. Rafael Díaz-Balart stated that "Fidel owes his life to Felipe Mirabal," for providing security at his wedding and escorting him to the Camagüey airport when MSR gunmen were hunting for him. Díaz-Balart, interview; Lt. Carlos Lazo Cuba, interview, Miami, Fla., July 2, 2004; Lt. Antonio Policarpo Ochoa Ferrer, interview, Miami, Fla., Dec. 23, 1974; "The Bitter Family," *Time*, July 10, 1964, 28; Latell, *After Fidel*, 58, 73–74; Geyer, *Guerrilla Prince*, 32; Blanco, *Todo el tiempo*, 208; and Raffy, *Castro el Desleal*, 616.

22. Katiuska Blanco's hagiography contradicts Fidel Castro by saying that his father "demonstrated tenderness" and did not frequently "chide or argue" with his children. See Blanco, *Todo el tiempo*, 89, 134, 184, 217; Betto, *Fidel y la religión*, 123, 160–61; Angela López, "Así nació, creció y amó Fidel Castro," *El Mundo* (Madrid), May 7, 2004; Geyer, *Guerrilla Prince*, 24; José Pardo Llada, *Fidel y el "Che"* (Barcelona: Plaza & Janes Editores, 1988), 13–14; Bourne, *Fidel*, 17.

23. Szulc, *Fidel*, 112–13; Coltman, *Real Fidel Castro*, 8; Bourne, *Fidel*, 18; Blanco, *Todo el tiempo*, 160; "Fidel Castro Wrote to FDR When He Was a Schoolboy," *Miami Herald*, December 4, 1977; "Fidel's Start: Castro Confirms He Won First Fame with Letter Asking FDR for $10 Bill," *Miami Herald*, December 7, 1977; Thomas, *Cuba*, 808.

24. Ramón Mestre Gutiérrez was expelled from Belén one year prior to graduation for bad grades. He became a successful building contractor and was elected senator from Pinar del Río in November 1958. Mestre joined a conspiracy against the government that led to his arrest on August 10, 1959. He received a twenty-year prison term and went into exile in Miami in 1979. See Betto, *Fidel y la religión*, 141; Blanco, *Todo el tiempo*, 195–98; Franqui, *Vida*, 36; Raffy, *Castro el Desleal*, 52; Ramón Mestre, personal interview, Miami, Fla., December 29, 2005; Enrique Ovares Herrera, personal interview, Key Biscayne, Fla., April 8, 1990.

25. *Time* magazine described the representative Benito Remedios Langaney as "a law unto himself" whose congressional immunity avoided prosecution from seventy-six charges that had accumulated against him. His explosive temperament was depicted on one occasion: "when a brand-new $7,500 Cadillac refused to start, he riddled its recalcitrant carburetor with bullets." Remedios was shot and killed on a Havana street in 1952 after drawing a pistol and scuffling with a policeman who had given him a parking ticket. See "Immunity Ended," *Time*, January 28, 1952, 37; Ovares, interview; Szulc, *Fidel*, 114, 123; Dorothy Bishop, "Castro's Rebellious Streak Evident in School," *Kansas City Times*, December 27, 1966.

26. *Hoy* quote in Pardo Llada, *Fidel y el "Che,"* 18. See Betto, *Fidel y la religión*, 145, 150, 156; Conte Agüero, *Los dos rostros*, 23, 25; Bourne, *Fidel*, 29.

27. Jaime Suchlicki, *Cuba: From Columbus to Castro and Beyond* (Washington, D.C.: Brassey's, 1997), 127; *New York Times*, March 16, 1941, E6; Coltman, *Real Fidel Castro*, 10–11; Bourne, *Fidel*, 26–31; Quirk, *Fidel Castro*, 20; Bonachea and Valdés, *Revolutionary Struggle*, 5; Thomas, *Cuba*, 810; Blanco, *Todo el tiempo*, 227; Díaz-Balart, interview.

28. Ramón de Armas, Eduardo Torres-Cuevas, and Ana Cairo Ballester, *Historia de la Universidad de La Habana 1930–1978* (Havana: Editorial de Ciencias Sociales, 1984), 2:522,

620; Enrique Ros, *Fidel Castro y el gatillo alegre: Sus años universitarios* (Miami: Ediciones Universal, 2003), 50, 83; Bourne, *Fidel*, 33; Blanco, *Todo el tiempo*, 224-27; Ovares, interview; Luis Conte Agüero, personal interview, Miami, Fla., August 26, 1988.

29. Manuel "Manolo" de Castro del Campo (1910-48), had graduated from Belén High School. After the fall of Machado, he was appointed police lieutenant and joined the Legión Revolucionaria de Cuba in 1934 to overthrow the Batista-backed government. In November 1935 Manuel de Castro was sentenced to death with five others for the kidnapping of the millionaire Antonio San Miguel, who was released unharmed and without paying ransom. He served two years in prison, where he met Rolando Masferrer Rojas, and later played football on the university team. He was president of the Engineering Students Association when he was elected FEU president on August 21, 1944. See *New York Times*, November 24, 1935, 28; Niurka Pérez Rojas, *El Movimiento Estudiantil Universitario de 1934 a 1940* (Havana: Editorial de Ciencias Sociales, 1975), 200-208, 220; Ros, *Fidel Castro*, 15, 31; Masferrer, interview; Duarte, *Historiología Cubana*, 2:576-77; Bonachea and Valdés, *Revolutionary Struggle*, 17; "Manolo Castro, 1910-1948," *Tiempo en Cuba*, February 27, 1949, 13.

30. Ramiro Valdés Daussá (September 5, 1909-August 15, 1940) was a founder of the University Student Directorate (DEU) and a political prisoner under the Machado regime that killed his two brothers. He was one of the signers of the September 4 revolutionary proclamation. José Noguerol Conde was sentenced to thirty years in prison for the murder of Valdés, and on May 31, 1945, he fled from a jail hospital ward to Mexico. Noguerol was later killed by Eufemio Fernández Ortega. Mario Salabarría Aguiar affirmed that moments before shooting *bonchista* Mario Sáenz de Buruhaga he warned him: "Stand up, because I am going to kill you." See Mario Salabarría Aguiar, personal interview, Miami, Fla., December 7, 1983; Mario Riera Hernández, *Historial obrero Cubano* (Miami: Rema Press, 1965), 178; Ramiro Arango Alsina, personal interview, Miami, Fla., March 1, 1988; Duarte, *Historiología Cubana*, 2:577-80; Raúl Aguiar Rodríguez, *El bonchismo y el gangsterismo en Cuba* (Havana: Editorial de Ciencias Sociales, 2000), 21-25, 145; de Armas et al., *Historia*, 505; *New York Times*, November 29, 1940, 7.

31. Mario Salabarría stated that in 1931, at the age of seventeen, he was incarcerated for a year because of his activities against the Machado regime. Eufemio Fernández Ortega resigned from the police force in May 1949. See Salabarría, interview; Duarte, *Historiología Cubana*, 3:17-18, 55; Masferrer, interview; Aguiar, *El bonchismo*, 165.

32. De Armas et al., *Historia*, 504; Thomas, *Cuba*, 811; Ernesto de la Fe Pérez, personal interview, Miami, Fla., April 10, 1990; "Violencia revolucionaria y degeneración," *Tiempo en Cuba*, April 24, 1948, 12; Rolando Masferrer, "Tres artículos contra el gangsterismo," *Tiempo en Cuba*, April 24, 1949, 12; CIA, Movimiento Socialista Revolucionario (MSR), January 8, 1948, FOIA.

33. Diego Vicente Tejera (March 3, 1914-July 10, 1991) was minister of education from October 27, 1945, to May 6, 1946. UIR members included Jesús Diéguez Lamazares, Vidal Morales Rodríguez, Rafael Lázaro del Pino Siero, José de Jesús Ginjaume Montaner, Luis Padierne Labrada, Armando Correa Morales, Guillermo "Billiken" García Riestra, Justo Fuentes Clavel, Herminio Díaz, Pedro Mirassou Tarnio, Santiago Touriño, and Orlando "Piro" Bosch Avila, among others. See Vidal Morales Rodríguez, personal interview, Miami, Fla., April 6, 1990; Quirk, *Fidel Castro*, 29; "Los atentados políticos durante el gobierno del Dr. Grau," *Bohemia*, October 10, 1948, 86-88; *Diario de la Marina*, January 2, 1948, 2.

34. Emilio Tro Rivero (1918–September 15, 1947) had been imprisoned in 1935 for a year convicted of illicit association and sabotage. He joined the National Revolutionary Alliance (ANR) and in 1939 was a member of Guiteras Revolutionary Action (ARG). Tro was arrested for attempting to assassinate the police official Mariano Faget. He fled to America, joined the U.S. Army, and served in the Pacific during World War II, where he was awarded the Purple Heart. Tro murdered the public works police chief Bruno Valdés Miranda and the secret police officer Julio Abril Rivas on July 28, 1946. See Vidal Morales, interview; "Los atentados políticos durante el gobierno del Dr. Grau," *Bohemia,* October 10, 1948, 86–88; Thomas, *Cuba,* 742; Mario G. del Cueto, "Unión Insurreccional Revolucionaria," *Bohemia,* June 15, 1947, 52–55.

35. Rolando Masferrer Rojas (January 12, 1918–October 31, 1975), Fidel Castro's lifelong nemesis, was born in Holguín and raised by one of his uncles, the Cuban army captain Alejandro Cano Rojas. In 1932 Cano was stationed at Fort Sam Houston, San Antonio, Texas, with the Civil Engineer Corps program. Rolando attended Hawthorne Junior High School in San Antonio, wore cowboy clothes, and played the harmonica. The family later moved to Fort Sill, Oklahoma, where his uncle lost his commission in September 1933 after the downfall of the Machado regime and settled in Miami, Florida. Masferrer returned to Cuba to live with another uncle, joined the Communist Party, and worked for the party newspaper *Hoy.* He later joined the revolutionary organization Joven Cuba and admitted that he "clandestinely misappropriated automobiles" that the organization used for armed attacks. Masferrer and three other Joven Cuba members were arrested on November 9, 1936, for plotting to assassinate Col. José Pedraza, chief of the national police. After his release, Masferrer enrolled in June 1937 in the International Brigades fighting for the republic during the Spanish Civil War. He achieved the rank of major, in charge of the 401st Battalion, 101st Brigade, Forty-sixth Division, Fifth Corps of the Ebro Army. Masferrer was wounded in action twice, first on the wrist and then having his heel blown away during a mortar attack, leaving him with a permanent limp and the moniker "El Cojo." After returning to Cuba in 1939, he became assistant editor of *Hoy* and graduated from the University of Havana Law School in 1945 with the Dolz Award, given to the most outstanding student. Masferrer and the novelist Carlos Montenegro founded the weekly magazine *Tiempo en Cuba* in January 1945. Eight months later they were expelled from the party for denouncing its leadership for its bourgeoisie and corrupt lifestyle. Montenegro admitted to the author that Masferrer temporarily received money from the American Embassy in Havana to promote the magazine's attacks against the Communist Party. Masferrer married Lucila Montero and had two children, Alejandro and Liudmila. In 1946 he was awarded a sinecure as English professor at Marianao High School. Masferrer was elected Republican Party representative from Oriente Province on June 1, 1948. He was elected in 1954 as Auténtico Party senator from Oriente. During the Sierra Maestra guerrilla campaign (1956–58), he created the Anti-Communist Peasant Militia, dubbed the "Tigers of Masferrer." The term originated after his group seized the abandoned army barracks at El Uvero in June 1957 and removed from its flagpole the military Fourth of September flag. It was replaced, as a jest, with the Marianao baseball team pennant, a blue banner with a tiger's head, to signify the evacuation of the army. Masferrer fled Cuba in his converted PT boat when Castro seized power on January 1, 1959, receiving asylum in the United States. He and a group of followers were arrested in Florida on January 2, 1967, for plotting with Haitian exiles to overthrow the Duvalier dictatorship. Masferrer

served two years in federal prison and was released on parole on December 4, 1972. He owned a security firm in Miami and published the controversial weekly tabloid *Libertad*. Masferrer was blown to bits by a C-4 bomb with a trip switch under his car on October 31, 1975, in spite of the *santería* amulets in his wallet to ward off evil. Investigators believe that this unsolved murder was ordered by an exiled double agent working for Fidel Castro, who instigated others to carry it out. See Rolando Masferrer, "El Movimiento Socialista Revolucionario," *Tiempo en Cuba*, May 1, 1949, 14–15; Masferrer, interview.

36. Leonel A. Gómez Pérez and Froilán Noroña had murdered former police chief Antonio Brito Rodríguez on November 28, 1945. As a result, Gómez briefly served time in the Torrens Youth Reformatory. Angel "El Gallego" Vázquez went into exile after Castro seized power. Isaac Araña Ahitó was sentenced by a revolutionary tribunal on March 29, 1960, to a nine-year imprisonment for conspiracy. See Bonachea and San Martín, *Cuban Insurrection*, 11; Franqui, *Vida*, 44; Ovares, interview; Díaz-Balart, interview; Aguiar, *El bonchismo*, 33–34; Ros, *Fidel Castro*, 69–70; Thomas, *Cuba*, 811–12; Bourne, *Fidel*, 36; Geyer, *Guerrilla Prince*, 54–55.

37. Vidal Morales, interview; Ros, *Fidel Castro*, 143–44; Aguiar, *El bonchismo*, 34–37.

38. Salabarría, interview; *Bohemia*, May 4, 1947; Blanco, *Todo el tiempo*, 230–32.

39. Díaz-Balart, interview.

40. The *Diario de la Marina*, on October 1, 1947 (28), and February 24, 1948 (25), identified Federico Marín as president of the Association of Law Students. Two days later the newspaper in a front-page article erroneously identified Fidel Castro with the same rank. Ovares pointed out that the conservative and pro-Catholic newspaper gave credence to any title that the Jesuit-educated Castro identified himself with. Castro admitted that because he had failed to register as a student that year, he had no political rights. Therefore, he could not aspire to or hold any student leadership position. See Ovares, interview. Robert Taber erroneously describes Fidel as "president of the FEU." See Taber, *M-26*, 44. The biographer Bourne, after interviewing Castro, wrote that he had been elected as the law school class representative during his first two years. See Bourne, *Fidel*, 36, 38; Ros, *Fidel Castro*, 121–24; Pablo Acosta, *Mi "compañero" Fidel* (Miami: Ediciones Universal, 2005), 38–39, 42; Blanco, *Todo el tiempo*, 237; "Universidad," *Bohemia*, June 15, 1947; Arturo Alape, *El Bogotazo: Memorias del Olvido* (Havana: Ediciones Casa de las Américas, 1983), 189.

41. *El Mundo*, June 5, 1947; *Prensa Libre* (Havana), June 6, 1947; *El País*, June 7, 1947.

42. Fidel Castro's perennial homophobia recently surfaced when during a prank call from a Miami radio broadcaster he called him a "maricón" and "mariconzón." See Wilfredo Cancio Isla, "Castro responde con insultos a una broma," *El Nuevo Herald*, June 18, 2003. These insults prompted gay organizations in Spain to denounce Castro. See Jaime Campmany, "Orgullo Gay," *ABC* (Spain), June 20, 2003; and Victor Llano, "Ademas de Asesino, Homofobo," *Libertad* (Spain), June 22, 2003. Castro's "loathing for homosexuality" is described in Quirk, *Fidel Castro*, 16. See also *El Crisol*, July 17, 1947; *Vanguardia Estudiantil*, July 30, 1947; Federación Estudiantil Universitaria de la Universidad de La Habana, Despatch 716, August 30, 1948, Department of State, FOIA; *El Mundo*, July 19 and August 31, 1947; Ros, *Fidel Castro*, 76–80, 91; Conte Agüero, *Los dos rostros*, 29; Dubois, *Fidel Castro*, 17; Ovares, interview; Thomas, *Cuba*, 811, which reiterates that Castro "failed to be elected either president of the Law Students or president of the FEU."

43. Mario Gajate Erro, personal interview, Miami, Fla., May 31, 1975; Masferrer, interview; Ovares, interview; Salabarría, interview; Charles D. Ameringer, *The Caribbean Legion:*

Patriots, Politicians, Soldiers of Fortune, 1946-1950 (University Park: Pennsylvania State University Press, 1996), 27, 32-34.

44. Gajate, interview; "Dominican Republic: Honored in the Breach," *Newsweek*, August 11, 1947, 50; Salabarría, interview; "Cuba: Filibuster's End," *Time*, October 13, 1947, 40; "Dominican Plot," *Newsweek*, November 3, 1947, 15; *Diario de la Marina*, September 30 and October 17, 1947; Ameringer, *Caribbean Legion*, 35-36.

45. Rafael Díaz-Balart is correctly identified as the president of the Committee for Dominican Democracy (CUDD), and not Fidel Castro, in Ameringer, *Caribbean Legion*, 30. Mario Gajate passed away in Miami on November 1, 1992. See Gajate, interview; Alape, *El Bogotazo*, 190; Szulc, *Fidel*, 155; Geyer, *Guerrilla Prince*, 61; Ovares, interview; Masferrer, interview.

46. U.S. Department of State, *Foreign Relations of the United States 1947, Vol. VIII, The American Republics* (Washington, D.C.: U.S. Government Printing Office, 1972), 644-50; Ameringer, *Caribbean Legion*, 40, 43-44, 47; Gajate, interview; "Cuba: Sandpit Revolution," *Newsweek*, October 13, 1947, 42; Masferrer, interview.

47. Mario Salabarría (April 4, 1914-March 10, 2004) received the maximum thirty-year prison sentence for murder on March 8, 1948, as a result of the Orfila shootout. Salabarría was released by the Castro regime on June 30, 1961, while in the Curie hospital after cancer surgery on his right leg. He was arrested again on June 22, 1965, accused of being part of a CIA plot to kill Fidel Castro, sentenced to thirty years, and released in August 1979. Seven months later Salabarría joined his wife and son in Miami. See *Diario de la Marina*, September 16, 1947, and February 10, 18, 20, 28, 1948; *New York Times*, September 16, 1947, 15, and March 9, 1948, 11; Mario García del Cueto, "Como murió Emilio Tro," *Bohemia*, September 21, 1947, 56-61; "Cuba: Death in Marianao," *Time*, September 29, 1947, 42; "Cuba: The Miramar Siege," *Newsweek*, September 29, 1947, 48; Salabarría, interview; Ros, *Fidel Castro*, 102-16; Duarte, *Historiología Cubana*, 3:56-58.

48. Genovevo Pérez Dámera (January 3, 1910-June 27, 1992) went into exile in 1959 and passed away in Miami, Florida. See Gajate, interview; Ameringer, *Caribbean Legion*, 54; Salabarría, interview; Masferrer, interview.

49. Some Cayo Confites expeditionaries later left for Costa Rica, where they formed the Caribbean Legion and helped José Figueres assume power in 1948. The next year the Caribbean Legion went to Guatemala and supported the Arévalo and Arbenz governments. In June 1953 rumors spread that they would invade Cuba with fifteen hundred men led by Eufemio Fernández Ortega. In 1954 the legion fled to Mexico after Arbenz was deposed, and the group disintegrated thereafter. See *Diario de la Marina*, September 28, 30, and October 3, 1947, 1; Szulc, *Fidel*, 156-57; Alape, *El Bogotazo*, 190; Geyer, *Guerrilla Prince*, 63; Conte Agüero, *Los dos rostros*, 30; Weyl, *Red Star over Cuba*, 68; Ameringer, *Caribbean Legion*, 56; Ros, *Fidel Castro*, 138-39; Masferrer, interview; *Havana Post*, October 2, 1947, 1; Jorge Yáñez, "Cincuenta y nueve días con los expedicionarios de Cayo Confites," *Bohemia*, November 16, 1947, 28-29; "Cuba: Filibuster's End," 40; "La Legión del Caribe," *Bohemia*, June 26, 1949, 67-70.

50. Alape, *El Bogotazo*, 190; Ovares, interview; Coltman, *Real Fidel Castro*, 19; Pérez, *El Movimiento Estudiantil*, 189.

51. The conservative *Diario de la Marina* erroneously identified Fidel Castro as FEU vice president and the next day as president of the Law School. This contradicts Castro's own admission that he had no student political rights that year after failing to register. See *Diario de la Marina*, November 4, 1947, 16, and November 7, 1947, 22; "En Cuba," *Bohemia*, November

9 and 16, 1947; *El Crisol,* November 4, 1947, 1; *El Mundo,* November 4, 1947, 1; Ovares, interview; Martin, *Early Fidel,* 40–41; Ros, *Fidel Castro,* 147–50; *Hoy,* November 4, 1947, 1.

52. The university policemen who assisted removing the Bell of La Demajagua were René Cano and Ramón "Mongo el Diablo" Quesada Ferra. See Ros, *Fidel Castro,* 154–55; *El País,* November 6, 1947, 1; *Diario de la Marina,* November 6, 1947, 1.

53. *Diario de la Marina,* November 7, 1947, 1; *El Mundo,* November 7, 1947, 1; Ros, *Fidel Castro,* 157–58.

54. *El Mundo,* November 7 and 8, 1947, 1; *Diario de la Marina,* November 7, 1947, 1; *Alerta,* November 7, 1947, 2; *Hoy,* November 7, 1947, 1; *Mañana,* November 7, 1947, 1; *El País,* November 7, 1947, 1; Ovares, interview; Ros, *Fidel Castro,* 161–62.

55. Manuel de Castro del Campo left a widow and two children. See "Slaying of Manolo Castro," Report R-35-48 of the U.S. Naval Attaché in Havana, February 26, 1948, Intelligence Division, Office of Chief of Naval Operations, Navy Department, FOIA; *Diario de la Marina,* February 24 and 26, 1948, 1; Szulc, *Fidel,* 167.

56. UIR gunman Gustavo Ortiz Fáez was later chief of Fidel Castro's G-2 political police in Matanzas. He went into exile in Venezuela with other UIR members and in 1963 was bodyguard to President Rómulo Betancourt. Ortiz was employed by the Venezuelan Directorate of Intelligence and Prevention Services (DISIP) political police. His comrades Guillermo "Billiken" García, Pedro Mirassou Tarnío, and Vidal Morales Rodríguez (January 9, 1918–January 2, 1996) also went into exile. See Thomas, *Cuba,* 761n7; *Diario de la Marina,* February 27, 1948, 15–16; Masferrer, interview; Enrique Ovares Herrera, "El Bogotazo," *El Nuevo Herald,* April 9, 1988, 11; *Diario de la Marina,* April 11 and 22, 1948, 32, and April 14, 1948, 30; Salabarría, interview; Vidal Morales, interview; Ros, *Fidel Castro,* 174; Acosta, *Mi "compañero" Fidel,* 44.

57. Szulc, *Fidel,* 168; Alape, *El Bogotazo,* 182; Santiago Touriño, "El Bogotazo," *El Nuevo Herald,* April 9, 1988, 11; Dubois, *Fidel Castro,* 17; Ovares, interview.

58. Ovares, interview.

59. Alfredo "El Chino" Esquivel Rodón (April 10, 1926–August 13, 2005) went into exile in New York in 1964 and passed away in Miami on Fidel Castro's birthday. See Ovares, interview; Alfredo Esquivel, "El Bogotazo," *El Nuevo Herald,* April 9, 1988, 11; Acosta, *Mi "compañero" Fidel,* 63–64; Franqui, *Diary,* 10; Touriño, "El Bogotazo," 11; Szulc, *Fidel,* 170–71; Raimundo, *Habla el Coronel Orlando Piedra,* 33–34; Gerardo Rodríguez Morejón, *Fidel Castro: Biografía* (Havana: P. Fernández y Cia., 1959), 14.

60. Rafael del Pino's passport is reproduced in Ramón B. Conte, *Historia oculta de los crímenes de Fidel Castro* (n.p., 1995), 28–29. He is erroneously identified as a student in Coltman, *Real Fidel Castro,* 40. See also Ovares, interview; Alape, *El Bogotazo,* 190, 192–93; Francisco Fandiño Silva, *La penetración Soviética en América y el 9 de abril* (Bogotá: Colección Nuevos Tiempos, 1949), 44; Ovares Herrera, "El Bogotazo," 11; Dubois, *Fidel Castro,* 18; Franqui, *Diary,* 12.

61. Franqui, *Diary,* 12; Alape, *El Bogotazo,* 188, 193, 195, 646; Blanco, *Todo el tiempo,* 248–49; Ovares, interview; Szulc, *Fidel,* 172–74; Ovares Herrera, "El Bogotazo," 11.

62. Blanco, *Todo el tiempo,* 247–51; Fandiño Silva, *La penetración Soviética en América,* 44–45; Alape, *El Bogotazo,* 193, 199–201, 648–49, 671; Gerardo Reyes, "Scotland Yard investigó a Castro por asesinato," *El Nuevo Herald,* April 10, 2001; Alberto Niño Heredia, *Antecedentes secretos del 9 de abril* (Bogotá: Editorial Pax, 1949), 54.

63. Franqui, *Diary*, 13; Alape, *El Bogotazo*, 180–81; Niño Heredia, *Antecedentes secretos del 9 de abril*, 54–55.

64. Alape, *El Bogotazo*, 181, 202, 304, 651; Ovares, interview; Mary Louise Wilkinson, "The Day Castro Ran Wild in Bogota Revolt," *Miami News*, November 11, 1966; Franqui, *Diary*, 13.

65. Ovares, interview; *New York Times*, April 10, 1948, 1.

66. Wilkinson, "Day Castro Ran Wild"; Ovares, interview; Alape, *El Bogotazo*, 316; Franqui, *Diary*, 9.

67. Although Rafael del Pino Siero never left Fidel Castro's side during most of the Bogotazo riot, in an extensive 1981 interview with Arturo Alape, Castro omitted mentioning his name and briefly referred to him as "the other Cuban." On September 15, 1948, the first anniversary of Emilio Tro's death, del Pino and others were involved in a second failed assassination attempt against Rolando Masferrer, resulting in one dead and five wounded. To elude MSR reprisals, del Pino, a World War II veteran who got a less than honorable discharge, went to live in the United States on December 6, 1948, and became a naturalized citizen in Los Angeles on June 9, 1950. On June 7, 1955, he was arrested in Miami, where he worked as a taxi driver, while in possession of forty-seven carbines and semiautomatic rifles. Del Pino was convicted in June 1956 for conspiracy to export arms and fined $150. He was in charge of purchasing weapons for Castro's Granma expedition, but after one of their safe houses was raided in Mexico on November 22, 1956, resulting in the loss of $56,000 worth of arms, Castro accused him of being a spy. After the Castro takeover in January 1959, del Pino flew several times from Miami to Cuba to drop leaflets calling Castro a Communist. When Castro visited New York and Washington in April, del Pino's Anti-Communist Movement of the Americas rallied 250 protesters. Del Pino, betrayed by Fernando Fuentes Cobas, was wounded and captured while making a clandestine flight into Cuba in July 1959, and he was sentenced to thirty years in prison. In August 1977, while U.S. senator Frank Church was attempting to negotiate the release of del Pino and other American citizens in Cuban jails, the Castro regime announced that he had committed suicide by hanging himself with a pair of socks in his cell. Mario Salabarría, imprisoned with del Pino, believes that "he hung himself because he was very perturbed and had previously attempted suicide a few times." See Rafael del Pino, MM 105-1738, April 6, 1959, FBI, FOIA; Salabarría, interview; Helga Silva, "Family Questions del Pino 'Suicide' in Cuban Prison," *Miami News*, August 30, 1977, 4; Franqui, *Diary*, 14–15; Ovares, interview; Alape, *El Bogotazo*, 309, 424; Dubois, *Fidel Castro*, 23–24; Duarte, *Historiología Cubana*, 3:77.

68. Dubois, *Fidel Castro*, 21; Franqui, *Diary*, 15–16; Alape, *El Bogotazo*, 373–75, 465–69, 679.

60. Ovares, interview; Wilkinson, "Day Castro Ran Wild"; Alape, *El Bogotazo*, 517–19.

70. Guillermo A. Belt (July 14, 1905–July 2, 1989) was minister of education in 1933 and mayor of Havana from 1935 to 1936, ambassador to the United States from 1944 to 1949 and concurrent representative to the OAS, and Cuban delegate to the United Nations during 1945–49. He left for exile in 1959 and later settled in Bethesda, Maryland, until his death. See Alape, *El Bogotazo*, 535–39; Franqui, *Diary*, 18–19; Dubois, *Fidel Castro*, 22–23; *Diario de la Marina*, April 20, 1948, 1; *New York Times*, April 12, 1948, 1; Ovares, interview.

71. A photograph of Fidel Castro, Enrique Ovares, and Jorge Menvielle Porte-Petit amidst the street rubble in Bogotá, taken from the Guayo newsreel, appeared in *Bohemia*, April 25, 1948, 7. The photo was later used by the Colombian police to identify Ovares as the foreigner

at the Kodak shop when Gaitán was murdered. See Alape, *El Bogotazo*, 534–35, 539; Dubois, *Fidel Castro*, 23; *Diario de la Marina*, April 14, 1948, 1; *Información*, April 15, 1948, 1; Kurt Singer, "I, Fidel Castro," *Illustrated Weekly of India*, December 18, 1960, 12; Helia D'Acosta, "Impresionante relato del 'Bogotazo,'" *Excelsior* (Mexico), May 6, 1948; Ovares Herrera, "El Bogotazo," 11.

72. Singer, "I, Fidel Castro," 12; Alape, *El Bogotazo*, 629, 675–78.

73. Fidel Castro's rap sheet with the national police, reproduced in Orlando Piedra's memoirs, identifies him as "one of the intellectual authors of the death of Manuel (Manolo) Castro" but does not link him to the murder of Sgt. Oscar Fernández Caral. See Raimundo, *Habla el Coronel Orlando Piedra*, 99. Police major Mario Salabarría Aguiar, imprisoned at the time for Emilio Tro's death, believes that Fidel Castro was not involved in Sgt. Oscar Fernández Caral's murder: "That was done in broad daylight. Fidel Castro was known in that neighborhood, and Fernández Caral would have spotted him coming. I do not think that Fidel is that brave to take that risk where it was very easy to detect him. The individual eventually arrested worked in a movie theater and looked a lot like Fidel." See *Hoy*, April 15, 1948, 1; Singer, "I, Fidel Castro," 12; "Bandidos Importados," *Tiempo en Cuba*, April 25, 1948; Ernesto Rodríguez Suárez, "Cuatro años de asesinatos impunes," *Tiempo en Cuba*, October 10, 1948, 51; *Prensa Libre*, July 10, 1948; *Diario de la Marina*, July 7, 1948, 30, and July 10, 1948, 20; Vidal Morales, interview; "Gangsterismo: El crimen semanal," *Tiempo en Cuba*, July 11, 1948.

74. Justo Fuentes Clavel and his chauffeur were murdered on April 2, 1949, by Orlando León Lemus and Policarpo Soler. Armando Galis-Menéndez Larraguechea (November 22, 1918–January 9, 1988) later became subsecretary of the interior during the Batista regime and went into exile in 1959. He joined Brigade 2506 during the Bay of Pigs invasion, was captured and imprisoned, and was returned to the United States during the 1962 prisoner exchange. Ernesto de la Fe (June 16, 1913–October 29, 1992) stated that was the last time he saw Castro in September 1948. He was arrested on January 4, 1959, and completed a fifteen-year prison sentence for having collaborated with the Batista government. De la Fe was not allowed to leave the island until January 1981, when he rejoined his wife and two offspring in Miami. See de la Fe, interview; Masferrer, interview; Díaz-Balart, interview; Franqui, *Vida*, 45; *Miami Herald*, January 23, 1981, C4; *New York Times*, June 9, 1981, B8; *El Nuevo Herald*, October 31, 1992, B4.

75. Díaz-Balart, interview; Franqui, *Vida*, 48; Coltman, *Real Fidel Castro*, 48; Geyer, *Guerrilla Prince*, 72–74; Raffy, *Castro el Desleal*, 83; Blanco, *Todo el tiempo*, 257–61.

76. After graduating in 1950 as an architect, Enrique Ovares abandoned politics and went into private practice. The *Bogotazo* experience kept him from joining Castro's revolution. Castro, in turn, had Ovares arrested in August 1959 and sentenced to six years of imprisonment for being a "counter-revolutionary." Ovares and his family settled in Key Biscayne, Fla., where he passed away on February 28, 2006. See Szulc, *Fidel*, 185; Geyer, *Guerrilla Prince*, 53, 66; Raimundo, *Habla el Coronel Orlando Piedra*, 98; Betto, *Fidel y la religión*, 163; Juana Castro, "My Brother Is a Tyrant," 27; Mario Mencia, *Time Was on Our Side* (Havana: Editorial Política, 1982), 147; Martin, *Early Fidel*, 68–69; Blanco, *Todo el tiempo*, 262–63; "Un lamentable y bochornoso incidente que conmovió a Cuba," *Bohemia*, March 20, 1949, 57; Díaz-Balart, interview; Blanco, *Todo el tiempo*, 219–21; Ros, *Fidel Castro*, 230–31; Baudilio Castellanos, "La historia me absolverá, documento esencialmente Marxista," *Revolución*, July 18, 1962, 6; Bourne, *Fidel*, 56; Ovares, interview.

77. Bourne, *Fidel*, 57; Coltman, *Real Fidel Castro*, 19, 48, 52; Federación Estudiantil Universitaria de la Universidad de La Habana, Despatch 716, August 30, 1948, Department of State, FOIA; Herminio Portell Vilá, *Nueva historia de la Republica de Cuba* (Miami: La Moderna Poesia, 1986), 635–36; Quirk, *Fidel Castro*, 31; Geyer, *Guerrilla Prince*, 93; Thomas, *Cuba*, 819; Blanco, *Todo el tiempo*, 278–79; Mencia, *El grito del Moncada*, 411; Martin, *Early Fidel*, 84; Szulc, *Fidel*, 202.

78. Luis Conte Agüero, *Eduardo Chibás: El adalid de Cuba* (Mexico City: Editorial Jus, 1955), 507, 526, 586; Suárez Rivas, interview; Charles D. Ameringer, *The Cuban Democratic Experience: The Auténtico Years, 1944–1952* (Gainesville: University Press of Florida, 2000), 37, 42; *New York Times*, April 28, 1946, sec. 2, p. 7; Thomas, *Cuba*, 767.

79. Pedro Emilio Castro Argota worked in the Communications Ministry, were he was arrested in possession of more than eleven thousand pesos in stolen checks and money orders by police major Mario Salabarría. He was charged with eighty counts of theft, but his father exerted political influence, and the case never went to court. See Salabarría, interview; Emilio Ochoa Ochoa, personal interview, Miami, Fla., December 2, 1983; Coltman, *Real Fidel Castro*, 4, 17.

80. Carlos Márquez-Sterling Guiral (September 8, 1898–May 3, 1991), a lawyer and statesman who presided over the drafting of the 1940 constitution, was Speaker of the Chamber of Representatives, minister of state (1941–42), and minister of education (1942–43). A journalist, historian, and political science professor at the University of Havana, he ran unsuccessfully for president in November 1958 under the peace platform of the Free Peoples Party (PPL). He sought asylum in the Venezuelan Embassy on July 13, 1959, and later settled in the United States. See Conte Agüero, *Eduardo Chibás*, 568–69; William S. Stokes, "The 'Cuban Revolution' and the Presidential Elections of 1948," *Hispanic American Historical Review* (February 1951): 72–74; *Diario de la Marina*, September 1, 1948, 12; Bonachea and Valdés, *Revolutionary Struggle*, 29; Quirk, *Fidel Castro*, 32; Bourne, *Fidel*, 53, 61–62; Ameringer, *Cuban Democratic Experience*, 45; Carlos Márquez-Sterling, telephone interview, Miami, Fla., December 4, 1982.

81. Díaz-Balart, interview; Thomas, *Cuba*, 818; Geyer, *Guerrilla Prince*, 100; Quirk, *Fidel Castro*, 29; "What Makes Fidel Run?," *Atlanta Journal*, May 12, 1963, B1.

82. In 1939 Eduardo Chibás was mysteriously shot in the stomach and claimed assailants tried to murder him. The publicity gained Chibás a vote of sympathy that elected him to the 1940 Constitutional Assembly. See Raúl Chibás Rivas, personal interview, San Juan, P.R., December 10, 1984; Conte Agüero, *Eduardo Chibás*, 765, 784–85, 798; Ameringer, *Cuban Democratic Experience*, 154–55; *New York Times*, August 17, 1951, 8.

83. Ramón Vasconcelos Maragliano (February 8, 1889–August 11, 1965) a Machado police confidant, survived an assassination attempt. He was elected as a liberal senator in 1936 and 1944. He served as minister of education in 1942 under Fulgencio Batista and later as minister without portfolio in Prío's cabinet until his resignation on August 25, 1950. He joined Batista's governing Council of Ministers in 1952. Vasconcelos went into exile in Spain on March 7, 1959, but after he developed a terminal illness, Castro allowed him to return to Cuba in 1964, a year before his death. *Alerta* newspaper, which he bought in 1949, had a daily circulation of thirty thousand. See "Yo Acuso," *Alerta*, January 28, 1952, 1; "El informe de Fidel Castro al Tribunal de Cuentas: $18,000 mensuales dan a las pandillas en Palacio," *Alerta*, March 4, 1952, 1; Suárez Rivas, interview.

84. Manuel Bisbé Alberni (December 28, 1906–March 20, 1961), a professor of Greek literature, was appointed by Fidel Castro on January 23, 1959, as Cuban ambassador to the

United Nations, where he died of a heart attack in the General Assembly building. See Quirk, *Fidel Castro*, 36; Conte Agüero, interview; Márquez-Sterling, interview.

85. "Frente a Todos!," *Bohemia*, January 8, 1956. Castro was replying to the article by Miguel Hernández, "La patria no es de Fidel," *Bohemia*, December 18, 1955.

86. Gay people in Cuba were interned in labor camps denominated Military Unit to Assist Production (UMAP) during 1965–67 and forced to watch pornographic movies in an attempt to alter their sexual preference. See Néstor Almendros and Orlando Jiménez-Leal, *Conducta impropia* (Madrid: Editorial Playor, 1984), 34, 185; Allen Young, *Gays under the Revolution* (San Francisco: Grey Fox Press, 1981), 20–25.

Chapter 2—"There is nothing unusual going on"

1. The legal document was reproduced in Mario Mencia, "¡Como mismo subió lo quitaremos!," *Bohemia*, July 6, 1973, 23, 27–28; Dirección Política de las FAR, *Moncada*, 65–67; Mencia, *El grito del Moncada*, 148–50; Autores varios, *Mártires del Moncada*, 258; Thomas, *Cuba*, 821.

2. The Tribunal of Constitutional and Social Guarantees had the powers to rule on all matters pertaining to the constitutionality of law, decrees, resolutions, or acts that would deny or restrict the normal functioning of the organs of the state. See Emilio Ochoa, interview; Dirección Política de las FAR, *Moncada*, 105, 116–19; Mencia, "¡Como mismo subió," 26; Mario Mencia, "El grito del Moncada," *Bohemia*, July 20, 1984, 84; "Al Tribunal de Urgencia," *Granma*, July 26, 1966, 5; *Mil fotos Cuba, territorio libre de América* (Havana: Comité Central del Partido Comunista de Cuba, 1967), 141; Suárez Rivas, interview; *El Mundo*, March 28 and April 1, 1952, 1; "Cronología de los cien años de lucha (1868–1968)," *Revista de la Universidad de La Habana*, October–December 1968, 230; Thomas, *Cuba*, 790; Leonel Antonio de la Cuesta, *Constituciones Cubanas desde 1812 hasta nuestros días* (New York: Ediciones Exilio, 1974), 338–39.

3. Héctor de Armas Errasti, personal interview, Miami, Fla., August 4, 1984; Dinorah Algarra Peralta, telephone interview, Miami, Fla., August 3, 1991; "Mario Muñoz, médico, combatiente, héroe," *Granma*, July 15, 1970, 2.

4. *Son los Mismos* was produced by Raúl Gómez García, Abel Santamaría, Jesús Montané, Juan Martínez Tinguao, Ricardo Valladares, and José Aceña. Another underground anti-Batista pamphlet was the Auténticos' *Ecos de la Resistencia*. See Despatch 795, November 19, 1952, U.S. Department of State, *Confidential U.S. State Department Central Files: Cuba, Internal Affairs, 1950-1954*, U.S. National Archives and Records Administration, Washington, D.C., hereafter cited as *Cuba Internal Affairs; A Sketch on the Clandestine and Guerrilla Press Covering the Period 1952-1958* (Havana: Instituto del Libro, 1971), 16; "Versión taquigráfica del programa 'Siempre es 26,'" *Granma*, June 29, 1973, 4; El Indio Nabori, "Raúl Gómez García: Poeta del '26 de julio' y de la generación del 'Centenario,'" *Bohemia*, July 27, 1962, 16; Luis Suardíaz, "Raúl Gómez García brilla en lo más alto," *Granma*, July 26, 2003; Jane McManus, *From the Palm Tree: Voices of the Cuban Revolution* (Secaucus, N.J.: Lyle Stuart, 1983), 19; Marta Rojas, *El que debe vivir* (Havana: Casa de las Américas, 1978), 85; Mencia, "¡Como mismo subió," 28; Mario Mencia, "En la tierra de Martí sin libertades," *Bohemia*, July 13, 1973, 29; Marta Rojas, "La gloria es de los precursores," *Bohemia*, August 2, 1963, 79.

5. Merle, *Moncada*, 78, 80; McManus, *From the Palm Tree*, 22, 24; Marta Rojas, *La Generación del Centenario en el Moncada* (Havana: Ediciones R, 1964), 47 [hereafter referred to as

La Generación del Centenario]; Fulvio Fuentes, "La morada de Abel," *Bohemia,* July 6, 1973, 61; Judas Pacheco, *Abel Santamaría y el Moncada* (Havana: Editora Política, 1983); *Granma,* July 24, 1973, 2, and July 23, 1988, 5; Ediciones Políticas, *Haydée habla del Moncada* (Havana: Instituto del Libro, 1967), 63; Franqui, *Diary,* 51; Geyer, *Guerrilla Prince,* 113; Raúl Martínez Ararás, personal interview, Miami, Fla., December 5, 1983; Orlando Castro García, personal interview, Miami, Fla., December 5, 1983; Autores varios, *Mártires del Moncada,* 273–74; Javier Rodríguez, "Habla el comandante Jesus Montane Oropesa," *Bohemia,* July 26, 1963, 61.

    6. "Lo que siguió el asalto del cuartel: Bestial reacción de la tiranía," *La Calle,* July 26, 1959, C8; Raúl Martínez, interview; Gerardo Pérez-Puelles Valmaseda, telephone interview, Miami, Fla., July 4, 1990; Emilio Ochoa, interview; Manuel Suardíaz Fernández, personal interview, Queens, N.Y., April 29, 1990; Alcides Iznaga, "La casa de Melba," *Bohemia,* July 6, 1973, 6.

    7. Algarra, interview; Héctor de Armas, interview; Franqui, *Diary,* 50; *Granma,* July 21, 1982, 2.

    8. Szulc, *Fidel,* 229; Franqui, *Diary,* 51; Jesús Montané Oropesa, "La Generación del Centenario libra sus primeros combates contra la tiranía," *Verde Olivo,* July 29, 1962, 9; Melba Hernández, "Siempre supimos que el asalto al Moncada culminaría en la victoria," *Verde Olivo,* July 28, 1963, 29–30; Mencia, "En la tierra de Martí," 29.

    9. *El Mundo,* September 18, 1959, 1; Montané Oropesa, "La Generación del Centenario libra," 10; Marta Rojas, "Justa indignación," *Verde Olivo,* July 25, 1965, 19; Bonachea and Valdés, *Revolutionary Struggle,* 147; Mencia, "En la tierra de Martí," 29; Dirección Política de las FAR, *Moncada,* 129–31; Chanes, interview; *Sketch on the Clandestine and Guerrilla Press,* 16; Héctor de Armas, interview.

    10. *El Mundo,* July 26, 1952; Montané Oropesa, "La Generación del Centenario libra," 11; "Versión taquigráfica del programa 'Siempre es 26,'" 4–5; Héctor de Armas, interview; Melba Hernández, "Siempre supimos que el asalto," 30; "Lo que siguió el asalto del cuartel," C8; Chanes, interview; Mario Mencia, "Con la tiranía descabezada a los pies (Segunda Parte)," *Bohemia,* July 23, 1976, 60; Szulc, *Fidel,* 230; Rojas, *El que debe vivir,* 36; Víctor Pérez-Galdós, "Antecedentes y preparativos de la acción del Moncada," *Bohemia,* June 10, 1983, 87; Suardíaz, "Raúl Gómez García brilla en lo más alto."

    11. Roberto D. Agramonte Pichardo (May 3, 1904–December 12, 1995) was a professor of philosophy and vice rector of the University of Havana. He served as Cuban ambassador to Mexico in 1947–48 and as revolutionary minister of state January–June 1959. He went into exile in San Juan, Puerto Rico, in 1960. The leaders of the Ortodoxo Youth were Max Lesnik Menéndez, secretary general; Omar Borges, national secretary; Luis López Pérez, propaganda secretary; José Iglesias Lastra, municipal secretary; Francisco Cardona Orta, finance secretary; Mario Rivadulla, national leader; Pedro Guzmán, national secretary of meetings; and Salvador Lew, organization secretary. None of them was invited to participate in the Moncada attack. See Rojas, *El que debe vivir,* 39–41; *El Mundo,* June 26, 1952, 7.

    12. Rojas, *La Generación del Centenario,* 42; Raúl Martínez, interview.

    13. Revolutionary activities and exile took a toll on many marriages, including Fidel Castro's, which ended in divorce. When this book was completed, Raúl Martínez Ararás and "Nenita" Varela had celebrated their sixtieth wedding anniversary. See Raúl Martínez, interview; Castro García, interview; and Pérez-Galdós, "Antecedentes y preparativos."

    14. The fourteen Afro-Cuban insurgents, making up less than 9 percent of the total, were two blacks, Agustín Díaz and Armando Mestre, and twelve mulattos, Juam Almeida, Enrique

Cámara, Giraldo Córdova, Rafael Freyre, Calixto García, Luciano González, Melba Hernández, Teodulio Mitchell, Isidro Peñalver, Ramón Pez, Osvaldo Socarrás, and Humberto Valdés. Merle, *Moncada*, identifies only ten attackers as black or mulatto. Thomas, *Cuba*, cites four blacks and fourteen mulattos. Alejandro de la Fuente, *A Nation for All: Race, Inequality, and Politics in Twentieth-Century Cuba* (Chapel Hill: University of North Carolina Press, 2001), 251, inflates the total number of nonwhite attackers to "between one-fifth and one-fourth," raising the number to forty Afro-Cuban rebels. Sketches of the dead rebels, depicting their racial composition, appeared in *Granma*, July 11–22, 1966, 2, and their photos appear in Autores varios, *Mártires del Moncada*. Rebels growing up without a father included the Martínez Ararás brothers, the Trigo López brothers, Gerardo Pérez-Puelles, Orlando Castro García, Reinaldo Boris Luis Santa Coloma, José Luis Tasende, Pedro Marrero, Raúl Gómez García, Hugo Camejo, Agustín Díaz Cartaya, Víctor Escalona, Juan Ameijeiras Delgado, Félix Rivero Vasallo, Tomás "Tocororo" Rodríguez Rodríguez, Gerardo Alvarez Alvarez, Rigoberto Corcho López, Juan Domínguez Díaz, Pablo Agüero Guedes, Rafael Freyre Torres, Raúl de Aguiar Fernández, José Madera Fernández, Armando Valle López, and Gilberto Barón Martínez. See Yolanda Mirabal Reyes, *El color de la Victoria* (Havana: Editora Abril, 1990), 17, 28, 43, 57, 69, 87, 109, 126, 130, 135, 172, 176, 181, 190, 201, 204; Szulc, *Fidel*, 224; Agustín Alarcón, "Papel revolucionario del grupo del Parque de la Fraternidad," *Revolución*, January 29, 1959, 2; Autores varios, *Mártires del Moncada*; Betto, *Fidel y la religión*, 171; Lockwood, *Castro's Cuba*, 146; Thomas, *Cuba*, 824, 1546–47; Bourne, *Fidel*, 68; Geyer, *Guerrilla Prince*, 107; Mencia, *El grito del Moncada*, 472; Carlos Moore, *Castro, the Blacks, and Africa* (Los Angeles: Center for Afro-American Studies, University of California, 1988), 33.

15. The lowly followers of Castro included Calixto García Martínez, a Johnson Pharmacy bicycle messenger; Antonio "El Gallego" López García, a plumber's helper; Juan Ameijeiras Delgado, a parking-lot attendant and cab driver; Generoso R. Llanes Machado, an illiterate maintenance man at the Biltmore Yacht Club; and Belén High School janitors Virginio and Manuel Gómez Reyes. Some insurgents, including Mario Martínez Ararás, Marcos "El Curro" Martí Rodríguez, José Testa Zaragoza, and Miguel Oramas Alfonso, had been in fistfights with the authorities. Those with criminal records were the stevedore Jacinto García Espinosa, a convicted marijuana addict and narcotics trafficker; the dairy worker Carmelo Noa Gil, jailed for attempted murder; and the twenty-three-year-old stonecutter Flores Betancourt Rodríguez, who had served one year in the youth reformatory. See Raúl Martínez, interview; Carlos A. Bustillo Rodríguez, personal interview, West New York, N.J., June 3, 1984; Julio Travieso, *Un nuevo día* (Havana: Editorial Letras Cubanas, 1984), 48, 54–57; Chanes, interview; Matthews, *Revolution in Cuba*, 52–53; Mirabal Reyes, *El color de la Victoria*, 122, 160, 208; "Attackers of Army Posts Identified as Criminals," *Havana Post*, July 31, 1953, 1; Díaz-Francisco, interview; Ovares, interview.

16. Díaz-Francisco, interview; "Relato del comandante Miret: Un Grupo Verdaderamente Heroico," *Verde Olivo*, July 29, 1962, 6; Ediciones Políticas, *Veintiseis* (Havana: Instituto del Libro, 1970), 134, 173, 174, 267; Raúl del Mazo Serra, telephone interview, Miami, Fla., August 9, 1984; Rojas, *La Generación del Centenario*, 43.

17. Centro de Estudios de Historia Militar de las Fuerzas Armadas Revolucionarias, *Moncada: La Acción* (Havana: Editora Política, 1981), 10; "Relato del comandante Miret," 7; Bustillo, interview; Díaz-Francisco, interview; Héctor de Armas, interview; Szulc, *Fidel*, 236; "La acción del Palacio de Justicia," *Verde Olivo*, July 26, 1964, 12.

18. After 1959, Nereida Rodríguez never received a government post and died in Havana in 2005. In 1971, Melba Hernández told Boris Junior that his father's last wish had been that his son bear his full name. Melba, using her power of attorney, then changed his name to Boris Luis Santa Coloma. Boris Junior served in the diplomatic corps and was third secretary of the Cuban Embassy in Berlin when the Berlin Wall came down. He returned to Havana a few months later but went back to Berlin in 1991 and sought asylum. *El Mundo,* December 31, 1952, 1; Carlos Nicot, "No hay problema, es el pollero," *Revolución,* July 25, 1963, 1; Autores varios, *Mártires del Moncada,* 353–59; Mencia, *El grito del Moncada,* 465; Suardíaz, interview.

19. Suardíaz, interview.

20. Merle, *Moncada,* 84; Travieso, *Un nuevo día,* 46; Mencia, "¡Como mismo subió," 28; "Relato del combatiente del Moncada Pepe Suarez," *Verde Olivo,* July 29, 1962, 83; Gerardo Granados Lara, personal interview, Orlando, Fla., August 10, 1984.

21. The Artemisa cell included Ciro Redondo García, Julio Díaz González, the butcher Antonio Betancourt Flores, café employee Severino "Vero" Rosell González, nineteen-year-old high school student Ramón Pez Ferro, and eighteen-year-old peasant Marcos "El Curro" Martí Rodríguez, who had already had various confrontations with the rural guard. See Granados, interview; Autores varios, *Mártires del Moncada,* 249–53; Merle, *Moncada,* 84; Juan Almeida Bosque, *La aurora de los héroes* (Santiago de Cuba: Editorial Oriente, 1999), 161; José Ponce Díaz, "Recuerdos del ataque," *Verde Olivo,* July 28, 1963, 17; Ana María Radaelli, "José Ponce Díaz," *Cuba Internacional,* July 1983, 62, in which Ponce exaggerated many of his previous statements; Mencia, "¡Como mismo subió," 23; Travieso, *Un nuevo día,* 26, 93; Marta Rojas, *La cueva del muerto* (Havana: Ediciones Unión, 1983), 101; Mariano Rodríguez Herrera, "Gudelia, de Marcos," *Juventud Rebelde,* July 21, 1987, 5.

22. Entry into the closed Artemisa Masonic lodge was provided by Ramón Pez Ferro, treasurer of the Association of Hopeful Youths of the Fraternity (AJEF) Masonic organization. Those present at the meeting included "Pepe" Suárez and group leaders Gerardo Granados Lara, Ramiro Valdés Menéndez, José Ponce Díaz, Julio Díaz González, Severino Rosell, and former AJEF member Mario Lazo Pérez. Other secret meetings were held in the Catholic Youth hall, with entry provided by cell leader Froilán Enríquez. See Granados, interview. Thomas, *Cuba,* 824, incorrectly states that José Ponce was a Freemason and provided his lodge for rebel meetings. Mario Chanes claims that Mario Lazo's memoirs contain "some truths, some lies and some exaggerations" (Chanes, interview). See also Mario Lazo Pérez, *Recuerdos del Moncada* (Havana: Editora Política, 1987), 17; Víctor Pérez-Galdós, "Moncada en el recuerdo de un combatiente," *Bohemia,* July 15, 1983, 77; Almeida Bosque, *La aurora de los héroes,* 162; *Revolución,* July 22, 1963; Ponce, "Recuerdos del ataque," 17.

23. Enrique Sanz Fals, "Los artemiseños en el Moncada," *Granma,* July 24, 1987, 3; Autores varios, *Mártires del Moncada,* 34, 182, 363; "Fidel Labrador habla de los días del Moncada," *Bohemia,* July 25, 1986, 6, 7; Mencia, *El grito del Moncada,* 421, 423; Granados, interview; Lazo, *Recuerdos,* 22–23; *Revolución* (Rotograbado), July 22, 1963, 7; Georgina D. Cuervo Cerulia and Ofelia Llenín del Alcazar, *Moncada: Epopeya heróica* (Havana: Instituto Cubano del Libro, 1973), 141; Jesús A. Portocarrero, *Cuba: Paradigma y destino de América* (Miami: Colonial Press, 1966), 106; Ponce, "Recuerdos del ataque," 17; Israel Tápanes, "26 de Julio," *Verde Olivo,* July 26, 1970, 27.

24. Marta Matamoros, "El asalto al Cartel de Bayamo," *Revista de Granma,* July 6, 1967; "Fernando Chenard, '... vístete de rojo que ha triunfado la Patria,'" *Granma,* September 7,

1978, 2; Chanes, interview; Mirabal Reyes, *El color de la Victoria,* 120–21; Eduardo Montano Benítez, personal interview, Passaic, N.J., June 17, 1995; Autores varios, *Mártires del Moncada,* 49–52, 76, 157–61, 346; *Granma,* June 26 and July 10, 1973, 2; Dirección Política de las FAR, *Moncada,* 246.

25. Raúl Martínez, interview; Mencia, *El grito del Moncada,* 458; Merle, *Moncada,* 87, 88; Osvaldo Ortega N., "Entrevista con Oscar Alcalde: Después del asalto," *Verde Olivo,* July 26, 1964, 33; Carmen Villar, "El asalto al Moncada visto por uno de los combatientes: Oscar Alcalde," *Juventud Rebelde,* July 21, 1966, 8; Juan Sánchez, "Las finanzas del movimiento," *Bohemia,* July 13, 1973, 4; Marta Rojas, "Ochenta pesos de tiros: Como se sufragaron los gastos para el ataque al Cuartel Moncada," *Verde Olivo,* July 29, 1962, 38.

26. The Nueva Paz cell included their leader, twenty-one-year-old albino Tomás "Tocororo" Rodríguez Rodríguez, Manuel M. Rojo Pérez, Manuel E. Isla Pérez, Rolando Guerrero Bello, Genaro Hernández Martínez, Guillermo Elizalde Sotolongo, Rubén Gallardo, and two other friends. See Horacio Hidalgo-Gato González, personal interview, Miami, Fla., June 10, 2004; Suardíaz, interview; Matamoros, "El asalto al Cuartel de Bayamo," 5; Margarita Torres, "Aquella primera práctica en la finca 'Santa Elena,'" *Granma,* July 24, 1969, 2; Cuervo and Llenín, *Moncada,* 141; Mencia, *El grito del Moncada,* 421; Lazo, *Recuerdos,* 23; Szulc, *Fidel,* 235, 244.

27. Merle, *Moncada,* 104; Duarte, *Historiología Cubana,* 3:256; Mario Mencia, "La concepción del asalto al Moncada," *Cuba Internacional,* July 1983, 15; Sánchez, "Las finanzas del movimiento," 4; Lisandro Otero, "Entrevista a Haydée Santamaría y Melba Hernández," *Bohemia,* September 9, 1966, 11; Franqui, *Diary,* 53–54; Lockwood, *Castro's Cuba,* 140–41.

28. Raúl Castro's goddaughter, Temis Tasende Dubois, who was fifteen months old when her father was killed, is today a lieutenant colonel in the Cuban Revolutionary Armed Forces. See Betto, *Fidel y la religión,* 229–30; Pedro A. García, "El pequeño motor que echó a andar el motor grande," *Granma,* July 25, 2000; Mencia, *El grito del Moncada,* 395; Autores varios, *Mártires del Moncada,* 87–93; Raúl Martínez, interview; Mencia, "¡Como mismo subió," 28; Raúl Castro Ruz, "VIII Aniversario del 26 de Julio," *Verde Olivo,* July 16, 1961, 6.

29. Fernando Chenard Piña, Emilio Albentosa Chacón, and Enrique Cámara Pérez abandonaron el PSP to join the Ortodoxo Party. See Mencia, *El grito del Moncada,* 462; Raúl Martínez, interview; Alape, *El Bogotazo,* 583; Betto, *Fidel y la religión,* 157–58; Centro de Estudios, *Moncada: La acción,* 11–13; Lockwood, *Castro's Cuba,* 163; Szulc, *Fidel,* 227, 257; Haydée Santamaría, *Moncada: Memories of the Attack That Launched the Cuban Revolution* (Secaucus, N.J.: Lyle Stuart, 1980), 87–88; Thomas, *Cuba,* 825.

30. Raúl Martínez, interview; Dr. Ricardo Martínez Serrera, personal interview, Miami, Fla., June 10, 2004; "Novias de Junio," *Diario de la Marina,* June 8, 1948, 13; Melissa Lee, "Socialite Whose Love Affair with Castro Produced a Daughter Prefers Not to Linger on Her Past," *Miami Herald,* September 28, 2003; Geyer, *Guerrilla Prince,* 102; Wendy Gimbel, *Havana Dreams: A Story of Cuba* (New York: Alfred A. Knopf, 1998), 48, 52–53, 106–7; Pablo Alvarez de Cañas and Joaquín de Posada, eds., *Libro de Oro de la Sociedad Habanera 1952* (Havana: Editorial Lex, 1951), 255; *Mundo social: Registro social de las familias Habaneras* (Havana: Impresos Pastor, 1954), 71; Merle, *Moncada,* 103.

31. Dr. Ricardo Martínez Serrera stated that among Natalia Clews's lovers were Matanzas representative Antonio de la Guardia, Dr. Julio Esnard, and Dr. Gabriel Casuso. Her brother, Heriberto Clews, was appointed Cuban consul in Kingston, Jamaica, by Fulgencio Batista in

1944. See Martínez Serrera, interview; Gimbel, *Havana Dreams*, 56–58, 70–71, 90–94; *Diario de la Marina*, June 20, 1948, 11.

32. Héctor de Armas, interview; Francisco Pita Rodríguez, "Las armas estaban en las armerías...," *Bohemia*, July 20, 1973, 5; Rojas, "Ochenta pesos de tiros," 38; Raúl Martínez, interview; Iznaga, "La casa de Melba," 6; Autores varios, *Mártires del Moncada*, 91, 259–60; Mencia, "¡Como mismo subió," 28; Conte Agüero, *Los dos rostros*, 37; Mirabal Reyes, *El color de la Victoria*, 39–40, 118; *Granma*, July 25, 1981, 2.

33. Isaac Santos Domínguez, alias "Professor Harriman," was arrested on May 5, 1956, after being implicated in an insurrectional plan headed by Justo Carrillo. Raúl del Mazo stated that after Castro seized power, Harriman was sentenced to twenty years of imprisonment. See del Mazo, interview; Ambassador Beaulac to Secretary of State, Despatch 338, January 15, 1953, *Cuba Internal Affairs*; Héctor de Armas, interview; Moisés Mafut Delgado, personal interview, Miami, Fla., August 7, 1984.

34. Luisa Margarita de la Cotera O'Bourke (October 26, 1898–December 26, 1978), a charity activist whose motto was "lift those who have fallen," passed away in Miami. See Luisa Margarita de la Cotera O'Bourke, *Los miserables de Cuba* (Havana: Imprenta Cuba Intelectual, 1938). See also Dirección Política de las FAR, *Moncada*, 238; Fidel Castro, "Asaltado y destruido el estudio del escultor Fidalgo," *Bohemia*, February 8, 1953; Teresa Andux González, Haydée Laborí Ripoll, and José M. Leyva Mestre, *La Capital en el Moncada* (Havana: Editorial de Ciencias Sociales, 1990), 36; Despatch 1832, May 25, 1953, *Cuba Internal Affairs*; Mencia, "El grito del Moncada," *Bohemia*, July 20, 1984, 82; Autores varios, *Mártires del Moncada*, 344; Szulc, *Fidel*, 238; José Lupiáñez Reinlein, *El Movimiento Estudiantil en Santiago de Cuba 1952-1953* (Havana: Editorial de Ciencias Sociales, 1985), 120; Mirabal Reyes, *El color de la Victoria*, 198.

35. *El Mundo*, July 8, 1952, 8; Llerena, *Unsuspected Revolution*, 49.

36. Llerena, *Unsuspected Revolution*, 49–50; Thomas, *Cuba*, 797; Despatch 1278, February 13, 1953, *Cuba Internal Affairs*.

37. Despatch 1556, April 6, 1953, *Cuba Internal Affairs*; *Diario de la Marina*, April 7 and 11, 1953, 1; *New York Times*, April 7, 1953, 18; Luis Ricardo Alonso, "'Es falso que intentara tomar Columbia el Domingo de Resurrección,' afirma García Bárcena," *Bohemia*, April 26, 1953, 52; Mencia, "El grito del Moncada," *Bohemia*, July 20, 1984, 82; Llerena, *Unsuspected Revolution*, 49.

38. Raúl Martínez, interview; Mencia, *El grito del Moncada*, 340–41.

39. "Relato del comandante Miret," 7; Víctor Pérez-Galdós and Carmen Alfonso, "Ernesto Tizol y Oscar Alcalde: Dos testimonios del Moncada," *Bohemia*, July 8, 1983, 88; Szulc, *Fidel*, 244; Merle, *Moncada*, 104; Fulvio Fuentes, "El Liceo de Prado 109," *Bohemia*, July 6, 1973, 44; Dirección Política de las FAR, *Moncada*, 142; Mencia, *El grito del Moncada*, 385.

40. Merle, *Moncada*, 105; Marta Rojas, "El asalto al Moncada," *Bohemia*, February 1, 1959, 28; José A. Tabares del Real, *Guiteras* (Havana: Instituto Cubano del Libro, 1973), 202–6, 267.

41. Jaime Sarusky, "La célula de Santiago," *Bohemia*, July 20, 1973, 35, 42, 44; Autores varios, *Mártires del Moncada*, 138–42; "Renato Guitart," *Cuba Internacional*, July 1967; Almeida Bosque, *La aurora de los héroes*, 163; Casero, interview; Manuel Bartolomé, personal interview, Miami, Fla., August 16, 1993.

42. Members of Acción Libertadora included Rafael Iglesias, Angel del Cerro, Andrés Suárez Ameneiro, René Díaz de Villegas, Calixto Sánchez White, Alvaro Barba, Danilo Baeza,

Marcelo Salado, and Israel Rodríguez. The group disintegrated in June 1954 after its leader Justo Carrillo Hernández went into exile. Until then, they had detonated a few dozen bombings, mostly in Oriente Province. The majority of its armed militants in Oriente, led by Frank País, then joined Fidel Castro's 26 of July Movement and participated in the November 30, 1956, uprising in Santiago de Cuba. See Justo Carrillo, *A Cuba le tocó perder* (Miami: Ediciones Universal, 1993), 44–45; del Mazo, interview; Lupiáñez Reinlein, *El Movimiento Estudiantil*, 73–77; Thomas, *Cuba*, 802, 862; "La célula de Santiago," 35; Mencia, *El grito del Moncada*, 217-27.

43. "La célula de Santiago," 35, 37, 38, 40; Lupiáñez Reinlein, *El Movimiento Estudiantil*, 160-61; del Mazo, interview; Autores varios, *Mártires del Moncada*, 142; Merle, *Moncada*, 116.

44. Robert Quirk erred in writing that Melba Hernández "persuaded an army sergeant" to supply the uniforms (Quirk, *Fidel Castro*, 51). See Sara Más, "Mi vida cambió," *Granma*, July 18, 2003; Merle, *Moncada*, 109–12; Mencia, *El grito del Moncada*, 426; Travieso, *Un nuevo día*, 27, 30–31, 51, 59–61; Florentino Fernández, "Los uniformes de los asaltantes al Moncada," *Verde Olivo*, July 26, 1964, 36–37; Pérez-Galdos, "Antecedentes y preparativos," 88; Pedro Trigo, "Antes del ataque," *Verde Olivo*, July 26, 1964, 11; Jaime Costa Chávez, personal interview, Miami, Fla., August 7, 1984; Sánchez, "Las finanzas del movimiento," 4; "Lo que siguió el asalto del cuartel," C8; Iznaga, "La casa de Melba," 7; Rojas, *La Generación del Centenario*, 97; Pita Rodríguez, "Las armas estaban en las armerías," 6; Autores varios, *Mártires del Moncada*, 281.

45. Juana Castro stated that after Fidel Castro was released from prison in May 1955, he did not visit his father, who passed away seventeen months later. Lina Ruz died on August 6, 1963. See Szulc, *Fidel*, 114–15, 241, 245; Pérez Galdós and Alfonso, "Ernesto Tizol y Oscar Alcalde," 85; Pita Rodríguez, "Las armas estaban en las armerías," 6; Raúl Martínez, interview; Quirk, *Fidel Castro*, 47; Mencia, *El grito del Moncada*, 410; Fernández, *Castro's Daughter*, 65; Lee, "Socialite."

46. *Diario de la Marina*, July 16, 1953, 20; Merle, *Moncada*, 106; Rojas, *La Generación del Centenario*, 48.

47. Rojas, *La Generación del Centenario*, 99; Raúl Martínez, interview.

48. Raúl Martínez, interview; Elio Rosete, telephone interview, Miami, Fla., February 28, 1988; Castro García, interview.

49. Pérez-Galdós and Alfonso, "Ernesto Tizol y Oscar Alcalde," 84, 88; Centro de Estudios, *Moncada: La acción*, 86; "La célula de Santiago," 40; Mencia, *El grito del Moncada*, 398–99; "Versión taquigráfica del programa 'Siempre es 26,'" 4; Raúl Martínez, interview; "La granjita Siboney: El cuartel general de los asaltantes," *Bohemia*, July 20, 1973, 49.

50. "La granjita Siboney," 50–51.

51. Rafael García-Bárcena Gómez (June 7, 1907–June 13, 1961) on January 20, 1959, was appointed as press secretary of the state ministry of the revolutionary government and ambassador extraordinary. He resigned on December 26, 1960, as ambassador to Brazil, six months before passing away in Havana. See *New York Times*, May 22, 1953, 5; Mencia, *El grito del Moncada*, 343, 358; Mirabal Reyes, *El color de la Victoria*, 197; Díaz-Francisco, interview.

52. The Guatemalan Communists accompanying Raúl Castro were Bernardo Lemus Mendoza and Ricardo Ramírez León. See Jorge García Montes and Antonio Alonso Avila, *Historia del Partido Comunista de Cuba* (Miami: Ediciones Universal, 1970), 446; Merle, *Moncada*, 120–21; Szulc, *Fidel*, 249; Thomas, *Cuba*, 826; *Carib*, June 1959, 49–50; Mencia, *El grito del Moncada*, 489; Raúl Castro, "Fragmentos de un diario escrito en el presidio," *Bohemia*,

July 26, 1963, 66; "Continua la labor de Mons. Pérez Serantes para una pacificación," *Diario de la Marina,* July 31, 1953, 23; Rojas, *La Generación del Centenario,* 285.

53. The Montreal Pact Ortodoxo faction participants were Emilio Ochoa Ochoa, José Pardo Llada, José Manuel Gutiérrez Planes, Isidro Figueroa, Raúl de Jan, and Javier Lescano. The Auténtico signatories were Carlos Prío, Guillermo Alonso Pujol, Manuel Antonio de Varona Loredo, Eduardo Suárez Rivas, Juan A. Rubio Padilla, Carlos Hevia, Tony Santiago Ruiz, Aracelio Azcuy, Luis Gustavo Fernández, and Rafael Izquierdo. See Emilio Ochoa, interview; Suárez Rivas, interview; Manuel Antonio de Varona Loredo, telephone interview, Miami, Fla., December 14, 1991; Despatch 1880, June 1, 1953, *Cuba Internal Affairs; El Mundo,* June 3, 1953, 1; *El Crisol,* June 3, 1953, 1; *Bohemia,* June 7, 1953, 69, 74–77; *El Mundo,* June 5 and 19, 1953, 7; Tony de la Hoza, "Ni Batista ni Prio constituyen una solución nacional (entrevista con Roberto Agramonte)," *Bohemia,* June 14, 1953, 82, 94; Thomas, *Cuba,* 796, 802.

54. Ariel Matos had joined the army in Camp Columbia in 1951 when his father, Juan Matos Rodríguez, and uncles Urbano and Anselmo were officers and another uncle, Faustino, was a sergeant at Moncada. Private Matos was not promoted after the March 10 coup and was soon transferred to Moncada. He indicated that his fellow conspirators were Pvts. Lenin Samá, Pedro Pérez Santana, and Idilo Leyva. See Emilio Ochoa, interview; Pvt. Ariel Matos Romero, personal interview, Miami, Fla., August 1, 2004.

55. "Priístas y Ortodoxos Acuerdan en Montreal la Insurrección," *Tiempo,* June 2, 1953, 1; Cpl. Néstor Reyes Martín, interview, West New York, N.J., June 17, 1989; "Una nueva tormenta: Una invasión armada en el Caribe," *Visión* (New York), June 26, 1953, 8 (although dated June 26, this *Visión* issue was distributed earlier on the 17th); *El Mundo,* July 7, 1953, 1; Varona, interview.

56. "Una nueva tormenta," 8; "Los conspiradores de Montreal compraron 8 aviones y millares de armas," *Alerta,* June 18, 1953, 1; Despatch 1901, June 3, 1953, *Cuba Internal Affairs;* Despatch 2019, June 24, 1953, *Cuba Internal Affairs.*

57. "La 'invasión del país XXVI': Cuba," *Bohemia,* July 5, 1953, 62–88.

58. "Nueva amenaza de invasión," *Alerta,* July 6, 1953, 1; Despatch 78, July 10, 1953, *Cuba Internal Affairs;* Despatch 98, July 14, 1953, *Cuba Internal Affairs.*

59. Santiago Cardosa Arias, "Ya nos vamos para la fiesta, señora," *Granma,* July 25, 1967, 4; "La granjita Siboney," 53–54; Susana Lee, "A 50 años del Moncada: Sus protagonistas en los recuerdos de Melba," *Granma,* July 26, 2003; Alfredo Reyes Trejo, "Del Moncada a las montañas," *Verde Olivo,* July 23, 1967, 42; "La célula de Santiago," 39; Cesar A. Marín, "A 35 años del Moncada," *El Nuevo Herald,* July 26, 1988, 7; Rubén Castillo Ramos, "En el Cuartel de Bayamo se escribió otra página heróica," *Bohemia,* July 23, 1961, 62; Joaquín Oramas, "Aquel 26 de julio en Bayamo, un testimonio vivo de nuestra historia," *Granma,* July 20, 1979, 2; Rubén Castillo Ramos, *Las avanzadas del cauto: El ataque al Cuartel de Bayamo* (Santiago de Cuba: Editorial Oriente, 1981), 18–19; Raúl Martínez, interview; Pérez-Puelles, interview; "Reportan absoluta normalidad en la capital de Oriente," *Diario de la Marina,* July 29, 1953, 24.

60. Raúl Martínez, interview; Pérez-Puelles, interview.

61. Autores varios, *Mártires del Moncada,* 72; "La acción del Palacio de Justicia," 12, 62; Enrique Canto Bory, *Mi vida* (Hato Rey, P.R.: Ramallo Bros. Printing, 1993), 174; Mencia, *El grito del Moncada,* 446; "La célula de Santiago," 42.

62. "La célula de Santiago," 41–42; Santiago Cardosa Arias, "26 de Julio de 1953: Ultima cena antes del asalto," *Granma,* July 20, 1994.

63. Autores varios, *Mártires del Moncada*, 81, 115, 189, 259; *Juventud Rebelde*, July 22, 1979, 2; *Havana Post*, August 6, 1953, 1; Raúl Martínez, interview; Duarte, *Historiología Cubana*, 3:290; Bonachea and Valdés, *Revolutionary Struggle*, 92n260; Rojas, "Ochenta pesos de tiros," 36–37; Villar, "El asalto al Moncada," 8; Pérez-Galdos and Alfonso, "Ernesto Tizol y Oscar Alcalde," 88; Carlos M. Piñeiro del Cueto, personal interview, Guaynabo, P.R., February 13, 1986.

64. The peso was equal in value to the dollar. "Forgery of Checks to Pay for Santiago Revolt Is Discovered," *Havana Post*, August 4, 1953, 1; "Defraudan a una compañía los asaltantes del Moncada," *Alerta*, August 5, 1953, 24; Rojas, "Ochenta pesos de tiros," 36, 38; Mencia, *El grito del Moncada*, 415; *El Mundo*, September 22, 1953, 8; Raúl Castro Ruz, "VIII Aniversario del 26 de Julio," 6; Raúl Martínez, interview; Rojas, "Como se sufragaron los gastos," 36.

65. Manuel Ugalde Carrillo (June 13, 1919–March 21, 1980) passed away in Los Angeles, Calif. See *Diario de la Marina*, July 28, 1953, 35; U.S. Department of State, *Foreign Relations of the United States 1952–1954*, 898.

66. Lt. Armando Acosta Sánchez, the son and grandson of Cuban army veterans, joined the service on January 7, 1941. He held the rank of major when he left Cuba on January 1, 1959, in the same airplane as Fulgencio Batista. See Lt. Armando Acosta Sánchez, personal interview, Los Angeles, Calif., June 26, 1989.

67. Bourne mistakenly stated that Haydée accompanied her brother on the trip "posing as husband and wife" (Bourne, *Fidel*, 73). Melba claimed in 2003 that the flower box she carried contained four rifles instead of a shotgun. See Lee, "A 50 años del Moncada"; "La célula de Santiago," 46; Mencia, *El grito del Moncada*, 518–19; Sánchez, "Las finanzas del movimiento," 4; "Las heroinas del Moncada: Relato de Haydee Santamaria," *Bohemia*, July 20, 1962, 46; Iznaga, "La casa de Melba," 10; Mencia, "¡Como mismo subió," 28; Melba Hernández, "Siempre supimos que el asalto," 32.

68. *Diario de la Marina*, July 29, 1953, 1; Marta Rojas, *La Generación del Centenario en el juicio del Moncada* (Havana: Editorial de Ciencias Sociales, 1979), 384; "La célula de Santiago," 42, 46; Melba Hernández, "Siempre supimos que el asalto," 32; Lee, "A 50 años del Moncada"; Merle, *Moncada*, 123; Armando Acosta, interview; "Jefes de regimientos de las provincias," *Bohemia*, April 20, 1952, 48; Col. Alberto R. del Río Chaviano, telephone interview, Dallas, Tex., November 26, 1974.

Chapter 3—"On Sunday, Cuba will be in flames"

1. Mafut Delgado, interview.

2. Ibid.; Almeida Bosque, *La aurora de los héroes*, 149; *Granma*, December 5, 1974, 2.

3. The grocery store owner had paid a traveling salesman with the worthless check signed by Fidel Castro. The day after the Moncada attack he located the person, recovered the check, and gave it to Mafut's wife, who burned it. The dime-store owner kept the smaller-amount check and later gave it back to Mafut as a memento. See Mafut Delgado, interview; Mencia, *El grito del Moncada*, 507–8; *Granma*, February 1, 1987, 4.

4. Mafut Delgado, interview.

5. Dirección Política de las FAR, *Moncada*, 207–8; Travieso, *Un nuevo día*, 66–67; "Versión taquigráfica del programa 'Siempre es 26,'" *Granma*, June 29, 1973, 3; Vicente Cubillas, "Los artemiseños en el 'Moncada,'" *Revolución*, July 22, 1963, 7; Merle, *Moncada*, 124; Carlos Franqui, *The Twelve* (New York: Lyle Stuart, 1968), 27.

6. The five rental cars were acquired by Ernesto Tizol, Raúl Martínez Ararás, and Héctor de Armas. Oscar Quintela was accompanied to Oriente by Argelio Guzmán, José L. López Díaz, Julio Trigo López, and René Bedia Morales. See Merle, *Moncada*, 132, 141; "El viaje de Fidel a Santiago aquel histórico julio de 1953," *Granma*, July 24, 1977, 4; Cpl. Norberto Batista Seguí, personal interview, Bronx, N.Y., August 22, 1988; Travieso, *Un nuevo día*, 18, 73–74; Mencia, *El grito del Moncada*, 505; "La acción del Palacio de Justicia," *Verde Olivo*, July 26, 1964, 12; Raúl Martínez, interview; Héctor de Armas, interview.

7. Juan Ameijeiras Delgado was accompanied by the peasant Gerardo A. "El Chino" Alvarez Alvarez, the busboy Pablo Cartas Rodríguez, bookstore messenger Roberto Mederos Rodríguez, the bartender Félix Rivero Vasallo, and parking-lot attendant Osvaldo Socarrás Martínez. All would perish that weekend. "Chucho" Montané Oropesa went with Gabriel Gil Alfonso, the carpenter Manuel Saíz Sánchez, brothers José and Horacio Matheu Orihuela, and Ernesto González Campos. See Mencia, *El grito del Moncada*, 495; Travieso, *Un nuevo día*, 69, 80, 89, 100–101, 103; "Versión taquigráfica del programa 'Siempre es 26,'" 3; Merle, *Moncada*, 128.

8. Reinaldo Boris Luis left Havana with Manuel Suardíaz, Orbeín Hernández, Ulises Sarmiento Vargas, and Vicente Chávez Fernández. Fernando Chenard went to Santiago de Cuba with Belén High School janitors Manuel and Virginio Gómez Reyes, amateur boxer Giraldo Córdova Cardín, and the barber Eduardo Montano Benítez, who would be the only survivor of the group. See Suardíaz, interview; Chanes, interview; Montano, interview; Mencia, *El grito del Moncada*, 493, 498.

9. Pedro Marrero was accompanied by Generoso R. Llanes Machado, Orlando Galán Betancourt, and two Artemisans. The novelist Robert Merle (August 28, 1908–March 28, 2004) erroneously places Armelio Ferrá [sic] in the car with Gildo Fleitas, instead of Raúl Gómez García. See Merle, *Moncada*, 130; Mencia, *El grito del Moncada*, 493–94, 500–502, 504; Autores varios, *Mártires del Moncada*, 160; Rosendo Gutiérrez, "Mi primer viaje a Santiago (entrevista con Carlos González)," *Verde Olivo*, July 24, 1966, 20; Travieso, *Un nuevo día*, 21–22, 53, 78, 86, 98; "Versión taquigráfica del programa 'Siempre es 26,'" 3; "26 de Julio," *Verde Olivo*, July 26, 1970.

10. Twenty years later, "Pepe" Ponce changed his story and claimed that they went to the home of Melba Hernández to pick up their passage. In 1999 Ponce gave yet another version, saying that Pepe Suárez provided their bus tickets. See Almeida Bosque, *La aurora de los héroes*, 163; "La acción del Palacio de Justicia," 62; José Ponce Díaz, "Recuerdos del ataque," *Verde Olivo*, July 28, 1963, 17; Ana María Radaelli, "José Ponce Díaz," *Cuba Internacional*, July 1983, 63; Gimbel, *Havana Dreams*, 110–11.

11. *Mártires del Moncada* credited Raúl Gómez García as the sole author of the "Manifesto to the Nation." In 2003 Marta Rojas admitted that Fidel Castro told her in January 1959: "That document reflected all of our ideas, but the one who wrote it was Raúl Gómez García." See Autores varios, *Mártires del Moncada*, 207; *Granma*, July 26, 2003.

12. The sixteen train passengers included six Nueva Paz peasants and Cayo Hueso neighborhood residents: Humberto Valdés Casañas; Isidro Peñalver O'Reilly; Armando Valle López, a twenty-three-year-old furniture maker; José J. Madera Fernández, a seventeen-year-old factory worker; Andrés Valdés Fuentes, a twenty-four-year-old baker with a fifth-grade education; and thirty-year-old Raúl R. de Aguiar Fernández, substituting for their cell leader Angel Pla Picette, a thirty-year-old ice deliveryman, who stayed behind with an asthma attack.

The Artemisa group departing with Léster Rodríguez were José Ponce, Julio Díaz, Rosendo Menéndez, Roberto "Bolo" Galán Betancourt, Fidel and José A. Labrador, Ramiro Valdés, and Ramón Callao Díaz. See Raúl Castro, "Fragmentos de un diario escrito en el presidio," *Bohemia*, July 26, 1963, 67; Autores varios, *Mártires del Moncada*, 120, 148, 202, 298; Andux et al., *La Capital en el Moncada*, 45; Mencia, *El grito del Moncada*, 400, 491–94; Chanes, interview; "Cuatro muchachos del Barrio de Cayo Hueso," *Bohemia*, July 31, 1960, 98–100; "Continua la labor de Mons. Pérez Serantes para una pacificación," *Diario de la Marina*, July 31, 1953, 23.

13. "Fidel Labrador habla de los días del Moncada," *Bohemia*, July 25, 1986, 6; Cubillas, "Los artemiseños en el 'Moncada,'" 7; Lazo, *Recuerdos*, 34; Merle, *Moncada*, 128, 130; Mencia, *El grito del Moncada*, 493; Bustillo, interview; Autores varios, *Mártires del Moncada*, 291; "Uno de los caídos en el Moncada," *Bohemia*, August 28, 1960, 99; "Alfredo Corcho Cinta: presencia campesina en el Moncada," *Granma*, June 26, 1973, 2.

14. Florentino Fernández, "Los uniformes de los asaltantes al Moncada," *Verde Olivo*, July 26, 1964, 38; Francisco Pita Rodríguez, "Las armas estaban en las armerías...," *Bohemia*, July 20, 1973, 6; Travieso, *Un nuevo día*, 18, 61, 99–100; Autores varios, *Mártires del Moncada*, 407–8; Merle, *Moncada*, 134, 136–37; Mencia, *El grito del Moncada*, 496, 497.

15. Agustín Díaz Cartaya's nickname of "Thompson" was due to his close resemblance to Major Leagues baseball player Hank Thompson, an African American married to a Cuban woman. Díaz Cartaya was raised in an orphanage until age eleven, when he began working for his upkeep. See Raúl Martínez, interview; "Pablo Agüero Guedes," *Granma*, July 10, 1973, 2; Rosete, interview.

16. The Marianao cell members accompanying Mario Martínez Ararás to Bayamo were Armando Arencibia Martínez, Adalberto Ruanes Alvarez, Calixto García Martínez, and "Ñico" López. During the trip, Ñico strummed his guitar and sang while Ruanes played the harmonica. The dentist Pedro Aguilera went with his assistant Oscar "Nito" Ortega Lora, Orestes Abad, unemployed cobbler Enrique Cámara Pérez, construction worker Lázaro Hernández Arroyo, and flower vendors Angel Guerra Díaz and José Testa Zaragoza. Ibrahím Sosa González was later implicated in the conspiracy and sought asylum in the Costa Rican Embassy with Calixto García Martínez and Luis Hernández Alvarez. See Dirección Política de las FAR, *Moncada*, 232, 241, 249, 253; Marta Matamoros, "El asalto al Cuartel de Bayamo," *Revista de Granma*, July 6, 1967, 5; Raúl Martínez, interview; Merle, *Moncada*, 139; Pita Rodríguez, "Las armas estaban en las armerías," 7; Mencia, *El grito del Moncada*, 509.

17. Mafut Delgado, interview.

18. Díaz-Francisco, interview; Arcos, interview; Centro de Estudios, *Moncada: La acción*, 77; Mencia, *El grito del Moncada*, 499.

19. Héctor de Armas drove to Santiago de Cuba with Humberto Valdés, Isidro Peñalver, and the brothers Alejandro and Antonio Ferrás Pellicer. The third brother, Armelio, departed with another group from Abel's apartment. See Héctor de Armas, interview; Orfilio Peláez, "Solo la casualidad impidió la toma del Moncada," *Granma*, July 22, 2003.

20. Robert Merle erroneously wrote that Reinaldo Benítez's mother lived in Bayamo instead of Camagüey. See Merle, *Moncada*, 131–32, 140; Cuervo and Llenín, *Moncada*, 32; Travieso, *Un nuevo día*, 88, 102; Mencia, *El grito del Moncada*, 505–6.

21. Mario Dalmau de la Cruz drove to Santiago de Cuba with Pepe Suárez, Severino Rosell, Gregorio Careaga Medina, and Ricardo Santana Martínez. The latter omitted Mario Dalmau

from his 1984 account, erroneously claiming that Pepe Suárez drove the car. See Travieso, *Un nuevo día*, 77; Mencia, *El grito del Moncada*, 500, 508; "Relato del combatiente del Moncada Pepe Suarez," *Verde Olivo*, July 29, 1962, 83; Merle, *Moncada*, 140; "El viaje de Fidel," 4.

22. Szulc, *Fidel*, 254, omitted Nito Ortega and Manuel Lorenzo as Fidel Castro's travel companions. See Merle, *Moncada*, 140; "El viaje de Fidel," 4; Dirección Política de las FAR, *Moncada*, 241; Autores varios, *Mártires del Moncada*, 35, 36; Mencia, *El grito del Moncada*, 495, 508; *Granma*, July 6, 1983, 2.

23. "El viaje de Fidel," 4; Merle, *Moncada*, 142–43; Marta Rojas, "El asalto al Moncada," *Bohemia*, February 1, 1959, 30; Mencia, *El grito del Moncada*, 509–10.

24. *Cuba en la mano: Enciclopedia popular ilustrada* (Havana: Imprenta Ucar, Garcia y Cia., 1940), 183–87; Casero, interview; Rodríguez Morejón, *Fidel Castro*, 61; Canto, *Mi vida*, 161; "Unos 70 muertos es el trágico balance del golpe contra los cuarteles de Santiago y Bayamo," *Diario de la Marina*, July 28, 1953, 25.

25. Pedro Miret arrived with Guanajay peasants Jaime "El Catalán" Costa Chávez, Abelardo García Ylls, Angel M. Sánchez Pérez, José R. Martínez Alvarez, Alfredo Corcho Cinta, and José F. Costa Velázquez. See Merle, *Moncada*, 145–46; Instituto Cubano del Libro, *Moncada: Edición homenaje al Vigésimo Aniversario del 26 de julio de 1953* (Havana: Editorial de Ciencias Sociales, 1973), 12; Costa, interview; "La célula de Santiago," 39; Mencia, *El grito del Moncada*, 515, 522; Santiago Cardosa Arias, "Ultima cena antes del asalto," *Granma*, July 20, 1994; "La acción del Palacio de Justicia," 62–63; Autores varios, *Mártires del Moncada*, 291; Chanes, interview; Raúl Castro, "Fragmentos de un diario," 68; Josefina Ortega, "El más joven de los moncadistas," *Juventud Rebelde*, July 24, 1988, S6; Javier Rodríguez, "Habla el comandante Jesus Montane Oropesa," *Bohemia*, July 26, 1963, 63; Travieso, *Un nuevo día*, 103; Ponce, "Recuerdos del ataque," 17; Suardíaz, interview; "Versión taquigráfica del programa 'Siempre es 26,'" 3.

26. Lt. Col. Angel González Alfonso, personal interview, Miami, Fla., April 18, 1975; Instituto Cubano del Libro, *Moncada*, 103.

27. Pvt. José Alberto Ferrá Mulet, personal interview, Orlando, Fla., June 13, 2004; Pvt. Rafael Morales Gros, personal interview, Queens, N.Y., September 12, 1974; Cpl. Eugenio Alcolea Ramírez, personal interview, Elizabeth, N.J., August 23, 1988.

28. Bustillo, interview; Lazo, *Recuerdos*, 36–37; "La célula de Santiago," 46–47; Mafut Delgado, interview; Almeida Bosque, *La aurora de los héroes*, 149; Osvaldo Ortega N., "Entrevista con Oscar Alcalde: Después del asalto," *Verde Olivo*, July 26, 1964, 33, 40; "La acción del Palacio de Justicia," 63; Chanes, interview.

29. Radaelli, "José Ponce Díaz," 63; "Fidel Labrador habla," 6; "La célula de Santiago," 45; Santiago Cardosa Arias, "Los combatientes hospedados en el 'Rex,'" *Granma*, July 26, 1967, 3; Díaz-Francisco, interview; Arcos, interview; Centro de Estudios, *Moncada: La acción*, 77; Montano, interview; Merle, *Moncada*, 147, 150; Travieso, *Un nuevo día*, 108; Mencia, *El grito del Moncada*, 514.

30. Mencia, *El grito del Moncada*, 516–18; Lazo, *Recuerdos*, 37; Mafut Delgado, interview; Rojas, *La Generación del Centenario*, 199; Rojas, *El que debe vivir*, 48; Fernández, "Los uniformes de los asaltantes," 38; Travieso, *Un nuevo día*, 109–10; "¿Qué ocurrió con Julio Trigo la noche del 25 de julio?," *Bohemia*, July 20, 1973, 43; Autores varios, *Mártires del Moncada*, 227.

31. Angel González, interview; Maj. Florentino E. Rosell Leyva, telephone interview, Hialeah, Fla., August 15, 2005; "Versión taquigráfica del programa 'Siempre es 26,'" 4; Canto, *Mi vida*, 161.

32. Ramón Callao Díaz returned to Havana, where he was arrested by the SIM a few days later and confessed his role. See Díaz-Francisco, interview; Almeida Bosque, *La aurora de los héroes,* 163; Montano, interview; "La célula de Santiago," 40; "La acción del Palacio de Justicia," 63; Lazo, *Recuerdos,* 38; Mencia, *El grito del Moncada,* 521–22; Mafut Delgado, interview; Merle, *Moncada,* 155.

33. The Fourth of September flag had five equal vertical stripes—blue, white, red, yellow, and green—representing all the branches of the armed forces and police. A 1934 presidential decree authorized the banner to be displayed alongside the national flag in all military and public buildings, and the Fourth of September hymn was always to be played immediately after the national hymn. President Grau abolished the decree in 1944, but it was reinstated by Batista in 1952. Mencia, *El grito del Moncada,* 513–15; Melba Hernández, "Setenta y dos horas," *Granma,* July 26, 1998; Franqui, *Diary,* 57; "El viaje de Fidel," 5; Merle, *Moncada,* 143, 158; Suardíaz, interview; Lazo, *Recuerdos,* 39; "La célula de Santiago," 47; "La acción del Palacio de Justicia," 63; Travieso, *Un nuevo día,* 115.

34. Rojas, *La Generación del Centenario,* 34; Instituto Cubano del Libro, *Moncada,* 214; Rodríguez Morejón, *Fidel Castro,* 76; Raúl Castro Ruz, "VIII Aniversario del 26 de Julio," *Verde Olivo,* July 16, 1961, 1; del Mazo, interview; Mencia, *El grito del Moncada,* 221; Travieso, *Un nuevo día,* 111.

35. Granados, interview; Montano, interview; Conte Agüero, interview; Melba Hernández, "Setenta y dos horas"; "Fidel Labrador habla," 6; Merle, *Moncada,* 159–60; Bourne, *Fidel,* 77; Luis Conte Agüero, *Fidel Castro—psiquiatría y política* (Mexico City: Editorial Jus, 1968), 140; Travieso, *Un nuevo día,* 102, 111, 113, 115; Israel Tápanes, "26 de julio," *Verde Olivo,* July 26, 1970, 27; Pedro Padilla, "Realizando tareas agrícolas honraremos este año a nuestros hermanos caídos en el Moncada," *Juventud Rebelde,* July 21, 1969, 2; Gutiérrez, "Mi primer viaje a Santiago," 22.

36. Magistrate Adolfo Nieto Piñeiro-Osorio, personal interview, Falls Church, Va., May 10, 1975; Rojas, "El asalto al Moncada," 166; Granados, interview; Chanes, interview; Montano, interview; Costa, interview; Szulc, *Fidel,* 255; Travieso, *Un nuevo día,* 115, 131.

37. Arcos, interview; "Relato del combatiente del Moncada Pepe Suárez," 84; Suardíaz, interview; Cubillas, "Los artemiseños en el 'Moncada,'" 7; Rojas, *La Generación del Centenario,* 212; Fernández, "Los uniformes de los asaltantes," 38; Chanes, interview; Autores varios, *Mártires del Moncada,* 110; Montano, interview; Díaz-Francisco, interview; Rodríguez Morejón, *Fidel Castro,* 76; Travieso, *Un nuevo día,* 114, 116, 117; Merle, *Moncada,* 166.

38. Travieso, *Un nuevo día,* 113–14; "El viaje de Fidel," 5; Merle, *Moncada,* 170–71.

39. "La acción del Palacio de Justicia," 63; Mencia, *El grito del Moncada,* 539; Bourne, *Fidel,* 79; Cubillas, "Los artemiseños en el 'Moncada,'" 7; Merle, *Moncada,* 166; Granados, interview; Lazo, *Recuerdos,* 44; Centro de Estudios, *Moncada: La acción,* 322.

40. Gutiérrez, "Mi primer viaje a Santiago," 20; Díaz-Francisco, interview; "El viaje de Fidel," 5.

41. Ediciones Políticas, *Haydée habla del Moncada,* 116; "Continua la labor," 23; Luis Conte Agüero, *Cartas del Presidio* (Havana: Editorial Lex, 1959), 21; Cubillas, "Los Artemiseños en el Moncada,'" 7; Granados, interview; Montano, interview; Merle, *Moncada,* 162; "El viaje de Fidel," 5; Radaelli, "José Ponce Díaz," 63; Ortega, "El más joven de los Moncadistas," S6; Franqui, *Diary,* 57; Bustillo, interview; Arcos, interview; Suardíaz, interview.

42. In 2003 Melba Hernández claimed for the first time that Dr. Muñoz changed out of his army uniform into his physician's outfit after Fidel Castro asked him to serve as a doctor and not as a combatant. See Susana Lee, "A 50 años del Moncada: Sus protagonistas en los recuerdos de Melba," *Granma*, July 26, 2003; Suardíaz, interview; Merle, *Moncada*, 157; Fidel Castro, *History Will Absolve Me* (London: Jonathan Cape, 1968), 32; Montano, interview; Díaz-Francisco, interview; Héctor de Armas, interview; Centro de Estudios, *Moncada: La acción*, 144; Algarra, interview.

43. The Almendares cell was composed of Víctor Escalona Benítez, Gilberto Barón Martínez, Félix Córdoba Alonso, Orlando Cortés Gallardo, Ramón Montes Cuba, and Eduardo Rodríguez Alemán. See Ediciones Políticas, *Haydée habla del Moncada*, 117; Rojas, *La Generación del Centenario*, 168; Chanes, interview; Bustillo, interview; Travieso, *Un nuevo día*, 115; Merle, *Moncada*, 168; Díaz-Francisco, interview; Arcos, interview.

44. Bustillo, interview; Suardíaz, interview; Travieso, *Un nuevo día*, 119.

45. Raúl Castro is erroneously identified as the leader of the Palace of Justice squad in Dubois, *Fidel Castro*, 32; Taber, *M-26*, 36, 40; Thomas, *Cuba*, 836; Geyer, *Guerrilla Prince*, 119; and Quirk, *Fidel Castro*, 53. See "La acción del Palacio de Justicia," 63; "Versión taquigráfica del programa 'Siempre es 26,'" 4; Melba Hernández, "Setenta y dos horas"; Lee, "A 50 años del Moncada"; Díaz-Francisco, interview; Cuervo and Llenín, *Moncada*, 64; Granados, interview.

46. Some rebel accounts claimed that Pepe Ponce was driving a vehicle. In 1999 he stated having been a passenger in the third car, which is incorrect. In 1959 Dubois erroneously wrote in *Fidel Castro*, 33, that the caravan had twenty-six vehicles. The mistake was repeated in Thomas, *Cuba*, 836; Bourne, *Fidel*, 81; and Geyer, *Guerrilla Prince*, 117. See Almeida Bosque, *La aurora de los héroes*, 163; Cuervo and Llenín, *Moncada*, 45, 91; "La acción del Palacio de Justicia," 12; Autores varios, *Mártires del Moncada*, 144, 185, 283, 346; Chanes, interview; Merle, *Moncada*, 172, 182; Mario Mencia, "El grito del Moncada," *Bohemia*, July 27, 1984, 86.

47. Mencia, *El grito del Moncada*, 542; Ortega N., "Entrevista con Oscar Alcalde," 33; Merle, *Moncada*, 178; "Fidel Castro, Rebel Leader, Surrenders," *Havana Post*, August 2, 1953, 9; Suardíaz, interview; Travieso, *Un nuevo día*, 128; Díaz-Francisco, interview; Cuervo and Llenín, *Moncada*, 45.

48. Víctor Pérez-Galdós, "Antecedentes y preparativos de la acción del Moncada," *Bohemia*, June 10, 1983, 88; "La acción del Palacio de Justicia," 63; Arcos, interview.

49. Nydia Sarabia, *Moncada: Biografía de un cuartel* (Havana: Editorial de Ciencias Sociales, 1984), 52–53; Travieso, *Un nuevo día*, 120–21; Centro de Estudios, *Moncada: La acción*, 39, 370.

50. Thomas, *Cuba*, 828; and Geyer, *Guerrilla Prince*, 114, erroneously have one thousand men in the barracks. Maj. Rafael Morales Alvarez correctly estimated "some 400." See Ernesto González Bermejo and Norberto Fuentes, "La otra cara del Moncada," *Cuba*, July 1968, 11; Instituto Cubano del Libro, *Moncada*, 103; "El asalto al Cuartel Moncada," *Granma*, July 20, 1973, 3; Angel González, interview.

Chapter 4—"Shoot at those wearing tennis shoes"

1. Teodulio "Lulo" Mitchell had provided the novelist Robert Merle and a *Granma* reporter with extensive and minute details of events leading to and after the Moncada attack but nothing about the actual combat. He was apparently among those led astray. See "El viaje de Fidel a Santiago aquel histórico julio de 1953," *Granma*, July 24, 1977, 4–5; Rojas, *La*

cueva del muerto, 26; Betto, *Fidel y la religión,* 177; Conte Agüero, *Los dos rostros,* 46; Carmen Villar, "El asalto al Moncada visto por uno de los combatientes: Oscar Alcalde," *Juventud Rebelde,* July 21, 1966, 8; Víctor Pérez-Galdós, "Antecedentes y preparativos de la acción del Moncada," *Bohemia,* June 10, 1983, 88; Víctor Pérez-Galdós and Carmen Alfonso, "Ernesto Tizol y Oscar Alcalde: Dos testimonios del Moncada," *Bohemia,* July 8, 1983, 89; Florentino Fernández, "Los uniformes de los asaltantes al Moncada," *Verde Olivo,* July 26, 1964, 38; Rojas, *El que debe vivir,* 50; Franqui, *Diary,* 59; Santamaría, *Moncada,* 46.

2. Pérez-Galdós and Alfonso, "Ernesto Tizol y Oscar Alcalde," 84; Raúl Martínez, interview; Díaz-Francisco, interview.

3. Fidel Castro was accompanied to the Moncada in his Buick by Reinaldo Benítez and Pedro Miret in the front seat, while Gustavo Arcos, Abelardo Crespo, Israel Tápanes, and Carlos González occupied the back seat. Bourne, *Fidel,* 82, mistakenly adds a lieutenant and a jeep to the roving patrol. See Montano, interview; "Anécdotas del Moncada: El Oldsmobile con la foto de Batista en el parabrisas," *Granma,* June 9, 1983, 2; Mencia, "El grito del Moncada," *Bohemia,* July 20, 1984, 86; Travieso, *Un nuevo día,* 128; Pvt. Alfonso Silva Domínguez, interview, Hialeah, Fla., July 10, 1974; Conrad Allain, "The Sorrow over the Tragedy of Santiago Is Nationwide," *Havana Post,* August 2, 1953, 1; Rafael Morales, interview; Reyes, interview.

4. Cpl. Eugenio Alcolea Ramírez was a former barber from El Cristo who joined the army in 1946. His brother-in-law, José Joaquín Vázquez, was the army orderly killed in the military hospital. When Batista was overthrown, Alcolea made his way to Havana and left the country on June 14, 1960, with his family. He was able to smuggle out his army identification card, which he proudly displayed to friends visiting his barbershop. He passed away on December 13, 1993. See Alcolea, interview.

5. Cpl. Isidro C. Izquierdo Rodríguez was a member of the Rosacruz fraternity, metaphysical star gazers who seek "intimate harmony with the universe." The vanguard rebel vehicle was occupied by Pedro Marrero, José Luis Tasende, and Artemisa natives Carmelo Noa, Rigoberto Corcho, Flores Betancourt, Pepe Suárez, and Ramiro Valdés. See Autores varios, *Mártires del Moncada,* 185, 346. Merle, *Moncada,* 172–73, 182, omits Flores Betancourt and includes Jesús Montané and Renato Guitart. See Cuervo and Llenín, *Moncada,* 91; Mencia, "El grito del Moncada," *Bohemia,* July 20, 1984, 87; Travieso, *Un nuevo día,* 126–27; Alcolea, interview; Pvt. Justo Ramón Martija, personal interview, Miami, Fla., August 28, 2000; Ferrá, interview; F. Fernández Rubio, "La Batalla del Cuartel Moncada," *Alerta,* July 29, 1953, 1; Rojas, *La Generación del Centenario,* 134, 474, 478; "Detenido Fidel Castro y enviado a la Prisión Provincial de Oriente," *El Mundo,* August 2, 1953, 1; Sgt. José Hidalezio Virués Moraga, interview, Caguas, P.R., August 14, 1988.

6. Pvt. José Ferrá and Cpl. Eugenio Alcolea agreed that the privates on duty at Post 3 were not harmed after being disarmed. See Ferrá, interview.

7. Centro de Estudios, *Moncada: La acción,* 18–19; Arcos, interview; Mencia, "El grito del Moncada," *Bohemia,* July 20, 1984, 86–87; Merle, *Moncada,* 183, 185; Taber, *M-26,* 37; Pedro Padilla, "Realizando tareas agrícolas honraremos este año a nuestros hermanos caídos en el Moncada," *Juventud Rebelde,* July 21, 1969, 2; Mencia, "El grito del Moncada," 547; Rosendo Gutiérrez, "Mi primer viaje a Santiago (entrevista con Carlos González)," *Verde Olivo,* July 24, 1966, 22; José Ponce Díaz, "Recuerdos del ataque," *Verde Olivo,* July 28, 1963, 17; Alfonso Silva, interview.

8. Sgt. Eulalio González Amador, personal interview, Miami, Fla., April 20, 1974; Alfonso Silva, interview; Szulc, *Fidel*, 267; Mencia, "El grito del Moncada," *Bohemia*, July 20, 1984, 87; Norberto Batista, interview.

9. Alfonso Silva, interview.

10. Eulalio González, interview; Melba Hernández, "Siempre supimos que el asalto al Moncada culminaría en la victoria," *Verde Olivo*, July 28, 1963, 32; Raúl Castro, "Fragmentos de un diario escrito en el presidio," *Bohemia*, July 26, 1963, 67. Mencia, *El grito del Moncada*, 535, confirms that at least two rebels wore two-toned shoes.

11. "Soldier Wounded in Rising in Santiago Is Decorated," *Havana Post*, August 27, 1953, 1, 10; Rojas, *La Generación del Centenario*, 471–72, 474; "Se esperan muchas libertades en el juicio por los sucesos del 26 en Moncada y Bayamo," *Diario de Cuba*, October 1, 1953, 3.

12. "Continua la labor de Mons. Pérez Serantes para una pacificación," *Diario de la Marina*, July 31, 1953, 23; "Habla un ex soldado de la tiranía: 'Yo custodiaba el día 26 la Audiencia en Santiago,'" *Revolución*, July 25, 1963, 4; "Brother of Fidel Castro Admits Hospital Murders," *Havana Post*, July 31, 1953, 10; Rojas, *La Generación del Centenario*, 327–28; "Declararon ante Urgencia en Santiago numerosos testigos," *Diario de la Marina*, October 3, 1953, 1; Centro de Estudios, *Moncada: La acción*, 125–26; Merle, *Moncada*, 192; Cuervo and Llenín, *Moncada*, 65, 68. This last version by Léster Rodríguez differs from the one he told in "La acción del Palacio de Justicia," *Verde Olivo*, July 26, 1964, 63–64.

13. After the rebels seized power, they dismissed Dr. Norberto Machirán Ortiz as Civil Hospital director, replacing him in March 1959 with Dr. José Ruiz Velazco. See Rojas, *El que debe vivir*, 91; Marta Rojas, *Los testigos del hospital* (Havana: Ediciones Granma, 1967), 47, 163.

14. The rebels firing on the Moncada from the rear of the Civil Hospital were Lawton cell members Remberto A. Alemán Rodríguez, Juan Domínguez Díaz, José W. Matheu Orihuela, Ramón Méndez Cabezón, and Manuel Saíz Sánchez; Artemisa natives Antonio Betancourt Flores, José F. Costa Velázquez, and Ramón Pez Ferro; and Juan M. Ameijeiras, Pablo Cartas Rodríguez, Roberto Mederos Rodríguez, Félix Rivero Vasallo, and Osvaldo Socarrás Martínez. Pvt. José W. Fonseca Martínez was described by Manuel Bartolomé as "a very influential Freemason." See "Declararon ante Urgencia," 1; Rojas, *El que debe vivir*, 44; Rojas, *La Generación del Centenario*, 260; Merle, *Moncada*, 189; Marta Rojas, "Combatientes del Hospital Civil asesinados mas tarde en el Moncada," *Granma*, July 15, 1967, 5; "Se esperan muchas libertades," 3; "Remberto Abad Alemán Rodríguez, el espirituano del Moncada," *Granma*, July 21, 1986, 2; Allain, "Sorrow over the Tragedy," 2; Bartolomé, interview.

15. Haydée Santamaría claimed that she broke the glass on the medicine cabinet. See McManus, *From the Palm Tree*, 10–11; Marta Rojas, "Golpearon a los heridos ante sus ojos," *Granma*, July 7, 1967, 8; Melba Hernández, "Siempre supimos que el asalto," 31; Dubois, *Fidel Castro*, 36; Gervasio G. Ruiz, "El asalto al Cuartel Moncada," *Carteles*, July 26, 1959, 53; Rojas, *La Generación del Centenario*, 322; Rojas, *El que debe vivir*, 51; Rojas, *Los testigos del hospital*, 84, 118–19, 137.

16. Second Lt. Pedro V. Feraud Mejías left a widow and three orphans. His brother Mauricio Feraud Mejías retired from the army with the rank of sergeant in December 1959 with a one-thousand-peso yearly pension from the revolutionary government. See Cástulo Feraud Mejías, telephone interview, Union City, N.J., June 5, 1984. At the time of the Moncada attack, the forty-six-year-old Cástulo Feraud was an alderman and president of Batista's Progressive Action Party (PAP) in Santiago de Cuba. He went into exile in 1963 and passed away in New

Jersey on September 15, 1987. See Ernesto González Bermejo and Norberto Fuentes, "La otra cara del Moncada," *Cuba*, July 1968, 9-10; "'Tenemos el deber de guardar el orden y la paz,' dijo Batista," *Diario de la Marina*, August 4, 1953, 28; Rojas, *El que debe vivir*, 57-58; Rojas, *Los testigos del hospital*, 83; McManus, *From the Palm Tree*, 14; Dr. Mauricio León Orúe, telephone interview, Plattsburgh, N.Y., January 24, 1988. Contacted twice by phone and once by mail, Dr. León did not want to provide his version of what transpired in the Civil Hospital and said, "It is best to leave those things tranquil." Dr. León went into exile in 1963 and passed away on August 11, 2000.

17. Rojas, *El que debe vivir*, 47-50, 59, 63-65; Autores varios, *Mártires del Moncada*, 226; Merle, *Moncada*, 200-201; Rojas, *Los testigos del hospital*, 44, 68, 71-73, 81-82, 85, 117, 119, 134; "Versión taquigráfica del programa 'Siempre es 26,'" *Granma*, June 29, 1973, 3; Rojas, "Golpearon a los heridos," 8; Ruiz, "El asalto al Cuartel Moncada," 53; Rojas, *La Generación del Centenario*, 474; "Un resumen de los dolorosos sucesos de Oriente," *Bohemia*, August 9, 1953, 71; "El dolor es de toda Cuba," *Diario de la Marina*, August 2, 1953, 29.

18. Rojas, *El que debe vivir*, 63-65; Rojas, *Los testigos del hospital*, 20; Mariano Rodríguez Herrera, "Desde dentro del Moncada," *Juventud Rebelde*, July 25, 1969, 2; José Tobío, personal interview, Miami, Fla., March 2, 1975.

19. Tobío, interview; Lazo, *Recuerdos*, 47; "Relato del combatiente del Moncada Pepe Suarez," *Verde Olivo*, July 29, 1962, 84.

20. "Lo que siguió el asalto del cuartel: Bestial reacción de la tiranía," *La Calle*, July 26, 1959, C8; Merle, *Moncada*, 61; Betto, *Fidel y la religión*, 181; Travieso, *Un nuevo día*, 132; Rojas, *La cueva del muerto*, 42; "'El gobierno debe ser sereno y justo, pero energico'" (Batista quoted in *Diario de la Marina*, July 28, 1953, 16); González Bermejo and Fuentes, "La otra cara del Moncada," 10; Rojas, *La Generación del Centenario*, 473; Mariano Rodríguez Herrera, "¿Qué Santiaguero nos guió a Santiago?," *Juventud Rebelde*, July 24, 1988, S7.

21. The third rebel car, driven by Fernando Chenard, contained Mario Chanes, Giraldo Córdova Cardín, "Pancho" González, Eduardo Montano, and the brothers Manuel and Virginio Gómez. The passengers in the fifth rebel vehicle, driven by Ricardo Santana, were Severino Rosell, Roberto and Orlando Galán, Marcos Martí, and Marino Collazo Cordero. See Chanes, interview; Montano, interview; Centro de Estudios, *Moncada: La acción*, 85; Cubillas, "Los artemiseños en el 'Moncada,'" *Revolución*, July 22, 1963, 7; Granados, interview.

22. Alejandro Ferrás Pellicer gave an apocryphal account in 1959, stating that the three brothers went to the Moncada in a vehicle driven by Léster Rodríguez (who led the Palace of Justice assault and did not drive), accompanied by Ramón Pez Ferro (the only survivor of the Civil Hospital event). He admitted killing an "officer" who had "many medals." The three Ferrás brothers were active in the 26 of July Movement underground. As a result, Alejandro and Armelio left for the United States in October 1957. Armelio returned four months later, and his brother went back after Batista's fall. Armelio passed away on October 12, 2005, at the age of eighty-two. Antonio Ferrás later served with the Cuban military in Angola. Two years after the Moncada attack, Pvt. José Humberto Olivares Pérez was stationed in Havana and befriended the rebel Antonio Ferrás, his boardinghouse neighbor, although he did not realize that Ferrás was a rebel at the time. Ferrás would ask Olivares about his Moncada combat role and persisted in inquiring if he had shot someone or recognized Fidel Castro or any of the attackers. After Batista's fall, Ferrás showed Olivares a government card identifying him as a veteran of the Moncada attack and described how his brother had killed Cpl. Nemesio Traba.

See Héctor de Armas, interview; Centro de Estudios, *Moncada: La acción*, 323; "Sepultado el combatiente del Moncada Armelio Ferrás Pellicer," *Granma*, October 16, 2005; Pvt. José Humberto Olivares Pérez, personal interview, Hialeah, Fla., June 7, 2004.

23. Medical lieutenant Erik Juan Pita, personal interview, Miami, Fla., December 21, 1974; medical lieutenant Rolando Pérez Sainz de la Peña, personal interview, Miami, Fla., January 19, 1975.

24. Israel Tápanes told Robert Merle in 1965 that he fired a rifle "when a soldier appeared at the window of the military hospital." In 1984 he gave a different account to Julio Travieso, claiming to have been issued a shotgun at the Siboney farmhouse, which he fired at a soldier in a window of the garrison. See Merle, *Moncada*, 185; Travieso, *Un nuevo día*, 116, 131; Rolando Pérez, interview; Juan Pita, interview.

25. The ophthalmologist Erik G. Juan Pita (September 24, 1924–March 27, 2002) joined the army in November 1951 due to unemployment. He was commissioned a medical lieutenant and never received promotion by the time he resigned in December 1956. As a civilian, in 1958 he clandestinely went to treat a wounded rebel in the Sierra Maestra. See Juan Pita, interview; Rolando Pérez, interview; Rojas, *La Generación del Centenario*, 471; Betto, *Fidel y la religión*, 181; Ray Brennan, *Castro, Cuba and Justice* (New York: Doubleday, 1959), 17; Héctor de Armas, interview; Rodríguez Herrera, "¿Qué Santiaguero nos guió a Santiago?," S7.

26. Norberto Batista, interview.

27. Ibid. Pedro Morejón Valdés was visiting Santiago de Cuba from Baracoa and was staying in the same La Mejor boardinghouse as the rebels. He was tried by a revolutionary tribunal on January 27, 1959, charged with murdering thirteen peasants. His three accusers individually picked the wrong man when brought face-to-face with the defendant. Rebel army chief of staff Camilo Cienfuegos, called as a technical witness, threatened to commit suicide if Morejón escaped execution. Morejón was sent to the firing squad on March 9, 1959. See "Batista Major Sentenced to Death," *Miami Herald*, January 28, 1959; "Batista Man Doomed," *New York Times*, January 28, 1959, 14.

28. Pvt. José D. Agüero was recommended for promotion two days later for his participation in the defense of the military hospital. See Merle, *Moncada*, 188; Mencia, *El grito del Moncada*, 554; Allain, "Sorrow over the Tragedy," 2; Rolando Pérez, interview; "Se esperan muchas libertades," 3; Centro de Estudios, *Moncada: La acción*, 18.

29. Juan Pita, interview; Allain, "Sorrow over the Tragedy," 2.

30. Pvt. Fredesvindo González and a Private Muñoz were among the soldiers sleeping on the cots under the stairway. Mario Chanes, who later in prison spoke about the events with Ramiro Valdés, Pepe Suárez, and Jesús Montané, believes that none of them entered the citadel. Valdés told Chanes that he was unable to lower the Post 3 gate chain due to the heavy gunfire. Montané and Valdés were in poor physical shape to be part of the agile vanguard team. Montané was an overweight, myopic, chain-smoking asthmatic with flat feet who was later unable to maintain the rigorous hike of the fleeing rebels. According to Gerardo Granados, Valdés was unemployed as an assistant truck driver due to a knee injury that left him with a permanent slight limp. Valdés stated to the novelist Robert Merle that he shot a "tall mulatto" sergeant in the chest with a pistol and that his victim then wounded him on the foot. Mario Mencia identified the victim as Sgt. Luis Oliva, the only sergeant to die inside the garrison. This version is disproved by Oliva's death certificate, showing that he died of a single small-caliber forehead wound. Lt. Mariano Cuello (July 23, 1906–November 4, 1997), Oliva's

half-brother, who retrieved the corpse, stated that Oliva was shot in the head inside the regimental quartermaster office as he looked out the window. Cpl. Eugenio García indicated that Oliva "fell at my feet" after being struck by a bullet in the forehead while peering out the quartermaster room window. Pepe Suárez, armed with a .45-caliber machine gun, alleged that he shot Cpl. Isidro Izquierdo three times, but the sentry's death record demonstrates that he was hit four times with small-caliber projectiles. Suárez provided other conflicting accounts that are far from the truth. He claimed that José Luis Tasende was shot in the leg while entering the garrison and that Pedro Marrero was cut down by a .50-caliber machine gun burst while ascending the stairway. Military accounts confirm that both men safely reached the administrative wing and were later captured alive. See Chanes, interview; Luciano Tejera Díaz, "Un dulcero artemiseño en el Moncada," *El Habanero,* July 26, 2003; Castro, *History Will Absolve Me,* 28; "Fidel Castro, Rebel Leader, Surrenders," *Havana Post,* August 2, 1953, 9; Merle, *Moncada,* 182–83; Mencia, *El grito del Moncada,* 550–52; Lt. Mariano Cuello, telephone interview, Miami, Fla., September 24, 1988; Cpl. Eugenio García, personal interview, Miami, Fla., February 28, 1975; Rafael Morales, interview; Rojas, *La Generación del Centenario,* 474, 477; "Relato del combatiente del Moncada Pepe Suarez," 84.

31. Lt. Angel Machado, medical lieutenant Rolando Pérez Sainz de la Peña, and Pvt. Alfonso Silva all stated that only five rebels managed to enter the garrison. Bourne, *Fidel,* 83, mistakenly calculates that "About fifty men had made it through the gate into the fort." Friends of Flores Betancourt recalled that he was an expert marksman, had a "rebellious character," and "became extremely violent" when offended. See "Attackers of Army Posts Identified as Criminals," *Havana Post,* July 31, 1953, 1; "Flores Betancourt Rodríguez: A cumplir la palabra empeñada con la patria," *Granma,* June 25, 1973, 2; Chanes, interview; de la Fe, interview; Mirabal Reyes, *El color de la Victoria,* 22; Merle, *Moncada,* 172–73, 182; Cuervo and Llenín, *Moncada,* 91; Autores varios, *Mártires del Moncada,* 185, 346; Mencia, *El grito del Moncada,* 533, 544, 547, 551–53; "Así se realizó el asalto a la posta número tres," *Granma,* July 20, 1971, 2; Mencia, "El grito del Moncada," *Bohemia,* July 20, 1984, 87; and "Lo que siguió el asalto del cuartel," C8.

32. Norberto Fuentes, "La guerra comenzó con el último disparo," *Cuba Internacional,* July 1977, 12, 14.

33. Renato Guitart's death certificate indicates that he was shot on the forehead by a large-caliber projectile and on the left buttock. Robert Taber incorrectly places Renato "dead at the door of the radio station." The rebel Mario Lazo erroneously states that Renato Guitart stayed behind after the attack to cover the retreat. See Rojas, *La Generación del Centenario,* 125; Alfredo Reyes Trejo, "Habla un combatiente del Moncada (Entrevista con Mario Lazo)," *Verde Olivo,* July 31, 1966, 14; Taber, *M-26,* 38; Autores varios, *Mártires del Moncada,* 144; "Fidel Labrador habla de los días del Moncada," *Bohemia,* July 25, 1986, 6; Rolando Castillo M., "Renato Guitart: El mártir de la posta 3," *Verde Olivo,* July 25, 1965, 10.

34. Police corporal Manuel Miras Mierez left a pregnant widow. See Pvt. Armando F. Oliva López, personal interview, Miami, Fla., April 6, 1975; Rojas, *La Generación del Centenario,* 475–77; Norberto Batista, interview.

35. Pvt. Justo Ramón Martija had been a peasant cane cutter for eleven years in Las Villas on the Macagual farm of Alejandro del Río Pérez, father of the regimental commander, before joining the army in April 1952. He left Cuba with his family in 1990. See Martija, interview; Pablo Mila Ortiz, "Termina la prueba de confesión," *El Mundo,* September 30, 1953, 8; Rojas, *La Generación del Centenario,* 473; Rafael Morales, interview.

36. Martija, interview; Ferrá, interview; Pvt. Orlando Morales Gros, personal interview, Tampa, Fla., December 14, 2005.

37. The policeman Evelio Xenis López (August 24, 1928–April 15, 1993) had joined the army in 1942 and later went into the Santiago de Cuba police force. His wife's cousin was the revolutionary William Gálvez. Xenis obtained asylum in the Colombian Embassy in Havana on January 1, 1959, and migrated from Colombia to the United States in 1967. See Evelio Xenis López, personal interview, Hialeah, Fla., March 1, 1988; Eugenio García, interview; Mariano Cuello, interview.

38. Reyes, interview.

39. Ibid; Rojas, *La Generación del Centenario*, 131.

40. The medical description of Cpl. Néstor Reyes Martín's wounds was reprinted in Rojas, *La Generación del Centenario*, 472–73. After recovering from his wounds, Reyes was transferred to the Holguín regiment. He was arrested in Banes on January 4, 1959, and sentenced to death for the killing of a rebel in Oriente during the April 9, 1958, general strike uprising. The conviction was reduced to thirty years of imprisonment and commuted on November 13, 1979, along with four hundred other political prisoners. Reyes arrived in the United States with his father on March 7, 1980. See Reyes, interview; Allain, "Sorrow over the Tragedy," 2.

41. Pvt. Ernesto Cuello Silveira was a relative of medical captain Edmundo Tamayo Silveira, director of the military hospital. He passed away on December 31, 1990. See Ernesto Cuello Silveira, telephone interview, Bronx, N.Y., September 25, 1988.

42. Virués, interview; Olivares, interview; Pvt. Juan Manuel Sánchez Pruna, personal interview, Miami, Fla., August 26, 1988.

43. On August 8, 1959, Ismael Valdés was among 130 people arrested for conspiring to overthrow the Castro regime and was sentenced to nine years of imprisonment. See Lt. Ismael Valdés Cabrera, personal interview, Miami, Fla., January 12, 1975; Rojas, *La Generación del Centenario*, 476; González Bermejo and Fuentes, "La otra cara del Moncada," 11.

44. Pvt. Argeo Sarmiento Moreno was executed by a rebel firing squad in Manzanillo on January 13, 1959. See Pvt. Antonio H. Rodríguez Pérez, personal interview, Miami, Fla., September 9, 2000; Matos, interview.

45. Alcolea, interview; Allain, "Sorrow over the Tragedy," 2; Norberto Batista, interview; Rojas, *La Generación del Centenario en el juicio del Moncada*, 328; Rojas, *El que debe vivir*, 52; Rojas, *Los testigos del hospital*, 54; Bermejo and Fuentes, "La otra cara del Moncada," 10; Pablo Mila Ortíz, "Duró cinco horas el combate en Santiago," *El Mundo*, July 28, 1953, 8; "Unos 70 muertos es el trágico balance del golpe contra los cuarteles de Santiago y Bayamo," *Diario de la Marina*, July 28, 1953, 25; "Relación de los civiles vecinos de Santiago muertos accidentalmente," *Oriente*, July 27, 1953, 1; "Civiles muertos y heridos en los sucesos de Santiago," *Tiempo*, July 28, 1953, 1; "Civiles heridos en el asalto al 'Moncada,'" *Prensa Universal*, July 31, 1953, 1.

46. Lt. Angel S. Machado Rofe, personal interview, Miami, Fla., December 31, 1974. Adj. Capt. Manuel E. Aguila Gil refused to talk about the events of the Moncada attack during a telephone conversation with the author in Miami, Fla., on August 5, 1984. Cpl. Norberto Batista Seguí believes that his negative attitude is because in 1959 Aguila Gil collaborated with the rebel commandant Manuel Piñeiro in reorganizing the Moncada regiment and was later allowed to leave Cuba without problems. Pvt. Radamés Reyes Romero, a radio telegraphist in the Manzanillo garrison who joined the rebels in the Sierra Maestra, in 1959 told

Batista Seguí that he received messages regarding army troop movements that Aguila Gil clandestinely sent nightly to the rebels before the downfall of the Batista regime.

47. Machine gun platoon 1st Sgt. Braulio J. Curuneaux was a mulatto orphan who managed to graduate from high school, when most peasants did not finish the sixth grade. After the Moncada attack, he was transferred to Holguín, where he became the leader of a gang of soldiers that carried out armed robberies. Curuneaux was convicted and sentenced to eight years in the Boniato Provincial Prison. While a trustee, on November 30, 1956, he led a daring escape, taking with him rebel prisoners including the future general Raúl Menéndez Tomassevich, who was incarcerated for forgery. Curuneaux joined the rebel forces fighting in Oriente Province, providing leadership and valuable military expertise that gained him the rank of captain. On November 23, 1958, Curuneaux was killed leading rebel troops in the Battle of Guisa. Fidel Castro described him in a radio broadcast that day as "the most outstanding Rebel officer . . . veteran of numerous actions who died gloriously defending his position on the highway of Guisa, where the enemy tanks were not able to pass" ("La batalla de Guisa," *Verde Olivo*, January 22, 1967, 11). His combat activities are chronicled in Franqui, *Diary*. See also Justo Estevanell, "Braulio Coroneaux," *Verde Olivo*, December 8, 1963, 31, where his photograph appears. Early rebel versions mistakenly spell his last name as "Coroneaux." In 1999 Juan Almeida correctly named him and detailed the prison break (Almeida Bosque, *La aurora de los héroes*, 253–57). Sgt. Bernabé González died in combat in Alto Songo during the Sierra Maestra campaign. See Reyes, interview; Oliva, interview; Mila Ortiz, "Termina la prueba de confesión," 8; Rojas, *La Generación del Centenario*, 302; Mencia, "El grito del Moncada," *Bohemia*, July 20, 1984, 87.

48. Pepe Ponce later exaggerated that he was wounded "in the chest and the arm," instead of on his shoulder and his hand. He also claimed twenty years later that he asked the taxi driver to take him to Havana instead of Siboney. See Ponce, "Recuerdos del ataque," 17; Ana María Radaelli, "José Ponce Díaz," *Cuba Internacional*, July 1983, 63; Almeida Bosque, *La aurora de los héroes*, 163; del Mazo, interview; Rojas, *La Generación del Centenario*, 248; Héctor de Armas, interview; Merle, *Moncada*, 195; Dr. René Eldidy Eljaiek, telephone interview, Miami, Fla., February 15, 1986.

49. Cubillas, "Los artemiseños en el 'Moncada,'" 7; Arcos, interview; Eldidy, interview; Merle, *Moncada*, 196–97; Mencia, *El grito del Moncada*, 573–74; Marta Rojas, "Abelardo Crespo: A quien dejaron por muerto, la solidaridad del pueblo santiaguero le salvó la vida," *Granma*, July 17, 1973, 4; Chanes, interview; Díaz-Francisco, interview. Díaz-Francisco indicated that Abelardo Crespo's small-caliber injury did not leave an exit wound. Although Crespo stated that he was shot in the chest, Rojas and Raúl del Mazo Serra affirm that he was shot in the back. See Rojas, *La curva del muerto*, 43; del Mazo, interview; "Continua la labor," 23.

50. The only three military deaths occurring on the streets outside the Moncada garrison were Lt. Pedro V. Feraud Mejías, in front of the Civil Hospital; 1st Sgt. Ramón V. Silveiro Enriquez, as he stepped out of his house; and Cpl. Nemesio A. Traba Montero, shot in the back as he got off a bus on the corner of Moncada Street and Victoriano Garzón Ave. See appendix 2. See also Merle, *Moncada*, 194–96; Mencia, *El grito del Moncada*, 569, 572–73.

51. Granados, interview; Iraida Moreno Careaga, "La historia de un mártir," *Verde Olivo*, July 8, 1962, 7; Autores varios, *Mártires del Moncada*, 223, 316; Merle, *Moncada*, 195; Mencia, *El grito del Moncada*, 573.

52. Dubois, *Fidel Castro*, 36, erroneously has Fidel Castro armed with a shotgun. The mistake is repeated in Bourne, *Fidel*, 82. Geyer, *Guerrilla Prince*, 118, wrongly states that

Castro jumped from his car with a submachine gun. See Granados, interview; Bustillo, interview; Héctor de Armas, interview; Mafut Delgado, interview; Szulc, *Fidel,* 268; Taber, *M-26,* 39.

53. Raúl Castro and Vilma Espín held their wedding at Rancho Club on January 26, 1959. Col. Orlando Piedra Negueruela (Dec. 18, 1917–July 12, 1999) passed away in Hialeah, Fla. See Lt. Teodoro Rico Boué, personal interview, Miami, Fla., March 2, 1988; Ferrá, interview; del Río Chaviano, interview; Raimundo, *Habla el Coronel Orlando Piedra,* 220; Alcolea, interview; Alfonso Silva, interview; Rodríguez, interview; Martija, interview; González Bermejo and Fuentes, "La otra cara del Moncada," 10.

54. Rafael Morales, interview; Mencia, *El grito del Moncada,* 567; Matos, interview; González Bermejo and Fuentes, "La otra cara del Moncada," 10–11.

55. González Bermejo and Fuentes, "La otra cara del Moncada," 11

56. Angel González, interview; Alfonso Silva, interview; Rojas, *La Generación del Centenario,* 297; Orlando Morales, interview; Nieto, interview; Olivares, interview.

57. Pvt. José Alberto Ferrá Mulet, a native of Banes, Oriente, had joined the army on April 1, 1952, to improve his life. He subsequently was stationed in Victoria de las Tunas, were he got married, and fought in the Sierra Maestra campaign. As a result, the revolutionary government detained him on January 18, 1959, charged him with burning the town of Sagua de Tánamo, and gave him a death sentence that was commuted to a thirty-year prison term. He was amnestied with a group of political prisoners in September 1986 and left for the United States. See Olivares, interview; Matos, interview; Ferrá, interview.

58. Angel González, interview; Rafael Morales, interview; Centro de Estudios, *Moncada: La acción,* 78.

59. Norberto Batista, interview; Rojas, *La Generación del Centenario,* 306; medical lieutenant Roberto P. Mas Renedo, telephone interview, La Canada, Calif., February 15, 1986. Mas Renedo (June 11, 1911–April 7, 1994) was brief and refused to go into details of the events that transpired.

60. Dr. Roberto Villalón Virgilí, telephone interview, Columbus, Ohio, February 1, 1986; Dr. Fernando Pedro Fornaris, telephone interview, Miami, Fla., February 1, 1986; Dr. Eduardo García-Ferrer Méndez, telephone interview, Crevecoeur, Mo., December 9, 1984.

61. Norberto Batista, interview; Alfonso Silva, interview.

62. The wounded Cpl. José Llanes León was promoted to sergeant in charge of the El Cobre post. After Castro seized power, he hid during seven months in the cane field of the Guayabo Viejo farm, Calabazar de Sagua, Las Villas, before being arrested with three others who awaited a ship on which to sail abroad. Llanes was sentenced to eight years in prison on December 14, 1961, for "mistreating the citizens of El Cobre." Dr. Fernando Pedro Fornaris (April 26, 1915–December 18, 1989) passed away in Miami, and Dr. Roberto Villalón Virgilí (July 25, 1925–November 28, 1999) died in Fairborn, Ohio. See "7 meses oculto en un cañaveral," *Revolución,* September 9, 1959; *Diario las Américas,* December 15, 1961, 1; Dr. Rafael Parladé, telephone interview, Daytona Beach, Fla., February 1, 1986; Villalón, interview; Dr. Héctor L. Ortíz Fernández, telephone interview, Miami, Fla., February 1, 1986; Fornaris, interview; García-Ferrer, interview; Norberto Batista, interview.

63. Norberto Batista, interview; Valdés, interview; Fernández Rubio, "La Batalla del Cuartel Moncada," 1.

64. Policeman Horacio Martínez Verdecia, personal interview, Miami, Fla., July 26, 1974.

65. Pvt. Angel Pupo Miranda passed away in Los Angeles, Calif., on March 25, 2000. See Pvt. Angel Pupo Miranda, personal interview, Glendale, Calif., March 14, 1990; Autores varios, *Mártires del Moncada,* 223; Valdés, interview.

66. Oliva, interview; Valdés, interview; Sánchez, interview; "Nuevo Comdte. de la Cruz Roja Pérez Almaguer," *Diario de la Marina,* October 13, 1953, 2; "Unos 70 muertos," 25.

67. Capt. Rosendo Abreu Jiménez, telephone interview, Miami, Fla., September 27, 1988; González Bermejo and Fuentes, "La otra cara del Moncada," 11.

68. González Bermejo and Fuentes, "La otra cara del Moncada," 11; Virués, interview; Ferrá, interview; Martija, interview.

69. Pvt. José Humberto Olivares Pérez, a native of Guantánamo, was a descendant of Cuban-independence general Pedro "Periquito" Pérez. Both of his grandfathers and his father were in the military. In 1948 he worked as a carpenter in the U.S. naval base at Guantánamo, and the following year he joined the Cuban army, serving at various posts in Oriente Province. Olivares was sent to Havana in December 1952 for a six-month aviation mechanic course and transferred to Moncada on June 15, 1953. In August 1953 he was assigned to Camp Columbia in Havana, where he remained until resigning from the army in 1959. Olivares and his family left Cuba for the United States in February 1969. See Olivares, interview.

70. José Tobío (March 21, 1903–October 15, 1983) passed away in Miami. The policeman Enrique Despaigne Noret was shot by a rebel firing squad at San Juan Hill on January 12, 1959, and a sequence of photographs of the execution appeared in *Time,* January 26, 1959, 40. See Tobío, interview.

71. Sgt. José H. Virués Moraga (March 22, 1921–July 29, 1999), a native of Cajimaya, Mayarí, was a heavy-equipment operator at the U.S. naval base at Guantánamo before joining the Cuban army during World War II. He was wounded in 1957 during the Sierra Maestra campaign and transferred to Havana. On the afternoon of January 1, 1959, Virués and another soldier fled the island by hijacking a commercial plane to Santo Domingo. He settled in Puerto Rico, where he passed away in Juncos. Pvt. Ernesto Cuello Silveira stated that his cousin Pvt. Angel L. Duvallón-Gilbert Cuello was murdered by rebels in Santiago de Cuba in 1957. See Rico, interview; Virués, interview; Alcolea, interview; Merle, *Moncada,* 230; Rojas, *La Generación del Centenario,* 134.

72. Pvt. Luis Enrique Naranjo was later dismissed from the army, moved to Venezuela, and was accidentally electrocuted. See Héctor de Armas, interview; Alcolea, interview; Rico, interview; Rojas, *La Generación del Centenario,* 134; Mila Ortíz, "Duró cinco horas," 8.

73. The rebel Pedro Marrero, captured alive and beaten, was killed that same day, and his corpse appears in a photograph of a room in the military hospital where the dead soldiers and attackers were placed together. See Editorial de Ciencias Sociales, *Moncada,* 172; Alcolea, interview; Olivares, interview.

74. Norberto Batista, interview; Juan Carlos Santos, "Jose Luis Tasende ... sus ultimas horas," *Granma,* July 21, 1977, 2.

75. Lts. Claudio Morales García and Marcelo Otaño Cookerman were killed during the Sierra Maestra campaign. The latter died when a soldier accidentally discharged his rifle. A court-martial later ruled that Cpl. Juan Silva Domínguez acted in self-defense when he killed two outlaws in La Maya. When the rebels seized power, Silva and his girlfriend fled from Holguín to Havana, where he was captured within a week. He was sent to a firing squad in August 1959. Cpl. José Gerardo Rosabal Rosales later lost a leg due to an assassination attempt

in Charco Redondo. See Reyes, interview; Alfonso Silva, interview; Pvt. Isidro Ferrer, telephone interview, Elizabeth, N.J., July 29, 1989; Matos, interview; Rojas, *Los testigos del hospital,* 137; Rojas, *El que debe vivir,* 54, 60; González Bermejo and Fuentes, "La otra cara del Moncada," 11; Angel González, interview; Rojas, *La Generación del Centenario,* 327.

76. "Brother of Fidel Castro Admits," 10; "La acción del Palacio de Justicia," 64; Cuervo and Llenín, *Moncada,* 66; "Sigue el juicio por el asalto al Cuartel Moncada y al de Bayamo," *Diario de la Marina,* October 4, 1953, 1; Centro de Estudios, *Moncada: La acción,* 127; Autores varios, *Mártires del Moncada,* 291.

77. Thomas, *Cuba,* 838, indicates that "[t]he battle had lasted about one hour." See Rojas, *Los testigos del hospital,* 10; Rojas, *El que debe vivir,* 54; Szulc, *Fidel,* 267; Bustillo, interview; Montano, interview; Mafut Delgado, interview; Chanes, interview; Granados, interview; Reyes Trejo, "Habla un combatiente del Moncada," 14–15; Gutiérrez, "Mi primer viaje a Santiago," 22; Centro de Estudios, *Moncada: La acción,* 84.

78. Montano, interview; Arcos, interview; Granados, interview; Centro de Estudios, *Moncada: La acción,* 18.

79. Jaime Costa Chávez published his memoirs, *El clarín toca al amanecer* (Barcelona: Ediciones Rondas) in 2003. The work has the literary style of the writer Jorge Valls, who penned the prologue, but Costa insisted that he wrote the book and that Valls only made the "corrections." Only 8 of the autobiography's 468 pages are devoted to the Moncada events, and these are fraught with disturbing errors. For example, Costa now claims that some rebels went to Santiago de Cuba in airplanes, that Jesús Montané was driving the car that took Fidel Castro to the Moncada, and that all the rebel vehicles "penetrated the Moncada." There is a fictitious battle account in which the attackers "advance on the barracks, making a great number of prisoners." Dr. Mario Muñoz, not Abel Santamaría, is depicted as the rebel combat leader in the Civil Hospital. Costa alleges that he and Gerardo Granados managed to escape in the countryside moments before Fidel Castro was arrested, instead of three days earlier. This published account contradicts the taped and transcribed version that I obtained from Costa twenty years earlier and does not adjust itself to the historical record. See Montano, interview; Merle, *Moncada,* 197, 215; Costa, interview; Chanes, interview; Rojas, "Abelardo Crespo," 4; Rojas, *La cueva del muerto,* 43; Mencia, "El grito del Moncada," *Bohemia,* July 20, 1984, 88; "Lo que siguió el asalto del cuartel," C8; Travieso, *Un nuevo día,* 135; Granados, interview.

80. Although Oscar Alcalde claimed that he shot a lieutenant on the street, the only casualties with that rank were Lt. Andrés Morales, mortally wounded inside the garrison, and Lt. Pedro Feraud, killed at the Civil Hospital. See Merle, *Moncada,* 216–17; Sara Más, "Mi vida cambió," *Granma,* July 18, 2003; Mafut Delgado, interview; Ruiz, "El asalto al Cuartel Moncada," 53; Travieso, *Un nuevo día,* 24, 133; Reyes Trejo, "Habla un combatiente del Moncada," 15; Lazo, *Recuerdos,* 51.

81. Héctor de Armas and Carlos Bustillo hid overnight in the garage of a friend's house, who asked them to leave the next day. A business acquaintance in Santiago de Cuba provided Bustillo with money and a letter of recommendation for both men so that they could safely return to Havana by bus. They had to pay a bribe to obtain asylum in the Mexican Embassy and departed for Mexico City on August 12, 1953. Both men returned to Cuba in 1955 under the general amnesty and opted for political discourse instead of revolutionary violence. In 1959 de Armas became military instructor in Matanzas and fought against the Bay of Pigs invaders before fleeing Cuba in a boat with his brother and his uncle on August 4, 1961. He

died of stomach cancer in Miami, Fla., on April 26, 1993, and was interred in Woodlawn Park Mausoleum. Carlos Bustillo went into exile in 1960 and died of a heart attack in Miami, Fla., on June 17, 2002. See Bustillo, interview; Héctor de Armas, interview.

82. The Fajardo siblings were Beralia, age twenty-two, engaged to Pvt. Armando Oliva López; Julián, twenty; Olga, eighteen; and Ana María, nine. See "Fidel Labrador habla," 7; Merle, *Moncada,* 196, 201, 205; Szulc, *Fidel,* 268; Autores varios, *Mártires del Moncada,* 75, 160; Sgt. Julián Fajardo Mendoza, personal interview, Miami, Fla., November 2, 1974; "Detenido Fidel Castro," 10; Allain, "Sorrow over the Tragedy," 2; Llerena, *Unsuspected Revolution,* 119; Thomas, *Cuba,* 837; Castro, *History Will Absolve Me,* 29.

83. Mencia, "El grito del Moncada," *Bohemia,* July 20, 1984, 89; Alfonso Silva, interview; Juan Pita, interview; Merle, *Moncada,* 206; Centro de Estudios, *Moncada: La acción,* 72; "Fidel Labrador habla," 7.

84. Juan Pita, interview; Rolando Pérez, interview; Rojas, *La Generación del Centenario,* 249; *Bohemia,* July 22, 1966, S-3.

85. Sgt. Julián Fajardo passed away in Orlando, Fla. on February 2, 1995. His wife, Ana Vázquez Rojas, was the sister of José Vázquez, the Siboney farmhouse owner. See Julián Fajardo, interview; Ana María Fajardo Vázquez, personal interview, Miami, Fla., December 28, 2005.

86. Rojas, *El que debe vivir,* 70–73; McManus, *From the Palm Tree,* 12; Dubois, *Fidel Castro,* 36; Rojas, *La Generación del Centenario,* 261; Rojas, *Los testigos del hospital,* 19–20, 97; "Versión taquigráfica del programa 'Siempre es 26,'" 5–6; Rojas, "Golpearon a los heridos," 8.

87. On July 2, 1959, Senén Carabia Carrey was sentenced to four years at hard labor in the Zapata Swamp for graft. He was also convicted of disloyalty and sentenced to death after Melba Hernández testified against him. Haydée, on the other hand, was unable to positively identify him. On appeal Carabia alleged that his name was confused with that of SIM agent Angel Esteban Garay González, who was executed on January 13, 1959. Carabia's sentence was commuted to thirty years of imprisonment. He was freed on October 18, 1978, and allowed to travel to the United States along with thirty-six hundred political prisoners. See Centro de Estudios, *Moncada: La acción,* 146; McManus, *From the Palm Tree,* 13; Bermejo and Fuentes, "La otra cara del Moncada," 10; Martija, interview; Rojas, *El que debe vivir,* 92–94; Rojas, *La Generación del Centenario en el juicio del Moncada,* 190; Travieso, *Un nuevo día,* 136; Norberto Batista, interview.

88. When the rebels seized power, Lt. Manuel Piña Martínez was shot by a firing squad on January 12, 1959, on San Juan Hill, along with more than 120 other Moncada soldiers, Santiago policemen, and civilians executed without a trial by orders of Raúl Castro. Future Watergate burglar Frank Fiorini Sturgis, wearing a rebel uniform, was photographed posing with a rifle on top of the mass grave. See Angel González, interview; González Bermejo and Fuentes, "La otra cara del Moncada," 10; Martija, interview; Rojas, *El que debe vivir,* 76–77, 83–84, 93–94, 96; Autores varios, *Mártires del Moncada,* 171, 205; *Granma,* July 11, 1967, 8; Rojas, *Los testigos del hospital,* 86, 157–61; Ruiz, "El asalto al Cuartel Moncada," 53.

89. Pvt. Antonio H. Rodríguez Pérez and Cpl. Eugenio Alcolea Ramírez agreed that Cpl. Orestes Pompa Castañeda killed Dr. Muñoz in revenge for the death of his brother Horacio at the Civil Hospital. Pvt. Ariel Matos Romero stated that it was Rural Guard corporal Suárez, who has since passed away, who murdered the physician. Pvts. Alfonso Silva and Justo Ramón Martija indicated that Muñoz's killer was a Pvt. Montes de Oca who later joined the rebels in

the Sierra Maestra Mountains. Pvts. Armando Oliva and Orlando Morales Gros heard that Pvt. Aquiles García Bell, executed by a rebel firing squad on January 11, 1959, had killed Dr. Muñoz. The rebels sent Cpl. Orestes Pompa Castañeda to the firing squad in Santiago de Cuba on April 27, 1959. Pvt. Antonio H. Rodríguez Pérez was imprisoned during 1962-67 for being a counterrevolutionary and migrated to Florida in 1972. See Víctor Pérez-Galdós, "Moncada en el recuerdo de un combatiente," *Bohemia*, July 15, 1983, 79; Rojas, *Los testigos del hospital*, 10, 121; Rojas, *El que debe vivir*, 60, 94, 98-100, 108; Rojas, "Golpearon a los heridos," 8; Orfilio Peláez, "Solo la casualidad impidió la toma del Moncada," *Granma*, July 22, 2003; Martija, interview; Matos, interview; Algarra, interview; Rodríguez, interview.

90. Rojas, *Los testigos del hospital*, 59, 91-92, 126; Cuervo and Llenín, *Moncada*, 73; Centro de Estudios, *Moncada: La acción*, 145; Rojas, *El que debe vivir*, 61.

91. Ediciones Políticas, *Veintiseis*, 120; Rojas, *El que debe vivir*, 111; Rojas, *La Generación del Centenario*, 127-28; Rafael Morales, interview; Ediciones Políticas, *Haydée habla del Moncada*, 33; Travieso, *Un nuevo día*, 147; Ruiz, "El asalto al Cuartel Moncada," 53; "Army Pursuit of Fleeing Rebels Continues; Death Toll Reaches Total of 75," *Havana Post*, July 30, 1953, 2.

92. Canto, *Mi vida*, 180; *New York Times*, July 27, 1953, 1; Matthews, *Fidel Castro*, 65.

93. Díaz-Balart, interview; Emilio Ochoa, interview.

94. The nine rebels killed in action were Flores Betancourt, Rigoberto Corcho, Gildo Fleitas, Manuel and Virginio Gómez Reyes, Guillermo Granados Lara, Renato Guitart, Carmelo Noa, and Miguel Oramas Alfonso. The eleven wounded were Tomás Alvarez Breto, Marino Collazo Cordero, Guillermo Elizalde Sotolongo, Fidel Labrador García, Horacio Matheu Orihuela, Ramiro Valdés, José Luis Tasende, Gustavo Arcos Bergnes, Reinaldo Benítez Nápoles, Abelardo Crespo Arias, and José Ponce Díaz, the last four being hit by friendly fire. See Conte Agüero, *Los dos rostros*, 48; Chibás, interview; "Califica el Doctor Carlos Prío 'de una tontería' el suceso ocurrido en Santiago de Cuba," *El Camagüeyano*, July 29, 1953, 1; Nieto, interview; "¡Sangre Cubana!," *Alerta*, July 27, 1953, 1.

Chapter 5—"We are going into history"

1. "El Cuartel de Bayamo," *Revolución*, July 18, 1964, 1; Pérez-Puelles, interview.

2. Castro García, interview; Pérez-Puelles, interview.

3. Castro García, interview; Rubén Castillo Ramos, "En el Cuartel de Bayamo se escribió otra página heróica," *Bohemia*, July 23, 1961, 63.

4. Pérez-Puelles, interview; Francisco Pita Rodríguez, "Las armas estaban en las armerías...," *Bohemia*, July 20, 1973, 7; Jaime Sarusky, "La célula de Santiago," *Bohemia*, July 20, 1973, 44; Dirección Política de las FAR, *Moncada*, 261; Castillo Ramos, *Las avanzadas del cauto*, 26-27; Centro de Estudios, *Moncada: La acción*, 75; "Entrevista con Antonio Darío López del asalto al Cuartel de Bayamo," *Verde Olivo*, July 26, 1964, 15; Marta Matamoros, "El asalto al Cuartel de Bayamo," *Granma*, July 6, 1967, S5; Travieso, *Un nuevo día*, 103; Merle, *Moncada*, 164.

5. Pedro Aguilera drove to Bayamo with Orestes Abad, Enrique Cámara Pérez, Angel Guerra Díaz, Lázaro Hernández Arroyo, and José Testa Zaragoza. See Merle, *Moncada*, 164-65; Lidice Valenzuela, "Los atacantes recuerdan: El 26 en Bayamo," *Cuba Internacional*, July 1981, 19; Dirección Política de las FAR, *Moncada*, 252; Raúl Martínez, interview.

6. Szulc, *Fidel*, 254, erroneously has Castro addressing all the combatants in the Gran Casino. See Castillo Ramos, *Las avanzadas del cauto*, 28-29, 31; Raúl Martínez, interview; Castro García, interview; Pérez-Puelles, interview.

7. Raúl Martínez, interview; Centro de Estudios, *Moncada: La acción*, 76, 175; Aldo Menéndez and Rubén Castillo Ramos, "El asalto al Cuartel de Bayamo," *Bohemia,* July 27, 1973, 75; Dirección Política de las FAR, *Moncada,* 243, 254–55; Castro García, interview; Pérez-Puelles, interview.

8. Elio Rosete's wife gave birth to a boy a few days after the attack. See Rosete, interview; Raúl Martínez, interview; Castillo Ramos, *Las avanzadas del cauto,* 24, 30; Méndez and Castillo, "El asalto al Cuartel de Bayamo," 75; Mencia, *El grito del Moncada,* 529; Dirección Política de las FAR, *Moncada,* 242, 256–61.

9. Castro García, interview; Raúl Martínez, interview; Centro de Estudios, *Moncada: La acción,* 77.

10. Merle, *Moncada,* 166; Rosete, interview; Raúl Martínez, interview.

11. Castro García, interview; Raúl Martínez, interview; Sarusky, "Las horas que precedieron," 38; Dirección Política de las FAR, *Moncada,* 258–59; Castillo Ramos, *Las avanzadas del cauto,* 33.

12. Castro García, interview; Pérez-Puelles, interview; Centro de Estudios, *Moncada: La acción,* 174; Mencia, *El grito del Moncada,* 531; Dirección Política de las FAR, *Moncada,* 253; Castillo Ramos, "En el Cuartel de Bayamo," 63; Raúl Martínez, interview.

13. Pvt. José Olivares Pérez was stationed in the Bayamo garrison for a few months in 1952 before being transferred to Moncada. See Olivares, interview; Carlos Manuel Pérez, "Declarado Monumento Nacional Parque Museo Ñico López," *La Demajagua* (Bayamo), April 19, 2004; Raúl Martínez, interview; Menendez and Castillo, "El asalto al Cuartel de Bayamo," 79; Castillo Ramos, *Las avanzadas del cauto,* 39; Pérez-Puelles, interview; Castro García, interview.

14. Pérez-Puelles, interview; Castro García, interview; Raúl Martínez, interview; Castillo Ramos, *Las avanzadas del cauto,* 35; Centro de Estudios, *Moncada: La acción,* 178; Alfredo Reyes Trejo, "Habla un combatiente del ataque al Cuartel de Bayamo (Entrevista con Antonio López García)," *Verde Olivo,* July 31, 1966, 18.

15. Menéndez and Castillo, "El asalto al Cuartel de Bayamo," 79–80; Castillo Ramos, *Las avanzadas del cauto,* 40–41; Diego Barcaz, "Asalto al Cuartel de Bayamo: Zeguen," *Revolución* (Rotograbado), July 22, 1963, 13; Raúl Martínez, interview.

16. Castillo Ramos, *Las avanzadas del cauto,* 41; Castro García, interview; Centro de Estudios, *Moncada: La acción,* 184; Menéndez and Castillo, "El asalto al Cuartel de Bayamo," 80; Raúl Martínez, interview.

17. Pérez-Puelles, interview; "El asalto al Cuartel de Bayamo: Relato del 'muerto vivo,'" *Revolución,* July 20, 1962, 1; Castillo Ramos, *Las avanzadas del cauto,* 41; Castro García, interview.

18. Pérez-Puelles, interview; Centro de Estudios, *Moncada: La acción,* 185; Castillo Ramos, "En el Cartel de Bayamo," 62–63; Barcaz, "Asalto al Cuartel de Bayamo: Zeguen," 14–15; Merle, *Moncada,* 214; Mencia, "El grito del Moncada," *Bohemia,* July 20, 1984, 88; Raúl Martínez, interview; Joaquín Oramas, "Aquel 26 de julio en Bayamo, un testimonio vivo de nuestra historia," *Granma,* July 20, 1979, 2; Castillo Ramos, *Las avanzadas del cauto,* 42, 44; Menéndez and Castillo, "El asalto al Cuartel de Bayamo," 79, 80.

19. Pérez-Puelles, interview; Raúl Martínez, interview.

20. When the revolutionaries assumed power, Lt. Juan A. Roselló Pando was accused of murdering the rebel prisoners by Cpl. Indalecio Estrada Calderón, who received a retirement pension after his testimony. Roselló was sentenced to death by a Bayamo revolutionary

tribunal, but the penalty was commuted on March 4, 1959, to twelve years at hard labor in the Sierra Maestra Mountains. A revolutionary Superior Tribunal of Special Appeal held in the Moncada fortress on April 30, 1959, resentenced Roselló to death by firing squad, but that sentence was later reduced on appeal to a thirty-year term. Roselló Pando was released under commutation decree number 8 of November 13, 1979, along with 399 other political prisoners, including Moncada soldiers Norberto Batista Seguí and Néstor Reyes. Pvt. Juan Pérez Castañeda was tried on January 14, 1959, by a Bayamo revolutionary tribunal presided by Commandant Manuel "Barbaroja" Piñeiro. See *El Mundo*, March 5, 1959, 7; and *Diario de la Marina*, May 1, 1959. See also Autores varios, *Mártires del Moncada*, 193–96; Castillo Ramos, "En el Cuartel de Bayamo," 82; "Veinte aniversario asalto al Cuartel Moncada," *Cuba Internacional*, June–July 1973, 43–44; Menéndez and Castillo, "El asalto al Cuartel de Bayamo," 80.

21. Merle, *Moncada*, 214–15; Centro de Estudios, *Moncada: La acción*, 182; Menéndez and Castillo, "El asalto al Cuartel de Bayamo," 77; Barcaz, "Asalto al Cuartel de Bayamo: Zeguen," 14; Mirabal Reyes, *El color de la Victoria*, 211–12; "Veinte aniversario asalto al Cuartel Moncada," 43.

22. Menéndez and Castillo, "El asalto al Cuartel de Bayamo," 76, 78–79; Castillo Ramos, "En el Cuartel de Bayamo," 63; Merle, *Moncada*, 268; Castillo Ramos, *Las avanzadas del cauto*, 51; Pedro Mora, "Cuartel Carlos Manuel de Céspedes," *Granma*, July 26, 2003; Centro de Estudios, *Moncada: La acción*, 172; Reyes Trejo, "Habla un combatiente del ataque al Cuartel de Bayamo," 18; "Reportan absoluta normalidad en la capital de Oriente," *Diario de la Marina*, July 29, 1953, 24; "Nosotros no debemos olvidar," *Granma*, July 26, 2003; "Fue asaltado el Cuartel de Bayamo," *Diario de Cuba*, July 28, 1953, 1.

23. Barcaz, "Asalto al Cuartel de Bayamo: Zeguen," 14; Matamoros, "El asalto al cuartel de Bayamo," S5; Castillo Ramos, *Las avanzadas del cauto*, 43–44; Reyes Trejo, "Habla un combatiente del ataque al Cuartel de Bayamo," 18; Rubén Castillo Ramos, "¡Aquí Bayamo!," *Revolución*, July 22, 1964, 1; Menéndez and Castillo, "El asalto al Cuartel de Bayamo," 76.

24. Years later Juan Olazábal gave another account, falsifying his own participation. He claimed that the two rebels gave him a .45-caliber pistol and that he returned with them to the garrison but did not fight after seeing the other attackers retreating. In 1979 Olazábal was the director of the Ñico López Museum on the grounds of the old Bayamo army garrison. See Castillo Ramos, *Las vanzadas del cauto*, 45, 49; Castro García, interview; "Dos testimonios sobre una acción," *Granma*, July 26, 1969, 10; Menéndez and Castillo, "El asalto al Cuartel de Bayamo," 79; Oramas, "Aquel 26 de julio en Bayamo," 2.

25. Castro García, interview; Castillo Ramos, *Las avanzadas del cauto*, 49; Centro de Estudios, *Moncada: La acción*, 309; Menéndez and Castillo, "El asalto al Cuartel de Bayamo," 79.

26. José Gabriel Guma, "Engañando a los esbirros durante 800 kilómetros," *Revolución*, July 25, 1963, 5; Centro de Estudios, *Moncada: La acción*, 172, 309–11; "Detenido Fidel Castro y enviado a la Prisión Provincial de Oriente," *El Mundo*, August 2, 1953, 10.

27. Castro García, interview.

28. Ibid.

29. The SIM photograph of the corpse of Rolando "Wiki" San Román was published in *Trabajo*, second fortnight of July, 1961, 16. See Autores varios, *Mártires del Moncada*, 177, 180, 319–22; Mirabal Reyes, *El color de la Victoria*, 150; Menéndez and Castillo, "El asalto al Cuartel de Bayamo," 79–80; Merle, *Moncada*, 252–54; Castillo Ramos, *Las avanzadas del cauto*, 50–51; Oramas, "Aquel 26 de julio en Bayamo," 2.

30. "Entrevista con Antonio Darío López," 51; Reyes Trejo, "Habla un combatiente del ataque al Cuartel de Bayamo," 18.

31. After returning to Havana, Ñico López sought asylum in the Guatemalan Embassy. Following the general amnesty of May 1955, Ñico went back to Havana. In 1956 he traveled to Mexico to join the Granma expedition, and three days after landing he was killed in the skirmish at Alegria de Pío on December 5, 1956. Antonio "El Gallego" López García followed Ñico Lopez into exile in Guatemala and returned to Cuba in an armed expedition into Pinar del Rio led by Menelao Mora, Raúl Martínez Ararás, and Gerardo Pérez-Puelles, two months before the amnesty. He later went to Mexico, returned in the Granma expedition, and was captured and imprisoned until 1959. Calixto García Martínez obtained asylum in the Costa Rican Embassy with Ibrahim Sosa González and Luis Hernández Alvarez. García, the former pharmacy bicycle messenger, later fought in the Sierra Maestra campaign and was eventually promoted to division general in the Cuban Revolutionary Armed Forces. See "Entrevista con Antonio Darío López," 51; Castillo Ramos, *Las avanzadas del cauto*, 57; and "Relación de los que se marcharon de Cuba el sábado por vía aérea a Costa Rica," *Oriente*, August 31, 1953, 1.

32. The squad was composed of Pvts. Félix Rodríguez, Agustín Torres, José Baldor, Santiago "El Barberito" Dávila, Lino Noriega, and one coincidentally named Camejo. In an interview in "El asalto al Cuartel de Bayamo: Relato del 'muerto vivo,'" *Revolución*, July 20, 1962, 1, Andrés García erroneously accused Cpl. Pedro A. Maceo Martí of participating with Sgt. de la Paz in the murders. Maceo was shot by a revolutionary firing squad in Santiago de Cuba on February 10, 1959. See "Hugo Camejo Valdes," *Granma*, July 10, 1973, 2; Rojas, *La cueva del muerto*, 125, 129–31, 155; and Merle, *Moncada*, 288.

33. On the night of July 27, 1956, Andrés García Díaz and Eugenio Véliz Hernández, covertly entered the Veguitas cemetery, exhumed the remains of Hugo Camejo and Pedro Véliz, washed the bones at a nearby farm, and took them back to Havana in a suitcase for reburial in the La Lisa cemetery. See Autores varios, *Mártires del Moncada*, 84–85; "El asalto al Cuartel de Bayamo: Relato del 'muerto vivo,'" 1; Mirabal Reyes, *El color de la Victoria*, 169; Castillo Ramos, *Las avanzadas del cauto*, 52; Rojas, *La cueva del muerto*, 143, 146.

34. According to Elio Rosete, when Fidel Castro made his triumphant journey from Santiago de Cuba to Havana in January 1959, he stopped in Bayamo but did not visit the six graves of his comrades fallen on July 26. Rosete, who never again got involved in revolutionary activities, went into exile in 1960. He passed away in Miami on September 14, 2002. See Rosete, interview; Mirabal Reyes, *El color de la Victoria*, 137; Barcaz, "Asalto al Cuartel de Bayamo: Zeguen," 15; Castillo Ramos, "En el Cuartel de Bayamo," 82; Menéndez and Castillo, "El asalto al cuartel de Bayamo," 77; "El trabajo que hizo posible la identificación de los cadáveres," *Granma*, July 26, 1969, 10.

35. Pérez-Puelles, interview; Raúl Martínez, interview; Castillo Ramos, *Las avanzadas del cauto*, 53–55.

36. Pérez-Puelles, interview; Raúl Martínez, interview; Castillo Ramos, *Las avanzadas del cauto*, 55–56.

37. Pérez-Puelles, interview; Raúl Martínez, interview; Castillo Ramos, *Las avanzadas del cauto*, 56.

38. Coralia Agustina Varela Pla, personal interview, Miami, Fla., August 4, 1984.

39. "Pide comprensión el arzobispo de Santiago," *El Crisol*, July 31, 1953, 1; Castillo Ramos, "En el Cuartel de Bayamo," 63; "Detenido el jefe de la policía de Bayamo," *Prensa Universal*, July

28, 1953, 1; Centro de Estudios, *Moncada: La acción,* 260; "Unos 70 muertos es el trágico balance del golpe contra los cuarteles de Santiago y Bayamo," *Diario de la Marina,* July 28, 1953, 25.

40. Manuel J. Norman García-Iñiguez, telephone interview, Ypsilanti, Mich., August 18, 2005.

41. Castro García, interview.

Chapter 6—"That savagery cannot be blamed on Batista"

1. The "Manifesto to the Nation" appears in appendix 5. Cosme de la Torriente (June 27, 1872–December 8, 1956), a Liberation Army colonel during the war of independence, had been a lawyer, diplomat, twice secretary of state, senator, and founder of the Conservative Party. Raúl Chibás Rivas (April 25, 1916–August 25, 2002) went into exile on August 2, 1960, and passed away in Miami. See Rosa Hilda Zell, "6 documentos del Moncada," *Bohemia,* July 27, 1962, 64; Chibás, interview; Merle, *Moncada,* 220.

2. Emilio Ochoa, interview; "Fugitive Rebels Begin to Surrender to Army," *Havana Post,* August 1, 1953, 10; "Batista Opens Terror Drive on Unions, CP," *Daily Worker* (New York), August 5, 1953, 3.

3. Ramiro Arango Alsina had been appointed chancellor of the Cuban legation in Stockholm, Sweden, in March 1947. Two years later he was detained in Stockholm with twelve thousand pairs of nylon stockings and accused of contraband. See *Diario de la Marina,* March 15, 1947, 11; Ignacio A. Fiterre Rivera, telephone interview, Miami, Fla., August 5, 1984; Arango, interview; "Ramiro Arango y Alsina; Unfavorable Reports," Office Memorandum from Harvey R. Wellman, May 27, 1953, *Cuba Internal Affairs.*

4. On the morning of July 26, the SIM arrested opposition senators Eduardo Suárez Rivas, Carlos Márquez-Sterling Guiral, Ramón Zaydín Márquez-Sterling, Pelayo Cuervo Navarro, José Manuel Gutiérrez Planes, José R. Andreu Martínez, Sergio Mejías Pérez, and Lomberto Díaz Rodríguez, along with political activists Manuel Bisbé Alberni, Orlando Castro Llanes, Aida Pelayo Pelayo, and Joaquín López Montes. Senators Mejías and Díaz were leaders of the Triple A organization. Ortodoxo leaders José Pardo Llada and Luis Conte Agüero escaped the dragnet. The rebels implicated by the paper targets in Nueva Paz municipality were Rolando Guerrero Bello, Tomás D. Rodríguez Rodríguez, Pablo Agüero Guedes, Rafael Freyre Torres, Jenaro Méndez, Andrés García Iglesias, Antonio Ferro, Mario Pérez, Angel Pla Picette, José Fosca, and Manuel Gutiérrez. Mario Hidalgo-Gato spent three weeks in El Príncipe prison in Havana before charges were dropped after bribing Urgency Tribunal secretary de la Ville. See Horacio Hidalgo-Gato, interview; Suárez Rivas, interview; Márquez-Sterling, interview; "En Cuba: Oriente," *Bohemia,* November 1, 1953, 73; "Unos 70 muertos es el trágico balance del golpe contra los cuarteles de Santiago y Bayamo," *Diario de la Marina,* July 28, 1953, 25; "'Tenemos el deber de guardar el orden y la paz,' dijo Batista," *Diario de la Marina,* August 4, 1953, 28; Varona, interview.

5. Norberto Batista, interview; Marta Rojas, "El asalto al Moncada," *Bohemia,* February 1, 1959, 166; Merle, *Moncada,* 233; Pedro de la Hoz, "En la vida de Marta Rojas hubo también un antes y un después del Moncada," *Granma,* July 26, 2003; *Revolución,* July 25, 1963, 5.

6. "Unos 70 muertos," 25; Angel González, interview; Horacio Martínez, interview; Tobío, interview; Ernesto Cuello, interview.

7. Tobío, interview; Ernesto Cuello, interview; Despatch 191, July 30, 1953, *Cuba Internal Affairs.*

8. Ernesto Cuello, interview; Tobío, interview; Ambassador Beaulac to Secretary of State, July 26, 1953, *Cuba Internal Affairs*.

9. Rafael Morales, interview; Conrad Allain, "The Sorrow over the Tragedy of Santiago Is Nationwide," *Havana Post*, August 2, 1953, 2.

10. Ramon Eduardo Ruiz, *Cuba: The Making of a Revolution* (New York: W. W. Norton & Company, 1970), 152, 158; Halperin, *Fidel Castro's Road to Power*, 89; Moore, *Castro, the Blacks, and Africa*, 32–33; Ramón M. Barquín, *Las luchas guerrilleras en Cuba: De la colonia a la Sierra Maestra*, vol. 1 (Madrid: Editorial Playor S.A., 1975), 98. See also de la Fuente, *Nation for All*, which neglects to analyze the role of Afro-Cubans in the armed forces during 1902–58.

11. Maj. Rafael Morales Alvarez (June 7, 1904–July 7, 1988), police major José Izquierdo, and Capt. Juan de Dios Ruiz Herrera acted honorably during the defense of the garrison. After Castro seized power, they were not persecuted or jailed and retired with pensions. Because they did not go into exile, some military personnel who sympathized with Col. Alberto del Río Chaviano have referred to the three as "traitors." Cpl. Norberto Batista claimed that Ruiz was actively conspiring with him against the Communist regime in the 1960s before he died of lung cancer in 1971. Rafael Morales Gros (October 14, 1932–November 11, 1985) died in Miami of complications from diabetes. See Norberto Batista, interview; Lt. Antonio Policarpo Ochoa Ferrer, personal interview, Miami, Fla., December 23, 1974; Lt. Carlos Lazo Cuba, personal interview, Miami, Fla., July 2, 2004; Rafael Morales, interview; Pvt. Osvaldo Toledo Niebla, personal interview, Carolina, P.R., August 14, 1988; Raimundo, *Habla el Coronel Orlando Piedra*, 48.

12. Capt. Rosendo Abreu Jiménez (March 1, 1912–April 17, 2001) retired from the army in August 1958 after thirty-three years and went to live in Europe. He moved to Florida in 1963 and passed away in North Bergen, N.J. Pvt. Roberto Lescano Lescano was sentenced to thirty years of imprisonment on April 17, 1959, by a revolutionary tribunal in Holguín (*El Mundo*, April 18, 1959, 6). See Norberto Batista, interview; Abreu, interview; Thomas, *Cuba*, 840.

13. Lt. Vicente Camps Ruiz, personal interview, Bronx, N.Y., September 10, 1974.

14. Eulalio González, interview; Olivares, interview.

15. Castro, *History Will Absolve Me*, 31; Canto, *Mi vida*, 164.

16. Lt. Jesús Yanez Pelletier, a mulatto of New Orleans Creole and Chinese descent, had obtained his Cadet School commission in July 1946. He was married to María del Carmen Querejeta, daughter of Afro-Cuban Gen. Gregorio Querejeta, and had a son, Jesús Gregorio. See Lt. Angel Machado Rofe, interview, December 31, 1974; Eulalio Gonzalez, interview; Rosell, interview; Lt. Jesús Yanez Pelletier, telephone interview, Havana, Cuba, May 6, 1997.

17. Lt. Alberto Alonso Martínez (December 14, 1924–July 1985) appeared on a photo with the Lenin book in "Aquel libro de Lenin," *Verde Olivo*, July 26, 1964, 41. Lieutenant Alonso went into exile in New York in 1959, worked at the *El Diario-La Prensa* newspaper, and was murdered in the street while resisting a holdup. See "Lenin Book Found on Attackers," *Havana Post*, July 28, 1953, 10; and Rojas, *La Generación del Centenario*, 50. After Fidel Castro announced in December 1961 that he had always been an avowed Communist, Marta Rojas alleged that prior to the Moncada attack the rebel leaders, who had mostly a primary education, had studied the voluminous and dense "*Communist Manifesto*, the *Works of Lenin*, *Das Capital*, and the *History of Political Ideas*, of the Academy of Sciences of the USSR." See Marta Rojas, "Los fundadores de la nueva Cuba," *Bohemia*, July 27, 1962, 30; Yanez, interview; Despatch 191, July 30, 1953, *Cuba Internal Affairs;* Capt. Agustín Lavastida Alvarez, personal interview, Miami, Fla., July 6, 1974; Brennan, *Castro, Cuba and Justice*, 27.

18. Ernesto González Bermejo and Norberto Fuentes, "La otra cara del Moncada," *Cuba*, July 1968, 10; Yanez, interview; Rojas, *La cueva del muerto*, 47.

19. Díaz-Francisco, interview.

20. "Detenido Manuel Lorenzo Acosta," *Prensa Universal*, August 27, 1953, 8; "Libertan a líderes del PRC y PPC," *El Mundo*, September 27, 1953, 4; Rojas, *La Generación del Centenario*, 168, 177; Merle, *Moncada*, 256; Autores varios, *Mártires del Moncada*, 427; "Gilberto E. Barón Martínez," *Bohemia*, December 30, 1983, 81; "Víctor Escalona Benítez: Obligado a cavar su propia tumba," *Granma*, June 28, 1973, 2; Mirabal Reyes, *El color de la Victoria*, 203.

21. Autores varios, *Mártires del Moncada*, 394; Carmen Villar, "El asalto al Moncada visto por uno de los combatientes: Oscar Alcalde," *Juventud Rebelde*, July 21, 1966, 8; Merle, *Moncada*, 272.

22. Teodulio "Lulo" Mitchell Barbán (April 17, 1924–November 10, 1992) in 1959 was appointed first lieutenant of the rebel army. In 1977 he was employed in the army transport base in Boyeros municipality. See "Teodulio Mitchell: Tengo 24 años porque yo nací aquel día . . . ," *Granma*, July 24, 1977, 5; Merle, *Moncada*, 274–77.

23. José Méndez Cominches, a member of the Catholic Youth, later joined the 26 of July Movement. In 1959 he headed the repressive G-2 State Security in Santiago de Cuba. See Canto, *Mi vida*, 375; Merle, *Moncada*, 251; Jaime Sarusky, "Una increible cadena de solidaridad humana," *Bohemia*, July 21, 1972, 6; Bartolomé, interview; Autores varios, *Mártires del Moncada*, 290; Lupiáñez Reinlein, *El Movimiento Estudiantil*, 168; Enrique Rubio Llerena, personal interview, San Juan, P.R., December 11, 1985; Cuervo and Llenín, *Moncada*, 88; "Sepultado el asaltante al Cuartel Moncada Mario Dalmau de la Cruz," *Granma*, October 1, 1990, 2.

24. Dr. René Eldidy (March 26, 1921–February 26, 1996) passed away in Miami. See Arcos, interview; Franqui, *Twelve*, 85; Mencia, *El grito del Moncada*, 575; Centro de Estudios, *Moncada: La acción*, 267–68; Eldidy, interview.

25. Sarusky, "Una increible cadena," 9; "No señor, de aquí no se llevan a nadie . . . ," *Granma*, July 18, 1969, 2; José Ponce Díaz, "Recuerdos del ataque," *Verde Olivo*, July 28, 1963, 17; Almeida Bosque, *La aurora de los héroes*, 163; Allain, "Sorrow over the Tragedy," 2; Centro de Estudios, *Moncada: La acción*, 268; Ana María Radaelli, "José Ponce Díaz," *Cuba Internacional*, July 1983, 63.

26. Oscar Quintela Bonilla was third secretary in the Cuban Embassy in Czechoslovakia from 1974 to 1978, and Ernesto Tizol Aguilera was third secretary there in 1978. See Gervasio G. Ruiz, "El asalto al Cuartel Moncada," *Carteles*, July 26, 1959, 53; Llerena, *Unsuspected Revolution*, 54–57; Travieso, *Un nuevo día*, 166–68; Raúl Martínez, interview; Autores varios, *Mártires del Moncada*, 408; Merle, *Moncada*, 135, 250, 267–68.

27. Mencia, "El grito del Moncada," *Bohemia*, July 20, 1984, 88; Suardíaz, interview; Mafut Delgado, interview; Franqui, *Diary*, 60–61; Autores varios, *Mártires del Moncada*, 359; Rojas, *La Generación del Centenario*, 261; Rojas, *El que debe vivir*, 103–5.

28. Oscar Alcalde later confirmed to Raúl del Mazo Serra in the Boniato Provincial Prison that Fidel Castro had put a pistol to his own head in the Siboney farmhouse after the failed attack. See Chanes, interview; Granados, interview.

29. Suardíaz, interview; Granados, interview; Marta Rojas, "Abelardo Crespo: A quien dejaron por muerto, la solidaridad del pueblo santiaguero le salvó la vida," *Granma*, July 17, 1973, 4; Travieso, *Un nuevo día*, 138; Chanes, interview; Mafut Delgado, interview.

30. Bourne, *Fidel*, 85, inflates to sixty the number of rebels returning to the farmhouse. Teodulio Mitchell claimed in 1977 that Fidel Castro asked him to take Nito Ortega away for treatment. On the road a group of rebels in an automobile picked up Nito, and according to Mitchell, all of them were captured and killed. This apocryphal account contradicts Mafut's statement. See "Teodulio Mitchell," 5; Reyes Trejo, "Habla un combatiente del Moncada," 15; Betto, *Fidel y la religión*, 175–76; Chanes, interview; Mafut Delgado, interview; Costa, interview.

31. The rebels who accompanied Fidel Castro into the countryside were Oscar Alcalde, Juan Almeida, Reinaldo Benítez, Mario Chanes de Armas, Francisco González Hernández, Emilio Hernández Cruz, Rosendo Menéndez, Armando Mestre, Jesús Montané, Eduardo Montano, José Suárez, Israel Tápanes, Jaime Costa Chávez, Orlando and Roberto Galán, Gerardo Granados Lara, Mario Lazo, Severino Rosell, and Ricardo Santana. The last seven eventually escaped capture. See Costa, interview; Chanes, interview; Granados, interview.

32. Manuel Suardíaz Fernández (December 8, 1924–June 29, 1992) went to work for the Cuban Institute of Sugar Stabilization in 1954. He was arrested after the April 9, 1958, general strike, tried, and found not guilty. Suardíaz organized the clandestine rebel First Column Angel Ameijeiras in Madruga with sixty-seven men. He was arrested on September 7, 1961, and sentenced to nine years of imprisonment in Case 567 for being a member of the anti-Castro Democratic Revolutionary Front. He was released in 1970 and left Cuba in the 1980 Mariel boatlift. Suardíaz became a naturalized American citizen and settled in Queens, N.Y., where he passed away. See Suardíaz, interview; and "Falleció Orbeín Hernández, asaltante al Moncada," *Granma*, July 31, 1985, 2.

33. Merle, *Moncada*, 259–60; Travieso, *Un nuevo día*, 142–43; Lázaro Barredo Medina, *Mi prisionero Fidel: Recuerdos del teniente Pedro Sarría* (Havana: Editorial Pablo de la Torriente, 1986), 85.

34. Gelasio Fernández Martínez, who killed Sgt. Ramón Silveiro, hid in the home of Rubén Pérez Proenza's father until Tuesday afternoon, July 28, when after receiving clothes, phony identification, and funds, he went by train to Havana. The carnival tourists with criminal antecedents killed by the soldiers were Francisco Viera Milián, a forty-three-year-old sugar mill worker; Eduardo A. Hernández Ravella, a thirty-two-year-old peasant; and Rubén Cordero Sánchez. See Centro de Estudios, *Moncada: La acción*, 268–69; Lupiáñez Reinlein, *El Movimiento Estudiantil*, 168; "Unos 70 muertos," 25; Rojas, *La cueva del muerto*, 19; Merle, *Moncada*, 227; Marta Rojas, "Esos heridos traían dos ropas," *Granma*, July 10, 1967, 8; Autores varios, *Mártires del Moncada*, 337, 349, 425; "Nueva relación de los muertos en la capital de Oriente," *Diario de la Marina*, August 14, 1953, 32; "Attackers of Army Posts Identified as Criminals," *Havana Post*, July 31, 1953, 1; Pablo Mila Ortíz, "Duró cinco horas el combate en Santiago," *El Mundo*, July 28, 1953, 8.

35. Merle, *Moncada*, 261–63; Autores varios, *Mártires del Moncada*, 386–89.

36. Lawton cell leader Gabriel Gil Alfonso during the past forty-five years has never clarified in various interviews his role in the Moncada attack or why he was not leading six of his seven men who were captured in the Civil Hospital and later executed. Humberto Valdés Casañas was acquitted in court of his participation in the Moncada attack. He was killed on November 17, 1958, while participating in a drive-by shooting with other comrades against the Fifteenth Precinct Police Station in Miramar. See Merle, *Moncada*, 261–63; "Unos 70 muertos," 25; and "Versión taquigráfica del programa 'Siempre es 26,'" *Granma*, June 29, 1973, 5.

37. Angel "El Gallego" Núñez received from Fidel Castro a Soviet Moskovich car in 1973 and a monthly guarantee of sixty free gallons of gas. See Canto, *Mi vida,* 465; Alfredo Reyes Trejo, "Del Moncada a las montañas," *Verde Olivo,* July 23, 1967, 42; Chanes, interview; Rojas, *La cueva del muerto,* 61; Guillermo Cabrera, "El comerciante de pollos de Siboney," *Juventud Rebelde,* July 18, 1969, 2; Sarusky, "Una increíble cadena," 7; Centro de Estudios, *Moncada: La acción,* 79; Rojas, "Abelardo Crespo," 4.

38. Mafut Delgado, interview; Rojas, *La cueva del muerto,* 44.

39. Reyes Trejo, "Del Moncada a las montañas," 53; Rojas, *La cueva del muerto,* 46–47; Mafut Delgado, interview; Almeida Bosque, *La aurora de los héroes,* 150.

40. Moises Mafut Delgado (March 11, 1922–March 25, 2005) left Cuba on the Mariel boat lift and passed away in Miami. Emilio Albentosa Chacón went into exile in Mexico with a few other Moncada veterans on August 9, 1955. He returned to Cuba sixteen months later on the Granma expedition. Albentosa was shot in the neck during the first encounter with army troops three days later. He managed to reach Santiago de Cuba and obtain medical treatment. Albentosa did not join his comrades in the Sierra Maestra and consequently did not receive a post in the revolutionary government. See Rojas, *La cueva del muerto,* 49; Mafut Delgado, interview.

41. Marta Rojas, "Julito Díaz permaneció en 'Las Múcuras' mientras Ciro Redondo y Marcos Martí estaban en 'La Cueva del Muerto,'" *Granma,* July 24, 1968, 5; Rojas, *La cueva del muerto,* 28, 32, 48; Sarusky, "Una increíble cadena," 10; Centro de Estudios, *Moncada: La acción,* 291.

42. "Unos 70 muertos," 25; "Jose Villa Romero: Sus antecedentes políticos y vida actual," *Granma,* July 24, 1973, 3; Rojas, *El que debe vivir,* 102.

43. Lt. Luis S. Gamboa Alarcón was executed before a revolutionary firing squad on January 12, 1959, at San Juan Hill. Lt. Antonio Barquet Aguiar met the same fate in Santa Clara on November 24, 1959. See Matthews, *Revolution in Cuba,* 61; Merle, *Moncada,* 236; Rico, interview; Pupo, interview; Martija, interview; Matos, interview; Olivares, interview; Rosell, interview.

44. José Luis Tasende's corpse was later dressed in a clean uniform, outfitted with shoes, and photographed on the barbershop floor with a shotgun next to him to simulate death in combat. The photo appeared in Editorial de Ciencias Sociales, *Moncada,* 177. His killer, Pvt. Manuel Avila Sánchez, died in Cuba of natural causes without his deed being known by the revolutionary government. Pvt. Mónico García, who carried Tasende to the first-aid clinic, was sentenced to three years at hard labor for "banditry" by a revolutionary tribunal in Santiago de Cuba on April 28, 1959. Gen. Martín Díaz Tamayo (November 11, 1904–March 4, 1995) was appointed director of the Bureau for the Repression of Communist Activities (BRAC) in July 1955. In April 1956 he became commander of the Moncada regiment. Díaz Tamayo was promoted the following year to major general and headed the SIM. He was forced to retire after participating in the Thanksgiving Day 1958 conspiracy against Batista. He was imprisoned for only a few hours after the rebels seized power. Díaz Tamayo confidently told his cell mate Ernesto de la Fe Pérez, "I just saw Fidel's mother and sister, who are indignant that I have been arrested and are going to obtain my release." He obtained asylum in the Peruvian Embassy and left the country on March 16, 1959. In 1972 Dr. Santiago Ramón Guillaume, of the Oriente Office of Historical Affairs, told the journalist Herbert Matthews that the Castro regime possessed a note from Fulgencio Batista to Martín Díaz Tamayo ordering "to kill ten rebels for every soldier killed." The apocryphal note has never been reproduced,

and it seems illogical that such a dastardly order would need to be written down. If the order were true, the revolutionary government would have executed the imprisoned former general and not have released him to seek asylum. See Merle, *Moncada*, 236; Rico, interview; Norberto Batista, interview; Martija, interview; Matos, interview; Mila Ortíz, "Duró cinco horas," 1; Rojas, *El que debe vivir*, 107; Castro, *History Will Absolve Me*, 64.

45. In 1959 the Castro regime sentenced former Oriente governor Waldo Pérez Almaguer to nine years in prison and confiscated his property for being a counterrevolutionary. The prosecutor had asked for a death sentence. His brother Osvaldo Pérez Almaguer was executed by a rebel firing squad in Holguín on January 19, 1959. See "Pérez Almaguer Resigns as Oriente Governor," *Havana Post*, September 3, 1953, 10; "Yo vi fusilar a mas de 30 revolucionarios," *La Calle*, June 3, 1955, 1; Nieto, interview; Rico, interview.

46. José Pujol Soler, personal interview, Miami, Fla., December 22, 1974.

47. Antonio Ochoa, interview; Rafael Morales, interview; Rojas, *La cueva del muerto*, 83; "Biografía de un asesino," *Bohemia*, August 30, 1968, 58–63; Despatch 525, October 5, 1953, *Cuba Internal Affairs*; Sarusky, "Una increíble cadena," 7; Rojas, *La Generación del Centenario*, 112; Merle, *Moncada*, 241; Col. Carlos Tabernilla Palmero, telephone interview, West Palm Beach, Fla., December 21, 2005; Col. Marcelo Tabernilla Palmero, telephone interview, Miami, Fla., December 29, 2005; "Unos 70 muertos," 27.

48. Díaz-Francisco, interview.

49. Merle, *Moncada*, 246; Alcolea, interview; Oliva, interview; Olivares, interview; Yanez, interview.

50. "Un resumen de los dolorosos sucesos de Oriente," *Bohemia*, August 9, 1953, 61; Marta Rojas, "Moncada 1953: Los fundadores de la nueva Cuba," *Bohemia*, July 27, 1962, 32, 97; Marta Rojas, "Itinerario y balance de un infame crimen," *Bohemia*, February 8, 1959, 42; Merle, *Moncada*, 244; "Gráficas de los trágicos y lamentables sucesos de Santiago de Cuba," *Bohemia*, August 2, 1953, 81.

51. "Cuba Government Troops Rout Rebels After Raids on Oriente Army Barracks," *Havana Post*, July 28, 1953, 2. Cpl. Elio Rizo Carbonell, who was photographed holding up an eighteen-inch kitchen knife purported to have been used by the attackers in the military hospital, became a teacher at Moncada after it was converted into a school on January 28, 1960. See "Unos 70 muertos," 25; "Gráficas de los trágicos," 75; and Editorial de Ciencias Sociales, *Moncada*, 212.

52. "En Cuba: Oriente," 74; de la Fe, interview.

53. "Derechos sin vigencia con la suspensión de las Garantías" and "Nombran censores para 4 periódicos," *Diario de la Marina*, July 28, 1953, 1; Despatches 167 and 173, July 29, 1953, *Cuba Internal Affairs*.

54. *Tribuna Médica*, July–December 1962; Merle, *Moncada*, 244–47; Travieso, *Un nuevo día*, 158–60.

55. Santiago de Cuba was divided into two instruction judicial districts. See *Tribuna Médica*, July–December 1962; Sarusky, "Una increíble cadena," 14; Merle, *Moncada*, 231; Conte Agüero, *Cartas del Presidio*, 15; Francisco Mendieta Tamayo, personal interview, San Juan, P.R., November 8, 1982.

56. José Tobío claimed that Manuel "El Niño" Cala Reyes was killed when he mouthed off to a group of passing soldiers and called them abusers. The policeman Evelio Xenis stated that Cala, "a dangerous person," was killed "needlessly" by Sgt. René Caso Pérez. Cpl. Norberto

Batista Seguí, whose father had been in the army with Cala, claimed that the soldier who murdered Cala was someone else who was never caught. Three of Cala's relatives who were in the army, César Cala Reytor and Antonio and Ramón Reytor, were executed by revolutionary firing squads in January 1959. See *Tribuna Médica*, July–December 1962; Travieso, *Un nuevo día*, 159; "Troops, Rebels Clash at Two Points," *Havana Post*, July 29, 1953, 10; Centro de Estudios, *Moncada: La acción*, 257; Rojas, *La Generación del Centenario*, 131; Tobío, interview; Xenis, interview; Horacio Martínez, interview; Bartolomé, interview.

57. Judge Manuel Urrutia Lleó (December 8, 1901–July 5, 1981) presided over the trial of the Granma expeditionaries in 1957. He voted for the acquittal of the rebels but was overruled by the two other magistrates, who gave them a six-year sentence. Urrutia went into exile in December 1957 and joined the revolutionary cause. He became provisional president of Cuba when the rebels seized power. On July 17, 1959, Urrutia resigned the presidency after Castro accused him of treason. He spent some time under house arrest and then obtained asylum in the Venezuelan Embassy until receiving a safe-conduct pass on March 25, 1963, when he went to the United States via Mexico. The following year he published *Fidel Castro and Company, Inc.: Communist Tyranny in Cuba* (New York: Praeger). He was a university professor in New York City, where he passed away. See Wolfgang Saxon, "Manuel Urrutia Lleo, 79, Dies; Was President under Castro," *New York Times*, July 6, 1981, D7; Centro de Estudios, *Moncada: La acción*, 260; Merle, *Moncada*, 265; "Tenemos el deber de guardar," 28; Editorial de Ciencias Sociales, *Moncada*, 214–15.

58. Lázara Sarah Pérez Cuesta alleged that she and Mario Burman were married in 1951. They went to Venezuela in 1957, and she returned to Cuba two years later after their separation. Pérez Cuesta remarried in 1959, and she and her husband were exiled in 1961. Burman remained in South America, where he passed away. See Lázara Sarah Pérez Cuesta, telephone interview, Miami, Fla., August 3, 1991; Domingo Estrada Beatón, telephone interview, Kansas City, Mo., July 29, 1984; McManus, *From the Palm Tree*, 17.

59. Cols. Fermín Cowley Gallegos (December 7, 1907–November 23, 1957) and Antonio Blanco Rico (July 4, 1917–October 28, 1956) were assassinated by revolutionaries during the Sierra Maestra campaign. On the same front page that the newspaper published Batista's speech, saying that the guards on Post 3 had been stabbed to death, the correspondent in Santiago de Cuba claimed that the sentinels were killed "by hand grenades thrown against Post 3" and that "seven members of the Armed Forces were killed in their beds in the Military Hospital." On p. 25 of that issue, army chief of staff major general Francisco Tabernilla Dolz said that the sentries on Post 3 were gunned down by contact shots. Of the thirty-six Moncada military and police personnel interviewed for this book, only three insisted that the rebels had stabbed soldiers to death: Col. Alberto del Río Chaviano, Capt. Agustín Lavastida, and Lt. Teodoro Rico Boué, all three directly involved in the execution of prisoners. See "Unos 70 muertos," 25; "'El gobierno debe ser sereno y justo, pero energico" (Batista quoted in *Diario de la Marina*, July 28, 1953, 1, 16); and Despatch 165, July 28, 1953, *Cuba Internal Affairs*.

60. "Unos 70 muertos," 25; Bartolomé, interview.

61. "Unos 70 muertos," 25; Alcolea, interview; Armando Acosta, interview; Reyes, interview; "Los muertos en Oriente," *El Crisol*, July 28, 1953, 1; "Noticias nacionales," *Diario de Cuba*, July 29, 1953, 2; Carlos A. Delgado Martínez, telephone interview, Miami, Fla., December 10, 2005.

62. José Medina Puig, telephone interview, Miami, Fla., February 1, 1986; Centro de Estudios, *Moncada: La acción,* 307; Rojas, *La Generación del Centenario en el juicio del Moncada,* 89; Bartolomé, interview.

63. Red Cross major José Manuel Diez gave an apocryphal account in 1984, claiming that the rebels were interred in groups of six or seven inside refrigerator packing crates. After her husband's death, Mrs. Muñoz moved with her two daughters to her mother's house in Havana. When she and the children went into exile on October 24, 1961, after paying a five-thousand-peso bribe for an exit permit, they were erased from all revolutionary accounts. The Muñoz home was converted into a museum. Younger brother Roberto Muñoz became an avid Castro supporter in 1959. Mrs. Muñoz described him as "an opportunistic bum" who was always jealous of his successful sibling. See Travieso, *Un nuevo día,* 155, 161–62; Bartolomé, interview; Cuervo and Llenín, *Moncada,* 134–35, 139; "Continúa la persecución de los asaltantes del Cuartel Moncada," *Avance,* July 28, 1953, 1; Algarra, interview; Centro de Estudios, *Moncada: La acción,* 142–43, 307; Rojas, "Itinerario y balance," 44; Rojas, *La Generación del Centenario,* 125–37; "Fuerzas de mar y aire apresaron y condujeron 2 buques a Puerto la Fe," *Diario de la Marina,* July 30, 1953, 17; Canto, *Mi vida,* 164; Sarusky, "Una increíble cadena," 12.

64. Lt. Vicente Camps Ruiz was sentenced to death by a revolutionary tribunal on January 29, 1959, which was later commuted to thirty years of imprisonment and a fifty-thousand-peso fine. He was released from the Isle of Pines penitentiary in 1962 and later went into exile. After this interview ended late at night, Camps, armed with a handgun, accompanied the author to a subway station in the Bronx, warning that he lived in a high-crime neighborhood. Nine months later Camps was murdered in front of his home by a drug addict. See "Continua la labor de Mons. Pérez Serantes para una pacificación," *Diario de la Marina,* July 31, 1953, 23; and Camps, interview.

65. Merle, *Moncada,* 296; Camps, interview.

66. Camps, interview; Centro de Estudios de Historia Militar, *Moncada: Motor de la Revolución* (Havana: Editora Política, 1986), 15.

67. "Brother of Fidel Castro Admits Hospital Murders," *Havana Post,* July 31, 1953, 1, 10.

68. "Reportan absoluta normalidad en la capital de Oriente," *Diario de la Marina,* July 29, 1953, 1; Rojas, *La cueva del muerto,* 114. "Fidel Castro, Rebel Leader, Surrenders," *Havana Post,* August 2, 1953, 9.

69. In February 1959 the revolutionary government named Max E. Figueroa Araújo (1913–96) as provincial inspector of urban schools in Oriente as well as director general of superior and secondary education. María Antonia Figueroa Araújo (1918–) later became an organizer for the 26 of July Movement. See Sarusky, "Una increíble cadena," 6, 11, 16; Lupiáñez Reinlein, *El Movimiento Estudiantil,* 166; and Centro de Estudios, *Moncada: La acción,* 294–95.

70. "Entregados a Urgencia los 21 detenidos por el asalto al Moncada," *Diario de Cuba,* July 28, 1953, 1; "Muertos once asaltantes," *Alerta,* July 29, 1953, 1; Lázara Pérez, interview; Díaz-Francisco, interview; Rojas, *Los testigos del hospital,* 26, 34; Merle, *Moncada,* 230; Alfredo Corcho Acosta, "Allí reconocimos el cadáver de nuestro hermano," *Granma,* March 14, 1973, 2.

71. Taber, *M-26,* 42, claims that not one but both of Abel's eyes were "gouged out." This falsehood is repeated in Bourne, *Fidel,* 88. In a 1977 interview with Sally Quinn, Haydée Santamaría propagated the myth that, "in order to make Santamaria and Santa Colona [sic] talk, the captors tore out Abel's *eyes* [author's emphasis] and crushed one of Boris' testicles, but the

captives still would not tell where Fidel was. So one eye and one testicle were brought to Haydee Santamaria to try to make her tell. She didn't." ("To Die Is Much Easier," *Washington Post*, March 21, 1977). See "Hablan los detenidos," *Prensa Universal*, July 28, 1953, 1; Ediciones Políticas, *Veintiseis*, 123; Franqui, *Diary*, 61; Ediciones Políticas, *Haydée habla del Moncada*, 33; Castro, *History Will Absolve Me*, 66; McManus, *From the Palm Tree*, 17; Rojas, *La Generación del Centenario*, 111, 262, 264; Kurt Singer, "I, Fidel Castro," *Illustrated Weekly of India*, December 18, 1960, 13; Fiterre, interview.

72. Forty-seven forensic reports published in Marta Rojas's *La Generación del Centenario*, 124–36, 218–23, indicate that the rebels all died of bullet wounds. None mentions signs of mutilation or torture. See Matthews, *Fidel Castro*, 71–72; Bonachea and Valdés, *Revolutionary Struggle*, 198n32, 223n3, 5; Raúl Martínez, interview; Bartolomé, interview.

73. The soldiers dubbed the revolutionaries Mau Maus, after the Kenyan nationalists who began a terrorist campaign in October 1952 against British colonialism. Forensic physician Manuel Prieto Aragón heard the soldiers on the night of the attack referring to the rebels as Mau Maus. The rebel Abelardo Crespo recalled being called a Mau Mau. Sgt. Eulalio "El Mulo" González never saw action during the Sierra Maestra campaign, serving in the security detail of the camp commander's residence. See Eulalio González, interview; Centro de Estudios, *Moncada: La acción*, 85; Travieso, *Un nuevo día*, 158; Castro, *History Will Absolve Me*, 68–69.

74. Marta Rojas, "Los últimos minutos de Abel Santamaría en los calabozos del Moncada," *Granma*, July 24, 1973, 3; Rojas, *La Generación del Centenario*, 264; Rojas, *El que debe vivir*, 105; Valdés, interview; Yanez, interview.

75. The bodies of Reinaldo Boris Luis and Fernando Chenard were photographed on the grounds of the Siboney farmhouse and appeared in Centro de Estudios, *Moncada: La acción*. See also Sarusky, "Una increíble cadena," 7; Yanez, interview; Bartolomé, interview; "Trasladan a El Caney los cadáveres de los 6 asaltantes muertos en 'Siboney,'" *Prensa Universal*, July 29, 1953, 1; Lavastida, interview.

76. "Otra víctima de la tiranía," *Bohemia*, April 3, 1960, 115; Tobío, interview.

77. Raúl de Aguiar Fernández, Armando Valle López, and Andrés Valdés Fuentes are sometimes erroneously identified as Bayamo combatants. Their killers, Sgt. Eliodoro Montes de Oca Mayea and Cpl. Pedro A. Maceo Martí, were executed by a revolutionary firing squad on January 12, 1959, at San Juan Hill. In November 1964 six former soldiers were found guilty in a Santiago de Cuba courtroom of Gregorio Careaga's murder. Three were shot by firing squad, and the others were sentenced to thirty years of imprisonment. One of them, Sgt. Vicente Alonso Cruz, died of cardiac arrest in prison in the late 1970s. See "Un resumen de los dolorosos," 62; Autores varios, *Mártires del Moncada*, 249–53; Travieso, *Un nuevo día*, 140–41; Mencia, *Time Was on Our Side*, 106; "Dos fechas históricas," *Bohemia*, July 13, 1984, 80; Mencia, *El grito del Moncada*, 491; "Andrés Valdés Fuentes," *Granma*, July 12, 1973, 2; Rojas, *La Generación del Centenario*, 435.

78. Rojas, *La Generación del Centenario*, 220–24; Rojas, *La cueva del muerto*, 166.

79. Thomas, *Cuba*, 840–41, erroneously has Archbishop Enrique Pérez Serantes personally meeting with Andrés Morales del Castillo. This mistake is repeated in Bourne, *Fidel*, 86. Although Robert Merle claims that the telephone call to Morales del Castillo was on Monday, some of those present said it was on Tuesday. Luis Savigne Pavón (November 3, 1902–March 27, 1998) passed away in Sarasota, Fla. See Merle, *Moncada*, 282; Conte Agüero, *Los dos rostros*, 49; Luis Savigne Pavón, telephone interview, Sarasota, Fla., February 15, 1986.

80. Carlos Piñeiro, interview.

81. Ibid; del Río Chaviano, interview; Rafael Morales, interview; Batista, *Cuba Betrayed*, 36.

82. Rolando Amador Hernández was sentenced to six years of imprisonment and had all his property confiscated by a revolutionary tribunal on February 11, 1960, for conspiracy against the powers of the state. See Rolando Amador Hernández, telephone interview, Miami, Fla., February 28, 1988; "Plan terrorista," *Tiempo,* July 29, 1953, 1; "Viene a Santiago la esposa de F. Castro," *Diario de Cuba,* July 30, 1953, 2; Despatch 191, July 30, 1953, *Cuba Internal Affairs.*

83. Jacob Canter (July 13, 1911–January 31, 2000) received a Ph.D. from Harvard University in 1940. He served in the navy during World War II before starting in 1946 his career as a public and cultural-affairs officer with both the State Department and the U.S. Information Agency. His postings included Nicaragua, Colombia, Cuba, Mexico, and Spain. At his retirement in 1971 Canter was visiting professor of public diplomacy at Tuft University's Fletcher School of Law and Diplomacy. Despatch 223, August 3, 1953, *Cuba Internal Affairs;* "Clausurado el Periódico 'Hoy,'" *Alerta,* July 27, 1953, 1.

84. Despatch 165, July 28, 1953, *Cuba Internal Affairs.*

85. Despatch 223, August 6, 1953, *Cuba Internal Affairs;* de la Fe, interview.

86. Enrique Pérez Serantes (November 29, 1883–April 18, 1968) was born in Tuy, Spain; obtained a doctorate in philosophy and theology from the Pontificia Universita Gregoriana in Rome; and was ordained into the priesthood at Havana on September 11, 1910. He became bishop of Camagüey on February 24, 1922, and was appointed archbishop of Santiago de Cuba on December 11, 1948. In his pastoral letter of February 2, 1959, he asked the revolutionary government to stop the firing squad executions and create a climate of forgiveness. In another pastoral letter two years later, Pérez Serantes accused the Castro regime of "initiating a battle against Christianity." Mariano Roca Gutiérrez (January 15, 1914–December 19, 1994) passed away in Miami. See "Un resumen de los dolorosos," 63–65; Juan Martín Leiseca, *Apuntes para la Historia Eclesiástica de Cuba* (Havana: Talleres Tipográficos de Carasa, 1938), 343; Medina, interview; Mariano Roca Gutiérrez, telephone interview, San Juan, P.R., February 1, 1986; "Propician Rotarios y Leones un clima de paz y concordia," *Diario de Cuba,* July 31, 1953, 1; "De Monseñor Pérez Serantes al Coronel Río Chaviano," *Alerta,* July 31, 1953, 8; Matthews, *Fidel Castro,* 67–68; Canto, *Mi vida,* 166.

87. Rector Felipe Salcines Morlote (June 12, 1903–March 1987) went into exile in West New York, N.J., in 1972, where he passed away. See Canto, *Mi vida,* 166; "Continua la labor," 1; Angel González, interview; and "Bando Militar No. 1," *Oriente,* July 30, 1953, 8.

88. Canto, *Mi vida,* 166–67; "Continua la labor," 23; Despatch 223, August 6, 1953, *Cuba Internal Affairs.*

89. Canto, *Mi vida,* 167–68.

90. When Ernesto Tizol was released from prison in 1955, he left for the United States with his wife and two children and did not participate in the guerrilla war against the Batista regime. He returned to Cuba in 1959 and held various minor government positions. Tizol later divorced and married a Russian woman before passing away on July 1, 1984. The official *Granma* newspaper did not publish his obituary. A list of the dead rebels is in appendix 1. See Alcolea, interview; Radaelli, "José Ponce Díaz," 63; del Mazo, interview; Raúl Martínez, interview; "Detenido Fidel Castro y enviado a la Prisión Provincial de Oriente," *El Mundo,* August 2, 1953, 10; Merle, *Moncada,* 286; "'Soy el único responsable' dice Fidel Castro en su declaración," *El Crisol,* August 3, 1953, 1.

Chapter 7—"You do not kill ideas"

1. Chanes, interview; Costa, interview; Granados, interview; Montano, interview; Centro de Estudios, *Moncada: La acción,* 15; N. Osvaldo Ortega, "Después del asalto," *Verde Olivo,* July 26, 1964, 33; Lazo, *Recuerdos,* 53; Alfredo Reyes Trejo, "Del Moncada a las montañas," *Verde Olivo,* July 23, 1967, 37, 41.

2. Mario Lazo, in *Recuerdos,* calls Leocadia "Chicha" García Garzón by the name "Eleocadia." Lazo had previously identified her as "Domitila" in Reyes Trejo, "Habla un combatiente," 15. See "Cuando Sarría detuvo a Fidel Castro y a sus dos compañeros el sábado 1ro. de agosto de 1953," *Revolución,* July 26, 1962, 15; Rojas, *La cueva del muerto,* 88; Lazo, *Recuerdos,* 58; Reyes Trejo, "Del Moncada a las montañas," 39; Merle, *Moncada,* 218; "La cueva del muerto," *Granma Resumen Semanal,* June 26, 1983, 12; Granados, interview; Montano, interview.

3. Lazo, *Recuerdos,* 56; Costa, interview; Rojas, *La cueva del muerto,* 85, 87, 90.

4. Lazo, *Recuerdos,* 59; Reyes Trejo, "Del Moncada a las montañas," 38, 49; Chanes, interview; Reyes Trejo, "Habla un combatiente," 15; Manuel Leizán Montero, personal interview, Rio Piedras, P.R., September 15, 1982.

5. Reyes Trejo, "Del Moncada a las montañas," 47, 52; Reyes Trejo, "Habla un combatiente," 15; Chanes, interview; Montano, interview; Gervasio G. Ruiz, "El asalto al Cuartel Moncada," *Carteles,* July 26, 1959, 53; Costa, interview.

6. Lazo, *Recuerdos,* 63; Reyes Trejo, "Del Moncada a las montañas," 47, 53; Montano, interview; Costa, interview; Granados, interview.

7. Lt. Randolfo Cossío was killed in an aviation accident in early 1959. See Conrad Allain, "The Sorrow over the Tragedy of Santiago Is Nationwide," *Havana Post,* August 2, 1953, 2; Rojas, *La cueva del muerto,* 34, 99; Carlos Lazo, interview; Despatch 7, August 10, 1953, *Cuba Internal Affairs;* Reyes Trejo, "Del Moncada a las montañas," 55, 56; Chanes, interview; Costa, interview; Montano, interview; Lazo, *Recuerdos,* 64, 67.

8. "Cuba Government Troops Rout Rebels After Raids on Oriente Army Barracks," *Havana Post,* July 28, 1953, 2; Lazo, *Recuerdos,* 64; Reyes Trejo, "Del Moncada a las montañas," 55.

9. Rojas, *La cueva del muerto,* 78; Lazo, *Recuerdos,* 69; Reyes Trejo, "Habla un combatiente," 15; Granados, interview.

10. Reyes Trejo, "Habla un combatiente," 15; Jaime Sarusky, "Una increible cadena de solidaridad humana," *Bohemia,* July 21, 1972, 12; Lazo, *Recuerdos,* 70; Chanes, interview.

11. Bourne, *Fidel,* 85, erroneously depicts Montané as being wounded. See Granados, interview; Merle, *Moncada,* 303; Reyes Trejo, "Del Moncada a las montañas," 55-56; Lazo, *Recuerdos,* 71-73.

12. After the revolution, the Arza family went into exile. See Lazo, *Recuerdos,* 170; Lázaro Barredo Medina, "En el vivac por los hechos del Moncada. ¡De pie los asaltantes!," *Juventud Rebelde,* July 4, 1971, 4; "Falleció Israel Tápanes," *Granma,* May 15, 1990, 2.

13. "Hablan los detenidos," *Prensa Universal,* July 30, 1953, 1; "Fidel Castro, Rebel Leader, Surrenders," *Havana Post,* August 2, 1953, 9.

14. Three years later, after landing with the Granma expedition, Jesús Montané would also passively surrender to the army after the government decreed a truce, and he stated, "I am convinced that the conditions for the insurrection have not been created." Montané married and later divorced Melba Hernández. See "Lo que nos dejaron seguir viendo," *Bohemia,* December 16, 1956, 52; "Lo que siguió el asalto del cuartel: Bestial reacción de la

tiranía," *La Calle,* July 26, 1959," C8; "Fidel Castro, Rebel Leader, Surrenders," 9; Ruiz, "El asalto at Cuartel Moncada," 53.

15. José Miró Cardona (August 22, 1902–August 10, 1974) became the prime minister of the revolutionary government on January 6, 1959, and resigned a month later. He went into exile in June 1960 and headed the Cuban Revolutionary Council, which orchestrated the Bay of Pigs invasion with U.S. government support in April 1961. Miró resigned from the council in March 1963 and taught law at the University of Puerto Rico. Humberto Sorí Marín joined the rebel forces in the Sierra Maestra in 1958. He drafted the rebel army penal code authorizing the execution of those considered "war criminals." Sorí Marín, sometimes called the "Cuban Robespierre," presided over the "war crimes" trials in 1959. He was designated the first revolutionary minister of agriculture and drafted the first agrarian reform program, which Castro rejected as "too mild." After six months Sorí Marín was dismissed from the cabinet and relegated to insignificant army posts. He went into exile in December 1960 and clandestinely returned on the eve of the Bay of Pigs invasion to coordinate an internal uprising. Sorí Marín was arrested with Eufemio Fernández Ortega and twenty-five other conspirators in a Marianao residence on April 17, 1961. Both men and five other plotters were executed by firing squad two days later. See "Continua la labor de Mons. Pérez Serantes para una pacificación," *Diario de la Marina,* July 31, 1953, 23; and "Designan Abogado Para Santiago," *El Mundo,* July 31, 1953, 5.

16. Chanes, interview; Montano, interview; René Celeiro, telephone interview, Miami, Fla., August 5, 1984; Carlos Lazo, interview; Rojas, *La cueva del muerto,* 169, 170.

17. Reyes Trejo, "Del Moncada a las montañas," 45; Rojas, *La cueva del muerto,* 173–74; Chanes, interview.

18. Chanes, interview; Reyes Trejo, "Del Moncada a las montañas," 52; Rojas, *La cueva del muerto,* 176.

19. Celeiro, interview; Chanes, interview; Montano, interview; Blanco, *Todo el tiempo,* 275; Canto, *Mi vida,* 169.

20. Amelia Fajardo was described by Marta Rojas as an "Ortodoxo sympathizer." She disavowed this, saying that she and her husband were apolitical. Fajardo stated that their friendship with the Campanals, who were Communists, ended before she and her husband went into exile in 1968. Arturo Campanal stated that he took his family to Santiago de Cuba on Wednesday, but Marta Rojas erroneously wrote that it occurred on Thursday. See Centro de Estudios, *Moncada: La acción,* 291; Rojas, *La cueva del muerto,* 165, 178–79; Amelia Fajardo, telephone interview, Miami, Fla., March 9, 1988.

21. The revolutionaries also sent the alcoholic "Carburo" to the firing squad in 1959. See Rojas, *La cueva del muerto,* 101, 186–88, 190; Centro de Estudios, *Moncada: La acción,* 291; Mariano Rodríguez Herrera, "Gudelia, de Marcos," *Juventud Rebelde,* July 21, 1987, 5; Sarusky, "Una increíble cadena," 10; Ariel Rojas, "El Caney: Testigo de una masacre," *Granma,* July 24, 1973, 5; "Ratifican la prisión y excluyen de fianza a sediciosos detenidos," *Prensa Universal,* July 31, 1953, 1; "Recorre sin descanso montañas, bosques y caminos S. I. Serantes," *Diario de la Marina,* August 1, 1953, 24.

22. "Un resumen de los dolorosos sucesos de Oriente," *Bohemia,* August 9, 1953, 65; Canto, *Mi vida,* 168–69.

23. Canto, *Mi vida,* 169; Matthews, *Fidel Castro,* 68.

24. Canto, *Mi vida,* 170–71.

25. Angel González, interview.

26. Reyes Trejo, "Del Moncada a las montañas," 45; Rojas, *La cueva del muerto*, 193; Chanes, interview; Leizán, interview.

27. Rojas, *La cueva del muerto*, 198; Chanes, interview; Montano, interview; Blanco, *Todo el tiempo*, 171; Reyes Trejo, "Del Moncada a las montañas," 59.

28. Manuela Montero died in Miami in May 1985, and her daughter Carmen also passed away there on August 3, 1999. Manuel Montero Moscoso died in San Juan, P.R., on July 5, 1994. See Leizán, interview; Manuel Montero Moscoso, interview, Rio Piedras, P.R., October 15, 1982; Rojas, *La cueva del muerto*, 199.

29. Leizán, interview; Rojas, *La cueva del muerto*, 200; Reyes Trejo, "Del Moncada a las montañas," 65; Manuel Montero, interview; "Cuando Sarría detuvo a Fidel Castro," 15.

30. Chanes, interview; Montano, interview; Rojas, *La cueva del muerto*, 201; Merle, *Moncada*, 305; Ortega, "Después del asalto," 31; Betto, *Fidel y la religión*, 182.

31. The lowest officer rank in the Cuban army was that of sublieutenant, below that of second lieutenant and first lieutenant. Sgt. Eulalio González called Sub Lt. Pedro Sarría a "shameless traitor" for later joining the rebel 26 of July Movement "after they killed so many of his comrades that he spent many years with in the army." See Oliva, interview; Sgt. Cesáreo Morales Herrera, personal interview, Miami, Fla., October 24, 1974; Julián Fajardo, interview; and Ernesto González Bermejo and Norberto Fuentes, "La otra cara del Moncada," *Cuba*, July 1968, 13.

32. Rafael Morales, interview; "Un resumen de los dolorosos," 70; Angel González, interview; Leizán, interview; Berta González, personal interview, Rio Piedras, P.R., September 15, 1982; Canto, *Mi vida*, 171.

33. "Un resumen de los dolorosos," 70; Leizán, interview; Canto, *Mi vida*, 171–72.

34. According to Cpl. Norberto Batista Seguí, when the revolutionaries seized power in 1959, El Cilindro farm owner Francisco Sotelo Piña was incarcerated in the Boniato Provincial Prison for having collaborated with the army, resulting in Fidel Castro's detention. Sotelo died in his cell, hanging from his belt, on July 10, 1959. See Oliva, interview; and González Bermejo and Fuentes, "La otra cara del Moncada," 13.

35. Chanes, interview; Montano, interview; Juan Emilio Friguls, "Culminaron en un éxito laudable las disposiciones patrióticas y nobles de Su Ilustrísima Mons. Pérez Serantes y de las Fuerzas Armadas," *Diario de la Marina*, August 5, 1953, 1; Canto, *Mi vida*, 172.

36. Barredo Medina, *Mi prisionero Fidel*, 89; Oliva, interview; González Bermejo and Fuentes, "La otra cara del Moncada," 13–14.

37. According to Cpl. Norberto Batista Seguí, during the Sierra Maestra campaign, Pvt. Leonardo Cala Cala was in charge of the Charco Mono dam that supplied water to Santiago de Cuba. After he was killed defending his position, the rebels cut off his head and displayed it on a dish on top of a radio at their headquarters in Margarita del Cristal farm. In a 1986 interview in Cuba, Cpl. Julio Corbea Monteagudo falsely claimed that it was Cala, instead of Luis Batista Seguí, who kicked in the door. See Barredo Molina, *Mi prisionero Fidel*, 89–90; Oliva, interview; Rojas, *La cueva del muerto*, 206; Reyes Trejo, "Del Moncada a las montañas," 59; "Cuando Sarría detuvo a Fidel Castro," 15; González Bermejo and Fuentes, "La otra cara del Moncada," 14; Merle, *Moncada*, 311.

38. Carlos Piñeiro del Cueto, the grand master (1949–59) of the Masonic Grand Lodge of Cuba, affirmed that Sub Lt. Pedro Sarría was not a Freemason. See Carlos Piñeiro, interview.

Although there has been much controversy as to whether or not Sarría stated that "You do not kill ideas" (*Las ideas no se matan*), Pvt. Armando Oliva never forgot that phrase. Oliva passed away in Miami on December 25, 2003. See Oliva, interview; Reyes Trejo, "Del Moncada a las montañas," 59; Rojas, *La cueva del muerto,* 207–9; Betto, *Fidel y la religión,* 184–85; Carlos Nicot Benítez, "La captura de Fidel Castro," *Carteles,* August 9, 1953, 33; Rodolfo Rodríguez Zaldivar, "Por qué Fidel Castro no fue asesinado al capturarlo el ejército en Oriente," *Bohemia,* March 8, 1959, 63; Ruiz, "El asalto al Cuartel Moncada," 53; González Bermejo and Fuentes, "La otra cara del Moncada," 14.

39. Chanes, interview; Thomas, *Cuba,* 851; Szulc, *Fidel,* 277; "Un resumen de los dolorosos," 70; Matthews, *Fidel Castro,* 68; Canto, *Mi vida,* 172–73; Betto, *Fidel y la religión,* 185.

40. Gerardo Abascal Berenguer, telephone interview, Miami, Fla., December 9, 1984; "Un resumen de los dolorosos," 70; Canto, *Mi vida,* 172–73.

41. In the 1960s in La Cabaña prison, Cpl. Norberto Batista Seguí met the rebel Mario Chanes de Armas, who was sentenced to thirty years in 1961 for conspiring against the Communist regime. Chanes told him that he had been given a cigarette by a soldier when he was captured. Norberto showed Chanes a photograph of his brother Luis that he had received from home, and Chanes identified this man as the person who had provided the cigarette. See Norberto Batista, interview; Chanes, interview; Oliva, interview; "Cuando Sarría detuvo a Fidel Castro," 15; González Bermejo and Fuentes, "La otra cara del Moncada," 14; Betto, *Fidel y la religión,* 185; Reyes Trejo, "Del Moncada a las montañas," 65; Merle, *Moncada,* 315.

42. Sub Lt. Pedro Sarría was charged with conspiracy on August 20, 1957, for betraying the identity of Capt. Agustín Lavastida's nephew, who was attempting to infiltrate a group of rebels who then murdered him on the Veguitas highway. Sarría was sentenced to one year, one month, and one day in prison. In January 1959 Sarría was appointed captain in the rebel army and bodyguard of provisional president Manuel Urrutia Lleó. Sarría died of cancer on September 29, 1972. See "Inhumado el capitán Pedro Sarría," *Granma,* October 2, 1972; Abascal, interview; "Un resumen de los dolorosos," 70; Canto, *Mi vida,* 173; Rojas, *La cueva del muerto,* 211–12; Angel González, interview; Montano, interview.

43. Lt. Antonio Policarpo Ochoa Ferrer's statement that he would have killed Fidel Castro and the others should not be dismissed as braggadocio. Ochoa (February 1903–January 1986), a fatherless mulatto, had joined the army in 1919 and had been an SIM henchman for the notorious Maj. Arsenio Ortíz. He fled Cuba after Machado's overthrow in 1933 and became a sergeant in the Dominican Republic army. Ochoa went to Havana in the 1940s and teamed up with the gangster Orlando León Lemus. After Batista's coup, Colonel del Río Chaviano asked him to rejoin the army and work for him. On December 27, 1958, Ochoa again fled to the Dominican Republic, accompanying del Río Chaviano and Lt. Teodoro Rico Boué. He subsequently settled in Miami, where in 1974 he was a construction laborer. See Antonio Ochoa, interview.

44. Student leaders Temístocles Fuentes Rivera and Orlando Benítez Hernández were cleared of charges and released the following month. See Canto, *Mi vida,* 173; "Un resumen de los dolorosos," 70; "Capturado Fidel Castro Ruz junto con dos compañeros por una patrulla militar cerca de Siboney," *Prensa Universal,* August 1, 1953, 1; González Bermejo and Fuentes, "La otra cara del Moncada," 14; Lupiáñez Reinlein, *El Movimiento Estudiantil,* 95, 169–70.

45. Pvt. Luis Manuel Batista Seguí moved to Havana in 1959. He later joined anti-Communist forces in the Sierra de los Organos Mountains in Pinar del Río under the

NOTES TO PAGES 192–194   337

command of former rebel officer Bernardo Corrales. They were captured and executed by firing squad. Batista Seguí was shot in Artemisa on September 7, 1961. See Oliva, interview; "Capturados Fidel Castro y 7 fugitivos más," *Avance*, August 1, 1953, 1; González Bermejo and Fuentes, "La otra cara del Moncada," 15; Chanes, interview; Orlando Morales, interview.

46. Rojas, *La cueva del muerto*, 214; "Vinimos a regenerar a Cuba," *Granma*, July 20, 1973, 6; Rojas, *La Generación del Centenario*, 310; Dubois, *Fidel Castro*, 39; Rafael Morales, interview; Cesar A. Marín, "A 35 años del Moncada," *El Nuevo Herald*, July 26, 1988, 7; Despatch 223, August 6, 1953, *Cuba Internal Affairs*.

47. "Un resumen de los dolorosos," 70; "Fidel Castro reveló todos los detalles," *Alerta*, August 3, 1953, 1; Fidel Castro, "Mientes, Chaviano," *Bohemia*, May 29, 1955, 57; Nieto, interview; Yanez, interview; "Vinimos a Regenerar a Cuba," 6; "Cuban Student Held as Leader of Revolt," *New York Times*, August 2, 1953, 29.

48. Lt. Jesús Yanez Pelletier was later tried by military court-martial, imprisoned, and dishonorably discharged from the army. Freed during the general amnesty of 1955, he later went into exile in the United States and in 1957 was a representative of the 26 of July Movement in the secret military subcommittee of the Junta de Liberación Cubana, a coalition organization against the Batista regime. He was active in smuggling weapons to Cuba on commercial airliners in the luggage of willing Cuban and American young women. In January 1959 Yanez returned to Cuba and was appointed captain and bodyguard of Fidel Castro, accompanying him to the United States that April. Yanez was later named military attaché to the Cuban Embassy in Italy until January 18, 1960. He was afterward assigned to give hush money to Castro's teenage mistress, Marita Lorenz, and was accused of pocketing half of the cash. The mentally unstable Lorenz said that in March 1960 Yanez and another man attempted to kidnap her in front of her apartment building in New York City to take her back to Cuba, and when she told police, Yanez was told to leave the United States. Under orders from Castro, Yanez was imprisoned on April 14, 1960, and later failed an escape attempt (*New York Times*, April 15 and June 24, 1960). He was accused in Case 280 of 1960 of embezzling, conspiracy, consorting with the mafia, and other charges and sentenced to fifteen years. His brother Bernabé Yanez was charged as accomplice accessory after the fact and sentenced to seven years. In 1971 Jesús Yanez was released and put to work as a French translator in the Cuban Book Institute. He remarried and in 1979 was denied permission to leave the country. Yanez died of a heart attack on September 18, 2000, on the sidewalk, after leaving the U.S. Interests Section in Havana. Lt. Angel S. Machado (March 1, 1913–March 9, 1999) passed away in Miami. See Yanez, interview; Angel Machado, interview; Conte Agüero, *Los dos rostros*, 51; "Desahoga su frustración un ex ayudante de Castro," *El Nuevo Día* (San Juan, P.R.), June 23, 1988, 34; Casuso, *Cuba and Castro*, 99, 155; Matthews, *Fidel Castro*, 78; Taber, *M-26*, 44–45; Llerena, *Unsuspected Revolution*, 137; "Girls Smuggled Guns for Castro," *New York Times*, January 4, 1959, 4; "Desde La Habana: Así paga Castro los favores," *El Nuevo Herald*, August 24, 1988, 6; Wilfredo Cancio Isla, "Concurrido entierro del disidente Yanez Pelletier," *El Nuevo Herald*, September 20, 2000; "Jesus Yañez Pelletier, Castro's Jailer, 83, Dies," *New York Times*, September 21, 2000, B14.

49. See appendix 1 for the list of the rebels dead, captured, and escaped. See also Chanes, interview; Rafael Morales, interview; Orlando Morales, interview; González Bermejo and Fuentes, "La otra cara del Moncada," 15; Conte Agüero, *Los dos rostros*, 49; Dubois, *Fidel Castro*, 40; Yanez, interview; Matos, interview.

50. Centro de Estudios, *Moncada: La acción*, 262; Cuervo and Llenín, *Moncada*, 116.

51. "Confesión de Marino Collazo Cordero," *Diario de Cuba*, August 8, 1953, 2; "Se presentó en Palma uno de los complicados," *Alerta*, August 8, 1953, 1; "Ratifícase prisión de Luis Casero," *Prensa Universal*, August 8, 1953, 1; Casero, interview; "Dos nuevos detenidos por el asalto al Moncada," *Prensa Universal*, August 12, 1953, 8; Rojas, *La cueva del muerto*, 153, 159; Canto, *Mi vida*, 176–77.

52. José Escala subsequently became a priest and went into exile after Castro seized power. See Canto, *Mi vida*, 177–78.

53. "'Tenemos el deber de guardar el orden y la paz,' dijo Batista," *Diario de la Marina*, August 4, 1953, 1, 28; "Un resumen de los dolorosos," 71; Despatch 223, August 6, 1953, *Cuba Internal Affairs*; Centro de Estudios, *Moncada: La acción*, 377.

54. Mabis Guilarte, daughter of the slain Pvt. Pedro Guilarte, graduated from the Ceiba del Agua Institute, excelling in sports, and became a member of the Cuban national volleyball team during the Castro regime. The wounded visited in the military hospital by General Batista were Lt. Juan Piña Martínez; Cpls. Eugenio Alcolea, Gerardo Hechavarría Granados, and Néstor Reyes Martín; and Pvts. José Fonseca, Clemente Godó, Miguel Ruiz, Emilio Reyes Rodríguez, Angel Duvallón-Gilbert, Lázaro Tejadilla, and Luis Enrique Naranjo. Cpl. Norberto Batista Seguí, accompanied by his mother, traveled to Havana in a military transport plane on September 16, 1953, and met with Batista in the Presidential Palace. Corporal Batista was transferred from Moncada in 1955 and later ascended to the position of SIM sergeant in Havana. He was arrested in Havana on December 8, 1963, for conspiring against the Communist regime and released from prison on November 19, 1979, under a sentence commutation for four hundred political prisoners. Three months later he departed for the United States. See Norberto Batista, interview; "Tenemos el deber de guardar," 28.

55. Enrique Canto Bory (December 24, 1909–January 2, 1982), a Phalangist admirer of the Spanish monarchy and the dictator Francisco Franco, had lived in Spain during 1918–33, where he attended Jesuit schools and dabbled in journalism. On returning to his native Santiago de Cuba, he worked as a clerk in his family's department store and organized the Catholic Youth (JC) in Oriente Province. Canto was also elected vice president of the Colonia Española Association in Santiago de Cuba. He provided safe houses, funds, and other assistance to underground activists of the 26 of July Movement during 1955–57. Canto served as national treasurer of the movement during May–August 1957 and had to go into exile in Spain when his role was discovered by the police. After the fall of the Batista regime, Canto assumed control of the Cuban Embassy in Madrid during January–September 1959. After returning to Cuba, he was regarded as adverse to Communism because of his Catholic activism and denied a government post. On April 6, 1962, Canto was sentenced in Santiago de Cuba to twenty years in prison for being a member of a counterrevolutionary organization, along with the attorneys Carlos Peña-Justiz, José Valls Tamayo, and Francisco Mendieta Tamayo and thirty other people. His department store and bank account were confiscated by the government. Canto was released after two years and, due to his Spanish citizenship, became chancellor of the Spanish consulate in Santiago de Cuba. After applying for permission to migrate, he was arrested on November 22, 1973, and released on April 1, 1974, and sent to Madrid. He went to live with a brother in Carolina, P.R., where he succumbed to cancer on January 2, 1982. Léster Rodríguez Pérez passed away in Havana on August 26, 1998. See Canto, *Mi vida*, 174, 179, 479, 480.

56. Higinio "Nino" Díaz Landrían and Teófilo Babún Selman supported Castro until he became totalitarian. The Babún family had their six enterprises, worth $15 million, confiscated in April 1960. Both men went into exile then dedicated the rest of their lives to fighting against the Castro regime. Babún's sons and Díaz joined the ill-fated Bay of Pigs invasion. In 1985 Díaz was arrested when the police found in his bedroom closet a mortar launcher, a machine gun, and a pistol silencer. See "Bay of Pigs Leader Gets 3-Year Probation," *Miami Herald*, August 27, 1985, C14; Granados, interview; Costa, interview; Centro de Estudios, *Moncada: La acción*, 303; Canto, *Mi vida*, 174.

57. Lazo, *Recuerdos*, 172; Reyes Trejo, "Como nos convertimos en carboneros," *Verde Olivo*, July 28, 1968, 94; Sarusky, "Una increíble cadena," 11–13; Reyes Trejo, "Del Moncada a las montañas," 34.

58. Mario Lazo stayed in Santiago de Cuba with Ibis Atala Medina until the general amnesty twenty months later. In his 1987 memoirs he omitted mentioning the visit to Gustavo Arcos, who at the time was languishing in a Castro prison. See Lazo, *Recuerdos*, 92–93, 95–97; Sarusky, "Una increíble cadena," 12; Canto, *Mi vida*, 176; Reyes Trejo, "Del Moncada a las montañas," 34; Granados, interview; Arcos, interview.

59. Florentino Fernández, "Los uniformes de los asaltantes al Moncada," *Verde Olivo*, July 26, 1964, 40; Merle, *Moncada*, 111, 274.

60. The seven defendants taken from Havana to the Boniato prison the day before the trial started were Oscar Alvarado González, Ramiro Arango Alsina, Aracelio Azcuy Cruz, José M. Gutiérrez Planes, Sergio Mejías Pérez, Lázaro Peña González, and Joaquín Ordoqui Mesa. See Emilio Ochoa, interview; Fiterre, interview; Arango, interview; "Trasladados a Oriente, Ochoa y Tellaheche," *El Crisol*, August 22, 1953, 1; "Political Prisoners to Be Moved to Oriente," *Havana Post*, September 20, 1953, 10.

61. Del Mazo, interview; Fiterre, interview; Chanes, interview; Arango, interview.

62. Del Mazo, interview; Casero, interview.

63. Despatch 525, October 13, 1953, *Cuba Internal Affairs;* "Appointment with Ambassador Concheso of Cuba," September 1, 1953, ibid.

64. Díaz-Francisco, interview.

65. Yanez, interview; Casero, interview.

66. Emilio Ochoa, interview.

67. Fiterre, interview; Chanes, interview.

68. Díaz-Francisco, interview; Fiterre, interview; Chanes, interview; Emilio Ochoa, interview; Casero, interview; McManus, *From the Palm Tree*, 27; Lázara Pérez, interview; Szulc, *Fidel*, 284; Centro de Estudios, *Moncada: La acción*, 286.

69. Centro de Estudios, *Moncada: La acción*, 286; Chanes, interview; McManus, *From the Palm Tree*, 27; Lázara Pérez, interview; Santamaría, *Moncada*, 68; del Mazo, interview.

70. Earl E. T. Smith, *The Fourth Floor: An Account of the Castro Communist Revolution* (New York: Random House, 1962), 165.

Chapter 8—"A leader is born"

1. See appendix 3 for the list of the 122 defendants. See also Mendieta, interview.

2. Camps, interview; Alcolea, interview; Fiterre, interview; Mendieta, interview.

3. When the rebels seized power, Judge Adolfo E. Nieto Piñeiro-Osorio (December 15, 1899–January 13, 1980) and other magistrates were imprisoned for a few months and

eventually released thanks to José Miró Cardona and José Alabau Trelles. Nieto said that provisional president Manuel Urrutia Lleó persecuted his former colleagues to the extreme of enacting a decree entitled "Magistrates who dishonored their robes serving the tyranny." Nieto went into exile in 1961 and passed away in Ft. Lauderdale, Fla. See Nieto, interview; "Actóa de magistrado en La Causa 37," *Prensa Universal,* September 21, 1953, 1; "El juicio por el asalto al 'Moncada,'" *Bohemia,* September 27, 1953, suplemento; Mendieta, interview.

4. Chief prosecutor Francisco Mendieta Hechavarría was also the prosecutor during the 1957 trial against the Granma expeditionaries. By then, his aversion to the Batista regime and his sympathy for the rebel cause prompted him to abstain from requesting a prison sentence for the accused revolutionaries. Yet, the government took no reprisals against him. When the revolutionaries seized power, Mendieta was not dismissed from his post as were all other judicial employees. He was forced into early retirement in 1961 for "lacking revolutionary qualities," a euphemism for not being a Communist. Mendieta Hechavarría died in Santiago de Cuba of a heart attack on August 3, 1967. His son, Francisco Mendieta Tamayo, completed law school and became a public defender in Santiago de Cuba. He joined the Sierra Maestra guerrillas one month before Batista was overthrown. After the rebels seized power, Mendieta Tamayo was appointed president of a revolutionary tribunal in Santiago de Cuba that sent scores of *batistianos* to the firing squad. In January 1962 he was arrested for being second-in-command and treasurer of the Movimiento de Recuperación Revolucionaria in Santiago de Cuba and given a thirty-year prison sentence. See Nieto, interview; Mendieta, interview; Centro de Estudios, *Moncada: Motor de la Revolución,* 22; Chanes, interview.

5. The six rebels declared fugitives by the tribunal were Gerardo Granados Lara, Orlando Galán Betancourt, Severino Rosell González, Mario Dalmau de la Cruz, "Ñico" López Fernández, and Antonio "El Gallego" López García. The last three, along with Armando Arencibia and Benjamín de Yurre, had obtenido asylum in the Guatemalan Embassy after the uprising and had departed for Central America on August 14. See Pablo Mila Ortíz, "Seguirán juzgando hoy a los 122 acusados de asaltar el 'Moncada,'" *El Mundo,* September 22, 1953, 1; Despatches 160 and 289, August 19, 1953, *Cuba Internal Affairs;* Rafael Mendoza Guanche, telephone interview, Miami, Fla., February 28, 1988.

6. Mila Ortíz, "Seguirán juzgando hoy," 8; Arango, interview; "Comenzó ayer el juicio contra los acusados por el asalto al 'Moncada,'" *Diario de Cuba,* September 22, 1953, 3; "Insurrection Trial Begins in Santiago," *Havana Post,* September 22, 1953, 1, 10.

7. Kurt Singer, "I, Fidel Castro," *Illustrated Weekly of India,* December 18, 1960, 12; "Insurrection Trial Begins," 1; "Comenzó ayer el juicio," 3; Nieto, interview.

8. "Insurrection Trial Begins," 1; "Comenzó ayer el juicio," 3; Rojas, *El que debe vivir,* 12; "Cuba Begins Trial of 100 for Revolt," *New York Times,* September 22, 1953, 19; Mila Ortíz, "Seguirán juzgando hoy," 8; Nieto, interview.

9. See appendix 4; Rojas, *La Generación del Centenario,* 73; and Suardíaz, interview.

10. Luis Casero Guillén (November 22, 1902–August 21, 1998) went into exile in 1971 with an exit visa granted by Juan Almeida Bosque. Prior to that, he had sent four of his daughters to the United States and stayed in Cuba with his wife and daughter Graciela because her husband, Francisco Mendieta Tamayo, the prosecutor's son, was a political prisoner. See Casero, interview; "Comenzó ayer el juicio," 3; Olance Nogueras, "Luis Casero Guillén izó en vida una bandera azul de honestidad," *El Nuevo Herald,* August 22, 1998.

11. Emilio Ochoa, interview; "All but One Witness Deny Participation in July 26 Revolt," *Havana Post*, September 23, 1953, 1; "Declaran en el juicio del Cuartel Moncada Millo Ochoa y J. M. Gutiérrez," *Avance*, September 22, 1953, 1; Pablo Mila Ortíz, "Hasta mañana no seguirá el juicio en Santiago," *El Mundo*, September 23, 1953, 1.

12. The physician Oscar Alvarado González left Cuba with the codefendant Aracelio Azcuy Cruz after they were acquitted. A week later they were arrested in Miami, Fla., with Oscar's brother Adalberto and Daniel Vázquez in possession of a large weapons cache they were preparing to forward to Cuba. Oscar Alvarado became embittered after his teenage son Juan Oscar Alvarado, a member of the 26 of July Movement, was killed by the police in 1958. Oscar Alvarado was a rebel army captain presiding over the revolutionary tribunals in La Cabaña fortress in 1959 that sent hundreds of *batistianos* to the firing squad. See "All but One Witness Deny Participation," 1; Marta Rojas R., "La Causa 37," *Bohemia*, February 15, 1959, 114.

13. Joaquín Ordoqui had been a congressional representative from Las Villas Province during 1940-52. Lázaro Peña was secretary general of the Cuban Workers Confederation (1939-47) and representative from Havana Province in 1940-44 and 1950-52. Luis Pérez Rey ran unsuccessfully for commissioner in Havana as a PSP candidate in 1950. See "All but One Witness Deny Participation," 10; Mila Ortíz, "Hasta mañana no seguirá," 8; Alfredo Gómez, "The Political Situation in Cuba," *Political Affairs*, October 1954, 49-59; Bonachea and San Martín, *Cuban Insurrection*, 25.

14. Aida Pelayo Pelayo, a former member of the Marxist Ala Izquierda Estudiantil, had lived in concubinage with Communist Party leader Juan Marinello. She was a prosecution witness on March 11, 1959, against a Havana policeman sentenced to death by a revolutionary tribunal and later held a minor government post. See *Diario de la Marina*, March 12, 1959, B7; García Montes and Alonso Avila, *Historia del Partido Comunista de Cuba*, 130, 363; "Remitida a esta ciudad y recluida en el vivac municipal la señora Aida Pelayo," *Oriente*, September 7, 1953, 1; "All but One Witness Deny Participation," 10; Fiterre, interview.

15. Marta Rojas, in *La Generación del Centenario en el juicio del Moncada*, omits mentioning the denial testimony of Guillermo Elizalde Sotolongo, Rolando Guerrero Bello, and Genaro Hernández Martínez or that Castro exculpated them. See Andrés Silva Adán, telephone interview, Columbus, Ohio, February 1, 1986; Mila Ortíz, "Hasta mañana no seguirá," 8.

16. Manuel Villa Romero went into exile with his family in Madrid, Spain, in 1958, returning to Cuba after the fall of Batista. See "All but One Witness Deny Participation," 10; Canto, *Mi vida*, 259.

17. Nieto, interview; Rojas, *La Generación del Centenario*, 138; Fiterre, interview; Centro de Estudios, *Moncada: Motor de la Revolución*, 95-96.

18. Camps, interview; Fiterre, interview; Conte Agüero, *Los dos rostros*, 50.

19. "Libertan a líderes del PRC y PPC," *El Mundo*, September 27, 1953, 1; Centro de Estudios, *Moncada: Motor de la Revolución*, 114; Rosa Hilda Zell, "6 documentos del Moncada," *Bohemia*, July 27, 1962, 67; Fiterre, interview.

20. Oscar Lorient Guerrero, "Nueva sesión del juicio por los sucesos del Moncada," *Oriente*, September 26, 1953, 2; Nieto, interview; Rojas, *La Generación del Centenario*, 161.

21. "Libertan a líderes del PRC y PPC," 4; Rojas, *La Generación del Centenario*, 166, 168.

22. Moto Mendel Weis at the age of thirteen had been sentenced to the reformatory Centro de Rehabilitación Infantil Torrens on July 10, 1948. After being acquitted, he traveled to Costa Rica, where he stayed in the same rented house with Orlando Castro García. Mendel was

arrested in Paris, France, on July 28, 1955, for passing false checks during the previous two months totaling eight thousand dollars. José M. Pérez Lamy had belonged to the Marxist Ala Izquierda Estudiantil, and in the 1950 elections he lost his bid as PSP candidate for Havana commissioner. In 1959 Pérez Lamy became prosecutor of the revolutionary tribunals. The attorney Lucas Morán Arce (August 15, 1919–March 13, 1999), a rebel officer during the Sierra Maestra campaign who later went into exile in 1960, claimed that he did not remember the charges against his client, nor did he mention that he had helped the rebel Mario Lazo. Morán wrote various lengthy articles regarding the Moncada events but failed to describe his personal involvement. See Lucas Morán Arce, personal interview, San Juan, P.R., September 10, 1982; Lucas Morán, "A treinta años del 26 de Julio," *El Nuevo Día (Revista Domingo)*, July 22, 1984, 18; Lucas Morán, "El último carnaval," *Diario las Américas*, July 26, 1989, 4; Carlos C. Hall to Henry A. Hoyt, Department of State, October 27, 1954, *Cuba Internal Affairs;* "Se esperan muchas libertades en el juicio por los sucesos del 26 en Moncada y Bayamo," *Diario de Cuba*, October 1, 1953, 3; "Libertan a líderes del PRC y PPC," 4; Rojas, "La Causa 37," 115; Chanes, interview.

23. The chauffeur Oscar Gras Escalona later became a fervent revolutionary. In 1961 he was a jailer in El Príncipe prison in Havana. See "Libertan a líderes del PRC y PPC," 4; Lázara Pérez, interview; Estrada, interview; del Mazo, interview.

24. Pedro Aguilera (1925–98) in 1955 became part of the National Directorate of the 26 of July Movement and participated in clandestine activities. After 1959 he joined the Cuban Revolutionary Armed Forces and was a general in the Ministry of the Interior. Raúl del Mazo was arrested on February 14, 1961, and accused in Case 64 of 1961 of conspiring with Holguín Squadron 77 and members of the Guantánamo police against the Castro regime. He served two years in prison and went into exile in 1969. See Autores varios, *Mártires del Moncada*, 394; Rojas, *La Generación del Centenario en el juicio del Moncada*, 50; del Mazo, interview.

25. Pablo Mila Ortíz, "Ratifican prisión a un ex Alcalde," *El Mundo*, September 16, 1953, 8; "Ordena urgencia citar a prío por lo del Moncada," *Avance*, September 26, 1953, 1; Andux et al., *La Capital en el Moncada*, 86–87; Rojas, *La Generación del Centenario en el juicio del Moncada*, 143.

26. The dissident rebels Orlando Cortés Gallardo and Eduardo Rodríguez Alemán later became active supporters of Castro's Communist regime. See Luis Gómez Domínguez, telephone interview, Miami, Fla., December 7, 2002; "Efectuado el sepelio del combatiente del Moncada Teniente Coronel Eduardo Rodríguez Alemán," *Granma*, September 13, 1980, 2; "Efectuado el sepelio de Orlando Cortés, asaltante al Moncada," *Granma*, March 6, 1989, 2; Rojas, *La Generación del Centenario en el juicio del Moncada*, 131–32; Díaz-Francisco, interview.

27. Those released on their own recognizance were Bayamo motel owner Juan Manuel Martínez and political leaders Ramiro Arango Alsina, José M. Gutiérrez Planes, Oscar Alvarado González, Joaquín Ordoqui Mesa, Lázaro Peña González, Arturo Hernández Tellaheche, Luis Casero Guillén, Emilio Ochoa Ochoa, Roberto García Ibáñez, Aracelio Azcuy Cruz, and Sergio Mejías Pérez. See Mendieta, interview; Marta Rojas, "En libertad provisional once líderes políticos," *Bohemia*, October 4, 1953, 68; "Oriente Court Frees Twelve Defendants in Rebellion Trial," *Havana Post*, September 27, 1953, 1.

28. Nieto, interview; Zell, "6 documentos del Moncada," 67.

29. "Celebrada ayer la cuarta sesión del juicio por el asalto a los cuarteles," *Diario de Cuba*, September 29, 1953, 3; Rojas, *La Generación del Centenario en el juicio del Moncada*, 140–41, 144–45.

30. Marta Rojas, in *La Generación del Centenario en el juicio del Moncada*, omits mentioning the denial testimony of Julio Díaz González, a martyr of the revolution killed during the Sierra Maestra campaign. José Ponce later joined the Granma expedition and was one of the first two expeditionaries captured after landing. He gave a full confession, detailing "the number and composition of the revolutionaries" who "left Mexico" and were "led by Fidel Castro." Ponce was sent back to the Isle of Pines penitentiary in May 1957 with a six-year sentence and released when the rebels seized power twenty months later. Ponce was interred in the Cuban Revolutionary Armed Forces Pantheon in Colón Cemetery, Havana, on February 18, 2001. Ciro Redondo was killed in Mar Verde on November 29, 1957, during the Sierra Maestra campaign by Sgt. Rafael Castillo Batista. See "Lo que nos han dejado ver," *Bohemia*, December 16, 1956, 107; Almeida Bosque, *La aurora de los héroes*, 167–68; Montano, interview; Chanes, interview; Pablo Mila Ortíz, "Confesaron 20 acusados en Santiago," *El Mundo*, September 29, 1953, 8; Rojas, "La Causa 37," 115.

31. "Sigue la vista del Moncada," *El Crisol*, September 29, 1953, 1; Rojas, "La Causa 37," 115; Rojas, "En libertad provisional," 68.

32. Pablo Mila Ortíz, "Terminada la prueba de confesión," *El Mundo*, September 30, 1953, 1; Rojas, *La Generación del Centenario en el juicio del Moncada*, 181.

33. Rojas, *La Generación del Centenario*, 259, 265; McManus, *From the Palm Tree*, 25.

34. Mila Ortíz, "Terminada la prueba de Confesión," 1; "Seven Remaining Defendants Testify in Treason Trial," *Havana Post*, September 30, 1953, 1, 10.

35. Angel González Alfonso served in the army for forty-three years and was stationed at Moncada from December 1952 until he retired in 1955. Born in 1890, he remembered seeing the Cuban flag hoisted for the first time on Independence Day, May 20, 1902. Three months after this interview, he died of bone cancer at the age of eighty-five. See Angel González, interview; Juan Pita, interview; Alcolea, interview; Alfonso Silva, interview; Lavastida, interview; Virués, interview; Mila Ortíz, "Terminada la prueba de confesión," 8.

36. "Seven Remaining Defendants Testify," 1, 10; Mila Ortíz, "Terminada la prueba de confesión," 8.

37. The fifteen lieutenants testifying on September 30 were Eladio Carrillo Morales, Angel Machado Rofe, Horacio York Botella, Marcelo Otaño Cookerman, Sigbiardo G. Prévez Carcellés, Antonio María López, Juan Piña Martínez, Pedro Morejón Valdés, Pedro Sarría Tartabul, Teodoro Rico Boué, Antonio Barquet Aguiar, Eugenio Rizo Viel, Claudio Morales García, Cándido Garrido Wilson, and Alberto A. Alonso Martínez. They were followed by the testimony of Sgts. Amarante Pagés Portuondo, Agustín González Le Blanch, and Rafael Castillo. The police major Bonifacio Haza Grasso was executed by a revolutionary firing squad at San Juan Hill on January 12, 1959. Forensic physician Manuel Prieto Aragón stated after the revolution that the forensic records showed that all the soldiers died of gunshot wounds. See Jaime Sarusky, "Una increíble cadena de solidaridad humana," *Bohemia*, July 21, 1972, 14; "Aceleran el juicio por el asalto al Moncada," *Alerta*, October 1, 1953, 1; Nieto, interview; Rolando Pérez, interview; "Se esperan muchas libertades," 3; "Declaran militares en el juicio por los sucesos de Oriente," *Diario de la Marina*, October 1, 1953, 1; Angel Machado, interview; Rico, interview.

38. According to medical lieutenant Rolando Pérez Sainz de la Peña, medical captain Mario Porro Varela died in 1957 of tetanus acquired from morphine addiction. See "Se esperan muchas libertades," 3.

39. "Defense Counsels in Treason Trial Ask Release of Clients," *Havana Post*, October 2, 1953, 10; Rojas, "La Causa 37," 116; "Inician prueba testifical en el juicio del Cuartel

Moncada," *Diario de la Marina,* October 2, 1953, 1; Rojas, *La Generación del Centenario,* 319; "Nueva sesión celebrada ayer en la audiencia del juicio por el asalto a cuarteles," *Diario de Cuba,* October 2, 1953, 3.

40. "Nueva sesión celebrada ayer," 3; Juan Pita, interview; Alfonso Silva, interview; "Inician prueba testifical," 1.

41. "Nueva sesión celebrada ayer," 3; McManus, *From the Palm Tree,* 14–15; Rojas, *La Generación del Centenario,* 322; "Inician prueba testifical," 32.

42. "Defense Counsels in Treason Trial," 10; "Inician prueba testifical," 32.

43. "46 Witnesses Testify in Santiago Treason Trial," *Havana Post,* October 3, 1953, 10; Valdés, interview; Horacio Martínez, interview; "Declaró ayer ante urgencia el jefe del distrito Coronel Chaviano sobre los sucesos del 'Moncada,'" *Diario de Cuba,* October 3, 1953, 3; "Declararon ante urgencia en Santiago numerosos testigos," *Diario de la Marina,* October 3, 1953, 1; Rojas, *La Generación del Centenario,* 326.

44. "Declararon ante urgencia," 1.

45. "Declararon ante urgencia," 1; "Declaró ayer ante urgencia el jefe," 3; "Emplearon granadas los atacantes del Moncada," *El Crisol,* October 3, 1953, 1; "Entraron asesinando, afirma el coronel A. del Río Chaviano ante el Tribunal," *Alerta,* October 3, 1953, 1.

46. "Experts at Trial Fix Revolt Damage at About $2,400," *Havana Post,* October 4, 1953, 1; "Sigue el juicio por el asalto al Cuartel Moncada y al de Bayamo," *Diario de la Marina,* October 4, 1953, 1.

47. Juan Pita, interview; "Sigue el juicio por el asalto," 1; "Terminó la prueba testifical y pericial en el juicio por el asalto al Cuartel 'Moncada,'" *Diario de Cuba,* October 4, 1953, 2.

48. "58 Treason Trial Defendants Freed by Santiago Court," *Havana Post,* October 6, 1953, 1; "Libertados otros 58 detenidos por los sucesos del 'Moncada,'" *Diario de la Marina,* October 6, 1953, 1.

49. Rojas, *La Generación del Centenario,* 337, 338.

50. The lawyers supporting the prosecutor's dismissal petition were José F. Valls Tamayo, Roberto García Ibáñez, Raúl Villavilla, Recaredo García Fernández, Andrés Silva Adán, Jorge Nariño Brauet, Juan J. García Benítez, José M. Pérez Lamy, Rubén Alonso Alvarez, Conrado Castell Cordero, Eduardo Eljaiek Eldidi, Lucas Morán Arce, Roberto Rosillo Rodríguez, Luis Pérez Rey, Rafael A. Cisneros Ponteau, Domingo Estrada de Beatón, and Ramiro Arango Alsina. José F. Valls Tamayo (May 29, 1906–November 11, 1987) was arrested on December 29, 1961, in Santiago de Cuba and sentenced to three years of imprisonment for "counterrevolutionary activities" in Case 50 of 1962. He went into exile in Puerto Rico in 1969 and passed away in Miami. See "58 Treason Trial Defendants," 10; "Libertados otros 58 detenidos," 1.

51. The attorney Luis Gómez Domínguez was sentenced by the Castro regime to twenty years of imprisonment for conspiracy against the powers of the state on May 7, 1964. He was released in 1979 and went into exile in the United States. See Gómez, interview; Rojas, *La Generación del Centenario,* 344; "58 Treason Trial Defendants," 10.

52. Fiterre, interview; "Santiago Court Sentences 28 of Accused in Treason Trial to Terms in Prison," *Havana Post,* October 7, 1953, 1; "Condenados por los sucesos del Cuartel Moncada 29 acusados," *Diario de la Marina,* October 7, 1953, 1.

53. "Santiago Court Sentences 28," 1; "Condenados por los sucesos," 1, 32; Rojas, *La Generación del Centenario,* 358, 359.

54. Mario Chanes de Armas and his brother Francisco were arrested on July 17, 1961, and later sentenced in Case 556-61 to thirty and twenty years respectively for conspiracy against the powers of the state. In prison Mario was notified of the birth and later the death of his only son, Mario, who died at the age of twenty-two while undergoing an appendectomy in Cuba. His wife Caridad believes that her son was murdered by the Castro regime. See Rojas, *La Generación del Centenario*, 370; Nieto, interview; "Condenados por los sucesos," 32; "Santiago Court Sentences 28," 10.

55. Nieto, interview; "Cuban Rebels Sentenced," *New York Times*, October 7, 1953, 9; "Dictó urgencia sentencia condenatoria contra los que asaltaron el 'Moncada,'" *Diario de Cuba*, October 7, 1953, 3; Rojas, *La Generación del Centenario*, 370.

56. Fiterre, interview. After the revolutionaries seized power, Ignacio Fiterre was appointed as ambassador to the Netherlands on November 2, 1959. He resigned his post on March 15, 1961, after stating that the Castro regime "did not grant justice, freedom and democracy."

57. Angel Díaz-Francisco (December 28, 1928–January 5, 1993) had his car recovered by the insurance company in poor condition. "Patachula" returned to his law studies at the University of Havana until it was closed in December 1956. He continued his revolutionary activities and was a founder of the Student Revolutionary Directorate (DRE). In early 1957 Díaz-Francisco went into exile in Miami, returning to Cuba in 1958. In January 1959 he was named assistant secretary of provisional president Manuel Urrutia Lleó, and he served until a few months after Urrutia resigned in July 1959. He then worked for the Treasury Department. In 1967 Raúl Castro used his influence so that Díaz-Francisco could leave for Miami, where he later passed away. See Díaz-Francisco, interview.

58. The attorney Ramiro Arango Alsina (March 11, 1924–March 14, 2002), his wife, and Leonel Gómez Pérez traveled to Paris on December 1, 1953, accompanied by the Haitian ambassador and a SIM official. Arango worked as an economic history teacher. He moved to Rome to work in show business in 1959 and then settled in Miami in 1972. Arango became a naturalized American citizen and advocated Cuban annexation to the United States. In 1982 he and his wife were sued in a stock deal and settled out of court. After failing the Florida Bar exam eleven times, in February 1983 Arango was sentenced to a year in jail for practicing law without a license. After his release he established a men's clothing store, but he was soon under investigation by federal agencies "for lying on a police report and in sworn documents, that he forged documents submitted to Customs and undervalued clothes when importing them." Arango was arrested in 1992 for laundering drug money and later sentenced by a federal court to thirty years of imprisonment. He renounced his American citizenship and was granted the Spanish citizenship of his parents. Arango applied for the foreign prisoner exchange program and on March 18, 2000, when he was seventy-six years old, was sent to Madrid's Prison V, from which he was released the following year. He then went to Cuba for inexpensive liposuction surgery, developed a massive infection from the procedure, and as a result died after returning to Madrid. See "El padre del anexionismo," *Réplica* (Miami), December 10, 1980; "Sentencian a un abogado Cubano por ejercer la profesión sin el título," *Diario las Américas*, February 17, 1983, B1; Lisa Getter, "Now, Suit Case Witness Being Investigated," *Miami Herald*, December 16, 1987, B1; "Revolucionario, novio de Ava Gardner, abogado de 'narcos' y recluso," *ABC* (Madrid), July 27, 2000; Arango, interview.

59. In 1986 the one-eyed Fidel Labrador García was still a peasant in Artemisa working the land from dawn to dusk. See "Fidel Labrador habla de los días del Moncada," *Bohemia*, July

25, 1986, 7; "Transfer of Political Prisoners Is Ordered," *Havana Post,* October 13, 1953, 10; "Trasladan a Isla de Pinos a los atacantes del 'Moncada,'" *El Mundo,* October 13, 1953, 1; "Moncada Attackers Sent to Isle of Pines Prison," *Havana Post,* October 14, 1953, 2; Rojas, *La Generación del Centenario,* 375.

Chapter 9—"History Definitively, Will Say It All"

1. "Señalado para el día 16 del presente mes el juicio contra el doctor Fidel Castro y otros dos acusados," *Oriente,* October 13, 1953, 1; "Comenzará hoy en el Hospital 'Lora' el juicio contra Fidel Castro," *Diario de Cuba,* October 16, 1953, 1; Camps, interview.

2. After the trial, the reporter Marta Rojas sent a congratulatory letter to the chief magistrate Adolfo Nieto. She later became the leading propagandistic writer of the Moncada affair as a newspaper reporter for *Revolución* in 1960 and for *Granma* in 1965. The Castro regime has bestowed on her numerous honors. See Rojas, *La Generación del Centenario,* 376; Camps, interview; Nieto, interview; Centro de Estudios, *Moncada: Motor de la Revolución,* 22.

3. On July 24, 1985, Radio Rebelde announced that the attorney's robe worn by Fidel Castro during his "History Will Absolve Me" defense speech would be on display in the Hall of Culture in Guantánamo Province. See Rojas, *La Generación del Centenario,* 377-78; "Castro Is Sentenced to 15 Years," *Havana Post,* October 17, 1953, 1; Mencia, *Time Was on Our Side,* 249.

4. Alcolea, interview; Rojas, *La Generación del Centenario,* 378, 379. Maj. Andrés Pérez-Chaumont was appointed military attaché to the Cuban Embassy in Mexico in early 1957. A copy of his intelligence reports to Cuba, on Communist assistance to the 26 of July Movement, were sent to the assistant military attaché in the U.S. Embassy in Mexico. Pérez-Chaumont remained abroad until moving to Houston, Tex., in 1959. He was called to testify on March 29, 1961, before a U.S. Senate subcommittee investigating Communist activities. When referring to the Moncada attack, he grossly exaggerated rebel strength at "295 men," of which they had "about 190 dead and 70-something captured, and the rest got away." He claimed that Moncada had only "49 or 50" soldiers when the attack began. Pérez-Chaumont described Haydée Santamaría as "an awful type of woman because she would talk and act even worse than the men." He passed away in Houston, Tex., July 14, 1988. See United States Senate, Committee on the Judiciary, Hearings before the Subcommittee to Investigate the Administration of the Internal Security Act and Other Internal Security Laws, *Communist Threat to the United States through the Caribbean,* March 29, 1961, part 13 (Washington, D.C.: U.S. Government Printing Office, 1962), 831-37.

5. Rojas, *La Generación del Centenario,* 380; "Comenzará hoy en el Hospital 'Lora,'" 1.

6. "Comenzará hoy en el Hospital 'Lora,'" 1; "Castro Is Sentenced," 10; Mencia, *Time Was on Our Side,* 251; Rojas, *La Generación del Centenario,* 381; "Julio: La guerra civil," *Bohemia,* December 27, 1953, 70.

7. Szulc, *Fidel,* 296, concurs that Castro's defense speech lasted for two hours. See Nieto, interview; Camps, interview.

8. Nieto, interview; Kurt Singer, "I, Fidel Castro," *Illustrated Weekly of India,* December 18, 1960, 12; "Julio: La guerra civil," 70.

9. See the last unnumbered page in Marta Rojas, *El juicio del Moncada* (Havana: Editorial de Ciencias Sociales, 1988). The original manuscript of Castro's courtroom defense speech

typed by Rojas from her notes has the last phrase crossed out and the penned-in correction "history will absolve me." It seems unlikely that if Rojas had originally quoted that phrase in her notes she would later type a different ending, afterward insert a written correction, and not retype the last page of the manuscript. See also Castro, *History Will Absolve Me*.

10. Adolf Hitler, *Mein Kampf* (Boston: Houghton Mifflin, 1943), 686; Nieto, interview; Camps, interview.

11. "Two Cuban Rebels Sentenced," *New York Times*, October 17, 1953, 4; Nieto, interview.

12. Nieto, interview; "Castro Is Sentenced," 1; Camps, interview.

13. Despatch 548, October 19, 1953, *Cuba Internal Affairs*.

14. Juan Marinello Vidaurreta (November 2, 1898–March 27, 1977) was a delegate from Las Villas to the 1940 Constituent Assembly, a representative from Havana Province (1942–44), a minister without portfolio in the Batista cabinet (1943–44), senator from Camagüey Province (1944–48), and elected president of the Communist Revolutionary Union (URC) in 1939 until its dissolution. In March 1959 the attorneys Carlos Peña-Jústiz Arrieta and Jorge Paglieri obtained the acquittal of forty-three former Batista airmen accused of genocide. When Fidel Castro disregarded the verdict and ordered a retrial, Peña-Jústiz warned the tribunal that if the flyers were subsequently convicted, Castro might become "a new Napoleon of the Caribbean." Castro blamed the defense lawyers of engaging in an "antirevolutionary campaign." Peña-Jústiz was later imprisoned during 1961–65 and passed away in Cuba in 1987. Gustavo Arcos Bergnes was transferred to the orthopedic hospital in Havana on December 22, 1953. After six months of therapy, as he was about to be transferred to prison, he escaped on the night of July 12, 1954. Arcos was assisted by Dr. Orlando Ventura Reyes, Jorge Alonso Fernández, and two other men disguised as hospital attendants. He was arrested in the home of the attorney Fernando Sánchez Amaya and sent to the Isle of Pines penitentiary in November 1954. After the May 1955 amnesty, Arcos helped organize the 26 of July Movement in Las Villas before going into exile in Mexico in January 1956. His brother Luis was killed during the Granma expedition landing. Arcos was appointed Cuban ambassador to Belgium on September 9, 1959. He was imprisoned by the Castro regime from March 15, 1966, to July 1969, charged with "incorrect attitude toward the revolution." Arcos was again jailed from January 1982 to March 1988 for attempting to leave Cuba clandestinely with his brother Sebastián. Arcos headed the islandwide dissident group called the Cuban Committee on Human Rights until his death on August 8, 2006. See "Castro a Napoleon?," *Miami News*, March 6, 1959; "A uno de los asaltantes del Cuartel 'Moncada' le impusieron diez años," *Avance*, October 23, 1953, 1; "Urgencia en el Sanatorio de Stgo. de Cuba," *Diario de la Marina*, October 24, 1953, 11; "Cuban Prisoner Escapes," *New York Times*, July 14, 1954, 13; Despatch 67, July 16, 1954, *Cuba Internal Affairs;* "In or Out of Jail, Castro's Old Ally Is a Defiant Foe," *New York Times*, August 11, 1988, 4; Arcos, interview; Conte Agüero, interview; Camps, interview; Rolando Pérez, interview; Centro de Estudios, *Moncada: Motor de la Revolución*, 21; Nieto, interview; "Cabinet Restores Guarantees; News Censorship Lifted," *Havana Post*, October 25, 1953, 1.

15. In contrast to the accommodating prison conditions experienced by Melba Hernández and Haydée Santamaría, under the Castro regime female political prisoners have been subjected to humiliation and brutal treatment and have been lodged with common criminals. See Ana Rodriguez and Glenn Garvin, *Diary of a Survivor: Nineteen Years in a Cuban Women's Prison* (New York: St. Martin's, 1995). See also de la Cuesta, *Constituciones Cubanas*, 339;

Mencia, *Time Was on Our Side*, 3; "... Correr la misma suerte que nuestros compañeros," *Bohemia*, July 26, 1974, 56–61.

16. Gerardo Mosquera, "El museo del presidio," *Revolución y Cultura*, July 1978, 21; Manuel Pereira, "Las ruinas circulares," *Cuba Internacional*, February 1974, 46.

17. "Fidel Castro Enters Isle of Pines Prison," *Havana Post*, October 18, 1953, 1; Franqui, *Diary*, 67; Montano, interview; "Fidel Labrador habla de los días del Moncada," *Bohemia*, July 25, 1986, 7; Francisco Pita Rodríguez, "Dos estampas de Isla de Pinos: Tinieblas del confinamiento, alborada de la libertad," *Bohemia*, August 10, 1973, 34; Marta Rojas, "Educación y solidaridad en los combatientes del Moncada," *Verde Olivo*, July 24, 1966, 3; Chanes, interview; Mencia, *Time Was on Our Side*, 10–11; Szulc, *Fidel*, 305; Singer, "I, Fidel Castro," 13.

18. Mario Chanes de Armas, later imprisoned in the Isles of Pines penitentiary under the Castro regime, stated that, in comparison, the Communist system prohibited conjugal visits and initially allowed one regular visit every six months. Prisoners who accepted the Camilo Cienfuegos Rehabilitation Plan were later given one visit every forty-five days. See Mencia, *Time Was on Our Side*, 11, 18; Conte Agüero, *Los dos rostros*, 80; Chanes, interview; Betto, *Fidel y la religión*, 190; Gimbel, *Havana Dreams*, 33, 34–35.

19. Montano, interview; Mencia, *Time Was on Our Side*, 21–22, 39.

20. Mencia, *Time Was on Our Side*, 152; Conte Agüero, *Cartas del Presidio*, 20–23.

21. Conte Agüero, *Cartas del Presidio*, 41–43.

22. The "26 of July Hymn" was composed on July 22, 1953, as the "March of Liberty Hymn" after Fidel Castro asked Agustín "Thompson" Díaz Cartaya to write a combat hymn to identify his movement. Díaz Cartaya did not participate in the Granma expedition nor did he join the rebels in the Sierra Maestra. He remained in obscurity for decades and only recently surfaced during 26 of July celebrations. See "Nosotros no debemos olvidar," *Granma*, July 26, 2003; Betto, *Fidel y la religión*, 190–91; Israel Tápanes, "26 de julio," *Verde Olivo*, July 26, 1970, 27; Chanes, interview; Piedra, interview; Szulc, *Fidel*, 308–9; Mencia, *Time Was on Our Side*, 66.

23. Isle of Pines penitentiary warden Juan M. Capote Fiallo and chief of internal order Lt. Pedro "Perico" Rodríguez Coto were sentenced to death by a revolutionary tribunal on April 28, 1959, and executed two days later. Salustiano "Cebolla" Rodríguez was sentenced to death on May 5, 1959. Eduardo Montano Benítez was dismayed by the execution of Capote, "because he treated us well during two years. I do not believe the accusations against him. Fidel should have sent Capote out of the country on a plane." See Montano, interview; Chanes, interview; Mencia, *Time Was on Our Side*, 71; Conte Agüero, *Cartas del Presidio*, 26, 36; Szulc, *Fidel*, 305–6.

24. In June and October 1954 homicide Cases 284 and 303 were forwarded from the Bayamo tribunal and added to the others in northern Santiago de Cuba. The charges were annulled when the Amnesty Law was decreed on May 15, 1955, granting freedom to the Moncada combatants. See Mencia, *Time Was on Our Side*, 75, 121; Singer, "I, Fidel Castro," 13; Conte Agüero, *Cartas del Presidio*, 17.

25. Jorge Mañach Robato (February 14, 1898–June 25, 1961) went into exile in 1959 in Puerto Rico, where he died of cancer. See Mendieta, interview; Conte Agüero, *Cartas del Presidio*, 23; Conte Agüero, interview; Mencia, *Time Was on Our Side*, 104; Rosa Hilda Zell, "6 documentos del Moncada," *Bohemia*, July 27, 1962, 67–69; Francisco de Armas, "Como se

edito en la clandestinidad la primera edición de la Historia me Absolverá," *Hoy,* July 21, 1963, 2-3; "Con la sangre de mis hermanos muertos," *Granma,* July 16, 1971, 2; Nieto, interview.

26. Szulc, *Fidel,* 312; Raúl Martínez, interview.

27. Conte Agüero, *Cartas del Presidio,* 37; Chanes, interview; Mencia, *Time Was on Our Side,* 124-25; Matthews, *Fidel Castro,* 73.

28. Conte Agüero, *Cartas del Presidio,* 20; Theodore Draper, *Castroism: Theory and Practice* (New York: Praeger, 1965), 6; Ruiz, *Cuba,* 13; Conte Agüero, interview.

29. According to Mario Llerena, when Castro was in Mexico in 1956, he received from Cuba an economic document consisting of about thirty to forty legal-size, double-spaced pages. "The document was a thesis on the economic bases and development of a new Cuba. The fundamental aspects of the economic thesis (that is what it came to be called: *Economic Thesis*) included control of foreign investments, state interventionism, revision of the United States-Cuba treaties, and diversification of industry." Llerena, *Unsuspected Revolution,* 89. An August 1957 issue of *Cuba Libre,* a magazine published by the 26 of July group in Costa Rica, carried an article attributed to Fidel Castro entitled "Socioeconomic Objectives of the 26 of July," which was made up of out-of-context passages from *History Will Absolve Me.* The publication also had a summary of *Our Reason,* along with a facsimile of the booklet's cover. See Llerena, *Unsuspected Revolution,* 77; Casuso, *Cuba and Castro,* 203; Nieto, interview; Arango, interview; Conte Agüero, *Los dos rostros,* 82.

30. Mencia, *Time Was on Our Side,* 150, 152, 164; Matthews, *Fidel Castro,* 79; Conte Agüero, *Cartas del Presidio,* 38.

31. "Excluyen de la amnistía los sucesos de Moncada," *Oriente,* May 24, 1954, 1; *El Mundo,* July 31, 1954, 1, and August 11, 1954, 4; Luis Conte Agüero, "Sin miedo y sin odio," *Bohemia,* April 3, 1955, 63; Conte Agüero, interview.

32. Conte Agüero, *Cartas del Presidio,* 35; Mencia, *Time Was on Our Side,* 126, 158-59.

33. Mencia, *Time Was on Our Side,* 142-43; Salabarría, interview; "El viaje de Fidel a Santiago aquel histórico julio de 1953," *Granma,* July 24, 1977, 4; Raúl Martín Sánchez, "Con los presos políticos en Isla de Pinos," *Bohemia,* July 9, 1954.

34. Conte Agüero, *Cartas del Presidio,* 30-31, 43, 45-46; Szulc, *Fidel,* 310.

35. Fidel Castro and Mirta Díaz-Balart were divorced on June 18, 1955. Emilio Núñez Blanco died in Madrid in August 2006 while his wife, Mirta, was in Havana visiting the ailing Fidel Castro. Aramís Taboada erroneously appears as a Moncada fighter in Szulc, *Fidel,* 154. He was jailed in 1980 and died in prison on November 20, 1985. See Conte Agüero, *Cartas del Presidio,* 47; Fernández, *Castro's Daughter,* 71; Casuso, *Cuba and Castro,* 177; Francisco Lorié Bertot, *Rafael Díaz-Balart: Pensamiento y acción* (Miami: Editorial Rex Press, 1978), 54; Szulc, *Fidel,* 316.

36. "Se entrevistó el Dr. Hermida con Fidel Castro," *El Crisol,* July 27, 1954, 1; Rafael J. Díaz-Balart, "La funesta actuación de Hermida," *Tiempo,* July 29, 1954, 1; Taber, *M-26,* 48; Mencia, *Time Was on Our Side,* 143-45, 213; Conte Agüero, *Cartas del Presidio,* 50, 55-57, 82; Lorié Bertot, *Rafael Díaz-Balart,* 33.

37. Conte Agüero, *Cartas del Presidio,* 63-64; Taber, *M-26,* 47; Mencia, *Time Was on Our Side,* 170; Szulc, *Fidel,* 318.

38. Mencia, *Time Was on Our Side,* 189-91.

39. The amnesty document was signed by Cosme de la Torriente, Carlos Márquez-Sterling Guiral, Manuel Antonio de Varona Loredo, Ramón Zaydín, Jorge Mañach, José R. Andreu, Pelayo Cuervo, José Gutiérrez Planes, Antonio Martínez Fraga, Néstor Carbonell, Manuel

Bisbé, Francisco Carone, Félix Lancís, Lincoln Rodón, José Pardo Llada, Héctor Pagés, Luis Casero Guillén, Alberto Saumell, Carlos M. Peláez, José Díaz, Rogelio Regalado, José Miguel Morales Gómez, Vicentina Antuña, Roberto Melero Juvier, Antonio G. Cejas, Luis Conte Agüero, Manuel Palacio Blanco, Eduardo Corona, Andrés Valdespino, Rafael Miyar, Luis Felipe Gutiérrez, Max Lesnik, Javier Lezcano, Aramís Taboada, Orlando de la Portilla, and Francisco Ramos Montejo. Most of these political leaders went into exile after 1959 in disagreement with Fidel Castro's policies. The amnesty text also appeared in *Bohemia,* February 27, 1955, 62; Mencia, *Time Was on Our Side,* 184; Marta Rojas, "Carlos Prío puede y debe regresar a Cuba, dice el general Batista," *Bohemia,* February 27, 1955, 59.

40. Lorié Bertot, *Rafael Díaz-Balart,* 52.

41. The El Pinero ferry has been converted into a revolutionary relic. See Conte Agüero, *Los dos rostros,* 88; Mencia, *Time Was on Our Side,* 47; Mario Mencia, "Con la tiranía descabezada a los pies," *Bohemia,* July 16, 1976, 61.

42. Ortodoxo leaders Raúl Chibás Rivas, Roberto Agramonte, and Max Lesnik and *Bohemia* reporter Agustín Alles Soberón, all went into exile in the United States by 1961. See Agustín Alles Soberón, "Del Moncada al presidio y a la libertad," *Bohemia,* May 22, 1955, 22, 73; Mencia, "Con la tiranía descabezada," 63.

43. Castro's love affair with Naty Revuelta produced an out-of-wedlock daughter, Alina Fernández Revuelta, on March 19, 1956. Naty eventually divorced her husband, who moved to West Virginia with their oldest daughter after the revolution. In 1991 Naty's mother, who lived with her in Havana, was still blaming her daughter "for everything that's happened in Cuba" and calling her a Communist. Alina escaped Cuba in 1993 with a phony Spanish tourist passport. Naty still resides in Havana, frequents the tourist hotels "stylishly dressed, heavily bejeweled," and travels abroad often. See Gimbel, *Havana Dreams,* 42, 72; "Quiere escaparse de Cuba una hija de Fidel Castro," *Diario las Américas,* July 1, 1988, 1; Antonio Valle Vallejo, "La hija rebelde de Fidel Castro," *El Nuevo Herald,* October 11, 1988, 7; Raúl Martínez, interview.

44. "Quieren matar a Fidel," *La Calle,* May 14, 1955, 1; "Réplica sobre los sucesos de Santiago," *Bohemia,* May 22, 1955; Fidel Castro, "¡Mientes, Chaviano!," *Bohemia,* May 29, 1955, 57; "Chaviano, el provocador," *La Calle,* May 30, 1955, 1.

45. Luis Orlando Rodríguez (1917–89) joined the rebel army in 1957, edited its newspaper, and in 1958 directed Radio Rebelde. After 1959 he spent more than two decades in the diplomatic service. See "Yo vi fusilar a más de 30 revolucionarios," *La Calle,* June 3, 1955, 1; "Manos asesinas," *La Calle,* June 7, 1955, 3.

46. Szulc, *Fidel,* 323; "¡Estúpidos!," *La Calle,* June 9, 1955, 3.

47. Jorge Agostini Villasana (February 5, 1910–June 8, 1955), the clandestine military chief of the Triple A, graduated from the Cuban Naval Academy in 1931. He went into exile in 1933 and fought with the Republicans in the Spanish Civil War. Agostini rejoined the Cuban navy in 1941, was minister of the navy in the Grau administration, and served as chief of the Presidential Palace Guard. In 1947 he was a liaison to the Cayo Confites expedition. On April 21, 1959, a revolutionary tribunal sentenced two ex-navy noncoms to twenty years of imprisonment at hard labor, and an ex-lieutenant and an ex-seaman received ten-year terms for denouncing Agostini's clandestine role to chief of naval intelligence Julio Laurent, resulting in Agostini's murder. Rebel terrorism reached its zenith on the "Night of One Hundred Bombs" in Havana on March 15, 1958. José "Pepe" Suárez Blanco (1927–91) was relegated to insignificant posts in

the revolutionary government. See "Four Sentenced in Agostini Case," *Havana Post,* April 22, 1959, 1; Santamaría, *Moncada,* 46; "Frente al terror y frente al crimen," *La Calle,* June 11, 1955, 3; Franqui, *Diary,* 62, 291; Hart, *Aldabonazo,* 94; Szulc, *Fidel,* 324; Mencia, "Con la tiranía descabezada a los pies (Segunda Parte)," *Bohemia,* July 23, 1976, 64.

48. Mencia, "Con la tiranía descabezada (Segunda Parte)," 61–63; Edmundo Desnoes, ed., *La Sierra y el llano* (Havana: Casa de las Américas, 1961), 7.

49. Cuba had 6,563,000 inhabitants in 1958, 77.9 percent of whom were literate. See Grupo Cubano de Investigaciones Económicas, *Un estudio sobre Cuba,* 794, 802.

Chapter 10—The "Grand Task of Cuban Reconstruction"

1. Fulgencio Batista Zaldívar (January 16, 1901–August 6, 1973) fled to the Dominican Republic on January 1, 1959, with his family and two planeloads of his closest collaborators. Eight months later, after being permanently denied admission into the United States, he moved to Funchal, Madeira, a remote Portuguese island off the northern coast of Africa. In 1963 the Batista family settled in a rented two-story villa in Estoril, an elite suburb of Lisbon, Portugal. Batista died of a heart attack in Marbella, Málaga, Spain, and is interred in San Isidro Cemetery, Madrid.

2. The twenty Moncada and Bayamo attack veterans who went on the Granma expedition were Emilio Albentosa Chacón, Juan Almeida Bosque, René Bedia Morales, Reinaldo Benítez Nápoles, Enrique Cámara Pérez, Raúl Castro Ruz, Mario Chanes de Armas, Jaime Costa Chávez, Julio Díaz González, Calixto García Martínez, Gabriel Gil Alfonso, Francisco González Hernández, Antonio "Ñico" López Fernández, Antonio D. López García, José R. Martínez Alvarez, Armando Mestre Martínez, Jesús Montané Oropesa, José Ponce Díaz, Ciro Redondo García, and Ramiro Valdés Menéndez.

3. Alberto del Río Chaviano was dismissed by Batista and fled to the Dominican Republic with his assistants Teodoro Rico Boué and Antonio Policarpo Ochoa Ferrer one week before Castro assumed power. Del Río Chaviano bought a cattle ranch that was later expropriated by the dictator Rafael Trujillo. In 1963 he settled in Dallas, Tex., as a college Spanish teacher before succumbing to bone cancer on April 26, 1978, in Miami, where he is interred in Woodlawn Park Mausoleum. Rico Boué left the Dominican Republic after ten months and settled in Miami. He passed away on December 6, 1989, and is interred in Flagler Memorial Park cemetery. See U.S. Department of State, *Foreign Relations of the United States, 1958–1960, Volume VI, Cuba* (Washington, D.C.: U.S. Government Printing Office, 1991), 299; Smith, *Fourth Floor,* 177–79; John Dorschner and Roberto Fabricio, *The Winds of December: The Cuban Revolution 1958* (London: Macmillan, 1980), 273–76; Raimundo, *Habla el Coronel Orlando Piedra,* 46.

BIBLIOGRAPHY

Interviews

Fourteen Rebels
Arcos Bergnes, Gustavo. Telephone interview. Havana, Cuba, May 6, 1997.*
Bustillo Rodríguez, Carlos A. Personal interview. West New York, N.J., June 3, 1984.*
Castro García, Orlando. Personal interview. Miami, Fla., December 5, 1983.
Chanes de Armas, Mario. Personal interview. Miami, Fla., August 12, 1993.*
Costa Chávez, Jaime. Personal interview. Miami, Fla., August 7, 1984.
de Armas Errasti, Héctor. Personal interview. Miami, Fla., August 4, 1984.*
Díaz-Francisco, Angel. Personal interview. Miami, Fla., March 3, 1988.*
Granados Lara, Gerardo. Personal interview. Orlando, Fla., August 10, 1984.
Mafut Delgado, Moisés. Personal interview. Miami, Fla., August 7, 1984.*
Martínez Ararás, Raúl. Personal interview. Miami, Fla., December 5, 1983.
Montano Benítez, Eduardo. Personal interview. Passaic, N.J., June 17, 1995.
Pérez-Puelles Valmaseda, Gerardo. Telephone interview. Miami, Fla., July 4, 1990.
Rosete, Elio. Telephone interview. Miami, Fla., February 28, 1988.*
Suardíaz Fernández, Manuel. Personal interview. Queens, N.Y., April 29, 1990.*

Forty-seven Military and Government Personnel
Abreu Jiménez, Capt. Rosendo. Telephone interview. Miami, Fla., September 27, 1988.*
Acosta Sánchez, Lt. Armando. Personal interview. Los Angeles, Calif., June 26, 1989.
Aguila Gil, Capt. Manuel. Telephone interview. Miami, Fla., August 5, 1984.
Alcolea Ramírez, Cpl. Eugenio. Personal interview. Elizabeth, N.J., August 23, 1988.*
Batista Seguí, Cpl. Norberto. Personal interview. Bronx, N.Y., August 22, 1988.*
Camps Ruiz, Lt. Vicente. Personal interview. Bronx, N.Y., September 10, 1974.*
Cuello, Lt. Mariano. Telephone interview. Miami, Fla., September 24, 1988.*
Cuello Silveira, Pvt. Ernesto. Telephone interview. Bronx, N.Y., September 25, 1988.*
del Río Chaviano, Col. Alberto R. Telephone interview. Dallas, Tex., November 26, 1974.*
Delgado Martínez, Sgt. Carlos A. Telephone interview. Miami, Fla., December 10, 2005.
Fajardo Mendoza, Sgt. Julián. Personal interview. Miami, Fla., November 2, 1974.*
Ferrá Mulet, Pvt. José Alberto. Personal interview. Orlando, Fla., June 12, 2004.

*Have passed away since being interviewed.

Ferrer, Pvt. Isidro. Telephone interview. Elizabeth, N.J., July 29, 1989.
Gajate Erro, Naval Capt. Mario. Personal interview. Miami, Fla., May 31, 1975.*
García, Cpl. Eugenio. Personal interview. Miami, Fla., February 28, 1975.*
González Alfonso, Lt. Col. Angel. Personal interview. Miami, Fla., April 18, 1975.*
González Amador, Sgt. Eulalio. Personal interview. Miami, Fla., April 20, 1974.*
Juan Pita, Med. Lt. Erik. Personal interview. Miami, Fla., December 21, 1974.*
Lavastida Alvarez, Capt. Agustín. Personal interview. Miami, Fla., July 6, 1974.
Lazo Cuba, Lt. Carlos. Personal interview. Miami, Fla., July 2, 2004.
Machado Rofe, Lt. Angel S. Personal interview. Miami, Fla., December 31, 1974.*
Martija, Pvt. Justo Ramón. Personal interview. Miami, Fla., August 28, 2000.
Martínez Verdecia, Policeman Horacio. Personal interview. Miami, Fla., July 26, 1974.*
Mas Renedo, Med. Lt. Roberto P. Telephone interview. La Canada, Calif., February 15, 1986.*
Matos Romero, Pvt. Ariel. Personal interview. Miami, Fla., August 1, 2004.
Morales Gros, Pvt. Orlando. Personal interview. Tampa, Fla., December 14, 2005.
Morales Gros, Pvt. Rafael. Personal interview. Queens, N.Y., September 12, 1974.*
Morales Herrera, Sgt. Cesáreo. Personal interview. Miami, Fla., October 27, 1974.
Ochoa Ferrer, Lt. Antonio Policarpo. Personal interview. Miami, Fla., December 23, 1974.*
Oliva López, Pvt. Armando Fidelio. Personal interview. Miami, Fla., April 6, 1975.*
Olivares Pérez, Pvt. José Humberto. Personal interview. Hialeah, Fla., June 7, 2004.
Pérez Sainz de la Peña, Med. Lt. Rolando. Personal interview. Miami, Fla., January 19, 1975.*
Piedra Negueruela, Col. Orlando. Personal interview. Miami, Fla., October 24, 1974.*
Pupo Miranda, Pvt. Angel. Personal interview. Glendale, Calif., March 14, 1990.*
Reyes Martín, Cpl. Néstor. Personal interview. West New York, N.J., June 17, 1989.
Rico Boué, Lt. Teodoro. Personal interview. Miami, Fla., March 2, 1988.*
Rodríguez Pérez, Pvt. Antonio Herminio. Personal interview. Miami, Fla., September 9, 2000.
Rosell Leyva, Maj. Florentino E. Telephone interview. Hialeah, Fla., August 15, 2005.
Sánchez Pruna, Pvt. Juan Manuel. Personal interview. Miami, Fla., August 26, 1988.
Silva Domínguez, Pvt. Alfonso. Personal interview. Hialeah, Fla., July 10, 1974.
Tabernilla Palmero, Col. Carlos. Telephone interview. West Palm Beach, Fla., December 21, 2005.
Tabernilla Palmero, Col. Marcelo. Telephone interview. Miami, Fla., December 29, 2005.
Toledo Niebla, Pvt. Osvaldo. Personal interview. Carolina, P.R., August 14, 1988.
Valdés Cabrera, Lt. Ismael. Personal interview. Miami, Fla., January 12, 1975.*
Virués Moraga, Sgt. José Hidalezio. Personal interview. Caguas, P.R., August 14, 1988.*
Xenis López, Policeman Evelio. Personal interview. Hialeah, Fla., March 1, 1988.*
Yanez Pelletier, Lt. Jesús. Telephone interview. Havana, Cuba, May 6, 1997.*

Fifty-four Civilians and Politicians
Abascal Berenguer, Gerardo. Telephone interview. Miami, Fla., December 9, 1984.*
Algarra Peralta, Dinorah. Telephone interview. Miami, Fla., August 3, 1991.*
Amador Hernández, Rolando. Telephone interview. Miami, Fla., February 28, 1988.*
Arango Alsina, Ramiro. Personal interview. Coral Gables, Fla., March 1, 1988.*
Bartolomé, Manuel. Personal interview. Miami, Fla., August 16, 1993.
Casero Guillén, Luis. Personal interview. Miami, Fla., August 9, 1984.*
Celeiro, René. Telephone interview. Miami, Fla., August 5, 1984.
Chibás Rivas, Raúl. Personal interview. San Juan, P.R., December 10, 1984.*

Bibliography

Conte Agüero, Luis. Personal interview. Miami, Fla., August 26, 1988.
de la Fe Pérez, Ernesto. Personal interview. Miami, Fla., April 10, 1990.*
del Mazo Serra, Raúl. Telephone interview. Miami, Fla., August 9, 1984.
Díaz-Balart Gutiérrez, Rafael. Personal interview. Miami, Fla., March 9, 1988.*
Eldidy Eljaiek, Dr. René. Telephone interview. Miami, Fla., February 15, 1986.*
Estrada Beatón, Domingo. Telephone interview. Kansas City, Mo., July 29, 1984.*
Fajardo, Amelia. Telephone interview. Miami, Fla., March 9, 1988.*
Fajardo Vázquez, Ana María. Personal interview. Miami, Fla., December 28, 2005.
Feraud, Cástulo. Telephone interview. Union City, N.J., December 9, 1984.*
Fiterre Rivera, Ignacio A. Telephone interview. Miami, Fla., August 5, 1984.*
Fornaris, Dr. Fernando Pedro. Telephone interview. Miami, Fla., February 1, 1986.*
García-Ferrer Méndez, Dr. Eduardo. Telephone interview. Crevecoeur, Mo., December 9, 1984.
Gómez Domínguez, Luis. Telephone interview. Miami, Fla., December 2, 2002.
González, Berta. Personal interview. Río Piedras, P.R., September 15, 1982.
Hidalgo-Gato González, Horacio. Personal interview. Miami, Fla., June 10, 2004.
Leizán Montero, Manuel. Personal interview. Río Piedras, P.R., September 15, 1982.*
León Orúe, Dr. Mauricio. Telephone interview. Plattsburgh, N.Y., January 24, 1988.*
Márquez-Sterling Guiral, Carlos. Telephone interview. Miami, Fla., December 4, 1982.*
Martínez Serrera, Ricardo. Personal interview. Miami, Fla., June 10, 2004.
Masferrer Rojas, Rolando. Personal interview. Miami, Fla., August 1, 1975.*
Medina Puig, José. Telephone interview. Miami, Fla., February 1, 1986.
Mendieta Tamayo, Francisco. Personal interview. San Juan, P.R., November 8, 1982.
Mendoza Guanche, Rafael. Telephone interview. Miami, Fla., February 28, 1988.*
Mestre Gutiérrez, Ramón. Personal interview. Miami, Fla., December 29, 2005.
Montero Moscoso, Manuel. Personal interview. Río Piedras, P.R., October 15, 1982.*
Morales Rodríguez, Vidal. Personal interview. Miami, Fla., April 6, 1990.*
Morán Arce, Lucas. Personal interview. San Juan, P.R., September 10, 1982.*
Nieto Pineiro-Osorio, Magistrate Adolfo. Personal interview. Falls Church, Va., May 10, 1975.*
Norman García-Iñiguez, Manuel J. Telephone interview. Ypsilanti, Mich., August 18, 2005.
Ochoa Ochoa, Emilio. Personal interview. Miami, Fla., December 2, 1983.
Ortíz Fernández, Dr. Héctor L. Telephone interview. Miami, Fla., February 1, 1986.
Ovares Herrera, Enrique. Personal interview. Miami, Fla., April 8, 1990.*
Parladé, Dr. Rafael. Telephone interview. Daytona Beach, Fla., February 1, 1986.
Pérez Cuesta, Lázara Sarah. Telephone interview. Miami, Fla., August 3, 1991.
Piñeiro del Cueto, Carlos M. Personal interview. Guaynabo, P.R., February 13, 1986.*
Pujol Soler, José. Personal interview. Miami, Fla., December 22, 1974.
Roca Gutiérrez, Mariano. Telephone interview. San Juan, P.R., February 1, 1986.*
Rubio Llerena, Enrique. Personal interview. San Juan, P.R., December 11, 1985.
Salabarría Aguiar, Mario. Personal interview. Miami, Fla., December 7, 1983.*
Savigne Pavón, Luis. Telephone interview. Sarasota, Fla., February 15, 1986.*
Silva Adán, Andrés. Telephone interview. Columbus, Ohio, February 1, 1988.*
Suárez Rivas, Eduardo. Personal interview. Miami Beach, Fla., May 13, 1974.*
Tobío, José. Personal interview. Miami, Fla., March 2, 1975.*
Varela Pla, Coralia Agustina. Personal interview. Miami, Fla., August 4, 1984.

Varona Loredo, Manuel Antonio de. Telephone interview. Miami, Fla., December 14, 1991.*
Villalón Virgilí, Dr. Roberto. Telephone interview. Columbus, Ohio, February 1, 1986.*

United States Government Documents

United States Department of State. *Confidential U.S. State Department Central Files: Cuba, Internal Affairs, 1950–1954*. U.S. National Archives and Records Administration, Washington, D.C.

———. *Foreign Relations of the United States 1947, Volume VIII, The American Republics*. Washington, D.C.: U.S. Government Printing Office, 1972.

———. *Foreign Relations of the United States 1952–1954, Volume IV, The American Republics*. Washington, D.C.: U.S. Government Printing Office, 1983.

———. *Foreign Relations of the United States, 1958–1960, Volume VI, Cuba*. Washington, D.C.: U.S. Government Printing Office, 1991.

United States Senate. Committee on the Judiciary. Hearings before the Subcommittee to Investigate the Administration of the Internal Security Act and Other Internal Security Laws. *Communist Threat to the United States through the Caribbean*. Pt. 13. Washington, D.C.: U.S. Government Printing Office, 1962.

Federal Government Freedom of Information Act Releases

Central Intelligence Agency
Movimiento Socialista Revolucionario (MSR), January 8, 1948.

Department of State
Federación Estudiantil Universitaria de la Universidad de La Habana. Despatch No. 716, August 30, 1948.

Federal Bureau of Investigation, U.S. Department of Justice
Rafael del Pino. MM 105–1738, April 6, 1959.

Intelligence Division, Office of Chief of Naval Operations, Navy Department
Slaying of Manolo Castro. Report R-35–48 of the U.S. Naval Attaché in Havana, February 26, 1948.

Periodicals

ABC (Madrid)
Alerta
ANAP
Ataja
Atlanta Journal
Avance
Bohemia
Bohemia Libre
Carteles
Casa de las Américas
Cuba
Cuba Internacional

Diario de Cuba (Santiago de Cuba)
Diario de la Marina
Diario las Américas (Miami, Fla.)
El Camagüeyano
El Crisol
El Habanero
El Mundo (Havana)
El Mundo (Madrid)
El País
El Nuevo Herald (Miami, Fla.)
El Siglo (Bogotá)
Excelsior (Mexico)
Granma
Havana Post
Hispanic American Historical Review
Hoy
Illustrated Weekly of India
Información
Juventud Rebelde
La Calle
Libertad (Spain)
Mañana
Miami Herald
Miami News
New York Times
Oriente (Santiago de Cuba)
Political Affairs
Prensa Universal (Santiago de Cuba)
Réplica (Miami, Fla.)
Revista de la Universidad de La Habana
Revista Moncada
Revolución
Revolución y Cultura
Tiempo en Cuba
Time
Tribuna Médica
Vanguardia Estudiantil
Verde Olivo
Vida Universitaria
Visión (New York)
Washington Post

Books

Acosta, Pablo. *Mi "compañero" Fidel*. Miami: Ediciones Universal, 2005.

Aguiar Rodríguez, Raúl. *El bonchismo y el gangsterismo en Cuba*. Havana: Editorial de Ciencias Sociales, 2000.

Alape, Arturo. *El Bogotazo: Memorias del Olvido*. Havana: Ediciones Casa de las Américas, 1983.

Almeida Bosque, Juan. *La Aurora de los Héroes*. Santiago de Cuba: Editorial Oriente, 1999.

Almendros, Néstor, and Orlando Jiménez-Leal. *Conducta impropia*. Madrid: Editorial Playor, 1984.

Alvarez de Cañas, Pablo, and Joaquín de Posada, eds. *Libro de Oro de la Sociedad Habanera 1952*. Havana: Editorial Lex, 1951.

Ameringer, Charles D. *The Caribbean Legion: Patriots, Politicians, Soldiers of Fortune, 1946–1950*. University Park: Pennsylvania State University Press, 1996.

———. *The Cuban Democratic Experience: The Auténtico Years, 1944–1952*. Gainesville: University Press of Florida, 2000.

Andux González, Teresa, Haydée Laborí Ripoll, and José M. Leyva Mestre. *La Capital en el Moncada*. Havana: Editorial de Cincias Sociales, 1990.

Asamblea Nacional de Amigos de Cuba. *Homenaje al 10mo. aniversario del asalto al Cuartel Moncada, 26–27–28 de julio de 1953*. Santiago de Cuba, 1963.

Autores varios. *Mártires del Moncada*. Havana: Ediciones Revolución, 1965.

Azcuy, Aracelio. *Cuba: Campo de concentración*. Mexico City: Ediciones Humanismo, 1954.

Baeza Flores, Alberto. *Las Cadenas vienen de Lejos*. Mexico City: Ediciones Letras, 1960.

Barquín, Ramón M. *Las luchas guerrilleras en Cuba: De la colonia a la Sierra Maestra*. Vol. 1. Madrid: Editorial Playor, 1975.

Barredo Medina, Lázaro. *Mi prisionero Fidel: Recuerdos del teniente Pedro Sarría*. Havana: Editorial Pablo de la Torriente, 1986.

Batista, Fulgencio. *Cuba Betrayed*. New York: Vantage Press, 1962.

Betto, Frei. *Fidel y la religión*. Santo Domingo: Editorial alfa y omega, 1985.

Blanco, Katiuska. *Todo el tiempo de los cedros: Paisaje familiar de Fidel Castro Ruz*. Havana: Casa Editorial Abril, 2003.

Bonachea, Ramón L., and Marta San Martín. *The Cuban Insurrection 1952–1959*. New Brunswick, N.J.: Transaction Books, 1974.

Bonachea, Rolando E., and Nelson P. Valdés, eds. *Revolutionary Struggle 1947–1958: Volume I of the Selected Works of Fidel Castro*. Cambridge: MIT Press, 1972.

Bourne, Peter G. *Fidel: A Biography of Fidel Castro*. New York: Dodd, Mead & Company, 1986.

Brennan, Ray. *Castro, Cuba and Justice*. New York: Doubleday, 1959.

Canto Bory, Enrique. *Mi vida*. Hato Rey, P.R.: Ramallo Bros. Printing, 1993.

Carrillo, Justo. *A Cuba le tocó perder*. Miami: Ediciones Universal, 1993.

Castillo Ramos, Rubén. *Las avanzadas del cauto: El ataque al Cuartel de Bayamo*. Santiago de Cuba: Editorial Oriente, 1981.

Castro, Fidel. *History Will Absolve Me*. London: Jonathan Cape, 1968.

———. *Pensamiento político, económico y social de Fidel Castro*. Havana: Editorial Lex, 1959.

Casuso, Teresa. *Cuba and Castro*. New York: Random House, 1961.

Centro de Estudios de Historia Militar de las Fuerzas Armadas Revolucionarias. *Moncada: La acción*. Havana: Editora Política, 1981.

———. *Moncada: Motor de la Revolución*. Havana: Editora Política, 1986.

Chester, Edmund A. *A Sergeant Named Batista*. New York: Henry Holt and Company, 1954.

Coltman, Leycester. *The Real Fidel Castro*. New Haven, Conn.: Yale University Press, 2003.

Comisión de Orientación Revolucionaria de la Dirección Nacional del PURSC. *Relatos del asalto al Moncada.* Havana: Empresa Consolidada de Artes Gráficas, 1964.

Conte, Ramón B. *Historia oculta de los crímenes de Fidel Castro.* N.p., 1995.

Conte Agüero, Luis. *Cartas del Presidio.* Havana: Editorial Lex, 1959.

———. *Eduardo Chibás: El Adalid de Cuba.* Mexico City: Editorial Jus, 1955.

———. *Fidel Castro—psiquiatría y política.* Mexico City: Editorial Jus, 1968.

———. *Fidel Castro: Vida y obra.* Havana: Editorial Lex, 1959.

———. *Los dos rostros de Fidel Castro.* Mexico City: Editorial Jus, 1960.

Costa, Jaime. *El clarín toca al amanecer.* Barcelona: Ediciones Rondas, 2003.

Cuba en la mano: Enciclopedia popular ilustrada. Havana: Imprenta Ucar, Garcia y Cia., 1940.

Cuervo Cerulia, Georgina D., and Ofelia Llenín del Alcázar. *Moncada: Epopeya heróica.* Havana: Instituto Cubano del Libro, 1973.

de Armas, Ramón, Eduardo Torres-Cuevas, and Ana Cairo Ballester. *Historia de la Universidad de La Habana 1930–1978.* Vol. 2. Havana: Editorial de Ciencias Sociales, 1984.

de la Cotera O'Bourke, Luisa Margarita. *Los miserables de Cuba.* Havana: Imprenta Cuba Intelectual, 1938.

de la Cuesta, Leonel Antonio. *Constituciones Cubanas desde 1812 hasta nuestros días.* New York: Ediciones Exilio, 1974.

de la Fuente, Alejandro. *A Nation for All: Race, Inequality, and Politics in Twentieth-Century Cuba.* Chapel Hill: University of North Carolina Press, 2001.

Desnoes, Edmundo, ed. *La Sierra y el llano.* Havana: Casa de las Américas, 1961.

Dirección Política de la FAR. Sección de Historia. *Moncada: Antecedentes y preparativos.* Havana: FAR, 1972.

Draper, Theodore. *Castroism: Theory and Practice.* New York: Frederick A. Praeger, Publishers, 1965.

Duarte Oropesa, José. *Historiología Cubana.* Vol. 3, *Desde 1944 hasta 1959.* Miami: Ediciones Universal, 1974.

Dubois, Jules. *Fidel Castro: Rebel-Liberator or Dictator?* Indianapolis: Bobbs-Merrill, 1959.

Ediciones Políticas. *Haydée habla del Moncada.* Havana: Instituto del Libro, 1967.

———. *Veintiseis.* Havana: Instituto del Libro, 1970.

Fandiño Silva, Francisco. *La penetración Soviética en América y el 9 de abril.* Bogotá: Colección Nuevos Tiempos, 1949.

Fernández, Alina. *Castro's Daughter: An Exile's Memoir of Cuba.* New York: St. Martin's, 1999.

Fernández Miranda, Roberto. *Mis relaciones con el General Batista.* Miami: Ediciones Universal, 1999.

Franqui, Carlos. *Diary of the Cuban Revolution.* New York: Viking, 1980.

———. *The Twelve.* New York: Lyle Stuart, 1968.

———. *Vida, aventuras y desastres de un hombre llamado Castro.* Mexico City: Planeta, 1989.

García-Calzadilla, Miguel. *The Fidel Castro I Knew.* New York: Vantage, 1971.

García-Carranza, Araceli. *Bibliografía del asalto al Cuartel Moncada: Suplemento (1973–1987).* Havana: Editora Política, 1989.

García Montes, Jorge, and Antonio Alonso Avila. *Historia del Partido Comunista de Cuba.* Miami: Ediciones Universal, 1970.

García-Pérez, Gladys Marel. *Insurrection & Revolution: Armed Struggle in Cuba, 1952–1959.* Boulder: L. Rienner Publishers, 1998.

Geyer, Georgie Anne. *Guerrilla Prince: The Untold Story of Fidel Castro.* Boston: Little, Brown and Company, 1991.

Gimbel, Wendy. *Havana Dreams: A Story of Cuba.* New York: Alfred A. Knopf, 1998.

Grupo Cubano de Investigaciones Economicas. *Un estudio sobre Cuba.* [Coral Gables, Fla.:] University of Miami Press, 1963.

Halperin, Ernst. *Fidel Castro's Road to Power: Cuban Politics from Machado to Moncada.* Cambridge: MIT Center for International Studies, 1970.

Hart, Armando. *Aldabonazo: Inside the Cuban Revolutionary Underground 1952-58.* New York: Pathfinder, 2004.

Hernández, Mirian. *Bibliografía del asalto al Cuartel Moncada.* Havana: Instituto Cubano del Libro, 1975.

Hitler, Adolf. *Mein Kampf.* Boston: Houghton Mifflin, 1943.

Imágenes de Cuba, 1952–1973. Havana: Instituto del Libro, 1973.

Instituto Cubano del Libro. *Moncada: Edición homenaje al Vigésimo Aniversario del 26 de julio de 1953.* Havana: Editorial de Ciencias Sociales, 1973.

Karol, K. S. *Guerrillas in Power: The Course of the Cuban Revolution.* New York: Hill & Wang, 1970.

La Charite, Norman. *Case Studies in Insurgency and Revolutionary Warfare: Cuba, 1953–1959.* Washington D.C.: Special Operations Research Office (SORO), 1963.

Latell, Brian. *After Fidel: The Inside Story of Castro's Regime and Cuba's Next Leader.* New York: Palgrave Macmillan, 2005.

Lazo Pérez, Mario. *Recuerdos del Moncada.* Havana: Editora Política, 1987.

Llerena, Mario. *The Unsuspected Revolution: The Birth and Rise of Castroism.* Ithaca, N.Y.: Cornell University Press, 1978.

Lockwood, Lee. *Castro's Cuba, Cuba's Fidel.* New York: Macmillan, 1967.

Lorié Bertot, Francisco. *Rafael Díaz-Balart: Pensamiento y acción.* Miami: Editorial Rex Press, 1978.

Lupiáñez Reinlein, José. *El Movimiento Estudiantil en Santiago de Cuba 1952-1953.* Havana: Editorial de Ciencias Sociales, 1985.

Martín Leiseca, Juan. *Apuntes para la Historia Eclesiástica de Cuba.* Havana: Talleres Tipográficos de Carasa, 1938.

Martin, Lionel. *The Early Fidel: Roots of Castro's Communism.* Secaucus, N.J.: Lyle Stuart, 1978.

Matthews, Herbert. *Fidel Castro.* New York: Simon and Schuster, 1969.

———. *Revolution in Cuba: An Essay in Understanding.* New York: Charles Scribner's Sons, 1975.

McManus, Jane. *From the Palm Tree: Voices of the Cuban Revolution.* Secaucus, N.J.: Lyle Stuart, 1983.

Mencia, Mario. *El Grito del Moncada.* Havana: Editora Política, 1986.

———. *Time Was on Our Side.* Havana: Editora Política, 1982.

Meneses, Enrique. *Fidel Castro.* New York: Taplinger, 1968.

Merle, Robert. *Moncada: Premier combat de Fidel Castro.* Paris: Robert Laffont, 1965.

Mil fotos Cuba, territorio libre de América. Havana: Comité Central del Partido Comunista de Cuba, 1967.

Mirabal Reyes, Yolanda. *El color de la Victoria.* Havana: Editora Abril, 1990.

Moore, Carlos. *Castro, the Blacks, and Africa.* Los Angeles: Center for Afro-American Studies, University of California, Los Angeles, 1988.

Mundo social: Registro social de las familias Habaneras. Havana: Impresos Pastor, 1954.

Niño Heredia, Alberto. *Antecedentes secretos del 9 de abril.* Bogotá: Editorial Pax, 1949.

Organización Nacional de Bibliotecas Ambulantes y Populares. *13 documentos de la insurrección.* Havana: ONBAP, 1959.

Pacheco, Judas. *Abel Santamaría y el Moncada.* Havana: Editora Política, 1983.

Pardo Llada, José. *Fidel y el "Che."* Barcelona: Plaza & Janes Editores, 1988.

Pérez, Louis A., Jr. *Army Politics in Cuba 1898-1958.* Pittsburgh: University of Pittsburgh Press, 1976.

Pérez Rojas, Niurka. *El Movimiento Estudiantil Universitario de 1934 a 1940.* Havana: Editorial de Ciencias Sociales, 1975.

Portell Vilá, Herminio. *Nueva historia de la República de Cuba.* Miami: La Moderna Poesia, 1986.

Portocarrero, Jesús A. *Cuba: Paradigma y destino de América.* Miami: Colonial Press, 1966.

Quirk, Robert. *Fidel Castro.* New York: W. W. Norton & Company, 1993.

Raimundo, Daniel Efrain. *Habla el Coronel Orlando Piedra.* Miami: Ediciones Universal, 1994.

Ray Rivero, René. *Moncada, Sierra Maestra: Libertad y revolución.* Havana, 1959.

Riera Hernández, Mario. *Cuba libre 1895-1958.* Miami: Colonial Press, 1968.

———. *Historial obrero Cubano.* Miami: Rema Press, 1965.

Roca, Blas. *The Cuban Revolution.* New York: New Century, 1961.

Rodriguez, Ana, and Glenn Garvin. *Diary of a Survivor: Nineteen Years in a Cuban Women's Prison.* New York: St. Martin's, 1995.

Rodríguez Morejón, Gerardo. *Fidel Castro: Biografía.* Havana: P. Fernández, 1959.

Rojas, Marta. *El juicio del Moncada.* Havana: Editorial de Ciencias Sociales, 1988.

———. *El que debe vivir.* Havana: Casa de las Américas, 1978.

———. *La cueva del muerto.* Havana: Ediciones Unión, 1983.

———. *La Generación del Centenario en el Juicio del Moncada.* Havana: Editorial de Ciencias Sociales, 1979.

———. *La Generación del Centenario en el Moncada.* Havana: Ediciones Revolución, 1964.

———. *Los testigos del hospital.* Havana: Ediciones Granma, 1967.

Rojas, Marta, et al. *Antes del asalto al Moncada.* Havana: Ediciones Unión, 1979.

Ros, Enrique. *Fidel Castro y el gatillo alegre: Sus años universitarios.* Miami: Ediciones Universal, 2003.

Ruiz, Ramón Eduardo. *Cuba: The Making of a Revolution.* New York: W. W. Norton & Company, 1970.

Sarabia, Nydia. *Moncada: Biografía de un cuartel.* Havana: Editorial de Ciencias Sociales, 1984.

A Sketch on the Clandestine and Guerrilla Press Covering the Period 1952-1958. Havana: Instituto del Libro, 1971.

Smith, Earl E. T. *The Fourth Floor: An Account of the Castro Communist Revolution.* New York: Random House, 1962.

Soto Acosta, Jesús. *Bibliografía prensa clandestina revolucionaria (1952–1958)*. Havana: Biblioteca Nacional "José Martí," 1965.
Suchlicki, Jaime. *Cuba: From Columbus to Castro and Beyond*. Washington, D.C.: Brassey's, 1997.
Szulc, Tad. *Fidel: A Critical Portrait*. New York: William Morrow and Co., 1986.
Tabares del Real, José A. *Guiteras*. Havana: Instituto Cubano del Libro, 1973.
Taber, Robert. *M-26: The Biography of a Revolution*. New York: Lyle Stuart, 1961.
Thomas, Hugh. *Cuba: The Pursuit of Freedom*. New York: Harper & Row, 1971.
Travieso, Julio. *Un nuevo día*. Havana: Editorial Letras Cubanas, 1984.
Urrutia Lleó, Manuel. *Fidel Castro and Company, Inc.: Communist Tyranny in Cuba*. New York: Praeger, 1964.
Weyl, Nathaniel. *Red Star over Cuba: The Russian Assault on the Western Hemisphere*. New York: Devin-Adair Company, 1960.
Young, Allen. *Gays under the Revolution*. San Francisco: Grey Fox Press, 1981.
Zeitlin, Maurice. *Revolutionary Politics and the Cuban Working Class*. New York: Harper Torchbooks, 1970.

INDEX

Abad, Orestes, 263, 304n16, 319n5
Abascal Berenguer, Gerardo, 190
ABC Organization, xiii, xxix, 205, 236, 238, 277
Abreu Jiménez, Capt. Rosendo, 106, 142, 324n12
Abril Rivas, Julio, 287n34
Acción Libertadora, 48, 72, 172, 198, 213, 299n42
Acción y Trabajo para un Orden Mejor (ATOM), 11, 26, 43, 92
Aceña, José, 294n4
Acosta, Alfredo, 220
Acosta, Pablo, 19–20
Acosta Sánchez, Lt. Armando, 57–58, 68–69, 161, 302n66
Afro-Cubans, 38, 42, 60–61, 64, 67, 78–79, 83, 85, 91, 94, 97–98, 102, 106, 115, 122, 130–32, 141–42, 144, 150, 157, 174–75, 177, 182–83, 186, 188–89, 191, 222, 240, 295n14, 324n10, 324n16, 336n43
Agostini Villasana, Jorge, 153, 245, 350n47
Agramonte Loynaz, Ignacio, 275
Agramonte Pichardo, Roberto D., 30, 32, 36, 52, 138, 234, 244, 295n11, 350n42
Agricultural and Industrial Development Bank of Cuba (BANFAIC), xxx, 48
Agüero, Pvt. José D., 91, 311n28
Agüero Guedes, Pablo "Machito," 64, 125, 134, 265, 296n14, 323n4
Aguila, Julio, 268
Aguila Cuevas, Pvt. Luis Cosme, 113, 267

Aguila Gil, Capt. Manuel E., 98, 156, 159–60, 218, 313n46
Aguilera González, Pedro C., 37, 50, 61, 65–66, 122–24, 126, 129, 172, 194, 198, 213, 246, 263, 274, 319n5, 342n24
Ala Izquierda Estudiantil, 341n14, 342n22
Alabau Trelles, José, 340n3
Alape, Arturo, 291n67
Albentosa Chacón, Emilio, 60–61, 69, 71, 152, 263, 298n29, 327n40, 351n2
Alcalde Sánchez, Emilio, 255
Alcalde Valls, Oscar, xv, 42–43, 47, 50, 56, 60–61, 65, 69–70, 77, 81, 111, 113, 144, 148–49, 175–76, 180, 182, 185–86, 188–89, 199–200, 215, 224, 235, 255, 260, 273, 317n80, 325n28, 326n31
Alcolea Ramírez, Cpl. Eugenio, 69, 82–83, 101, 108, 156, 161, 172, 217, 267, 308nn4, 6, 318n89, 338n54
Alegría de Pío, Oriente, 251, 322n31
Alemán, José Manuel, 15–16
Alemán Rodríguez, Remberto A., 265, 309n14
Alerta (newspaper), 30, 32, 54, 119, 157, 293n83
Alfonso Cruz, Sgt. Vicente, 219
Algarra Peralta, Dinorah, 33, 35, 67, 116, 162, 330n63
Allain, Conrad, 170
Alles Soberón, Agustín, 244, 350n42
Almeida Bosque, Juan xv, 60–61, 70, 73, 76, 111–12, 178, 180, 183–85, 199–200, 224,

Almeida Bosque, Juan (*continued*)
    235, 255, 260, 273, 295n14, 314n47,
    326n31, 340n10, 351n2
Almendares, Havana, 41, 46
Almendares rebel cell, 66, 76, 145, 214,
    307n43
Alonso Alvarez, Rubén, 273, 344n50
Alonso Cruz, Sgt. Vicente, 167, 331n77
Alonso Fernández, Jorge, 347n14
Alonso Lemus, Capt. Manuel F., 171
Alonso Martínez, Lt. Alberto A., 324n17,
    343n37
Alonso Pujol, Guillermo, 1–2, 301n53
Alto Cedro, Oriente, 163, 167
Alvarado, Juan Oscar, 341n12
Alvarado González, Adalberto, 341n12
Alvarado González, Oscar, 198, 208, 271,
    273, 339n60, 341n12, 342n27
Alvarez Alvarez, Gerardo A. "El Chino," 86,
    88, 115, 265, 296n14, 303n7
Alvarez Breto, Tomás, 86–88, 115, 265,
    319n94
Alvarez Morgado, Pvt. Manuel I., 97, 105,
    220, 267
Amador Hernández, Rolando, 169, 332n82
Amador Rodríguez, Juan, 243
Amaya López, Bernardo, 133–34
Ameijeiras Delgado, Efigenio, 246
Ameijeiras Delgado, Juan M., 62, 77–78,
    172, 246, 265, 296nn14, 15, 303n7,
    309n14
Ameijeiras Romo, Gustavo, 172, 246, 271,
    273
Americas Watch, 255
Amnesty International, 255, 280
Andino Hotel, Havana, 27, 32
Andreu Martínez, José R., 323n4, 349n39
Anglada, Francisco, 87
Anglada, Oscar, 182–83, 187
Antonetti Fernández, Fausto "Paco," 12
Antuña, Vicentina, 350n39
Aranda, Aranda Castillo, Reinaldo, 26
Arango Alsina, Ramiro, 139, 198, 205–6,
    225–26, 239, 271, 274, 323n3, 339n60,
    342n27, 344n50, 345n58
Arango Bustamante, Rafael, 204
Araña Ahitú, Isaac, 12–14, 288n35
Ararás, Rosaura, 37, 42, 45
Arbenz, Jacobo, 240, 289n49

Arcos Bergnes, Gustavo: activism, 4, 65;
    ambassador to Belgium, 279, 347n14; dissident, xxiii; flees Moncada, 110, 146;
    hospitalized, 146–47, 197, 226; imprisoned, 168, 240, 347n14; jailed by Castro,
    254, 279, 339n58, 347n14; letter from
    Cuba, July 26, 2003, 279–80; MNR member, 51; rides with Castro to Moncada,
    xxii, 77–78, 83, 308n3; shoots Pvt.
    Frómeta, 84–85; sentenced, 232, 260;
    Siboney farmhouse, 75–76; trial of, 205,
    217, 228, 232, 274; wounded by friendly
    fire, xiii, 99, 319n94
Arcos Bergnes, Luis, 347n14
Arcos Bergnes, Sebastián, 280, 347n14
Arencibia García, Armando, 129, 132–33,
    263, 304n16, 340n5
Arévalo, Juan José, 20, 289n49
Argentina, 20–21
Argentine Embassy in Havana, 132, 135
Argota Reyes, María Luisa, 4, 6–7, 284n16
Armaignac, Dr. Quinidio, 164
Arpa Ceballo, Lt. Manuel, 98, 155, 191
Arrastía Navarrete, Luis, 271, 273
Arroyo Naranjo, Havana, 41, 60
Arroyo Naranjo rebel cell, 61, 65, 69, 250
Arteaga, Cardinal Manuel, 168–69
Artemisa, Pinar del Río, xv, 40–41, 66, 116,
    179, 182, 255, 337n45, 346n59
Artemisa rebel cell, xvii, 40–41, 63–64, 68–
    69, 89, 92, 111, 115, 140, 143, 149, 167,
    178, 182, 196, 297n21, 304n12
Aruca, Juanita, 65
Arza, Benjamín, 179, 196
Association of Law Students, 9, 13–14,
    288n40
Ataja (newspaper), 163, 245
Atala Medina, Ibis, 197, 339n58
Atala Medina, Nayibe, 197
Auténtico activists, 3–4, 28, 39–40, 43, 52–
    53, 57, 118–19, 139, 209
Auténtico Party, 1–2, 12, 26, 28–29, 45–46,
    52, 159, 164, 171, 173, 194, 204, 206–8,
    213, 232, 238, 242, 244, 257, 277, 287n35,
    294n4, 301n53
Avila Sánchez, Pvt. Manuel, 154, 327n44
Azcuy Cruz, Aracelio, 208, 271, 301n53,
    339n60, 342n27
Azpiazo Núñez de Villavicencio, Jorge, 28

INDEX 365

Babún Selman, Teófilo, 171, 196, 339n56
Babún Serret, Pvt. Farik, 182
Badell, Domingo, 179
Badell Romero, José M., 223, 273
Baeza, Danilo, 299n42
Baire, Oriente, 126, 169
Balart, Barbara, 179
Baldor, Pvt. José, 322n32
Baldor School, Havana, 33
Balgán Fresco, Idelisa, 218
Banes, Oriente, 27, 313n40, 315n57
Barajagua, Oriente, 29
Barba, Alvaro, 299n42
Baró Melodio, Pvt. Eusebio, 94, 105, 141, 267
Barón Martínez, Gilberto, 66, 145, 265, 296n14, 307n43
Barquet Aguiar, Lt. Antonio, 153, 327n43, 343n37
Barquín López, Col. Ramón M., 142
Barrancas, Oriente, 167
Bartolomé, Antonio, 146, 161
Bartolomé, Manuel, 48, 158, 161–62, 165–66, 173, 309n14
Bartolomé Funeral Home, 48, 146, 157, 160–61
Barzaga Vázquez, Humberto, 86, 267
Batabanó, Havana Province, 243
Batista Lotti, José A., 211, 271, 274
Batista Rubio, Rubén, 45, 48
Batista Seguí, Cpl. Norberto, xxii, 91, 103–4, 141–42, 195, 267, 313n46, 321n20, 324n11, 328n56, 335nn34, 37, 336n41, 336n45, 338n54
Batista Seguí, Pvt. Juan, 141
Batista Seguí, Pvt. Luis Manuel, 141, 188–91, 202, 335n37, 336n41
Batista Zaldívar, Fulgencio, xxii, 74, 133, 144, 279–80; Afro-Cuban support, 141–42, 150, 189; awards medals to Moncada soldiers, 195; betrayed by generals, 143, 254, 327n44; Col. del Río Chaviano and, 168, 170–71; contribution to Santiago carnival, 68; controls supreme court prosecutor, 203; coup d'état xiv, xxvi, 1–3, 31–32, 50, 70, 131, 192, 241, 249; denounced by Castro, 59, 206, 222, 236, 240; elections of 1954, 52, 237, 242; flees Cuba, 250, 302n66, 351n1; grants

amnesty to political prisoners, 239, 242–43, 247; hailed by soldiers during Moncada combat, 84, 91, 102; halts execution of prisoners, 154, 168, 245; Kuquine residence, 1–2, 29; leads raid on weapons cache, 57; lifts press censorship, 231; Luisa Margarita de la Cotera and, 46, 199, 207; March 1935 strike, 119; major general, 282n1; Montreal Pact, 53–54; orders sparing Fidel Castro's life, 168, 171, 191, 202, 252; PAU leader, 212; photo used by rebels as ruse, 82; president during 1940–44, xxix, 11, 298n31; rebels in combat proclaim his overthrow, 85, 87, 105, 127, 130; receives U.S. Ambassador Gardner, 232; repression, 253, 255; senator, 29; sergeant, xxix, 120; speech after Moncada attack, xi, 160, 173, 177; U.S. retires support for, 201, 254; Varadero national regatta, xii, 62, 80, 157, 252; visits Holguín, 210; visits Isle of Pines prison, 235; visits wounded Moncada soldiers, 195, 338n54; wedding gift to Fidel Castro, 27
Bayamo, Oriente, xxvi, 50, 55, 57, 64–66, 74, 77, 121–24, 128, 130–32, 134–36, 139, 145, 161, 167, 169, 172, 192, 194–96, 200, 209, 211, 213, 219, 237, 242, 250–51, 258, 304n16
Bayamo attack: duration of combat, 128; strategy, 124–25, 136–37
Bayamo attack casualties: rebel wounded in action, 127, 137; rebels executed or murdered by soldiers, 128–29, 132–34; soldiers and policemen wounded or murdered by rebels, 127–28, 130, 137
Bay of Pigs invasion, 54, 292n74, 317n81, 334n15, 339n56
Bayamo Cemetery, 134
Bayamo garrison, see Carlos Manuel de Céspedes Rural Guard garrison
Bayamo River, Oriente, 122, 125–26, 128, 134, 137
Bayona, Pvt. Luis, 94, 161, 267
Beaulac, Willard L., 169
Bécquer, Gustavo, 131
Bécquer, Nelson, 131–32
Bedia Morales, René, 72, 147, 215, 224, 260, 273, 303n6, 351n2

Bejar, "Chicho," 131–32
Bejar, Rafaela, 132
Belén High School, 8–9, 45, 184, 285n29, 286n28, 296n15
Belize, 19
Bell of la Demajagua, 17–18, 290n52
Belt, Guillermo A., 18, 23–25, 291n69
Benítez, Sgt. Miguel, 108
Benítez Hernández, Orlando, 191, 336n44
Benítez León, Cecilio T., 208, 224, 271, 273
Benítez Nápoles, Reinaldo, 62, 100, 111, 148, 175–76, 178–79, 198, 215, 224, 260, 304n20, 308n3, 319n94, 326n31, 351n2
Betancourt, Rómulo, 20–21, 290n56
Betancourt Castillo, René, 197, 209, 219, 223, 271, 274
Betancourt Flores, Antonio, 265, 297n21, 309n14
Betancourt Rodríguez, Flores, 92, 265, 296n15, 308n5, 312n31, 319n94
Betto, Frei, 9, 284n17
Biltmore Yacht Club, Havana, 44, 296n15
Birán, Oriente, 5, 7, 29, 110, 167
Bisbé Alberni, Manuel, 30, 54, 293n84, 323n4, 350n39
Black Legend myth of rebel prisoner torture and mutilation, xi, xiii, xvi–xviii, xix, xxvii, 165–66, 173, 227, 234, 330n71, 331n72
Blanc Corbín, Fernando, 229
Blanco Alba, Jesús "Garabato," 65, 76–77, 164, 214, 263, 273
Blanco Rico, Col. Antonio, 160, 195, 329n59
Blanco Rodríguez, Pvt. Antonio T., 128, 268
Bogotá, Colombia, 19–22, 25, 256
Bogotazo, xxviii, 23–25, 31, 37–38, 54, 57, 234, 291n67, 292n76
Bohemia (magazine), xii, xvii, xxvii, 1–2, 13, 20, 27, 45, 54, 138, 140, 156, 177, 192–93, 216, 230, 235–36, 238, 240, 244, 247
Bonachea, Ramón, xv
Bonachea, Rolando E., xv
Bonche thugs, 10–12, 16
Boniato Provincial Prison, Oriente, 144, 165, 193–94, 197–99, 203, 216, 223, 225, 232, 236, 314n27, 325n28, 335n34, 339n60; description, 198
Bonito, Luis, 246
Borges, Omar, 295n11

Bosch, Juan, 15, 20, 284n16
Bosch Avila, Orlando "Piro," 286n33
Bourne, Peter G., xvii, xviii, 8, 288n40, 302n67, 308n3, 312n31, 333n11
Bóveda González, Sgt. Emilio, 162
Bragaña, Lola, 142
Brennan, Ray, 144
Brito Oquendo, Silverio E., 211, 271, 274
Brito Rodríguez, Antonio, 288n36
Bueno, Miriam, 194
Bureau of Investigations, 133
Buey River, Oriente, 133
Burman Corman, Mario, 159–60, 199, 212, 271, 274, 329n58
Bustillo Rodríguez, Carlos, 38, 64, 69, 75–76, 80, 89, 100, 110, 112, 244, 263, 317n81

Caballero de la Luz fraternity, 150
Cabrales Arjona, Dr. José Ramón, 158, 194, 220
Cabrera, José A., 212, 271, 274
Cadena Oriental de Radio, 157, 163, 193, 235
Café Raúl, Marianao, 65–66
Cala Cala, Pvt. Leonardo, 188, 335n37
Cala Reyes, Manuel "El Niño," xiii, 158–59, 268, 328n56
Cala Reytor, César, 329n56
Calabazar, Havana Province, 15, 41, 49, 60, 213, 215, 223–24
Calabazar rebel cell, 48, 61, 64, 70, 81, 111, 147, 194, 215
Callao Díaz, Ramón, 71, 213, 263, 273, 304n12, 306n32
Camacho, César, 225
Camagüey Province, 16, 27, 55, 58, 62, 67, 74, 97, 131, 133, 135, 139, 207, 232
Camajuaní, Las Villas, 160
Cámara Pérez, Enrique, 130–32, 214–15, 224, 260, 273, 295n14, 298n29, 304n16, 319n5, 351n2
Camejo Valdés, Hugo: activism, 56; background, 42, 265; departs for Bayamo, 64; deserted, xv, 125, 136; fatherless, 296n14; Marianao cell leader, xvi, 42, 50; murdered, 133–34, 209–10
Camp Columbia, Havana, 2–3, 17, 46–47, 53, 85, 124, 138, 157, 169, 192, 197, 206, 208, 225, 232, 241, 301n54, 316n69

Campa Delgado, Ramón, 271
Campanal, Arturo, see Arturo González del Río
Campanal, Arturo "Turín," 152
Campechuela, Oriente, 133
Campos Delgado, Ramón, 211, 274
Campos Pontigo, Cpl. Narciso, 7, 284n21
Camps, Police Sgt. Godofredo, 106
Camps Ruiz, Lt. Vicente, 143, 162–63, 203–4, 210–11, 228, 230–32, 330n64
Canciano Labory, Héctor, 223, 273
Canet Comas, Lt. Rafael, 157
Cano, Francisco "Panchito," 140
Cano, René, 290n52
Cano Rojas, Alejandro, 287n34
Canter, Dr. Jacob, 169, 332n83
Canto Bory, Enrique, 118, 143, 170–71, 181–83, 186–87, 189–90, 194–97, 338n55
Capote, Sgt. Buenaventura, 219
Capote Fiallo, Major Juan M., 232, 234–35, 348n23
Carabia Carrey, Senén, 57, 106, 115, 318n87
Carbó, Sergio, 138
Carbonell Andricaín, Néstor, 350n39
Cardona Orta, Francisco, 295n11
Careaga Medina, Gregorio, 40, 167, 219, 265, 304n21, 331n77
Caribbean Legion, 53–54, 59, 250, 289n49
Carlos Manuel de Céspedes Rural Guard garrison, Bayamo, 125–30, 257, 321n24
Carone, Francisco, 350n39
Carpintero River, Oriente, 167, 175
Carrillo Hernández, Justo, 48, 299n33, 300n42
Carrillo Morales, Lt. Eladio, 103, 343n37
Cartas Rodríguez, Pablo, 265, 303n7, 309n14
Carter, Jimmy, xvii
Casa de Socorro First Aid Clinic, Santiago de Cuba, 149
Casa Granda Hotel, Santiago de Cuba, 142, 145, 159–60, 169, 225
Casals Fernández, Rafael, 28
Casamayor Caballero, José, 150, 268
Casamayor Martínez, Baudilio, 150, 268
Casate Funeral Home, Bayamo, 134

Casero Guillén, Luis, 2, 48, 194, 198–200, 207, 211, 271, 274, 340n10, 342n27, 350n39
Casino Español, Havana, 139
Caso Pérez, Sgt. René, 105, 154, 328n56
Castell Cordero, Conrado, 273, 344n50
Castellanos García, Baudilio, xv, xvii, 27, 198, 210–12, 214, 223–24, 226, 228, 230, 273
Castelló, Vicente, 182
Castillo, Felipa, 98, 269
Castillo, Sgt. Mauricio, 94
Castillo Batista, Lt. Rafael, 343nn30, 37
Castillo Ramírez, Alicia, 98, 269
Castro Argiz, Angel María, 4–7, 28–29, 49, 283n15
Castro Argota, Lidia, 1, 32, 237, 241–42, 244, 246
Castro Argota, Pedro Emilio, 4, 29, 242, 293n79
Castro del Campo, Manuel "Manolo" de, 10–11, 13–15, 18–20, 31, 249, 286n28, 290n55, 292n73
Castro Díaz-Balart, Fidel Angel, 1, 27, 240, 246
Castro Fernández, Reinaldo, 263
Castro García, Orlando, xxii; background, 263; Bayamo combat role, 127; Bayamo plan a folly, 137; breaks with Fidel Castro over autocracy, 244, 256–57; describes Moto Mendel, 212; exiled, 135, 341n22; fatherless, 296n14; flees and hides after attack, 130–32; harangues citizenry to revolt, 129; imprisoned under Fidel Castro, xxi; joins movement, 37; prepares Bayamo attack, 121–26; revolutionary rank, 50, 123, 136–37, 258; reconciliation, xxiv; residence, 34
Castro Llanes, Orlando, 323n4
Castro Martínez, Gerardo, 219
Castro Ruz, Agustina, 7
Castro Ruz, Angela, 6
Castro Ruz, Emma, 6, 192, 246, 284n20
Castro Ruz, Fidel Alejandro: accused of trickery by rebels, 150, 179; anti-Americanism of, xiii, xxvi, xxviii, 4, 18, 20–21, 31, 234, 238, 247, 283n11; articles by, 30, 32, 35–36, 45, 244–46; assumes his

Castro Ruz, Fidel Alejandro *(continued)*
own legal defense, 205–10, 226, 229–31, 246, 252, 274; as athlete, 8–9; attempted murder of rivals by, 12, 15, 26, 31, 209; attains international recognition, 119, 252; attorney, xxvi, 28, 31–32, 39, 45; avoids cross-examination of Col. del Río Chaviano, 229, 246; avoids verbal provocation, 18, 26, 204–5; Batista gift to, 27; Batista meets with, 29; Batista orders sparing the life of, 168, 171, 191, 252; Bayamo rebel meeting, 123, 319n6; Bogotazo, 23–25, 31, 201, 234, 291n71; called Napoleon of the Caribbean, 347n14; Cayo Confites expedition, 15–17, 31, 169, 201, 234; celebrates fiftieth anniversary of Moncada attack, xxiii; character of, 6–8, 30–31, 46, 194, 198, 206, 234–35, 239–41, 247; charisma and prestige of, 35, 37, 44, 227; childhood of, xxviii, 6–8, 30; compared to Adolf Hitler, xxx, 172, 231, 252–53; compared to Augusto César Sandino, 249; commits perjury in court, 206, 209, 226, 229, 246, 252; concerned about brother Raúl's fate after attack, 148, 184; confesses his role in attack, 192, 206, 229; death threat from Col. del Río Chaviano, 210, 229; defense speech in court, 230–31, 246; denies Communist involvement in movement, 206; described by U.S. Embassy, 169, 198, 252; despondent, 183, 201; devious manipulation by, xii, xxii, 7–8, 13, 15–18, 20–21, 25, 29–30, 34–35, 37–38, 42–43, 45, 49, 58–59, 61, 66, 71–77, 80, 92, 108, 111–12, 118–20, 143, 163–65, 172–74, 177–78, 181, 184, 192–93, 201–2, 210–11, 234–35, 239, 241–44, 247, 251–52, 284n17, 291n67; divorce of, 241, 247, 283n15, 349n35; electoral fraud accusation against, 30; faked attempted suicide, 148, 175, 201, 253, 325n28; family of, 1, 4–5; Fascist ideology of, 9; and fear, 1, 18, 20, 25, 32, 188, 211, 229; final preparations for revolt, 60–66; first Communist manifestations, 234; flees from Moncada skirmish, 110–12, 147–48; flees to the hills after Moncada attack, 151, 164, 170–71, 174–85, 252; four-month solitary confinement in prison, 235–36, 240;

gangsterism, xv, xxviii, 12–13, 29–30, 169, 194, 227; granted a separate trial, 211, 216–17, 225; height and weight of, 10; homophobia of, 31, 45, 241, 288n42, 294n86; hypocritical, 246; illegitimacy of, 6–7, 284n16; implicated by rebels in Moncada attack, 103, 143, 154, 159; in foster home, 6; incarcerated in Boniato prison, 194, 198–200, 232; incarcerated in *vivac* jail, 191–93; incarcerated in the Isle of Pines, 233–43; indicted by Urgency Tribunal, 180; insurrectional strategy, 40–41, 43, 47–48, 50–51, 54, 57–58, 73–76, 80, 121, 124; issues worthless checks, 61–62, 66, 302n3; judicial writ of, 30, 32; lacks religious faith, 9; leaves for Mexico, 246; letter to Franklin D. Roosevelt, 8; Marxist, xvi, 22, 25, 247; military ineptitude, xxvi, 42, 113, 117–18, 136, 172–73, 201, 250–52; Moncada attack role, xii–xiii, 81–84, 89, 91, 100, 110, 117–18, 250–51, 308n3; murder suspect, 18–19, 25–26, 30, 169, 292n73; Naty Revuelta and, xiv, 44, 144, 241, 244, 246, 350n43; nearly killed after capture, 188–191, 336n43; nicknames of, 8; organizes 26 of July Movement, 237, 246; parental economic assistance, 27; perceived as not being Communist, xiii, 27, 144; poisoning attempt while incarcerated, xxii, 193; police rap sheet of, 292n73; political aspirations of, 28–30, 52; praises the dead Moncada soldiers, 193, 206, 243; praises his judicial proceedings, 211, 226, 230–31; praises officers who arrested him and his brother, 229, 246; projected revolutionary government after Moncada victory, 206, 234, 247; and Puerto Rican independence, 20, 31; refused paraffin test after arrest, 194, 251; rejects revolutionary rank for himself, 75, 123; revolutionary internationalism of, xxviii, 31, 257; schooling of, 6–7; sentenced to 15 years, 231, 246, 260; Siboney farmhouse, 71–77, 143; social resentment of, 7–9, 26, 30, 194, 235, 239, 254; speeches of, xii, xxv, 9, 14, 17–18, 23, 32, 73; sports, 9–10; student elections, 10, 14, 31, 288n40, 289n51; surrenders without resistance,

INDEX

188–93; tobacco smoker, 10, 236; trial of, 204–11, 228–31; university student, 9, 16, 289n50; unaffectionate father, 8, 26, 49, 284n16, 300n45; wedding of, 26; well treated in prison, 192, 210, 236, 241–42, 280; wife pleads for his life and safety, 168–69, 214
Castro Ruz, Juana, 6, 284n18, 300n45
Castro Ruz, Ramón, 6–7, 167, 236
Castro Ruz, Raúl Modesto: armed forces minister, 255; arrested in Havana with Communist propaganda, 52; arrested after Moncada attack, xiv, 162–63, 168, 185, 203; attends Socialist Youth festival in Europe, 52, 196; birth of, 6, 284n16; biological father, 7, 285n21; cashed forged checks, 56; charged with bombing a theater, 246; denounces Fidel Castro after Moncada attack, 163; denounces Ortodoxo Party, 163, 234; departs for Mexico, 246; erroneously identified as Palace of Justice raid leader, xii–xviii, xxvii, 307n45; goddaughter of, 298n28; Granma expeditionary, 351n2; ideology of, 43; incarcerated in *vivac* jail, 191; incarcerated in Boniato prison, 198, 200; incarcerated in the Isle of Pines, 240–42; joins University Socialist Committee, 52; lacking a Moncada attack leadership role, 43, 52, 117, 216, 226, 251; learns of Moncada attack plan from Tasende, 63–64; MNR activist, 52; orders 1959 executions without trial, 318n88; Palace of Justice raider, 85, 90, 110; paraffin test negative, 163, 251; prankster, 199; public statement after capture, 74, 163, 172; schooling of, 6, 39; sentenced, 224, 260; Siboney farmhouse, 73, 76, 163; travels to Santiago de Cuba with rebels, 63–64, 68; trial of, 211, 215–16, 273; wedding of, 315n53; well treated in prison, 163, 173, 192, 210
Casuso, Gabriel, 298n31
Casuso, Teresa, 238, 241
Catalina de Güines, Havana Province, 66
Catholic Action (AC), 170
Catholic University Association (ACU), 14
Catholic Youth (JC), 14, 187, 195–96, 297n22, 325n23, 338n55

Cauto Cristo, Oriente, 122, 126, 132, 196
Cauto Embarcadero, Oriente, 135, 204
Cauto River, Oriente, 50, 135–36, 167
Cayo Confites, xxviii, 16, 20, 31, 37, 92, 158, 234, 289n49, 350n47
Cayo Espino, Oriente, 132
Cayo Hueso, Havana, 29, 41, 167, 303n12
Cayuga Company, 44
Ceiba del Agua Institute, 94, 195, 338n54
Cejas, Antonio G., 14, 350n39
Celda Street safehouse, Santiago de Cuba, 56, 58, 61, 64, 68–71
Celeiro, René, xix, 181
Central Highway, 50, 78, 81–82, 123, 134, 140, 144–45, 149
Central Intelligence Agency (CIA), 11–12, 25, 54, 201, 240, 289n47
Central Miranda, Oriente, 5, 167
Centro Gallego Clinic, Santiago de Cuba, 151
Centro Médico Quirúrgico, Havana, 44–45
Céspedes, Carlos Manuel de, xxix, 75, 257
Céspedes Park, Bayamo, 121
Céspedes Park, Santiago de Cuba, 72, 145, 159
Chamber of Representatives, xxix, 7, 9, 30, 208, 242–43, 293n80
Chanes de Armas, Francisco, 345n54
Chanes de Armas, Mario, xvi, xxii, 4, 36, 41, 62–63, 69, 72–73, 76–77, 89, 92, 100, 110–11, 147–48, 151, 174–75, 177–78, 180–81, 183–85, 189–90, 192, 198–200, 205, 212, 215, 224, 233, 235, 237, 254, 260, 273, 297n22, 310n21, 311n30, 326n31, 336n41, 345n54, 348n18, 351n2
Chaprón, Gisel, 98, 268
Charco Redondo, Oriente, 50, 124, 317n75
Chauvín, Cpl. Carlos, 85, 220
Chávez Fernández, Vicente, 77, 145, 213, 263, 274, 303n8
Chenard Piña, Fernando, xvi, 36, 41, 45, 69, 75–77, 110, 112, 150–51, 166, 265, 298n29, 303n8, 310n21, 331n75
Chibás Rivas, Eduardo, xvii, 27–29, 32, 36, 44, 53, 63, 66, 74, 80, 112, 138, 234, 238, 244, 275, 293n82

Chibás Rivas, Raúl, xx, 119, 244, 323n1, 350n42
Chicago Tribune, xii, 19
Chomat Fetué, Dr. Liam, 87, 114, 220
Church, Frank, 291n67
Cid, Georgina, xxii
Ciego de Avila, Camagüey, 65, 213
Cienfuegos, Camilo, 311n27
Cienfuegos carnival, 49, 249
Cigues Morales, Sgt. José, 217
Cisneros Ponteau, Rafael A., 212, 274, 344n50
Ciudamar Beach, Santiago de Cuba, 144, 146
Civil Hospital, xi, xiv–xvi, xxi, 56, 74, 76–79, 81–82, 85–88, 96–98, 101–2, 107, 109–10, 113–17, 136, 144, 147, 150, 153, 156, 158–59, 164, 199–200, 216–21, 228, 251, 256, 309nn13, 14, 310n16, 314n50, 317nn79, 80, 318n89, 326n36; description, 85–86
Clews Alvarez, Heriberto, 298n31
Clews Alvarez, Natalia, 44–45, 298n31
Club Aponte, Santiago de Cuba, 142
CMKR radio station, Santiago de Cuba, 191–92
Cold War, xxvii, 19, 173, 248, 252
Coll, Heberto, 44
Collada Alonso, José, 130
Collazo Cordero, Marino, 99–100, 111, 194, 213, 263, 273, 310n21, 319n94
Colombia, xxviii, 20, 313n37, 332n82
Colón, Matanzas, 33, 35–37, 42, 64–65, 67, 129, 162
Colón Cemetery, Havana, 32–33, 46, 241, 343n30
Colonia Española Clinic, Santiago de Cuba, 99, 146, 197, 228, 232
Coltman, Leycester, xix
Combinado del Este prison, Havana, 285n20
Cominches, Micaela, 146, 164
Committee for Dominican Democracy (CUDD), 15, 289n45
Communist Revolutionary Union, (URC) xxix, 144, 347n14
Compañía Cubana de Refrigeración Eléctrica, 34, 39
Compañía Lechera dairy, 60
Congress of Cuban Writers and Artists, xii

Conservative Party, 205, 323n1
Constitution of 1940, xxvi, xxix, 7, 59, 65, 119, 208, 224, 230, 242, 251, 255, 257–58, 278, 293n80
Constitution of 1976, xxv
Constitutional Code of April 4, 1952, 157, 224, 232
Conte Agüero, Luis, xxvi, 10, 30, 72, 74, 81, 118, 232, 234–40, 247, 251, 273, 323n4, 350n39
Contramaestre, Oriente, 169
Corbea Monteagudo, Cpl. Julio, 149, 186, 188–89, 335n37
Corcho Cinta, Alfredo, 64, 75, 80, 265, 305n25
Corcho López, Rigoberto, 92, 108, 151, 164, 265, 296n14, 308n5, 319n94
Cordero Sánchez, Rubén, 268, 326n34
Córdoba Alonso, Félix, 263, 307n43
Córdova Cardín, Giraldo, 41, 265, 296n14, 303n8, 310n21
Corinthia yacht, 256
Corona, Eduardo, 350n39
Corona Fernández, José Desiderio, 129
Corral, Miguel, 219
Corrales, Bernardo, 337n45
Correa Morales, Armando, 286n33
Cortés Gallardo, Orlando, 66, 145, 150, 213–14, 223–24, 260, 274, 307n43, 342n26
Cossío, 2nd Lt. Randolfo, 177, 180, 333n7
Costa Chávez, Jaime "El Catalán," xiii, xxi, xxiv, 72, 111, 148, 174–78, 196, 254, 263, 305n25, 317n79, 326n31, 351n2
Costa Rica, 20, 135, 196, 256, 289n49, 304n16, 322n31, 341n22, 349n29
Costa Velázquez, José F., 41, 265, 305n25, 309n14
Council of Ministers, 157, 195, 242, 293n83
Cowley Gallegos, Col. Fermín, 160, 329n59
Crain, Earl T., 232
Crespo Arias, Abelardo "El Perico," 38, 51, 65, 69, 76, 99–100, 103, 111, 148, 151, 164, 205, 217, 226, 228–31, 246, 256, 260, 273, 308n3, 314n49, 319n94, 331n73
Cruz, Pvt. Francisco, 219
Cuadrado Barrueco, Manuel, 182
Cuba Aeropostal, 155
Cuba Mining baseball team, 48

INDEX

Cuban Communist Party, xxvi, xxx, 3, 17, 27–28, 43, 52, 54, 138, 159, 164, 172–73, 198–200, 206–8, 237, 247, 287n35, 298n29, 341nn13, 14, 342n22; denounce Moncada attack, 139, 172, 208, 212, 227, 234, 242, 252, 254. *See also* Popular Socialist Party
Cuban Congress, xxix, 3, 16, 28, 242–43, 282n1
Cuban-Haitian Cultural Association, 167
Cuban Institute of Friendship with the Peoples (ICAP), 283n10
Cuban Missile Crisis, 253
Cuban National Party (PNC), 1–2
Cuban Navy, 14–16, 75, 131, 140
Cuban People's Party, see Ortodoxo Party
Cuban Revolutionary Party. *See* Auténtico Party
Cuban War of Independence, 37, 44
Cuban Workers Confederation (CTC) 3, 20, 171, 341n13
Cubana Airlines, 66, 138
Cubela, Rolando, 254
Cuello, Lt. Mariano, 311n30
Cuello Silveira, Pvt. Ernesto, 96, 140–41, 313n41, 316n71
Cuervo Navarro, Pelayo, 32, 138, 241, 323n4, 350n39
Cueto, Oriente, 7, 162, 284n16
Cu-Mex Petroleum Company, 65
Curuneaux, Sgt. Braulio J., 95, 99, 107, 109, 314n47

Daiquirí, Oriente, 167, 177
Dalmau de la Cruz, Mario, 51, 66, 69, 77–78, 85, 146, 263, 304n21, 340n5
Damajayabo, Oriente, 167
Dau, Rosa, 145, 211
Dávila, Santiago "El Barberito," 322n32
Daytona Beach, Fla., 27
de Aguiar Fernández, Raúl R., 66, 167, 265, 296n14, 303n12, 331n77
de Armas Errasti, Héctor, xix, 33, 35–36, 39, 45, 66, 69–70, 75, 77, 89–90, 99–100, 108, 112, 263, 303n6, 304n19, 317n81
de Armas Laucira, Héctor, 33, 35
de Cárdenas Armenteros, Manuel, 92
de Céspedes, Carlos Manuel, 222, 275
de Feria Mora, Dr. Arturo, 229

de Jan, Raúl, 301n53
de la Cotera O'Bourke, Luisa Margarita, 46, 199, 299n34
de la Fe Pérez, Ernesto, 11, 26, 57, 157, 170, 292n74, 327n44
de la Guardia, Antonio, 298n31
de la Paz, Sgt. Abraham, 133, 322n32
de la Portilla, Orlando, 350n39
de la Torriente, Cosme, 138, 323n1, 349n39
de la Torriente Brau, Pablo, 144
de la Vega, Benjamín, 253
de Varona Loredo, Manuel Antonio, 139, 301n53, 349n39
de Varona Loredo, Roberto, 139, 232, 301n53
de Yurre, Benjamín, 271, 340n5
Dead Man's Cave, Oriente, 153, 182
del Cerro, Angel, 299n42
del Mazo Serra, Raúl, 45, 48, 50, 172, 198, 200, 213, 271, 274, 299n33, 314n49, 342n24
del Pino Siero, Rafael, 18, 20–26, 286n33, 290n60, 291n67
del Pozo García, Abelardo, 213, 222, 271, 274
del Río Chaviano, Col. Alberto Roberto, xvi, xviii; background of, 58; carelessness of, 58, 68–70; character of, 106, 167; commands Moncada after attack, 143–44, 161, 197; condones execution of prisoners, 154, 166, 173, 236, 245; corruption, xxi, 142–43, 244; denounced by Fidel Castro, 244–45; denounced by Waldo Pérez Almaguer, 245; dismissed from the army, 254, 336n43, 351n3; falsified report of attack, 155–57, 159, 173, 205, 218, 227, 246, 329n59; furious at Fidel Castro's statements, 193, 210, 226; interrogates Fidel Castro, 192–93; letter in *Bohemia*, 244; meets with archbishop Enrique Pérez Serantes, 170–71, 183; message of pacification, 171, 181, 186, 191; reputation, 142; reproached by Fulgencio Batista, 168, 171, 202; rehearsed court testimony of military witnesses, 217; rescinds city curfew, 194; supports Batista coup, 3; testifies at trial, 220–21,

del Río Chaviano, Col. Alberto Roberto: testifies at trial (*continued*) 226–27, 229; whereabouts during attack, 98, 101–2, 114, 140–41
del Río Pérez, Alejandro, 312n35
del Valle, Raúl, 168–69
Delgado Cortez, Herminia, 218
Delgado Martínez, Sgt. Carlos A., 161
Dellundé, Carlos, 167
Dellundé Puyáns, Buenaventura, 30
Democratic Party, 2, 283n7
Despaigne, Agustín, 177
Despaigne, Basilia, 176
Despaigne, Eduardo, 177
Despaigne, Efigenia, 176
Despaigne, Felipe, 176
Despaigne, Gilberto, 176
Despaigne Grave de Peralta, Leoncio, 157–58
Despaigne Noret, Enrique, 107, 316n70
Despaigne Vinent, Pedro, 177–78
Despradel, Roberto, 16
Diario de Cuba, 140, 225, 228
Diario de la Marina, 9, 96, 100, 149, 187, 219, 288n40, 289n51
Diario Nacional, 138
Díaz, Herminio, 286n33
Díaz, José, 350n39
Díaz Cartaya, Agustín "Thompson," 64–65, 125, 129, 131, 213, 224, 235, 256, 260, 273, 295–96n14, 304n15, 348n22
Díaz Castelar, Armando, 212, 271, 274
Díaz Cominches, Alfredo, 146
Díaz Conde, Amalia, 86, 218
Díaz de Villegas, René, 299n42
Díaz González, Julio, 41, 89, 111, 149, 151–52, 164, 173, 215, 223–24, 260, 274, 297nn21, 22, 304n12, 343n30, 351n2
Díaz Landrían, Higinio "Nino," 196, 339n56
Díaz Lanz, Pedro, 254
Díaz Lorenzo, Elizardo, 223, 274
Díaz Olivera, Ricardo, 204, 228
Díaz Quintero, Ramón, 220
Díaz Rodríguez, Lomberto, 323n4
Díaz Tamayo, Gen. Martín, xvi, 154, 160–61, 236, 327n44
Díaz-Balart Gutiérrez, Frank, 10, 13, 19

Díaz-Balart Gutiérrez, Mirta, 1, 26–27, 168–69, 179, 192, 204, 214, 234, 236–37, 240–41, 247, 283n15, 349n35
Díaz-Balart Gutiérrez, Rafael Lincoln, 1, 10, 12–13, 15, 26–27, 29, 119, 169, 240–41, 243, 285n21, 289n45
Díaz-Balart Gutiérrez, Waldo, 1, 204
Díaz-Francisco, Angel L. "Patachula," xiv, 4, 38, 51, 65, 69–71, 73–77, 82, 100, 144–45, 155, 164, 199, 205, 214, 225, 263, 273, 345n57
Diéguez Lamazares, Jesús, 286n33
Diez, José Manuel, 330n63
Dolores School, Santiago de Cuba, 7, 48
Domínguez Díaz, Juan, 265, 296n14, 309n14
Dominican Republic, xxviii, 12, 46, 336n43, 351nn1, 3
Dominican Revolutionary Party (PRD), 15
Dos Caminos, Oriente, 162
Drago Grajales, Pvt. Poliano, 96
Draper, Theodore, 238
Duany, Julio "Mongolé," 151–52
Duarte Oropesa, José, 54
Dubois, Jules, xii, xiii
Duvallón-Gilbert Cuello, Pvt. Angel L., 108, 268, 316n71, 338n54

Echevarría, Mariano, 196
Ecos de la Resistencia, 294n4
El Acusador, xvi, xvii, 35–36, 58
El Caney, Oriente, 57, 144, 148, 166, 182, 184, 215
El Caney Cemetery, Oriente, 166, 182
El Cerro, Havana, 66
El Cerro Hunting Club, 42
El Cilindro farm, Oriente, 183, 186–87, 335n34
El Cobre, Oriente, xvii, 64, 67, 72, 149, 169, 216, 315n62
El Crisol (newspaper), 135, 157, 193
El Cristo, Oriente, 162, 196, 308n4
El Maracas, Santiago de Cuba, 142
El Príncipe prison, Havana, 36, 52, 323n4, 342n23
El Salvador, 20
El Vedado, Havana, 1, 34–35, 45, 60, 65, 135, 244
Eldidy, Dr. René, 99, 146–47, 325n24

INDEX

Elizalde Sotolongo, Guillermo, 91, 149–50, 209, 263, 274, 298n26, 319n94, 341n15
Eljaiek Eldidi, Eduardo, 274, 344n50
Emergency Hospital, Santiago de Cuba, 109, 209
England, 136
Enríquez, Froilán, 64, 297n22
Eros Sánchez, Angel, 213, 271, 274
Escala, José, 195, 338n52
Escalona Benítez, Víctor, 43, 66, 76, 145, 150, 265, 296n14, 307n43
Escandel Hill, Oriente, 51, 176
Esnard, Julio, 298n31
Espín Guillois, Nilsa, 52, 196
Espín Guillois, Vilma, 315n53
Espín Vivar, José, 196
Esquivel Rodón, Alfredo "El Chino," xvii, 18–20, 290n59
Estrada Calderón, Cpl. Indalecio, 126–27, 221, 320n20
Estrada de Beatón, Domingo, 212, 274, 344n50

Faget, Mariano, 287n34
Fajardo, Amelia, 182, 334n20
Fajardo Mendoza, Sgt. Julián, 112–14, 186, 318n85
Fajardo Vázquez, Ana María, 114, 318n82
Fajardo Vázquez, Beralia, 156, 318n82
Fajardo Vázquez, Julián, 114, 318n82
Fajardo Vázquez, Olga, 318n82
Falkland Islands, 19
Feal, General, 180
Feal Despaigne, Alfonso, 180–81, 183, 185
Federal Bureau of Investigation (FBI), 11
Federation of University Students (FEU), xiii, 3–4, 10, 12–15, 17–21, 27, 31, 38, 48, 239, 286n29
Feldman, Arthur W., 155, 198, 225
Feraud Mejías, Cástulo, 309n16
Feraud Mejías, Cpl. Mauricio, 87, 113, 141, 220, 268, 309n16
Feraud Mejías, 2nd Lt. Pedro V., 87, 113, 141, 158, 216, 218–21, 267, 309n16, 314n50, 317n80
Feraud Mejías, Sgt. René, 113, 141, 191
Fernández, Capt. Adolfo, 122, 130, 135
Fernández, Luis Gustavo, 301n53
Fernández Alfonso, Julio C., 64, 263

Fernández Caral, Oscar, 10, 26, 31, 292n73
Fernández Catá, Fernando, 55, 121–22, 135, 209, 219, 271, 274
Fernández Febles, Major Gumersindo, 140
Fernández Ferrer, Orlando, 44
Fernández León, Florentino, 48–49, 64, 69–71, 73, 81, 145, 197, 215, 263
Fernández Martínez, Gelasio, 60, 89–90, 150, 263, 326n34
Fernández Miranda, Lilia, 168
Fernández Miranda, Marta, 171
Fernández Miranda, Roberto, xi
Fernández Ortega, Eufemio J., 11, 14–18, 53, 159, 286nn29, 30, 31, 289n49, 334n15
Fernández Revuelta, Alina, 350n43
Fernández Revuelta, Natalie, 44
Ferrá Mulet, Pvt. José, xxii, 69, 83, 95, 100, 102, 308n6, 315n57
Ferrándiz Millán, Roberto, 85, 267
Ferrás Pellicer, Alejandro, 73, 89–90, 147, 263, 304n19, 310n22
Ferrás Pellicer, Antonio, 73, 89–90, 147, 263, 304n19, 310n22
Ferrás Pellicer, Armelio, 89–90, 147, 263, 303n9, 304n19, 310n22
Ferreira, Desiderio, 12
Ferrer, Pvt. Isidro, 109
Ferro, Antonio, 323n4
Fiallo, Amalio, 244
Fidalgo Rodríguez, José Manuel, 45
Figueres, José, 289n48
Figueroa, Isidro, 301n53
Figueroa, Lt. Luis, 203
Figueroa Araújo, María Antonia, 164, 330n69
Figueroa Araújo, Max E., 164, 330n69
Fiterre Rivera, Ignacio A., 139, 165, 173, 197–98, 200, 203, 208–11, 223, 225, 271, 274, 345n56
Fleitas López, Gildo, 45, 51, 55–56, 62–63, 66, 72, 77, 112, 114, 155–56, 252, 265, 303n9, 319n94
Fontecha refinery, Marianao, 41
Fonseca, Ibis, 141, 167
Fonseca Martínez, Pvt. José W., 86, 268, 309n14, 338n54
Fornaris, Dr. Fernando Pedro, 103–4, 315n62

Fosca, José, 323n4
Fourth of September flag, 63, 71, 82, 122, 257, 287n35, 306n33
Fraga Moreno, René, xix
Franco, Francisco, 9, 338n55
Franqui, Carlos, 5
Fraternity Park, Havana, 62
Freemasonry, xiv, xviii, 40, 53, 56, 142, 150, 167–68, 170, 172–73, 188, 211, 252, 297n22, 309n14, 335n38
Freyre de Andrade, Fernando "La Vaquita," 12
Freyre Torres, Rafael, 56, 134, 265, 296n14, 323n4
Frías, Luis A., 213, 271
Friguls García, Juan Emilio, 187, 189
Frómeta Naranjo, Pvt. Luis E., 83–85, 161, 268
Fuentes Clavel, Justo, 18, 26, 286n33, 292n74
Fuentes Cobas, Fernando, 291n66
Fuentes Rivera, Temístocles, 191, 198, 336n44

Gaitán, Jorge Eliécer, 21–22, 292n71
Gajate Erro, Capt. Mario, 14–15, 289n44
Galán Betancourt, Orlando, 112, 178, 196, 263, 303n9, 310n21, 326n31, 340n5
Galán Betancourt, Roberto "Bolo," 112, 175, 178, 196, 263, 304n12, 310n21, 326n31
Galano Liranza, Pvt. Efraín, 83, 104, 267
Galano Rodríguez, Sgt. Mario, 105
Galis-Menéndez Larraguechea, Armando, 18, 26, 292n74
Gallardo, Rubén, 63, 263, 298n26
Gallegos, Rómulo, 21
Gálvez, William, 313n37
Gamboa Alarcón, Lt. Luis S., 153, 186, 327n43
Gangsterism, 2–3, 11–13, 52
Garay, Angel Esteban, 88, 115, 318n87
García, Pvt. Dionisio Jorge, 126
García, Cpl. Eugenio, 95, 312n30
García, Pvt. Mónico, 109, 327n44
García, Col. Pilar, 229
García Baez, Col. Irenaldo, 138
García Bell, Pvt. Aquiles, 319n89
García Benítez, Juan José, 207, 274, 344n50

García Díaz, Andrés: attempted murder of, 133, 322nn32, 33; deserted, 125; incarcerated in Boniato prison, 200; leads Fidel Castro to Bayamo safehouse, 123; sentenced, 224, 260; surrenders, 134, 194–95; trial of, 209–10, 273
García Espinosa, Jacinto, 51, 265, 296n15
García Fernández, Recaredo, 274, 344n50
García Ferrer, Dr. Eduardo, 104
García Garzón, Leocadia "Chicha," 174–75, 333n2
García Ibáñez, Roberto, 205–7, 271, 274, 342n27, 344n50
García Iglesias, Andrés, 323n4
García Inclán, Guido, 18, 45, 177, 233
García Iñiguez, Calixto, 136
García Martínez, Calixto, 125, 129, 132–33, 242, 255, 263, 296nn14, 15, 304n16, 322n31, 351n2
García-Pérez, Gladys Marel, xviii, xix
García Riestra, Guillermo "Billiken," 286n33, 290n56
García Tudurí, Elpidio, 203, 214
García Ylls, Abelardo, 41, 85, 146, 164, 263, 305n25
García Zulueta, Andrés, 62
García-Bárcena Gómez, Rafael, 46, 51, 58, 139, 213, 239, 300n45
García-Ferrer Méndez, Eduardo, 104
Gardner, Arthur, 232
Garrido Wilson, 2nd Lt. Cándido, 83, 153, 343n37
General Motors Inter-American Corporation, 34
Geyer, Georgie Anne, xviii, 34
Gil Alfonso, Gabriel, 61, 149–51, 216, 224, 260, 273, 303n7, 326n36, 351n2
Ginjaume Montaner, José de Jesús, 26, 286n33
Godó Estenóz, Pvt. Clemente, 94, 268, 338n54
Godoy, Gastón, 241
Gómez Báez, Máximo, 250
Gómez Domínguez, Luis A., 214, 223, 274, 344n50
Gómez García, Raúl, xvi, 33, 35–36, 62–63, 66, 73, 86–87, 115, 156, 265, 294n4, 296n14, 303nn9, 11
Gómez Ochoa, Leopoldo, 132, 196

Index

Gómez Pérez, Leonel A., 12, 31, 209, 217, 225, 271, 274, 288n36, 345n58
Gómez Reyes, Manuel, 100, 265, 296n15, 303n8, 310n21, 319n94
Gómez Reyes, Virginio, 100, 265, 296n15, 303n8, 310n21, 319n94
González, Angelina, xx, 84
González, Anibal, 271
González, Sgt. Bernabé, 98, 217, 314n47
González, Berta, 186–87
González, Pvt. Fredesvindo, 311n30
González, Sgt. José, 220
González, Pvt. Rafael, 219
González, Ramón, 162–63
González Alfonso, Lt. Col. Angel, 68, 70, 78, 103, 118, 183, 191, 217, 343n35
González Amador, Sgt. Eulalio "El Mulo," xx, 84–85, 105, 143, 165–66, 331n73, 335n31
González Calderín, Francisco, 188
González Camejo, Luciano, 43, 134, 265, 296n14
González Campos, Ernesto, 263, 303n7
González Cuadra, Joaquín, 36
González del Río, Arturo (alias Arturo Campanal), 152–53, 182, 334n20
González Hernández, Francisco "Pancho," 62, 72, 180, 185, 198, 224, 260, 273, 310n21, 326n31, 351n2
González Le Blanch, Sgt. Agustín, 343n37
González Machado, Sergio, 135, 209, 271, 274
González Ruiz, José Luis, 212, 271, 274
González Seijas, Carlos, 51, 62, 110, 256, 263, 308n3
Good Neighbor Policy, xxix
Gran Casino Motel, Bayamo, 55, 67, 121–26, 129, 133, 209, 213, 257
Gran Piedra Mountain, Oriente, 166–67, 175, 178, 181
Granados Lara, Gerardo, 40, 49, 64, 71–72, 75, 89, 100, 110–11, 148–49, 174–75, 177–78, 196, 244, 263, 297n22, 311n30, 317n79, 326n31, 340n5
Granados Lara, Guillermo, 40, 89, 100, 111, 265, 319n94
Granma expedition, 250–51, 253–54, 257, 291n67, 322n31, 327n40, 329n57, 333n11, 340n4, 343n30, 347n14, 348n22, 351n2
Gras Escalona, Oscar, 159–60, 212, 271, 274, 342n23
Grau, Paulina, 19
Grau San Martín, Ramón, xxix, 11, 14–17, 24, 28, 48, 52–53, 209, 237, 242, 306n33
Grobart, Fabio, 208
Guach Ovieto, Dr. Vicente, 147
Guanabo Beach, Havana Province, 147
Guanajay, Pinar del Río, 41, 49, 71, 166, 213, 233
Guanajay rebel cell, 64, 68, 305n25
Guanche, Dr. Carmelina, 233
Guane, Pinar del Río, 284n16
Guantánamo naval base, 20, 31, 169, 316nn69, 71
Guantánamo Rural Guard post, 82
Guaro, Oriente, 4
Guas Inclán, Rafael, xxix, 242
Guatemala, 20, 46, 53, 232, 240, 289n49, 322n31
Guerra, Cpl. Argelio, 82
Guerra Cisneros, Antonio, 182
Guerra Díaz, Angel, 132, 265, 304n16, 319n5
Guerrero Bello, Rolando, 100, 209, 263, 274, 298n26, 323n4, 341n15
Guevara Valdés, Alfredo, 14, 17, 20–25, 52
Guilarte, Mabis, 338n54
Guilarte, Pvt. Pedro, 98, 104, 267, 338n54
Guillaume, Dr. Santiago Ramón, 327n44
Guin, Ramón, 254
Güines, Havana Province, 32, 56
Guitart, René, 161
Guitart Rosell, Renato M., 43, 48, 50–51, 55–58, 68–72, 77, 93, 120–21, 153, 156, 158, 161–62, 206, 209, 265, 308n5, 312n33, 319n94
Guiteras Holmes, Antonio, 35, 47–48, 59, 80, 249, 275
Guiteras Revolutionary Action (ARG), 65, 158, 208, 287n34
Gutiérrez, Luis Felipe, 350n39
Gutiérrez, Manuel, 323n4
Gutiérrez Menoyo, Eloy, 254
Gutiérrez Planes, José Manuel, 43–44, 207–8, 241, 271, 273, 301n53, 323n4, 339n60, 342n27, 350n39

Gutiérrez Santos, Pedro, 147, 263
Guzmán, Argelio, 64, 303n6
Guzmán, Pedro, 295n11
Guzmán, Samuel, 60–61

Hague Convention of 1899, 90
Hall, Carlos C., 212
Halperin, Ernst, xiv
Hart Dávalos, Armando, xxv, 246
Havana, xii, 1–3, 6, 16, 19, 25, 27–28, 30–31, 34–35, 37, 39–41, 44, 47, 50–51, 53, 55–58, 61, 64–65, 68, 70–72, 92, 97, 101, 105, 110–12, 116, 121, 123, 129, 131–33, 135–36, 138–40, 142–43, 145–47, 150, 152, 155, 157, 159–61, 164, 167–70, 172, 180, 194–97, 200, 207–8, 213–14, 217, 225, 232–34, 240–41, 246, 250, 253, 316n75, 336n43
Havana Bar Association, 180, 207, 211, 239
Havana Institute, 10, 12
Havana Post, 82, 85, 116, 138, 147, 156–57, 163, 208–9, 216, 220, 229
Haza Grasso, Capt. Bonifacio, 160, 217, 343n37
Hechavarría Granados, Cpl. Gerardo, 97, 268, 338n54
Heredia, Sgt. Diógenes, 109, 217
Heredia, Feliciano, 177
Hermida Antorcha, Ramón O., 225, 240–41
Hernández, Delia, 218
Hernández, Col. Octavio, 37
Hernández, Víctor Manuel "Baracoita," 94, 161, 268
Hernández, Victoriano, 220
Hernández Alvarez, Luis, 304n16, 322n31
Hernández Arroyo, Lázaro, 134, 265, 304n16, 319n5
Hernández Cruz, Emilio, 111, 174, 177, 265, 326n31
Hernández Díaz, Orbeín, 39, 62, 71, 77, 148–49, 263, 303n8
Hernández Enríquez, Florentino, 194, 213, 215, 223–24, 263, 273
Hernández Font, Pvt. Gerardo, 90
Hernández Hernández, Bernardo, 212, 272, 274
Hernández Martínez, Genaro, 209, 263, 274, 298n26, 341n15
Hernández Ravella, Eduardo A., xiv, 268, 326n34

Hernández Rodríguez, Pvt. Alberto, 268
Hernández Rodríguez, Melba, xii, xiv–xviii, 300n44; activism, 35–37, 49, 197, 239, 241, 243, 253, 302n67, 318n87; attorney, 33–34, 143, 207, 297n18; at Civil Hospital, 86–88, 114–16, 218, 220, 307n42; demanded paraffin test after arrest, 117; depicted as desiring to be First Lady, 164; diplomat, 256; ethnicity, 34, 296n14; founder of 26 of July Movement, 246–47; grateful for treatment after capture, 117; ideology, 43; incarcerated in *vivac* jail, 164, 192–93; incarcerated in Boniato prison, 165, 199–200, 280; incarcerated in National Women's prison, 233, 257, 347n15; marriage of, 333n14; Reinaldo Boris Luis and, 85, 147; released from prison, 237; reputation of, 34; residence used for rebel meetings, 55–58, 62 66–67, 303n10; sentenced, 224, 261; at Siboney farmhouse, 70–71, 76–77, 216; trial of, 207, 211, 216, 223, 274; views Moncada exequies, 160
Hernández Rodríguez, Pvt. Alberto, 268
Hernández Suárez, Eduardo "Guayo," 16, 25
Hernández Tellaheche, Arturo, 139, 197–98, 207, 211, 243, 272, 274, 342n27
Hernández Vera, Gerardo, 222, 274
Hernández Vilaret, Med. Lt. Pedro, 103
Herrera Fritot, René, 10
Hevia, Carlos, 212, 301n53
Hevia Ruiz, Rolando, 272, 274
Hibbert, Luis Hyppolyte Alcides, 5
Hidalgo-Gato González, Horacio, 42
Hidalgo-Gato González, Mario, 42, 140, 323n4
Hispanidad, 9
History Will Absolve Me (Fidel Castro), xi–xiii, xv, xix, xxv–xxvii, xxx, 18, 43, 75, 92, 154, 165, 198, 227, 230–31, 236–39, 244, 246–47, 257–58, 346n3
Hitler, Adolph, xxx, 172, 231, 252–53
Hodelín Angulo, Pvt. Luis H., 96, 161, 268
Holguín, Oriente, 51, 53, 64, 66–67, 88, 124, 128, 132–33, 136, 138–39, 145, 147, 155, 166, 169, 172, 207, 210–11, 214–15, 287n35, 313n40, 314n47, 316n75, 324n12, 328n45, 344n44

INDEX

Holy, Dr. Guillermo, 146
Honduras, 20, 54, 196
Hoy (Communist newspaper), 9, 17, 25, 139, 208, 287n35

I Street safehouse, Santiago de Cuba, 55, 58, 68–69, 71
Ibarra Martínez, Francisco, 167
Iglesias, Rafael, 299n42
Iglesias Betancourt, Pedro, 30
Iglesias Lastra, José, 295n11
Iglesias Mónica, Carlos, 20, 24–25
Imperial Hotel, Santiago de Cuba, 225
Inglaterra Hotel, Havana, 18
Ingenieros, José, 144
Instituto de Segunda Enseñanza, Havana, 34
Isla Pérez, Manuel E., 77, 149, 265, 298n26
Isle of Pines, 34, 225, 232
Isle of Pines penitentiary. *See* National Men's Prison
Izquierdo, Rafael, 301n53
Izquierdo Rodríguez, Cpl. Isidro C., 82–83, 95–96, 102, 141, 217, 267, 308n5, 312n30
Izquierdo Rodríguez, Major José, 102, 114–16, 142, 192, 217, 324n11

Jaimanitas, Havana Province, 48, 145, 197
Jesuits, xxviii, 7–9
Jiguaní, Oriente, 126
Jiménez, Emilia, 88
Jobabo sugar mill, Oriente, 39
Joaquín Castillo Duany Military Hospital, 78, 82–85, 91–92, 99, 103, 106, 109, 112–13, 118, 151, 156, 158–59, 209, 217, 220, 316n73; description, 90
Jones-Costigan Act, xxix
Jonestown, Guyana, 76
Joven Cuba, 45, 48, 50, 167, 212, 277, 287n35
Juan Pita, Med. Lt. Erik G., 90–91, 103, 113, 217–18, 221, 258, 311n25
Juraguá Iron Company, 176

Karol, K. S., xiv
Korean War, xxx, 155

La Cabaña Fortress, 2, 53, 149, 155, 165, 197, 224–25, 232, 336n41, 341n12

La Calle (newspaper), 154, 244–46
La Ceiba, Marianao, xvi, 41
La Ceiba rebel cell, 45, 55, 62, 69
La Maya, Oriente, 109, 316n75
La Mejor boardinghouse, Santiago de Cuba, 66, 68–70, 72, 311n27
La Perla de Cuba Hotel, Santiago de Cuba, 68–69, 143
La Polar brewery, Santiago de Cuba, 91
La Progresiva Presbyterian Business School, Matanzas, 48
La Rotonda bar, El Vedado, 64, 66
La Salle Catholic School, Santiago de Cuba, 6–7
La Víbora Institute, Havana, 10, 139
Labañino, Publio, 97
Labrador Díaz, José A. "Toño," 148, 151–52, 265, 304n12
Labrador García, Fidel, 41, 71, 89, 93, 112–13, 151, 164, 215, 223–24, 226, 233, 261, 274, 304n12, 319n94, 346n59
Lamadrid, Alfredo, 194–95
Lamothe Coronado, Humberto, 213, 272–73
Lancís, Félix, 350n39
Larrea, Dr. Darío, 109
Larrusea, Miguel, 8
Las Delicias farm, Oriente, 184–85, 187, 190, 215
Las Guásimas, Oriente, 51
Las Múcaras, Oriente, 151–52
Las Villas Province, 33, 58, 139, 158, 208, 254, 341n13
Laurent, Julio, 350n47
Lavastida Alvarez, Capt. Agustín "Bebo," xviii, xxi, 142, 144, 150–51, 153, 160, 166, 171–72, 179–80, 191, 197, 201, 217, 225, 329n59, 336n42
Lavastida Martínez, Pvt. Daniel, 161, 268
Lawton, Havana, 41
Lawton rebel cell, 61–62, 68, 122, 149, 309n14, 326n36
Lazo Cuba, Lt. Carlos, 142, 284n21
Lazo Pérez, Mario, xv, 41, 64, 69, 88, 92, 110, 112, 148, 174–79, 196–97, 212, 256, 263, 297n22, 312n33, 326n31, 333n2, 339n58, 342n22
Legión Revolucionaria de Cuba, 286n29
Leizán, Manuel, 184, 190

Leizán Montero, Alfredo, 184
Leizán Montero, Carmen, 184, 335n28
Leizán Montero, Juan, 184–87, 190
Leizán Montero, Manuel "Lelín," 184–87
Lemes González, Sgt. José, 91
Lemus Mendoza, Bernardo, 300n52
Lenin, Selected Works of Vladimir, 144, 206
León Lemus, Orlando, 292n74, 336n43
León Orúe, Dr. Mauricio, 86–87, 114, 219, 310n16
Lescano, Javier, 301n53
Lescano Lescano, Pvt. Roberto, 142, 324n12
Lesnik Menéndez, Max, 244, 295n11, 350nn39, 42
Lew, Salvador, 284n18, 295n11
Leyva, Idilo, 301n54
Lezcano, Javier, 350n39
Liberal Party, 2, 242, 283n7
Limia Rodríguez, Fernando, 213, 272, 274
Lions Club, Santiago de Cuba, 170
Llanes León, Cpl. José "Pancho Villa," 98, 104, 268, 315n62
Llanes Machado, Generoso R., 89, 213, 263, 273, 296n15, 303n9
Llerena, Mario, 5, 46–47, 113, 238, 349n29
Llorente, Amando, 9
Llosas Perera, Juan M., 212, 272, 274
Lobo, Julio, 44
López, Lt. Antonio María, 343n37
López, Narciso, xxviii, 49, 59, 80, 249
López, Pedro Angel, 98, 269
López Alvarez, Lt. Juan, 219
López Betancourt, Sgt. Jonás, 99
López Blanco, Marino, 241
López Díaz, José L., 64, 263, 303n6
López Fernández, Antonio "Ñico," xiv–xvii; activism, 46; Bayamo attack, 122, 124, 126, 137, 304n16; exiled, 242; flees Bayamo, 129, 132–33, 340n5; founder of 26 of July Movement, 246; Granma expeditionary, 257, 322n31, 351n2; illiterate, unskilled worker xix, 38, 242, 263; ideology, 43; murders a police sergeant, 130; museum dedicated to, 321n24
López García, Antonio "El Gallego," 65, 126, 129, 132–33, 263, 296n15, 322n31, 340n5, 351n2
López Migoya, Manuel, 282n1

López Montes, Joaquín, 323n4
López Pérez, Luis, 295n11
Lorenz, Marita, 337n48
Lorenzo Costa, Manuel, 66–67, 76, 118, 145, 211, 223, 224, 240, 261, 273, 305n22
Los Angeles Clinic, Santiago de Cuba, 103–4, 115, 140, 188, 195
Los Libertadores Avenue, Santiago de Cuba, 86, 98, 109, 154
Los Palos, Nueva Paz municipality, 42, 56, 140
Loynaz del Castillo, Enrique, 18
Loynaz Hechevarría-Cordovés, Porfirio, 272–73
Ludwig, Emil, 29
Luis Rodríguez, Boris, 39, 297n18
Luis Santa Coloma, Reinaldo Boris, xv, 39, 43, 62, 68, 77, 81, 85, 110, 146–47, 164–66, 182, 213, 265, 296n14, 303n8, 330n71, 331n75
Luna, Emilio, 162

Mabay, Oriente, 126
Maceo Grajales, Antonio, 50, 174, 222, 250, 275
Maceo Martí, Cpl. Pedro, A., 167, 322n32, 331n77
Machado Morales, Gerardo, xxviii, 47, 168, 244, 336n43
Machado Rofe, Lt. Angel S., xx, 98, 143, 155, 167, 193, 312n31, 337n48, 343n37
Machirán Ortiz, Dr. Norberto, 86, 309n13
Madera Fernández, José J., 265, 296n14, 303n12
Madruga, Havana Province, 39, 62, 149, 326n32
Madruga rebel cell, 62, 149
Maffo, Oriente, 110, 167
Mafobrio Prieto, Isabel, 115
Mafut Delgado, Moisés "El Moro," xxii, 60–61, 65, 100, 110–11, 147–48, 151–52, 251, 254, 263, 302n3, 327n40
Magariño, Primitivo, 221
Magín Hernández, Lt. Luis, 146
Malaparte, Curzio, 29
Mamprivá farm, Oriente, 184, 186
Manacas plantation, Oriente, 5–6
Manifesto to the Nation, xvi, xvi, xxii, xxvi, xxvii, xxx, 43, 63, 73, 138, 257–58, 303n11
Manzanillo, Oriente, 17, 30, 69, 130–31, 133–34, 139, 145, 195, 210, 313nn44, 46

INDEX

Mañach Robato, Jorge, 236, 239, 348n25, 349n39
Marcané, Oriente, 27, 162
Marianao municipality, 8, 38, 41, 56, 66, 129, 131–32, 213, 215, 245, 256, 334n15
Marianao rebel cell, xvi, 41–42, 50, 56, 64–65, 125, 133, 136, 304n16
Mariel, Pinar del Río, 15, 256
Marín, César A., 192
Marín Robaina, Federico, 13–14, 288n40
Marinello Vidaurreta, Juan, 9, 28, 138, 159, 180, 208, 232, 272, 274, 341n14, 347n14
Marjorie Webster Junior College, Washington, D.C., 44
Márquez, María Antonia, 218
Márquez Rodríguez, Juan Manuel, xv, 245, 272
Márquez-Sterling Guiral, Carlos, 29–30, 293n80, 323n4, 349n39
Marrero Aizpurúa, Pedro: activism, 46; background, 41, 265; drives to Siboney farmhouse, 62, 66, 71, 303n9; drives vanguard car to Moncada, 77–78, 82–83, 308n5; enters Moncada, 92, 312n30; fatherless, 296n14; killed, 316n73; surrenders, 108; takes weapons to Oriente, 55
Marshall, George C., 19, 24
Martí Pérez, José, xxviii, 9, 27, 45, 49, 59, 63, 74, 80, 192, 206, 215, 222, 230, 236–37, 247, 250, 256, 275, 277
Martí Rodríguez, Marcos "El Curro," 73, 100, 148, 151–52, 182, 215, 265, 296n15, 297n21, 310n21
Martija, Pvt. Justo Ramón, 94, 101, 115, 154, 312n35, 318n89
Martín, Félix, 30
Martin, Lionel, xvi
Martínez, Juan Manuel, 55, 121, 124, 130, 135, 209, 214, 219, 272, 274, 342n27
Martínez, Lt. Cándido, 105
Martínez Alvarez, José R., 85, 164, 263, 305n25, 351n2
Martínez Ararás, Elvira, 42
Martínez Ararás, Emma, 42
Martínez Ararás, Mario, xiv, xix; background, 42, 65, 265, 296nn14, 15; drives to Bayamo, 65, 122, 304n16; drives to Bayamo garrison, 125–26; murdered, 129, 134–35
Martínez Ararás, Raúl, 264; Abel and Haydée Santamaría and, 34; Bayamo rebel gathering, 123–25; breaks with Fidel Castro over autocracy, 244, 256–57; commands Bayamo combat, 126–28; coordinates with Fidel Castro in Bayamo, 67; discredits rebel torture theory, 165, 173; Ernesto Tizol and, xxi, 42, 51, 81; estimates rebel expenses, 57; exiled in Mexico City, 237, 244; family, 37, 56, 295n13; fatherless, 296n14; flees Bayamo, 134–35; joins armed expedition in 1955, 322n31; joins movement, 36; leadership role, xii, xvi, xxvi, 42–43, 50–51, 55, 64–65, 74, 122–25, 136, 250, 303n6; Ñico López and, 38; omitted from historical accounts, xvii, xix; revolutionary rank, 123; visits Castro estate, 49
Martínez Arbona, Lt. Mario, 105, 115, 217
Martínez Aruca, Mario, 65
Martínez Bles, Pvt. Diocles, 84, 94, 268
Martínez Fraga, Antonio, 350n39
Martínez Pimienta, Dr. Aurelio, 129
Martínez Serrera, Ricardo, 44, 298n31
Martínez Tinguao, Juan, 36, 294n4
Martínez Varela, Ana Lourdes, 237
Martínez Varela, Raúl, 37
Martínez Varela, Tatiana, 37
Martínez Verdecia, Horacio, 105, 158, 220
Martiniano, Cpl. Generoso, 98, 217
Martorell García, Juan, 214
Mas Renedo, Med. Lt. Roberto P., 103, 218, 315n59
Mascaró Yarini, Raúl, 158, 205, 210, 220, 228
Masferrer Rojas, Rolando, 4, 10–12, 15–19, 25–27, 31, 53, 249, 286n29, 287n35, 291n67
Masonic Grand Lodge of Cuba, 60, 167–68
Massó, José Luis, 14
Matanzas province, xix, 3, 17, 139, 207–8, 317n81
Matheu Orihuela, Horacio, 86, 88, 115, 265, 303n7, 319n94
Matheu Orihuela, José W., 265, 303n7, 309n14
Matos Benítez, Huber, 254

Matos Rodríguez, Anselmo, 301n54
Matos Rodríguez, Col. Urbano, 301n54
Matos Rodríguez, Faustino, 301n54
Matos Rodríguez, Juan, 301n54
Matos Rodríguez, Urbano, 53, 301n54
Matos Romero, Pvt. Ariel, xxiv, 53, 101–2, 142, 153–54, 193, 301n54, 318n89
Matthews, Herbert, xiv, xvi, 119, 165, 237, 327n44
Mayarí, Oriente, 5, 29, 284n16
Mederos Rodríguez, Roberto, 265, 303n7, 309n14
Medina, Marino, 29
Medina, Waldo, 233
Medina Puig, José, 161, 170
Medrano, Humberto, 138
Mejías, Irma, 228
Mejías Pérez, Sergio, 198, 208, 210, 272–73, 323n4, 339n60, 342n27
Mejías Valdivieso, Juan F., xv, 204, 226, 228, 232
Melero Juvier, Roberto, 350n39
Mella, Julio Antonio, 45, 275
Mencia, Mario, xvii, 311n30
Mendel Weis, Moto, 212, 272–73, 341n22
Méndez, Jenaro, 323n4
Méndez Cabezón, Ramón, 265, 309n14
Méndez Cominches, José, 146, 325n23
Méndez García, Rosendo, 304n12
Mendieta Hechavarría, Francisco: background, 204, 340n4; closing arguments and rebuttal, 222, 224, 254; and *History Will Absolve Me*, 237; prosecutor in first trial, 206–7, 213–14, 218–21; prosecutor in second trial, 228–30; Rotary Club member, 190
Mendieta Montefur, Carlos, xxix
Mendieta Tamayo, Francisco, 204–5, 338n55, 340n4, 340n10
Mendoza Guanche, Rafael "Pilin," 205, 272
Menéndez García, Rosendo, 112, 174, 177–79, 215, 224, 261, 273, 326n31
Menéndez Tomassevich, Raúl, 314n47
Menvielle Porte-Petit, Jorge, 22, 25, 291n71
Merille Acosta, Carlos A., 65, 76–77, 155, 214, 264, 273
Merle, Robert, xiii, xiv, xvii, 111, 153, 188, 303n9, 304n20, 311n30, 331n79
Mesa González, Cpl. Doris, 93, 219

Mestre de Arango, Corina, 171
Mestre Gutiérrez, Ramón, 8, 285n24
Mestre Martínez, Armando, 60, 111–12, 175, 180, 183, 185, 189, 224, 261, 273, 295n14, 326n31, 351n2
Mexico, 20, 46, 53, 253, 260, 286n30, 289n49, 291n67, 295n11, 322n31, 327n40, 332n82, 347n14
Mexico City, 3, 12, 237, 244, 317n81, 346n4
Miami, Fla., 3, 27, 157, 256, 287n35, 291n67, 341n12
Miami Beach, Fla., 27, 37
Milet Alavo, Josefina, 114, 218
Military Hospital. *See* Joaquín Castillo Duany Military Hospital
Military Intelligence Service (SIM), xii, 36, 39, 46, 57–59, 68, 88, 106, 115, 123, 131–32, 135, 138–40, 156–57, 161, 166, 170, 173, 197, 213–14, 225, 306n32, 327n44, 336n43, 338n54
Ministry of Education, 11, 13
Ministry of Information, 54, 170
Ministry of the Treasury, 42
Mirabal Mirabal, Lt. Felipe, 7, 27, 284n21
Miranda Montes de Oca, Armando, 268
Miras Mierez, Cpl. Manuel, 94, 160, 267, 312n34
Mirassou Tarnio, Pedro, 18, 286n33, 290n56
Miret Prieto, Pedro, xvii, 4, 38, 43, 47, 52, 65, 68, 71, 99, 112–13, 151, 164, 215, 224, 236, 246, 255, 261, 273, 305n25, 308n3
Miró Cardona, José, 180, 334n15, 340n3
Miró Ríos, Pvt. Felino, 98, 267
Mitchell Barbán, Teodulio "Lulo," xvii, xix, 61, 66–67, 71, 73–74, 81, 145–46, 264, 296n14, 307n1, 325n22, 326n30
Miyar, Rafael, 350n39
Moisés, Violeta, 87
Molina, Raúl, 62
Molina Amores, Pvt. Orlando, 83
Molinari, Diego Luis, 19–20, 24
Molino Arrocero de Matanzas, 45
Moncada, Gen. Guillermo, 78
Moncada and Bayamo rebels: accuse Castro of trickery, 150, 179; amnesty campaign, 235, 349n39; background, xiv, 37–38, 56, 64–66; command staff, 43, 250; Communist book, 144, 160, 324n17; Communist indoctrination, xxiii, 324n17; criminal

record, 92, 182; defectors and deserters, 62–66, 71, 75–77, 80, 82, 125, 137, 145, 214, 251; defy Batista at Isle of Pines prison, 235; disoriented at Moncada, 81–82, 86, 89–90, 99, 103–4, 110, 118, 251; disoriented during escape route, 178–84; dubbed Mau Maus, 165, 331n73; fatherless, 296n14; finances, 42–45, 49, 56–57, 206, 215, 250; five who penetrated Moncada, 83, 92, 98, 101; flee from Moncada, 81, 110–12; grateful for treatment after capture, 117, 163, 173, 179–80, 191–92; ideology and motivation, 43, 119–20, 215, 227, 234–35, 251; incarcerated in Boniato prison, 198–200; nineteen acquitted in court, 224, 226; proclaim in combat Batista's overthrow, 85, 87, 105, 127, 130; revolutionary ranks, 55, 75; Siboney farmhouse, 71–77; special treatment as political prisoners, 232–33, 247, 280; torture and mutilation (*see* Black Legend); training, 38–42; trial of, 203–26, 246, 252; unaware of enemy strength, 126, 250, 307n50; uniforms, 49, 123, 179; use hollow-point bullets, 90, 94, 104, 183, 221, 251; weaponry, 45, 49, 56, 64, 72, 117, 123, 206, 221

Moncada and Bayamo soldiers: background, 141–43, corruption, 142–43

Moncada attack: alleged Communist plot, 139, 144, 160, 173; amnesty for convicted rebels, 243; amnesty for soldiers accused of crimes, 239; considered a feud between military factions, 97, 102–3, 105, 118, 143, 155, 250; defective planning, 117–18, 163–64, 172–73, 192, 206, 250–52; denounced by Communists, 139, 172, 208, 234; duration of combat, 110; meaning of, xxv, 117–120, 250; military exequies, 160–61; projected revolutionary government after Moncada victory, 137, 206, 234, 247; strategy, 73–76, 137

Moncada attack casualties: civilians killed or wounded, 98, 150, 326n34; rebels killed or wounded in action, 91, 93, 100, 109, 112–14, 119, 149, 161; rebels executed or murdered by soldiers, 109, 141, 143, 145, 153–56, 158, 162, 169, 171–74, 177, 194, 236, 244–45, 252; rebels wounded by friendly fire, xiii, xxvi, 99–100, 118, 146–47, 229, 250; soldiers and policemen wounded or killed by rebels, 85–91, 93–100, 102–5, 107–8, 113, 119, 141, 143, 147, 158; military physicians testify in court of no stab wounds, 218–19, 221, 227; soldiers purportedly stabbed to death by rebels, xi, 119, 156–57, 159–60, 173, 329n59

Moncada fortress, 3, 47, 50–51, 53, 67, 71, 81, 88, 94, 97, 100–101, 104–6, 109, 112, 116, 135–36, 140–41, 145, 149–50, 153–57, 160–61, 163, 165, 169, 179, 190, 193, 195, 197, 206, 237, 256, 279; anticipating attack, 53, 57–58, 68–69, 80, 82, 118, 170, 173; armament, 80; Bureau of Press and Radio, 140; command structure, 79–80; communications room, 93, 97, 105–6; description, 78–80; Enlisted Men's Club, 79, 98; Fusilier Company, 69, 82–83, 87, 96, 102, 109; Guard Corps, 68–70, 78–79, 83, 98, 101–2, 105–6, 109, 140, 150, 153, 155, 172, 186; Headquarters Company, 94–95, 97; Mariana Grajales theater, 79; military housing complex, 78, 80, 89, 98, 100, 102, 108, 111–13, 118, 215; Officers' barbershop, 93, 96, 107–8, 156, 158, 164; Officers' Club, 79, 109, 116, 150, 157; Operations and Training Section office, 92–93, 107–9; Police adjutant office, 93, 108; Post 1, 78; Post 2, 68, 78, 85, 94, 102, 106–7, 117, 140, 154, 156; Post 3, xii, xv, xvi, 51, 74, 76–78, 80–85, 88–89, 92–96, 98, 100–103, 105, 109–14, 117–18, 137, 156, 158, 192, 209, 217, 220, 223, 229, 250–52, 311n30, 329n59; Post 4, 79, 86, 96–97, 109, 116, 219; Post 5, 58, 78–79, 98, 101, 105, 107, 172, 220; regimental quartermaster room, 92–95, 106–7, 117–18, 166; Regimental Intelligence Service (SIR), 79, 95, 109, 142, 144, 150, 153, 160, 166, 172, 179, 197, 217, 223; Rural Guard 11th Squadron, 79, 98; Service Company, 82, 93–94, 96, 102, 105, 109

Moncada Street, Santiago de Cuba, 78, 80, 82, 89–91, 95–96, 99, 103–4, 110–12, 146

Montané, Yotuhel, 255
Montané López, Sergio, 255
Montané Oropesa, Jesús "Chucho," xiii, xiv, xvi, xviii, 33–36, 42–43, 47, 62, 67–68, 71, 76–77, 89, 92, 111, 122, 174–76, 178–80, 200, 215, 224, 243, 246, 252, 255, 257, 261, 273, 294n4, 303n7, 308n5, 311n30, 317n79, 326n31, 333nn11, 14, 351n2
Montané Oropesa, Mireya, 255
Montano, Santa, xxiii, 41, 234
Montano, Yolanda, xxiii, 41
Montano Benítez, Eduardo, xxiii, 41, 70, 73, 75, 89, 110–11, 174–77, 180–81, 184–85, 187, 191, 198, 215, 224, 234, 261, 273, 303n8, 310n21, 326n31, 348n23
Montenegro, Carlos, 287n34
Montero, Lucila, 287n35
Montero, Manuela, 184, 335n28
Montero Moscoso, Manuel, 184–85, 335n28
Montes Cuba, Ramón, 264, 307n43
Montes de Oca Mayea, Sgt. Eliodoro, 167, 331n77
Montreal, Canada, 52, 54, 159
Montreal Conference Pact, 52–54, 59, 102, 119, 139, 157, 159, 173, 205–8, 227, 250, 301n53
Monzón, Pvt. Walfrido, 83
Moore, Carlos, 38
Mora, Menelao, 322n31
Morales Alvarez, 2nd Lt. Andrés D., 94, 102–3, 141, 158, 197, 267, 317n80
Morales Alvarez, Major Rafael, xiii, xxi, 101–2, 109, 114, 141–42, 192–94, 217, 307n50, 324n11
Morales Castillo, Evelio, 158
Morales del Castillo, Andrés Domingo, 168, 331n79
Morales García, Lt. Claudio, 109, 155, 316n75, 343n37
Morales Gómez, José Miguel, 350n39
Morales Gros, Pvt. Orlando, 94, 142, 192–93, 319n89
Morales Gros, Pvt. Rafael, 69, 94, 142, 168, 186, 192–93, 324n11
Morales Rodríguez, Vidal, 11–12, 19, 26, 286n33, 290n56
Morán Arce, Lucas, 196–97, 212, 274, 342n22, 344n50

Morejón Valdés, Lt. Pedro, 91, 311n27, 343n37
Moreno, Carlos, 20
Moreno Rubio, Patricio "El Chino," 105, 161, 268
Morgan, William, 254
Morín Dopico, Antonio, 10–11, 16
Mount St. Joseph's Academy, Philadelphia, 44
Mujal Barniol, Eusebio, 171
Muñoz Algarra, Dinorah, 33
Muñoz Algarra, María Teresa, 33
Muñoz Monroy, Dr. Mario, xviii, xix; activism, 35, 43; airplane pilot, 33, 132; background, 33, 37, 266; burial, 161–62; at Civil Hospital, xiv, 81, 86–87, 96, 114, 317n79; drives to Oriente, 67; murdered, 116 156, 158, 318n89; rejects combat role, 75, 80, 307n42; at Siboney farmhouse, 72, 75–77
Muñoz Monroy, Roberto, 330n63
Mussolini, Benito, 37, 253

Nager Rodríguez, Pablo, 229
Naranjo, Pvt. Luis Enrique, 108, 161, 268, 316n72, 338n54
Nariño Brauet, Jorge, 274, 344n50
National Bank of Cuba, xxx
National Civic Front, 32, 42
National Federation of Sugar Workers, 26
National Insane Asylum, Mazorra, Havana, 212
National Men's Prison, Isle of Pines, xvii, xxiii, 225, 232–36, 239–40, 243, 257, 343n30, 347n14, 348nn18, 23
National Police Marching Band, 88, 91–94, 98, 104, 105, 107, 140, 160, 219
National Rebellion Day, xxv
National Revolutionary Alliance (ANR), 287n34
National Women's Prison, Guanajay, Pinar del Río, 224, 233, 257
Navarro Molina, Pvt. Juan P., 126–27, 268
New York City, N.Y., 21, 27, 45, 157, 329n57, 337n48
New York Daily Worker, 139
New York Times, 28, 119, 224, 253
Nicaragua, 20, 332n82
Nieto Piñeiro-Osorio, Adolfo: background, 204; Fidel Castro and, 206, 210–11, 231–32; *History Will Absolve Me* and, 230–31,

237, 239; imprisoned and exiled, 339n3; letter from Marta Rojas, 346n2; military vengeance, 154; praised by Mario Chanes, 205; presides Case 37 revolt trial, 204–6, 209, 218–20, 222–23; presides trial in Civil Hospital, 228–32; prohibits political propaganda during trial, 205–6, 212; revolt purpose, 119; sentences Fidel Castro, 231; sentences rebels, 224–25; visit from Mirta Díaz-Balart, 214
Ninth Inter-American Conference (OAS), 19–21, 23–24
Nipe Bay, Oriente, 4, 16
Noa Gil, Carmelo, 92, 266, 296n15, 308n5, 319n94
Noguerol Conde, José, 286n30
Noriega, Pvt. Lino, 322n32
Noriega Plaza, Santiago, 232
Norman García-Iñiguez, Manuel J., 136
Noroña, Froilán, 288n36
Nueva Gerona, Isle of Pines, 34, 232, 236, 243, 257
Nueva Paz rebel cell, 42, 209, 298n26, 303n12, 323n4
Nuevitas, Camagüey, 208
Nú ez Blanco, Emilio, 241, 283n15, 349n35
Núñez Carballo, José A., 232
Núñez Cinta, Miguel, 86
Núñez Jurjo, Angel "El Gallego," 51, 151, 155, 166, 174, 327n37
Núñez Leyva, Rafael, 194, 272–73
Núñez Portuondo, Emilio, 5, 283n15

Ocaña Heights, Oriente, 174–75
Ochoa Ferrer, Lt. Antonio Policarpo, 142, 153, 155, 191, 285n21, 336n43, 351n3
Ochoa Ochoa, Emilio "Millo," 28–29, 32, 34, 40, 42, 52–53, 69, 119, 138, 159, 180, 197–200, 207, 211, 272, 274, 301n53, 342n27
Ojeda Sancho, Fernando, 161
Olazábal Garcés, Juan, 130, 132, 321n24
Oliva, Pvt. Cristino, 219
Oliva, Sgt. Luis, 95, 267, 311n30
Oliva López, Pvt. Armando, xxi, 94, 106, 156, 186, 188–92, 318n82, 319n89, 336n38

Olivares Pérez, José Humberto, 96–97, 101–2, 107, 109, 143, 153–54, 156, 310n22, 316n69, 320n13
Omaja, Oriente, 135
Oppositionist National Union, 1
Oramas Alfonso, Miguel A., 41, 62, 72, 112, 266, 319n94
Ordoqui Mesa, Joaquín, 198, 208, 212, 272, 274, 339n60, 341n13, 342n27
Orfila, Marianao, 16, 30
Organization of American States (OAS), 19, 33, 291n70
Oriente (newspaper), 167, 191
Oriente Province, 26, 29, 53, 56–57, 60–61, 66, 75–76, 80, 106, 135, 137–38, 140–41, 155, 158, 169, 195, 197, 205, 207–8, 211, 213, 216, 232, 245, 250–51, 253, 257, 300n42, 314n47
Oriente University, Santiago de Cuba, 164
Orta, Juan, 119, 135
Ortega Lora, Oscar "Nito," 66, 148, 151, 154, 266, 304n16, 305n22, 326n30
Ortiz, Maj. Arsenio, 336n43
Ortiz Fáez, Gustavo, 18–19, 290n56
Ortiz Fernández, Dr. Héctor L., 104
Ortiz Quintero, Cpl. José, 109
Ortiz Rodríguez, José Antonio, 103
Ortodoxo Party, xiv, xxvi, 28–30, 33–40, 42–43, 46, 49, 52, 63, 66, 118–19, 131–32, 135, 137–39, 159, 163–64, 172–73, 184, 197, 205–7, 212, 214, 232, 234, 238, 241, 244–45, 247, 250–51, 277, 298n29, 301n53, 323n4
Ortodoxo Radical Action (ARO), 29
Ortodoxo Youth, 4, 28–29, 33, 36–37, 39–41, 43, 48, 58, 67, 146, 184, 295n11
Osorio, René Domingo, 86, 220
Ospina Pérez, Mariano, 21, 24
Otaño Cookerman, Lt. Marcelo, 102, 109, 316n75, 343n37
Otero, Adolfo, 29
Ovares Herrera, Enrique, 8–10, 12–25, 27, 38, 288n40, 291n71, 292n76

Pacheco, Hebrecinio, 98, 269
Padierne Labrada, Luis, 286n33
Padrón Ferrer, Dr. Carlos M., 157–58
Pagés, Sgt. Alberto, 94, 268
Pagés, Héctor, 350n39

Pagés Portuondo, Sgt. Amarante, 88, 343n37
Paglieri Cardero, Jorge, 207, 223, 274, 347n14
País, Frank, 300n42
Palace of Justice, xii, xiii, xv, xvii, xviii, xxvii, 56, 74, 76–78, 256; seized by rebels, 85 106, 109, 112; 117, 146, 158, 196; and trial of rebels, 203–4, 210, 220–21, 251
Palacio Blanco, Manuel, 350n39
Palma, María Luisa, 87–88
Palma Soriano, Oriente, 58, 61, 64, 67, 105, 110, 122, 139, 142, 144–46, 160, 163, 169, 194, 196–97, 211, 213
Palmero, María del Carmen, 171
Pan American Conference. *See* Ninth Inter-American Conference (OAS)
Pan American Union, 19
Panama, xxviii, 20–21
Panama Canal, 20, 31
Panamanian Embassy in Havana, 164
Paneque, Robert, 134
Pardo Llada, José, 8, 33, 36, 52–53, 135, 203, 272, 301n53, 323n4, 350n39
Parladé, Dr. Rafael, 104
Pedraza, José, 155, 287n34
Peláez, Carlos M., 350n39
Pelayo Pelayo, Aida, 208, 272–73, 323n4, 341n14
Pellicier, Victoriano, 162
Penabaz, Chano, 29
Peña González, Lázaro, 198, 212, 272, 274, 339n60, 341n13, 342n27
Peña-Jústiz Arrieta, Carlos, 232, 274, 338n55, 347n14
Peñalver O'Reilly, Isidro, 150, 198, 221, 264, 273, 296n14, 303n12, 304n19
Pérez, Emma, 87
Pérez Jr., Louis A., xix
Pérez, Mario, 323n4
Pérez, Pedro "Periquito," 316n69
Pérez, Romelia, 229
Pérez Acosta, Dr. Francisco, 104
Pérez Almaguer, Osvaldo, 328n45
Pérez Almaguer, Waldo, 106, 109, 150, 154, 160, 167, 195, 244–45, 328n45
Pérez Cabrejas, Luis, 212, 272–73
Pérez Castañeda, Pvt. Juan, 128, 321n20
Pérez Cuesta, Lázara Sarah, 159–60, 164, 199–200, 212, 272, 274, 329n58

Pérez Dámera, Gen. Genovevo, 16, 289n48
Pérez Díaz, Lt. Roger, 243
Pérez Hernández, Faustino, 246
Pérez Hernández, Nicolás, 195
Pérez Lamy, José M., 212, 274, 342n22, 344n50
Pérez Mujica, Antonio, 212, 272, 274
Pérez Mujica, Elda, 33, 58
Pérez Proenza, Rubén, 146, 150, 196, 326n34
Pérez Rey, Luis, 274, 341n13, 344n50
Pérez Rodríguez, Manuel, 217
Pérez Sainz de la Peña, Med. Lt. Rolando, 78, 90–91, 103, 217, 312n31, 343n38
Pérez Santana, Pedro, 301n54
Pérez Serantes, Enrique, 6, 170–71, 181–83, 185–87, 189–91, 194–95, 201, 331n79, 332n86
Pérez-Chaumont Altuzarra, Major Andrés, 101–2, 144, 155, 166, 171–72, 183, 190–92, 219, 226–27, 229, 346n4
Pérez-Puelles Valmaseda, Gerardo, 34, 44, 55, 121–23, 125–28, 134–35, 257, 264, 296n14, 322n31
Perla de Cuba Hotel, Santiago de Cuba, 57
Perón, Juan Domingo, 19–20, 135
Pez Ferro, Ramón, 115–16, 213, 256, 264, 274, 296n14, 297nn21, 22, 309n14, 310n22
Piedra Negueruela, Col. Orlando, xi, 101, 142, 195, 235, 315n53
Piedra Villadroin, Julio, 42
Pijirigua, Pinar del Río, 41
Pila Teleño, Augusto, 200
Pila Teleño, José F., 198, 200, 213, 272, 274
Pinar del Río Province, 41, 47, 53, 140, 150
Pinares de Mayarí, Oriente, 5
Pino Santos, Fidel, 4, 7–8, 181–82
Piña, Julio, 187
Piña, Luis, 184–85, 187
Piña Martínez, Lt. Juan, 84, 91, 108, 113, 161, 268, 338n54, 343n37
Piña Martínez, Lt. Manuel, 94, 98, 114–15, 153, 186, 318n88
Piñeiro del Cueto, Carlos, 56, 168, 335n38
Piñeiro, José Ramón, 132
Piñeiro Losada, Manuel "Barbaroja," 256, 313n46, 321n20
Pla Picette, Angel, 264, 303n12, 323n4

INDEX

Placetas, Las Villas, 67
Platt Amendment, xxviii, xxix
Plaza de Dolores, Santiago de Cuba, 51
Plaza de Marte Park, Santiago de Cuba, 68, 70–71, 78, 101, 103, 149–51, 229
Poll Cabrera, Gerardo, 217, 226, 228–29, 231, 272, 274
Pompa Castañeda, Cpl. Orestes, 141, 318n89
Pompa Castañeda, Cpl. Pedro H., 88, 115, 141, 218, 221, 267, 318n89
Ponce Díaz, José "Pepe," xiv, 40, 63, 99, 146–47, 172, 215, 223–24, 261, 273, 297n22, 303n10, 304n12, 307n46, 314n48, 319n94, 343n30, 351n2
Ponte, José, 272
Popular Socialist Party (PSP). *See* Cuban Communist Party
Porro Varela, Med. Capt. Mario, 86, 116, 218, 343n38
Porto Chacón, Pvt. Pedro, 268
Portuondo, Dr. Aurelio, 214
Posada Gómez, Dr. Alejandro, 146
Posada Recio, Dr. Alejandro, 146–47
Poveda, Arquimides, 14
Prada, Ricardo, 151–52
Prensa Libre, 35, 138
Prensa Universal, 192
Preston sugar mill, Oriente, 4
Prévez Carcellés, Lt. Sigbiardo G., 343n37
Prieto Aragón, Dr. Manuel, 157–58, 162, 331n73, 343n37
Primo de Rivera, José A., 9
Princeton Theological Seminary, N.J., 13
Prío, Mireya, 209
Prío Socarrás, Carlos, xiii, 1–3, 29, 30, 32, 52–54, 57, 70, 119, 139, 157, 159, 177, 180, 203, 205–8, 272, 301n53
Procter & Gamble, 37
Professional Accountants Association, 37
Professor Harriman. *See* Isaac Santos Domínguez
Progressive Action Party (PAP), 162, 282n1, 309n16
Puentes Grandes, Marianao, 4, 41
Puerto Boniato, Oriente, 51, 145
Puerto Rico, 20, 316n71
Pujol Soler, José "Pepín," 154–55
Pujol Soler, Juan, 154–55

Punta Blanca, Santiago de Cuba, 106, 140
Pupo, Lt. Manuel A., 101
Pupo Miranda, Pvt. Angel, 105, 153, 316n65

Quemado de Güines, Las Villas, 212
Querejeta, Gen. Gregorio, 324n16
Querejeta, María del Carmen, 324n16
Quesada Ferra, Ramón "Mongo el Diablo," 290n52
Quesada Granados, Anibal, 212, 272, 274
Quevedo, Miguel Angel, 20, 138, 235–36
Quintana Riverí, Genaro, 85, 110
Quintela Bonilla, Oscar, 61, 64, 70, 77, 81, 147, 256, 264, 303n6, 325n26
Quintero Heights, Santiago de Cuba, 81, 101, 111, 143, 145
Quirk, Robert, xviii, 300n44

Radical Liberation Movement (MRL), 244
Ramírez Corría, Dr. Filiberto, xv, 42
Ramírez León, Ricardo, 300n52
Ramírez Santiesteban, Pvt. Saturnino, 161, 267
Ramos Montejo, Francisco, 350n39
Ramsden, Concha, 194
Rancho Boyeros, Havana Province, 20, 41, 60, 66, 250
Rancho Club, Santiago de Cuba, 101, 143, 315n53
Ravelo Ravelo, Miguel A., 268, 166–67
Reciprocity Treaty of 1934, xxix
Redondo García, Ciro, 64, 72–73, 77, 89, 91, 100, 103, 111–12, 147–49, 151–52, 182, 215, 224, 261, 273, 297n21, 343n30, 351n2
Regalado, Rogelio, 350n39
Remedios Langaney, Benito, 9, 285n25
Remedios Oliva, Carlos, 9
Remedios Oliva, Jorge, 9
Reporters Association, 56
Republican Party, 2, 283n7, 287n35
Resende Viges, Rafael, 28
Revolutionary Insurrectional Union (UIR), 11–15, 17–19, 24–27, 29–30, 37, 65, 80, 201, 209, 286n33
Revolutionary Nationalist Movement (MNR), 46–47, 51, 65, 75, 139, 191, 213, 238–39

Revuelta, Manuel, 44
Revuelta Clews, Natalia "Naty," xiv, xv,
　　xxvii, 44–45, 49, 63, 66, 138, 144, 234,
　　241, 244, 246, 350n43
Rex Hotel, Santiago de Cuba, 56, 62–63, 66,
　　68–69, 71, 144
Reyes Cairo, Julio M., 67, 72, 86–87, 266
Reyes Martín, Cpl. Néstor, xxii, 95–96, 98–
　　99, 109, 161, 268, 313n40, 321n20,
　　338n54
Reyes Rodríguez, Pvt. Emilio, 161, 268,
　　338n54
Reyes Romero, Pvt. Radamés, 313n46
Reytor, Antonio, 329n56
Reytor, Ramón, 329n56
Rico Boué, Lt. Teodoro, 101, 107–8, 142,
　　153–56, 218, 226–27, 329n59, 336n43,
　　343n37, 351n3
Ricondo Fernández, Ismael, 41, 149–50, 266
Riera Hernández, Mario, xi
Rigel Boris, Felipe, 175–76, 181
Rigel Boris, Justino, 176
Rigual, Vicente, 219
Río Cauto, Oriente, 126
Rivadulla, Mario, 295n11
Riveiro Suárez, Eduardo, 217
Rivera Ruá, Esmérido, 175
Rivero, Raúl, 138
Rivero Vasallo, Félix, 266, 296n14, 303n7,
　　309n14
Rives, Miguel, 241
Rizo Carbonell, Cpl. Elio, 157, 328n51
Rizo Viel, Lt. Eugenio, 97, 343n37
Roa García, Raúl, 11
Roa Sierra, Juan, 23
Robaina, Alberto, 115
Roca, José Antonio, 196
Roca Calderío, Blas, 138–39, 159, 203, 208,
　　212, 272
Roca Gutiérrez, Mariano, 170, 332n86
Rodón Alvarez, Lincoln, 350n39
Rodríguez, Camelia, 116, 218
Rodríguez, Carlos, 28, 33
Rodríguez, Carlos Rafael, 9, 27
Rodríguez, Eladio, 196
Rodríguez, Pvt. Félix, 322n32
Rodríguez, Pvt. Filiberto, 128
Rodríguez, Israel, 300n42
Rodríguez, José "Pepe Secundino," 180

Rodríguez, Luis Orlando, 244, 350n45
Rodríguez, Nereida, 39, 297n18
Rodríguez, Rolando, 122, 128, 134–35, 264
Rodríguez, Salustiano "Cebolla," 235,
　　348n23
Rodríguez Alemán, Eduardo, 66, 145, 150,
　　213–14, 223–24, 261, 274, 307n43,
　　342n26
Rodríguez Coto, Lt. Pedro "Perico," 232,
　　235, 348n23
Rodríguez Cruz, René, 4, 283n10
Rodríguez García, Juan, 15
Rodríguez Gutiérrez, Marcial, 228, 230, 274
Rodríguez López, Dr. Alipio, 158, 220
Rodríguez Medrano, Capt. Pedro A., 203,
　　228, 232
Rodríguez Morejón, Gerardo, xii
Rodríguez Pérez, Léster, xxvii, 38–39, 52,
　　55–56, 61, 63, 65, 68, 76–78, 85, 110, 117,
　　196, 216, 237, 256, 264, 304n12, 309n12,
　　310n22, 338n55
Rodríguez Pérez, Pvt. Antonio H., 97, 101,
　　116, 318n89
Rodríguez Rodríguez, Tomás D.
　　"Tocororo," 77, 264, 273, 296n14,
　　298n26, 323n4
Rojas Ortiz, Sgt. Carlos, 84, 112
Rojas Rodríguez, Marta, xii, xiv, xvii, 110,
　　140, 216, 228–29, 231, 238, 242, 247,
　　303n11, 324n17, 346n2
Rojo Pérez, Manuel M., 150, 266, 298n26
Romaguera, Capt. Armando, 105
Romero Díaz, Zoila, 217
Romero Fonseca, Pedro, 268
Roosevelt, Franklin D., xxix, 8–9
Roosevelt Corollary, xxviii
Ros, Enrique, xxiv
Rosabal, 2nd Lt. Miguel D., 199–200
Rosabal Rosales, Cpl. José Gerardo, 109,
　　316n75
Rosell González, Severino "Vero," 73–74,
　　89, 178–79, 196, 264, 297nn21, 22,
　　304n21, 310n21, 326n31, 340n5
Rosell Leyva, Major Florentino E., 70, 143–
　　44, 153
Roselló Pando, Lt. Juan A., 128–29, 219,
　　320n20
Rosete, Elio, 50, 64, 123–25, 134, 136,
　　320n8, 322n34

Rosillo Rodríguez, Roberto, 274, 344n50
Rotary Club, Santiago de Cuba, 161, 170, 190
Route 80 bus station, Santiago de Cuba, 68, 88, 107, 150, 167
Ruanes Alvarez, Adalberto, 122–23, 132, 264, 304n16
Rubio Llerena, Enrique, 146
Rubio Padilla, Juan A., 301n53
Ruiz, Pvt. Miguel Mariano, 147, 161, 268, 338n54
Ruiz Herrera, Capt. Juan de Dios, 102, 107, 113, 142, 217, 324n11
Ruiz Leiro, Humberto, 13–14
Ruiz Velazco, Dr. Ramón, 309n13
Ruiz, Ramón Eduardo, 238
Rural Guard, 27, 40, 42, 47, 83, 85, 89, 90, 95, 99, 122, 129, 133, 139–40, 144, 176, 182–83, 186
Rural Guard 11th Squadron, Santiago de Cuba, 79, 98, 183
Rural Guard 13th Squadron, Bayamo, 125, 128
Rural Guard 14th Squadron, Palma Soriano, 98, 167
Rural Guard 57th Squadron, Isle of Pines, 232, 243
Russia, 143, 257–58
Ruston Academy, Havana, 44
Ruz, Francisco, 5
Ruz González, Fidel Casiano, 7. *See* Castro Ruz, Fidel
Ruz González, Fidel Hipólito, 6. *See* Castro Ruz, Fidel
Ruz González, Lina, 5–7, 49, 192, 284n16, 300n45

Sabatés, 37, 121, 131
Sáenz, Paquita, 196
Sáenz de Buruhaga, Mario, 286n30
Sagua de Tánamo, Oriente, 315n57
Sagua la Grande, Las Villas, 214
Saíz Sánchez, Manuel, 266, 303n7, 309n14
Salabarría Aguiar, Mario, 10–16, 19, 26, 286nn30, 31, 289n47, 291n67, 292n73, 293n79
Salado, Marcelo, 300n42
Salas Ca izares, Rafael, 1–2, 4, 28, 32
Salas Humara, Dr. Carlos, 168

Salazar, María Elvira, xxiv
Salcines Morlote, Felipe, 167, 170–71, 332n87
Samá, Lenin, 301n54
San Antonio, Texas, 287n35
San Francisco de Sales Trade School, Havana, 45
San Juan River, Oriente Province, 77, 112, 196
San Lázaro, Havana, 41
San Leopoldo rebel cell, 62
San Luis, Oriente, 162, 203
San Luis Rural Guard outpost, 47
San Martín, Marta, xv
San Miguel, Antonio, 286n29
San Pedrito airport, Santiago de Cuba, 155, 195, 197
San Pedro del Cotorro, Havana, 42, 56, 61, 65
San Román de las Llamas, Antonio, 272–73
San Román de las Llamas, Rolando "Wiki," 132, 266, 321n29
Sánchez, Ana Rosa, 181
Sánchez, Bienvenido, 115
Sánchez, Tomás, 115
Sánchez Abalos, Pvt. Urbano, 94, 267
Sánchez Amaya, Fernando, 347n14
Sánchez Arango, Aureliano, 29, 52–53, 65, 119, 139, 159, 180, 203–4, 209, 225, 272
Sánchez del Campo, Ciro, 157
Sánchez Domínguez, Cpl. Narciso D. "Nacho," 145–46
Sánchez Domínguez, Ramiro, 122, 125, 127–28, 134–35, 264
Sánchez López, Roberto, 88
Sánchez Manduley, Celia, xvi
Sánchez Pérez, Angel M., 85, 146, 164, 264, 305n25
Sánchez Pruna, Pvt. Jesús R., 96–97, 106, 109, 267
Sánchez Tamayo, Eriberto, 211, 272, 274
Sánchez White, Calixto, 299n42
Sandino, Augusto César, 16, 249
Santa Clara, Las Villas, 53, 67, 106, 135–36, 150, 228–29
Santa Clara Institute, Las Villas, 139
Santa Cruz del Sur, Camagüey, 139
Santa Ifigenia cemetery, Santiago de Cuba, 160–62, 195

Santa Rita, Oriente, 126
Santamaría Cuadrado, Abel B., 266; bookkeeper xvii, xix, 33, 45; character, 34, 42–43, 50, 114; at Civil Hospital, 85–87, 98, 115, 256, 317n79; detained after Moncada attack, 153, 166; executed, xx, xxi, 164–66; ideology, xvi, 34, 43, 144, 206; irresolute, 50, 114, 117, 136, 251; leadership role, 43, 47, 51, 54–58, 75–78; lodges rebels in Santiago, 66–70; meets Fidel Castro, 33; meets Dr. Mario Muñoz, 35; mentioned at trial, 213, 216; prior arrest, 36; residence, xviii, 34, 60–62, 64, 304n19; Siboney farmhouse, 71–72, 166, 211; *Son los mismos*, 294n4; torture legend, xiii–xv, 165–66, 330n71; training, 41
Santamaría Cuadrado, Haydée, xviii, 58, 318n8; activism, xii, 241, 243; at Civil Hospital, 81, 86–88, 114, 116, 218, 220, 309n15; commits suicide, 255; demanded paraffin test after arrest, 117; detonated bombs, 246; domineers brother Abel, 76, 114, 117, 136; description of, 34, 346n4; detained in Moncada, 160; founder of 26 of July Movement, 246–47; grateful for treatment after capture, 117; ideology, 43; incarcerated in Boniato prison, 165, 199–200, 280; incarcerated in National Women's prison, 233, 257, 347n14; incarcerated in *vivac* jail, 164, 193; meets Fidel Castro, 33; Reinaldo Boris Luis and, 39, 147; released from prison, 237; resides with Melba Hernández, 55; sentenced, 224, 261; Siboney farmhouse, 57, 71, 74; torture legend, xiii–xiv, xvi, xxvii, 164–66, 173, 216, 330n71; trial of, 216, 226, 273
Santana Martínez, Ricardo, 77, 111, 178, 196, 264, 304n21, 310n21, 326n31
Santiago de Cuba, Oriente, xii, xxv, xxvi, 3, 6, 29, 48, 50–51, 53, 55, 57–67, 70–72, 74–75, 77–78, 81–82, 104, 106, 118, 123–25, 129–32, 134, 136–40, 143–50, 152–53, 157–64, 166–70, 174, 176, 178–85, 190–91, 194–98, 201, 203, 207–9, 212–17, 219–20, 225, 228–29, 234, 236, 242, 250–51, 254, 300n42, 317n81, 325n23, 335n37, 338n55, 340n4; description of, 67
Santiago de Cuba Bar Association, 180, 200, 206–7

Santiago de Cuba carnival, 50, 55, 61, 67–70, 82, 88, 91, 93–94, 96–98, 105, 106, 112, 124, 130, 140, 143, 151, 155, 157, 162, 179, 182, 205, 212, 214–15
Santiago de Cuba naval headquarters, 103, 106, 140, 257
Santiago de Cuba *vivac* jail, 117, 163, 180, 182, 191–93, 208, 224, 256, 284n20
Santiago de las Vegas, Havana Province, 41, 60, 80, 213, 220, 250
Santiago Ruiz, Tony, 17–18, 301n53
Santos Domínguez, Isaac "Professor Harriman," 38–39, 45, 59, 299n33
Santos Suárez, Havana, 39, 41
Sarabia, Leida, 186–87
Sardinero, Oriente, 151
Sarmiento, Domingo, 188
Sarmiento Moreno, Pvt. Argeo, 97, 268, 313n44
Sarmiento Vargas, Ulises, 36, 77, 111, 149–50, 216, 264, 273, 303n8
Sarría Tartabul, Lt. Pedro, xiii, xviii, xix, 186–92, 202, 252, 335nn31, 38, 336n42, 343n37
Saturnino Lora Civil Hospital. *See* Civil Hospital
Saumell Soto, Alberto "Beto," 135, 350n39
Savigne Pavón, Luis, 167–68, 331n79
Sears, xii, 39, 42, 56
Sed Arias, 2nd Lt. Julio M., 129
Selva Yero, Carlos, 192–93
Serrano Alfonso, Ramón, 212, 272, 274
Sevilla, Oriente, 179, 182–83, 186, 190
Sevilla-Biltmore Hotel, Havana, 15
Siboney, Oriente, xviii, 51, 57, 65, 69, 92, 99, 141, 154, 164, 166, 177, 190, 196, 199, 219
Siboney Beach, Oriente, 51, 57, 70, 149, 151, 178, 184–85, 191
Siboney farmhouse, xvii, 51, 55–58, 62, 65, 67, 70–77, 81, 112, 143–45, 147–52, 155, 161, 163, 165–66, 172–75, 179, 182, 184, 201, 206, 211, 214–16, 223, 251–52, 256, 318n85, 325n28, 331n75
Siboney highway, Oriente, 77–78, 81, 112, 144, 146–47, 149, 151–52, 164, 174, 179, 183–84, 187, 189–90
Sierra Maestra, xix, 132, 237, 255, 287n35, 311n25, 314n47, 315n57, 316nn71, 75, 319n89, 322n31, 327n40, 329n59,

INDEX 389

331n73, 334n15, 335n37, 340n4, 342n23, 343n30, 343n44, 348n22
Sigas, Manuel, 160
Silano, José "Pepín," 132
Silva, Mercedes, 179
Silva Adán, Andrés, 209, 274, 344n50
Silva Domínguez, Cpl. Juan, 109, 316n75
Silva Domínguez, Pvt. Alfonso, 82, 84, 101, 104, 113, 217, 219, 312n31, 318n89
Silveiro Enríquez, Sgt. Ramón V., 89, 160, 267, 314n50, 326n34
SIM. *See* Military Intelligence Service
Singer, Kurt, 165
Smith, Earl E. T., 254
Socarrás Martínez, Osvaldo, 144, 266, 296n14, 303n7, 309n14
Social Defense Code, 32
Socialist Revolutionary Movement (MSR), 12–15, 17–20, 25
Sogo Hernández, Col. Dámaso, 241
Soler, Policarpo, 292n73
Son los Mismos, 33–35, 294n4
Sorbonne University, 198
Sorí Marín, Humberto, 180, 254, 334n15
Sosa Aguilar, Delio, 129
Sosa González, Elpidio C., 55, 58, 65, 71, 266
Sosa González, Ibrahim, 65, 304n16, 322n31
Sosa Hernández, Gerardo, 62, 77, 111, 149–50, 216, 264, 273
Sosa Jurado, José, 86, 221
Sotelo Piña, Francisco, 187, 335n34
Soto, María, 142
Soto Prieto, Lionel, 17
Sotús, Jorge, 254
Spain, xxviii, 4, 51, 184, 332n82, 338n55, 341n16, 351n1
Spanish Civil War, 152, 287n35, 350n47
Spanish-American War, xxviii, 4, 51, 67, 190
Stakeman Gómez, Anibal Celso, 60
Standard Oil Company, Havana, 44
Story, Henry, 141
Sturgis, Frank Fiorini, 318n88
Suardíaz Fernández, Manuel, xxii, 34, 37, 39, 62, 68, 71, 73, 75, 77, 147–49, 207, 254, 264
Suárez Ameneiro, Andrés, 299n42
Suárez Blanco, José "Pepe," xvii, 40, 73, 88, 92–93, 111, 148, 175–76, 180, 184, 186, 188–89, 224, 246, 262, 273, 297n22, 303n10, 304n21, 308n5, 311n30, 326n31, 350n47
Suárez Camejo, Police Sgt. Gerónimo R., 130, 160, 267
Suárez Espinosa, Lt. Domingo, 133
Suárez González, Cpl. Pedro E., 188
Suárez Rivas, Eduardo, 2, 28, 30, 32, 52, 301n53, 323n4
Suárez Suárez, Mauro, 172, 272–73
Subirats de Quesada, José M., 167–68, 170–71, 182
Sueño neighborhood, Santiago de Cuba, 55, 68, 105–6, 182, 186
Superior War College, 46
Szulc, Tad, xvii, xviii, 110, 241, 305n22, 319n6

Taber, Robert, xiii, 101, 288n40, 312n33
Tabernilla Dolz, Carlos, 25
Tabernilla Dolz, Gen. Francisco, 2, 46, 58, 143, 169, 236, 254, 329n59
Tabernilla Palmero, Col. Carlos, 155
Tabernilla Palmero, Col. Francisco "Silito," 54, 155, 195
Tabernilla Palmero, Col. Marcelo, 155
Taboada González, Aramís, xvii, 13, 20, 241, 349n35, 350n39
Taboada Bernal, Augusto B., 200, 214
Tamayo, Manuel, 129
Tamayo Silveira, Med. Capt. Edmundo, 103, 113, 158, 217, 313n41
Tandrón Femenías, Capt. José C., 183, 186
Tápanes Vento, Israel, 62, 73, 84, 90, 100, 111, 175, 178–79, 215, 224, 235, 256, 262, 273, 308n3, 311n24, 326n31
Tasende Dubois, Temis, 298n28
Tasende de las Muñecas, José Luis: activism, 45; background, 43, 266; enters Moncada, 83, 92, 308n5, 312n30; executed, 154, 327n44; fatherless, 296n14; morbid comment, 50; Raúl Castro and, 52, 63–64; Siboney farmhouse, 71, 73; travels to Oriente, 63–64, 68; wounded by grenade, 108–9, 319n94
Tejadilla Suárez, Pvt. Lázaro "Tirilo," 97, 141, 161, 219, 268, 338n54
Tejeda, Tomasa, 177, 179

Tejera, Diego Vicente, 11, 286n33
Ten Years' War, xxviii, 39, 50, 222, 249
Testa Zaragoza, Guillermo, 128
Testa Zaragoza, José, 128–29, 134, 266, 296n15, 304n16, 319n5
Thion Laboratory, xv, 42, 56
Thomas, Hugh, xiv, xv, 113
Tiempo en Cuba (magazine), 4, 11, 25–26, 53, 287n35
Tiempo (newspaper), 53
Tizol Aguilera, Ernesto: background, 42, 332n90; buys weapons, 45; deserted, xxi, 81, 117, 145, 213, 251; diplomat, 256, 325n26; drives to Oriente, 61, 63, 66–67, 303n6; erroneous portrayal of, xii–xiii, xv, xvii; incarcerated in Boniato prison, 199–200; incarcerated in the Isle of Pines, 235; rebel military committee member, 43; Siboney farmhouse, 51, 71, 77; surrenders, 172; trial of, 211, 213, 215, 273; sentenced, 224, 262
Tobío, José, 88, 107, 140–41, 167, 316n70, 328n56
Toledano, Migdalia, 98, 269
Toledo, Tomás, xviii
Toledo Niebla, Pvt. Osvaldo, 142
Tornés, Marino, 134
Torrens Youth Reformatory, 288n36, 341n22
Torres, Pvt. Agustín, 322n32
Torres Sánchez, Maximino, 106, 160–62, 166
Touriño, Santiago, 19–20, 286n32
Traba Montero, Cpl. Nemesio A., 90, 104, 111, 267, 310n22, 314n50
Trejo González, Rafael, 275
Triana Manzo, Pvt. Eulogio, 85
Triay, Pvt. Luis "Cara de Chivo," 82, 84, 219
Tribunal of Constitutional and Social Guarantees, 33, 294n2
Trigo Crespo, Julio, 256
Trigo López, Julio, 70–71, 81, 87, 147, 215, 266, 296n14, 303n6
Trigo López, Pedro, 48–49, 60, 64, 72, 77, 111, 147, 197, 244, 256, 264, 296n14
Trinidad Street, Santiago de Cuba, 78, 89, 93, 95–96, 98, 105–6, 108–9, 115–16
Triple A (organization), 53, 65, 132, 139, 153, 209, 323n4, 350n47
Tro Rivero, Emilio, 11–12, 16, 18, 26, 287n34, 291n67
Trujillo, Pvt. Juan, 85

Trujillo, Rafael, 12, 14, 16, 20, 351n3
26th of July flag, xxv
26 of July hymn, xxv, 235, 258, 348n22
26 of July Movement, xi, 118, 237, 246–47, 253–54, 257, 300n42, 310n22, 325n23, 330n69, 335n31, 337n48, 338n55, 341n12, 342n24, 346n5

Ugalde Carrillo, Col. Manuel, xviii, 2, 57–58, 161, 195, 236, 302n65
Unión de Reyes, Matanzas, 63
Union of Electrical, Radio and Machine Workers of America (CIO), 21
Unitary Action Party (PAU), 1, 212, 282n1
United Fruit Company, 4–5
United Nations, 16, 18, 255, 291n70, 294n84
United States–Cuba relations, xxvii, xxviii, xxix, 3, 141, 144, 199, 232, 238, 252, 254, 257, 291n66
United States Congress, xxviii, 253
United States Department of State, xxii, 8, 11, 15–16, 46, 54, 57, 139, 157, 169, 173, 198, 201, 212, 232, 252, 254, 332n83
United States Embassy in Havana, xvii, xxii, xxvii, 11, 14, 28, 31, 44, 46, 54, 63, 138, 141, 157, 169–70, 173, 198, 201, 205, 212, 225, 252, 287n35
University of Havana, xix, 3–4, 9–10, 13–14, 16–17, 27, 36, 39, 41, 45–46, 193, 196, 204, 209, 214, 287n35, 293n80, 295n11, 345n57
University of Miami Archives, xviii, xxi
University of Oriente, 167, 169, 207
University Student Directorate (DEU), xxix, 46, 286n30
Urgency Tribunal, 32, 158–59, 180, 203, 205, 213, 228, 232, 236, 254, 323n4
Uruguayan Embassy in Havana, 196
Urrutia Lleó, Manuel, 158–59, 205, 254, 329n57, 336n42, 345n57
USS *Maine*, xxviii

Valdés, Nelson P., xv
Valdés Cabrera, Lt. Ismael, 97, 105–6, 166, 220
Valdés Calvo, Rafael "Onay," 213, 220, 272–73
Valdés Casañas, Humberto, 150, 256, 264, 273, 296n14, 303n12, 304n19, 326n36
Valdés Daussá, Ramiro, 10, 286n30
Valdés Fuentes, Andrés, 167, 266, 303n12, 331n77

Valdés Menéndez, Ramiro, xiii, xvii, 40, 64, 92, 103, 110, 112, 146, 182, 215, 224, 255, 262, 273, 297n22, 304n12, 308n5, 311n30, 319n94, 351n2
Valdés Miranda, Bruno, 287n34
Valdés Puentes, Ramiro, 255
Valdés Rodríguez, Angel, 272–73
Valdespino, Andrés, 350n39
Valladares, Ricardo, 294n4
Valle López, Armando, 167, 266, 296n14, 303n12, 331n77
Valls, Jorge, 317n79
Valls Tamayo, José F., 207, 274, 338n55, 344n50
Valmaseda, Inocencio, 135
Varadero Beach, Matanzas, xii, 50, 57, 62, 80, 252
Varela, Antonio, 134
Varela Pla, Coralia "Nenita," 37, 135, 295n13
Vargas Machuca, Ernesto, 142
Varona Loredo, Manuel Antonio de, 53
Varona Loredo, Roberto de, 232
Vasconcelos Maragliano, Ramón, 30, 119, 293n83
Vázquez, Angel "El Gallego," 12, 288n36
Vázquez, Daniel, 341n12
Vázquez, Pvt. José Joaquín, 90–91, 267, 308n4
Vázquez Martínez, Mario, 158
Vázquez Rojas, Ana, 318n85
Vázquez Rojas, José, 51, 81, 155, 211, 215, 272, 274, 318n85
Vázquez Tió, Manuel, 76–77, 145, 214, 225, 264, 273
Vedado Tennis Club, 44
Veguitas, Oriente, 126, 133–34, 194–95, 336n42
Velasco Montalvo, José, 136
Velazco, Dr. Luis, 226
Velázquez, Mariano, 161
Véliz Hernández, Eugenio, 322n33
Véliz Hernández, Pedro "Caro": activism 56; background, 266; deserted, 125; murdered, 133–34, 210
Venero Agudo, Aurora "Chia," 154
Venezuela, 20–21, 46, 290n56, 316n72
Ventura Reyes, Dr. Orlando, 347n14

Vera Serafín, Aldo, 254
Verdecia, Cpl. Erico, 91
Victoria de las Tunas, Oriente, 65, 135, 149, 169, 315n57
Victoriano Garzón Avenue, Santiago de Cuba, 51, 56, 68–69, 78, 81–82, 90, 98, 104, 111, 115, 229
Viera Milián, Francisco, xiv, 268, 326n34
Villa Blanca. *See* Siboney farmhouse
Villa Romero, José Manuel, 153, 159, 166, 209, 272, 274, 341n16
Villalón Virgilí, Dr. Roberto, 103–4, 315n62
Villalvilla Carbonell, Raúl, 212, 217, 274, 344n50
Villegas, Juan, 64, 264
Viñas Batista, Fernando, 134
Virués Moraga, Sgt. José Hidalezio, 96, 106–7, 217, 316n71
Visión (magazine), 53–54, 177
Vista Alegre, Santiago de Cuba, 104, 112, 146, 171, 182, 190

Walters, Barbara, 241
War of Independence, xxvii, 80, 204, 227
Washington, D.C., 33, 44
Welles, Sumner, xxix
Women's Civic Front of the Martí Centenary, 208
Woodward, Robert F., 198–99
World Student Congress, 21
World War II, xxx, 11, 24, 38, 54, 287n34, 291n67, 316n71, 332n83

Xenis López, Evelio, xxii, 95, 268, 313n37, 328n56

Yanez Pelletier, Bernabé, 337n48
Yanez Pelletier, Lt. Jesús xxii, 144, 156, 166, 193, 199, 202, 252, 324n16, 337n48
Yanez Querejeta, Jesús Gregorio, 324n16
Yara, Oriente, 132
York Botella, Lt. Horacio, 107, 144, 218, 343n37

Zambrano, Zenaida, 196
Zamora, Filiberto, 60
Zaydín Márquez-Sterling, Ramón, 323n4, 349n39